# Women in the American Civil War

# Women in the American Civil War

## VOLUME I

*Lisa Tendrich Frank*

### Editor

Santa Barbara, California    Denver, Colorado    Oxford, England

Library of Congress Cataloging-in-Publication Data
Women in the American Civil War / Lisa Tendrich Frank, editor.
   v.  cm.
   Includes bibliographical references and index.
   ISBN 978-1-85109-600-8 (hard copy : alk. paper) — ISBN 978-1-85109-605-3 (ebook)   1. United States—History—Civil War, 1861–1865—Women—Encyclopedias.   2. United States—History—Civil War, 1861–1865—Participation, Female—Encyclopedias. 3. United States—History—Civil War, 1861–1865—Biography—Encyclopedias.   4. United States—History—Civil War, 1861–1865—Social aspects—Encyclopedias.   5. Women—United States—History—19th century—Encyclopedias.   6. Women—United States—Biography—Encyclopedias.   I. Frank, Lisa Tendrich.
   E628.W655   2008
   973.7082'03—dc22

2007025822

12 11 10 9 8  1 2 3 4 5 6 7 8 9 10

Production Editor: Alisha Martinez
Production Manager: Don Schmidt
Media Editor: Julie Dunbar
Media Production Coordinator: Ellen Brenna Dougherty
Media Resources Manager: Caroline Price
File Manager: Paula Gerard

This book is also available on the World Wide Web as an eBook.
Visit www.abc-clio.com for details.

ABC-CLIO, Inc.
130 Cremona Drive, P.O. Box 1911
Santa Barbara, California 93116–1911

This book is printed on acid-free paper ∞

Manufactured in the United States of America

*For Daniel*

# Contributors

Adgent, Nancy L.
Rockefeller Archive Center

Allred, Randal
Brigham Young University,
    Hawaii

Anderson, Joe L.
University of West Georgia

Antolini, Katharine Lane
West Virginia University

Bair, Barbara
Library of Congress

Barber, E. Susan
College of Notre Dame of
    Maryland

Beilke, Jayne R.
Ball State University

Blake, Debra A.
North Carolina State Archives

Blalock, Kay J.
St. Louis Community College-
    Meramec

Boccardi, Megan
University of Missouri, Columbia

Bohanan, Robert D.
Jimmy Carter Library

Boswell, Angela
Henderson State University

Broussard, Joyce L.
California State University,
    Northridge

Brown, William H.
North Carolina Office of
    Archives and History

Bruns, Gabrielle
Independent Scholar

Burin, Nikki Berg
University of Minnesota

Campbell, Jacqueline Glass
University of Connecticut

Carter, María Agui
Iguana Films

Castagna, JoAnn E.
University of Iowa

Cole, N. Scott
Longwood University

Coles, David
Longwood University

Confer, W. Clarissa
California University of
    Pennsylvania

Coryell, Janet L.
Western Michigan University

Cox, Karen L.
University of North Carolina at
    Charlotte

Crist, Lynda L.
Rice University

Dunn, Kristina K.
South Carolina Confederate
    Relic Room and Military
    Museum

Eliassen, Meredith
San Francisco State University

Engle, Nancy Driscol
Independent Scholar

Eye, Sara Marie
University South Carolina

Eylon, Dina Ripsman
University of Toronto

Foroughi, Andrea R.
Union College

Frank, Andrew K.
Florida State University

Frank, Ed
University of Memphis

Gallman, J. Matthew
University of Florida

Gerard, Gene C.
Tarrant County College

Gigantino, James
University of Georgia

Graves, Donna Cooper
University of Tennessee at
    Martin

Gross, Jennifer Lynn
Jacksonville State University

Halloran, Fiona Deans
Eastern Kentucky University

Hartsock, Ralph
University of North Texas
    Libraries

Haynes, Robert W.
Texas A&M International
    University

Hinton, Paula Katherine
Tennessee Technological
    University

Holcomb, Julie
Navarro College

Hudson, Linda S.
East Texas Baptist University

Jepsen, Thomas C.
Independent Scholar

Kehoe, Karen A.
Saint Vincent College

Kelsey, Sigrid
Louisiana State University
    Libaries

Kinzey, Karen
Arlington House

Kuipers, Juliana
Harvard University Archives

Lancaster, Jane
Brown University

Lane, Yvette Florio
Monmouth University

Larson, Kate Clifford
Independent Scholar

Lause, Mark A.
University of Cincinnati

Lewis, Elizabeth Wittenmyer
Independent Scholar

Long, Alecia P.
Louisiana State University

Marszalek, John F.
Mississippi State University

Martinez, Jaime Amanda
University of Virginia

Mays, Gwen Thomas
North Carolina State Archives

McDevitt, Theresa R.
Indiana University of
    Pennsylvania Libraries

Minton, Amy
Marymount University

Moody, Wesley
Gordon College

Myers, Barton A.
University of Georgia

Nester, Thomas
Texas A&M University

Neumann, Caryn E.
Ohio Wesleyan University

Nguyen, Julia Huston
Independent Scholar

Nichols, Jennifer Jane
Michigan State University

Nickeson, Dawn Ottevaere
Michigan State University

Nussel, Jill M.
Indiana/Purdue University
    Fort Wayne

Nytroe, Sarah K.
Boston College

Oglesby, Catherine
Valdosta State University

Olsen, Christopher J.
Indiana State University

Ott, Victoria E.
Birmingham-Southern College

Prushankin, Jeffrey S.
Pennsylvania State University
    Abingdon

Quigley, Paul D. H.
University of Edinburgh

Richard, Patricia
Metropolitan State College
of Denver

Ritter, Charles R.
College of Notre Dame
of Maryland

Roberts, Giselle
La Trobe University

Ross-Nazzal, Jennifer
NASA Johnson Space Center

Rouse, Kristen L.
Independent Scholar

Rubin, Anne Sarah
University of Maryland,
Baltimore County

Sacher, John M.
University of Central Florida

Schoonmaker, Nancy Gray
University of North Carolina
at Chapel Hill

Schroeder, Adriana
University of Central Oklahoma

Schurr, Nancy
University of Tennessee,
Knoxville

Scroggins, Eloise E.
Indiana Historical Society

Selby, Kelly D.
Kent State University

Shaffer, Donald R.
University of Northern Colorado

Sheehan-Dean, Aaron
University of North Florida

Sherman, Dawn M.
Independent Scholar

Smith, Lisa M.
University of Akron

Stabler, Scott L.
Grand Valley State University

Streater, Kristen L.
Collin County Community
College

Sullivan, Regina D.
Independent Scholar

Taylor, Robert A.
Florida Institute of
Technology

Todras, Ellen H.
Independent Scholar

Tolley-Stokes, Rebecca
East Tennessee State University

van Zelm, Antoinette G.
Tennessee Civil War National
Heritage Area Center for
Historic Preservation
Middle Tennessee State
University

Vincent, Thomas
North Carolina Department of
Archives and History

Wamsley, E. Sue
Kent State University-Salem

Warner, Jay
Independent Scholar

Wayne, Tiffany K.
Cabrillo College

Wells, Cheryl A.
University of Wyoming

White, Jonathan W.
University of Maryland, College
Park

Wilkerson, Jessie
Pellissippi State Technical
Community College

Williams, David
Valdosta State University

Wongsrichanalai, Kanisorn
University of Virginia

Wooton, Sarah
South Carolina Confederate
Relic Room & Museum

Wyatt-Brown, Bertram
Richard J. Milbauer Professor
Emeritus, University of
Florida and Visiting Scholar,
Johns Hopkins University

Younger, Karen Fisher
Pennsylvania State University

# Contents

# List of Entries

# Introduction

Until the past few decades, most scholars would have agreed with Margaret Mitchell's narrator, who asserted in *Gone with the Wind,* that war "is men's business, not ladies" (Mitchell, *Gone with the Wind,* 8). Indeed, until recently, only a few scholars dared to treat women as central players in the American Civil War. Instead, the bulk of the scholarship on the war pushed women to the margins, discussing them only as a sidebar to the "important" work done by men on the battlefields and in the political arena. In most accounts, the women stayed at home as unnamed civilians, while the men in their worlds fought the battles that defined the outcome of the war. A few nurses were recognized for their valor, but their wartime efforts remained overshadowed by those of military men, such as William Tecumseh Sherman, Ulysses S. Grant, Thomas "Stonewall" Jackson, and Robert E. Lee, as well by those of politicians like Abraham Lincoln and Jefferson Davis. This book reflects the growing and increasingly sophisticated literature on women during the American Civil War that demonstrates the need to acknowledge women's central roles in pursuing the war and in determining its outcome. Rather than auxiliaries, women across all racial, class, ethnic, religious, and geographic lines were an essential component of the action. Slave women and their white female owners shaped and were shaped by the war, as were female abolitionists, yeoman farmers, recent immigrants, widows, and domestic laborers. Whether living in the North, South, or West or in the countryside or city, women of all classes and backgrounds found ways to involve themselves in the events shaping their lives.

Although this volume focuses on women in the Civil War period, it does not glorify them for the sake of noticing them. Instead, the entries in this encyclopedia offer a nuanced view of how women survived, contributed to, undermined, and lived through the Civil War. This approach contrasts sharply with that of the literature about Civil War women appearing throughout the nation immediately after the war. These accounts typically elevated women, particularly elite white women, to a mythical status as self-sacrificing feminine patriots. To create this mythology, the accounts, written by both men and women, emphasized women's nurturing roles on the homefront, especially as nurses, seamstresses, and fundraisers for their men on the battlefield. The women of these extensive volumes provided the necessary support for politicians and soldiers, but they rarely played any independent role in the conflict. Instead, they willingly gave up their food, fancy clothes, comfort, homes, and loved ones in support of a cause that they believed in. They never stepped outside the boundaries of what was then considered proper womanhood, but rather performed their wartime tasks with the knowledge that they did them for the men. Those who took on the extraordinary roles as soldiers and spies were often portrayed as doing so in the name of the men they loved.

The reality of women's wartime experiences, however, was much more complicated than this self-sacrificing feminine image suggests. As women stepped outside their traditional roles as sweethearts, wives, mothers, sisters, and daughters, many willingly took on roles that, at the time, some classified as unfeminine. Some white Southern women, for example, vehemently supported or opposed disunion, engaged in political debates, attended secession conventions, and otherwise eagerly participated in the political sphere. Some Northern women similarly joined and helped form abolitionist organizations, petitioned Congress to limit the expansion of slavery, and otherwise became political actors. Once the war began, Northern and Southern women took government jobs, served as spies and soldiers, wrote political and fictional accounts of events, took themselves to the battlefield as frontline nurses, ran farms and plantations to varying degrees of success, worked as doctors, hid deserters and shirkers, protested conscription and wartime shortages, provided information and supplies to enemy soldiers in their midst, offered advice to husbands in military command, and otherwise demonstrated that they made their own choices throughout the war. Enslaved African American women helped turn the war into a fight for emancipation, claiming safety behind Union lines, reuniting with family members, and otherwise pursuing freedom. Free black women helped raise Union regiments, nursed injured and sick soldiers as necessary, and formed aid societies to help the soldiers and widows of their communities. Others remained leery of stepping outside the boundaries of femininity and instead remained on the sidelines as support staff to the men of their families. Many women, regardless of their stances, kept diaries of their experiences and observations of the war and of the people involved. Women of all backgrounds sent letters—filled with words of support, complaint, or requests—to their men at the front. In all cases, however, women could not escape a war that had such wide reaching effects.

To best explore how women experienced and affected the course of the Civil War, this title contains a mixture of types and lengths of entries. The fourteen contextual essays at the beginning outline the general contours of the war, the different types of women, the wartime issues, as well as the experiences of women in particular. These extended entries, appearing at the start of the volume and separated from the traditional alphabetical entries, provide an overview of how various groups of women experienced the era and how women in general shared similar experiences. Specifically, the essays explore abolitionism and Northern reformers, African American women, the Confederate homefront, female spies, female combatants, military invasion and occupation, Northern women, nurses, politics, religion, Southern women, the Union homefront, wartime employment, and wartime literature. Collectively, these essays provide an overview of the female experience during the war. They offer a broad outline of the war experience that is augmented by the individual shorter entries throughout the rest of the volume.

The bulk of the volume consists of more than three hundred entries that detail the experiences of women during the American Civil War without necessarily glorifying them, as was done in the postwar literature. They explore topics that traditionally fall under the headings of military affairs, social life, labor issues, politics, and culture. Some of the entries are explicitly about women, often biographical sketches of well-known and not so well-known participants and observers. Other entries explore famous military and political events, like the Battle of Gettysburg or the wartime elections, introducing and emphasizing the traditionally neglected participation of women. Women's roles in the recruitment of soldiers, the protest of wartime policies, the care of wounded men, and the creation of supplies for the men of both armies are highlighted. In addition, the volume details the cross-dressing women who served as soldiers in the Confederate and Union armies, as well as the employment of women in government and private-sector jobs. It also contains details about emancipation, slave life, and the enlistment of African American soldiers. Even women's homefront lives and roles are explored from various viewpoints. In short, this volume details the contributions and experiences of women across the social, ethnic, and racial spectra.

Each of the alphabetical entries contains the basic components of an encyclopedia—details, dates, names, and the other essential facts for the term—with special attention paid to how the topic relates to the experiences of women during the war. Biographical entries detail the milestones of the person's entire life, but the bulk of their information relates to the individual's wartime experiences. Similarly, entries on battles and other traditional military topics contain the outline of maneuvers and tactics, with special attention paid to the contributions of female spies, civilians, nurses, and soldiers as well as to how women experienced or reacted to the event. Each entry also contains cross references to allow users to flesh out the contours of the wartime experience through a reading of related entries. Finally, all the entries contain a list of specialized books and articles that will allow readers to further explore the topics covered.

The twenty-four primary sources included in the volume offer a first-hand look at women's wartime experiences. They cover a wide array of viewpoints and events, including the Richmond bread riots, the capture of Union spy Pauline Cushman, the formation of United States Sanitary Commission–sanctioned aid societies, the life of a slave woman, the education of freed people by Northern women, and the evacuation of Atlanta. In addition, they offer a brief glance at some of the contemporary popular literature, North and South. The disparate experiences outlined in these sources lend credence to the need for an encyclopedia that examines women's individual wartime experiences. Although these sources are all by or about women, they each offer a specific viewpoint on the war, on its effects, and on women's involvement, demonstrating the impossibility of casting women's wartime experiences in monolithic terms.

Exploring this volume, readers discover the centrality of the Civil War to the lives of American women and American society. Indeed, many scholars paint the Civil War as a defining moment in the history of the United States. Military historians stress its importance as the first modern war—a statement about the tactics, technology, and interaction of civilians. Social historians have uncovered the transformative nature of the war in a host of areas. Many women's historians argue that the wartime participation of Northern women in abolitionism, nursing, and aid societies led to the coales-

cence of a woman's movement in the Northern states. Even scholars of tourism demonstrate how the unprecedented movement around the nation by military troops helped to develop more of a nationwide tourism industry than had existed in antebellum America; soldiers wanted to revisit and bring their loved ones to the places they had fought, and widows and other family members wanted to visit the places where their loved ones had lost their lives. The Civil War did, in fact, alter the lives of all who lived through it. However, individual backgrounds, as well as locations, wartime experiences, and expectations, resulted in lingering effects that each person felt differently.

Readers may also be surprised by the connections between the homefront and the warfront, between civilians and soldiers, and between women and men that this encyclopedia illuminates. Although scholars have often ignored women in their military treatments of the Civil War because they were not on the battlefield, women's omnipresence on the homefront shaped how officers directed their military campaigns and determined what soldiers would eat and wear. Northern and Southern women's often unpaid work as nurses, recruiters, fundraisers, seamstresses, cooks, and laundresses provided essential functions for the waging of war. By performing these tasks, women fulfilled a need for labor and goods that would have otherwise drawn men from their positions on the battlefront. Consequently, women—whether they were rich or poor, black or white, Native American or immigrant, Southern or Northern, rural or urban—helped determine the outcome of the war and in turn were shaped by the events around them.

In addition, for many women, the homefront became the battlefront. Communities in the Shenandoah Valley, for example, constantly shifted between Union and Confederate control, and the residents there found themselves dealing with soldiers on a daily basis. They had to find a way to survive, retain their loyalties, and support their own troops. Similarly, in occupied Southern cities such as Vicksburg, Mississippi, women had to choose between loyalty oaths and possible starvation when occupying Union troops vowed not to do business with Confederates. Some women chose to take loyalty oaths while harboring Confederate allegiance, and others found their fervor for the Southern nation dampened by the realities of war and occupation. In New Orleans, Union officials dealt directly with what they saw as Southern women's insolence. Fed up with the behavior of the city's women, General Benjamin Butler issued the Woman Order to bring Confederate women under control and to force them to behave like ladies with the occupying troops. African American women, who expected the Union army to bring freedom from slavery and its horrors, often found themselves confronted with Northern racism. Much to their surprise, these women faced rape as well as the loss or destruction of their property by those they thought would be their liberators. Northern women, for their part, assumed themselves safe from invasion. However, some faced Confederate soldiers when the troops pushed northward, most notably into Gettysburg, Pennsylvania. Like their Southern counterparts, these women were forced to find ways to protect themselves and their families from enemy soldiers.

Even when they did not face enemy troops, women's roles on the homefront remained essential to the course of the Civil War. As many scholars and participants have noted, women's moral and material support allowed men to leave home for military duty. Women's objections to the course of the war or to the cause that their men supported often proved

equally powerful. Some women, unable to handle the business at home on their own, urged their husbands to desert. Other women created underground groups of protest in their communities, such as the secret Unionist circle in Atlanta frequented by Cyrena Stone. In more drastic instances, women took to the streets to make their voices heard. In cities across the South, for example, hundreds of women participated in food riots in 1863, drawing attention to their needs in a time of shortage. That same year, many Northern women participated in draft riots throughout Northern cities.

In addition to the contextual essays and alphabetic entries, this volume also contains two additional resources to help readers understand the experience of women and the Civil War. At the start of the volume, there is a chronology that integrates women's participation in the Civil War with the traditional military and political events. At the end of the volume, an extensive bibliography offers researchers a way to begin their search for information on the topics covered and on the Civil War in general.

Margaret Mitchell may have penned her famous and misleading words about the Civil War a couple of generations ago, but her message resonates to this day. Hopefully, this encyclopedia helps illuminate the falsehood of treating war as men's work and of ignoring women in our interpretations and understandings of the Civil War. This volume, as well as the growing literature on women and the war, should make it clear that war is also women's work.

# Chronology

**January 1831**
Abolitionist William Lloyd Garrison publishes the first issue of *The Liberator*.

**December 1833**
The American Anti-Slavery Society forms in Philadelphia.

**July 1840**
Abby Kelly is elected to the board of the American Anti-Slavery Society. Subsequent debate over the role of women in the abolitionist movement results in some members forming the separate American and Foreign Anti-Slavery Society. William Lloyd Garrison remains with the American Anti-Slavery Society.

**July 1848**
Lucretia Mott, Elizabeth Cady Stanton, and other supporters of women's rights hold a convention at Seneca Falls, New York, and issue a Declaration of Sentiments.

**September 1850**
President Millard Fillmore signs a series of bills that deals with states' rights and the extension of slavery into the new territories of the United States that becomes known as the Compromise of 1850.

**May 1851**
Sojourner Truth delivers her "Ain't I a Woman?" speech at a women's rights convention in Akron, Ohio.

**June 1851**
Washington-based abolitionist newspaper, *The National Era*, begins publishing in serial form Harriet Beecher Stowe's *Uncle Tom's Cabin; Or, Life among the Lowly*.

**March 1852**
*Uncle Tom's Cabin; Or, Life among the Lowly* is published in book form.

**April 1853**
Harriet Tubman begins working on the Underground Railroad.

**May 1854**
Congress passes the Kansas-Nebraska Act.

**March 1857**
The Supreme Court makes its *Dred Scott v. Sanford* ruling.

**October 1859**
Abolitionist John Brown leads a raid on the federal arsenal at Harper's Ferry, Virginia, hoping to initiate a slave rebellion.

**April 1860**
Anna Dickinson delivers "The Rights and Wrongs of Women" at a Quaker meeting.

**November 1860**
Abraham Lincoln is elected president of the United States.

**December 1860**
South Carolina secedes from the Union.

**January 1861**
Mississippi, Florida, Alabama, Georgia, and
  Louisiana secede.
Harriet Jacobs [Linda Brent] publishes *Incidents
  in the Life of a Slave Girl*.

**February 1861**
Texas secedes.
Seceded states hold convention in Montgomery,
  Alabama, where they adopt a Confederate Con-
  stitution and elect Jefferson Davis president of
  the Confederate States of America.

**March 1861**
Abraham Lincoln is inaugurated as president of
  the United States.

**April 1861**
Rebecca Harding Davis publishes "Life in the Iron
  Mills" in *The Atlantic Monthly*.
Confederates fire on and capture Fort Sumter in
  South Carolina.
Lincoln calls for troops to put down the insurrec-
  tion, and he orders a naval blockade of Confed-
  erate seaports. Virginia secedes. Lincoln also
  orders all civilian employees within the execu-
  tive branch to take a loyalty oath.
Riots erupt in Baltimore, Maryland.
New York City women form the Women's Central
  Association of Relief.
Dorothea Dix is appointed Superintendent of the
  United States Army Nurses.

**May 1861**
Arkansas and North Carolina secede.
Dorothea Dix organizes the first military hospitals
  in the United States.

**June 1861**
The Women's Central Association of Relief is sanc-
  tioned by Lincoln, and it becomes the United
  States Sanitary Commission.

After speaking at a pro-Union rally, Sojourner
  Truth is arrested for breaking a state law that
  prohibited African Americans from entering
  Indiana.
Mary Ann Bickerdyke begins her work at Union
  hospitals.
Western counties in Virginia secede from the state
  and form West Virginia.

**July 1861**
Congress authorizes the enlistment of half a million soldiers and passes the Crittenden Resolution, which declares that the United States was
  waging war to reunify the nation rather than to
  eliminate or restrict slavery.
The Confederate and Union armies face each
  other for the first time at the Battle of Bull Run
  (Manassas). During that battle, Anne Blair
  Etheridge and other women witness their first
  combat as frontline nurses.

**August 1861**
Lincoln declares the Confederate states to be in a
  state of insurrection.
Congress passes the first Confiscation Act.
The United States Secret Service arrests and
  imprisons Rose O'Neal Greenhow for spying on
  behalf of the Confederacy.
Anne Ella Carroll publishes *Reply to the Speech of
  Honorable John C. Breckinridge*.

**September 1861**
Sally Louisa Tompkins becomes a commissioned
  Confederate officer in order to keep Robertson
  Hospital open in Richmond, Virginia.

**October 1861**
Charlotte Forten goes to Port Royal, South Car-
  olina, to work as a teacher for recently freed
  African Americans.

**November 1861**
General Winfield Scott resigns his post as head of
  the United States Army. Lincoln appoints
  George B. McClellan to replace him.

The Young Men's Christian Association establishes the United States Christian Commission.

**January 1862**
The Port Royal Experiment begins on the Union-occupied Sea Islands in South Carolina.

**February 1862**
Julia Ward Howe publishes "The Battle Hymn of the Republic" in *The Atlantic Monthly*.

**March 1862**
The Confederate ironclad *Merrimac* and Union ironclad *Monitor* fight to a draw.
The Peninsular Campaign begins.
The United States Congress passes the Impressment Act.

**April 1862**
The Battle of Shiloh takes place.
Congress abolishes slavery in the District of Columbia.
The Confederacy passes its first Conscription Act.

**May 1862**
Union General Benjamin Butler takes command of occupied New Orleans, Louisiana. He issues his General Order Number 28, the Woman Order.

**June 1862**
Virginian Robert E. Lee assumes command of the Confederate army.

**July 1862**
Lee and McClellan face each other at the Seven Days Battle.
General Henry Halleck takes control of the Union army.
Confederate spy Belle Boyd is imprisoned at the Old Capital Prison.

**August 1862**
Confederate soldiers defeat the Union army at the Second Battle of Bull Run.

**September 1862**
Lee's Army of Northern Virginia invades the North. The deadliest day of fighting occurs when twenty-six thousand soldiers die at the Battle at Antietam in Maryland.
Lincoln issues a preliminary Emancipation Proclamation.
Laura M. Towne establishes a school for freedmen and freedwomen on St. Helena Island, South Carolina.
An explosion at the Allegheny Arsenal kills seventy-eight workers, mostly young women.

**November 1862**
General Ambrose E. Burnside replaces McClellan as commander of the Union's Army of the Potomac.

**December 1862**
Confederates defeat Union forces at the Battle of Fredericksburg.
Louisa May Alcott begins work at Union Hospital in Washington, D.C.

**January 1863**
Lincoln's Emancipation Proclamation goes into effect.
General Joseph Hooker replaces Ambrose Burnside, and Union General Ulysses S. Grant takes control of the Army of the West.
Recruitment begins for the Fifty-fourth Massachusetts Infantry Regiment, the nation's first African American unit.

**March 1863**
An explosion at an ordnance lab in Richmond, Virginia, kills thirty-four women.
Women in Salisbury, North Carolina, riot in response to their shortage of salt and flour.
Mary Abigail Dodge [Gail Hamilton] publishes "A Call to My Country-Women" in *The Atlantic Monthly*.

**April 1863**
Women in Richmond, Virginia, engage in bread riots to protest the wartime shortages.

The Battle of Chancellorsville begins.

Confederate Mary Frances "Fanny" Battle is arrested for spying.

The Union's policy of conscription goes into effect.

### May 1863

Lee defeats Hooker at Chancellorsville.

The National Women's Loyal League meets for the first time.

Louisa May Alcott begins to publish in serial form her *Hospital Sketches*.

Fanny Kemble publishes her *Journal of a Residence on a Georgian Plantation* while in England; it is published in the United States that July.

Union spy Pauline Cushman is captured.

### June 1863

Lee again invades the North, and General George G. Meade becomes the Union commander of the Army of the Potomac.

Residents of Vicksburg, Mississippi, evacuate to nearby caves to avoid Union shelling.

Western Virginia separates from Virginia and re-enters the Union.

### July 1863

The Union army defeats Lee at the Battle of Gettysburg.

Union forces under Grant capture Vicksburg and takes control of the Mississippi River.

The Battle of Honey Springs takes place in Indian Territory.

Draft riots in New York expose homefront frustrations. Similar riots occur in Boston, Massachusetts, Holmes County, Ohio, and elsewhere across the Union.

### August 1863

Confederate William C. Quantrill and four hundred and fifty supporters raid Lawrence, Kansas.

### September 1863

Confederates win the Battle of Chickamauga.

### October 1863

Lincoln calls for a national day of thanksgiving to be held in November.

Grant takes control of all operations in the Western theater.

The United States Sanitary Commission holds one of its most successful sanitary fairs in Chicago.

### November 1863

Lincoln delivers the Gettysburg Address at the dedication of a national cemetery.

Grant repels the Confederate siege at Chattanooga, Tennessee.

### February 1864

Confederates win the Battle of Olustee in Florida.

The National Women's Loyal League presents Congress with a petition demanding the abolition of slavery.

Rebecca Lee becomes the first African American woman to earn an M.D. degree.

### March 1864

Grant takes control of all the armies of the United States, and General William T. Sherman assumes control of Union forces in the West.

Women protest for peace in High Point, North Carolina.

### April 1864

The United States Sanitary Commission holds a three-week fundraising fair in New York that raises $1 million.

A bread riot erupts in Savannah, Georgia.

### May 1864

Union troops under Grant's command fight Confederate forces led by Lee at the Battles of the Wilderness and Spotsylvania.

Sherman advances toward Atlanta and the Army of the Tennessee.

### June 1864

Confederates win the Battle of Cold Harbor.

Grant begins a nine-month siege of Petersburg, Virginia.

**July 1864**
Sherman forcefully evacuates female workers and
their families from the textile mill town of
Roswell, Georgia.

**September 1864**
Sherman captures Atlanta and issues Special Field
Orders, Number 67, evacuating the city of all
civilians. The order primarily affects the city's
women and children.
Frustrations lead to bread riots in Mobile,
Alabama.

**October 1864**
Union General Philip H. Sheridan defeats General
Jubal Early's Confederate troops in the Shenan-
doah Valley.

**November 1864**
Lincoln defeats McClellan in the presidential race.
Sherman burns Atlanta and begins his March to
the Sea.

**December 1864**
General George H. Thomas defeats the Army of
the Tennessee.
Sherman captures Savannah, Georgia.

**January 1865**
Freed slaves obtain control of the Sea Islands
between Jacksonville, Florida, and Charleston,
South Carolina, when Sherman issues Special
Field Order, Number 15. Sherman marches
through South Carolina, destroying much
of Charleston, Columbia, and the
surrounding areas.
Before Sherman arrives, the women of Columbia
hold the Confederacy's largest fundraising
bazaar.
Freed slave and Union spy Mary Elizabeth Bowser
flees from Confederate President Jefferson
Davis's Richmond home.

**February 1865**
African American Julia C. Collins begins publishing "The Curse of Caste; or, The Slave Bride" as

a serial in the *Christian Recorder,* a weekly
newspaper run by the African Methodist Episcopal Church.

**March 1865**
Grant defeats Lee at the Battle of Petersburg.
Congress creates the Freedmen's Bureau to help
former slaves in their transition to freedom.
Clara Barton establishes the Office of Correspon-
dence with Friends of the Missing Men of the
United States Army.

**April 1865**
Confederate forces evacuate Richmond, Virginia.
Lee surrenders to Grant at Appomattox Court-
house, Virginia.
John Wilkes Booth assassinates President Lincoln
at Ford's Theater in Washington, D.C.
Andrew Johnson becomes president.

**May 1865**
General Oliver Otis Howard becomes head of the
Freedmen's Bureau.
Northerners celebrate the Union victory with
a parade down Pennsylvania Avenue in
Washington, D.C.

**July 1865**
Mary Surratt is hanged for her involvement in the
conspiracy to assassinate Lincoln.

**November 1865**
Mississippi passes the first black code.

**December 1865**
Congress ratifies the Thirteenth Amendment,
abolishing slavery.
The Ku Klux Klan forms in Pulaski, Tennessee.

**March 1866**
Congress enacts the Civil Rights Act of 1866.

**May 1866**
Susan B. Anthony and Elizabeth Cady Stanton
organize the Eleventh National Women's Rights
Convention in New York City.

**July 1866**
A race riot erupts in New Orleans.

**July 1867**
The Ladies' Memorial Association unveils the first monument to the Confederate dead in Cheraw, South Carolina.

**July 1868**
The Fourteenth Amendment is ratified. It grants citizenship to all men born or naturalized in the United States. The amendment introduces the term "male" to the Constitution.

**November 1868**
Ulysses S. Grant is elected president.

**February 1869**
Congress passes the Fifteenth Amendment that prevents states from denying voters the right to voice on the basis of race, color, or previous condition.

**May 1869**
Susan B. Anthony and Elizabeth Cady Stanton establish the National Woman Suffrage Association.

**December 1869**
Wyoming passes the first women's suffrage law in the United States.

**April 1871**
Congress passes the Civil Rights Act of 1871, also known as the Ku Klux Klan Act.

**June 1872**
Congress abolishes the Freedmen's Bureau.

**March 1875**
The United States Supreme Court, in *Miner v. Happersett,* concludes that citizenship does not guarantee suffrage.
The Civil Rights Act of 1875 guarantees that African Americans receive equal treatment in public facilities.

**November 1876**
Rutherford B. Hayes is elected president.

**April 1877**
Hayes orders the last federal troops to leave South Carolina, and Reconstruction comes to a formal end.

**May 1881**
Former Civil War nurse Clara Barton forms the American Association of the Red Cross.

**September 1894**
The United Daughters of the Confederacy is formed.

# Contextual Essays

## Abolitionism and Northern Reformers

Abolitionism is commonly dated from the 1830s; however, the movement has its earliest origins in the Enlightenment doctrine of human rights and in the evangelical attack on slavery during the Great Awakening of the eighteenth century. In the United States, this early stage of abolitionism peaked in the last quarter of the eighteenth and early years of the nineteenth centuries with the abolition of slavery in the Northern states and a ban on the international slave trade. In 1831, William Lloyd Garrison initiated a new era in the abolitionist movement with the publication of *The Liberator*. Garrison's call for the immediate abolition of slavery was influenced by the religious revivals of the 1820s and early 1830s. Revivalist ministers exhorted their followers to renounce their sinful ways and seek divine salvation through good deeds and a close, personal relationship with God. The reform movements of the nineteenth century began or were deeply influenced by the revivals of the Second Great Awakening. Abolitionism was the most extreme of the reform movements in the antebellum North, often operating at the margins of political and social life.

In the early nineteenth century, sweeping changes transformed American society. The development of manufacturers, cities, transportation, and wealth in the North altered American society, often in dramatic ways. Manufacturing first took hold in New England. Power and transportation provided by the extensive waterways of the region, as well as the steady influx of immigrant laborers, facilitated the growth of the factory system. Prior to the development of the factory system, manufacturing had been completed in home-based artisan workshops. As industrialization took hold in New England and elsewhere in the North, small mills were replaced by large factories, labor became an impersonal market commodity, and the social controls inherent in home-based manufacture disappeared.

The growth of an urban working class, economic instability, improvements in communication and transportation, and the development of a mass culture and popular publications impacted every aspect of American life. Universal suffrage also contributed to the extreme social dislocations of early nineteenth-century American life. After 1815, state after state revoked property qualifications for voting and holding elected office. Suffrage was generally extended only to white males, however, as states limited or, in some instances, denied political rights to black men and all women. Nevertheless, the expansion of political rights transformed spectators into citizens as more and more eligible voters turned out at the polls. By 1840, nearly 60 percent of eligible voters went to the polls.

The early nineteenth century was also a time of great religious excitement. The Second Great Awakening emerged partly as a result of the social dislocations of early nineteenth-century American life. Revivalist ministers like Charles Grandison Finney and Lyman Beecher encouraged followers to seek a more personal relationship with God. Sin, they preached, was the result of selfish choices made by men and women who possessed free will to choose otherwise. The social evils that revivalists and reformers believed had penetrated American society were not the result of any one event or person or institution. Rather the collective sinfulness of society contributed to social evils like drunkenness, lewd behavior, intemperate husbands, and poor work habits. Therefore, redeeming the individual would redeem society. The religious revivals of the 1820s and 1830s attracted a broad range of converts, including women, blacks, and Native Americans. Women, in particular, were frequent participants in the revivals. Inspired by this renewed religious spirit, converts formed movements to reform and educate Americans. Movements for the abolition of slavery, educational reform, penal reform, temperance, women's rights, and moral reform (i.e., the elimination of prostitution, lewdness, and obscenity) all grew out of the religious ferment and the social dislocations of the early nineteenth century.

Northern middle-class Whigs were the most prominent reformers. Motivated by the religious revivals and the sin and disorder they saw throughout American society, Northern reformers established institutions and social movements to improve the morals of individuals and of society. Educational reform led to the establishment of tax-supported public schools. Reformers like Calvin Stowe of Ohio and Horace Mann of Massachusetts proposed public schools that would be controlled by the states and that would require attendance by all children. They emphasized teaching reading, writing, arithmetic, and good citizenship. Reformers believed that establishing public schools would open education to the masses and build the character of individual students who in turn would become good citizens. The extension of suffrage to all free males helped advance the educational reform movement because politicians worried about the effects of an illiterate electorate exercising the right to vote. Throughout the North, public schools were established along the lines advocated by Mann and other educational reformers. In the South, however, educational reform made little progress.

Prison reform was another significant movement of the era. Rather than punishing the prisoner through whippings, incarceration, or execution, prison reformers sought to improve the soul of the convict. Prison reformers believed crime was the result of prisoners' childhood neglect. Rehabilitation therefore was the only way to counteract the trauma of such an upbringing. Rehabilitative programs emphasized instruction, personal discipline, and order. Reformers believed that former prisoners, once rehabilitated, would exercise the self-discipline necessary to become productive members of society. The prison reform movement also sparked an effort to reform how the mentally ill were treated. Until the 1840s, the mentally ill were incarcerated in poor houses or more often in prisons, which only worsened their conditions. Reformer Dorothea Dix helped lead a movement to establish insane asylums to rehabilitate the mentally ill.

The temperance movement was the largest and most sustained of all the social movements of the period. The social upheaval in early nineteenth-century America contributed to a remarkable rise in the production and consumption of alcohol. Northern Whig evangelicals, concerned over the rising popularity of drinking, established temperance organizations, most prominently the American Temperance Society formed in 1826. Reformers believed drinking led to a host of social evils, including poverty, crime, family violence, and poor child rearing. As the movement expanded in the 1830s, more and more workers joined the movement out of concern over the effects of alcohol consumption on job performance. By 1835 reformers had established more than five thousand temperance societies throughout the United States. By the 1840s, the temperance movement had successfully reduced alcohol consumption, and by the 1850s many states had limited or prohibited the sale of alcohol.

Abolitionism was the most prominent and probably the most controversial of the reform movements that emerged in the 1820s and 1830s. In the Revolutionary era, antislavery societies were generally organized by white elite males, often members of the Society of Friends (the Quakers). The New York Manumission Society (NYMS) and the Pennsylvania Abolition Society (PAS) were among the earliest and most prominent of these first-generation abolitionist organizations. The NYMS and the PAS fought for gradual emancipation, which they believed would be achieved after the international slave trade was abolished. Early abolitionist efforts were strikingly different from the abolitionist movement under way just before the Civil War. The NYMS and the PAS, along with other early abolition societies, did not emphasize the sinfulness of slavery, seeking instead to mediate the conditions of slavery and bring about its eventual demise through gradual emancipation.

After the 1808 abolition of the international slave trade, abolitionist activity waned until the founding of the American Colonization Society (ACS) in 1817 by abolitionists who hoped to establish an American colony in Africa for freed slaves and free blacks. Addressing concerns over the presence of a large, free black population should slavery be abolished, colonizationists hoped that slaveholders could be encouraged to free their slaves if, once emancipated, they would emigrate to Africa. Members of the ACS believed that blacks and whites could not live together and that blacks would be assured of their rights only if they were settled in their own colony. Though racist in its worldview, the ACS gained the support of Christian antislavery activists. However, the ACS failed to win the support of black activists, who feared forced emigration to Africa. Black and white antislavery activists believed the ACS to be antiblack, not antislavery, because of its racist intentions and numerous concessions to slaveholders. Throughout the 1820s and 1830s, black and white abolitionists organized to fight the colonization movement. This organizational activity against the ACS encouraged participation in the abolitionist movement by women and African Americans, two groups that generally had been excluded from early organizations established to fight slavery.

The 1831 publication of the first issue of William Lloyd Garrison's *The Liberator* is often used to date the start of the nineteenth-century abolition movement. With this inaugural issue, Garrison helped birth a new, radical abolitionist movement that called for an immediate end to slavery and equality for African Americans. Influenced by the revivals of

the 1820s, Garrison declared slavery a sin that had to be abolished without delay. Slavery prevented blacks from exercising their innate free will to make good choices. Slavery also corrupted the slaveholder by sanctioning brute force, lust, and hatred of an entire group of people. To fight slavery, Garrison established the New England Anti-Slavery Society in 1832. In 1833, Garrison also helped form the American Anti-Slavery Society (AASS), the first such national organization. By 1840, abolitionists had established more than fifteen hundred local organizations.

The abolitionist movement of the 1830s, like other reform movements of the period, drew from a broad base of support, including women, blacks, and white men of all classes. However, the evangelical middle class of New England, upstate New York, and the Old Northwest, particularly Ohio, provided the movement's primary constituency. Garrison dominated the New England group, while Arthur and Lewis Tappan dominated the New York group and James G. Birney, Elizur Wright, and Theodore D. Weld dominated antislavery activity in Ohio. The evangelical middle class lived in a reform society that saw social evils closing in all around them. Moral free will and Christian love were locked in battle against brutality and power, particularly in the institution of slavery, and it was the reformers' responsibility to take that fight to the masses.

Unlike other nineteenth-century reform movements, abolitionism constituted a minority of the reform movement and occupied the margins of American political and social life. Abolitionists were often confronted by mobs of angry proslavery supporters who sought to silence the reformers. In 1835, the abolitionists' postal campaign sparked a wave of mob violence throughout the North and South. Abolitionists targeted ministers, politicians, and newspaper editors throughout the South, inundating them with thousands of pieces of abolitionist literature. If slaveholders could be convinced of the hostility of world opinion, abolitionists believed, they would realize the futility of their fight against the antislavery movement. By the end of 1837, the AASS estimated that more than a million pieces of antislavery literature had been sent south. However, any hopes of peacefully converting slaveholders to an antislavery position were dashed in the wave of violence that followed the postal campaigns. In 1835, angry South Carolinians broke into the Charleston post office and destroyed the antislavery literature. The mob later hanged Garrison and Arthur Tappan in effigy before burning the effigies and the abolitionist newspapers in a massive bonfire. Throughout the South, slaveholders established vigilance societies to search incoming mail and to confiscate and destroy any abolitionist literature.

Similar antiabolitionist riots broke out in the North. In 1835, British abolitionist George Thompson was greeted by mobs everywhere he went. Later that year in Boston, antiabolitionist mobs looking for Thompson found Garrison instead and dragged him through the city streets. Violence peaked with the murder of Elijah P. Lovejoy, a printer in Alton, Illinois, who had refused to back down from his antislavery stand. In November 1837, mobs set fire to the warehouse where Lovejoy and his supporters had gathered to guard his press. When Lovejoy ran from the burning building he was shot, making him the movement's first martyr.

In the mid-1830s, abolitionists also began an intensive national antislavery petition campaign. Abolitionists had already petitioned Congress for an end to slavery in Washington, D.C., and for an end to the interstate slave trade. The national campaign launched in 1835 emphasized local effort as volunteers went door to door, gathering signatures on antislavery petitions bound for Congress. The grassroots approach of the petition campaign appealed to women and to others who found signing the petitions a safe and effective way to voice their support for the abolitionist cause. By May 1838, the AASS reported that it had sent more than four hundred and fifteen thousand petitions to Congress. Over half of those petitions bore the signatures of women; however, no Congressional action was taken because the petitions were automatically tabled as a result of the gag rule, implemented in 1836. The gag rule was passed during the height of antislavery violence when Northern and Southern politicians, with various motives, sought to quell sectional hostilities. In force until 1844, the gag rule ironically contributed to the growing sectionalism of American politics and did much to politicize the American abolition movement.

Mob violence was not limited to the cause of antislavery itself. Women, who were particularly prominent in the temperance and antislavery crusades, were taking an increasingly active stand in both movements. However, women's involvement in the abolitionist effort provoked the greatest controversy. Women had been involved from the beginning of the second-generation abolitionist movement, and they had been involved in benevolent organizations since the 1790s, caring for widows and orphans, assisting the aged, and providing medical care for pregnant women. However, women's involvement in reform movements, especially abolitionism, was markedly different from their work in benevolent organizations. Benevolent organizations adhered to a deferential mode of politics. Women active in such organizations used private influence to gain the financial and political support necessary for their work. Benevolent organizations focused on improving the moral character of the individual and on promoting social order. Women's reform groups, however, drew members from more varied social backgrounds, organizing across both race and class lines. Women reformers also sought political support from a large group of politicians and citizens, employing controversy to publicize their work and to bring out about sweeping social changes. Furthermore, women reformers and their supporters called on other women to identify with fallen, poor, or enslaved women. Garrison and other abolitionists used this tactic to recruit women for the antislavery movement by using real or implied images of women in bondage and subject to indiscriminate whippings.

Women responded in large numbers to the call for the immediate abolition of slavery. They participated in local, state, and national organizations and formed antislavery societies that served as auxiliaries to larger, male-dominated organizations. The Boston Female Anti-Slavery Society (BFASS), formed in 1833 as auxiliary to the Massachusetts Anti-Slavery Society, is an example of female abolitionist activity in the 1830s. Counting prominent members like Helen Garrison and Lydia Maria

Text of "Make the slave's case our own" anti-slavery speech of Susan B. Anthony, ca. 1859. (Library of Congress)

Child among its membership, the group also recruited working-class women and black women to join in the fight. The BFASS followed the traditional pattern of women's involvement in antislavery societies by organizing antislavery fairs to raise funds for the state society, circulating petitions, aiding in the creation and distribution of antislavery literature, and establishing institutions like the Samaritan Asylum for indigent black children.

By the mid-1830s women took on more public roles in the fight against slavery. In 1836, Garrison hired Angelina and Sarah Grimké as lecturers for the AASS. As members of a well-known slaveholding South Carolina family, the Grimké sisters proved powerful spokespersons for the antislavery cause and quickly became favored speakers on the antislavery lecture circuit. Within a short time, the women were attracting mixed-sex audiences, which shocked the general Northern public. The Congregational clergy rebuked them in 1837, declaring

that, when women like the Grimkés assumed the public role of men, they risked shame and dishonor.

The growing activism of women in the antislavery movement brought the issue of women's rights to the fore. The temperance and antislavery movements had given women a chance to be publicly involved in reforming society. Women reformers soon began agitating for their own rights as well as for temperance and abolition. The Grimké sisters, Elizabeth Cady Stanton, and Lucretia Mott had all been active in the antislavery movement. These women and their supporters, including William Lloyd Garrison, argued that men and women were created equal and should be treated as equals under the law. The movement for women's rights, like abolitionism, was more radical than mainstream reform movements like temperance, education, and prison reform. Equal rights for women carried serious implications for black civic rights if slavery were abolished. If women and blacks achieved full civic rights, opponents predicted social chaos.

The debate over the place of women's rights within the antislavery movement split the movement in 1840. Conservatives like Lewis and Arthur Tappan worried that the controversy over women's rights would taint the abolitionist cause. After years of fighting with Garrison and other radicals in the movement, the Tappan brothers and other conservatives left the AASS and formed the American and Foreign Anti-Slavery Society (AFASS). Garrison assumed leadership of the AASS, which maintained a broad reform platform that included women's rights. Garrison recruited all abolitionists regardless of religious, social, or political views. He was a particularly avid supporter of women's involvement in the abolitionist movement. Lewis Tappan, however, argued that mixing abolitionism with other reform movements threatened the antislavery cause. Antislavery must remain orthodox, he argued. Failure to remain compatible with traditional views of issues like women's rights might alienate the general Northern public. Abolitionists should instead focus on a single reform movement.

In addition to establishing organizations to reform American society, Northern reformers organized national and international gatherings to further publicize their cause. For example, in the late 1830s, women abolitionists organized three Anti-Slavery Conventions of Women. The conventions, held in 1837, 1838, and 1839, signaled the growing involvement of women in the antislavery movement. The convention speeches encouraged traditional antislavery activism, and delegates passed resolutions to abolish slavery in Washington, D.C., and the territories. Delegates also passed a resolution calling on women to play a more public role in the abolition of slavery. The 1837 convention drew two hundred women. A year later, more than three hundred women attended the second convention; however, the success of the event was marred by mob violence. The violence of the second convention made locating the third convention difficult, and a much smaller crowd attended in 1839.

As reformers sought to broaden their humanitarian efforts, international gatherings became a logical step forward in the progression. The first World's Anti-Slavery Convention inaugurated numerous international gatherings on a variety of reform issues. Prior to the 1840 convention, the only international meetings were church-organized councils. In addition to the antislavery conventions of 1840 and 1843, other international congresses were held focusing on peace, temperance, prison reform, agriculture, and free trade. The first World Peace Convention in 1843 and the first World Temperance Convention in 1846 were part of a growing trend to organize reformers on an international level. Prison reform and free trade congresses were held in 1846 and 1847. Motivating these international gatherings was the reformers' desire for international cooperation in all manner of social and moral reform.

The idea for the World's Anti-Slavery Convention began in 1839, when the newly formed British and Foreign Anti-Slavery Society (BFASS) began discussing the possibility of hosting such a convention to bring together representative abolitionists from throughout the world. Members of the BFASS, particularly British abolitionist Joseph Sturge, organized the world gathering of abolitionists. Dubbed the London Committee, the organizers gathered information and statistics about slavery and the slave trade from around the globe.

Additionally, the Committee provided convention tickets only to recognized members of antislavery organizations and made it clear that only male delegates would be seated. The AASS selected a prowoman's rights delegation including Lucretia Mott, Wendell Phillips, and Garrison. However, Garrison and many of his close associates delayed their departure for the convention because of the mid-May meeting of the AASS, which ultimately gave the more radical Garrison control of the society. Garrison arrived on the fifth day of the convention to find that the London Committee had refused to seat the organization's women delegates. In protest Garrison sat in the balcony with the ladies rather than enter the convention and be seated with the other delegates.

The first World's Anti-Slavery Convention included discussions of free labor versus slave labor, endorsing the former as a means of combating slavery, and the role of the church in supporting slavery in the United States. Delegates issued admonitions, memorials, and addresses to the people of Great Britain and the United States, but ultimately the convention could do little more than continue the moral and political campaign against slavery where it existed.

A second World's Anti-Slavery Convention was held in London in 1843. Planners had considered holding the convention in the United States but decided conditions were not favorable for an international gathering of abolitionists. The second convention was not as well attended as the first, and only sixteen of the three hundred delegates were from the United States. Garrison and his supporters had not been invited. Instead, Lewis Tappan led the American delegation. As in the earlier convention, delegates discussed the use of slave labor versus free labor and the church's role in supporting U.S. slavery. They also discussed the possible annexation of Texas by the United States. While other reform movements continued to hold international gatherings throughout the 1840s, the second World's Anti-Slavery Convention marked the end of any organized international gathering of abolitionists.

While antislavery activists continued their fight during the politically charged 1850s, it was not until the Civil War that the abolitionist movement was reenergized with a new sense of purpose that allowed it to transcend some of the 1840s divisions. Early wartime abolitionist and reform activities resembled those of the antebellum era, as abolitionists conducted petition drives and held conventions. Abolitionists also called on President Abraham Lincoln to make the war about slavery rather than just the preservation of the Union. Most abolitionists saw the Civil War as the culmination of decades of work aimed at abolishing slavery and gaining civic rights for blacks. When the Emancipation Proclamation took effect on January 1, 1863, abolitionists' work took on even greater urgency.

During the Civil War, hundreds of abolitionists went south to teach freed slaves and tend to their material needs. When Union soldiers occupied South Carolina's Sea Islands in late 1861, abolitionists saw an opportunity to bring literacy to the freed slaves and to refute the commonly held view that blacks were inherently inferior. For abolitionists, educating the freed slaves was an extension of their antislavery activities. By war's end, more than nine hundred Northerners, including agents of Lewis Tappan's American Missionary Association (AMA), were teaching in the South. During the war, the AMA began schools for freed slaves throughout the South, and by 1867 it had established hundreds of schools in every Southern state. Women also headed south, as agents for the Freedmen's Aid Commission, to tend to the various physical, spiritual, and mental needs of the freed slaves.

During the Civil War, other antebellum Northern reformers turned their focus to raising regiments for the Union and then sustaining the soldiers. Throughout the North, women collected medical supplies and other sundries for soldiers on the battlefield. New York women established the Women's Central Association of Relief (WCAR) to coordinate the wartime relief work of women throughout the state. The WCAR eventually became a regional branch of the United States Sanitary Commission (USSC), a male-led national organization established in 1861 to coordinate women's war work throughout the North. Women also formed local soldiers' aid societies to gather

and send much needed supplies to the men in the field. The United States Christian Commission (USCC), also established in 1861, brought ministers and tracts to tend to the spiritual needs of soldiers. Building on the earlier work of evangelical ministers and the American Tract Society, the Christian Commission often clashed with the Sanitary Commission. The Christian Commission was established and operated under an older style of benevolence based in traditional grassroots evangelicalism, whereas the Sanitary Commission embraced a new style of reform, developed during the Civil War, that placed greater emphasis on the efficiency and centralized control of relief work.

The end of the Civil War resulted in the adoption of the Thirteenth Amendment abolishing slavery. The American Anti-Slavery Society continued under the direction of Wendell Phillips until 1870 and the passage of the Fourteenth and Fifteenth amendments guaranteeing black citizens protection of their civil rights.

*Julie Holcomb*

***See also*** Aid Societies; Antislavery Societies; Child, Lydia Maria Francis (1802–1880); Dix, Dorothea Lynde (1802–1887); Education, Northern; Education, Southern; Emancipation Proclamation (January 1, 1863); Factory Workers, Northern; Fairs and Bazaars; Fifteenth Amendment; Fourteenth Amendment; Garrison, William Lloyd (1805–1879); Grimké (Weld), Angelina (1805–1879); Grimké, Sarah Moore (1792–1873); Lincoln, Abraham (1809–1865); Mott, Lucretia Coffin (1793–1880); Northern Women; Politics; Quaker Women; Religion; Stanton, Elizabeth Cady (1815–1902); Teachers, Northern; Thirteenth Amendment; United States Christian Commission; United States Sanitary Commission.

**References and Further Reading**

Fladeland, Betty. 1972. *Men and Brothers: Anglo-American Antislavery Cooperation.* Urbana: University of Illinois Press.

Geisberg, Judith Ann. 2000. *Civil War Sisterhood: The U.S. Sanitary Commission and Women's Politics in Transition.* Boston: Northeastern University Press.

Ginzberg, Lori D. 1990. *Women and the Work of Benevolence: Morality, Politics, and Class in the Nineteenth-Century United States.* New Haven, CT: Yale University Press.

Hansen, Debra Gold. 1993. *Strained Sisterhood: Gender and Class in the Boston Female Anti-Slavery Society.* Amherst: University of Massachusetts Press.

Jeffrey, Julie Roy. 1998. *The Great Silent Army of Abolitionism: Ordinary Women in the Antislavery Movement.* Chapel Hill: University of North Carolina Press.

Kraditor, Alison. 1967. *Means and Ends in American Abolitionism: Garrison and His Critics on Strategy and Tactics, 1834–1850.* New York: Random House.

Newman, Richard S. 2002. *The Transformation of American Abolitionism: Fighting Slavery in the Early Republic.* Chapel Hill: University of North Carolina Press.

Stewart, James Brewer. 1997. *Holy Warriors: The Abolitionists and American Slavery.* New York: Hill and Wang.

## African American Women

The American Civil War was a defining event for African American men and women. Most drastically, the war turned slaves into freed people, emancipating nearly 4 million black slaves from generations of bondage. Although many of the freedoms that emerged during and after the war would be temporary, African Americans used the war to secure the legal and social rights that had long been denied them. The Civil War also created crises for black women; they suffered from wartime shortages, the dangers of invasion, race- and gender-based hiring policies, refugee life, and the absence of many loved ones. The era of Reconstruction that followed eradicated their race-based form of bondage but confirmed that patriarchy would continue in a postslavery American society.

When the American Civil War began, the United States contained 4.4 million African Americans. Nearly half a million were free blacks, whereas the majority were enslaved in the Southern and border states. African Americans comprised approximately 31 percent of the total Southern population, and Mississippi and South Carolina had slave majorities. Although most slaveholding Southerners owned fewer than five slaves, the majority of slaves lived on large plantations growing staple crops like cotton, rice, and tobacco. Within this context, African American slaves created vibrant yet precarious communities. About 10 percent of African American slaves lived in the nation's towns and cities. There they intermingled with the free black population, working as craftspeople, manual laborers, and domestics.

Even before the Civil War, African Americans recognized that they had a tremendous stake in the sectional conflict. Black abolitionists and former slaves like Frederick Douglass, Harriet Jacobs, and Sojourner Truth used their firsthand experiences to help the cause. In their oral and written narratives, Jacobs and Truth offered a feminine voice on the abuses of slavery and the particular problems faced by slave women. Jacobs, in her *Incidents in the Life of a Slave Girl*, described the problems of sexual assault in a society that denied black women protection from white men. Jacobs hoped that her descriptions of her abuse by her white master would help persuade middle-class women to join the abolitionist cause. Similarly, in her speeches, Truth pointed to the sexual injustices of slavery. Denied the rights of a mother, sister, and wife, Truth went on the lecture circuit and famously asked, "ar'n't I a woman?" (Gilbert 1968, 134).

When the Civil War began in 1861, African Americans played an increasingly active role in shaping its ideological direction. Although emancipation was not recognized as a war aim at the beginning of the conflict, many African Americans took steps to push President Abraham Lincoln and the federal government in this direction. Through their actions and words, free and enslaved blacks worked to end the institution of slavery. At the start of the war, returning runaway slaves to their owners was the official policy of the United States. Despite this reality, as Union troops approached slaveholding homesteads and occupied Confederate territory, hundreds of African Americans pressed the issue by fleeing to Union lines.

Although Lincoln refused to incorporate an antislavery and abolitionist stance in his policies, some of his commanders realized the utility of freeing Southern slaves as a way of impeding the Confederacy. On August 30, 1861, John C. Frémont, commander of the Western Department, proclaimed the slaves of all Confederates in Missouri to be free. Although Lincoln asked Frémont to modify this order and only confiscate property, including slaves, that Confederates directly used to aid their war effort, Frémont refused to comply with the president's wishes. In response, Lincoln removed Frémont from command and revoked the emancipation order. Lincoln's actions outraged abolitionists, who understood the need to strike down slavery in order to win the war.

The path to official emancipation remained a slow one, however. Eventually, the growing numbers of slaves running to Union lines forced the issue. When three slaves escaped to General Benjamin Butler's lines in Virginia in May 1861, he ruled that the state's decision to secede released him from the terms of the Fugitive Slave Act. He consequently determined the runaways to be contraband of war, including them in a category that applied to any enemy property used in the pursuit of the Confederate war effort. Lincoln approved the policy and by July approximately one thousand contrabands—men, women, and children—had run to Union lines. The congressional vote on the issue allowed the confiscation of property but still refused to recognize contrabands as free people. Even so, once they escaped to Union lines, these African Americans lived under the protection of the United States government and were not eligible to be returned to their owners. It was not until Lincoln's 1863 Emancipation Proclamation that freeing the slaves became a war aim and tactic.

At the start of the war, many African Americans volunteered to serve in the army only to be turned away. Instead, Northern free blacks frequently found their labor impressed by the Union cause. Even before they were permitted to enlist in the Union army, local officials forced them to perform unpaid menial labor on behalf of the Union cause. In the fall of 1862, for example, Cincinnati officials used the threats of bayonets and jail to coerce a group of free blacks to perform hard labor. The policy concerning the enlistment of African Americans changed in the summer of 1862, with the creation of the First Kansas Colored Infantry. After the Union formed

the Louisiana Native Guards and the First South Carolina Infantry, it turned its attention to forming a Northern black regiment. In January 1863, the Union mustered the Massachusetts Fifty-fourth, and other black regiments formed throughout the remainder of the war. By the end of the war, approximately two hundred and sixteen thousand African American men had enlisted in the Union army and navy. Although many soldiers were single men, many left wives behind to manage the household and other chores. For the wives and mothers of the more than thirty-seven thousand black soldiers who were killed, the war brought immeasurable emotional pains.

With the establishment of black regiments, many African American women became unofficial recruiters for the Union army. Harriet Jacobs and Josephine St. Pierre Ruffin, for example, both helped raise troops for the Massachusetts Fifty-fourth. They, like most African American women, recruited for the Union army as volunteers. An exception to this rule was Mary Ann Shadd Cary. In August 1864, Indiana Governor Levi P. Morton made her the only paid female recruiting officer for the Union army, when he commissioned Cary to raise a black regiment. Later in the war, Cary also worked as a paid fundraiser for Chicago's Colored Ladies Freedmen's Aid Society. Ironically, the success of black recruiters led to the increased workload on female African Americans on the Northern homefront.

Economic needs and political desires led many African American women to perform a myriad of tasks to assist the United States in its war effort. Whether slave or free, African Americans were accustomed to working in a variety of contexts when the war began. As a result, many free black women took jobs with the federal government to provide themselves with the basic necessities. About a quarter of a million African Americans officially worked for the Union and Confederate armies as laborers, servants, and laundresses. Many of these workers were women whose husbands or fathers had enlisted in the Union army and who therefore could not completely provide for their families. African American women worked as nurses, cooks, seamstresses, teachers, and relief workers. They nursed wounded soldiers, raised money and supplies to aid troops, and recruited soldiers to enlist in the Union army. African American women received lower wages than did African American men and white women who performed comparable work. In 1864, African American female nurses and cooks received $10 per month plus rations. In addition to the relatively low wages, the federal government routinely treated its black workers with disregard and failed to meet their economic obligations. As a result, many African American women filed formal applications to be paid for the work that they did. Most of these petitions failed to secure the promised wages. In addition, some African American women performed labor without pay in relationships that nearly paralleled Southern slavery. In these cases, African American women provided their labor under the knowledge that their hard work might secure the freedom of the nation's African Americans.

Many African American women volunteered to educate the swelling population of freed people. Although most of the teachers hired by the American Missionary Association were white, the association also hired black teachers. Most of the black teachers came from wealthy and well-connected families and frequently believed that they could force a more radical vision of what postemancipation society might resemble. As a result, African American teachers often focused much of their efforts on teaching their students about the importance of voting, racial uplift, and African American history. Charlotte Forten, for example, worked as a teacher in the North prior to the war and went to Port Royal, South Carolina, to teach recently freed slaves from 1862 to 1864. She, like many other Northern black teachers, thought education could eradicate the myths that pervaded society about black ignorance, laziness, and intellectual inferiority. In addition, poor African American women, unable to obtain employment with schools, served as teachers in an informal fashion, tutoring within their communities. Others taught African American soldiers who served with their husbands.

Just as the United States was slow to enlist African American soldiers, it was also slow to hire African American women for certain professions. The United States, for example, did not hire African American nurses until January 16, 1864. Even after hiring black nurses, the Union often relegated them to jobs doing menial hospital tasks. Rather than tending to the sick and wounded, many black nurses did laundry, cooked meals, cleaned, and performed other domestic tasks. Nevertheless, African American women increasingly found employment with the federal government during the war.

Some black women worked directly for the Union military. Hundreds of African American women risked their lives to assist the Union war effort, serving as spies and scouts. These courageous women passed Confederate secrets on to Union soldiers, informing them of maneuvers, troop numbers, and other vital information. For example, in addition to leading hundreds of slaves to freedom during the war, Harriet Tubman served as a scout or spy on several occasions. The intelligence Tubman provided to Colonel James Montgomery, the African American commander of the Second South Carolina Volunteers, allowed Montgomery to destroy several Confederate warehouses and ammunition depots. In addition, many African American women provided tactical assistance while they performed domestic chores. For example, Susie Baker, who later became Susie King Taylor, routinely cleaned guns and taught soldiers to read while she officially served as a laundress and nurse.

A few black women served as soldiers in the Union army. To do so, African American women, like other female soldiers, had to hide their sex. As a result, the number of female black soldiers remains uncertain. Scholars have discovered that Virginian Maria Lewis served with the Eighth New York Calvary, yet most of her life remains obscure. Other African American women fought without officially enlisting in the Union army. On several occasions, the Union army received military assistance from the scores of African American refugee families who followed the Union army as it advanced through the South. Similarly, many African American women marched alongside their husbands when they went off to battle, helping out with various chores and otherwise suffering from the discomforts of wartime marches. Confederate soldiers, outraged by the presence of African American soldiers, sometimes took out their fury on black women as well. For example, at the Fort Pillow massacre, one woman was killed after the battle as she retrieved the body of her slain husband.

Like their white counterparts, many black women formed organizations to help their enlisted loved ones, provide assistance for the widows of killed soldiers, and otherwise help the Union war effort. Women's aid societies tended to be segregated, and black women's organizations formed out of a fear that other Union relief groups would not assist black soldiers. Some aid societies were extensions of African American churches, whereas others grew out of abolitionist organizations. These societies collected and donated food, clothing, cooking utensils, bandages, cash, and other goods to help muster and support black regiments. In addition, just as did white women, black women formed sewing circles to create uniforms, socks, and regimental flags for their men. They also wrote letters to soldiers for illiterate members of the community, assisted at local hospitals by comforting and caring for wounded soldiers, and raised money in their communities through fairs, bazaars, and solicitations.

Many African Americans became refugees during the Civil War. Once white slaveholding civilians abandoned their homes, their slaves frequently left to find loved ones and otherwise experience freedom. Many of these refugees congregated in the nation's cities. Refugee and urban populations consequently flourished as the war progressed. In 1862, for example, approximately four hundred escaped slaves had congregated in Washington, D.C. At the end of the war, the refugee population swelled to forty thousand.

Refugee camps were established across Union-occupied areas to shelter these former slaves. Life was difficult in the camps; African American women were expected to support themselves despite the dearth of employment opportunities. Black women frequently leaned on one another for support, pooling resources, sharing food, living together, and tending to communal gardens. In many Northern cities, black women formed relief organizations to assist local and distant refugees. Some African American groups collaborated with white organizations by creating auxiliary associations or by joining them. For example, Elizabeth Keckley, first lady Mary Todd Lincoln's seamstress, was a member of the integrated National Association for the Relief of Destitute Colored Women and Children in Washington, D.C. Keckley was also a founder of the Contraband Relief Association, an all-black organization formed in August 1862. Others joined and assisted with integrated abolitionist organizations that extended their missions to deal with the refugees.

The war provided African American women the opportunity to expose many of the racial inequities that existed in Northern society. Using the enlistment of their husbands and sons as leverage, these women confronted various forms of mistreatment. In the summer of 1864, for example, African American women, who were refused seats on the train when they traveled to Camp William Penn to tend to wounded black soldiers, protested their treatment on trains. This protest led to few changes during the war, and Philadelphia did not prohibit discrimination on streetcars until 1867. Elsewhere, African American women were more successful in their protests. In 1864 New York, for example, an African American widow of a killed black soldier had a conductor arrested for assault after he forced her off the streetcar. This and other victories were closely watched by the African American press and brought renewed confidence to the courts to institute social change.

For numerous reasons, most slaves remained on Southern plantations and farms throughout the war, despite opportunities to escape. Many stayed out of fears that stemmed from rumors of abuse by federal soldiers or from concern about retribution by owners for running away. Others remained out of a general reluctance to abandon gardens and homes that they had built and lived in all their lives. Perhaps the most compelling reason to remain where they were, however, was family; many African American women believed that, if they left their homes, their loved ones would not be able to find them. As a result, most Southern African Americans lived as slaves during the war.

Slaves of Confederate General Thomas F. Drayton at his plantation on Hilton Head Island, South Carolina, during May 1862. (Library of Congress)

In some ways, life on the plantation initially remained unchanged for slave women at the start of war. Slave masters continued to treat slave women as their sexual property and abused them as they had for generations. Slave sales continued for years into the war, and physical beatings continued for any woman caught defying the wishes of her owner. The war, though, compounded many of the abuses associated with slave life and created new ones. Many slaves put slave women at risk when they decided to run away, stop working, or disobey their owners. Many slave women were punished for these actions, even when they were not the perpetrators. In other instances, slave women were brutally punished by their masters and mistresses in their desperate attempts to maintain control of a society that seemed to be crumbling from within.

The lives of slave women also underwent tremendous changes during the war. Many disruptions resulted from wartime shortages and the enlistment of Confederate men; others resulted directly from actions within the slave community. Many slaves found ways to fight for their freedom without leaving the plantation. They committed acts of arson, vandalism, and generally sabotaged the Southern economy. In some instances, they intentionally poisoned livestock and generally slowed down the pace of work in the fields. Others stole food and other valuable supplies and sneaked them to Union soldiers. Slave women also helped captured Union soldiers escape, and they cared for wounded and sick Union soldiers without the knowledge of their owners. In short, slave women helped destroy any sense of tranquility on the Southern homefront.

Slave masters frequently disrupted the lives of slave women by impressing them and, more often, their husbands into wartime service. The impressment of slave labor did not end with the arrival of Union troops, which often brought new hardships. As they foraged and looted their way through the South, Union soldiers frequently failed to distinguish between the private property of Confederate families and items that belonged to the slave community. In addition to stealing the property of slaves, some Union soldiers also committed acts of rape and sexual assault on slave women. Union soldiers raped slave women more often than they sexually assaulted white Confederates. These actions, which were comparable to the treatment of slave women by Confederate deserters and returning soldiers, often surprised slave women who had initially come to see Union soldiers as natural allies and emancipators. Similar acts of abuse occurred as slave refugees left their homes for the presumed safety of Union camps.

As the Southern economy and social structure strained in the face of the war and Southern civilians suffered increased prices as well as shortages of food and basic supplies, African American women found themselves in a precarious position. Although surrounded by cotton, Southern civilians increasingly faced a scarcity of cloth. Consequently, the custom of providing slaves with new clothing came to an end. At the outset of the war, for example, slaves on one South Carolina plantation received pants but no coat. By the final months of the war, new clothing was provided to very few. Shoes were equally hard to come by, as were some tools and refined foods. In addition, slave women found that their workloads changed and increased as a result of the war. The impressment of horses and mules left them with fewer work animals to perform routine fieldwork. Furthermore, the confiscation, sale, and wartime killing of livestock left them with even less meat than was normal. As a result, slaves often ate and wore only what they could create themselves. Several coastal plantations, for example, included only rice in the allotted wartime rations for the slaves. As a result, Union soldiers frequently saw hungry, malnourished, half-naked slaves as they marched through the Southern countryside.

Workloads on plantations also changed as a result of the war. On some plantations, masters increased or changed the agricultural tasks to cope with the naval blockades. With the diets and fashion of white Southerners tied to slave production, workloads increased for slave women. They spun more cotton into homespun, wove more cloth, made more clothing, and otherwise performed more domestic tasks than they had prior to the war. With many slave men impressed into the Confederate army to perform labor, many female domestic slaves found themselves working in the fields during the day and sewing at night.

At the same time, with many white men and overseers gone, many female slaves discovered a more autonomous life during the war. Many plantation mistresses and overseers watched as their slaves routinely ignored directives and otherwise chose when to work and what work to do. During the war, slave women frequently traveled to other plantations to visit loved ones and to get information. It was within this realm of autonomy that many slave women were able to pass military information to Union officers. In addition, a general inability to govern the wartime plantation allowed for the expansion of illicit trade among slaves. During the Civil War, the slaves' clandestine trade of crafts and food with poor whites and free blacks extended to trade with Union soldiers. In many cases, it also extended to wealthy white Southerners who were suffering from shortages as well. The expansion of autonomy was especially true in areas like Port Royal, South Carolina, where thousands of slaves gradually obtained their freedom when the Union occupied their lands.

When the war ended, African American women took the opportunity to reunite with husbands, children, and other loved ones from whom they had been separated prior to and during the war. They waited for soldiers to return home, scavenged for information about where their families were, and frequently made plans to legally sanctify their relationships. In this postslavery society, marriage became synonymous with freedom for many Southern black women. Officially barred to them in slavery, marriage became a way to secure and demonstrate their new rights as citizens. As a result, in the immediate aftermath of the war, thousands of African American couples recorded marriages that had been socially established years beforehand.

African Americans celebrated the end of the Civil War and their emancipation nationwide. In many towns and cities, African Americans held orchestrated parades and other festivities. They welcomed home soldiers, made speeches that pointed to the possibilities lying ahead, and otherwise celebrated the contributions of blacks to the war. As in many of the vigils that took place on December 31, 1862—the eve of the Emancipation Proclamation—women figured prominently in many of these celebrations.

The passing of the Thirteenth, Fourteenth, and Fifteenth Amendments brought a legal end to slavery and established a new place for African American citizens and voters. The Fifteenth Amendment, however, did not provide suffrage to African American women. Much to the dismay of many white and black women, it specifically extended the vote to African American men and refrained from leaving any misunderstanding by including the term "male." African American women further suffered from the Union's decision to provide few means for economic freedom. Although Africans Americans shook off the shackles of slavery, a race-based economy remained. In this postbellum society, whites provide the capital and blacks provided the hard labor.

*Andrew K. Frank*

***See also*** Abolitionism and Northern Reformers; Aid Societies; Antislavery Societies; Camp Followers; Cary, Mary Ann Shadd (1823–1893); Civilian Life; Confederate Homefront; Contraband Relief Association; Contrabands; Courtship and Marriage; Destruction of Personal Property; Douglass, Frederick (ca. 1817–1895); Emancipation Proclamation (January 1, 1863); Enlistment; Fairs and Bazaars; Farm Work; Female Combatants; Female Spies; Fifteenth Amendment; Flags, Regimental; Food; Foraging, Effects on Women; Forten (Grimké), Charlotte L. (1837–1914); Fourteenth Amendment; Free Blacks; Freedmen's Bureau; Frémont, Jessie Benton, (1824–1902);

Fundraising; Homespun; Hospitals; Impressment; Jacobs, Harriet Ann [Linda Brent] (1813–1897); Keckley, Elizabeth Hobbs (ca. 1818–1907); Lincoln, Abraham (1809–1865); Military Invasion and Occupation; Northern Women; Nurses; Politics; Rape; Reconstruction (1865–1877); Refugees; Religion; Rural Women; Sherman Land (Special Field Orders Number 15); Shortages; Slave Families; Southern Women; Teachers, Northern; Thirteenth Amendment; Truth, Sojourner [Isabella Baumfree] (1797–1883); Tubman, Harriet [Araminta Ross] (1822–1913); Union Homefront; Wartime Employment; Widows, Union.

**References and Further Reading**

Bercaw, Nancy. 2003. *Gendered Freedoms: Race, Rights, and the Politics of Household in the Delta, 1861–1875.* Gainesville: University Press of Florida.

Berlin, Ira, and Leslie Rowland, eds. 1997. *Families and Freedom: A Documentary History of African-American Kinship in the Civil War Era.* New York: New Press.

Edwards, Laura F. 2000. *Scarlett Doesn't Live Here Anymore: Southern Women in the Civil War Era.* Urbana: University of Illinois Press.

Faulkner, Carol. 2004. *Women's Radical Reconstruction: The Freedmen's Aid Movement.* Philadelphia: University of Pennsylvania Press.

Forbes, Ella. 1998. *African American Women During the Civil War.* New York: Garland Publishers.

Gilbert, Olive. [1878] 1968. *Narrative of Sojourner Truth: A Bondswoman of Olden Time.* New York: Arno Press.

Gutman, Herbert G. 1976. *The Black Family in Slavery and Freedom, 1750–1925.* New York: Vintage.

Hunter, Tera W. 1997. *To 'Joy My Freedom: Southern Black Women's Lives and Labors After the Civil War.* Cambridge, MA: Harvard University Press.

Jones, Jacqueline. 1985. *Labor of Love, Labor of Sorrow: Black Women, Work and the Family from Slavery to the Present.* New York: Vintage.

McPherson, James. 1965. *The Negro's Civil War.* New York: Pantheon Books.

White, Deborah Gray. 1985. *Ar'n't I a Woman? Female Slaves in the Plantation South.* New York: W. W. Norton.

## Confederate Homefront

The Confederate homefront has attracted a great deal of attention among historians of the Civil War, in large part because the overwhelming majority of military engagements took place on Confederate soil. Moreover, a profusion of newspapers and the voluminous correspondence between soldiers and their family members kept those on the homefront well aware of events on the battlefield. In no other war did Americans experience such sustained and regular contact between soldiers and civilians, although Confederate homefront experiences varied widely across space and time. Those who lived in remote areas generally faced fewer difficulties than civilians in close proximity to the armies. As the war progressed, the widespread scarcity of goods and civilian discontent began to threaten the stability of the Confederate war effort, factors that many historians cite when explaining the collapse of the Confederacy. Because the Confederacy lost the war, nearly every aspect of its homefront experience is the subject of great debate.

The Confederacy was roughly the size of continental Europe, so it is difficult to describe its homefront as a single entity. It is possible, however, to make a few key generalizations about the seceded states—Alabama, Arkansas, Florida, Georgia, Louisiana, Mississippi, North Carolina, South Carolina, Tennessee, Texas, and Virginia. The eleven Confederate states were overwhelmingly rural, with economies based on the sale of crops like wheat, cotton, rice, and sugar cane. During the 1850s, wealthy Southerners had invested most of their capital in land and slaves, which were wise long-term investments but difficult to liquidate and reinvest in the industry needed to support a war. The fledgling industrial centers of the South, among them Richmond, Virginia and Atlanta, Georgia, had expanded during the late antebellum years, but in 1860 the number of factories in the Northern states still exceeded the total number of factory workers in the Southern states. Yet perhaps the most impressive feature of this predominantly agricultural nation was the speed and success with which it developed war-related industries. Private industrial manufacturers rapidly expanded production to meet the needs of the Confederate armies, and the government built and operated many additional factories. By 1864, Southern factories were producing impressive amounts of iron and gunpowder in particular.

Unfortunately, these manufactured goods did not always get to the armies. Southern railroad construction had proceeded at a rapid pace in the 1850s, but a uniform standard had not governed construction, and the Confederacy lacked the machinery and skilled workers to maintain tracks, cars, and engines once the war began. Since the government was unable to control the railroads or keep them in good repair, the manufactured and agricultural goods the armies needed at the front often sat waiting in the interior of the country. Thus, though economically strong in 1861, the Confederate States were at a comparative disadvantage as the war became a prolonged conflict dependent on the combatants' capacity to manufacture and distribute war materiel.

The Confederate government also failed to create a viable financial infrastructure for the new nation. Struggling to negotiate the twin impulses of state sovereignty and basic survival, the Confederate Congress created several modest sources of tax revenue, including a property tax, a personal income tax, and small levies on wholesalers' profits and consumer goods. Combined, these taxes never accounted for more than 5 percent of the government's income. The state and national governments also sold bonds, and Confederate bond sales yielded about 35 percent of the revenue the government needed to fund its armies. The remaining 60 percent came through paper currency. The Confederacy printed massive amounts of paper money but never enacted legislation to make this paper currency legal tender, thus fueling inflation rates that exceeded 9,000 percent by April 1865. Some historians have suggested that this inflation constituted an indirect tax on Confederate citizens, because they paid ever increasing prices for consumer goods and food. Modest national taxes, the indirect tax of inflation, and eventually a 10-percent tax-in-kind on agricultural products were the basic means through which Southerners on the homefront financially supported their new government.

The new burdens of inflation and taxation combined with widespread shortages of many key goods. The Union blockade of Confederate ports, though never fully enforceable, severely restricted the flow of European manufactured goods into the Confederacy. New and expanded factories, though impressive in their growth, devoted all of their energies to war production rather than to goods for home consumption. The loss of important agricultural areas like northern Virginia, coastal Georgia and South Carolina, western Tennessee, and the Mississippi delta in the first two years of the war caused shortages of basic food items like wheat, corn, rice, and sugar. Moreover, chronic salt shortages made it difficult, if not impossible, for farmers to preserve meat. These shortages were exacerbated by the departure of most able-bodied white men for the front and the intransigence of slave laborers, as chronicled by both diarists and historians. Southern newspaper editors—though hampered by dwindling supplies of paper and ink as well as by a dearth of skilled woodcutters and printers—encouraged discontent among citizens, who blamed scarcity and high prices on incompetent politicians and ruthless speculators.

These tensions erupted in the spring of 1863, as women publicly protested high prices and shortages on the streets of several Southern towns and cities. The largest of these protests, the Richmond bread riot of April 2, 1863, comprised several hundred people. These were mostly white women, many of them soldiers' wives, refugees, or workers in the city's expanded factories. The women marched toward the capital square, breaking into stores to steal bread, flour, bacon, and clothing, as they demanded the attention and assistance of municipal, state, and national lawmakers. Accompanied by Richmond Mayor Joseph Mayo and Virginia Governor John Letcher, President Jefferson Davis ordered the women to disperse, giving them five minutes before he would have the public guard fire into the crowd. The crowd quickly left the square, and the guard arrested sixty-eight of the protesters. Although the city government moved quickly to make examples of these protesters, they also worked to allay the discontent that had fueled the riot in the first place, setting up free markets to distribute food and clothing to poor residents of the city. Similarly,

state and county governments across the Confederacy created or broadened relief programs for the families of poor soldiers, although these failed to meet fully the needs of most families.

Confederate politicians, in general, were ill equipped to handle the economic and social dislocations that the war caused. Many Confederate lawmakers, especially at the state levels, had little or no legislative experience, often because the more experienced politicians entered the army. Similarly, most talented, ambitious, well-educated young men sought their futures in the Confederate officer corps, which seemed more exciting and patriotic than political service. Confederate legislators who had served in the United States Congress during the antebellum years, moreover, had inherited a tradition of legislative obstructionism that hindered effective lawmaking in the early days of the Confederacy. Finally, both houses of the Confederate Congress met in secret and published no records, creating an atmosphere of distrust among their constituents.

With all of these factors working against the success of Confederate politicians, their list of accomplishments becomes even more impressive. First and foremost, they established the physical trappings of a working government, appropriating buildings as national institutions, dispatching ambassadors to European capitals, and selecting a national flag. They quickly created a massive national army out of disparate groups of state militia; they even enacted the first conscription law in North America in April 1862. This Conscription Act contained a controversial clause exempting one man on every plantation with twenty or more slaves, prompting bitter denunciations from yeoman farmers across the South. Still, though less than comprehensive, the Confederate draft was a vital step in both filling the army's ranks and increasing the power of the central government. The central government also impressed animals, wagons, agricultural produce, and black male laborers—both slave and free—to supply the army.

Confederate economic policies, though spectacularly unsuccessful at limiting inflation, represented a similarly huge departure from the idea of a limited central government. The modest income and property taxes that citizens paid to the Confederacy were shocking to Southerners, as most had never paid any kind of direct tax to the United States government. The tax-in-kind, requiring citizens to hand over 10 percent of their produce to Confederate agents, was an even greater limitation of state sovereignty. Furthermore, the War Department's management of clothing factories, arsenals, ordnance works, mines, and railroads ensured that the national government remained intimately involved in the economy. State governments also actively intervened in the economic activities of the homefront, enacting their own legislation for impressment, taxation, price controls, and crop management.

Conscription and taxation are merely two examples of the growth of the central Confederate government. President Davis suspended the writ of habeas corpus, which requires that a person not be imprisoned without being formally charged with a crime, and instituted martial law when he considered it a necessity. Most controversially, Davis urged the Confederate Congress to enact legislation that would enroll male slaves as Confederate soldiers and then provide for their manumission after the war. Certainly, a great deal of innovation and flexibility characterized the Confederate approach to politics, despite the fact that the Confederacy ultimately lost the war. However, none of these innovations came without intense debate between lawmakers who favored a strong national government and those who wanted power to remain with the individual states.

Political dissent in the Confederacy, like so many other topics connected to the Confederate homefront, has attracted quite a bit of attention from historians. For years, they pointed to the lack of political parties in the Confederacy as a weakness. Confederate politicians deliberately avoided creating a two-party system when they developed their political culture, hoping thus to forestall partisanship. This lack of organized political competition, historians have asserted, made all opposition personal rather than political. Often, these historians suggested that the existence of a two-party system in Northern politics allowed for a loyal opposition to develop in the Union, while the Southern politi-

cal opposition became increasingly obstructionist. More recent studies of Confederate politics have undermined this argument, suggesting that all Confederates—regardless of class status—shared a common political culture that rejected partisanship and sought a return to an idealized vision of eighteenth-century republicanism. By this formulation, even those who resented the strength of the central government, like North Carolina Governor Zebulon Vance, maintained an interest in a unified, harmonious political culture that championed white supremacy and thus did not actively seek to undermine the Confederacy.

Whether loyal or obstructionist, partisan or political, opposition to President Davis's policies abounded, although it is not clear that he faced significantly more opposition than did United States President Abraham Lincoln. Because the Constitution of the Confederate States of America allowed the president a single, six-year term, Davis did not face a reelection campaign during the war, but he did need to defend his policies over the course of numerous congressional and gubernatorial elections. These elections produced mixed results for Davis. Historians have lavished a great deal of attention on Vance's reelection on a peace platform in the spring of 1863 and his subsequent disagreements with Davis, but other elections seemed to vindicate Davis's nationalist agenda. Virginians, for example, voted in large numbers for former Whigs in their May 1863 elections, thus sending to Congress and the General Assembly men who favored strong central governments.

The struggle to understand why the Confederacy lost has led many historians to question the depths of Confederates' commitment to their new polity. One very common argument suggests that class divisions between the planter class and the nonslaveholding farmers always plagued the Confederacy and that Confederate politicians were unable to unite these two discordant groups with a sense of common political or cultural identity. Other historians argue that, while Confederate citizens possessed a sense of common purpose at the beginning of the war, they lost faith in their new nation and gave up hope, thus precipitating the end of the conflict. One

Confederate bread riots as depicted in *Frank Leslie's Illustrated Newspaper* on May 23, 1863. The mothers, daughters, and wives of Confederate soldiers grew more desperate for food as their sons, fathers, and husbands died on the battlefields and inflation increased on the home front. This desperation resulted in riots throughout the South during the Civil War. (Library of Congress)

strain of this argument suggests that Southern women were central to this loss of faith. Certainly, the Confederate government's apparent inability to protect them angered many white women, especially those who experienced short-term Union army occupations or who had to leave their homes as refugees. Others reacted to economic deprivation with acts of civil disobedience—some by participating in bread riots but far more by writing to their husbands in the army, urging them to come home. Yet it is not clear that these dissatisfied women were willing to give up and accept a Union victory.

While some historians associate hardship on the Southern homefront with a defeatist attitude, an equal number have suggested that, rather than inducing despair and capitulation, hardship and occupation often increased Confederates' will to resist. These historians argue that Confederate citizens did feel a sense of common identity, one centered around their military institutions and thus lost faith in victory only with the surrender of the Confederate armed forces, particularly Robert E. Lee's Army of Northern Virginia. Others have proposed that the deprivation people experienced when in the proximity of Union armies actually increased Confederate nationalism, since it gave them an external enemy to blame for their problems, rather than concentrating all their frustration on the government in Richmond. Indeed, Southerners living in occupied areas may have outwardly capitulated to the United States government, but their personal papers often showed evidence of strong internal affiliation with the Confederacy. In addition, while many women wrote to their husbands, sons, and brothers, begging their return from the Confederate armies, others regularly urged the men in their families to remain at the front.

The debate over Confederate nationalism on the homefront remains open because so much evidence exists to support both sides. There were pockets of Union supporters scattered throughout the Confederacy, particularly in the mountainous areas of eastern Tennessee, western North Carolina, and northern Alabama. There were also communities of conscientious objectors and draft resistors, and even local militias that conducted guerrilla raids against Confederate units. Yet there were also civilians who endured severe economic hardship and even physical danger but remained committed to the Confederacy until the end of the war. Indeed, it seems that those people living the closest to Union armies were also the most willing to endure sacrifice to achieve a Confederate victory. This debate will no doubt continue to attract the attention of future generations of historians.

While the motivations and loyalties of white Southerners may still be open to debate, historians have found the loyalties of black Southerners much easier to understand. Those slaves who lived in areas near the Atlantic coast or close to Union army operations began running away from their masters even before the fall of Fort Sumter. Slaves in the interior remained at home but used the departure of white men for the Confederate army to gain autonomy from their mistresses. Although the much feared mass uprising of slaves never materialized, many slaves engaged in small acts of disobedience and disloyalty that undermined the agricultural, industrial, and even military capacities of the Confederacy. When slaves refused to work—or worked poorly—they deliberately limited the productive capability of the Confederate homefront. Free blacks, like slaves, had to be circumspect in their actions, but many welcomed Union victory. Free black communities in urban areas faced extra scrutiny early in the war and at low points in the military status of the Confederacy, but they also took advantage of the disarray of war to strengthen their community institutions, building a tradition of black collective activism that they would turn to political ends after the war.

Since the overwhelming majority of white Southern men served in the Confederate armies, any story of the Confederate homefront tells a great deal about the wartime experiences of women. Most studies have focused on the experiences of elite white women because they left behind the greatest quantity and variety of written records. Women of the planter class struggled to maintain control over their enslaved labor force, especially the male slaves. Although they had help from exempted men and those men too old for military duty, asserting authority over the agricultural work force was a new and challenging role for elite women, particularly as slaves sought to take advantage of this new situation. Elite women from occupied areas along the Atlantic coast and the Mississippi River often left their plantations and became refugees. Some left their slaves behind and went to cities like Richmond and Charleston. Others helped shepherd large numbers of slaves into more remote areas of the Piedmont or Texas. Although the refugee experience was difficult for all the families who left their homes, the women of the planter class had greater economic resources with which to face these dislocations.

In addition to their newfound economic responsibilities during the war, elite white women were the most likely of all Southern women to engage in patriotic and voluntary endeavors. Although the Confederacy did not have a formal organization similar to the United States Sanitary Commission, Southern women organized fairs, concerts, and other fundraising activities to send medical supplies and reading materials to the soldiers. They also had less formal involvement in the nursing profession than Northern women, but many Southern women served as nurses on an ad hoc basis whenever a battle occurred near their homes. Wealthier Southern women collected food to provide holiday celebrations to the soldiers or basic necessities to their neighbors. And in the aftermath of the war, white Southern women formed numerous cemetery and memorial associations to celebrate the valor of Confederate soldiers. As several historians have noted, in doing so these women usually obscured their own contributions to the Confederate war effort. Indeed, the basic continuity of gender roles in the South over the course of the Civil War seems due to deliberate choices on the part of elite white women to maintain their traditional roles in ideology if not in reality.

Nonslaveholding white women had always played key roles in the Southern economy, and so initially their wartime experiences represented a less dramatic change than those of elite women. The wives and daughters of yeoman farmers had always participated in agricultural labor, and so taking over the farm during the war was not, in the beginning, a huge departure for them. But the scarcity of hired labor, the shortages of seeds and implements, the impressment of farm animals, and the Confederate tax-in-kind all combined to create great hardship for women running the small farms that constituted the majority of the Confederate homefront. Moreover, while Northern farm women benefited from a wide variety of agricultural machinery designed to maintain production with a reduced work force, Southern factories concentrated all their energies on war materiel. Working-class women faced even greater difficulties, as real wages declined rapidly due to inflation and scarcity constantly increased the price of food.

Southern women's vocal maintenance of a conservative gender ideology, both during and after the war, greatly obscured the array of new opportunities that the war offered for white women in the wage work force. Despite the rapid depreciation of their wages, white women made significant—if often temporary—inroads into the Southern wage labor force during the war. Although most nursing took place on a volunteer basis, some women received paid positions as nurses and hospital matrons, particularly in the large, formal hospitals like Chimborazo Hospital outside Richmond. Educated young women of the middle and upper classes worked as clerks in government offices and signed bond certificates for the Treasury Department. Poorer women sewed uniforms or wrapped cartridges in ordnance factories. This last job could be especially dangerous. In March 1863, an explosion in an ordnance lab on Brown's Island in Richmond killed thirty-four women and injured several dozen others.

The women least likely to receive attention in the literature on the Confederate homefront are enslaved black women. Aside from hagiographic paeans to "Mammy," black women are noticeably absent from most stories of the Civil War. Yet they were undeniably vital to the Confederate war effort, however unwillingly. Like black men, slave women worked in the fields on most farms and plantations; indeed, when the state and national governments impressed black men to build fortifications, slave women took on an even greater proportion of the agricultural labor in the Confederacy. Most of the slaves who ran away to the Union lines were men, leaving behind women and children to perform all the farmwork. In addition, when their husbands ran away, slave women faced retribution from their masters and mistresses. Finally, female slaves who were forced into the Confederate hinterlands as refugees may have left behind friends and relatives on neighboring farms. Free black women faced the same economic hardships as white women, along with the knowledge that their free status was always precarious, especially during the disorder of war.

Obviously, the Confederate homefront was a vast and complex entity. The experiences of Southern civilians varied greatly with race, class, and gender, as well as with shifting qualities like proximity to the armies, the strength of local governments, and the health of local economies. What makes the Civil War so fascinating is the ability to examine the components of Confederate homefront experiences in such detail and even perhaps to compare the Confederate homefront to that of the Union. Furthermore, the intimate and sustained relationship between battlefront and homefront in the Confederacy makes its example quite distinct in the history of the United States.

*Jaime Amanda Martinez*

**See also** African American Women; Aid Societies; Atlanta, Evacuation of (Special Field Orders Number 67); Bread Riots; Civilian Life; Columbia Bazaar (January 17–21, 1865); Conscription; Davis, Jefferson (1808–1889); Desertion; Destruction of Homes; Destruction of Personal Property; Diaries and Journals; Domesticity; Enlistment; Factory Workers, Southern; Fairs and Bazaars; Family Life, Confederate; Food; Foraging, Effects on Women; Free Blacks; Fundraising; Government Girls; Guerrilla Warfare; Homespun; Hospitals; Impressment; Ladies' Memorial Associations; Letter Writing; Military Invasion and Occupation; Monuments; Morale; Nationalism, Confederacy; Nonslaveholding Southerners; Nurses; Plantation Life; Politics; Rape; Refugees; Rural Women; Secession; Separate Spheres; Sewing Bees; Shortages; Slave Families; Slaveholding Women; Southern Unionists; Southern Women; Treasury Girls; Union Homefront; United States Sanitary Commission; Urban Women, Southern; Wartime Employment; Widows, Confederate; Woman Order (General Order Number 28); Wounded, Visits to.

**References and Further Reading**

Ash, Steven V. 1995. *When the Yankees Came: Conflict and Chaos in the Occupied South, 1861–1865.* Chapel Hill: University of North Carolina Press.

Blair, William A. 1998. *Virginia's Private War: Feeding Body and Soul in the Confederacy, 1861–1865.* New York: Oxford University Press.

Campbell, Jacqueline Glass. 2003. *When Sherman Marched North from the Sea: Resistance on the Confederate Home Front.* Chapel Hill: University of North Carolina Press.

Faust, Drew Gilpin. 1996. *Mothers of Invention: Women of the Slaveholding South in the American Civil War.* Chapel Hill: University of North Carolina Press.

Freehling, William W. 2001. *The South vs. the South: How Anti-Confederate Southerners Shaped the Course of the Civil War.* New York: Oxford University Press.

Gallagher, Gary W. 1997. *The Confederate War: How Popular Will, Nationalism, and Military Strategy Could Not Stave Off Defeat.* Cambridge, MA: Harvard University Press.

Mohr, Clarence L. 1986. *On the Threshold of Freedom: Masters and Slaves in Civil War Georgia.* Athens: University of Georgia Press.

Rable, George. 1989. *Civil Wars: Women and the Crisis of Southern Nationalism.* Urbana: University of Illinois Press.

Rable, George. 1994. *The Confederate Republic: A Revolution against Politics.* Chapel Hill: University of North Carolina Press.

Schwalm, Leslie. 1997. *A Hard Fight for We: Women's Transition from Slavery to Freedom in South Carolina.* Urbana: University of Illinois Press.

Thomas, Emory M. 1971. *The Confederacy as a Revolutionary Experience.* Columbia: University of South Carolina Press.

Thomas, Emory M. 1979. *The Confederate Nation, 1861–1865.* New York: Harper & Row.

## Female Combatants

Despite public sensitivity, gender constraints, and government policy, hundreds of young women disguised themselves as men, enlisted, and served the Confederacy and the Union as combatants during the American Civil War. The exact number of female combatants is impossible to determine, however, because only the women who were discovered as such can be found in the records. In an age when dress, more than anything else, determined one's gender, women easily passed the superficial physical exams required for enlistment. In addition, if the men with whom they lived, slept, and fought recognized a female combatant among their ranks, they seldom reported the impostors to their superiors. Instead, capture by the enemy, the treatment of certain wounds, as well as pregnancy or birth led to the discovery and discharge of women soldiers. Often discharge did little to curb women's wartime service. Records indicate that several discharged women soldiers went to other regiments to reenlist. Women's motivations for enlistment ranged from a desire to remain with a lover, husband, or other family member, to a need for money or a thirst for adventure. For the most part, women, like their male counterparts, joined the armed forces for the social and economic opportunities that enlistment provided as well as out of a devotion to their country or region. However, female combatants, unlike men, could easily get released from their enlistment if they so desired. By outing themselves to the proper authorities or by discarding their disguises, they could return home and resume their civilian lives.

Women in uniform fought from the beginning of the war in 1861 to its conclusion in 1865. Women fought not only in minor scrimmages, but also in major confrontations in every theater of the war. Records of female combatants include their service in the Battles of First Manassas (Bull Run), Wilson's Creek, Fort Donelson, Shiloh, Murfreesboro, Antietam, Gettysburg, Vicksburg, Petersburg, Cold Harbor, the Shenandoah Valley and Peninsular campaigns, and the final conflicts near Appomattox Court House, where Robert E. Lee surrendered to Ulysses S. Grant. Ten women are known to have fought at Antietam, including a mother-to-be, and at least five known women made their contributions on the battlefield at Gettysburg, a battle that some scholars argue marked the turning point of the war. Two Confederate women died from wounds suffered during Pickett's Charge at Gettysburg, and one Southern female combatant survived the three-day battle after having her leg amputated by surgeons. Scholars can pinpoint these female combatants but are left to guess at the numbers of unknown women who fought. Although most documented female combatants were white, at least one woman on record served with the Twenty-ninth Connecticut Infantry (Colored).

As early as 1882, estimates of women soldiers surfaced. In their *History of Woman Suffrage,* Susan B. Anthony, Matilda Gage, and Elizabeth Cady Stanton wrote of "hundreds of women" who served as soldiers during the American Civil War. They noted that these women served out of their patriotism and loyalty, either to the Union or for the cause of the Confederacy. Considerable debate continues to exist over the actual number of female combatants who served in the Union and Confederate armies. Recent historians argue that one of the earliest estimates from the 1880s, that posited four hundred female soldiers, included only those discovered, and it may have referred only to women who served in the Union army. More recent estimates put the number of Civil War female combatants between five hundred and one thousand.

Scholars' exploration of female combatants have revealed vital details of these Civil War soldiers from official records and contemporary accounts. According to one study of over two hundred and forty discovered female combatants, over twice as many women served in the Union army as did in the Confederate army. In addition, 15 percent of female combatants suffered wounds; many women received more than one wound in the course of their military service. This detail illuminates how women were forced out of the armies. The location of a female combatant's wound could lead to the discovery of her sex and her subsequent discharge from service. Furthermore, according to this study, a greater percentage of female soldiers, as compared to men, died on the battlefield or from wounds than they did from disease. Additionally, statistically 2 percent more women than men found themselves captured. Many captured female combatants were exchanged or sent back to be handled by the armies they fought for, and most found themselves discharged upon their return. However, several women maintained their disguises during their time as prisoners of war. The study also revealed that female combatants served for an average of sixteen months, and approximately 10 percent of them mustered out of the army without their secret being discovered. Female combatants proved themselves as soldiers, and their promotion rate was 14 percent higher than that of their male comrades in arms.

Details about women who served as female combatants are found not only in government records, but also in more personal contemporary sources. Once discovered, a woman soldier became newsworthy. Local newspaper accounts provide details not found elsewhere. However, these accounts, often sensationalized and critical, also contain inaccuracies. In addition, letters written home by a female combatant's male comrades offer another perspective.

Despite prevailing social norms and nineteenth-century sensibilities, the young women who chose the soldier's life did so for a variety of reasons. For many, the excitement of military life seemed a cure to their homefront boredom. By the midnineteenth century, the popularity of cross-dressing female heroines in fictional and semifictional accounts had inspired the imagination of the reading public for hundreds of years. With limited opportunities in the social and economic realms, young women often envied the less traditional life of these literary characters. Additionally, in an era when society expected women to be pious and submissive and to remain within the private sphere of the home, the lure of a more active, exciting public life must have appealed to many young women. Few acted on the lure of a man's world, but many of those who became soldiers sought a life different from the one their sex mandated. With the outbreak of the Civil War, a few of these young women decided to find their own adventures. Their ability to fool physicians who performed the initial physical examination, as well as their commanders and comrades, tells as much about the time in which they lived as about their abilities to act like men.

Necessity rather than adventure contributed to the decision of some young women to become soldiers. The economic advantages of being a soldier persuaded numerous men and quite a few women to join the armies of the North and South. Though some young women found work outside the home for wages, employment opportunities were limited for working- and lower-class women. Occupations such as cook, laundress, or domestic worker provided little pay and few advantages; women might expect to earn a small percentage of what a man could earn as a farmer, the predominant occupation for men of the same socioeconomic level. Posing as a man in either the civilian or the military realm provided a logical way for a woman to alleviate the conditions of poverty. A few young women, even before the outbreak of the Civil War, had taken the opportunity to find better-paying jobs by seeking work disguised as men. Well-known female combatants Sarah Edmonds (Franklin Thompson), Jennie Hodgers (Albert D. J. Cashier), and Sarah Rosetta Wakeman (Lyons Wakeman) all earned a living as men in a male occupation before joining the army. In fact, peer pressure may have been an enlistment motivation for any female living as a male in a particular community.

Joining the army proved monetarily advantageous for women who did so. As a soldier, a woman could earn anywhere from two to four times more than a man in a civilian occupation. Many women took advantage of this economic opportunity and, like Sarah Rosetta (Lyons Wakeman), sent money home to help their families.

In their quest for economic survival, some women chose combat over prostitution, another last resort for economic survival, proving ridiculous local newspapers' claims that women combatants enlisted to serve as prostitutes. Journalists, in an attempt to condemn cross-dressing women, especially those who refused to admit the error of their ways, insisted that women must have disguised themselves as soldiers to better take advantage of the needs of male soldiers. In addition, women could be found in every regiment serving as cooks, laundresses, nurses, and prostitutes. Wives and other women, so-called camp followers, found an acknowledged place in the military life of the camps. Despite these realities, nineteenth-century notions about womanhood allowed the accusations that maligned women soldiers as prostitutes.

While money may have attracted a number of women to infantry, artillery, or cavalry positions in both the Union and Confederate armies, other factors also promoted enlistment. Some female combatants enlisted to escape an abusive relationship or home environment. At the same time, other women chose to enlist to remain with or to follow husbands, lovers, fathers, or brothers. Upon discovery, some revealed that the family member or members with whom they had enlisted were the only ones they had, and they did not wish to, or could not, remain behind. Often, their significant others remained the only ones who knew the true identity of the female combatant. A few officers ensured the enlistment of their wives, who then served under their husbands' commands. One woman who joined with her husband left her children in her sister's care. Another woman left her children in her husband's care and joined in his place. That these cases prove the exception remains unlikely. Although a few women revealed their identities to get out of military duty when the men they enlisted with died or mustered out, several women finished their enlistments despite the death or discharge of loved ones.

Whether joining with someone or not, women, like their male counterparts, cited patriotism as a reason for becoming a soldier. For both men and women, preserving the Union or protecting one's homeland resulted in a desire to join the army. Even revenge could serve as a motivating force; many soldiers on both sides sought satisfaction by fighting an enemy who had caused the death of a loved one. Whatever their initial motivation, women's reasons for reenlisting or continuing to serve after facing combat, more often than not, like men's, changed. The adrenaline rush of battle may have sufficed as a reason to remain despite the possibility of death. Women combatants may have feared battle less than they feared discovery, which could call into question their morals and reasons for becoming soldiers.

Nothing, including pregnancy, seemed to deter a woman who chose to fight. Records reveal that one veteran sergeant fought at the Battle of Murfreesboro even though she was five months pregnant; she was not unique. An unnamed New Jersey enlistee contributed to the fighting in the Seven Days' Battles during her first trimester. The second trimester found her at Antietam, where she suffered from a wound from which she recovered to return to her regiment to fight at Fredericksburg. After earning a promotion to sergeant at Fredericksburg, she remained in the ranks until she gave birth to a baby boy. As these cases indicate, some female combatants successfully hid their pregnancy as long as possible, often until childbirth.

A number of factors, unique to nineteenth-century America, allowed women soldiers to succeed in their deception. Clothing expectations and perceptions of capabilities contributed to the ease of disguise in which many females became men for military purposes. Attire rather than physical appearance determined gender in the nineteenth century. By nineteenth-century logic, if it wore pants and carried a gun, it must be male. No one expected to find a female in the ranks—soldiers cared more about whether their comrades in arms could fight than what sex they might be. It is no wonder that one of the first things required of a captured female soldier was that she get appropriately dressed in female attire.

Additionally, the enlistment of so many boys whose hairless faces could be seen and whose high-pitched voices could be heard in every regiment masked the fact that several smooth-faced youths were female rather than male. Although a few women gave themselves away by unintentionally displaying womanly mannerisms, other females secured their disguises by exhibiting "male" personal habits, including drinking, smoking, fighting, swearing, womanizing, and gambling. Some female combatants, such as Jennie Hodgers (Albert Cashier), dated women.; Señora Loreta Janeta Velazquez (Lieutenant Harry Buford) was considered an unashamed flirt with the ladies, much to the disdain of later accounts that found this characteristic of the cross-dressing self-promoter of more concern than that she fought and led others into battle. Whether these female combatants engaged and entertained women to enhance their disguises or to suit their personal preferences remains difficult to determine. In any case, their behavior certainly helped in their quest to be seen as male soldiers.

Although women, like all Civil War soldiers, had to pass a physical exam to gain entry into the army, most of the exams were superficial, and few physicians followed government directives. Enlistment numbers mattered more than policy, and many women joined a regiment already in the field, thereby bypassing the process entirely. The need for soldiers prompted many examiners to offer a cursory once-over, focusing instead on the needs of the military. As long as a prospective soldier could shoot—or had all ten fingers—he—or she—could easily pass the physical examination. In addition,

Albert D. J. Cashier of the 95th Illinois Regiment, aka Jennie Hodgers. (Courtesy of the Abraham Lincoln Presidential Library)

most of the skills required by the armies for combat were gender neutral. The majority of women who enlisted had worked on farms or performed other chores that aided physical adaptability to army life, such as carrying gear weighing between 40 and 50 pounds. Subsequently, they easily passed their physical and joined the ranks.

Despite the care taken by female combatants to remain undetected, it appears that other women could often see through a disguise. Female combatants may have felt comforted in finding other women in the same situation. They could work together to keep their sex hidden as they tried to survive military service. Although evidence suggests that a few female combatants had male companions who kept their secret, as well as relatives or acquaintances who aided their deceptions, occasionally a disgruntled relative or family friend could cause dismissal upon recognizing a woman he knew in the ranks and reporting her to the authorities.

For the most part, however, only close scrutiny could unmask a female combatant.

The modesty of the times allowed women soldiers enough space and privacy to attend to personal matters. As for menstruation, most female combatants' monthly cycle stopped altogether due to the physical demands of soldiering. Furthermore, the "evidence" of women's monthly cycles blended in with the items generated by the daily treatment of wounded soldiers.

A female combatant often found herself participating in duties other than combat. In addition to fighting, drilling and marching became a part of her daily existence. Other duties to which women soldiers, as well as men, found themselves assigned included guard duty, scouting, and occasionally hospital duty. The rate by which women rose in either the enlisted or the officer ranks attests to their abilities as soldiers and leaders. Though a woman, like a man, more than likely entered the enlisted ranks as a private, several women, by the time of their discovery and outing, had risen to the rank of sergeant. Most of the women whose disguise fell away when they gave birth were listed as sergeants, suggesting evidence of field promotion due to their courage under fire; several letters sent home by fellow male soldiers attest to these women's abilities as soldiers, as well as to their comrades' surprise at their abilities to become mothers. Although many female officers held their rank due to the influence of husbands under whom they served, one woman gained her husband's rank and command after his death. It is unlikely that this would have happened had she not been capable of fulfilling the position's duties and of holding the increased responsibility, and had she not proven herself worthy to those she commanded. Although for the most part women commanded as lieutenants and captains, one female prisoner of war was a major.

Many female combatants could not, or chose not to, uphold their disguise. Once revealed as women, most female combatants were mustered out of the army. No female combatants were court-martialed for crimes, incompetence, or disgrace. In addition, although scholars have found three female combatants who deserted, two of them reenlisted. As the war continued into its third and fourth years, several women, especially those in Southern regiments, found it unnecessary to continue to disguise themselves as men, finding that discovery did not bring an automatic mustering out; by this point in the war the need for man, or woman, power far outweighed gender sensitivities and ideals. Female combatants who served in the Western theater found regulations less restrictive as well because frontier ideals did not necessarily comply with traditional societal expectations.

Several women reenlisted after being released as prisoners of war. Neither the Union nor the Confederate army had any regulations to deal with women prisoners. The experiences of captured female combatants must be understood on a case-by-case basis, because individual commanders dealt with the situation as best they knew how and often with individual biases in place. More often than not, once it was discovered that a prisoner was not a man, she was provided with appropriate female attire, paroled, and sent on her way, unless she was ill or injured, after promising to return home. Some released women quickly discarded the dress for trousers and reenlisted. If injured or ill, women whose disguises had been discovered more likely than not found themselves segregated from their male comrades and retained in the same prison or sent to a civilian hospital. Some women used the fact that they were women to gain either release from the military or from the horrific conditions under which most prisoners lived; these women seldom reenlisted. Several others withheld their true identities and suffered along with their comrades. In prison and on the battlefield, a woman often refused treatment to keep her secret. When men on burial detail detected a female combatant, they usually buried her separately, whether she died on the battlefield or in prison, occasionally marking her grave, while mass and unmarked graves served well enough for fallen men.

At the end of the war, many female combatants returned home and took up the life they had lived before the war. The resumption of their prewar lifestyle was especially the case for those who had joined and served with their husbands or sweethearts. Several of these women had children, raised their families, and went on with their life as if nothing had happened. They never dwelled on their wartime battlefield experiences.

A few female combatants, such as Velazquez and Edmonds, whose disguises seemed to fluctuate throughout the war, published their memoirs afterward. Their elaborated and sensationalized details brought to question the true sacrifices of many other unnamed or unrecognized fellow female combatants. After the war, the public wanted to believe the less accurate though culturally acceptable tales of romanticized female soldiers—perhaps heartbroken, crazed, or morally bereft. These sensationalized tales held more appeal than any true account of female combatants whose motivations differed significantly or who had shown boldness and strength and proved themselves worthy soldiers and human beings.

Female combatants who had taken up male disguises prior to the war also returned to the lives that they had led before their enlistment. For example, female Civil War veterans and combatants such as Albert Cashier (Jennie Hodgers) of Illinois and Otto Schaffer (actual name unknown) of Kansas returned to the lives they had more than likely lived prior to their military service. Although, unlike other female combatants, these women continued to dress as men, they did so having lived as men for most, if not all, of their adult lives. It is unlikely that these two individuals were the only female veterans who led full lives as men after their wartime experiences. Other cross-dressed women who were never discovered likely continued as men after the war.

The female identity of Cashier was not discovered for decades after he mustered out of the army. Injured in an accident in 1911 and discovered by the physician who treated her, Cashier's secret was not revealed by the doctor or by the senator for whom she worked. In addition, once the news of Cashier's sex became general knowledge, her former comrades in arms maintained a loyal and somewhat protective response. Forced by her true identity to finally become a woman, the state of Illinois placed Jennie in the woman's wing of the mental hospital at the age of seventy. The state also determined that Jennie should look the part and dress as a woman. Unaccustomed to female attire— she had worn men's clothes her entire adult life— she tripped, fell, and broke her hip, an injury from which she never recovered. A woman who had fought tirelessly and without wounds through the Civil War succumbed to old age and a long skirt. The continued support of former comrades in arms ensured, however, that she be buried with full military honors.

Some female combatants applied for and received military pensions for their service, often with the support of former comrades who had come to know the true identity of their fellow soldier. The high level of support that came from former comrades in arms, even after a soldier had been identified as a female, might suggest that many men knew during the war that some of their fellow soldiers were women. As long as they fought bravely, did not complain any more than expected, and took on their assigned duties, their sex did not matter to other soldiers. Fellow soldiers, as well as community members, recognized and honored the Civil War service of female combatants in the postwar era.

*Kay J. Blalock*

***See also*** Antietam/Sharpsburg, Battle of (September 17, 1862); Bull Run/Manassas, First Battle of (July 21, 1861); Camp Followers; Confederate Soldiers, Motives; Courts Martial; Desertion; Disease; Domesticity; Edmonds, Sarah Emma [Franklin Thompson] (1841–1898); Enlistment; Family Life, Northern; Family Life, Southern; Female Spies; Fredericksburg, Battle of (December 13, 1862); Gettysburg, Battle of (July 1–3, 1863); Hodgers, Jennie [Albert D. J. Cashier] (ca. 1843–1915); Imprisonment of Women; Letter Writing; Morale; Murfreesboro, Battle of (December 31, 1862–January 2, 1863); Nationalism, Confederate; Nationalism, United States; Northern Women; Peninsular Campaign (1862); Petersburg Campaign (June 1864–April 1865); Prostitution; Separate Spheres; Sheridan's Shenandoah Valley Campaign (1864); Shiloh, Battle of (April 6–7, 1862); Southern Women; Union Soldiers, Motives; Velazquez, Loreta Janeta [Harry T. Buford] (1842–n.d.); Wakeman, Sarah Rosetta [Lyons Wakeman] (1843–1864); Wartime Employment; Wartime Literature.

**References and Further Reading**

Blanton, DeAnne, and Lauren M. Cook. 2002. *They Fought Like Demons: Women Soldiers in the Civil*

*War.* Baton Rouge: Louisiana State University Press.

Burgess, Lauren Cook, ed. 1994. *An Uncommon Soldier: The Civil War Letters of Sarah Rosetta Wakeman, Alias Pvt. Lyons Wakeman, 153rd Regiment, New York State Volunteers, 1862–1864.* Pasadena, MD: Minerva Center.

Clinton, Catherine, and Nina Silber, eds. 1992. *Divided Houses: Gender and the Civil War.* New York: Oxford University Press.

Dannett, Sylvia G. L. 1960. *She Rode with the Generals: The True and Incredible Story of Sarah Emma Seelye, Alias Franklin Thompson.* New York: Thomas Nelson & Sons.

Hall, Richard. 1993. *Patriots in Disguise: Women Warriors of the Civil War.* New York: Paragon House.

King, Wendy A. 1992. *Clad in Uniform: Women Soldiers of the Civil War.* Collingswood, NJ: C. W. Historicals.

Larson, C. Kay. 1990. "Bonnie Yank and Ginny Reb." *Minerva, Quarterly Report on Women and the Military* 8 (1).

Larson, C. Kay. 1992. "Bonny Yank and Ginny Reb Revisited." *Minerva, Quarterly Report on Women and the Military* 10 (2).

Leonard, Elizabeth D. 1999. *All the Daring of the Soldier: Women of the Civil War Armies.* New York: W. W. Norton.

Lowry, Thomas P., M.D. 1994. *The Story the Soldiers Wouldn't Tell: Sex in the Civil War.* Mechanicsburg, PA: Stackpole Books.

Velazquez, Loreta. 2003 [1876]. *The Woman in Battle: The Civil War Narrative of Loreta Velaquez, A Cuban Woman and Confederate Soldier,* with introduction by Jesse Aleman. Madison: University of Wisconsin Press.

## Female Spies

Female spies joined other women across the country during the Civil War in performing duties previously unimaginable for women. Even though they could not vote and were in most respects subservient to men, women who became spies were well educated and had long participated in family decisions and in church benevolent societies. As talk of war intensified, these women discussed the major issues—secession, slavery, and sedition—with their families, friends, and neighbors. Once the war began, they took on more active roles to support their nation.

Initially, most people in the North and South expected the conflict to end in a matter of months, if not days. Before either side conscripted troops, men with stanch convictions volunteered to fight. Their daughters, sisters, and wives later emerged as spies. In the Deep South, where secessionist sentiment raged, the minority white male population diverged along class lines. Plantation owners, who were exempt from service, often donated money to Confederate coffers and raised companies of soldiers that included their own sons. Concurrently, many masters sent their slaves to the most remote areas of their holdings in an attempt to insulate them from talk of freedom and to discourage escape or rebellion, while they either moved north or west to avoid harm or went into voluntary exile farther south. Some left their wives and children behind, assuming their dependents would be protected by their status and the ubiquitous code of male paternalism and chivalry. In the Upper South and Midwest, where small farmers with only a few or no slaves dominated the rural landscape, families worked alongside their servants in the fields. These men were less inclined to abandon their homes for what they perceived as a rich man's war until forced by the draft, lured by money, or persecuted by neighbors.

After the Union and Confederacy instituted conscription, women in rural middle-class families of necessity stayed at home to protect their children and property, no small feat when guerrilla violence plagued areas outside Federal or Confederate protection. Poor women moved in with family members or neighbors when possible; otherwise, they became refugees, finding food and shelter as they roamed from place to place. Black women, free and slave, fled the South to the North and Canada or to the safety of Union lines when possible. A few remained in their Southern homeland. Because the soldier-aged white male population in Northern states was larger than that in the South, Northern communities were not as bereft of men as Southern ones. In addition, because battles and troop movements took place primarily in the South, Northern women, black and white, contended with less disruption and deprivation than did Southern women. After the Union army began accepting black men as soldiers in 1863, their female dependents followed when allowed. Otherwise, Northern black women's experiences paralleled those of Southern women more closely than those of Northern white women. By the war's third year, women in Southern states felt the effects of feeding two armies, hosting battles, and the lack of male protection and assistance. Shortages of food, clothing, medicine, firewood, salt, labor, and work animals affected rural women more than residents of Union-occupied towns. Since one army or the other appropriated most beasts of burden, only the most fortunate women retained a horse. Women spies experienced the same hardships, although not as extensively or as early in the conflict as poorer and older women. Even though female spies sewed, tended wounded soldiers, and otherwise made contributions similar to those of other women, their wealth supplied the leisure time, social contacts, and transportation necessary for spying.

Even before the Civil War officially started, some spymasters planned their networks and strategies. Female spies close to central governments in Washington, D.C., and Richmond, Virginia, extracted critical information from elected and appointed office-holders in the legislative and executive branches and from other government employees, often funneling it via female friends and relatives. Socialite Rose O'Neal Greenhow, for example, cultivated U.S. cabinet and congressional members privy to presidential and military decisions. Because departments like the Secret Service and Federal Bureau of Investigation did not exist on the eve of the war, individual generals, Union and Confederate, bore responsibility for their own intelligence work. Even if he hired a civilian to head his espionage efforts, the general retained the authority to decide whether to obtain information from citizens, prisoners, refugees, deserters, or anyone, as well as how much credence to give each source. Union General George B. McClellan, who retained former Chicago railroad detective Allan Pinkerton as his first intelligence chief, experimented with a variety of information-gathering techniques, including balloons and

Rose Greenhow was a spy for the Confederacy during the American Civil War. She is reported to have continued her intelligence activity even after her capture by the Union in 1861. (Library of Congress)

signal corps in addition to people. While official records use the term "spy," military documents also refer to persons who performed the same functions as scouts, guides, and couriers. Ideally, commanders delegated spy duties to their cavalry units. Muster rolls show soldiers on "detached service," "courier duty," or "special service"—all terms used to describe their absence while on undercover missions. Later, generals on both sides integrated local civilian spy groups into their networks. The Confederacy continued to rely on each general to organize his own band of spies; however, Confederate President Jefferson Davis occasionally entertained and supported singular secret missions. Not all generals considered women capable of or suitable for spying.

During the first year or so of war, men on both sides failed to recognize the potential for harm that women presented. As Union generals conquered new territory, they hoped to cultivate latent nationalist sentiments among the local populace, as well as to improve troop morale by inviting area women to army-sponsored balls—perfect opportunities for female spies to coax secrets from unsuspecting soldiers. Even officers proudly escorted small parties of area women around fortifications or through manufacturing operations like the Confederate Tredegar Iron Works. Female spies capitalized on such opportunities. Gradually military police units realized that women were hiding smuggling and spying activities behind their charm. Nevertheless, the notion that women were incapable of treason persisted among military leaders. Actress turned Union spy Pauline Cushman convinced Confederate General John Hunt Morgan that she was a raging secessionist, yet fellow General Nathan Bedford Forrest failed to fall for her act. Tennessee Governor Andrew Johnson ordered the release of two "harmless belles" arrested for spying.

By its nature, espionage is a solitary activity rarely generating written records; thus, a person's participation can be speculative, based on circumstantial evidence. Consequently, what scholars know of Civil War espionage is a composite of the *Official Records of the War of the Rebellion,* provost marshal records, newspaper articles, papers of intelligence chiefs and military officers, family papers, civilians' memoirs, and soldiers' diaries. Because many female spies operated at least one or two links removed from the male spies who reported to a spymaster or a general, their names do not appear in documentation created by the higher echelon. While payment records certainly validate a woman's service, the absence of a woman's name does not prove that a woman never spied. She may have volunteered; her name may have been changed, shown as initials, or omitted; or the record may be missing. Before Richmond fell, Confederate Secretary of War Judah Benjamin burned stacks of documents, likely including those containing information about covert operations.

Whether her service consisted of a single incident or a series of tasks, whether she was an organizer or a link in the spy chain, a female spy usually associated with family members, friends, former classmates, or neighbors rather than infiltrating a

circle of strangers. Some women smuggled goods or assisted refugees, escapees, or fugitives, while awaiting a spying opportunity. A few diaries and memoirs by credible women spies exist, usually published only after their deaths. Veiled entries such as "visited Dr. Hudson" or "Mr. Wilson here" indicate contact with male members of the clandestine network. After the War, both Union and Confederate officials encouraged operatives to continue their silence because exposing surreptitious activities could have endangered lives for years.

Women acknowledged as spies were typically young, white, well-to-do, and unmarried, as well as attractive, charming, intelligent, and quick-witted—desirable characteristics when eliciting information from soldiers. Since few able-bodied men or servants remained in communities, especially in the South, married and widowed women usually were too preoccupied with caring for family, neighbors, and soldiers to consider becoming involved in surreptitious activities. The majority of female spies volunteered; however, occasionally women were officially recruited even if they had previously been operating independently. Virginian Elizabeth Van Lew, who spied for the Union, and Washington, D.C. socialite Rose O'Neal Greenhow, who aided the Confederacy, were two of the most well-known who were sought out by spymasters. Some, like Belle Boyd, stepped forward because they happened upon valuable information, while others, such as Mary Overall, wanted to assist a friend. Those who sought public acclaim after their escapades via published memoirs or in traveling lectures were some of the least effective as spies, in part because the very publicity ended their usefulness and that of their contacts as spies. Openly discussing their actions or the failure to use coded messages while the country was still at war not only exposed their comrades and methods to the enemy, but also jeopardized future operations.

Although women on both sides participated in spying and smuggling, most battles occurred on Southern soil; thus Unionist and Confederate Southern women had the advantage of being near knowledgeable sources and commanders who needed information. Confederate sympathizers in the North and Unionists in the South found it much more difficult to form or join networks of like-minded spies. Intelligence groups were most active between Union encampments or occupied territory and the closest Confederate boundary. Male spies for both sides regularly traveled between Union and Confederate lines, corridors plagued with foragers, deserters, and bushwhackers. To meet with or to leave messages for other members of their network, women traversed the same territory, often without the required travel passes. Having a horse was critical for female spies, who operated outside the towns, a necessity that excluded poor women from spy networks.

Careful to maintain ladylike behavior in normal times, women pushed the boundaries of acceptable conduct when engaging in covert activities. Arranging to meet a male conspirator in a hotel lobby, admitting men into one's home late at night, or taking an unescorted horse or buggy ride created, at the least, speculation about a woman's virtue. Rose Greenhow attracted suspicion and criticism early in the war due to the steady stream of men visiting her house. Others invited censure by openly flirting, as in Belle Boyd's case, or by flashing pistols and sleeping with male cohorts, as did Frankie Abells. Northern and Southern newspapers branded any woman charged with treasonous acts as a prostitute unless her wealth or social position was significant enough to temper reporters' rhetoric. The same adventurous spirit that attracted women to spying also caused them to disregard their reputations. More dangerous and socially isolating, however, was assisting the army that her neighbors considered the enemy. Women who possessed the courage and determination required for covert operations were not intimidated.

What constituted spying changed as the war escalated. In 1863 Union commanders issued orders defining spies or traitors as anyone who transported or wrote secret mail as well as extreme female secessionists. Secret mail included letters to soldiers in the opposite army. A woman could be arrested for spying when a letter found on a dead man was signed with a code name similar to hers. Anyone caught carrying newspapers across military lines was automatically considered a spy. Traveling with a forged travel pass also led to arrest. Initially, United States and Confederate investigators refrained from searching women bodily in deference to the prevailing codes of chivalry. Women's elaborate hairstyles, dress bodices, hems, and large hoop skirts concealed maps, battle plans, troop strength and movement details, and accounts of army supplies, among other confidential information. Unable to find evidence to support a charge of spying, officers arrested women for smuggling. By mid-1863, the Union employed female guards to find documents and contraband goods that women spies carried.

Women used a variety of spying techniques. Those who avoided detection used cipher codes or invisible ink for written correspondence and entrusted only a few well-known contacts with their true purpose. Rose Greenhow's contemptuous disregard for the Union led to her arrest when she carelessly left uncoded messages and her cipher key easily accessible to Pinkerton's detectives. Coded want ads in newspapers provided clues regarding travel and rendezvous. Messages written in tiny script, further reduced by photography and then concealed inside buttons, were later deciphered using strong magnifying glasses. Many spy rings used Vigenere Tableau, court, route, or other ciphers based on text, pictographs, or numbers. Often only the sender and receiver could interpret the message. When personal contact was too risky or inconvenient, operators left messages at a designated street corner, in a rural hollow stump, or inside objects such as books, napkins, newspapers, and chairs in public places.

Men and women differentiated spying tasks based on gender. Men could easily wander about enemy camps in the uniform of the other army or in the guise of peddlers or other civilians, whereas women charmed post commanders and pickets so that they could readily obtain passes to and from garrisoned towns. Male military officers garnered information from interrogating prisoners, deserters, and contrabands; men operated surveillance balloons and formed the signal corps. Women's assignments involved gathering information about troop numbers and movements, obtaining maps and newspapers, determining fortifications, and conveying letters across enemy lines; however, they spent much of their time transferring messages from one male operative working between Confederate and Union lines to another inside occupied towns. They also kept track of other spies in their chain, searching or substituting for them when they failed to appear at the expected time, advising their intelligence network chief of changes in operating methods and of problems, assisting male spies in escaping from prison, and claiming the bodies of male spies killed in the line of duty.

Occasionally a female spy adopted a disguise. Self-proclaimed Union spy Emma Edmonds allegedly posed at various times as a soldier, a slave boy, a black woman, and an Irish peddler. Elizabeth Van Lew dressed like a working-class woman. In the chaotic milieu of war and with many young boys joining the military, other soldiers rarely scrutinized a beardless face. Unless wounded, a woman's gender could remain undetected. Nor was her race questioned because both armies used black women as cooks and laundresses. Women, along with blacks, preachers, physicians, and photographers, were "invisible" in that soldiers talked freely around them as though they were not present. Invisibles could travel across enemy lines with little interference and did not have to hide during the day, as did male spies. Thus, women spies often gathered more information and delivered messages more quickly than did their male counterparts.

Countless nameless male and female blacks, free and enslaved, facilitated the work of white spies, and their number doubtless exceeded that of their white colleagues. African American women, most notably Harriet Tubman, and some white women acted out of abolitionist convictions; they saw spying as a means of fighting slavery. Slaves accompanied their owners on secret missions and acted as lone couriers. They provided food, shelter, and transportation when needed, found horses, hid horses, and relayed overheard conversations. Perhaps their most valuable contribution was using their superior knowledge of roads and wooded trails to hide spies or to lead spies from one contact point to another. When Confederate officials suspected blacks of aiding treasonous whites, black

associates received disproportionately harsh treatment, including the loss of freedom, physical abuse, imprisonment, and death, for keeping their secrets.

The reasons females spied are as diverse as the women themselves, but patriotism was a common denominator. Those with Confederate sympathies believed their first loyalty was to their homeland, the South, perhaps instinctively and subconsciously realizing that their lives would be easier during and after the war if they held the same political philosophy as their neighbors. Spies for the North believed the Rebels had no right to secede, and many also wanted to end slavery. North and South, religious leaders encouraged patriotism. Consequently, women, considered more pious than men, had a sacred duty to do whatever they thought necessary to assist the cause. Contemporary accounts frequently mention Confederate women's zeal, so strong that they ridiculed men who were reluctant warriors. A large part of their fervor came from Southern ministers who assured women that not only was God aligned with the South, but also that He sanctioned women's efforts in support of His chosen land and people. Loyalty to family and friends was another factor, although some spies alienated themselves from their loved ones' over differing political views. For other women, the risk, adventure, excitement, or challenge presented a rare opportunity to step outside traditional roles at a time when life would otherwise have been quite dismal.

Until the Union began its hard war campaigns in mid-1863, the consequences of spying for both Confederate and Union women were mitigated by a paternalistic system, socioeconomically stratified by class, that excluded wealthy white women from suspicion of immoral or illegal behavior and that insulated them from harsh treatment. Although neither side executed female spies, some women received death sentences that were later commuted. Wealthy women, though sometimes arrested and imprisoned, generally were not treated as cruelly as were poor women, blacks, and male spies. From Old Capitol Prison in Washington, D.C., to Gratiot Street Prison in St. Louis, imprisoned female spies described almost universally squalid physical environments, contending with rats, bad food, and uncomfortable, unsanitary cells. Nevertheless, women's conditions were considerably less crowded and unpleasant than those that male spies encountered. Women convicted of spying for the Confederacy were exiled to the Deep South, usually hundreds of miles from their families. Occasionally, a particularly valuable or well-connected female spy was exchanged for male Union prisoners held in the South, but more typically women prisoners were exchanged for other women in a one-to-one ratio. Deserved or not, women who garnered bad reputations had difficulty shedding them after the war.

Whether the memories were too painful or the deeds too sensitive, most women who spied refused to discuss or publicize their roles. Recognizing their significance, descendants published some women spies' papers decades later. A few female spies received accolades during or immediately following the war. Rose Greenhow funneled information to Confederate General Pierre G. T. Beauregard that enabled him to prepare for the Battle of Bull Run. Another female spy in the same ring with Greenhow warned the Confederacy of an impending naval attack on Port Royal. Although Belle Boyd's well-reported and public rush to convey Federal troop positions to Brigadier General Richard Taylor enabled General Thomas "Stonewall" Jackson to rout Union forces at Front Royal, Virginia, historians discredit her other espionage claims.

After the war, male spies and military officers publicly acknowledged certain women spies' importance to their operations, although rarely revealing details. Alfred Douglas, cofounder of Confederate General Braxton Bragg's Coleman Scouts, commended Mrs. Doctor Patterson and Miss Fannie Battle, while another Coleman Scout lauded Kate Patterson and Robbie Woodruff for saving men from capture as well as for identifying opportune times and places to attack Federal forces. That particular network, which included several women, contributed to raids by Generals John Hunt Morgan and Nathan Bedford Forrest. The fact that Union General Grenville Dodge gave orders specifically to capture Coleman Scouts indicates the effectiveness of the group and indirectly

compliments the women. Confederate President Jefferson Davis and numerous Missouri officers acknowledged Belle Edmondson's sacrifices and devotion. Near the end of the war, Union spies in Richmond relayed precise information to General Ulysses S. Grant in time for him to capture Fort Harrison and weaken Confederate General Robert E. Lee's troop strength. Union Generals Grant and Butler and Colonel George H. Sharpe praised Elizabeth Van Lew's work, and Congress awarded her partial compensation for wartime expenses. That women spies were arrested validates their power even though a particular woman's information may not have contributed to winning or losing a battle.

How female spies fared after the war depended to some extent on their political persuasion and place of residence. Elizabeth Van Lew, for instance, continued to live in Richmond, suffering social ostracism because she spied for the Union in the midst of a Confederate majority population and continued to assist blacks after the war. Benefiting from her wartime alliance with General Grant, she used her appointments to the Freedmen's Bureau and as Postmaster to help blacks move to the North and to hire blacks as postal clerks. Most former female spies who had aligned with the dominant cause in their area chose postwar marriage and a traditional domestic life. In addition, many former Confederate spies were active in the organization that became the United Daughters of the Confederacy, raising money to place memorials to fallen soldiers, ensuring that school children learned the "true history" of the war, and otherwise contributing to the Lost Cause campaign. Some women spies joined socially acceptable occupations, primarily teaching, until they married. A few women spies opted to remain unwed and to teach or enter fields newly opened to women, such as nursing and positions as office, shop, or government clerks, because they had performed those jobs during the war. Some participated in the burgeoning women's club, temperance, and suffrage or antisuffrage movements. Most participated in their church benevolent society, and a few delved into what eventually became social work. The handful who traveled recounting their exploits or who quickly published memoirs brought sorely needed attention to women's capabilities and contributions, sometimes exaggerating their own deeds and thereby instilling doubt about other female spies' achievements.

The extent to which female spies impacted life during and after the Civil War is debatable. Significantly, a sizeable number of women risked their reputations and lives as activists for their cause in an era when such behavior was unexpected and, during peacetime, socially unacceptable. Their wartime assertiveness presaged women's late nineteenth-century move toward attaining higher education, working outside the domestic sphere, engaging in activism for causes, and choosing to delay or forgo marriage—transformations that may not have come as quickly or spread as widely without women's Civil War experiences.

*Nancy L. Adgent*

**See also** Abolitionists and Northern Reformers; African American Women; Battle, Mary Frances "Fannie" (1842–1924); Boyd, Belle (1844–1900); Bull Run/Manassas, First Battle of (July 21, 1861); Civilian Life; Confederate Homefront; Conscription; Cushman, Pauline [Harriet Wood] (1833–1893); Domesticity; Edmondson, Belle (1840–1873); Enlistment; Female Combatants; Freedmen's Bureau; Guerrilla Warfare; Greenhow, Rose O'Neal (ca. 1814–1864); Imprisonment of Women; Lee, Robert Edward (1807–1870); Military Invasion and Occupation; Nationalism, Confederate; Nationalism, United States; Northern Women; Nurses; Politics; Refugees; Religion; Separate Spheres; Shortages; Southern Unionists; Southern Women; Teachers, Northern; Teachers, Southern; Tubman, Harriet [Araminta Ross] (1822–1913); Union Homefront; United Daughters of the Confederacy; Van Lew, Elizabeth (1818–1900); Velazquez, Loreta Janeta [Harry T. Buford] (1842–n.d.); Wartime Employment.

**References and Further Reading**

Ash, Stephen V. 1995. *When the Yankees Came: Conflict and Chaos in the South, 1861–1865.* Chapel Hill: University of North Carolina Press.

Clinton, Catherine. 1998. *Civil War Stories.* Athens: University of Georgia Press.

Clinton, Catherine, and Nina Silber, eds. 1992. *Divided Houses: Gender and the Civil War.* New York: Oxford University Press.

Cox, Karen L. 2003. *Dixie's Daughters: The United Daughters of the Confederacy and the Preservation of Confederate Culture.* Gainesville: University Press of Florida.

Edmonds, S. Emma E. 1865. *Nurse and Spy in the Union Army.* Hartford, CT: W. S. Williams and Company.

Faust, Drew Gilpin. 1996. *Mothers of Invention: Women of the Slaveholding South in the American Civil War.* Chapel Hill: University of North Carolina Press.

Fishel, Edwin C. 1996. *The Secret War for the Union: The Untold Story of Military Intelligence in the Civil War.* Boston: Houghton-Mifflin.

Galbraith, William, and Loretta Galbraith, eds. 1990. *A Lost Heroine of the Confederacy: The Diaries and Letters of Belle Edmondson.* Jackson: University Press of Mississippi.

Greenhow, Rose. 1863. *My Imprisonment and the First Year of Abolition Rule at Washington.* London: Richard Bentley.

Grimsley, Mark. 1995. *The Hard Hand of War: Union Military Policy toward Southern Civilians, 1861–1865.* Cambridge, UK, and New York: Cambridge University Press.

Headley, John W. 1906. *Confederate Operations in Canada and New York.* New York: Neale Publishing Company.

Leonard, Elizabeth. 1999. *All the Daring of a Soldier: Women of the Civil War Armies.* New York: W. W. Norton.

Stern, Philip Van Doren. 1959. *Secret Missions of the Civil War.* Chicago: Rand McNally.

Varon, Elizabeth R. 2003. *Southern Lady, Yankee Spy: The True Story of Elizabeth Van Lew, A Union Agent in the Heart of the Confederacy.* New York: Oxford University Press.

Velazquez, Loreta Janeta. 1876. *The Woman in Battle: A Narrative of the Exploits, Adventures, and Travels of Madame Loreta Janeta Velazquez, Otherwise Known as Lieutenant Harry T. Buford, Confederate States Army,* edited by C. J. Worthington. Richmond, VA: Dustin, Gilman & Co.

## Military Invasion and Occupation

During the Civil War, Union and Confederate women experienced military invasion and occupation differently. For women in the Union, citizens initially expected an aggressive Confederate military to make raids into Northern states. Such fears proved largely unfounded; with the exception of the Gettysburg campaign, no real organized Confederate invasion materialized. Union women's interaction with Confederate troops was largely limited to dealing with foraging and raiding parties, as well as guerrilla attacks. Women of both sympathies living in the border states had greater contact with the troops than their Northern counterparts, because their territory frequently became contested terrain between the two forces. Since the majority of battles took place in the Southern states, Confederate women's lives were the most affected by invading military forces. Homefront resistance flourished, and Union military strategy had to evolve to include relations with enemy civilians. While many instances of courtesy and protection are on record, most Confederate women could expect to suffer some loss of property, slaves, dignity, honor, and even life as the Union army conquered and subdued the rebellious region.

Regardless of where a woman lived or where her sympathies rested, fears about confrontations with enemy troops existed among the female population. With traditional male protectors absent from the homefront and the line between battlefield and home blurring, women's trepidations were many. The general pattern of invasion was well known: rumors preceded the arrival of troops, the military suddenly appeared and embarked on a brief pillaging period, and then the enemy just as suddenly evacuated. Once rumors of an invasion began to spread, panic and flight often followed. For those who remained to face the enemy, the protection of person and property took precedence. Anxieties about sexual assault dominated women's minds, and psychological stress either abounded while waiting for an attack or emerged after the devastation occurred. When the enemy finally arrived, women's reactions ranged from calm acceptance to hysterical panic, and their attitudes swung from courteous to hateful.

Once the war began, Union women faced few actual encounters with an invading army. Of greater concern for these women than fear of occupation, particularly in the border states, was contact with guerrilla forces or Confederate cavalry raiders. Guerrilla attacks were frequently damaging and bloody, with William Quantrill and his raiders among the most notorious in Missouri and Kansas. These men were often not associated with either the Union or the Confederacy's legitimate military force; as a result, many viewed them as rabble and composed of a lower class of men bent on selfish purposes. Their wide-ranging attacks targeted civilian populations without remorse, and their purpose was often to instill fear and intimidation. Again, Union women's interaction with organized Confederate forces was limited. The Confederate military sent regiments of cavalry into the North on scouting and scavenging missions. In these instances, the troops arrived in towns to search for food and supplies for the trailing army or to intimidate the local population into supporting the Confederate cause. As a result, Union civilians often had their crops and livestock commandeered or their personal safety threatened. If payment for supplies was promised, it often never came. The most prominent of such raiders were J.E.B. Stuart and Jubal Early in Maryland and the Shenandoah Valley region, as well as John Hunt Morgan in the Ohio Valley.

Confederate women's experiences were different. With the war being fought on their doorsteps, Southern women's interaction with an invading, and eventually occupying, military force was frequent. Contact between women and the military depended on the strategic importance of the region. In areas of high strategic value, such as major Southern cities and ports, the military kept a constant presence once it had secured possession. In the area surrounding such armed camps, the Union made occasional appearances while on patrol, foraging, or searching for the enemy. In remote or frontier territories in the Confederacy, citizens' contact with the military was sporadic.

The Union's military attitude toward enemy civilians evolved from an initial policy of conciliation to a policy of total war. Given early beliefs in a quick resolution to the sectional conflict, the official military guidelines urged noninterference with civilians. Southerners' rights were to be respected, their property left untouched, and their slaves unprovoked. The rationale was that most civilians only tacitly approved of secession and that, if the Union could demonstrate its respect for Southern life and property, a speedy reunion would ensue. Such a position dominated policy through the early stages of the war, until Union military reversals in 1862 forced a reexamination of policy. At that point, securing military victory became paramount, and concern for civilians became a consideration only so far as interaction affected the outcome of the battle. By 1864, with continued Confederate resistance among civilians, especially from women, Union military policy again shifted. A hard war policy developed, in which civilians became targets of the Union military in an effort to demoralize any fighting spirit that remained and to ruin the economic infrastructure that was sustaining the Confederacy.

As the interaction with Confederate civilians increased, the Union military needed a set of guidelines for conduct in the field. In 1863, the military issued General Order Number 100, also known as Lieber's Code for Francis Lieber, the lone civilian on the committee and primary author of the guidelines. The Code distinguished three categories of civilians: (1) those who were truly loyal and would support the Confederacy only if compelled to do so by force; (2) noncombatants who did not interfere in military affairs; and (3) openly hostile citizens determined to resist the invasion. Each group required different treatment. The military tried to protect loyal citizens' property as much as possible; if troops took supplies, payment was offered. For noncombatants, the Union would not harass them as long as they continued to not interfere. Their property, however, was subject to impressment if the military needed it. Any attempt by those in this group to aid the enemy would result in greater property seizures and strict punishment for offenders. The Union military treated citizens who were aggressively resisting Union occupation the most severely, subjecting them to property seizure and destruction, confinement, or expulsion from their homes and communities.

General Order Number 100 also provided a guideline for determining which property or action could be considered a military necessity: specifically, the material or action needed to facilitate the end of the war. With such latitude, soldiers could destroy property, obstruct travel and commerce, and take supplies needed to sustain their efforts. However, the Code did not advocate "wanton" destruction or any action that would create such resentment as to make peace difficult to attain. The Union wanted to conquer the Confederate territory, not produce lasting bitter feelings. Nonetheless, the message behind the guidelines was that the burden of the war was to fall on disloyal citizens.

As the army approached Confederate cities, commanders frequently issued formal warnings to the citizens. They urged people to evacuate the region to avoid unnecessary civilian casualties. Confederate city officials also encouraged women, children, and the elderly to flee the city limits, freeing up more men, provisions, and facilities for overall defense. For those who chose to leave, the roads and railroads were often congested with refugees struggling to flee with the few possessions they could carry. Those ignoring the warnings often suffered when the battle began. Not only did they have to avoid becoming casualties of the battle, but they also had to contend with reduced ability to provision themselves. One of the best examples of this was during the siege of Vicksburg. Women who stayed in the city were eventually forced to live in caves and feed their families on mule and rat meat due to the devastation of battle. Unfounded rumors of an attack became so frequent in some areas, often with no attack coming, that women frequently ignored the warnings, realizing too late when the danger proved real.

Choices existed for citizens as the enemy approached. Evacuation from homes and communities was a decision many Confederate sympathizers frequently made. When rumors were the only signs of approach and no one knew how the enemy would behave, the fear of harsh punishment, prison, or even death motivated many citizens to leave their property unattended in the face of invasion and become refugees. Often families of the elite classes chose this alternative, having the means and personal connections to transport themselves and their property to another location. In many communities, this caused a vacuum in local leadership, making the resistance by those who remained more difficult to sustain. For most of the population, the desire to protect their own property shored up their failing courage. Women often hid as many valuables as possible before the enemy raiders arrived in town. Hiding places ranged from cellars and attics (although those proved insecure and were usually the first places the soldiers searched), to wells, cisterns, mattresses, and even their own persons. Often suspicious of the loyalty of their slaves, Confederate women frequently changed their hiding spaces, even to the point of entering the woods and reburying items in the middle of the night.

When soldiers and civilians came into contact with one another, troop behavior varied. In some instances, the formal surrender of a town took place in a quiet, orderly ceremony. The conquering military officers announced their intentions and expectations, and then they began to work on winning over the population's favorable sentiments. Bodily harm would rarely come to middle- and upper-class white women, with officers punishing soldiers who physically abused the women they encountered. Rape also proved to be rare for upper-class women, with African American women the more frequent victims of sexual assault. In the early years of the war, the outright looting and destruction of property often occurred only if the home was abandoned, and in many instances, straggling soldiers or guerrillas, wandering slaves, or retreating Confederate troops did the most damage. Once the policy of total war guided the army's behavior, Union soldiers became more aggressive in their interactions with Confederate sympathizers. As the Union armies increasingly relied on the region for provisions rather than on supply lines from the North, property destruction increased. Exterior buildings and fences were always susceptible to impressment by passing troops, as were women's crops and livestock for sustenance. As the war dragged on, soldiers were less likely to be compassionate and leave a few supplies behind for the family's benefit. Search and seizure in women's homes also rose with each passing year. Women were shocked by the invasiveness of the men, and their images of Yankees as barbarous and inhuman were solidified when soldiers maliciously destroyed personal

effects. While physical rapes were rare and never officially sanctioned, soldiers became adept at symbolic rape when they entered a woman's home. Entering a woman's bedroom and taking her clothing and undergarments, often parading around the house in them or sending them back to their own female relatives, was a definitive violation of a Confederate woman's privacy and dignity. Soldiers also made obscene or lewd gestures or comments to women and their daughters, stole or destroyed family mementos, or forced women to cook meals for them, all in the effort to demonstrate women's helplessness and force them into humiliating submission.

Some good came with enemy occupation. Federal troop presence often brought a return of stability, improved law enforcement, job opportunities, a steady supply of food and provisions, and care for the indigent and refugees. In most cases, access to this care required all citizens, including women, to swear an oath of allegiance to the United States. Failure to do so not only made survival in an occupied region more difficult, but it could also mean expulsion from the area altogether. The shared experience of suffering helped to unite the Confederates, often across class lines. The devastation reduced many wealthy citizens to an impoverished status, and dependency on fellow citizens and Federal assistance gradually emerged. While some resistance remained, as the war lingered, more Confederate citizens swallowed the bitter pill and took the oath when survival became paramount.

Women's responses to invasion varied, ranging from passive avoidance to aggressive confrontation with the troops. Because their men had left for the battlefields or had gone into hiding to avoid capture, Confederate women frequently faced the invading Union forces alone. Prior to the war, women had been left alone to manage their farms and plantations when business took the men away, so that situation was not necessarily unusual. The strength of resistance women offered was what shocked many Union troops, who expected women to be passive and sheltered from the hostile world of men. Indeed, many women believed that civilian and military affairs were distinctly separate from each other and that soldiers would not cross that border and invade women's homes. Once troops arrived, however, such notions were quickly disabused, and women worked to have their homes, personal property, and persons protected. In early interactions, with the conciliatory policy in place, soldiers hesitated or were apologetic when searching women's homes or removing property for military use. In many ways this lulled women into believing that they could be defiant without suffering repercussions, that their gender would shield them. Thus, when attitudes hardened and soldiers became more demanding and punitive, women became bolder and their level of defiance increased. Since society prevented women from facing their foes on the battlefield, they seized the opportunity to actively attack the enemy on the homefront. Popular beliefs held that Yankees were contemptible, without honor, and unworthy of respect, and Confederate women used this rationale to behave in unladylike ways. Gender conventions could be cast aside since the targets of contempt were deemed unworthy, although the unchristian attitude and behavior that some women exhibited proved shocking. From sneering and insulting men, to spitting on and emptying the contents of chamber pots on passing soldiers, to physically attacking the men with fists and guns, women could behave badly.

Other Confederate women chose to negotiate with or manipulate the Union troops they met. In seeking protection for their homes and property, some women offered proof of their Northern birth or connections to Northern relatives or influential Northern friends, and in some cases this tactic proved successful. Some women continued to use their femininity to secure what they wanted. Practical needs often warred with women's emotional hatred for the enemy. Many women became two-faced, publicly flattering and flirting with the troops, pretending to be helpless and ignorant, and appearing to cooperate with Union authorities, while privately continuing to resist and promote the Confederate cause. Confederate women's dedication remained strong throughout the conflict, but survival often dictated a hypocritical demeanor in occupied regions.

When contact with the enemy went on for long periods of time, despite the instinct to hate the invader, many women found themselves grudgingly respecting them instead. Soldiers' humanity emerged, and some women found themselves attending to sick and wounded Union troops as tenderly as they would for their own men. Friendships developed, and genuine affection existed between some of the conquerors and the women citizens. With their own men absent and the need for social activity and the desire for beaux still present, many Confederate belles turned their affections toward the Union troops. On occasion, romance and marriage resulted, although both sides criticized many such unions as unacceptable.

One of the early and most infamous interactions between a Union occupying force and resistant Confederate women happened in New Orleans. That city fell under Union control by April 1862, and General Benjamin Butler bore the initial responsibility of maintaining peace and order in the city. His most difficult challenge came from Confederate-sympathizing women. Angered at the desertion of their own troops and seemingly determined to sustain the resistance, the women frequently and publicly displayed their displeasure toward their occupiers in very gendered ways. Feminine decorum evaporated, and women did everything from flouncing out of theaters, churches, and restaurants when a Yankee soldier entered, to spitting on the troops and dumping chamber pot contents on soldiers as they passed below residents' windows. Women believed that their gender—their being women—gave them immunity from punishment for such acts of aggressive resistance. However, General Butler made it clear that enemy combatants would not be tolerated, regardless of gender. In May 1862, he issued General Order Number 28, known by Confederates as the Woman Order. It stated that, if such disrespectful and disorderly behavior continued, the woman responsible would be treated as "a woman of the town plying her trade." Outrage over the implications of the Order broke out among the women of New Orleans and among sympathizers throughout the Confederacy. For Confederates, the Order renewed fears about rape or the violation of female purity. However, Butler was attempting

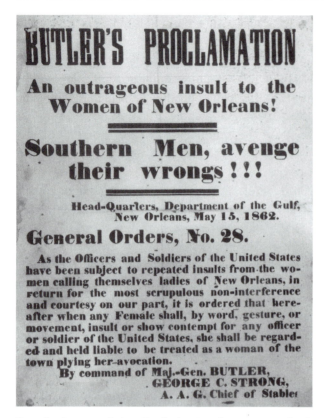

Broadside attacking Butler's Proclamation, which declared that any New Orleans woman who offended a member of the Union army would be treated as a common prostitute and thrown in jail, May 15, 1862. (MPI/Getty Images)

to make women accountable for their public behavior, demonstrating that such symbolic acts of protest carried as much significance as overt resistance by the Confederate military.

Women's resistance in New Orleans quieted following Butler's order, but, when General Nathaniel Banks replaced Butler in November 1862, renewed defiance emerged. In the so-called Battle of the Handkerchiefs in February 1862, a conciliatory policy toward women resurfaced. When a group of Confederate officers was being transported from New Orleans to Baton Rouge as part of a prisoner exchange, the women of the city gathered to support their men. In the Union's attempt to quiet the women, troops were faced with women waving parasols and handkerchiefs who refused to disband. The troops were hesitant to impose a forceful removal of the mob, although some women were slightly injured in the dispersal. The confrontation was considered a victory for the Confederates, because it seemed that Union policy would revert to seeing women as noncombatants or beyond the realm of political responsibility or retribution.

Perhaps the most complete implementation of the Union's total war policy came from troops under the command of General William T. Sherman as they marched through Georgia and into the Carolinas in 1864 and 1865. On Sherman's March to the Sea, from Atlanta to Savannah, Union soldiers lived off the land, taking supplies from homes and working to devastate the region's economy and ability to execute the war. This practice continued as the men turned north into the Carolinas. As the army moved to conquer South Carolina, inflicting vengeance on the population many believed to be responsible for the war was foremost in many soldier's minds. Renewed attention was focused on hurting civilians' ability to find food and shelter; homes came under more frequent attack, and verbal assaults on the female occupants also increased. Theft of property took precedence over physical attacks on women. The Union perspective held that, by encouraging the rebellion rather than nurturing productive civic-minded citizens, these women had violated the tenets of Republican Motherhood, which was women's role in the national political scene. Nonetheless, Confederate women in the state held fast to their commitment to the cause of Southern independence, and they defied their invaders with silent stares, accusations of immoral behavior, shaming, and physical assault. While the physical devastation weakened women's ability to sustain the conditions of their previous lives, in many cases it also renewed their drive to survive and resist. The enemy remained demonized, more so after actually experiencing the damage the army could do, and many women renewed their commitment to continue the fight, motivated by the desire for revenge.

For African Americans, the invasion of the Confederacy by Union troops offered a mixed blessing. On the one hand, many slaves associated the advent of the Union army with emancipation and fled their masters at the first rumor of approaching troops.

On the other hand, slaves were also victimized by their supposed saviors. Black women were more frequently raped than white women, and they were more likely to be the targets of verbal and physical abuse. African American property was not immune from military confiscation either. The treatment of loyal slaves who remained with their masters was severe as well, with threats of violence made to encourage the disclosure of the whereabouts of valuables or the owners. Racism remained within the ranks of the Union army, preventing absolute joy and harmony among African Americans, who had anticipated freedom as the Union armies forged through the Confederacy.

*Kristen L. Streater*

*See also* African American Women; Atlanta, Evacuation of (Special Field Orders Number 67); Border States; Butler, Benjamin F. (1818–1893); Camp Followers; Civilian Life; Columbia Bazaar (January 17–21, 1865); Confederate Homefront; Contrabands; Destruction of Homes; Destruction of Personal Property; Diaries and Journals; Domesticity; Family Life, Confederate; Family Life, Union; Food; Foraging, Effects on Women; Gettysburg, Battle of (July 1–3, 1863); Guerrilla Warfare; Honor; Impressment; Imprisonment of Women; Letter Writing; Loyalty Oaths; Morale; Northern Women; Nurses; Politics; Quantrill, William Clarke (1837–1865); Rape; Separate Spheres; Sheridan's Shenandoah Valley Campaign (1864); Sherman, William Tecumseh (1820–1891); Sherman's Campaign (1864–1865); Southern Women; Union Homefront; Woman Order (General Order Number 28); Wounded, Visits to.

**References and Further Reading**

Ash, Stephen V. 1995. *When the Yankees Came: Conflict and Chaos in the Occupied South, 1861–1865.* Chapel Hill: University of North Carolina Press.

Campbell, Jacqueline Glass. 2003. *When Sherman Marched North from the Sea: Resistance on the Confederate Home Front.* Chapel Hill: University of North Carolina Press.

Edwards, Laura F. 2000. *Scarlett Doesn't Live Here Anymore: Southern Women in the Civil War Era.* Urbana: University of Illinois Press.

Faust, Drew Gilpin. 1996. *Mothers of Invention: Women of the Slaveholding South in the American Civil War.* Chapel Hill: University of North Carolina Press.

Fellman, Michael. 1990. *Inside War: The Guerrilla Conflict in Missouri during the American Civil War.* New York: Oxford University Press.

Grimsley, Mark. 1995. *The Hard Hand of War: Union Military Policy toward Southern Civilians, 1861–1865.* Cambridge, UK, and New York: Cambridge University Press.

Leslie, Edward E. 1998. *The Devil Knows How to Ride: The True Story of William Clarke Quantrill and His Confederate Raiders.* New York: Da Capo Press.

Massey, Mary Elizabeth. 1994. *Women in the Civil War.* Lincoln: University of Nebraska Press.

Rable, George C. 1991. *Civil Wars: Women and the Crisis of Southern Nationalism.* Urbana: University of Illinois Press.

## Northern Women

The stories of the over 2 million men who fought for the Union during the American Civil War have been told many times, but the accounts of the women they left behind and the ways in which the war impacted their lives have often been overlooked. Whereas the majority of Northern women did not experience the war firsthand, as did many of their Southern counterparts, a great number participated in the war effort by contributing to soldiers aid societies or by providing nursing services to wounded soldiers. Many more took on new duties at home, running businesses and farms in the absence of their husbands, brothers, and fathers. A small but interesting group of Northern women sought out unusually direct roles in the war effort by disguising themselves as men and enlisting in the army or serving as spies. Finally, women who had been involved in the abolitionist movement and most black women felt the impact of the war in ideological ways, striking a blow for the freedom of African Americans throughout the nation. Whether in response to patriotic feelings or unromantic necessity, the war forced Northern women to undertake new roles and to expand their influence in ways they had never imagined.

The role of women in the Civil War has been underrepresented in most accounts since the first publication of the war's histories. Exceptions to this rule are notable. In 1867 Frank Moore published

*Women of the War: Their Heroism and Self Sacrifice,* a biographical account of Northern women who supported the war effort in various ways. While Moore recounted the deeds of dozens of women, his views were circumscribed by the mores of his time. Moore overlooked black women entirely. His belief that a lady would not seek out publicity for her good works colored his interpretation and led him to downplay women's public impact on the war. He also deleted the accounts of some women at the request of male relatives who, when they heard of Moore's upcoming work, wrote to make sure he did not include the ladies from their families. After Moore's work, the contributions of women during the Civil War period were largely ignored by the scholarly community until nearly one hundred years later. The centennial of the war in the 1960s coincided with the rise of the women's movement and brought women's achievements during the Civil War to the forefront. The centennial of the war was also responsible for the publishing of many women's diaries from the war, which helped to bring their stories out of the attics and into the hands of historians and the general public alike. Out of this newfound information came studies of women during the Civil War, predominately those of elite, white, Southern women. Still, until relatively recently, studies of Northern women during the Civil War were few in number.

The women of the Civil War era came of age between 1830 and 1860, a period that marked the emergence of the American middle class, a rapid expansion of manufacturing, and the idea of "separate spheres." With the rise of industrialization, traditional women's work lost monetary value, and men became the sole breadwinners for the family. As such, men were associated with the public sphere, the world outside the home. Women began to disappear from their already limited role in the public world as their household production became devalued in the new industrial society. Since middle-class women came to be less and less relied on to produce the basic household articles necessary for survival, the image and ideal of the American home came to be seen more and more as a haven for the feminized values excluded from public life, including piety and morality. A domestic sphere shorn of its productive value and market relationships came to be seen as a symbol of status and respectability, and a new ideology of gender emerged, giving expression to and supporting this ideal. Historian Barbara Welter first termed this change in gender ideals a "cult" of domesticated women, and since then historians have referred to the midnineteenth century Cult of True Womanhood or Cult of Domesticity as shorthand for large changes in class dynamics, work, and the operation of gender in women's lives at this time. This ideal must be taken into account when considering how Northern women impacted the waging of the war and when assessing the impact of the war on them.

In the decades preceding the Civil War, women began to be perceived as being morally superior to men and as the moral guardians of society. The cult of true womanhood focused on four foundational traits: domesticity, submissiveness, piety, and purity. Whereas gender segregation had long been a part of many American traditions, the cult of true womanhood gave new impetus to the idea of separate spheres for men and women. According to its ideology, since women were innately more emotional, domestic, modest, religious, and submissive than men, it was only natural that they belonged in the home, safe and protected from the outside world. The most important consequence of this ideology as it relates to the Civil War is that it obliged many middle-class Northern white women, who might otherwise feel little affinity for enslaved black women, to decry the market relationships that invaded the home through the mechanism of plantation slavery. Paradoxically, the same middle-class women, whose status depended on their divorce from the public realm, demanded public roles on the basis of the moral stature that the divorce had lent them.

Other paradoxes that hinged on the contradictions embedded in the separate sphere ideology also abounded during the war. With their fathers, husbands, and sons off in the Union armies, many Northern women stepped up to fill the traditionally male role as head of the household and thereby found themselves challenging the notion of separate spheres. Women not only ran their households, but in many cases oversaw the farm or family business as well. In the early days of the war, women relied heavily on the guidance, through letters, of their husbands or other male heads of households, to govern their actions with regard to how farms and businesses should be run. However, as the war lengthened, women became more confident in their abilities to make business decisions. Consequently, many came to rely less and less on input from their male relatives and depended more on their own ability to make the correct decisions. While letters from the battlefield continued to be filled with advice for running the farm, business, and other aspects of homefront life, women independently handled day-to-day affairs. Women who had previously written to their husbands about "your" fields or "your" business now claimed ownership for themselves when they wrote of "our" fields or even "my fields."

Northern women who assumed the task of running their family's farm or business also had a decided advantage over their counterparts in the South. Women in the North, with the notable exceptions of the border states, did not have to deal with the severe shortages or battles in their communities, faced by their Southern counterparts. Even so, Northern women had to cope with rising wartime prices and labor shortages as well as with other hardships such as illness, pregnancy, and the loss of family members while continuing to manage their family's assets. While not every woman who assumed the task of running farms and businesses did so willingly or even with much success, for many others it became the opportunity to loosen or abandon traditional gender restrictions and prove to themselves and others that they were capable of managing their family's assets.

In addition to assuming the duties of running their homes, farms, and businesses, many Northern women also joined soldiers' aid societies. The first official soldiers' aid society in the North was founded on April 15, 1861, in Bridgeport, Connecticut, and it was soon followed by thousands more throughout the North. The majority of these aid societies were overseen by the leading women

of the community and were most often made up of members of the middle class. For many aid societies, there was no official network through which they worked. Instead they were founded to supply the men from the community with food, clothing, blankets, and bandages. The ladies of the community held fairs, raffles, concerts, lectures, and dances to raise money to pay for supplies for their soldiers. In hopes of consolidating the goods produced by local aid societies, national aid societies like the United States Sanitary Commission (USSC) were created and began to centralize the aid efforts of Northern women. In spite of some resistance, the Sanitary Commission became the most successful aid society during the war, creating over ten thousand branch societies, producing goods worth over $15 million, and collecting monetary donations of nearly $50 million. The great success was achieved mainly due to the abilities of their female aid workers.

Not only did women supply food, clothing, and bandages to the soldiers, but they also kept the soldiers connected to the homefront. Letter writing was extremely important throughout the war, and letters from soldiers were eagerly awaited and sometimes published in local newspapers. Through letters, women kept male family members informed of community and family news, the latest happenings at home, and what the children were doing; letters essentially kept soldiers connected to their prewar lives.

Other women took their writing a step further and wrote not only for family members but also to the larger Northern population. The war forced women to step outside their traditional roles and to look beyond the family for solutions to their problems, and many women turned to writing as a solution. Some Northern women used their writing skills in an effort to get their loved ones home. Women wrote letters to commanding officers and even to the president detailing their hardships and asking that male family members be excused from military obligations to help their family. Most of the women who sent these letters had very little education, but they understood the gender roles of the time. In their barely literate letters, they wrote of their weakness as women, their inability to support their children, and their need to have their male providers returned home. Women of the middle and upper classes also used letter writing in hopes of mobilizing the war effort. Soldiers' aid societies created networks of women who, through correspondence, attempted to organize relief work, ensured that soldiers received the goods they needed, and offered encouragement to other aid workers, stressing the importance of their work.

Other women supported the war effort through nursing. Although many women saw nursing wounded and ill soldiers as an extension of their traditional family duties, there was opposition to female nurses in the military hospitals. Many male surgeons were concerned that ladies' delicate sensibilities would be disturbed by the sights, sounds, and smells of battlefield hospitals. Male doctors also balked at the idea of female hospital matrons because they frequently perceived the women as a threat to traditional male authority. In spite of these obstacles, over twenty thousand women from the North served in hospitals during the war. Many society women, including First Lady Mary Lincoln, frequently visited military hospitals, dispensing treats to the wounded soldiers, reading to them, and writing letters home for those who were unable to write for themselves.

Visiting was one of the common ways in which Northern women involved themselves in caring for the wounded, but it was not the only way. The majority of Northern women associated with military hospitals were there as hospital workers. Contrary to popular opinion, these female hospital workers cannot be categorized as white, educated, middle-class women. Northern female hospital workers represented all classes of women and included a larger than acknowledged population of African American women. In June 1861, Union Surgeon General R. C. Wood appointed well-known humanitarian Dorothea Dix to oversee female nurses officially associated with the Union army. The women hired by Dix to be nurses were paid $12 a month (40¢ a day) and given a food ration. Dix was well known for her demands that all nursing volunteers be plain in appearance and dress, be

between the ages of thirty-five and fifty, and have several letters of recommendation testifying to their moral character. Women rejected by Dix found other opportunities to serve; women with family connections could secure nursing appointments, and many women without powerful friends simply headed for Washington, D.C., hoping they would not be turned away from the hospitals once they arrived. Still other women bypassed the hospitals completely and went directly to the front to care for the wounded there. Women like Clara Barton from Massachusetts raised their own money and supplies and worked unofficially as nurses on the front lines, helping in field hospitals and providing food as well as medical care to the wounded.

Female hospital workers included more than just nurses; thousands of Northern women found work in military hospitals as cooks, laundresses, seamstresses, and cleaners. Nearly 10 percent of all Northern female hospital workers were African American. The majority of female African American hospital workers were to be found doing menial, yet vital, jobs such as laundry, cooking, and cleaning.

A small group of Northern women felt that traditional avenues of wartime support did not go far enough. These women wanted a more direct way to become involved in the war. Many were also looking for excitement and for something they could do outside the realm of their traditional sphere. For these women, serving as spies for the Union army or disguising themselves as men to fight in combat offered them unique opportunities to serve their country. Others became official "daughters of the regiment" and supported the troops through domestic work.

A considerable number of women traveled with the Union army during the war. Many were wives of officers; others were there in official capacities as laundresses, cooks, or nurses. Still others, especially during the early days of the war, were daughters of the regiment—generally younger women who wore military style dress and served mainly in an ornamental fashion with newly formed regiments. They also performed camp chores and cared for the wounded. Some drilled with the male soldiers and marched with them in parades and some, like Kady

Brownell of Rhode Island, saw combat action. Brownell accompanied her husband when he enlisted in the First Rhode Island regiment in 1861. She drilled with her husband's regiment, wore a military uniform with a knee-length skirt over the trousers, and became proficient in the use of the carbine and sword. She was praised for her bravery under fire and remained with the regiment until her husband was wounded at the Battle of New Bern, North Carolina.

Other women were not content simply to accompany the army; they wanted a more active role and became soldiers themselves. It was surprisingly easy for some women to pass themselves off as men and enlist in the army. The most obvious thing a woman had to do was to disguise her female characteristics, and many did so by cutting their long hair and tightly binding their chests to hide any unmanly curves. Also, with the rush to volunteer for service, many recruitment officers were more interested in filling their regiment rosters than in making sure their recruits were physically able to withstand the hardships of being a soldier. If a physical exam was administered to the new recruits, it often consisted of little more than a cursory look for obvious physical defects that might hinder marching or firing a rifle. As a result, many young boys enlisted in the army, and it was not unusual to see recruits with boyish faces in uniform. Since such little attention was paid to many of the new recruits, a woman could easily pass the physical exam and find herself enlisted. While it was fairly easy for some women to join the military, the difficulty was not in appearing to be a man but in acting like one, and in several accounts female soldiers were successful in disguising their appearance but were discovered when they were unable to disguise their feminine mannerisms and behaviors.

Estimates range from anywhere from four hundred to over one thousand women who disguised themselves as men and fought in the Civil War. Their motivations for enlisting vary from the desire to serve their country—which they believed they could do better as a soldier than through any outlet available to them as a female—or simply a desire for adventure. Whatever their motivation, nearly four hundred examples of female soldiers have

been documented. Of those, the most well-known is that of Sarah Emma Edmonds. Edmonds disguised herself as Franklin Thompson and enlisted in the Flint Union Greys, which was later absorbed into the Second Michigan Infantry. She served in the regimental hospital as a male nurse as well as at the front. She served until April 1863, when she became ill and deserted so that her true identity would not be discovered. She had served without incident and apparently without anyone suspecting her secret for two years. Later in life she petitioned the government for Frank Thompson's pension for his military service during the war and became the only female soldier to receive a veteran's pension under her own name.

Other women, who wanted to serve their country but not become soldiers, served as spies. Women often made perfect spies because they were rarely suspected as such. Nineteenth-century gender ideals assumed that women had no interest in or understanding of military matters, and female spies often used these assumptions to their advantage when gathering vital information. Also, women were rarely searched thoroughly as they traveled through military lines, especially during the early days of the war, so it was relatively easy for them to smuggle supplies or information without being detected. The Pinkerton Agency was among the first to use female operatives as a source of information, and, when the war began, hundreds of women with no training took it upon themselves to pass what they considered valuable information to those in positions of authority. While much of the information gathered by these amateurs had little or no value, there were several female spies who provided valuable service to the Union army. Northern actress Pauline Cushman used her position in a theater troupe to travel throughout areas of the South and pass information on Confederate positions, troop movements, and the names of Confederate spies to Union officers in Kentucky and Tennessee. Her career as a spy came to an end when she was captured by Confederate General Nathan Bedford Forrest and sentenced to death near Shelbyville, Tennessee. She was rescued by Union troops before her sentence could be carried out, but her usefulness as a spy was over.

Pauline Cushman (1833–1893), Union spy. (Library of Congress)

Perhaps the group of Northern women whose wartime experiences are the least known are African American women. These women lived as second-class citizens based on their race, yet many worked to support the Union war effort, hoping to end slavery and improve the status of African Americans in the United States. A few African American women played a large part in the Union's fight against slavery. The names of a few of these women have become well known. For example, Sojourner Truth, born a slave in New York, obtained her freedom and became well recognized as an abolitionist. During the Civil War, she took part in recruiting African American men for military service and in caring for wounded African American soldiers. Another former slave, Harriet Tubman of Maryland, served the Union cause as a

spy, scout, and nurse but gained her greatest fame as a conductor on the Underground Railroad, leading hundreds of slaves to freedom. Less celebrated black women, like Charlotte Forten of Philadelphia, grew up as part of the small free black middle class and during the war traveled to the Sea Islands in South Carolina to set up schools for the newly freed slaves. Other members of the black middle class, after being excluded from aid societies created by white women, created their own benevolent and soldiers' aid societies to support African American soldiers.

In addition to facing racism, many Northern African American women, especially those in border areas, lived with the fear that Confederate soldiers would seize them or their family members and take them into slavery in the Confederacy. This fear was not unfounded. There are accounts of between thirty and several hundred African American men, women, and children being kidnapped by Confederate soldiers during the Gettysburg campaign and taken south into slavery. Many of those taken had never been slaves but were part of the free black community in Pennsylvania.

African American women of the North, whether they were freeborn or had escaped from slavery, contributed to the Union war effort. In spite of being excluded from many avenues of participation, black women persevered and created their own institutions to aid African American soldiers and to care for those who were wounded. Others took on more dangerous roles as spies and scouts and were very successful in working behind Southern lines. Other elite black women went south to serve as teachers to newly freed slaves or helped to provide the funding to make such work possible.

The war thrust black and white women into new roles on the homefront, such as running business and farms, or closer to the battle, such as serving as nurses in military hospitals. Many women expanded their traditional roles to create soldiers' aid societies and nursing corps to aid the men who had gone off to war. Others, searching for more adventurous ways to aid the Union, served as spies or disguised themselves as men and fought. However, not every woman in the North supported the war effort.

Some, especially those living in border areas, were Confederate sympathizers, and still others who were members of pacifist religious communities did not actively support the war effort. What can be said for nearly all Northern women, though, is that the Civil War opened new roles and offered new opportunities for them to participate in public life.

*Lisa M. Smith*

**See also** African American Women; Aid Societies; Barton, Clara (1821–1912); Border States; Brownell, Kady (1842–n.d.); Camp Followers; Civilian Life; Cushman, Pauline [Harriet Wood] (1833–1893); Diaries and Journals; Dix, Dorothea Lynde (1802–1887); Domesticity; Edmonds, Sarah Emma [Franklin Thompson] (1841–1898); Factory Workers, Northern; Fairs and Bazaars; Family Life, Union; Female Combatants; Female Spies; Fiction Writers, Northern; Forten (Grimké), Charlotte L. (1837–1914); Free Blacks; Fundraising; Gettysburg, Battle of (July 1–3, 1863); Government Girls; Hospital Ships; Hospitals; Letter Writing; Morale; Mourning; Nationalism, United States; Nurses; Rural Women; Separate Spheres; Shortages; Southern Women; Teachers, Northern; Treasury Girls; Truth, Sojourner [Isabella Baumfree] (1797–1883); Tubman, Harriet [Araminta Ross] (1822–1913); Union Homefront; United States Christian Commission; United States Sanitary Commission; Urban Women, Northern; Wartime Employment; Wartime Literature; Widows, Union; Women's Central Association of Relief; Wounded, Visits to.

**References and Further Reading**

Attie, Jeanie. 1998. *Patriotic Toil: Northern Women and the American Civil War.* Ithaca, NY: Cornell University Press.

Blanton, DeAnne, and Lauren Cook. 2002. *They Fought Like Demons: Women Soldiers in the American Civil War.* Baton Rouge: Louisiana State University Press.

Cashin, Joan, ed. 2002. *The War Was You and Me: Civilians in the American Civil War.* Princeton, NJ: Princeton University Press.

Cimbala, Paul, and Randall Miller, eds. 2002. *An Uncommon Time: The Civil War and the Northern Home Front.* New York: Fordham University Press.

Clinton, Catherine, and Nina Silber, eds. 1992. *Divided Houses: Gender and the Civil War.* New York: Oxford University Press.

Edmonds, Sarah Emma. 1999. *Memoirs of a Soldier, Nurse and Spy: A Woman's Adventures in the Union Army.* DeKalb: Northern Illinois University Press.

Leonard, Elizabeth. 1994. *Yankee Women: Gender Battles in the Civil War.* New York: W. W. Norton.

Mitchell, Reid. 1993. *The Vacant Chair: The Northern Soldier Leaves Home.* New York: Oxford University Press.

Richard, Patricia. 2003. *Busy Hands: Images of the Family in the Northern Civil War Effort.* New York: Fordham University Press.

Schultz, Jane. 2004. *Women at the Front: Hospital Workers in Civil War America.* Chapel Hill: University of North Carolina Press.

Sizer, Lyde Cullen. 2000. *The Political Work of Northern Women Writers and the Civil War, 1850–1872.* Chapel Hill: University of North Carolina Press.

## Nurses

The effort to provide adequate medical care during the Civil War involved thousands of women and men and provided a way for noncombatants to demonstrate their patriotism. For many women the experience of wartime nursing proved to be personally definitive, and, in the process of being changed, they left a woman's imprint on Civil War hospitals and camps. While most of the women who got involved did not continue working as nurses during the postwar era, nevertheless their wartime efforts became an important experimental proving ground. Women's wartime experiment as workers in the medical field helped inspire a movement in the United States to professionalize nursing. Ultimately it helped create a place in the public sector in which women could work.

In Victorian America, expectations regarding what a nurse should do were varied. Hospitals dedicated to the care for the sick were limited to the biggest cities and thus were relatively inaccessible to a nation still largely rural. Of those hospitals, two offered small and rudimentary training programs for nurses before 1859. Most nurses in antebellum America were men, because society assumed their natures were better suited to hospital work.

Although nuns were beginning to branch into public nursing on the eve of the Civil War, Protestant women were usually the caregivers for ailing

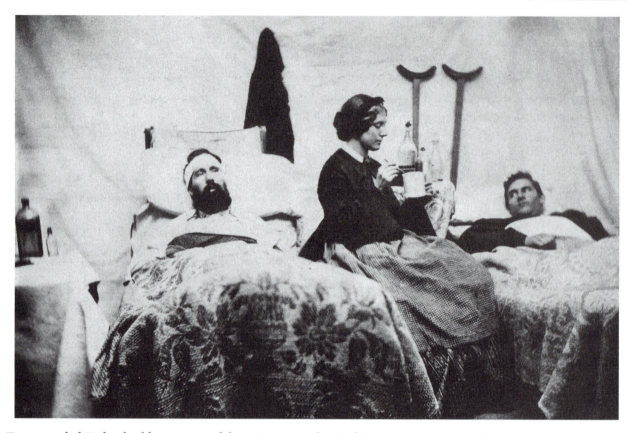

Two wounded Federal soldiers are cared for in Tennessee by Civil War nurse Anne Bell. Thousands of civilians took up their nations' call to help wounded soldiers. (Corbis)

family members. They were accustomed to applying motherly nurturing and comforting skills and to providing food, water, comfort, home remedies, and companionship for the sick within the confines of family and community. Widely accepted gender restrictions, however, made many women and their families, especially those of the upper classes, think twice before taking up medicine in the public realm.

One of the earliest women in the United States to begin formal studies in the medical field was Elizabeth Blackwell. In 1853, after completing medical school and finding that gender prejudice made it difficult for her to get a job, she opened a clinic in the slums of New York City. That year in England, Florence Nightingale, although criticized by members of her own family, finished a three-month nursing course, then began working in a hospital for women. A year later, with her country embroiled in the Crimean War, she worked to

improve the medical treatment available to soldiers. Her success made Nightingale a household name in England and gave her a reputation abroad. It also demonstrated that women could fill a vital position in wartime hospitals.

In the United States, gender expectations hindering women's entrance into public nursing were the most stringent among the South's upper classes. War did little to change the long-standing prohibitions against women's involvement in medicine. For example, Kate Cumming, of Mobile, Alabama, had to go against her family's wishes when she followed her brother to the front lines after the Battle of Shiloh in 1862. Although Cumming ultimately found respectability as a nurse in Confederate hospitals, she was angered to see that nuns were allowed a measure of freedom from the same conventional gender restrictions that limited what she could do for the wounded soldiers.

At the same time, the progressive urge to professionalize nursing was gaining momentum in the United States and Europe. For example, by the 1840s medical doctors were creating standards for themselves and their colleagues, while attempting to exclude those they viewed as uneducated practitioners, including homeopaths and midwives, both medical professions in which women had long been active.

Nevertheless, the majority of women who enjoyed elite hospital positions during the Civil War were influenced by this progressive move to create new professional standards. They were women who sought to maintain the values of Victorian female culture, which upheld qualities like submissiveness and self-sacrifice, while seeking to create professional standards for nurses that corresponded with the traditionally male qualities of confidence, action, and assertiveness. Whether Jane Hoge, the elite nurse from Illinois, or the South's Fannie A. Beers, they brought gendered ideas into professional culture.

However, if they influenced professional standards for medical personnel during peacetime, progressive ideals did not shape the reality of conditions in army hospitals during the war. Civil War battles left fields full of injured soldiers, unsanitary conditions in camp helped spread infectious diseases like influenza and smallpox, and inadequate army rations led to widespread illnesses caused by nutritional deficiencies. These specific conditions meant that military medical personnel could emulate peacetime standards, but they could not duplicate them. More specifically, progressives might insist on using only properly trained nurses, but conditions often demanded that any able-bodied person be put to work as a nurse. This meant that matronly, sufficiently responsible women were deemed qualified for the job. In some cases, convalescing soldiers, qualified only by the fact that they were less incapacitated than their fellow patients and that they had time to tend the sick since they were still too ill to be pressed back into battle, were similarly put to work as nurses.

Further complicating the situation, nineteenth-century medical technology was rudimentary and limited. With no way to sterilize wounds and no X-rays to help diagnose problems, surgeons routinely amputated injured arms and legs. Ether, chloroform, and alcohol were the only medications available to ease a patient's pain.

Nurses comforted and fed patients, wrote letters by the thousands for sick and wounded soldiers, and often prayed with them. They also assisted surgeons in changing bandages and performing operations. Some obtained supplies and distributed them. Others cooked and did laundry. A small number of well-to-do nurses worked on transport ships. Elite women in the North helped manage branches of philanthropic commissions, such as the United States Sanitary Commission (USSC) and the United States Christian Commission (USCC).

Patriotic women and men, in both the North and South, recognized the enormous medical needs created by war. Those who did not muster up for battle saw aiding the infirm as a way to make their personal contribution to the effort. For example, Dorothea Dix, the fifty-nine-year-old native of Massachusetts became the Union's Superintendent of Female Nurses in June 1861. She had already earned a reputation as a tireless advocate for establishing humane, state-controlled asylums for the insane. A native of Massachusetts, Dix had crusaded to improve the conditions of prisons and other institutions stretching from New England to Illinois and south to the Carolinas. When hostilities broke out in 1861, she immediately headed for Washington and volunteered to aid the Union cause.

There was no precedent in the United States for Dix to follow as she defined the responsibilities of her job. Consequently, she combined Victorian gender conventions with progressive ideas to create guidelines for appointing nurses. Just as progressives feared an outpouring of what they called benevolent chaos, Dix believed that tight control over who would become nurses would prevent the enthusiastic but ill-prepared masses from creating serious problems in army hospitals. She asserted that a female nurse must be in good health and observe high moral standards. To help ensure that only the best women work in military hospitals, she declared that successful candidates for nurse must be at least thirty-five years of age, dress simply, and not be too attractive. Finally, Dix preferred giving appointments to white middle- and upper-class women.

In attempting to reserve nursing jobs for the economically comfortable, Dix was demonstrating a value that was shared by many in Victorian America. The wartime philanthropic commissions also filled their most responsible positions with middle- and upper-class women. For example, Louisa Lee Schuyler, who helped establish the parent organization of the USSC, was from a prominent New York family. So were Georgeanna and Jane Woolsey, who had been turned down by Dix because of their youthfulness but who, through family connections, gained jobs on hospital transport ships operated by the USSC.

Dix herself enjoyed some economic advantages. Throughout the war she used her own money to finance her position. In addition to processing the applications of thousands of women, she rented two large houses in Washington, D.C., that doubled as supply depots and homes for soldiers in transit. She employed two secretaries, dispensed a myriad of needed supplies, operated her own ambulances, and distributed circulars—all while she traveled extensively.

Although her economic position proved an asset, Dix did not enjoy unlimited power because she did not appoint or supervise the army surgeons, and the nurses she placed in hospitals often struggled to work amid conflicting authorities. Moreover, some of her selection criteria destined her nurses to have difficulty with a number of local surgeons. For example, she preferred appointing Protestant women, but many surgeons wanted nuns, who were typically more experienced than Dix's nurses. In 1863, Dix lost what control she had managed to establish over nurses in hospitals, because the exigencies of the war convinced Union officials that surgeons should be able to select nurses at the local level. Dix, nevertheless, helped more than three thousand women gain nursing appointments in military hospitals during the war.

Dix's strict standards meant that she rejected a significant number of applicants. Several of those she turned away had enough personal initiative and

wherewithal to create positions for themselves in local hospitals. For example, Esther Hill Hawks of New Hampshire, a trained physician who was a bit too young and probably too attractive to become one of Dix's nurses, found her way to the front line hospitals and served in the South Carolina Sea Islands. There she tended injured black soldiers and local residents who needed medical assistance. Helen Gilson, a native of Boston, found a job working under her prominent uncle, the Honorable Frank Fay, a former mayor of Chelsea, Massachusetts. Dr. Elizabeth Blackwell's application to be a nurse was turned down by Dix and her negotiations with the USSC came to naught. She went back to New York and established a school to train women who wanted to nurse in military settings.

Women in elite positions with the USSC, such as Mary Livermore in Chicago, adopted Dix's guidelines as they screened nursing applicants from the region in which they lived. Yet applying Dix's rigid standards was not always that easy and occasionally these women found they had to compromise. For example, they sometimes certified women as official nurses who were already working in army hospitals. Those who had proved their value as workers could, if they so chose, gain official appointments without going through Dix.

One of the most colorful of these was Mary Ann Bickerdyke, a widow in her forties who was at home with two young sons when the war began. She quickly placed her children under the care of another and headed to the battlefields in the West, where she worked diligently as nurse, cook, and mother extraordinaire. Her ability to connect with the common soldier endeared her to many and ensured that she would have a long, acclaimed role in the war. She was in the field as early as the conflicts at Fort Donelson in late 1861, and she stayed in the war until after William Tecumseh Sherman's march through Georgia. At some point in her army career, she agreed to become affiliated with the Sanitary Commission and its smaller counterpart, the Christian Commission, because they allowed her to do what she wanted to, and they promised her much needed resources.

Bickerdyke's experiences demonstrate that nurses could, and sometimes did, enjoy more authority in the hospitals than did Dix. Quickly earning the respect of the rank and file as well as that of Sherman, Mother Bickerdyke, as she became known, could and did arrange to get specific doctors dismissed. In one case, a disgruntled surgeon whom she had been instrumental in ousting complained to Sherman, but he refused to intervene. Moreover in 1864, when Sherman set off on his march through Georgia, Bickerdyke accompanied his troops.

Of course, Bickerdyke understood the limits of her authority. She enjoyed real influence in the hospitals, but she would not have retained her power had she attempted to impose her authority over things like battle plans. Moreover, if she had gone into the army hospitals imitating the behavior of a crusty general rather than using the mannerisms of a bighearted mother, she would not have enjoyed the success that she did. In short, when nurses held their own in military hospitals and in camp, it was because they were at least superficially upholding gender conventions, and they recognized when it was best to accede to the prevailing authorities. Bickerdyke's unblemished reputation with the soldiers and officials of the USSC allowed her to expand her own authority in the military hospital and camp. She created for herself a comfortable place within the confines of military discipline.

Even if one found a satisfactory place in the larger military hierarchy, there were times when a woman encountered and recognized real injustices that she could not get changed. Esther Hill Hawks found herself in this uncomfortable position when the Sea Islands fell under Union control in 1862. Enraged to find that some military personnel were molesting local women, she noted in her diary that she was treating several black women in her hospital for injuries they had received while resisting unwanted sexual advances. Since both officers and enlisted men were guilty of perpetuating this outrage, Hawks found no one who would address her concerns.

Besides having to live with things they preferred not to deal with, female medical personnel found themselves isolated in military hospitals. Unlike men who joined the army, the women who worked near the front lines often did so without the benefit of female companionship. Some nurses filled this

void by establishing deep friendships with the men they worked with. But those who were seeking to avoid romantic involvement often had to distance themselves from everyone around them.

Economic, racial, and religious differences among hospital workers further divided them. Nuns, working-class whites, and blacks all found themselves pushed into menial jobs. For example, they were more likely to be assigned to caring for the soldiers with the most serious communicable diseases, such as smallpox and typhoid. Not surprisingly, the nurses who worked among the most ill patients were the most likely to contract communicable diseases, which could and did sometimes lead to their deaths.

In the South, racial prejudice kept slaves serving in the lowest tiers of hospital workers. Slaves might be pressed into work by their elite white owners. Others, who became cooks and laundresses, were referred to as camp followers. Even free blacks thought they were better than slaves and sometimes merited more elite jobs. Slaves, nevertheless, often worked in the same hospitals as elite nurses did, and thus they were likely to have the responsibilities associated with nursing, giving medicine to the sick and wounded when they were done with their primary responsibilities or when the demands of war prevailed over race and class divisions.

In the North, blacks and whites were less likely to work together. Black women did the heavy chamber work, worked as laundresses or cooks, and were confined to the most menial jobs. For example, black women employed by the Union navy were assigned to flush ship decks of blood and mud. However, when the soldiers being treated were black, African American women were appointed as their nurses.

If working in a military hospital required women to perform a delicate balancing act, it also required self-confidence and emotional fortitude. Women who might have fainted at the sight of blood only months earlier found that nursing in a military hospital demanded them to cultivate the strengths that were most often associated with masculinity. Physical stamina, personal initiative, and the ability to control their emotions were all necessary for nurses who needed to work among a never ending sea of sick and wounded men. If a woman could gather the strength to continue work in a military hospital for even a few months, she could easily marvel at the different person she had become.

Despite the real contributions that women were making to the war effort, both Union and Confederate officials had difficulty placing a monetary value on nurses. The Union government paid white women $12 a month and black women up to $10. The philanthropic commissions paid slightly more, but the pay was never more than just above subsistence levels. Women physicians got better paid, but often still received less than $500 annually, while their male counterparts got as much as $1,000 per year.

Elite Southern women, such as Phoebe Yates Pember, did not get paid for nursing. But the majority of workers in Southern hospitals, most of whom came from the working class, benefited in 1862 when Confederate officials standardized wages for nurses, paying chief matrons $40 per month. White women earned the same as free black women did. Slaves got paid nothing or had to turn over their small wages to their mistresses. Whatever Southern women received, the growing weakness of the Confederate dollar meant that their wages translated into minimal buying power.

The problem of paying female hospital workers was complicated by upper- and middle-class women's fears that receiving a paycheck would undermine their economic status. They believed that their labor must be offered with a sense of noblesse oblige, and thus their wartime service should not be motivated by the need for payment. For example, although she received a small monthly check for her work at the Patent Office, Clara Barton of Massachusetts boasted that she worked without need of reward. The independently wealthy Katharine Prescott Wormeley of New York disdained paychecks but joined the Sanitary Commission and landed the elite job of nursing aboard a transport ship. The prominent Southerner Sara Rice Pryor did not publicly discuss wages, but an incident during her first hospital experience demonstrated a similar sentiment. She struggled to prove herself worthy to nurse at a hospital in Richmond, until after she brought in a basket of fresh

bandages that had been fashioned from her private stock of household linens.

Besides devaluing the work of paid nurses, the middle- and upper-class women's insistence that they not work for pay complicates estimating the numbers of women who served as nurses during the Civil War. Only those women who received paychecks had their names listed in official Union records. Thus, although twenty-one thousand hospital workers were listed in the official records, hundreds of additional women worked in Northern Civil War hospitals.

The women who sought payment fell into two groups. A relatively small number of women, like Hawks, who had been trained as physicians or other medical professionals, expected to be paid for the services they rendered. Many more simply needed the money to survive during the war. Just as men from the lower classes were likely to become rank-and-file soldiers, less economically advantaged women were likely to become hospital workers in the hopes of earning the money to support their families.

Estimating the numbers of Confederate women who nursed is even more difficult than determining the numbers of Union nurses. There was no official counterpart to Dorothea Dix in the South. At the same time, no organizations there matched the North's huge privately operated philanthropic commissions. Prominent Southern citizens, such as Juliet Opie Hopkins in Alabama, created state hospitals near battle sites in Virginia, North Carolina, Arkansas, and Florida.

Nevertheless, much about Southern nurses' hospital experiences mirrored the daily lives of their Northern counterparts, and they faced many of the same challenges. The physical and emotional needs of patients bore the distinct imprint of war, and the situation of the military camps and of the state of medical technology available at the time remained the same, regardless of region. These conditions made up the primary characteristics of the Civil War experience for nurses, defining the tasks they must do and creating similar conditions in many hospitals.

In addition, Southern nurses had to contend with conditions that were specific to the region. The task of garnering supplies for hospitals was more challenging in the South. Procuring the medicines and necessary food for patients became increasingly difficult as the war destroyed resources across the South. Even elite nurses felt the crunch of dwindling supplies. For example, in April 1862, when a man in Corinth, Tennessee, asked the Confederate nurse Kate Cumming for food, she gladly helped collect coffee, bread, and meat to take to some injured men who were at the depot awaiting transportation. By September 1864, however, she felt the strain of not having enough food to share. With Sherman's men cutting a bloody path through Georgia, she blamed Abraham Lincoln and the North for the horrendous conditions that she had witnessed at Andersonville Prison. Southerners, she asserted, could not be expected to feed prisoners of war when they could scarcely feed their own citizens. Wartime exigencies could render any hospital short of food supplies. In 1864 a Northerner, Harriet Eaton, complained that she could not keep patients healthy when all they had to eat was hard tack and salt pork.

Moreover, at sites throughout the Confederacy, the battle lines intersected the boundaries of private property. Nursing the wounded often meant creating a hospital in one's home or in the local courthouse. Cornelia McDonald found herself working as a nurse in her hometown of Winchester, Virginia, one day after she and her youngest children had crouched in the cellar listening to the sounds of battle that raged just over the hill from their farmhouse. And following the first Battle of Manassas, Sally Louisa Tompkins used her own wealth to transform a friend's home in Richmond into a hospital, creating an elite private institution that lasted for the war's duration. Perhaps more typical for Southern nurses was Fannie Beers' experience. She lived in New Orleans when the war began and nursed in Alabama, as well as in Newman, Ringgold, and Fort Valley, Georgia.

Because they lived in the region where most of the battles were fought, Southern nurses were more likely to care for the most critically wounded soldiers than their Northern counterparts. Occasionally Northern nurses worked within earshot of battles; for example, Mother Bickerdyke's reputation shone the most brightly while working near the front lines. But Southern women from many locations could have related to McDonald's experience. A resident of the Shenandoah Valley in 1862, she kept track of where the armies were stationed, by the different military personnel who were using her home and property for a base of operations.

At the end of the Civil War, female nurses found themselves more courageous, better in control of their emotions, and otherwise steeled to offer aid to their patients. Motivated by a mixture of patriotism, necessity, and self-interest, they created a movement that was larger than any one philanthropic commission or government agency. Women of all classes, regions, races, and religions had worked in hospitals, combining comforting feminine ways with masculine professional standards. Although few of them went on after the war in the medical field, their combined efforts set the stage for a movement in the late nineteenth century to professionalize nursing and rid it of gendered interpretation, creating a standard for nursing in twentieth-century America.

*Nancy Driscol Engle*

**See also** Barton, Clara (1821–1912); Bickerdyke, Mary Ann Ball "Mother" (1817–1901); Blackwell, Elizabeth (1821–1910); Camp Followers; Catholic Women; Civilian Life; Cumming, Kate (ca. 1836–1909); Confederate Homefront; Disease; Dix, Dorothea Lynde (1802–1887); Domesticity; Hawks, Esther Hill (1833–1906); Hoge, Jane Currie Blaikie (1811–1890); Hopkins, Juliet Opie (1818–1890); Hospitals; Hospital Ships; Letter Writing; Livermore, Mary Ashton Rice (1820–1905); McDonald, Cornelia Peake (1822–1909); Military Invasion and Occupation; Northern Women; Pember, Phoebe Yates Levy (1823–1913); Pryor, Sara Agnes Rice (1830–1912); Rape; Schuyler, Louisa Lee (1837–1926); Sherman, William Tecumseh (1820–1891); Sherman's Campaign (1864–1865); Shiloh, Battle of (April 6–7, 1862); Shortages; Southern Women; Tompkins, Sally Louisa (1833–1916); Union Homefront; United States Christian Commission; United States Sanitary Commission; Wartime Employment; Woolsey, Jane Stuart (1830–1891); Wormeley, Katherine Prescott (1830–1908); Wounded, Visits to.

**References and Further Reading**

Brockett, L. P., and Mary C. Vaughan. 1867. *Woman's Work in the Civil War: A Record of Heroism, Patriotism and Patience.* Philadelphia, PA: Zeigler McCurdy & Co.

Cumming, Kate. 1959. *Kate: The Journal of a Confederate Nurse,* edited by Richard Barksdale Harwell. Baton Rouge: Louisiana State University Press.

Jones, Katharine M. 1962. *Ladies of Richmond, Confederate Capital.* Indianapolis, IN: Bobbs-Merrill.

McDonald, Cornelia Peake. 1992. *A Woman's Civil War: A Diary with Reminiscences of the War from March 1862,* edited by Minrose C. Gwin. Madison: University of Wisconsin Press.

Schultz, Jane E. 2004. *Women at the Front: Hospital Workers in Civil War America.* Chapel Hill: University of North Carolina Press.

## Politics

Party politics during the Civil War followed patterns and alignments from the antebellum years and in turn profoundly shaped the decades that followed. The war's immediate cause, secession, resulted from the election of a Republican president, the leader of a party that did not even exist in 1855. Throughout the war, United States President Abraham Lincoln and his party struggled to maintain political support for the military effort, threatened by some wavering Republicans but primarily a large body of Democrats who favored a negotiated peace. Confederate President Jefferson Davis faced no real partisan opposition because such organizations did not develop in the Confederacy. Instead, his critics focused on specific unpopular policies that tended to divide Southern voters along class lines. More broadly, the nation's political culture was participatory, and public spokesmen repeated endless paeans to white male democracy. Nearly all white men twenty-one and older were eligible to vote, and black men could vote only in several New England states. Voter turnout normally topped 80 percent in presidential elections. In each campaign season, the parties organized community events that fostered socialization and included women and other nonvoters. Politics, in short, was something of a national pastime, and,

although voting was restricted by race and sex, it allowed women to participate in myriad ways short of casting a ballot.

The partisan realignment of the 1850s led directly to Southern secession in 1860 and 1861. From the mid-1830s Whigs and Democrats had competed as national parties. Whigs predominated in New England and the Northeast, evolving as the party of native-born white Anglo-Saxon Protestants and particularly of the evangelical middle class. Democrats usually held sway in the Southern states and in Northern cities, espousing a doctrine of personal liberty and independence that appealed to immigrants, particularly Catholics, and to Southerners who feared those they saw as moralizing New Englanders.

The leaders of both organizations tried to avoid slavery-related issues to preserve intersectional harmony and cooperation. Until the late 1840s, they largely succeeded, but the American war with Mexico reopened the question of slavery's expansion when a large tract of new territory was added to the country in 1848. After the tenuous Compromise of 1850, Democratic Senator Stephen A. Douglas (Illinois) pushed through the fateful Kansas-Nebraska Act in 1854. This measure, strongly supported by Democrats and Southerners, repealed the Missouri Compromise (1821) and potentially allowed slavery to expand into the new territories of Kansas and Nebraska, both carved from the old Louisiana Purchase.

The Kansas-Nebraska Act outraged many Northern voters and led to formation of the free soil, Northern-only Republican Party in late 1855 and 1856. At about the same time, a growing fear of Catholic immigrants sparked the creation of the Nativist American, or Know-Nothing, Party that surged to prominence in Northern cities in late 1854 and early 1855. Thus, two powerful political forces—Nativism and Free Soil—operated simultaneously to disrupt the old Whig and Democratic Parties. In the Northern states both the Know Nothings and Republicans drew many native-born WASPs, weakening the Whigs beyond recovery.

In the 1856 presidential election Northern Know Nothings and Republicans came together, winning eleven states behind their candidate John C. Frémont. Throughout the rest of the 1850s, Republicans expanded the appeal of free soil and attracted more Northern voters. By 1860 it was the dominant party among native-born Northerners, and it was particularly powerful in the Northeast and upper North. Democrats remained strong in urban centers and in parts of the Midwest, especially southern Ohio, Illinois, and Indiana, as well as the border slave states: Delaware, Maryland, Kentucky, and Missouri.

In the future Confederate states, meanwhile, voters drifted to the Democrats, while both the Whigs and the Know Nothings died off as national organizations. By 1860 Democrats made up a sizable majority of voters in the lower South, while the upper South remained more divided as a mixture of Democrats, Know Nothings, and even surviving Whigs vied for power. Republican Abraham Lincoln's election in 1860 united men in the lower South, most of whom were unwilling to accept a free soil president; upper South voters waited for the attack at Fort Sumter and Lincoln's call for troops—presumably to invade the Confederate states—to leave the Union.

When the war began, Northern voters largely united behind Lincoln's insistence that the Union was perpetual and secession unconstitutional. Prominent Democrats, led by Stephen Douglas, supported Lincoln's call for troops and helped with recruiting. This bipartisan war effort lasted until August 1861, when Republicans in Congress passed the first Confiscation Act. The act allowed Union military commanders to seize runaway slaves as contraband of war, based on the logic that slave workers aided the Confederate war effort. Northern Democrats broke with Republicans, opposing any measure that seemed to threaten slavery and alter the war goal from simple reunification to something they saw as more radical. The Democrats' position drew from several sources: the party's profound racial conservatism and lack of reform tradition; historic ties to the South and Southerners; an ingrained suspicion that all Republicans secretly wanted abolition; and the economic fears of lower-class immigrant voters who did not want ex-slaves coming north in search of work. From this beginning and throughout the war, issues related to slavery and race united Democrats in seeking to maintain the antebellum status quo.

Most Republicans supported the Confiscation Act and anything else that weakened the Confederate war effort. While many issues, particularly those related to emancipation and racial equality, divided Lincoln's party, Republicans united behind the war effort. Essentially three factions emerged in the Republican ranks. First, the smallest in number were Conservatives, who dominated the party in border slave states and in some southern areas of Ohio, Indiana, and Illinois. Conservative Republicans, some of whom owned slaves, opposed emancipation when the war began, and many remained uncertain for much of the conflict; generally they did not support equality or civil rights for African Americans. Second, moderate Republicans controlled the party's agenda and platform in 1861. They claimed Lincoln as their leader and nearly perfect representative of their majority positions. Many hoped to restore the Union quickly with minimum destruction of Southern property and loss of life. Most did not expect that the war would lead to emancipation, and few believed in racial equality. Finally, Radical Republicans controlled many of the party's state organizations in New England, and most were abolitionists, although not all believed in equality or civil rights. Many Radicals perceived that the war offered a chance to strike at slavery. They argued consistently that slavery caused the war, and, as the war lengthened, they insisted that its primary cause must be addressed. These three Republican factions vied for party supremacy, with Radicals gaining strength as the conflict wore on.

Throughout the war, the overriding issue in the North remained the progress of Union forces and the prospects for victory. Military fortunes rose and fell, and thus did Republican political fortunes. The other important political issues—including emancipation, the enrollment of African American men in the army, conscription, civil liberties, and Reconstruction policy—arose directly from the one great issue of military conflict. Republicans advocated and enacted other legislation, including the Homestead Act (1862) to facilitate settlement in the West,

LINCOLN—"*I'm sorry to have to drop you, Sambo, but this concern won't carry us both!*"

Two years before the Emancipation Proclamation, political cartoons satirized Abraham Lincoln for his reluctance to include abolition as a Union war aim. (Library of Congress)

the Morrill Land Grant Act (1862) that supported agricultural colleges, a higher tariff on manufactured goods, and measures to help build a transcontinental railroad.

The war dominated Union politics. In 1862, the first full year of fighting, Union armies made no measurable progress in the Virginia theater but advanced significantly in Tennessee and along the Mississippi River. Victories in the West never captured public attention to the extent that defeats in the East sapped Northern morale. Both Union and Confederate leaders also recognized that 1862 was an election year. In September, Robert E. Lee's Army of Northern Virginia invaded Union territory for the first time, clearly hoping to influence the fall elections and encourage Democratic candidates. Union forces turned back Lee's Army at the Battle of Antietam Creek, giving Republicans a boost. More momentous and controversial was the preliminary Emancipation Proclamation that Lincoln issued on September 22, five days after the battle.

Lincoln's Emancipation Proclamation changed the nature of the war, even though it did not take effect until January 1, 1863 and exempted the Border States and most occupied portions of the Confederacy. It built on Congress's Second Confiscation Act, passed in July 1862, which declared slaves who ran away from rebel masters "forever free." Lincoln rationalized the proclamation as a war measure to weaken the Southern war effort, not an end in itself. His justification could not hide its transforming power, though. Democrats, who had previously opposed the Confiscation Acts, protested and accused Lincoln of lying from the beginning and secretly working for abolition all along. Radical Republicans were overjoyed, while moderates and conservatives rallied to the proclamation as an effective war measure. Lincoln worried that Union soldiers would desert nearly en masse rather than fight to free slaves. From September 1862 to the end of the war, opposition to emancipation and all related race issues united Democrats, forming the core of their political strategy in all wartime elections.

The proclamation united a large group of Northern women—primarily abolitionists and women's rights activists—who determined to get a constitutional amendment that would end slavery in the United States forever. They created the National Women's Loyal League (NWLL) in May 1863 and began a campaign to collect signatures supporting the amendment. In August 1864, the NWLL presented a petition of approximately four hundred thousand signatures to Congress.

The fall 1862 elections provided voters their first chance to pass judgment on Lincoln's and the Republicans' war leadership. Democrats attacked Lincoln as incompetent and the Republicans as radical abolitionists determined to legislate racial equality and intermarriage. Republicans defended their war effort but downplayed the proclamation, emphasizing its conservative exemptions and the underlying motive to weaken the Confederate war effort, not to abolish slavery everywhere. Results were mixed. Republicans held their own in New England and in most of the upper North. Ironically they gained in the border states, where many Democrats had gone south to fight for the Confederacy. Democrats gained in the crucial, heavily populated states from New York west to Illinois, all of which voted for Lincoln in 1860 but two years later went narrowly Democratic. Democrat Horatio Seymour won the governor's office in New York, the largest and arguably most important Union state. Fortunately for Lincoln, Republican governors in Illinois, Indiana, and Ohio were not up for reelection in 1862, and they blunted the power of Democratic-controlled legislatures. Overall, Democrats added thirty-five seats in the House of Representatives.

In the Confederacy, as in the Union, the dominant political issue was military success or failure. From that came all related issues that ultimately divided Southerners. In 1862 Southern armies lost ground in the West; Nashville and Baton Rouge became the first state capitals retaken by the Union, and the largest port, New Orleans, fell in February. Victories in Virginia made Lee, J.E.B. Stuart, and Thomas "Stonewall" Jackson heroes, and, like Northerners, Confederate voters paid more attention to the Eastern theater than the Western.

Politically, conscription dominated public debate in 1862. The Confederacy enacted the first compulsory military service in American history in April, encompassing white men between the ages of eighteen and thirty-five. Conscription itself was unpopular, but most divisive were specific provisions that favored wealthy men over the yeomen farmers and poor whites. The "twenty-slave rule" allowed one white man exempted for every twenty slaves owned; substitution allowed any man who could afford it to hire someone else to take his place. More than any other single measure, conscription prompted nonslaveholding men and women to question Confederate leadership and the cause and slowly undermined support for Jefferson Davis and his administration. Southern women helped thousands of men evade conscription officials—their own form of political protest.

In the winter and spring of 1862 and 1863, the Union Peace Movement, led by a growing body of Peace Democrats, reached a new height. Typically, Union military failures provided the context for antiwar sentiment. Offensives in Tennessee and Mississippi stalled, and humiliating defeats in Virginia brought Northern morale to a new low by June 1863. A draft law passed on March 3 made men from twenty to forty-five liable for service. It went into effect only if or when a district did not meet its quota (the number of men it was obligated to furnish for the Union army). Democrats led the opposition. Their leading spokesman, Ohio Congressman Clement Vallandingham, openly encouraged men to ignore their draft notices. For these sentiments, Vallandingham was convicted of disloyalty and transported out of the United States. Anti-draft sentiment also mixed with opposition to the Emancipation Proclamation and to the enrollment of African American men into the Union army. The latter development worried some Northerners more than the proclamation because military service had always carried an implication of equality and certain obligations on the part of society at large. By late spring and summer of 1863, anti-draft violence was common across the Northern states.

In New York City, all of these anti-Republican elements came together in a critical mass. A Democratic stronghold, the city's immigrant population, particularly Irish Catholics, resented and feared emancipation and were outraged at the draft. The Union draft—like the Confederate one—afforded wealthier men ways to avoid service. Most odious to poor Northerners was commutation, a straightforward fee of $300 that satisfied a man's obligation. In the first draft calls during the summer of 1863, more than fifty-two thousand men paid the commutation fee, in effect a tax to support the army, and another twenty-six thousand provided substitutes. Nearly forty thousand men simply failed to report when their names were called. New Yorkers, encouraged by Democratic Governor Horatio Seymour, believed their own quota was set too high and that conscription itself was unconstitutional. Starting July 11, when the first names were drawn in the city, and for several days after, the city's poor men and women rioted, targeting African Americans in particular but also ransacking Republican homes and recruiting offices. Approximately a dozen black men and women were killed and hundreds wounded, thousands more simply left New York. Finally, on July 16 Union troops arrived, most of them from the battlefield at Gettysburg, and put down the mob, killing more than one hundred rioters.

The New York City riots crippled the Peace Movement. They occurred just after the Union's two greatest victories—the Battle of Gettysburg (July 1–3) and the surrender of Vicksburg (July 4)—and were soon followed by the dramatic engagement of African American troops in the assault at Fort Wagner in South Carolina. Covered widely in the press, the service of black men in combat for the Union served as a natural and dramatic counterpoint to the mainly Democratic, immigrant rioters in New York City. Fall elections in several key states, particularly Ohio and Pennsylvania, provided another test of partisan strength. Still split into peace and war wings, Democrats united by attacking Republicans as radical race mixers. They also hammered Lincoln for his suspensions of the writ of habeas corpus, printing paper money, and higher taxes, all of which Democrats labeled as executive tyranny. Republicans, however, sounded a more confident note than they had in 1862, and African American military service seemed the key to their new approach. Lincoln blistered Democrats in a public letter written during the campaign, chastising them for their opposition to fight to free African Americans who were fighting themselves to save the Union.

The election results revealed that the Peace Movement had fizzled since June. Clement Vallandingham, who had returned to the United States, lost the Ohio gubernatorial race by one hundred thousand votes, and Republicans rolled up big victories elsewhere, winning every gubernatorial race contested that year. Union military victories in the summer and fall gave Northern voters great hope that victory was near. The Peace Movement seemed dead or at least irrelevant if the Union could complete a quick victory.

In the Confederacy, the fall 1863 elections for the Confederate Congress revealed growing opposition to Davis's administration. The effects of Union invasion, the naval blockade of Southern ports, the shortages and inflation, as well as heavy losses, led many Confederate men and women to question the war. Interpreting Confederate election returns are extremely difficult, considering that many areas were occupied by fall 1863 and that no party lines existed to make sense of the political landscape. By any measure, however, the opposition to Davis's leadership had grown considerably, and about 40 percent of the congressional representatives in Richmond were hostile to the president. In state elections as well, some strident secessionists were replaced by more moderate leadership. Mississippi's fire-eating Governor John Jones Pettus, for instance, declined to run for reelection and was succeeded by Whiggish planter Charles Clark. The new governor pledged that Mississippi's men should no longer be expected to lead invasions, but only repel them. Desertion from Confederate armies reached new heights in the depressing aftermath of Union victories. Because of the disorganized political climate across the Confederacy and the relatively few elections held, no organized peace movement developed. Instead, thousands of men and women registered their political opinions in the streets as they rioted for food or sheltered deserters from conscription agents. In 1863 thousands of Southern women participated in bread riots across the Confederacy, in cities that included Richmond, Atlanta, Mobile, and many other smaller cities.

The presidential election of 1864 was the political climax of the Civil War. Confederate strategists pinned their last hopes on a Democratic victory, and military events again revived the Northern Peace Movement. Union offensives in Virginia and Georgia faced stiff resistance, and the heavy casualties meant great disappointment among Northern voters. From the beginning of May through September 1, Union forces suffered one hundred thousand casualties. When Lincoln called for half a million more volunteers on July 18, Peace Democrats rejoiced. Thus, although the year started with great optimism, by midsummer Lincoln's chances for reelection looked bleak. Republican movements to replace Lincoln with Salmon Chase, John C. Frémont, or Ulysses Grant spoke to the uncertainty among party leaders. Lincoln controlled the convention, however, and was re-nominated easily on June 7 in Baltimore. Republicans replaced Vice President Hannibal Hamlin with Tennessee's Andrew Johnson, the only Confederate state senator to remain loyal to the Union when his state seceded. They intended his nomination to attract the votes of War Democrats, of which Johnson was the ultimate representative. Even after the Republican convention, New York's powerful editor Horace Greeley helped lead a movement for a second party meeting that he hoped would reconsider Lincoln's nomination. Despite these fears, however, most Republicans came together after the Democrats nominated former General George McClellan in their convention at the end of August.

McClellan was a War Democrat, although his running mate, George Pendleton, and the party's platform came from the Peace wing. The party's split personality, evident during the previous two years' elections, became even more problematic in 1864. Democrats presented McClellan as a sort of statesman-warrior, above party politics—posters and ballots often included him with George Washington and Andrew Jackson. Personally he favored winning the war first, then making peace, and he continued to oppose emancipation. The platform called for a quick end to the war and a restoration of peace. McClellan's reference to the war as a failure (a plank written by Peace Democrat Clement Vallandingham) cost him the votes of many soldiers, veterans, and their families. Other Democratic planks attacked Lincoln and the Republicans for suspending the writ of habeas corpus and for other violations of civil liberties. Finally, Democrats united behind their opposition to emancipation and racial equality. One manifestation of this was the prisoner of war issue. Prisoner exchange had broken down in 1863, in part because Lincoln insisted that African American prisoners be treated equally. Democrats therefore blamed the miserable state of Union prisoners on the Republicans' insistence on their own version of "radical racial equality."

Republicans defended their war effort, Lincoln's leadership, and the Emancipation Proclamation. Their platform demonstrated how far the party had come and included several strong planks that commended African American wartime contributions and that demanded equal treatment for black prisoners. Republicans blamed slavery for the war and stressed its inconsistency with the ideals of the nation. They also praised Lincoln's Emancipation Proclamation and supported the proposed constitutional amendment to eliminate slavery from the United States. Separate planks praised Lincoln's decision to enroll African American men into the Union army and defended the party's position that all soldiers, regardless of color, deserved to be treated as such. Republicans also called for a railroad to the Pacific Ocean, a liberal policy to encourage immigration, and the redemption of the public debt to maintain national credit.

Both parties knew the campaign turned largely on Union military fortunes. The other issues, most importantly emancipation and African American troops, were tied to the war and had been debated during the previous two years. By late August, Lincoln expected to lose the election. Grant's army, weakened daily by disease, was stuck in a seemingly endless siege outside Richmond and Petersburg; William T. Sherman's army was stuck outside Atlanta; and Union forces in southern Mississippi and the trans-Mississippi West made no progress against smaller but stubborn Confederate forces. On August 23, Lincoln urged his cabinet members to cooperate with the incoming administration and to pledge to work for military victory before the new president was sworn in. Mary Todd Lincoln packed many of their personal belongings for the anticipated move back to Springfield. The president even sketched out a peace offer to Jefferson Davis that would have required reunion but not necessarily complete abolition of slavery; Lincoln reconsidered, however, and never sent the letter. Democrats staked their fortunes on the Peace Movement, despite McClellan's contrary stance. Confederates watched the campaign closely and hoped for a Republican defeat.

Lincoln finally got good news from the battlefield. On August 23 the last fort guarding the entrance to Mobile Bay and the port of Mobile was taken by the U.S. navy, closing the city to blockade runners. More important, Union forces captured and occupied Atlanta on September 3. Besieged for over a month, the Confederates finally evacuated the city rather than risk starving, surrendering, and being captured. A grateful Lincoln thanked Sherman in a personal telegram. It was the breakthrough that Lincoln and the Republicans needed.

Early voting in Pennsylvania, Indiana, and Ohio on October 11 foretold a Republican victory, although balloting was very close. Lincoln carried all three of these important states. The vote was close in Pennsylvania and Indiana, and soldiers probably gave Lincoln his small margin of victory in the latter state. The soldier vote was decisive in several places, and Republicans owed much to new provisions that allowed for absentee balloting. Most states had passed legislation that allowed troops to vote in the field, although several Democratic-controlled legislatures—including Indiana's—refused to allow it. In those states Lincoln and Secretary of War Edwin Stanton gave furloughs to thousands of soldiers so that they could vote in their home towns. Eventually Lincoln and the Republicans garnered over 85 percent of the soldier vote, which provided the edge in several states, including New York and Connecticut. Lincoln won two hundred twelve electoral votes to McClellan's twenty-one; the popular vote was closer, about 55 to 45 percent. Even more impressive for the Republicans was their new dominance in Congress: forty-two to ten in the Senate and one hundred forty-five to forty in the House of Representatives.

Lincoln's victory in 1864 ensured that the war would be fought to its conclusion. The Republican landslide also meant that Republicans could impose whatever version of Reconstruction they wanted. In particular, radicals gained momentum for the Constitutional amendment to guarantee emancipation and to further legislation for civil rights. The elections in 1864 confirmed Republicans as the dominant party in the North and completed the partisan realignment that began in the mid-1850s. Democrats needed to wait for the end of Reconstruction and the return to politics of former Confederates before they could compete nationally.

*Christopher J. Olsen*

**See also** Abolitionism and Northern Reformers; African American Women; Bread Riots; Confederate Homefront; Conscription; Davis, Jefferson (1808–1889); Desertion; Draft Riots and Resistance; Emancipation Proclamation (January 1, 1863); Enlistment; Fort Sumter (April 12–14, 1861); Gettysburg, Battle of (July 1–3, 1863); Lincoln, Abraham (1809–1865); Lincoln, Mary Todd (1818–1882); Military Invasion and Occupation; National Women's Loyal League [Women's National Loyal League]; Northern Women; Reconstruction (1865–1877); Secession; Sherman, William Tecumseh (1820–1891); Southern Women; Thirteenth Amendment; Union Homefront; Union Soldiers, Motives; Vicksburg, Siege of.

**References and Further Reading**
Baker, Jean. 1983. *Affairs of Party: The Political Culture of Northern Democrats in Mid-Nineteenth-Century America.* Ithaca, NY: Cornell University Press.
Escott, Paul D. 1978. *After Secession: Jefferson Davis and the Failure of Confederate Nationalism.* Baton Rouge: Louisiana State University Press.
Frank, Joseph Allen. 1998. *With Ballot and Bayonet: The Political Socialization of American Civil War Soldiers.* Athens: University of Georgia Press.
Gienapp, William. 1987. *The Origins of the Republican Party, 1852–1856.* New York: Oxford University Press.
McPherson, James M. 1982. *Ordeal by Fire: The Civil War and Reconstruction.* New York: Alfred A. Knopf.
Oates, Stephen B. 1977. *With Malice toward None: A Life of Abraham Lincoln.* New York: Harper & Row.
Paludan, Philip Shaw. 1988. *"A People's Contest": The Union and the Civil War, 1861–1865.* New York: HarperCollins.
Rable, George. 1994. *The Confederate Republic: A Revolution against Politics.* Chapel Hill: University of North Carolina Press.
Silbey, Joel. 1977. *A Respectable Minority: The Democratic Party in the Civil War Era.* New York: W. W. Norton.
Thomas, Emory. 1979. *The Confederate Nation: 1861–1865.* New York: Harper & Row.

## Religion

Religion played significant roles in the lives of American women during the Civil War. Engagement in their faith and worship helped women sustain themselves in a time of severe emotional and physical strain and offered them opportunities to engage in activity to support the war effort. At the same time, the war profoundly altered religion in both the North and South.

Protestant Christianity, especially evangelical denominations, had become increasingly visible in

American society during the antebellum years, as well as extremely important in the lives of many American women. By 1860, the Baptist and Methodist denominations, considered marginal sects by many at the beginning of the century, had become socially and spiritually powerful bodies, ministering to a significant minority of the nation's population and claiming many prominent Americans as members and ministers. At the same time, Catholicism was also growing, fueled by the massive influx of Irish and German immigrants in the 1840s and 1850s.

Although barred from the clergy in nearly every denomination, women made up the bulk of antebellum American congregations and sustained both the churches and the religious revivals of the Second Great Awakening. Women were active participants in church services, and they often drew their families to religious practice as well. Many antebellum women, especially in the Northern states, also looked beyond the church and home worship in their religious observance. In the decades before the Civil War, numerous women engaged in benevolent work that grew out of their religious commitment. They involved themselves with activities that ranged from the church's sewing, tract, or missionary society to orphanages and antislavery organizations. The reforming spirit of Northern women during the antebellum period grew out of the religious revivals of the Second Great Awakening, which drew thousands of women to the evangelical churches and preached about the need to create a godly society on earth. Many Southern women, too, became involved in religiously motivated benevolent activities, though not at the same level as their Northern sisters.

Religion, like other aspects of American society, was not immune from the growing sectionalism of the antebellum period. Religious justifications were prominent in both proslavery and antislavery arguments. Ministers such as Henry Ward Beecher of Brooklyn's Plymouth Church and Benjamin Palmer of New Orleans's First Presbyterian Church played prominent parts both in the religious lives of their congregants and in the broader social discourse of their towns, states, and nation. In the North, a small but vocal number of Protestant ministers reached the conclusion that Christianity and slavery were fundamentally incompatible. Building on the theological arguments of the late eighteenth- and early nineteenth-century Baptists and Methodists, the Quakers, and the Second Great Awakening, men like Beecher preached against slavery from their pulpits. Many ministers also became actively involved in the antislavery movement, where they worked and debated alongside some of their congregants. Although abolitionists represented a small minority of Northerners even by 1860, they were extremely vocal and laid persuasive claim to the egalitarian message of Northern evangelical Protestantism. Many, though by no means most, Northern women found these arguments persuasive and became themselves involved in the antislavery movement.

Southern ministers, too, addressed slavery in their sermons. While some early Southern evangelicals, the numbers and influence of whom are still a matter of debate among historians, questioned slavery, by the 1830s Southern religion had made its peace with the peculiar institution. Ministers across the South, like Palmer, provided proslavery advocates with powerful arguments in favor of slavery, pointing to the existence of slavery in biblical societies, Jesus's failure to condemn slavery, and Paul's treatment of the slave Onesimus. Hearing these views aired at Sunday services, Southern women could take comfort, knowing that their church upheld the institution that served as their region's economic and social cornerstone.

These arguments often threatened the denominations themselves. In the Presbyterian Church, sectional animosity over the institution of slavery exacerbated disagreements over theology and led to the 1837 split between Old School and New School groups. The arguments in the Methodist and Baptist Churches were even more explicit about slavery. In 1844, the Methodist Episcopal Church divided into Northern and Southern institutions in an argument about the election of a slaveholding bishop, and the Baptist denomination split a year later. With secession and the beginning of the war, religion became even more closely intertwined with political questions. Denominations, like the Episcopal Church, that had resisted the sectional pressures of the pre-war years found that they could not remain whole as the nation ripped itself apart, and they too split as the Southern states left the union.

At the same time, clergy in both the North and South preached about the political situation, calling on their congregations to take a stand in the national crisis. Women in the pews were no less moved by what they heard than their male kin. Although some women criticized the political uses of the pulpit and feared that preachers were inflaming dangerous political passions, many others were reassured by and took comfort from the support that their ministers and their religion gave to their cause, whether Union or Confederate, that was consuming so much of their lives.

Politically themed sermons also served to increase feelings of nationalism among the civilian populations of both North and South. On both sides of the conflict, nationalism on the part of homefront civilians was a vital component of the war effort. Northern and Southern leaders alike couched their war aims in nationalistic terms: restore the Union or establish Confederate independence. Women were just as concerned with the course of events as were their male kin, and the sermons that they heard in church helped them come to terms with what was happening and reinforce their support of the national cause.

This nationalist function of religion was especially important in the South, where many women felt torn pledging allegiance to a new Confederate nation while retaining their established identity as Americans. Many Southern women did not know what to think in the chaotic winter and spring of 1861–1862. The nation that had been theirs was disintegrating, and they now found themselves embarking on the process of building a new state. Women across the South turned to their faith for answers and support during this troubling and confusing time. Religion had another role to play as well, and, through the sermons of Southern ministers, many women recognized that their new allegiance should be to the Confederacy. It was vital that Southern civilians, no less than the military, support the Confederacy and turn away from old

associations and love for the United States. The sermons that upheld the Confederate nation as blessed by God and following in the glorious footsteps of the Revolutionary generation helped many women make that transition, as their old national identity was destroyed and a new one created.

Religion also played a part in the early months of the war, as companies formed and prepared to leave for the front. Here, too, women occupied an important place in the preparations. Churches in both the Union and the Confederacy held special services in which they asked God's blessing for the troops and their cause. Female members of the congregations sewed the regimental banners that decorated the church sanctuaries, and they prayed alongside their male kin for a quick and glorious end to the war. Union and Confederate soldiers took both banners and prayers with them as they headed to the front and to the battles that would follow, powerful reminders that the women of their society stood behind them.

With many men gone into the armed forces, women became the primary recipients of the nationalistic sermons that had begun during the secession crisis. Northern ministers generally kept to this nationalist message throughout the war, continuing to see God's plan in the conflict. Union losses on the battlefield and war weariness might test their optimism and patience, but they could also see that the United States was in little danger of collapse and that much of the nation had the will to keep going until victory was secured. They could therefore cleave to their message, which was a vital part of ensuring that the national will would hold. In the later years of the war, some Northern ministers expanded on this message as the Union's war aims evolved, adding the eradication of slavery to their interpretation of God's plan for the American nation. After the 1863 Emancipation Proclamation, it was clear that a Federal victory would destroy slavery at the same time that it saved the Union. For those ministers who had embraced the antislavery cause before the war, the prospect of emancipation was the fulfillment of the promise of evangelical Protestantism, the hand of God working with man to purify the American nation of the sin of slavery, and they preached this message joyfully from the pulpits.

As the war stretched on and conditions in the Confederacy grew worse, Southern ministers found that they had to alter the message they presented in sermons. While they, like their Northern counterparts, viewed the war as part of God's plan for the American people, they had fewer and fewer Confederate victories to interpret as proof of God's support for their cause. They also had to come to terms with the increasing hardships of shortages, inflation, and destruction that Southern women faced on the homefront. Thus, in sermons across the South, the benevolent God of the war's early years, who would safeguard and bolster the fledgling nation, gave way to a severe, chastising deity who was punishing Southerners. In the words of Southern ministers, however, the punishment was not for slavery, as their Northern brethren claimed, but for arrogance, materialism, and lack of piety. The congregations listening to these sermons, almost exclusively female by the later years of the war, took these words to heart as they lamented the fate befalling their society.

For many American women, religion became a means of support, helping them deal with the absence, injury, and death of their loved ones as well as with the strains of living on the homefront. Religious faith, bolstered by the sermons they heard in church, also sustained women as the war stretched into its second, third, and fourth years. In church and in their prayers at home, women could ask God to aid their cause and to bring their husbands, sons, brothers, and sweethearts home safely. They could mourn those who had died and receive sympathy and help from both clergy and fellow worshipers. They could also celebrate victories, hoping for God's blessing and an end to the war.

In addition to regular Sunday worship, prayer services and fast days were special times that helped women during the war years. Churches and communities often held special services to pray for the war and the troops. At the same time, both Abraham Lincoln and Jefferson Davis appointed days of fasting and prayer, on which women abstained from food and attended church. These

occasions brought women together in common cause as they prayed fervently for the end of the war and victory for their nation. The value of these services was even greater, however, because they also provided time and space for women to commiserate with each other and to worship as part of a community of believers who were experiencing similar absences, losses, fears, and struggles to support their families.

Confederate women found themselves in an even more precarious position than their Northern sisters. In addition to the danger facing their husbands, sons, brothers, and sweethearts, Southern women had to deal with the privations caused by the Union blockade, marauding armies from both sides of the conflict, and the disintegration of the institution upon which their society had been built. As conditions in the Confederacy worsened with each passing year and Confederate victories came less and less frequently, women found solace in their faith.

Many American women, however, were not content merely to pray for victory and relief. They wanted to help their cause in more concrete ways, and religion offered them a means to do so. Women who had been active in church-sponsored benevolent work before the war, such as the church sewing circle or missionary society, turned their skills and contacts to the support of the war effort. Beginning during the secession crisis and extending through the war years, women and their churches organized fundraising and relief efforts.

Northern women, who had a more extensive history of organized benevolent activity, were especially vigorous. Almost as soon as the war began, women gathered in churches, homes, and civic buildings to roll bandages, knit, sew, and collect supplies for Union troops. They also mounted bazaars and other fundraisers. As organizations like the United States Christian Commission and the United States Sanitary Commission were founded to tend the spiritual and physical needs of the troops, Northern women stepped in to help. Whereas both groups were run primarily by men, women were extremely active in their daily operations. The Sanitary Commission, though founded by Unitarian minister Henry Bellows and connected to influential liberal denominations like the Episcopal and Unitarian Churches, remained the more secular of the two organizations, focusing on meeting the physical needs of Union soldiers. Women played important roles in the organization of local chapters and in the collection of supplies, and many women also served as nurses in the army and in convalescent homes.

The Sanitary Commission involved the clergy and congregants from liberal denominations, but the Christian Commission was founded by the Young Men's Christian Association (YMCA) and maintained ties to the North's evangelical denominations, especially the Baptist and Methodist Churches. The Christian Commission also retained a more religious outlook, focusing primarily on the spiritual needs of Union soldiers. In many ways, the functions of the Christian Commission resembled those of the Sanitary Commission. Women organized to raise money, serve as nurses, and collect much needed supplies like bandages and blankets. The women of the Christian Commission, however, also concerned themselves with fostering religious feeling among the troops. They worked tirelessly to send Bibles and other religious literature to soldiers, and they sponsored missionaries who worked among the Northern armies. The Sanitary and Christian Commissions both received widespread recognition and government support for their efforts, and they represented the largest aid organizations in the United States. Northern women, however, could also become involved in countless smaller, church- or community-based groups that allowed them to channel their religious impulses into help for the Union cause.

Some Northern women also traveled South as church-sponsored missionaries, part of the Northern churches' attempts to reform and remake Southern society. They converged on the occupied territories and began their work almost as soon as Federal forces had established control. The Baptist and Methodist denominations were especially prominent in this activity, and the African Methodist Episcopal Church and African Methodist Episcopal Church Zion also sent male and female missionaries to help former slaves build churches. Male missionaries came to occupied territories as ministers and chaplains, and female missionaries often worked as teachers, especially in schools and Sunday schools for the freedpeople. Although missions to white Southerners found little success, freedmen and freedwomen were often more receptive. Northern evangelicals saw in the acquisition of Confederate territory an opportunity to replicate their society, and women were often active participants in this endeavor.

In the Southern states, relief activity occurred on a more local level than in the North. The Confederacy did not have large, organized groups like the Sanitary Commission or the Christian Commission to coordinate efforts. In addition, antebellum Southern women had not been as active in benevolent causes as their Northern sisters. They were determined, however, to aid their troops, and they worked tirelessly through local churches and community groups to raise money, gather supplies, and nurse the wounded and convalescing.

The Civil War also brought significant changes in how American women approached and experienced religion, influencing how women, both Northern and Southern, participated in their chosen religions. They were accustomed to making up the majority of antebellum congregations, but the war exacerbated the imbalance, especially in the Confederacy where almost all able-bodied men entered the service. Men were notably absent in the pews and in the running of the church. Offices that men had often filled, like Sunday school teacher, became the province of female members, many of whom delighted in their newfound responsibility and took seriously their new task of helping the church continue to function.

Wartime changes were perhaps more significant in the South, where the effects of the war were more immediate and severe than in the North. The vast majority of Civil War battles were fought in Southern states, and a passing army—whether Union or Confederate—could wreak considerable destruction on a farm in its quest for food, firewood, or revenge. Thousands of Southern women and their families became refugees, fleeing the relentless march of Union forces across the Confederacy, and

Group in front of Christian Commission storehouse in Washington, D.C., April 1865. (Library of Congress)

Southern women were also more likely to suffer the loss or injury of a loved one, since a much larger proportion of the Southern male population served in the armed forces. In their day-to-day living, Southern women found themselves faced with the privations wrought by inflation, blockade-induced shortages, and the collapse of the cotton economy. All these factors affected the relationship that Southern women had with religion and their ability to engage in frequent worship.

Many churches across the South struggled to remain open during the war years, and a large number could not survive once most of their male members—and in many cases their ministers—had joined Confederate service. Church had been one of the central points in the lives of numerous South-

ern women, and the suspension of services due to the lack of funds, of a congregation, or of a minister served to underscore how much the Civil War had changed their lives for the worse. The closing of a church also pushed women to take on increased responsibility for their religious lives. Many Southern women had no intention of giving up the expression of their faith because they could no longer attend services, and so they began to worship at home with their families and neighbors, guided by such aids as the Episcopal *Book of Common Prayer* or by their own souls.

For many Northern and Southern women, the increased sphere of activity, whether in one of the large relief organizations, in a church-sponsored charitable group, in Sunday school teaching, or in missionary work, gave them an outlet for religious expression and work that they would continue after the close of hostilities.

Religion was no less important to enslaved women during the war. Slaves recognized the significance of the war, and many determined to help the Union war effort in any way they could. A number of slave women rendered aid through the secret religious services that mushroomed across the Confederacy, giving them a place to speak freely about their hopes for a future without slavery and to add their prayers to countless others for a Union victory. Enslaved women also used clandestine religious services to pass along any information they might have about the course of the war, the approach of Union troops, or the fate of those who had left home for freedom and Union service.

Religion played an equally important role in the lives of slave women who lived in areas of Union occupation or who left their homes for the Union lines. Once safely in Union territory, slave women found themselves able to engage in religious activities with unprecedented openness and freedom. They no longer had to ask permission to attend worship services or sneak off to secret prayer meetings. Women who had lived for decades in extralegal marriages could now have their weddings performed in churches—often by Union chaplains—and recorded by the government. These women, though in many cases still caught in a legal limbo that recognized their autonomy but did not yet declare them free, relished the ability to control their religious lives and express their faith more openly than in the past.

Once the end of slavery became official, freedwomen often couched their celebrations in religious terms. Many freedwomen saw the hand of God in Union victory and in the end of slavery, and they flocked to churches and prayer services to give thanks for the long-awaited answer to their prayers. Emancipation also brought new religious opportunities as freedmen and freedwomen gathered to form their independent churches. Finally, freedwomen could worship openly, on their own terms, and they could celebrate the significant events of their lives—weddings, baptisms, funerals, holidays—in churches that were legal and free from white control.

Many white women also found that they experienced the end of the war from a religious perspective. For Northern women, Confederate surrender was a vindication of the message that they had heard preached for four long years: God blessed their endeavor and safeguarded the Union. Northern women, whatever their personal losses and sacrifices, could take solace in the belief that their society was both godly and victorious.

Southern women had no such consolations. They, too, saw God's hand in the outcome of the war, but that hand was punishing and severe. The Confederate nation had been defeated, and slavery, the defining economic and social institution of the Southern states, had been eliminated. Southern women looked around themselves and saw little but destruction. Religion became for them the comfort that was missing in so many other aspects of their lives.

At the end of the war, American women found that their experience of religion and worship had changed. The denominations that had splintered during the sectional crisis rejoined slowly. While the Episcopal, Catholic, and Lutheran Churches reformed at the end of hostilities, the major evangelical denominations did not reconcile until the twentieth century, if at all, and many women continued to worship in an atmosphere of sectional conflict. A large number of Northern women also continued or joined the church-sponsored missionary work begun during the war, coming to teach in schools and Sunday schools and to remake the South in the North's godly image.

In the postwar period, religion became closely intertwined with the memory of the war, and church became a place to venerate the past. Women on both sides of the conflict commemorated the struggles and sacrifices of the war years in distinctly religious ways. Women often took the lead in decorating graves, organizing memorial services, and raising money for monuments. They embarked on campaigns to enshrine the memories of the war, its veterans, and especially its dead. This impulse was especially strong in the Southern states, where honoring the Confederate cause became a moral imperative for white women.

*Julia Huston Nguyen*

**See also** Abolitionism and Northern Reformers; African American Women; Aid Societies; Baptist Women; Catholic Women; Churches; Civilian Life; Confederate Homefront; Congregationalist Women; Emancipation Proclamation (January 1, 1863); Enlistment; Fairs and Bazaars; Family Life, Confederate; Family Life, Union; Flags, Regimental; Foraging, Effects on Women; Free Blacks; Fundraising; Jewish Women; Ladies' Memorial Associations; Methodist Women; Military Invasion and Occupation; Monuments; Morale; Mourning; Nationalism, Confederate; Nationalism, United States; Northern Women; Nurses; Politics; Presbyterian Women; Quaker Women; Refugees; Secession; Sewing Bees; Shortages; Southern Women; Union Homefront; Unitarian Women; United States Christian Commission; United States Sanitary Commission.

**References and Further Reading**
Faust, Drew Gilpin. 1996. *Mothers of Invention: Women of the Slaveholding States in the American Civil War.* Chapel Hill: University of North Carolina Press.

Goen, C. C. 1985. *Broken Churches, Broken Nation: Denominational Schisms and the Coming of the American Civil War.* Macon, GA: Mercer University Press.

Leonard, Elizabeth. 1994. *Yankee Women: Gender Battles in the Civil War.* New York: W. W. Norton.

Miller, Randall M., Harry S. Stout, and Charles Reagan Wilson, eds. 1998. *Religion and the American Civil War.* New York: Oxford University Press.

Rable, George. 1991. *Civil Wars: Women and the Crisis of Southern Nationalism.* Urbana: University of Illinois Press.

Raboteau, Albert J. 2004. *Slave Religion: The "Invisible Institution" in the Antebellum South.* New York: Oxford University Press.

Shattuck, Gardiner. 1987. *A Shield and Hiding Place: The Religious Life of the Civil War Armies.* Macon, GA: Mercer University Press.

Stowell, Daniel. 1998. *Rebuilding Zion: The Religious Reconstruction of the South, 1863–1877.* New York: Oxford University Press.

Wiggins, William H., Jr. 1987. *O Freedom!: Afro-American Emancipation Celebrations.* Knoxville: University of Tennessee Press.

Wilson, Charles Reagan. 1983. *Baptized in the Blood: The Religion of the Lost Cause, 1865–1920.* Athens: University of Georgia Press.

## Southern Women

Women living in the southern region of the United States encompassed a variety of social, economic, and cultural backgrounds. From the bayous of Louisiana to the hills of Tennessee, Southern women experienced life in the nineteenth century as active participants in their households, in their communities, and in the overall framework of the South. During the Civil War, the lives of these women dramatically changed as their families and homes were torn apart by invasive and unforgiving warfare. For women across the South, the war would offer new opportunities, new experiences, and new challenges as they faced the horrors of a national crisis.

The imagery associated with nineteenth-century Southern women often shapes modern descriptions and interpretations of them. Idyllic stories of belles at balls with handsome gentlemen skew the reality of Southern life. However, women of the pre-war South also fell victim to the power of imagery and the creation of the ideal woman. Women across the South were brought up with a strict notion of their place in antebellum culture. A woman of the South was expected to be a combination of submission, piety, compassion, purity, and domesticity. The ideal image was of a good mother, wife, and daughter, whose purpose in life was to submissively care for her husband and to manage the household and children with little outward expression of effort. The reality of Southern life was far less picturesque; very few women lived in an environment that allowed them to fulfill this perfect ideal. In reality, many women lived in busy homes that required hard work and dedication for the success of the family. The actuality of life for the majority of Southern women was therefore much less pleasant than the ideal.

The defining characteristic of Southern culture, and therefore the lives of women, was the household. The household was the center of both public and private interaction, the medium through which Southerners addressed the outside world. Southern culture functioned through a complex system of hierarchy that involved race, class, gender, and even age. The household functioned as the basis for this hierarchy, the most basic of structures through which a community of family members and laborers was organized. At the top of the structure was the patriarch or head male, usually the father or husband. The patriarch was the head of household, managing the private world of the home, and also interacting with the public world of economics or politics. Underneath the patriarch were his dependents, who included his wife, children, and perhaps even slaves. The wealthier families were able to afford slaves to help with the economic success of the household. Plantation owners, Southern farmers with twenty or more slaves, managed the largest and most complex households. Women were often left to negotiate the relationships among themselves, their children, and their slaves as part of their household responsibilities. White yeoman farmers who did not own slaves presided primarily over their wives and children. Like the plantation household, the yeoman household focused on the relationship between the patriarch and his "laborers" and was still the means of interaction in Southern society. While class separated the two groups, the hierarchy of the household and the dominance of the patriarch allied them in their culture. More important, their whiteness placed Southerners of any class above slaves.

The strict hierarchy in the South placed white women in a restrictive environment. Women were expected to fulfill specific tasks in the home, from normal household drudgery to the management of the domestic slaves. Part of their position as women dictated that they accept their roles without complaint as obedient wives and mothers. Upper-class Southern women might be exposed to greater freedom in the home because of the privileges of wealth and the slave system. Some young women were able to attend female academies that offered them a basic education. Many planters felt that the education of a young woman helped to create a well-behaved wife as well as a better mother. Consequently, many female academies focused their educational efforts not only on subjects such as mathematics or science, but also on skills that would be useful in the home, such as needlework. However, even the wealthiest farmer might not allow his daughters to be educated, considering formal education an unnecessary expense. Yeoman farmers often lacked the income and labor to let daughters attend school. Not only were their hands needed to help ensure a productive farm, but also most small farmers could not afford the tuition of an academy.

Whether or not Southern women received a formal education, their participation in the workings of the household was fully expected. Although the type and amount of work that women participated in varied according to class and location, all women performed vital tasks. The wives of yeoman farmers often worked alongside their husbands, laboring in the fields or performing household tasks. Unlike elite women, these women worked with their hands, cooking, cleaning, and farming. Women privileged enough to have slave labor still took part in the management of their homes. It was their job to maintain order in the home and to direct the work of domestic slaves. Additionally, elite women were often responsible for their own sewing, mending, and weaving. Other tasks included caring for the sick, making household goods such as soap or butter, and overseeing the cooking for the day. Although slave ownership often relieved elite women from the burdens of field work, they were still active in the home.

One of the most challenging tasks that elite women faced was the management of slaves, whose supervision required constant attention to ensure that work was completed correctly. Women were also responsible for the care of slaves, rationing food and clothing. Slaveholding women cared for sick slaves, birthed their children, and generally managed human relations. These tasks alone kept a woman busy all day long. Additionally, women had to negotiate the relationships between themselves and the slave community, maintain authority, but not overstep their boundaries as wives, mothers, and dependents. Although elite women worked to preserve this balance during the Civil War, many struggled with the increased difficulty of managing slaves without male authority figures around.

Although marriage played an important role in the lives of most women, some did not marry or were widowed. To be single in the South placed a woman in a precarious role. Because the South was a rigid structure of patriarchy, these women often fell outside the system, living on their own. Widowed women were often left with little or no opportunity to earn a living for their family. Although husbands left estates to their wives, they also frequently left large amounts of debt or assigned the estate to an executor, leaving little financial control to their widow. Most widows faced a steadily declining income, with little hope for upward social mobility. Single women lacked even the promise of an entailed estate and many depended on the aid of family members. Finding employment could lessen a woman's dependence on her male kin, but employment opportunities for Southern women were scarce. Most jobs available to women were domestic positions, such as those as seamstresses or washerwomen. Few single women from elite families would willingly take on these types of jobs. Teaching was also available, but it did not guarantee constant wages or permanent posts. These positions therefore left women precariously dependent on men.

The Civil War shattered the long-standing notions of place, class, and hierarchy. As the war impacted the region, women and men faced the devastation of their society and the need to adapt to the trials of battle. Being at home did not expose Southern women any less to the conflict. In fact, Southern women faced the Civil War head-on both at home and on the front lines. Their efforts became critical to the success or failure of the Confederate war effort.

As husbands and fathers left home to fight for the Confederacy, women confronted a variety of emotional, physical, economic, and political issues alone. Emotionally, women felt torn between their love for family members and their devotion to the Confederate States. Their dedication to the newfound nation often was demonstrated through the stoic acceptance of a son's or a father's departure. In many cases, Southern women encouraged male loved ones to enlist in the Confederate army and provided them with supplies to do so. They saw the soldiers off with celebrations and community-made flags. At other times, women rushed into marriage to support a departing beau before war.

Despite their initial enthusiasm, anxiety plagued Southern women, as it did people across the nation. Many women turned to religion to guide them through the war years. Religion served as a source of comfort and also provided consolation as more military defeats guaranteed the death of family and community members. Others simply begged military and political leaders for their husbands' return. Some women's dedication to the Confederacy did not outlast the trials of the Southern homefront during the war.

Women left on the Confederate homefront experienced the impact of warfare not only emotionally, but economically as well. The wartime economy of the South created immediate shortages of goods and the inflation of prices. Many women, previously unaware of financial issues, became acutely aware of the cost of clothes and fabric. To substitute for the expensive goods that could not be purchased, women began to make their own cloth and sew their own clothing. Homespun became a staple of dress across the region. Clothing was not the only item to increase in cost. By 1862, food shortages were widespread across the South, and by 1863 many families were on the brink of starvation. Often small farms that were financially strapped before the war faced extreme poverty, causing women to beg and depend on wealthy neighbors for food. Although class privilege protected women and their families from starvation, scarcity affected every home, causing misery and despair.

Whereas life on the homefront was often challenging, women of the South did not sit by idly. The war served as a catalyst for change in the South, offering women new opportunities and responsibilities that were previously left to men. The management of farms and plantations fell to the hands of women who were frequently inexperienced in this area. Early in the war, women depended heavily on the advice of their husbands or sons through letters, but soon they learned that decisions needed to be made without advice. The economic success of the farm depended on bookkeeping and management, which meant figuring ledgers and tallying accounts. In the years before the war, women rarely had the opportunity to perform these tasks, but they grew in experience and confidence during the war, becoming adept at running their homes.

While the management of a home or business often became more familiar during the war years, women faced the growing crisis of slavery as well. The absence of men deteriorated the complex system of patriarchy and paternalism in the South. Additionally, the chaos of war allowed more opportunities for slave resistance and freedom. Slavery gradually fell apart, not through the failure in management of women but through the decay of the entire system. As Northern troops rolled through the South, slaves left farms and homes for the promise of freedom. In addition to the growing economic crises, women felt increasingly threatened by the unruliness of their slaves. Rebellion became a fear for many women living alone. However, the larger problem was the disruption of labor. With husbands and sons away, plantations depended on slave labor more than ever to keep functioning. Without slaves, elite women who previously avoided manual labor were forced to labor in the fields, clean the home, or slaughter animals. While class differences were not erased during the war, labor and hardship brought the experiences of women of the South closer together.

The labor of Southern women was not limited to the plantation or farm; to support their families and themselves, many women worked as paid laborers during the war. Although jobs were limited in the antebellum years, the necessities of war provided new employment opportunities. Southern women, like their Northern counterparts, often filled in at posts previously held by men in peacetime. Women were needed to work in the Confederacy's few factories to help produce matériel for the war. Additionally, women turned to teaching in even greater numbers than they had prior to the war; these positions had greater consistency and longevity than they had before. Women were needed to continue education if men could not. One of the most significant opportunities for women was the availability of jobs for them in the Confederate government. The creation of a new government, combined with the exodus of men to the military, required women

to work for the Treasury, Post Office, and even War Departments. Women spent time printing and signing banknotes, delivering mail, and sewing uniforms. Single and widowed women found increased acceptance during wartime because of the value of their labor. Wartime moved domestic women into expanded roles outside the home and, more important, led to social acceptance, even if temporary, of the changes.

War had a drastic impact on the homefront. However, Southern women also experienced the war on the front lines. Because the Civil War was fought primarily in the South, many Southern women could not escape its direct impact. The war was fought in their backyards and fields. Cornfields became battlefields, and homes became command centers. Consequently, Southern women became part of the internal actions of war. They served as spies, soldiers, couriers, nurses, letter writers, cooks, and laundresses for the army. Southern women took an active role in their communities by feeding and clothing local soldiers, warning their husbands of danger, and facing the threat of assault by opposing forces. Left at home, women were open to attack to by anyone, from deserters to military officers. The devotion that women felt toward their families and friends led them to defy typically accepted behavior and actively involve themselves in the war effort.

The line between friend and foe blurred in the local communities and even on battle lines as civilians became soldiers and friends became enemies. Raiding and robbing homes was commonplace during the war. Fighting during the Civil War took place not only between large numbers of troops, but also in localized skirmishes. Lacking in numbers, small bands of men were often more effective for the South than larger corps, but Confederate guerrilla fighters were not regular troops and therefore depended heavily on their wives and other female kin to support them during the war. Such tactics led to harsh responses from the Union military, and, knowing of the close ties between guerillas and civilian supporters, Union officials responded by engaging the entire population, including women and children, in efforts to root out the enemy aggressors. Women were often caught in the middle. Many felt defenseless in their homes because of the fear of constant invasion by soldiers, sometimes Southern and sometimes Union. Ultimately, women of all classes and backgrounds struggled to defend themselves on the homefront and to deal with all the change and pressure.

Remaining at home as their men went off to join the Confederate army or to live in the bush as guerrilla fighters, women came face to face with many difficulties. To protect their families, some women tried to separate themselves from the war, but localized conflict brought the war home and made it unavoidable. The aggressive nature of guerrilla conflict forced women to become full participants in the war because it pervaded their homes and personal lives. In response to their involvement in the war, women were also treated harshly and became subject to interrogation and punishment. In Union-occupied areas across the South, banishment became a common punishment for women supporting the Confederacy. For example, Union officials banished women whose male family members were discovered to be guerrillas. Banished women were forced to leave their homes and communities and travel to a new location, where they would pose less of a threat to the Union army. Female-headed households became particular targets of banishment, because the Union suspected, often correctly, that the men of these families were most likely aiding the Confederate cause. Union officials recognized that women aided their husbands simply out of loyalty and love for their family, if not their devotion to the Southern cause. Banishment was a harsh reprisal to the actions of women in the war effort, but, Union officials rationalized, Southern women's importance to the Confederate war effort justified the action.

Southern women also faced invading Union troops, who often terrorized them, destroyed their crops and homes, and left with many personal treasures. For example, women in Virginia's Shenandoah Valley dealt with an ever changing landscape, as Union and Confederate forces traded control of the area. In addition, elite women in Georgia and the Carolinas personally dealt with William Tecumseh Sherman's invading force.

Union soldiers in the 1864 campaigns invaded not only Southern territory, but also Southern homes, taking women's letters, diaries, clothes, and other personal treasures as souvenirs.

In Union-occupied areas such as New Orleans and Vicksburg, Southern women had to find ways to coexist with the enemy troops or to escape to Confederate territory. Many women took loyalty oaths as a means to survive. Others, especially those who had conflicting loyalties at the outset of the war, were relieved upon the arrival of Union troops.

Many Southern women enthusiastically volunteered in service jobs during the war, aiding the Confederacy as hospital employees. The proximity of Civil War battles to Southern communities and homes also impacted women's roles as nurses and caregivers. From the outset of the war, Southern women opened their homes to injured soldiers, creating makeshift hospitals and offering as much care as they could provide. Frequently schools and churches also served as field hospitals, where local women cared for the wounded. Although it was not until 1862 that the Confederacy authorized female employment in hospitals, women often found opportunities to aid wounded men even in the early days of the war. Elite Southern women often found jobs as nurse managers, organizing the volunteers in the hospital, while working-class and slave women were left to menial and laborious tasks. Army regulations and gender conventions prohibited women from nursing on the front lines, so most women were active off the battlefield.

For many Southern women, hospital work consisted of more than health care duties. These women, like their Northern counterparts, brought food and water to soldiers in bed, wrote letters for soldiers, and helped them stay cool in the heat. Many women also raised funds for hospitals or volunteered their services making bandages or food. Some women, seeing themselves as unfit for medical service because of their class and gender, did not want help in the direct care of the injured. Other women volunteered to care for wounded soldiers despite issues of respectability.

While some women of the South set limits on their interaction with soldiers and the front lines,

Hospital laundry yard in Nashville, Tennessee, ca. 1861–1865. (Corbis)

others sacrificed themselves completely to the war effort. Women served as spies for the South, and some dressed as soldiers to join the men on the battlefields. Women participated in these ways for a variety of reasons, including their dedication to their nation and their need to remain close to their husbands. Problems arose when women became injured and their sex was discovered. Local militias presented a better opportunity for Southern women to involve themselves in the war. Women banded together to protect themselves and their community, and they acquired skills such as marksmanship and drills to enable them to act if necessary.

Women also served as able participants in espionage and smuggling for the Confederacy. Letting their gender act as a form of protection, many women used their femininity to get information or

to procure needed goods. Although gender allowed many women to succeed in their goals, they still were susceptible to capture and jail. Some women spent time incarcerated, but very often well cared for by their captors. Southern women were able to transform their domestic and submissive position in Southern society to one of strength that allowed them to break away from their roles and involve themselves directly in the war effort.

Although not all women took up arms against the enemy, many Southern women asserted themselves in ways that demonstrated their new power and independence. Women's use of community networks to create wartime organizations revealed Southern women's ability not only to work within the confines of antebellum gender expectations but also to stretch them as necessary. These tasks did not necessarily challenge traditional responsibilities, but they revealed the importance of women to the Confederate war effort. A new self-awareness developed for these women, who understood the importance of their sacrifices and contributions to their nation and to the soldiers.

As the military hostilities ended, women had to deal with the consequences of a war that had torn apart their families, communities, way of living, and culture. The end of Southern slavery required a new economic system and a new source of labor. It also created an upheaval in the South's traditional hierarchy. Southerners were forced to deal with the end of the plantation system and freedom for their slaves. For many the war brought about financial disaster and the need to rebuild their farm, homes, and families.

After the Civil War, many Southern women had lost husbands, brothers, and sons. Soldiers who returned often needed their wives' support—physically, economically, and emotionally—and the war provided Southern women with experiences that allowed them to face postwar challenges. Although some women longed for their antebellum lives, others embraced their new roles as businesswomen, managers, and leaders in the community. Some Southern women began memorializing the Confederacy and its fallen soldiers. In addition, many continued their work in voluntary organizations and sought out new opportunities to involve themselves in activities outside the home. Although the Civil War challenged many Southern women, it also created the opportunity for change. Many Southern women redefined themselves after the war.

*Megan Boccardi*

**See also** African American Women; Aid Societies; Bread Riots; Camp Followers; Civilian Life; Columbia Bazaar (January 17–21, 1865); Confederate Homefront; Confederate Surrender (1865); Courtship and Marriage; Destruction of Homes; Destruction of Personal Property; Diaries and Journals; Disease; Domesticity; Education, Southern; Enlistment; Fairs and Bazaars; Family Life, Confederate; Farm Work; Female Combatants; Female Spies; Flags, Regimental; Food; Foraging, Effects on Women; Fundraising; Girlhood and Adolescence; Guerrilla Warfare; Gunboat Societies; Homespun; Honor; Hospital Ships; Impressment; Imprisonment of Women; Ladies' Memorial Associations; Letter Writing; Loyalty Oaths; Military Invasion and Occupation; Monuments; Morale; Mourning; Nationalism, Confederate; Nonslaveholding Southerners; Northern Women; Nurses; Pensions, Confederate Widows; Plantation Life; Poets, Southern; Politics; Prostitution; Rape; Reconstruction (1865–1877); Refugees; Religion; Rural Women; Secession; Separate Spheres; Sewing Bees; Sheridan's Shenandoah Valley Campaign (1864); Sherman's Campaign (1864–1865); Shortages; Slaveholding Women; Southern Unionists; Teachers, Southern; Treasury Girls; United Daughters of the Confederacy; Urban Women, Southern; Wartime Employment; Wartime Literature; Widows, Confederate; Woman Order (General Order Number 28); Wounded, Visits to.

**References and Further Reading**

Bynum, Victoria E. 1992. *Unruly Women: The Politics of Social and Sexual Control in the Old South.* Chapel Hill: University of North Carolina Press.

Clinton, Catherine, ed. 2000. *Southern Families at War: Loyalty and Conflict in the Civil War South.* New York: Oxford University Press.

Edwards, Laura. 2000. *Scarlett Doesn't Live Here Anymore: Southern Women in the Civil War Era.* Urbana: University of Illinois Press.

Faust, Drew Gilpin. 1996. *Mothers of Invention: Women of the Slaveholding South in the American Civil War.* Chapel Hill: University of North Carolina Press.

Fellman, Michael. 1989. *Inside War: The Guerilla Conflict in Missouri During the American Civil War.* New York: Oxford University Press.

Fox-Genovese, Elizabeth. 1988. *Within the Plantation Household: Black and White Women of the Old South.* Chapel Hill: University of North Carolina Press.

McCurry, Stephanie. 1995. *Masters of Small Worlds: Yeoman Households, Gender Relations, and the Political Culture of the Antebellum South Carolina Low Country.* New York: Oxford University Press.

Rable, George. 1989. *Civil Wars: Women and the Crisis of Southern Nationalism.* Urbana: University of Illinois Press.

Roberts, Giselle. 2003. *The Confederate Belle.* Columbia: University of Missouri Press.

Schultz, Jane E. 2004. *Women at the Front: Hospital Workers in Civil War America.* Chapel Hill: University of North Carolina Press.

Scott, Anne Firor. 1970. *The Southern Lady: From Pedestal to Politics, 1830–1930.* Charlottesville: University of Virginia Press.

Whites, LeeAnn. 1995. *The Civil War as Crisis in Gender: Augusta, Georgia, 1860–1890.* Athens: University of Georgia Press.

## Union Homefront

The Union homefront, much like the Confederate homefront, was first and foremost a society caught in the exigencies of war. Generally, most Northerners were touched by the war in one way or another. Certainly those who volunteered to fight felt a direct effect, as did their relatives. Very few citizens remained completely untouched by the war because most had relatives enlisted in the army or working for the government. In addition, everyone felt the effects of increased prices, lower wages, patriotic pressures, and restricted freedom to travel. After the surrender of Fort Sumter, members of Northern communities felt the effects of war ideologically, physically, and financially.

With President Abraham Lincoln's call for troops on April 15, 1861, Northern citizens had to decide which cause to side with. Some Northerners, usually Democrats, sympathized with the Confederacy. Even though they took no action, they were seen as traitors by Unionists and by the Lincoln administration, and they were labeled Copperheads, after the snake of the same name. Other Northern citizens chose not just to sympathize, but actually to side with the Confederates. These Northerners usually left for the South to help the cause there. However, some, like the antebellum hostess Rose O'Neal Greenhow, stayed in Washington, D.C., and became a spy for the Confederates. Greenhow in particular took advantage of her political connections.

For most Northern women, like their Southern sisters, the decision of which side to support was an easy one. They followed their hearts, usually siding with their families and their home state. But the war also tore families apart. In some instances, one son, cousin, or uncle fought for the North while other close relatives fought in the Confederate armies. Despite the fact that these decisions were often out of women's control, they were often blamed for their relatives' choices. Some women from families with divided loyalties were seen as traitors. For them, the war was spent trying to cope from day to day in a hostile environment. Perceived traitors, male and female, became targets of physical and verbal abuse as well as property destruction.

Northern civilians did not experience the war in the same way as did their Southern counterparts for several reasons. First, with the exception of Northern communities like Gettysburg, Pennsylvania, Sharpsburg, Maryland, and Border State communities, few Northern women saw war firsthand. The majority of Civil War battles took place in the South, so Northerners were rarely touched by the hard hand of war. The people on the Union homefront rarely experienced the disruption of armies camping near their homes and "requisitioning" their livestock or crops. Also, few Northern women had to fear a wayward cannonball crashing into their home or a stray bullet coming through their windows. In addition, they never had to endure enemy occupation, and few had to cope with the difficulties that a large wartime refugee population, troops marching through towns, or a scarcity of supplies brought to the Confederate homefront.

However, some people on the Union homefront faced constant disruptions throughout the war. In the Border States of Missouri and Kentucky, citizens endured frequent raids by both armies as well as by guerrillas. In addition, those who lived near army camps had to endure the antics of drunken soldiers let loose in town with a day's pass. The civilians also lost chickens and crops to the troops. In addition, because prostitution thrived in the large cities during the Civil War, citizens in these areas encountered more of these "loose" women on their streets.

The types of products available to Northern civilians changed during the war. Less cotton and tobacco were available to them than had been in the antebellum years. However, they did not have to deal with a blockade that restricted imports. While the Southern economy strained under the Union blockade, the Northern economy thrived. With less cotton coming their way, Northern textile owners had to make a decision. Some, like those in Connecticut, chose to convert their textiles mills to arsenals to make bullets and explosives for the War Department.

Other businesses thrived through government contracts. Quartermaster General Montgomery C. Meigs cleverly devised a system that allowed civilian companies to bid on supplying the Union's armed forces. Despite some corruption, the government contracts worked well and stimulated all parts of the Northern economy. Farmers benefited by providing grain, vegetables, and livestock to the army. Factory owners sold wool uniforms and blankets as well as tenting and camping equipment. Wagon manufacturers, harness makers, and barrel makers all saw increased profits by providing for an army whose voracious appetite seemed to have no end.

Northern women also benefited from this strong homefront economy. Jobs previously closed to them opened up during the war. Women took the places left empty by the men who had gone off to fight. Women were hired by the Treasury and War Departments as clerks. In these government jobs, women made more money than they could in most other jobs open to them. In addition, some women became lighthouse keepers, teamsters, steamboat captains, bankers, brokers, and morticians. They worked as saleswomen in department stores and shops.

Many of the jobs open to women during the Civil War were in factories, especially those that manufactured war matériel. Women who worked in arsenals took on a hazardous job. Explosions due to dangerous work conditions and accidents killed and injured female munitions workers during the war.

Northern women also continued to work in traditional jobs. They remained as keepers of saloons and boarding houses. They also continued their work in the needle trades. The need for seamstresses increased during the war, and so did the competition among seamstresses. Because the War Department contracted this work to the lowest bidder, the company that gained the contract in turn hired the cheapest seamstresses it could find. Consequently, any seamstress who tried to hold out for higher pay usually found herself unemployed. Ironically, seamstresses actually earned less during the war than they had in 1860. This put tremendous financial pressures on women during a time when their husbands' pay did not arrive regularly or the war widowed them. Although the thriving economy benefited many people, war inflation often offset the increased pay.

The Northern homefront experienced wartime inflation of 80 percent. Although this was little compared to the 9,000 percent increase in the Confederacy, the rise in wartime prices affected the lives of all Union civilians. In Washington, D.C., the prices were so high that higher wages barely met the basic needs of government workers. Despite these problems, the Northern economy remained relatively stable throughout the war as a result of the greenback, the National Bank Act, an income tax, and a diversified economy. To control wartime inflation, the United States Congress made the greenback national legal tender and used it to finance the war. Congress also began standardizing the banking system, ensuring that individual banks could not print their own money. The passage of an income tax on incomes over $600 helped supplement government revenue and put the burden on those who could most afford it.

Even though inflation in the Union seemed under control, wartime prices kept many civilians from adequately supporting their families. Poor white women and black women suffered the most from these economic circumstances. Without the resources to supplement their meager wages and those of their soldier husbands, these women struggled to keep their families fed and clothed. Many moved in with relatives to ease their financial burdens, but in doing so they gave up their privacy. Women economized by feeding their families simple meals and by growing supplemental vegetables in corner gardens. They mended, refitted, and reused clothes to keep themselves warm and presentable. Keeping their children clothed, however, presented a continual problem. Growing children's need for clothes and shoes put a strain on family finances and women's ingenuity.

As the lowest-paid members of Northern society, black families suffered the most during this economic constriction. Hopes that economic woes would be alleviated by a soldier's pay were crushed. When the Union army enlisted black men in 1863, many black families suffered even more than they had before. The government tended to be six months behind on soldiers' pay and, adding to this hardship, the Union refused to pay African American soldiers the full pay of soldiers. Consequently, soldiers' families suffered without their male loved ones and without the benefits of a regular and sufficient paycheck.

Many needy civilian families were too proud to ask for help. However, when the situation became dire, women could turn to benevolent societies in their towns. Antebellum Northern communities had instituted benevolent work to help the poor, but wartime needs and increasing difficulties pressured an already strapped system. Civilians were torn between donating their time and money to benevolent groups that worked for the less fortunate in their towns and giving to soldiers' aid societies. Devoting time to charitable work and taking care of their families pushed some women beyond their capacities and they usually minimized the stress by quitting one of the groups. Other women were able to meet all their commitments, despite the exhaustion.

Work for soldiers' aid societies on the homefront became a common experience for most Northern women. Although some women offered only a couple of hours a week for the society or only helped by selling things at a booth during a sanitary fair, most women did some kind of work for these societies during the war. Work in soldiers' aid societies exhibited women's response to their nation's call to arms. They saw that they, too, had a duty to do something for the cause. Early in the war, it became apparent that the government would not be able to meet the troops' supply needs. Consequently, women helped to equip the men of their families and communities with blankets, food, and toiletries to get them to camp. Although they assumed that the government would take over the task of supplying the troops once they arrived in camp, women eventually helped outfit the soldiers at all stages of their service. The enormous army quickly tapped the skeletonlike governmental infrastructure, and supply needs could not be met.

In response to the soldiers' ongoing need for supplies, Northern women organized aid societies and pledged their commitment until the cessation of hostilities. Generally, the upper-class women of the community began the societies and provided the much needed funds, while middle-class women ran the day-to-day business of the societies. Poorer women of the communities also worked to help the soldiers' aid societies, giving as much time as they could, making a small cash donation, or giving a small portion of their garden harvest to enliven the meals of the soldiers. Society managers loved to advertise the participation of the community's poor citizens in the hopes of making the wealthy citizens feel guilty about their lack of financial support.

In April 1861, women in New York City gathered to create the Women's Central Association of Relief (WCAR). They hoped to organize women's efforts around the New England area and have them channel their goods to their New York office. From there the New York women would use their communication with army officials to decide what supplies were needed where. In this way, the New York volunteers hoped to organize women's war efforts, make the system more efficient, and bring about a feeling of nationalism among Northern women.

Men often took charge of women's efforts to aid Union soldiers. They created larger organizations to direct the collection and distribution of supplies to the troops. A group of New York physicians and ministers headed to Washington, D.C., for a meeting with President Abraham Lincoln about the need for a national benevolent organization that would aid the army's Medical Department. As this group of prominent men recognized, the small and understaffed Medical Department was in no shape to meet the medical needs of the growing armed forces. Although the head of the department and Lincoln viewed the civilian group as both meddlesome and unnecessary, the president gave it government sanction in June 1861. The United States Sanitary Commission (USSC), as it was named, became the liaison between the army and the Union homefront. Sanitary agents would travel to army camps, give army officials advice about sanitation in the camps and personal hygiene among the soldiers, and learn about the supply needs of the individual regiments. The USSC would also provide supplies for military hospitals, furnish transportation and temporary medical care for wounded soldiers, and assist soldiers in numerous other ways.

The New England soldiers' aid societies, fostered by the WCAR, eventually merged with the USSC when the WCAR became a branch of the USSC. Although the USSC established branches, it never fully gained the confidence of many Northern women. Consequently, hundreds of aid societies remained independent, donating their supplies to their local and state regiments as well as to national groups like the USSC and its rival, the United States Christian Commission.

The United States Christian Commission (USCC) similarly worked to supply Union troops. This organization was established by men from the Young Men's Christian Association (YMCA) in November 1861. Although they claimed that they were concerned only with the spiritual well-being of the soldiers, it quickly became clear that the USCC was distributing more than religious pamphlets to the young recruits. This organization, too, offered desperately needed supplies on the battlefield, in camp, and at the hospitals. To meet their demands, the USCC, like the USSC, depended on supplies made and sent by soldiers' aid societies across the North. Men may have been the officers of national organizations, like the USSC and the USCC, but women served as the backbone of their success. Without the work of hundreds of thousands of women across the North, the USSC and USCC would have failed in their primary goals.

The aid societies that sent their goods to the USSC and the USCC shared similar structures. The typical Union aid society had a dozen primary members and several women who occasionally offered their services. Societies had elected officers, dues, constitutions, and regular meetings. Members might meet on a weekly or monthly basis, depending on the size of the society and the amount of work to be done. The society's work was divided among the women in committees, which usually included a cutting committee, a packing committee, a sewing committee, and a purchasing committee. Children of society members also contributed by scraping lint for packing into wounds

and starting their own Juvenile Societies to raise money. The ladies planned their work as they responded to requests for supplies from their local regiments, state agencies, the USSC, and the USCC. They donated their goods to each group depending on need and on the organization's desire to help the particular group.

Black women also participated in and formed soldiers' aid societies. Before the Union army enlisted African American men, some black women worked in the offices of their communities' white soldiers' aid society. Once the Union army began enlisting black men into colored regiments in 1863, many black women established their own soldiers' aid societies to help their husbands, sons, and fathers in the military. As did the white societies, these "colored" groups elected officers, established work committees, collected dues, met weekly or monthly, and sent supplies to their local regiments. Black societies, however, did not usually have as much money or supplies available to them as did white soldiers' aid societies. Nor did their members have as much free time to devote to the society. Instead of funneling their handiwork through the USSC and the USCC, members of African American soldiers' aid societies often reserved the supplies they made for individual regiments. The USSC and USCC claimed that they gave supplies to all Union soldiers regardless of class, race, or region. However, although they provided for black soldiers, it was not completely without discrimination.

Regardless of race or organization, all soldiers' aid societies relied on their own funds to help supply and aid Union troops. Some members dedicated themselves to making goods, others helped raise money through donations and or fundraisers. To do so, many organizations held fundraisers. Society fundraisers served a dual purpose. First and foremost, the events generated desperately needed money and helped subsidize a society's efforts with activities that included concerts, oyster dinners, tableaux, and dances. Their success helped fund relief efforts and allowed women to continue their work for the troops. Second, fundraisers became a source of entertainment for citizens at war. Wartime Northern society ran more smoothly than Southern society, but there were still vivid reminders that the country was at war. Most notably, the absence of male loved ones not only gave women increased duties at home, but it also curbed their social activities. Victorian etiquette placed restrictions on women's public interactions and required that single women be chaperoned at times. Although war loosened society's morals, proper women still did not engage in certain activities without being accompanied by male relatives or friends. This meant fewer social engagements for Northern women during the war. Society fundraisers were not only patriotic; they also were within women's proper sphere of influence and so women got to participate without jeopardizing their propriety.

Perhaps the most financially successful Union fundraiser was the USSC's Chicago Sanitary Fair in October 1863. The Sanitary Fair was the brainchild of a group of Milwaukee and Chicago women determined to get everyone involved in raising money for Union soldiers. Local businesses and schools closed so that citizens could attend the grand opening of the fair. During the fair, visitors browsed among booths that included flower arrangements, art collections, historic artifacts, military equipment, and a trophy room filled with captured Confederate battle flags, muskets, and cannon balls. Visitors dined in the fair's restaurant, posted letters at the fair's post office, and played in the Children's Department. The overwhelming success of the Chicago Sanitary Fair in terms of communal response and money raised prompted women in other cities to begin plans for their own sanitary fairs. Even children began holding their own "fairs" in their backyards. The most financially successful of the later fairs was the Metropolitan Fair in New York City, whose organizers raised more than $1 million for the benefit of Union troops.

As financially successful as these fairs were, some contemporaries believed that they had detrimental aftershocks that aid societies felt long after the fair ended. Some women argued that precisely because of the enormous amounts of money raised in these large-scale events, the Northern public got the wrong impression about the ongoing needs of the

Home workers for Sanitary Commission, photographed for souvenir sales to secure money for the cause in connection with the New York Sanitary Fair. (Miller, Francis Trevelyan and Robert Sampson Lanier, *The Photographic History of the Civil War*, vol. 7, 1911)

USSC and other aid societies. Critics argued that some citizens presumed that no more money or individual help was needed by the societies on a regular basis. However, the opposite was true. The costly battles of 1864 required more hospital supplies and taxed the USSC storehouses. Likewise, the preparation and execution of the Sanitary Fair was so time-consuming and physically taxing that the ladies of the host communities were too exhausted to contribute any more of their time to the society after the end of the event. Aid society officers eventually convinced their communities that the fairs served a valuable and necessary purpose in the continued work of the USSC. However, sanitary fairs may have been most successful in releasing tension for a society at war and giving citizens tangible evidence that they were doing something for the cause.

Fundraising fairs and bazaars offered Northern civilians one way to attach themselves directly to the war and to their loved ones at the front. Yet, at times, Northerners felt disconnected from the war, or at least from the pageantry of the battles, encampments, and soldiers. To overcome this feeling, some women visited military hospitals in and around their communities. Most towns with military camps had hospitals. However, there were also several general military hospitals in Jeffersonville, Indiana, Philadelphia, Pennsylvania, New York City, and Washington, D.C. Local aid societies had a close relationship with these hospitals, their members providing supplies, sometimes appointing matrons and nurses, and regularly visiting the sick and wounded soldiers.

Women who visited wounded Union soldiers often brought with them flowers, jams, pies, reading material, and wholesome games. Visitors helped to break up the dull hours of recuperation by talking and listening to the patients and by engaging the men in singing and praying. These visits usually brightened the soldiers' days and helped the aid society ladies feel more connected to the war and to their loved ones at the front.

Other Northern women worked as nurses at military hospitals. Most lived on site, were expected to be available around the clock, and had to endure the nauseating smells, the sight of horrid wounds, and the soldiers' incessant moaning. Their personal sacrifices in enduring exhausting work that ruined the health of many women and their willingness to expose themselves to contagious diseases without a care for their own well-being led the soldiers to feel a special tie to these women, whom they saw as sister comrades.

African American women also made sacrifices for Union soldiers. Not allowed to work as nurses to white soldiers, black women often worked as laundresses and cooks. Their opportunities to dispense medicine and change dressings came with the enlistment of African American soldiers. Black soldiers did not usually receive immediate medical attention, and the medical corps segregated hospital transports. Some white nurses and doctors treated black soldiers, who often received very little care. However, African American women were allowed to nurse black soldiers and took up the medical aid of their men.

Northern civilians—white and black, men, women, and children—experienced the war through enlisted loved ones, national economic shifts, and the ideological choices they made. The Northern homefront may have undergone fewer disruptions caused by battles and marauding armies than its Southern counterpart, but Northern citizens nevertheless sacrificed, endured, and suffered as a result of the war. They found ways to support their families and their nation.

*Patricia Richard*

***See also*** Aid Societies; Border States; Civilian Life; Confederate Homefront; Confederate Sympathizers, Northern; Domesticity; Draft Riots and Resistance; Factory Workers, Northern; Fairs and Bazaars; Family Life, Union; Female Spies; Food; Foraging, Effects on Women; Free Blacks; Fundraising; Government Girls; Greenhow, Rose O'Neal (ca. 1814–1864); Hospitals; Letter Writing; Military Invasion and Occupation; Morale; Nationalism, United States; Northern Women; Nurses; Politics; Prostitution; Refugees; Rural Women; Separate Spheres; Sewing Bees; Shortages; United States Christian Commission; United States Sanitary Commission; Urban Women, Northern; Wartime Employment; Widows, Union; Women's Central Association of Relief; Wounded, Visits to.

**References and Further Reading**

Attie, Jeanie. 1998. *Patriotic Toil: Northern Women and the American Civil War.* Ithaca, NY: Cornell University Press.

Forbes, Ella. 1998. *African American Women During the Civil War.* New York: Garland Publishing.

Gallman, J. Matthew. 1994. *The North Fights the Civil War: The Home Front.* Chicago: Ivan R. Dee.

Leonard, Elizabeth D. 1999. *Yankee Women: Gender Battles in the Civil War.* New York: W. W. Norton.

Marten, James. 1998. *The Children's Civil War.* Chapel Hill: University of North Carolina Press.

Massey, Mary Elizabeth. [1966] 1994. *Women in the Civil War.* Lincoln: University of Nebraska Press.

McPherson, James. 1988. *Battle Cry of Freedom: The Civil War Era.* New York: Ballantine Books.

Richard, Patricia L. 2003. *Busy Hands: Images of the Family in the Northern Civil War Effort.* New York: Fordham University Press.

## Wartime Employment

The Civil War coincided with a radical change in the role of American women in the economy and in the work force. How much of a coincidence this was remains an unresolved area of Civil War history, women's history, and labor history. In addition, scholars' understanding of female employment in the Civil War period reflects the innate constraints of the historical sources' bias by gender, section, race, and class. Historians' grasp of what women were doing in these years becomes more tenuous as they move from white, relatively privileged urban women in the North to the wage-earning, non-white, rural, and Southern women.

In an age before household appliances, much of the day's women's work centered on the home. Household duties like cooking, cleaning, and laundry were time-consuming and arduous in the best of circumstances. Yet the standards and strains of doing these chores in the families of the poor, of the workingmen, or of the farmers remained limited, making them all the more laborious.

Middle-class homes required more than what the females of the family could provide single-handedly. Such households either hired vast numbers of women who boarded with their employers, or they made do if they were not able to afford help. With the prosperity of the growing number of middle-class households, the demand for servants became even greater. Most servants were younger women who could be spared from their own families, but domestic service increasingly became a relatively permanent kind of work.

Urbanization transformed employed housework, even before labor-saving devices mechanized it. In the generation before the Civil War, the explosive growth of American cities proportionately surpassed the already unprecedented increase of the population as a whole. According to the 1860 U.S. Federal Census, at least 6,217,000 Americans lived in 392 "urban places" with populations of 2,500 or more. Of those places, thirty-five communities had more than 25,000 residents, eight had populations of more than 160,000, and metropolitan New York's population reached a total of nearly a million and a half.

The commensurate increase in wealth raised middle-class domestic aspirations, increasing the need for household labor. It also provided the workers who made it easier for employers to meet the demand. Meeting the demand for domestic service in slaveholding communities was quite straightforward. Elsewhere, the chores in the cities were much less arduous than farmwork, reducing the roles of family relations and friendships in providing the labor. The anonymity of wage labor placed it directly at the center of domestic servitude.

Moreover, the ethnically stratified realities of nineteenth-century American life meant that domestic labor would disproportionately become the lot of female immigrants and African Americans. Respectable middle-class families who used domestic servants functioned with these hired women and girls going about their duties entirely in the background.

Many women may have begun their working lives in, and certainly always participated in, farmwork, although the demand for this kind of labor fluctuated widely and seasonally. At the most basic level, enslaved women of color participated alongside males from a very young age in the backbreaking field labor on the plantations. Conditions for slave women doing fieldwork were never easy, because their work was always ruthlessly driven by demand. In addition, slave women's work often involved simultaneously preparing food and managing the master's children as well as their own. The scale and intensity of plantation labor changed with the growing importance of cotton production, fueled by the demands of the new textile industries in England and the North. Unlike hemp, tobacco, and other crops grown by slaves, cotton fostered massive new plantations with hundreds of slaves on the lucrative estates of the Mississippi delta. The paternalist ideology of the slave owners necessarily meant less in practice, as the scale of work grew, driven increasingly by unrelenting exploitation.

Women work in the laundry room of the Philadelphia Citizens Volunteer Hospital, which was established during the Civil War to alleviate the other local hospitals of wounded, 1862. (Library of Congress)

Farm labor in nonslaveholding states rarely, if ever, implied the absolute ownership and power of mastery that it did in a slaveholding system. Nevertheless, the physical work was intense and arduous drudgery. Women participated fully in the work—the oldest division of labor.

The expansion and unprecedented prosperity of agriculture became contingent on its increasing scale and responsiveness to the market economy, which was rapidly expanding through steam technology over waterways, roads, and railroads. Because this technology had only begun to transform agricultural labor itself, the work on the expanding farms came to rely increasingly on poorly paid workers who were disproportionately women and children. With the notable exceptions of Native peoples and African slaves in the slaveholding states, land ownership and farming tended to reflect the duration of the family's presence in the New World.

The numbers of women involved in non-agricultural labor in the Civil War era remained subject to annual fluctuations that were less dramatic than,

but often mirrored, the seasonal nature of farm labor. The 1860 U.S. Federal Census counted 270,357 women nationally in non-agricultural labor. This represented 20.7 percent of all workers in this field. The proportions of women remained much higher in places and consistently ran near a third of all non-agricultural workers across New England, except Vermont. In more rural areas, men clearly preferred agricultural pursuits, and women actually constituted the majority of non-agricultural employees in Androscoggin (51.1 percent) and York (55.7 percent) counties, Maine. Notwithstanding the proportions, the absolute numbers of women workers in urban areas was very impressive. The counties of Philadelphia had 30,633, and those of New York had 24,721, while Boston and the neighboring counties of Essex, Middlesex, and Worcester contained nearly 48,000 working women.

The mothers, wives, and sisters of some artisans had been learning craft skills and performing artisan work for years. However, their general exclusion from the formal process of apprenticeship, the accepted means of attaining the required skills, caused the workingmen of most trades to see this simply as a further degradation of craft labor. Still, although women rarely performed artisan work, a growing number had begun to do so, particularly in the domestic and less prestigious crafts.

The needle trades epitomized how the industrialization of artisan labor eroded its status and blurred the lines not only between the traditional crafts and sweated labor, but also between traditional women's work and the labor that was vital to modern industrial life. Through subcontracts and piecework, middlemen contracted for the production of a set amount of product, purchased the raw material, and then subcontracted the labor to as many as could perform the work. This arrangement not only allowed for the expansion and contraction of the workforce to meet demand, but it also offered a seemingly unlimited level of profit through the ongoing erosion of wages and living conditions. The industries that mechanized the factory system achieved the same effect by radically increasing production through the use of machinery and a reorganized division of labor. Work in such places reduced all workers, regardless of gender, to the status of hands.

Industrialization had been under way in the New England textile industry for decades by the time of the Civil War, but the factory system expanded in an uneven way throughout the economy. Still, some workplaces, heavily dependent on female labor, employed thousands of workers, enough by 1860 to raise the average numbers of workers per workplace in New Haven County to nearly thirty.

The Civil War had an immediate and transformative impact on every aspect of American life, including the position of women in society and in the workplace. Military needs ultimately took about 5 million men out of the American workforce, even as it created or increased the demand for just about everything. Women and children disproportionately met the labor demands for this radical expansion of demand for products.

Agricultural demands increased as those left on the Union and Confederate homefronts had to provide food for soldiers in the field. Food production strained at the traditional production techniques, and mechanization began to change life on the farm. However, the war also stripped rural America of much of its livestock. The production of horses and mules increased in the Midwest but still resulted in a net loss. In the rural South, the direct devastation of the war destroyed the antebellum stability of this productive capacity. All these changes bore most heavily on women. In the case of farm work, the demand for hired labor, which usually tends to increase wages, did not have nearly such an impact because of the gender and age difference in the new workforce.

The Civil War also increased the need for industrial production. The war immediately produced an unprecedented demand for uniforms, foodstuffs, weapons, and equipage of all sorts. The demand fell on the shoulders of a workforce deprived of its traditional male breadwinners. Almost overnight, the exodus of men to the battlefields created the need for and the development of a massive new female workforce. At Philadelphia, the workforce at the Schuylkill Arsenal included over five thousand women, most laboring on uniform production, with more laboring out of the Girard House. Wages rose over the course of the war, but never enough to meet household needs. Compared to the North, the production of wartime goods in the less industrialized South entailed even greater problems. White Southern men were disproportionately in the ranks, and the women left at home faced less technologically experienced employers who were generally unwilling and unable to reward labor amply. Certainly, insofar as the war imposed a rapid and forced industrialization on the region, Southern women bore an even greater portion of the burden than did their Northern sisters.

In addition, the disruption of working life in the South proved particularly extreme and dramatic, ranging from the perpetual shortage of raw materials to the arrival of invading Union armies. As the conflict intensified, strategic planners came to understand that industrial labor represented an enemy asset and began to treat it accordingly. For example, when the troops in Union General William T. Sherman's army seized the Roswell Mills in Georgia, they not only burned the establishment but also took hundreds of the female employees and their children into custody. They exported the workers to Kentucky to keep them out of the Confederate workforce.

Aside from the rare artisan women, female self-employment remained marginal throughout the nineteenth century. However, the Civil War period marked the arrival of a few pioneering women doctors and clergy. In that conflict, a Congressional Medal of Honor was awarded to Dr. Mary Edwards Walker, although her labors probably attained less fame than her fearless adoption of masculine dress. Furthermore, President Abraham Lincoln's personal intervention gained a chaplaincy for Ella Gibson Hobart.

The emergence of spiritualism as a mass movement during the 1850s allowed women to assume a great leadership role. Although spirit communication was rare in the South and banned in several states, the numbers of Americans who dabbled in it is estimated in the millions. The prevailing means for reaching the spirits was to create a psychologically suggestive atmosphere through a séance, under the direction of a particularly sensitive medium, usually a woman. More than almost any other antebellum social movement, spiritualism represented the cultural response of women to the new imperatives of the secular market economy. It refined traditional religious assumptions into vehicles for major social change. Most abolitionist women drew inspiration from it, as did advocates of women's equality in general.

Almost from its onset, the war was a conflict of peoples in which the lines between civilian and soldier blurred. Both sides experienced serious political change. The North sought to follow a political party that had not been a majority party, and the political elite of the South attempted to transform the nature and identity of the nation itself. Tens of thousands of white Southerners were driven from their homes, the first of many who would be displaced by the the war. By 1862, some Southern counties had become virtually depopulated. The newspapers of the time attest to the fact that almost all cities or towns had informal refugee encampments in their parks, along the rivers or railroads, or just beyond the cities themselves. The refugee population depended almost entirely on the resourcefulness of women in finding sources of income. In such circumstances, the adult male population almost always entered the army, leaving the women and children to make their own arrangements. As was the norm in American society, as the populations grew, these communities became increasingly segregated by race.

The Federal expansion of its war goals to include slave liberation effectively invited African Americans to run away to these floating communities. They did so. Many of the Federal volunteers of "African Descent" were recruited from runaways, which left women to fend for themselves and to negotiate arrangements with the local military and civilian authorities. Many of these floating communities moved with the armies. Employment with the military provided an important alternative to a sedentary refugee life. Cooks, laundresses, clerical workers, teachers, and other women provided the Civil War armies and their floating communities with vital functions. In addition, some women—nobody knows exactly how many—actually cross-dressed and joined the military, often being discovered only when being medically treated.

The Civil War also saw the growth of the sex industry. The postwar hegemony of Victorian values among the respectable middle and upper classes later obscured the extent to which the sex industry provided an essential alternative for many women. An evening of prostitution could earn more than a week of factory or domestic labor. Estimates suggest that about 5 to 10 percent of young females in large cities engaged in prostitution at some point. Sources indicate that most of these were single, native-born, and recently arrived in the city. For most, prostitution represented a temporary expedient, to which they resorted until they could maintain themselves and any dependents through more socially acceptable employment or marriage. Clearly, many poor and working-class people, not yet overwhelmed by middle-class aspirations and values, tended to accept prostitution as a pragmatic measure. Among them, it did not permanently mar a woman or exclude her as a proper subject for courtship, marriage, and motherhood.

In the generation before the war, the unregulated boardinghouse subculture of young men created a market among "sporting males." By the time of the war, New York had over five hundred brothels catering to the high end of this market, advertising in guidebooks and the newspapers. Proportionate numbers appeared in cities and towns across the country, in the North and South. Wartime conditions created an immensely expanded market for prostitution by removing millions of men from their families and depriving millions of women of the support of male breadwinners. The problem became particularly acute in the devastated border and Southern communities, with their large populations of displaced persons. On the most pragmatic level, the Union army sought to protect the health of its troops through well regulated and medically serviced prostitution, notably in Nashville and Memphis, but also in Washington where General Joseph Hooker concentrated the industry in "Hooker's division" at the nation's capital.

Not all women turned to prostitution to support themselves. Many middle-class women had pursued a series of philanthropic projects in the generation leading up to the Civil War. These women focused their energies on causes such as the relief and moral elevation of the poor and "fallen women." With the war, philanthropic women extended their efforts to aid the soldiery, the families of soldiers, and refugees. Organizations like the United States Sanitary Commission and the United States Christian Commission took form in the Northern states to aid Union troops. While clergy and other prominent men associated their names with such efforts, women performed almost all of the associations' work, including their management. Southern women engaged in similar aid work, albeit without creating such overarching organizations.

The war largely subsumed the efforts of women's rights advocates like Susan B. Anthony and Elizabeth Cady Stanton, who had long been ardent abolitionists. With the start of 1863, Federal war goals expanded to include slave emancipation. On May 14, Anthony, Stanton, and others formed the National Women's Loyal League, which eventually claimed five thousand members and organized the "Mammoth Petition" to Congress, with some four hundred thousand signatures advocating an amendment to the Constitution to abolish slavery. The petition process contributed to the permanent transformation of the labor of African Americans and raised the question of equal rights. The experience and its ideological dynamic shaped the postwar emergence of the woman suffrage movement in the North.

However clear the impact of the Civil War was on race, gender, and labor, the limits of that impact remained uncertain. Emancipation became national and extended to formal civic equality for African Americans, but equality did not apply to African American women, who found their position no more equal in relation to men than that of free women of all races before the war. The elimination of slavery refocused the labor question on wage labor. Yet the extent to which formal citizenship and voting could address the problems of labor remained uncertain. After all, voting had proved inadequate to resolving the question of slavery.

Working women had participated in strikes and short-lived labor organizations since the 1820s, but the Civil War coincided with the explosive appearance of women in the labor movement. Under the protection of paternalistic expectations, working-class women had long participated in some of the most militant strike activities, events that would have brought the law down on the strikers themselves, like the efforts to prevent strikebreaking. For example, faced with an escalating wartime cost of living, coal miners near Kewanee, Illinois, went on strike in 1863, only to find that the employers were recruiting scabs and trying to keep the mines operating. At that point, the miners' wives and female family members threatened the strikebreakers with stones and other objects. They successfully chased off the strikebreakers and attacked one of the owners.

However, the war years also saw massive numbers of working women striking for themselves. Some two to three thousand women dramatically made their appearance as participants in the shoe strike of fifteen to eighteen thousand workers in

New England. Starting in February 1860, the strike lasted for weeks and spread across the region, though it centered in Lynn, Massachusetts, where a large contingent of women marched through the streets under banners demanding their rights as women as well as workers.

In addition, the local press of Philadelphia, New York, Washington, and other Northern cities recorded accounts of activism among women workers throughout the war. The government reduction of wages for women employed at Philadelphia's Schuylkill Arsenal inspired a protest meeting at Temperance Hall in September 1861. However, their protest was aimed not at a wartime wage reduction for those employed at government workshops, but at the expanding reliance on private contractors. Similar concerns inspired the 1863 formation of the New York Working Women's Protective Union. Led by middle-class women and clergymen, the organization sought to address the problems of the lowest-paid contract working women. They functioned as something of a benevolent society and also as an employment agency to encourage the better-paying contractors. The organization continued for decades.

Such efforts had a positive impact. In November 1863, about three hundred young women producing haircloth went on strike at some of the New York City shops for an additional 5¢ per yard. The *New York Times* noted that some of them were making as little as $1.50 per week and urged support not only for the women workers but for the underpaid females generally in the workforce. Nowhere in the Union was the cost of living more devastating than in Washington. Also in late 1863, employees at the Government Printing Office and on various construction projects demanded a wage increase to keep up with growing expenses. Among the former were about six hundred bookbinders, male and female.

The similar desire to adjust wages because of the increasing cost of living swept the country the following spring. The March and April 1864 strike movement in St. Louis, Missouri, involved tailors, shoemakers, machinists, and blacksmiths, and it led to military intervention against the strikers by the local authorities. A key issue among the tailors was the new wartime practices of hiring girls as apprentices. Largely led by socialists, the St. Louis tailors objected not to the introduction of female labor into the shops, but to their being paid less than men. However, after a month, the employers offered a pay increase but refused to recognize the union or change the practice of paying women less than men. The Typographical Union at Chicago proved to be less enlightened. In an effort to undercut the union, the "Copperhead" Democratic *Chicago Times* trained women as typesetters and then provoked a strike. When the union went on strike, the *Times* discharged the strikers and hired forty women. The presence of women in the printing trades would only grow; the postwar Typographical Union's decision to establish separate women's locals proved inadequate, but it represented a logical extension of the paternalism among male trade unionists that would take time to fade.

One of the features of the wartime American labor movement was that some women from privileged backgrounds with adequate leisure time began taking an active interest in the questions of social class and poverty. They did so not merely as philanthropists but as active labor reformers in their own right, ready to encourage workers to elevate their own condition through collective action. In so doing, these activists also planted the seeds of division within the women's movement.

The Civil War resolved on the battlefield sectional rivalries that reflected pervasive social tensions. Although the changing status of women in society and its economy was part of the process, the conflict centered on the political survival of the United States and on the enslavement of African Americans. However, the necessities of war accelerated these changes, alternately coaxing and forcing women into new roles, although the nature and pace of the changes varied with sectional, community, racial, and ethnic considerations. At the same time, the abolition of slavery opened the opportunity for an egalitarian rethinking of gender and labor, as well as of race. The Civil War also established a common national set of white, Christian, and middle-class values that idealized womanhood in a way that left the concerns of most women in continued obscurity.

*Mark A. Lause*

*See also* African American Women; Aid Societies; Anthony, Susan B. (1820–1906); Bread Riots; Camp Followers; Confederate Homefront; Contrabands; Domesticity; Factory Workers, Northern; Factory Workers, Southern; Family Life, Confederate; Family Life, Union; Farm Work; Female Combatants; Immigrant Women; Military Invasion and Occupation; National Women's Loyal League [Women's National Loyal League]; Nonslaveholding Southerners; Northern Women; Nurses; Politics; Prostitution; Refugees; Roswell Women; Rural Women; Separate Spheres; Sherman, William Tecumseh (1820–1891); Slaveholding Women; Southern Women; Stanton, Elizabeth Cady (1815–1902); Teachers, Northern; Teachers, Southern; Thirteenth Amendment; Treasury Girls; Union Homefront; United States Christian Commission; United States Sanitary Commission; Urban Women, Northern; Urban Women, Southern; Walker, Mary Edwards (1832–1919).

**References and Further Reading**

Clinton, Catherine. 1984. *The Other Civil War: American Women in the Nineteenth Century.* New York: Hill and Wang.

Clinton, Catherine, and Nina Silver, eds. 1992. *Divided Houses: Gender and the Civil War.* New York: Oxford University Press.

Cutter, Barbara. 2003. *Domestic Devils, Battlefield Angels: The Radicalization of American Womanhood, 1830–1865.* DeKalb: Northern Illinois University Press.

Delfino, Susanna, and Michele Gillespie, eds. 2002. *Neither Lady Nor Slave: Working Women of the Old South.* Chapel Hill: University of North Carolina Press.

Faulkner, Carol. 2003. *Women's Radical Reconstruction: The Freedmen's Aid Movement.* Philadelphia: University of Pennsylvania Press.

Faust, Drew Gilpin. 2004. *Mothers of Invention: Women of the Slaveholding South in the American Civil War.* Chapel Hill: University of North Carolina Press.

Leonard, Elizabeth D. 1999. *Yankee Women: Gender Battles in the Civil War.* New York: W. W. Norton.

Lowry, Thomas P. 1994. *The Story the Soldiers Wouldn't Tell: Sex in the Civil War.* Mechanicsburg, PA: Stackpole Books.

Richard, Patricia L. 2003. *Busy Hands: Images of the Family in the Northern Civil War Effort.* New York: Fordham University Press.

Schultz, Jane E. 2004. *Women at the Front: Hospital Workers in Civil War America.* Chapel Hill. University of North Carolina Press.

Silber, Nina. 2005. *Daughters of the Union: Northern Women Fight the Civil War.* Cambridge, MA: Harvard University Press.

## Wartime Literature

The Civil War inspired authors in the North and South. Literally thousands of works of Civil War literature have been published since the war erupted in 1861. In 1986 Albert Menendez identified no less than 1,028 works of "patriotic gore," as Edmund Wilson fittingly called them. In the twenty years since Menendez's catalogue emerged, the numbers have only grown. Moreover, many works of Civil War literature are nonfictional accounts, excluding them by definition from Menendez's tally.

Though the Civil War spawned a distinct genre of literature written by both Northern and Southern authors in relatively equal numbers, the tone and tenor of such literature depended greatly on the region from which the author emerged. Even among authors from the same region, there were many variations. For example, two distinct patterns can be seen among white Southern authors. Some treat the Civil War as a starting point from which to look forward to the future with hope and excitement; for others, a nostalgic but prolific minority, the Civil War was the tragic end of an era. The latter authors' writings were dominated by a romanticized view of the past that was "gone with the wind." By contrast, among African American Southerners and many white Northern authors, wartime literature, especially that written during and immediately after the war, was characterized by a focus on the institution of slavery and its ills, and African American authors often included the continued condemnation of the situation of African Americans in America or looked with excitement to a future of equality.

Regardless of the author's place of residence, Civil War literature can be categorized according to three criteria: form, date of publication, and theme. At times the categories coincide; at other times they do not. For example, one can find many works that deal with the battles of the war and that are based on personal reminiscences in the works appearing in the first wave of publication. Yet it cannot be said that all battle-themed works or even all works based on personal reminiscences were published in the 1860s. Mary Johnston's *Long Roll* (1911) and *Cease Firing* (1912) are examples of battle-themed works that appeared during the second phase of publication.

Civil War literature can also take two forms. The first includes novels or works of nonfiction in which the author writes based on his or her own recollections of war or on the collective recollections of his or her family or community. Mary Johnston's works are examples of this form of Civil War literature. She based her novels on the battlefield experiences of her father, Confederate General Joseph E. Johnston. Mary Chesnut's nonfiction writings, *Diary from Dixie* (1904), also belongs to the first form of Civil War literature.

The second form of Civil War literature includes works in which the author uses the war to provide the background for developing the novel's characters. Most of the works that comprise this form of Civil War literature are by definition fiction. The war in these works is secondary to the other details of the novel. Writing much later than Johnston, Caroline Gordon's *None Shall Look Back* (1937) is an example. She uses the war only as background material for the development of her characters, and the war does not figure into the plot of the novel. Grace King's *The Pleasant Ways of St. Médard* (1916) is another example of work that epitomizes this form.

Civil War literature can also be categorized according to the wave of publication. Although Civil War literature has emerged in every decade since the 1860s, there are three distinct waves of publication. The first includes works published during and immediately after the war. Very often, the authors of this period were women who wrote in the sentimental tradition, justifying the actions of their armies and celebrating the Christian sacrifice and pride of the citizens and armies of their section. Among many Northern writers, specific focus was often placed on the persecution of Unionists in the South and the rightness of the goal of abolition, as demonstrated in Louisa May Alcott's "The Brothers." Among many Southern authors, honoring the heroism of Confederate troops in the midst of defeat was common.

The second phase of Civil War literature includes works published during the years after the close of Reconstruction through the turn of the century. Though not the longest, the second phase was the most prolific in terms of works published in proportion to the length of the publication period. Although not all the authors of this period were Southern, the Southern point of view dominated it. Not coincidentally, the second phase coincided with the emergence of Jim Crow laws, the rise of Confederate patriotic groups like the United Daughters of the Confederacy, and the New South Movement. Multitudes of novels and short stories, along with numerous diaries, memoirs, and personal reminiscences, were published during this phase, especially just before the turn of the century. Many female authors, both professional and amateur, wrote during this phase. Although published authors of this period often had a tenuous connection to the actual experiences of the war, their writings were still tinged by the viewpoints, traditions, and lore of their hometowns, counties, states, or regions.

The third phase of publication is the modern period. It began just after World War I and it continues today. Because of the temporal distance from the war era, most works published by modern authors use the war merely as a background to develop characters, although numerous memoirs, diaries, journals, and reminiscences were published during this period by historians or descendants of the original authors.

In addition to categorizing works by their form or their phase of publication, one can also categorize Civil War literature by the themes explored. Among the numerous themes, subthemes, and variations of themes in Civil War literature, there are at least eight prominent themes or subjects. The first three themes, all of which emerged during and in the immediate aftermath of the war, are interconnected. The first theme includes unabashedly partisan reactions to the war. Literature with this theme emanated primarily from female authors writing in the sentimental tradition. The works often sprang up almost immediately after the start of the war, and Southern women were especially talented at utilizing the theme. The second and third themes, abolitionism and Southern Unionism, also emerged during and immediately after the war. Works employing these themes came almost exclusively from Northern authors.

Wartime literature was not always confrontational or explicitly political. The reunion of the country through North–South love is the fourth theme. Works using this theme promoted a peaceful national reunion through the romantic reunion of a Northern man and a Southern woman. Judged by the frequency of its occurrence, it was the most popular theme during the second phase of publication, when there was a wave of interest in works dominated by ideas of sectional reconciliation. This theme became especially popular in stories published after the war by Southern authors or in Southern literary journals. Southern author Thomas Nelson Page especially excelled at this theme, though the theme of North–South love appeared in the works of Northern authors as well. Such works most often used the symbolism of marriages between Southern female characters and Northern male characters to promote the idea that sectional reconciliation was possible and even desirable. Within works dominated by the symbolism of reconciliation was embedded the assumption that there was glory enough to go around to all soldiers regardless of which side they supported.

The fifth and sixth themes are closely linked: costume fiction, or the casting of ordinary male and female characters into incredible situations of bravery and daring, and the recounting of military campaigns or battles to highlight characters' heroism. As these themes grew in popularity, especially during the second phase of publication, the exploits of heroes and heroines often became more and more incredible. Modern authors have also utilized these themes in works published during the third phase of publication.

The seventh theme, sentimental romanticism about the prewar era, generally appeared in conjunction with another theme, usually that of reconciliation through North–South love. It was especially popular among Southern authors during the

second phase of publication. Through works invoking sentimental romanticism, the history of the antebellum South was virtually rewritten, primarily because the Old South had indeed passed away. Whether authors portrayed it realistically became irrelevant to readers. The land of beautiful Southern belles, gallant Southern gentlemen, and happy slaves, as often portrayed by Southern authors, did not need to have actually existed. It needed only to have existed in the authors' minds and thus in the reading public's minds. As such romanticism thrived among Southern authors, interestingly, among many white Northern authors, African American characters and any mention of slavery or abolition as the major accomplishment of the war all but disappeared. Indeed, after the first phase of publication ended, African American characters were rarely the focus of any Civil War literature, save works written by African American authors, until the civil rights movement. When white authors employed African American characters, they were generally auxiliary and too often fell into the "happy darky" stereotype. These images were effectively utilized during the second phase of publication by Thomas Nelson Page and Joel Chandler Harris.

The eighth theme of wartime literature is that of divided loyalties within families and among kin, friends, and communities. Similar to the conflicts highlighted in the theme of reconciliation, familial divisions were often healed as the characters were reunited in the aftermath of the war. The image of the family was perhaps the most often employed literary device in Civil War fiction. How the family, defined not only as the nuclear unit but also as the extended family of ancestors and future generations, was affected by the war serves as the focal point for many war novels. Furthermore, this theme can be found in all three phases of publication.

In fact, the characters' sense of family is persistently the key to both Southern and Northern authors' group portrayals of their societies. For many of these writers, the family served as a symbol of the Union. When the Union entered a crisis, the family unit did so as well, both in practice and in prose. The previously entrenched roles of male breadwinner and female domestic goddess faced a critical test as men marched off to war and women found themselves alone to provide for themselves and their children. Among Northern authors, stories of home and family portrayed the house—both individual homes and the metaphorical national one—as divided. Southern novelists had a different take: In their depictions, by contrast, the North invaded the peaceful Southern "home," and individual families were invaded by the loss and eventual death of husbands and sweethearts. In this portrayal of the Southern wartime family, the experiences of women almost always involved bereavement and loss. There is a constant concern with the death, in fact or symbol, of loved ones and how it will affect women's lives. For Southern authors, the defeat of the Confederacy in the war parallels the end of the familial tradition as Southerners knew it, or at least as they imagined they knew it.

Whether well-known or unknown, both professional and amateur writers can be found among the authors of Civil War literature. While many of the United States's major literary figures writing during the war's era paid little attention to the conflict in their works, for others the war was a central motif. Even so, while some authors may have written Civil War literature at one time or another in their careers, very few of them dedicated their entire literary efforts to the genre. Walt Whitman, for example, is best known for his poetry collected and published in *Leaves of Grass* (1855), but he also wrote about the Civil War. The prose work *Memoranda during the War* (1875) and the poems published under the title of *Drum Taps* (1865), *Sequel to Drum Taps* (1865–1866), and *Specimen Days and Collect* (1882) all document his experience of the Civil War in which he served as a clerk and a nurse. Louisa May Alcott also published work on the Civil War, chronicling her war experiences as a nurse for the Union army in Washington, D.C., in *Hospital Sketches* (1863). Although less known than her novels *Little Women* and *Little Men*, which had very little to do with the war, her descriptions in *Hospital Sketches* remain one of the most insightful looks at women's experience in this wartime experience.

Although one might assume that most authors of Civil War literature are male, since battlefields are very often the exclusive arena of men, many women can be found among any comprehensive list of Civil War authors. Women were especially prolific at writing war-themed poetry, and they can be found among the authors of Civil War fiction and nonfiction. Some of the most representative Civil War novels written by women include Louisa May Alcott's *Hospital Sketches* (1863) and *Work, a Story of Experience, 1861–73* (1873); Rita Mae Brown's *High Hearts* (1986); Willa Cather's *Sapphira and the Slave Girl* (1940); Ellen Glasgow's *The Battleground* (1902); Caroline Gordon's *None Shall Look Back* (1937); Frances Ellen Watkins Harper's *Iola Leroy, or Shadows Uplifted* (1892); Mary Johnston's *The Long Roll* (1911) and *Cease Firing* (1912); Margaret Mitchell's *Gone with the Wind* (1934); Mary Noailles Murfree's *The Storm Center* (1905); Evelyn Scott's *The Wave* (1929); Molly Elliott Seawell's *The Victory* (1906); Margaret Walker's *Jubilee* (1967); Augusta Jane Evans Wilson's *Macaria; Or, Altars of Sacrifice* (1864); and Lydia Collins Wood's *The Haydock's Testimony: A Tale of the American Civil War* (1907).

Regardless of whether women are the authors of Civil War fiction, they can be found among the main characters in many works of Civil War literature: John Peale Bishop's *Many Thousands Gone* (1931); George Washington Cable's *Dr. Sevier* (1885), *Kincaid's Battery* (1908) and *The Cavalier* (1901); Winston Churchill's *The Crisis* (1901); John William De Forest's *Miss Ravenel's Conversion from Secession to Loyalty* (1867) and *The Bloody Chasm* (1881); Thomas Cooper De Leon's *John Holden, Unionist: A Romance of the Days of Destruction and Reconstruction* (1893); Clifford Dowdey's *Where My Love Sleeps* (1945); William Faulkner's *The Unvanquished* (1938); Colonel William C. Faulkner's *The White Rose of Memphis* (1881); F. Scott Fitzgerald's "The Night before Chancellorsville" (1935); Harold Frederic's *The Copperhead* (1892); Allen Gurganus's *The Oldest Living Confederate Widow Tells All* (1989); Bret Harte's *Clarence* (1896); DuBose Heyward's *Peter Ashley* (1932); John Jakes's *North and South* (1982); Henry James's "The Story of a Year" (1865), "Poor Richard" (1865), and "A Most Extraordinary Case"

Frances Ellen Watkins Harper (1825–1911) was an African American abolitionist, suffragist, and poet. (Library of Congress)

(1868); Sydney Lanier's *Tiger-Lilies; A Novel* (1867); Thomas Nelson Page's *Meh Lady: A Story of the War* (1893), *Red Rock* (1898), and *Two Little Confederates* (1923); Joseph Stanley Pennell's *The History of Rome Hanks and Kindred Matters* (1944); Allen Tate's *The Fathers* (1938); Albion Winegar Tourgée's *Toinette: A Novel* (1864); Robert Penn Warren's *Band of Angels* (1955); and Stark Young's *So Red the Rose* (1934). The female characters in these works all belie the notion that war is men's domain.

Although some major American literary figures wrote about the war, many more works of Civil War literature were written by amateur authors, most of whom experienced the war firsthand and told their stories in short stories or nonfiction vignettes published during and after the war to a welcoming reading public. These stories and vignettes often told the story of a home invaded by the realities of war—

death and destruction—although most sought to reassure Americans that reunion and restoration were possible. There were ample serial publication opportunities for amateur authors of this type of Civil War literature. During the 1860s and 1870s alone, some three hundred such stories appeared in seventeen different literary magazines. Even *Godey's Lady's Book* published a Civil War story, "Thanksgiving," which appeared in 1863. Writers actively pursued the publication of their war stories in literary outlets that ranged from the Southern-oriented *Scott's Monthly* (Atlanta), *Land We Love* (Charlotte), *The Southern Literary Messenger*, *Eclectic* (and *New Eclectic*), and *Southern Illustrated News*, *Southern Opinion* (Richmond), *Southern Magazine*, *Southern Review* (Baltimore), *The Southern Bivouac* (Louisville), *The South-Atlantic* (Wilmington), *Southern Monthly* (Memphis), *Home Monthly* (Nashville), and later *The Confederate Veteran* (Nashville) to the Northern-based and nationally distributed *Atlantic Monthly* and *Continental Monthly* (Boston), *Old Guard*, *Appleton's*, *Round Table*, *Scribner's Monthly* (which became *Century Magazine* in 1881), *Harper's Weekly*, *Harper's Monthly*, *The Knickerbocker*, *Putnam's*, *The Galaxy*, (New York), and *Lippincott's* (Philadelphia).

Additionally, Southern as well as Northern publishers, especially after the close of Reconstruction, eagerly sought out book-length memoirs, journals, and reminiscences. Just as there were innumerable editions of war-centered fiction by professional and amateur authors, there was also a seemingly insatiable public appetite for published war reminiscences throughout the nation. Although Mary Boykin Chesnut's memoir, *Diary from Dixie* (1904, reissued in 1981 as *Mary Chesnut's Civil War*) is perhaps the best known of women's wartime remembrances, other female diarists also published their journals in the years after the war. Some of the better-known such works include *Belle Boyd in Camp and Prison* (1865) by Confederate spy Belle Boyd; Eliza Frances "Fanny" Andrews' *The Wartime Journal of a Georgia Girl* (1908); Union spy Pauline Cushman's *An Inside View of the Army Police: Thrilling Adventures of Pauline Cushman, the Distinguished American Actress and Famous Federal*

*Spy of the Department of the Cumberland* (1864) and *The Romance of the Great Rebellion: The Mysteries of the Secret Service: Pauline Cushman, the Famous Federal Scout and Spy, in the Department of the Cumberland* (1864); Rachel A. Stewart Cline's *1861–1862 Diary* (1862); Pauline DeCaradeuc Heyward's *Journals of Pauline DeCaradeuc (Mrs. J. Gerard Heyward) 1863–1867, 1875–1888* (1928); Lizzie Welcker's *Diary* (1865); Judith W. McGuire's *Diary of a Southern Refugee during the War, by a Lady of Virginia* (1867); Mary Ann Loughborough's *My Cave Life in Vicksburg, with Letters of Trial and Travel* (1864); Kate Cumming's *The Journal of Hospital Life in the Confederate Army in Tennessee* (1866); and Cornelia Phillips Spencer's *The Last Ninety Days of the War in North Carolina* (1866). Additionally, Confederate first lady Varina Howell Davis wrote and published a two-volume biography of her husband, *Jefferson Davis, Ex-President of the Confederate States of America; a Memoir* (1890), whereas Katherine Sherwood McDowell (Sherwood Bonner) published the loosely autobiographical novel, *Like unto Like* (1878).

Many more such diaries have been edited and published by historians or descendants of the diarists in the past few decades, making them available to a still welcoming public. These journals allow scholars and others an inside look at daily life inside the Confederacy and Union both in the battles and on the homefronts. Diaries by spies, nurses, and female soldiers offer details of the warfront by those who experienced it. For example, *A Yankee Spy in Richmond: The Civil War Diary of "Crazy Bet" Van Lew* (1996) offers an inside look at Union espionage in the Confederate capital. *A Woman Doctor's Civil War: Esther Hill Hawk's Diary* (1984) highlights the author's role as both a medical professional and a teacher to freedpeople. Published primary sources also allow an exploration of women's experiences in reconstructing the South during and after the Civil War. In *The Journals of Charlotte Forten Grimké* (1988) and *Sarah Jane Foster, Teacher of the Freedmen: The Diary and Letters of a Maine Woman in the South after the Civil War* (2001), the diarists detail their experiences teaching freedpeople. In addition, many other Northern and Southern women left accounts of their lives on the homefront. These journals illuminate the difficulties faced by women throughout the war, including shortages, invasion, and the loss of loved ones. Many also wrote about their work on behalf of their nation. Some of the better-known of these recently published works include *The Secret Eye: The Journal of Ella Gertrude Clanton Thomas 1848–1889* (1990); *The Civil War Diary of Sarah Morgan* (1991); Cornelia Peake McDonald's *A Woman's Civil War: A Diary with Reminiscences of the War from March 1862* (1992); *A Plantation Mistress on the Eve of the Civil War: The Diary of Keziah Goodwyn Hopkins Brevard, 1860–1861* (1993); *A Confederate Lady Comes of Age: The Journal of Pauline DeCaradeuc Heyward, 1863–1888* (1992); *A Heritage of Woe: The Civil War Diary of Grace Brown Elmore, 1861–1868* (1997); *Sanctified Trial: The Diary of Eliza Rhea Anderson Fain, a Confederate Woman in East Tennessee* (2004). Almost a century and a half after the Civil War, firsthand accounts of the conflict fascinate readers.

Despite the differences in form, the phase of publication, or the theme, what most works of Civil War literature have in common is an emphasis, implicit or explicit, on the experiences of women during the Civil War. Because the Civil War disrupted the homefront, it had the potential to change women's expectations and their roles. During the war, women found themselves facing new choices in terms of their behavior and attitudes. Many of the books, stories, diaries, and memoirs reveal the options that opened up to women because of the war and the life choices that they made as a result.

*Jennifer Lynn Gross*

**See also** Abernathy, Martha Stockard (1832–1878); African American Women; Aid Societies; Alcott, Louisa May (1832–1888); Andrews, Eliza Frances ["Elzey Hay"] (1840–1931); Blalock, Malinda [Sam Blalock] (ca. 1842–1901); Boyd, Belle (1844–1900); Breckenridge, Lucy Gilmer (1843–1865); Brevard, Keziah Goodwyn Hopkins (1803–1886); Buck, Lucy Rebecca (1842–1918); Burge, Dolly Sumner Lunt (1817–1891); Chesnut, Mary Boykin (1823–1886); Civilian Life; Confederate Homefront; Cumming, Kate (ca. 1836–1909); Cushman, Pauline [Harriet

Wood] (1833–1893); Davis, Varina Banks Howell (1826–1906); Diaries and Journals; Dickinson, Emily (1830–1886); Domesticity; Elmore, Grace Brown (1839–1912); Evans, Augusta Jane (1835–1909); Family Life, Confederate; Family Life, Union; Female Combatants; Female Spies; Fiction Writers, Northern; Fiction Writers, Southern; Forten (Grimké), Charlotte L. (1837–1914); Foster, Sarah Jane (1839–1868); Gilman, Caroline Howard (1794–1888); Harper, Frances Ellen Watkins (1825–1911); Holmes, Emma Edwards (1838–1910); Hospitals; House (Fletcher), Ellen Renshaw (1843–1907); Kemble (Butler), Frances "Fanny" Anne (1809–1893); Letter Writing; McDonald, Cornelia Peake (1822–1909); McGuire, Judith White Brockenbrough (1813–1897); Military Invasion and Occupation; Morgan, Sarah Ida Fowler (1842–1909); Northern Women; Nurses; Pickett, LaSalle Corbell (ca. 1843–1931); Plantation Life; Poets, Northern; Poets, Southern; Politics; Religion; Separate Spheres; Slaveholding Women; Southern Women; Southworth, Emma Dorothy Eliza Nevitte (1819–1899); Stone, Sarah Katherine (Kate) (1841–1907); Teachers, Northern; Thomas, Ella Gertrude Clanton (1834–1907); Union Homefront; Van Lew, Elizabeth (1818–1900); Wartime Employment.

## References and Further Reading

Diffley, Kathleen. 2002. *To Live and Die*. Durham, NC: Duke University Press.

Fahs, Alice. 2001. *The Imagined Civil War: Popular Literature of the North and South, 1861–1865*. Chapel Hill: University of North Carolina Press.

Gardner, Sarah E. 2003. *Blood and Irony: Southern White Women's Narratives of the Civil War, 1861–1937*. Chapel Hill: University of North Carolina Press.

Higonnet, Margaret R. 1989. "Civil War and Sexual Territories." In *Arms and the Woman: War, Gender, and Literary Representation*, edited by Helen M. Cooper, Adrienne Auslander Munich, and Susan Merrill Squier, 80–96. Chapel Hill: University of North Carolina Press.

Lively, Robert A. 1957. *Fiction Fights the Civil War: An Unfinished Chapter in the Literary History of the American People*. Chapel Hill: University of North Carolina Press.

Menendez, Albert J. 1986. *Civil War Novels: An Annotated Bibliography 1986*. New York: Garland Publishing.

Rubin, Louis D. 1958. "The Image of an Army: Southern Novelists and the Civil War." *Texas Quarterly,* 1: 17–34.

Silber, Nina. 1993. *The Romance of Reunion: Northerners and the South, 1865–1900*. Chapel Hill: University of North Carolina Press.

Sullivan, Walter. 1953. "Southern Novelists and the Civil War." In *Southern Renascence: The Literature of the Modern South*, edited by Louis D. Rubin Jr. and Robert D. Jacobs, 123–125. Baltimore, MD: Johns Hopkins University Press.

Skaggs, Merrill Maguire. 1972. *The Folk of Southern Fiction*. Athens: University of Georgia Press.

Wilson, Edmund. 1984. *Patriotic Gore: Studies in the Literature of the American Civil War*. Boston: Northeastern University Press.

# Entries

# A

## Abernathy, Martha Stockard (1832–1878)

Martha Stockard Abernathy's Civil War diaries offer a contemporaneous depiction of the everyday life of a Southern woman whose husband fought in the war. The diaries portray an intimate Southern perspective of the events in a small Tennessee town, give detailed descriptions of military camps, and provide transcripts of sermons and letters of the time.

Martha James Stockard was born September 18, 1832, in Maury County, Tennessee. She was the daughter of James R. Stockard and Euphence Gilmer Stockard. Her father died when she was young, after which she lived with her aunt, Mary Gilmer, for several years. During this time she received a primary education at the Pulaski Female Academy.

In June 1850, Martha graduated from Columbia Institute with honors. On August 18, 1851, she married Dr. Charles Clayton Abernathy, who had courted her for three years. The couple had three children, two of whom survived into adulthood. Their first child, Charles, born October 7, 1856, died at five weeks of age. Mary Gilmer, or Mollie, was born on October 13, 1857, and Elizabeth Lee (Lizzie) was born January 28, 1860.

When the war broke out, Martha was a twenty-nine-year-old mother of two. The published diary begins on May 7, 1861, with an entry in which she bitterly writes about the North praying for divine help to defeat the South. In her mind, the South was defending its rights and the North had no right to divine intervention. Her strong allegiance to the South is apparent throughout the diaries, but the tone changes as the war progresses. At first optimistic that the South will prevail, her words reveal her growing discouragement and sadness. By August 1862 her journal reflects hopelessness, except for the hope that divine intervention will keep the South from destruction.

A devoutly religious woman, having been converted in 1858 at a revival meeting, Abernathy includes in her diaries prayers, transcribed sermons, and Bible verses that are meaningful to her. Her conviction that God would help the South win the war comes across in an April 1862 entry, written after the Battle of Shiloh. In this and other entries, she asserts her knowledge that God would see to it that the "good" South overcomes the "evil" North.

Two months later, on June 17, 1862, she bid her husband good-bye as he departed to join the Confederate army. Dr. Abernathy's service in the war included a December 3, 1862 appointment to surgeon in the Provisional Army of the Confederate States. He was held as a prisoner of war three times over the course of his tour of service.

Martha Abernathy discontinued her journal sometime in 1862 because of a physical ailment that lasted until her May 14, 1878 death.

*Sigrid Kelsey*

**See also** Diaries and Journals; Religion; Shiloh, Battle of (April 6–7, 1862); Southern Women.

**References and Further Reading**

Dargan, Elizabeth Paisley. 1994. *The Civil War Diary of Martha Abernathy: Wife of Dr. Charles C. Abernathy of Pulaski, Tennessee*. Beltsville, MD: Professional Printing.

## Aid Societies

The American Civil War forever changed Northern and Southern women's lives. Any prewar activities in which women may have engaged—temperance, suffrage, abolition, and religious—were quickly altered by the wartime needs of society. Women formed and joined soldiers' aid societies to provide relief to soldiers and their communities. In the North, many of these local groups supported the United States Sanitary Commission, raising money through a variety of efforts, including sanitary fairs, to help the families, widows, and orphans of soldiers, as well as injured veterans.

Southern women's lives were particularly affected by the war in ways unique to their region. In addition to the fact that the war was primarily fought in the South, the region lacked the industry needed to produce the material for sustaining soldiers and thereby forced women to assume new public roles in the larger war effort. Women offered assistance in large part through the formation of soldiers' aid societies, also known as ladies' aid societies, in communities throughout the South. Southern women immediately went to work for their soldiers, organizing aid societies as the men organized and marched off to war.

Numerous women joined soldiers' aid societies in their locales. These women and their organizations proved critical in sustaining the Confederacy throughout the war. The aid societies' membership included white women from the middle and upper classes who rarely suffered deprivation of any kind. They were women who, in less trying times, complained about having to wear a dress from last season. However, during the war, these women recognized the need to curtail such extravagances, although they managed to maintain the appearance of their class and status in Southern society.

The contributions of soldiers' aid societies were numerous. Members sewed and knitted articles of clothing for soldiers, provided food for them, made cartridges for firearms, assisted with hospital work, and wrote letters for soldiers. They also wrote letters for the illiterate wives of men who had gone to war and read to them letters from the front.

Throughout the war, women's most important role was to "cheer and encourage" soldiers and to do their best to sustain men's morale. When Confederate troops marched through their towns, women lined the road to strew flowers and cheer them on. Their work to provide clothing, sew flags, knit socks, and send food was not simply about supplying troops with materials; it also served to boost soldiers' morale.

As the war neared an end and the social and economic landscape of the South was devastated, soldiers' aid societies continued to tend to the needs of the wounded and dying in their towns. Indeed, before the war had officially ended, women had begun the grisly task of burying the Confederate dead—raising money to build coffins and selecting property in town cemeteries. And it was there, in those cemeteries, that the first monuments to Confederate soldiers were erected.

The Civil War ended in April 1865, but the activity of women did not. North and South, women were irrevocably changed by their wartime efforts. Their work as homemakers and nurturers of children remained important, but women had entered the public arena during the war in an unprecedented way, and they were cognizant of their ability to accomplish good in their communities. Moreover, in the wake of Confederate defeat, the need for women's participation in the rebuilding of the South, especially the morale of white men, took on added importance. Soldiers' and ladies' aid societies did not fold at war's end but were reinvented as memorial associations. Thus began women's new public role as keepers of the faith of Southern nationalism and as preservers of Confederate memory—a role that continued well into the twentieth century.

*Karen L. Cox*

**See also** Civilian Life; Columbia Bazaar (January 17–21, 1865); Confederate Homefront; Fairs and Bazaars; Food; Fundraising; Ladies' Memorial Associations; Monuments; Morale; Northern Women; Nurses; Sewing Bees; Shortages; Southern Women; Union Homefront; United Daughters of the Confederacy; United States Sanitary Commission; Wounded, Visits to.

**References and Further Reading**
Cox, Karen L. 2003. *Dixie's Daughters: The United Daughters of the Confederacy and the*

*Preservation of Confederate Culture.* Gainesville: University Press of Florida.

Faust, Drew Gilpin. 1996. *Mothers of Invention: Women of the Slaveholding South in the Civil War.* Chapel Hill: University of North Carolina Press.

## Alcott, Louisa May (1832–1888)

Abolitionist author Louisa May Alcott recounted her experiences as a wartime nurse in a Georgetown hospital in *Hospital Sketches* (1863). She later published *Little Women* (1868), a novel of four New England sisters coping with the absence of their father during the Civil War.

Born in Germantown, Pennsylvania, on November 29, 1832, Louisa was one of Bronson and Abigail May Alcott's four daughters. The family moved to Boston, where Bronson set up the Temple School. In 1840 they moved to Concord, near friend Ralph Waldo Emerson, but returned to Boston in 1849. Growing up in a progressive abolitionist household greatly influenced the course of Louisa's life.

Alcott began writing at a young age and published her first poem in 1852. Her first book, *Flower Fables*, was published in 1855.

Alcott's frustration with sitting on the sidelines during the war led her to become a nurse for Union soldiers in Washington, D.C. In November 1862, she applied for a nursing position to support the war effort. She accepted a position at Georgetown's Union Hotel Hospital in December. Alcott arrived soon after the Battle of Fredericksburg and served for six weeks as a nurse at the Union Hotel, an early general hospital established during the Civil War to care for soldiers stationed in the vicinity and those wounded on Virginia's battlefields. The hospital could accommodate only two hundred and twenty-five patients at a time. The conditions at the three-story hospital, or Hurly-burly House as Alcott called it, were deplorable. Cold, damp, and dirty, the hospital was filled with odors from wounds, kitchens, washrooms, and stables. Alcott complained that there was no competent leadership to improve conditions and that the indifference of hospital staff only complicated matters. A July 1861

Louisa May Alcott, Civil War nurse and author, well known for *Little Women*, her novel about four New England sisters coping with the war (1832–1888). (Library of Congress)

United States Sanitary Commission report on hospital conditions concurred with Alcott's assessment. The Commission found that the building was old and out of repair. In addition, there were no provisions for bathing, the bathrooms were insufficient and defective, and there was no proper morgue.

Dorothea Dix, the Superintendent of Women Nurses in the Union army, assigned Alcott to work with hospital matron Hannah Ropes at the Union Hotel Hospital. Each nurse was assigned ten patients and worked a day or night shift. Alcott's regular duties included administering medicines and dressing wounds as instructed; cleaning and mending linens; singing lullabies to patients, as well as reading and writing letters for them; and making other preparations for the night.

As the war continued, death from disease grew, and typhoid, malaria, and dysentery became major threats to soldiers and civilians. Typhoid fever, which accounted for 17 percent of patients' deaths in 1861, would cause 56 percent of patients' deaths in 1865. Furthermore, working conditions in military hospitals compromised the health of many nurses. On January 7, 1863, Alcott contracted typhoid fever, and she returned to her family in Concord, Massachusetts. Typhoid ended Alcott's hospital career and killed her mentor Ropes. To cure Alcott of typhoid, doctors prescribed heavy doses of a mercurous chloride laxative, called calomel. She recovered but felt the poisoning effects of mercury for the rest of her life. The drug also caused Alcott to have dramatic dreams and visions.

Alcott's bout with typhoid may have ended her nursing career, but it allowed her the opportunity to reflect on hospital conditions and wartime life. Her experiences in Washington proved to be pivotal in shaping her life and writing. The harsh realities of nursing broadened Alcott's views and gave her new insights to the human condition. Unable to pursue a nursing career, Alcott was confined to her hospital room, where she sewed, sitting near a window. Her impressions were recorded in her letters and journals, and she formed the foundation for *Hospital Sketches*, the first public account of hospital conditions during the Civil War. The volume contained a provocative and insightful description of the unprecedented work of Northern women as wartime nurses, and it highlighted hospital practices during the war. First serialized in *The Commonwealth* in May and June 1863, *Hospital Sketches* was published in book form in August 1863. The public's outcry about the conditions revealed in the book led to hospital reform.

The timely publication and positive reception of *Hospital Sketches* created a demand for some of her other short stories written during the war. Alcott further documented her impressions as a nurse in "The Brother, or, My Contraband" (*The Atlantic Monthly*, November 1863) and in "The Hospital Lamp" (*Drum the Beat*, February 24–25, 1864). A collection of her stories was published in 1863 as *On Picket Duty*. In addition, Alcott published *Moods* in 1864.

After the war, Alcott enjoyed huge literary successes. When her publisher asked her to write a "girls story," she fictionalized her experiences growing up with her sisters in Civil War America. Pub-

lished in 1868, *Little Women,* also published as *Good Wives* in England, delighted readers and became an immediate hit. It became the first enduring classic in American children's literature. Audiences clamored for more, and Alcott continued the story of the fictional March sisters in future volumes. In all, Alcott published more than thirty books and collections of stories.

In the 1870s, Alcott became involved in the woman's suffrage movement. She went from door to door to get women to register to vote. She also contributed articles on the subject to *The Woman's Journal.*

Louisa May Alcott died in Boston on March 6, 1888, two days after her father's death.

*Meredith Eliassen*

***See also*** Abolitionists and Northern Reformers; Disease; Dix, Dorothea Lynde (1802–1887); Domesticity; Family Life, Union; Fiction Writers, Northern; Northern Women; Nurses; Separate Spheres; Union Homefront; Wartime Literature.

**References and Further Reading**

Alcott, Louisa May. [1863] 1960. *Hospital Sketches,* edited by Bessie Z. Jones. Cambridge, MA: Harvard University Press.

Eiselein, Gregory, and Anne K. Phillips, eds. 2001. *The Louisa May Alcott Encyclopedia.* Westport, CT: Greenwood Press.

Ropes, Hannah Anderson. 1980. *Civil War Nurse: The Diary and Letters of Hannah Ropes.* Knoxville: University of Tennessee Press.

Sizer, Lyde Cullen. 2000. *The Political Work of Northern Women Writers and the Civil War, 1850–1872.* Chapel Hill: University of North Carolina Press.

## Alexander, Charles Wesley [Wesley Bradshaw] (1837–1927)

Under the pseudonym Wesley Bradshaw, Charles Wesley Alexander wrote and published romantic and melodramatic Civil War stories of women spies. His mostly Northern heroines are beautiful, brave, and charming.

Born in 1837, little is known about Bradshaw other than his writing. During the war, he lived in Philadelphia, whose city records show his career development: In 1861 he worked as a clerk, in 1862 as an advertising agent, in 1863 as a reporter, in 1864 as an author, and in 1865 as a publisher. His wartime literary work focused on war-related fiction, history, and biography. His wartime books include *Pauline of the Potomac, or General McClellan's Spy* (1862), *Maud of the Mississippi, a Companion to Pauline of the Potomac* (1863), *The Volunteer's Roll of Honor* (1863), *The Picket Slayer* (1863), *General Sherman's Indian Spy* (1865), and *Angel of the Battle-field: A Tale of the Rebellion* (1865). He also published several broadsides and in 1865 a periodical, *Soldier's Casket.*

There is little evidence that the author's Civil War characters were based on real people. However, at the beginning of *Pauline of the Potomac* (1862), Bradshaw hinted at a basis in fact, asserting that in the tale he had merged stories from real wartime incidents. Some believe that Civil War spy Pauline Cushman served as inspiration for Bradshaw's Pauline D'Estraye, but the two share little in common other than their first names and service as Union spies.

All of Bradshaw's female characters are fearless. They can ride horses and handle guns, and they are athletic as well as beautiful. *General Sherman's Indian Spy* tells the story of Wenonah, a young Indian maiden who assists General William T. Sherman in his 1865 march from Atlanta to Raleigh. In *The Picket Slayer*, Bradshaw introduced one of his few Confederate characters, Mary Murdock. Unlike his glorification of his Northern female characters, Alexander painted Mary as a villain, who displays supernatural powers of evil. Although courageous, she is a "beautiful demon."

Bradshaw's fictional characters display brave devotion to their national causes and patriotic motivations for their spy work. Melodramatic and didactic, the stories never lack high adventure with a moral purpose. Bradshaw's strong female characters served as nurses and spies, and they displayed little fear no matter what their situation. In the postwar era, Alexander continued to venerate women. For example, in *Mattie Stephenson, the Sweet Young Martyr of Memphis: An Account of the Devotion of Miss Martha Stephenson, of Towanda, Illinois* (1873), he told the story of a woman who

traveled to Memphis to nurse yellow fever victims. She contracted the fever and died within a month.

Charles Wesley Alexander died in 1927.

*Sigrid Kelsey*

**See also** Female Spies; Wartime Literature.
**References and Further Reading**
Fahs, Alice. 2001. *The Imagined Civil War: Popular Literature of the North and South, 1861–1865.* Chapel Hill: University of North Carolina Press.
Leonard, Elizabeth D. 1999. *All the Daring of the Soldier.* New York: W. W. Norton.

## Allegheny Arsenal, Explosion at (September 17, 1862)

On September 17, 1862, an explosion at Allegheny Arsenal, one of the largest producers of Union munitions, killed seventy-eight workers, nearly all of them young women between the ages of sixteen and twenty.

Between 1861 and 1864, the Arsenal's workforce expanded and diversified. In the summer of 1861, administrators dismissed nearly two hundred boys who had repeatedly disregarded prohibitions against matches and smoking, replacing them with girls and young women, who administrators recognized could work as well as boys but were likely to be more compliant than the boys. Female cartridge makers were the lowest-paid workers in the Arsenal, earning 50¢ a day for their tedious and hazardous work. Most were employed in the main lab, the location of the industrial disaster.

Colonel of Ordnance John Symington and his lieutenants, John Edie and Jasper Myers, ran the Arsenal. Located in Pittsburgh's Lawrenceville community, the Arsenal included a number of buildings. The main laboratory building was separated from the other buildings by a cobblestone roadway that connected the buildings. However, the roadway was made of flinty stone that sparked when horses and wagons delivering materials drove on it. In addition, barrels of gunpowder could leak in the transportation process, and during munitions production gunpowder commonly rose in a fine dust that settled in the buildings and on the roadway. Under such conditions, the likelihood of an explosion was ever present, but administrators ignored the dangers in a drive to maintain a high level of production.

After a dry September in 1862, conditions were ripe for an explosion. On September 17, at approximately 2 p.m., a wagon caused sparks that ignited loose gunpowder on the roadway. The explosion set off the Arsenal's main supply of gunpowder. Blasts, which could be heard for miles, occurred in three parts of the building, causing the roof and walls to fall inward.

Employees in the main laboratory rushed the doors to exit the building after the first explosion. Tragically, the rush of people to the inward-opening doors prevented escape and trapped workers. Numerous employees were blown apart, parts of their clothes and bodies found in trees nearby. Many who escaped the building ran from it covered in blood and with their clothes aflame. Family members rushed to the scene to help sisters, mothers, daughters, and friends.

By the end of the afternoon, the explosion and the fire it caused had reduced the laboratory to a smoldering pile of rubble and killed or fatally wounded seventy-eight workers. Fifty-four bodies were so disfigured that they could not be identified. The community buried the unidentified remains in a mass grave in the nearby Allegheny Cemetery. Local newspapers lauded the dead young women as patriotic martyrs.

A coroner's hearing found Symington and his lieutenants guilty of gross negligence for allowing loose gunpowder to accumulate near and in the buildings, but a military investigation exonerated them.

*Theresa R. McDevitt*

**See also** Civilian Life; Immigrant Women; Northern Women; Union Homefront; Urban Women, Northern; Wartime Employment.

**References and Further Reading**

Fox, Arthur B. 2002. "United States Allegheny Arsenal, 1860–1865." In *Pittsburgh during the American Civil War, 1860–1865*, 99–131. Chicora, PA: Mechling Books.

Wudarczyk, James. 1999. *Pittsburgh's Forgotten Allegheny Arsenal*. Apollo, PA: Closson Press.

## Alleman, Matilda "Tillie" Pierce (1848–1914)

Born in 1848 in Gettysburg, Pennsylvania, Matilda J. Pierce wrote the quintessential civilian account of the battle there.

The first daughter of butcher James Pierce and Margaret McCurdy Pierce, Tillie and her family lived a comfortable life above James's butcher shop in the town's commercial district. She grew up, as did many of her friends, surrounded by culture, education, and the lure of the outdoors. During her formative years, Tillie played in the gardens and hills surrounding the town with her two brothers, James and William, and her sister, Margaret.

After the Civil War began and Tillie's two brothers enlisted in Pennsylvania regiments, Tillie seemed little bothered by national events. She also had little concern about a possible invasion of Gettysburg, assuming that wartime rumors always proved false. Life in Gettysburg went on during the Civil War much as it had in the antebellum era. Tillie continued her education at the Young Ladies' Seminary until late June 1863.

As soldiers passed through town in late June and early July 1863, Tillie's excitement at the unexpected events grew. Simultaneously, concern for her safety lead Tillie's parents to move her to a more secure area. Ironically, they entrusted Tillie to the care of a neighbor who moved the child to the supposed safety of Jacob Weiker's farm. The Weiker farm lay close to the Roundtops, and as a result Tillie ended up dangerously close to the battle that raged around these hilltops. As the battle progressed and the wounded began to pour into the Weiker farm, Tillie's initial enthusiasm turned to horror. She busied herself bringing water to the men, including General George Meade, and with nursing and comforting the wounded and dying, including Generals Gouverneur K. Warren and Stephen Hinsdale Weed. When the shelling came dangerously close to the farm, Tillie, like many civilians, retired to the basement until it sounded safe to emerge. Tillie also could hear the end of the battle as cheers of joy replaced screaming shells.

Gettysburg was changed forever by the battle. Tillie found the landscape, the architecture, and the population scarred. The experience also scarred her psychologically. Following the battle, she busied herself caring for the remaining wounded. In 1871, she married attorney Horace P. Alleman and moved to the small town of Selinsgrove, Pennsylvania, where they raised a family. Despite her new domestic responsibilities, Tillie never forgot her experiences and in 1888 decided to share them by writing her memoirs *At Gettysburg or What a Girl Saw and Heard of Battle.* Tillie died in 1914 and is buried in Selinsgrove's Trinity Lutheran Cemetery.

*Cheryl A. Wells*

**See also** Diaries and Journals; Gettysburg, Battle of (July 1–3, 1863); Northern Women; Union Homefront.

### References and Further Reading

Alleman, Tillie Pierce. 1994. *At Gettysburg or What a Girl Saw and Heard of Battle.* Baltimore, MD: Butternut & Blue.

Young, Agnes. 1959. *Women and the Crisis: Women of the North in the Civil War.* New York: McDowell.

## American Colonization Society

The American Society for Colonizing the Free People of Color of the United States, later known as the American Colonization Society (ACS), was formed in 1817, the culmination of more than forty years of debate among black and white intellectuals. The organization proposed sending free and enslaved African Americans to Africa as a way to gradually emancipate slaves and end slavery.

The colonization movement reflected white Americans' optimism about resolving racial problems in American society, their profound ambivalence about African Americans in their midst, and their confident religious convictions. Colonizationists believed that white prejudice against African Americans was so corrupting and absolute that African Americans could never attain equality unless they were removed from white society. Initially, most supporters were convinced that colonization would result in the safe, gradual, and voluntary abolition of slavery, and they argued that colonization would revolutionize African society by introducing republican government and Christian religion. Over the coming decades, however, the colonization

movement lost its drive for slavery reform, instead seeking a moderate position between the extremes of immediate abolition and perpetual slavery.

Generally the most active colonization societies were in cities along the Atlantic seaboard. Although there were colonization organizations in rural communities, villages, and small towns, colonization thrived in areas with large or growing numbers of free African Americans and in cities with a close economic connection to the South.

Initially, colonization leaders gave little thought as to how women might contribute to the cause. Despite its posture as a religious and benevolent organization, the colonization society promoted itself as a political movement. The group, headquartered in the nation's capital, held annual meetings in the Hall of the House of Representatives and recruited the political elite as leaders and figureheads. For two decades, ACS members sought Federal support for colonization so aggressively and intently that they made only weak attempts to build local organizations and no appeals to women.

By 1825, with only limited assistance from the Federal government and in need of funds, the ACS finally turned to the public for support while continuing to press the Federal and state legislatures for endorsements and money. When leaders began to recast colonization as a national benevolent movement in the late 1820s, their first appeals were to ministers and women.

As early as 1819, scores of women in the Upper South and Mid-Atlantic states supported colonization with money and goods. Merging missionary convictions and colonization goals, female supporters interpreted their efforts as chiefly religious. Female involvement in colonization in the 1820s was relatively unorganized and confined to a few geographic areas, primarily in the Upper South. By the mid-1830s, however, women's colonization efforts had become more associational and had expanded into the North and West.

The most effective female colonization societies focused on the "feminine" project of education in Liberia. By the mid-1830s, the majority of women's groups looked to societies like the Philadelphia Ladies' Liberia Association as their model and focused their efforts on education. As a national association with auxiliaries around the country, the Philadelphia Association was the largest female colonization association. The exceptional organizational skills of several dozen women sustained two girls schools for African American colonists, a school for African children and adults, a manual labor school for boys, and a high school for young men.

Besides forming auxiliary groups, women banded together to raise money for colonization, most often through their churches. Individual women gave small and large sums of money to city and state colonization societies and directly to the ACS. Still others formed African educational societies. While female monetary contributions were mostly small, collectively their contributions provided important assistance to a movement that was often plagued by debt and controversy. Perhaps more importantly, female cooperation legitimized the colonization platform and reinforced the moral and religious claims of the society.

The mobilization of white women that began in the late 1820s culminated not in the formation of a widespread colonization movement among women, but in the active support of denominational missions to Africa. Over the 1830s, the enemies of colonization multiplied in the North and in the South, and internal strife plagued the society. The battle with abolition forces stripped away supporters and confused others. Beset by debt and mismanagement, the society limped through the 1840s. Some female groups continued to gather donations, but annual receipts fluctuated, and many groups dissolved. Even as the ACS declined as a dynamic movement, interest in Africa intensified. Ironically, the idea of colonization as a solution to the race question remained popular even though the society did not.

*Karen Fisher Younger*

**See also** Abolitionism and Northern Reformers; African American Women; Aid Societies; Antislavery Societies; Free Blacks; Northern Women; Politics; Religion.

### References and Further Reading
Staudenraus, P. J. 1961. *The African Colonization Movement, 1816–1865*. New York: Columbia University Press.

Dorsey, Bruce. 2002. *Reforming Men and Women: Gender in the Antebellum City*. Ithaca, NY: Cornell University Press.

## Andrews, Eliza Frances [Elzey Hay] (1840–1931)

Eliza Frances "Fanny" Andrews, the daughter of a distinguished Georgia planter and jurist who opposed secession, kept a diary recording her experiences in an area increasingly disturbed near the end of the Civil War.

An enthusiastic Confederate, Andrews expressed her own shock and disappointment at the events transforming her world. Her lively narrative style and her involvement with conspicuous events and personalities make her story a particularly valuable account of the last days of Southern plantation society. The drama of her life was made even more complex by the ideological conflict between Eliza and her beloved Unionist father, as well as by her ongoing desire to retain a clear sense of her own identity as she perceived the disintegration of the universe in which she had enjoyed a privileged status.

As the Confederacy fought and lost its last battles, she was forced to make her way home from the southwestern part of the state to Washington, Georgia, across a region disorganized and disrupted by Union incursions and by breakdowns of authority on all levels. On her frenetic way home, she encountered the controversial governor of Georgia, Joseph Brown, the mother-in-law of Jefferson Davis, and a host of other people seeking refuge from the coming chaos. Upon her arrival in Washington, she soon endured the humiliation and danger of a hostile military occupation. In all of her diary entries, however, whether she gloomily lamented the demise of a society she loved or rejoiced in a successful evening with her friends, she was characteristically vigorous, impulsive, and eloquent.

Eliza Andrews was born in 1840 and reached adulthood during a turbulent period first of political conflict and then of outright war. Disturbed by what she and her friends saw as the tyranny of the United States government, she was caught up in the secessionist craze and rejoiced as the Southern states

Eliza Frances Andrews (1840–1931) kept a diary during the Civil War, recording life in Georgia as the Confederacy collapsed. (Andrews, Eliza Frances, *The War-Time Journal of a Georgia Girl*, 1908)

formed their own government and went to war against the North. As the Confederacy's early military successes gave way to a war of attrition and it became clear that the North would prevail, Andrews remained ardently devoted to the values based on the old traditions of her plantation society. As the Confederacy messily collapsed, she raged against the Yankees and the newly freed slaves, but she also began making quiet but necessary adjustments. For example, she described an early effort to master the skill of housecleaning, an effort that brought her some good-natured ridicule from her aristocratic friends. She also recorded her father's suggestion that she offer for publication in the North an account of the ineptitude and misbehavior of the Federal troops who occupied their neighborhood. She followed his suggestion, and the success of "Romance of Robbery" no doubt confirmed her own sense of competence as a writer, a strength much needed in the postbellum days of disempowerment.

Andrews in fact published extensively during her life, including three novels written under the assumed name of Elzey Hay. Her first novel, *A Family Secret* (1876), was followed by *A Mere Adventurer* (1879) and *Prince Hal; or, The Romance of a Rich Young Man* (1882). During an illness that struck her in 1881, she found comfort in the study of botany, in which field she developed such expertise as to enable her to publish two books on the subject.

Having graduated from LaGrange College in western Georgia, Andrews was well qualified as a teacher, and she taught school in various locations during her life. In 1885, she joined the faculty of Wesleyan College, remaining there until 1896, after which she became a public lecturer, traveling widely both in the United States and abroad. She continued to publish articles well into her old age, and she died in 1931 and was buried with her family in Washington.

*Robert W. Haynes*

*See also* Diaries and Journals; Fiction Writers, Southern; Refugees; Sherman's Campaign (1864–1865); Southern Women.

**References and Further Reading**

Andrews, Eliza Frances. 1908. *The War-Time Journal of a Georgia Girl, 1864–1865*. New York: D. Appleton & Co.

Andrews, Eliza Frances. 2002. *Journal of a Georgia Woman 1870–1872*, edited with an introduction by S. Kittrell Rushing. Knoxville: University of Tennessee Press.

Willingham, Robert M., Jr. 1976. *No Jubilee: The Story of Confederate Wilkes*. Washington, GA: Wilkes Publishing.

## Andrews, Orianna Moon (1834–1883)

Dr. Orianna Moon Andrews, a Virginia native and 1857 graduate of the Female Medical College in Philadelphia, treated the wounded and supervised nurses in army hospitals in Virginia from 1861 to 1862. Dr. Andrews was the only Virginia woman to hold an M.D. and was likely the only Southern female physician who treated soldiers during the conflict.

A native of Albemarle County, Virginia, Orianna Moon was born into a prominent planter family in 1834. She received her earliest education from tutors and decided to study medicine. To prepare for entry into the Female Medical College in Philadelphia, which opened in 1850, she matriculated at the Troy Female Academy in Troy, New York, one of the few women's institutions that provided the necessary courses in mathematics and science. After spending a year at Troy, she returned to Virginia. At age seventeen, she was described as hostile to religion, an opponent of slavery, and a supporter of women's rights. The following year she entered the Medical College with its fourth group of students, becoming only the third Southern woman and the only Virginian to do so. She submitted her thesis in 1856 and graduated the following February. Her graduation made her part of an extremely small cohort of female physicians; only thirty-eight women (including Orianna) had received medical degrees by 1857.

After her graduation, Dr. Moon spent two years traveling abroad in the Middle East and Europe before returning home. In the spring of 1861 she saw a flyer recruiting doctors for the war effort. She began writing letters to Virginia's military commanders offering her services. In late spring, General J. H. Cocke met with her at her home and then spoke about her to Brigadier General P. G. T. Beauregard, commander of the Northeast Virginia Army. Soon afterward Dr. Moon became superintendent of a ward of nurses at a makeshift hospital on the grounds of the University of Virginia in Charlottesville.

Dr. Moon hoped to be closer to the battlefield and in July 1861 informed General Cocke that she was willing to forgo remuneration to follow the army and treat the wounded. Her sister—famous Southern Baptist missionary Charlotte "Lottie" Moon—also wrote to the general asking him to move Dr. Moon closer to the "action of the war." Dr. Moon was never sent to the front, but she continued working in Charlottesville. She left Charlottesville after marrying a hospital colleague, Dr. John Summerfield Andrews, in November 1861 and moving with him to Richmond. There they both worked in an army hospital. Orianna returned to Albemarle County in 1862 to give birth to her first son.

After the war, Orianna and her family moved to rural Tennessee, where she ran a school for the children of freed slaves. A nighttime visit from the local Ku Klux Klan soon prompted the family to relocate. In 1881, they moved back to Albemarle County, where she and her husband set up a joint medical office.

Orianna Moon Andrews died of cancer in 1883.

*Regina D. Sullivan*

**See also** Baptist Women; Nurses; Southern Women.
**References and Further Reading**

Sullivan, Regina Diane. 2002. "Woman with a Mission: Remembering Lottie Moon and the Woman's Missionary Union." Ph.D. diss. University of North Carolina, Chapel Hill.

Warren, Edward. 1885. *A Doctor's Experiences in Three Continents.* Baltimore, MD: Cushings and Bailey.

## Anthony, Susan B. (1820–1906)

Abolitionist, temperance, and women's rights reformer Susan B. Anthony was born in Adams, Massachusetts, to Daniel Anthony and Lucy Read.

As a child, Anthony attended home school and later became a student at Deborah Moulson's Female Seminary near Philadelphia. She worked as a teacher in New York until 1849, when she quit to run her father's farm in Rochester. Living at home, she became friends with the leading abolitionists who sometimes attended meetings at the Anthony farm, where they would often discuss women's rights and the abolition of slavery.

Anthony's interest in women's rights blossomed when she met Elizabeth Cady Stanton in the early 1850s. Together they fought for women's rights in New York. To secure married women's property rights, Anthony toured the state, circulated petitions, and gave lectures on the subject. Anthony's hard work paid off in 1860, when the New York State Legislature passed the Married Women's Property Act. Recognizing her organizing and speaking abilities, the American Anti-Slavery Society offered Anthony a position as the chief agent for New York State in 1856. She accepted.

The start of the Civil War halted Anthony's abolition and women's rights work. Abolitionists cancelled scheduled meetings, and she called off the 1861 National Woman's Rights Convention. The following year Anthony and other abolitionists returned to their work, speaking in favor of the immediate emancipation of slaves, which stood in stark contrast to President Abraham Lincoln's gradual emancipation policy. On January 1, 1863, Lincoln signed the Emancipation Proclamation, freeing slaves in the Confederate states but exempting these in the Union.

The proclamation did not satisfy Anthony or her abolitionist colleagues, who wanted freedom for all slaves. They believed that the United States Congress needed to secure the emancipation of slaves by amending the Constitution. Anthony and Stanton agreed to organize women to stir up interest for a constitutional amendment. They issued a call for a meeting of the women of the Republic, and they assembled in New York in May 1863.

Those who attended the convention formed the National Women's Loyal League; delegates elected Stanton president and Anthony secretary. The goal of the league was to distribute petitions and to obtain signatures of those in favor of a Federal amendment to the Constitution to abolish slavery. Anthony headed the league's effort by writing letters, raising the necessary funds to print and mail petitions, and sending out field-workers. Less than nine months later, the league submitted petitions to Congress bearing the signatures of one hundred thousand individuals. Convinced of the proposal's overwhelming public support, the United States Senate passed the Thirteenth Amendment in April 1864, but the issue went down to defeat in the House of Representatives that June. By August 1864, the league had gathered nearly four hundred thousand signatures, and Anthony closed the league's office. In 1865, the House voted in favor of the Thirteenth Amendment, which was ratified the same year.

In the spring of 1864, as Anthony was working for the league, the American public began to discuss the upcoming presidential election. Although she could not vote, Anthony had a strong interest in the campaign. She believed that the Civil War was a war for freedom, and she opposed the reelection of Lincoln, believing him too conciliatory toward the Confederates. Instead, Anthony favored John C. Frémont, a Union general who had, in 1861, issued

Hailed as "the Napoleon of the woman's rights movement," Susan B. Anthony helped lead the fight for women's suffrage for more than 50 years. (Library of Congress)

an edict freeing the slaves of those who supported the Confederacy in Missouri. She was enthusiastic about his presidential candidacy in 1856 and remained a loyal supporter in 1864. Her support of Frémont was not unusual; other abolitionists like Wendell Phillips and Stanton backed his campaign. Throughout the spring, Anthony and Stanton tried to drum up interest in a Frémont presidency, and, in May 1864, a small group of supporters nominated him. He withdrew from the presidential race in September, and Lincoln was reelected to a second term in 1864.

With the work of the league behind her and the presidential election over, Anthony traveled to Leavenworth, Kansas, where she worked on her brother's newspaper. She returned home when she learned about the Fourteenth Amendment, which would, for the first time, introduce the word "male" into the Constitution. Anthony and Stanton opposed the amendment, a decision that put both women at odds with their former allies who had previously supported women's enfranchisement. Abolitionists and many Republicans declared the postwar period the Negro's hour and refused to support universal suffrage, that is, voting rights for African Americans and women.

Daunted but not dismayed, Anthony and Stanton held the first women's rights convention since the start of the Civil War. Delegates to the convention agreed to form the American Equal Rights Association, linking the causes of African Americans' and women's suffrage. The group began a campaign to remove the racial and sex-related restrictions placed on voters in their state constitutions. Anthony began to circulate petitions to delete the word "male" from the New York State Constitution. The issue was defeated. Later she headed to Kansas with Stanton, where they battled to secure the passage of two amendments to the state constitution: one to enfranchise African Americans and another to enfranchise women. Kansas voters opposed both issues in 1867, and the Kansas campaign helped to divide suffragists. Anthony, Stanton, and their allies began to recognize that the abolitionists would not support woman suffrage, and, as a result, the Kansas campaign helped foster an independent feminist movement.

In spite of their opposition to the Fourteenth Amendment, it was ratified and became part of the Constitution in 1868. When the Fifteenth Amendment—providing that a citizen may not be excluded from voting because of race, color, or "previous condition of servitude"—was introduced in Congress, Anthony and Stanton denounced it, using racist and elitist arguments to oppose it. The issue of African American suffrage and the Fifteenth Amendment split suffragists into those who favored the Fifteenth Amendment and those who opposed it. In 1869, the split led to the creation of two separate suffrage associations: the National Woman Suffrage Association (NWSA) and the American Woman Suffrage Association. Anthony and Stanton headed the NWSA, and they continued to work for woman suffrage. Anthony died in 1906.

*Jennifer Ross-Nazzal*

*See also* Abolitionism and Northern Reformers; Fifteenth Amendment; Fourteenth Amendment; National Women's Loyal League [Women's National Loyal League]; Northern Women; Stanton, Elizabeth Cady (1815–1902); Thirteenth Amendment.

**References and Further Reading**

Barry, Kathleen. 1988. *Susan B. Anthony: A Biography of a Singular Feminist.* New York: New York University Press.

Dorr, Rheta Childe. 1970. *Susan B. Anthony: The Woman Who Changed the Mind of a Nation.* New York: AMS Press. Reprint.

DuBois, Ellen Carol. 1978. *Feminism and Suffrage: The Emergence of an Independent Women's Movement in America 1848–1869.* Ithaca, NY: Cornell University Press.

Harper, Ida Husted. 1898. *The Life and Work of Susan B. Anthony.* Vol. 1. Indianapolis, IN: Hollenbeck Press.

Lutz, Alma. 1959. *Susan B. Anthony: Rebel, Crusader, Humanitarian.* Boston: Beacon Press.

## Antietam/Sharpsburg, Battle of (September 17, 1862)

The bloodiest one-day battle in the American Civil War, the Battle of Antietam, also known as Sharpsburg, resulted in a standstill in Maryland. Several women fought in the battle, and in its aftermath civilian aid workers, including many women, rushed to the scene. Among them was Clara Barton, whose dedication to the wounded exemplified the work of hundreds of nurses.

General Robert E. Lee initiated the Antietam campaign, in part to spare Virginians from the ravages of a harvesttime campaign. Lee crossed the Potomac into Maryland on September 4, 1862. Realizing that his supply line with the Confederacy would be threatened by the Union garrison at Harpers Ferry, Lee detached a segment of his command under General Thomas J. "Stonewall" Jackson to capture the town along with its munitions and supplies. Union General George B. McClellan protected Washington and was ordered to eject Confederate invaders from Maryland.

On September 14, while the armies of Lee and McClellan met at South Mountain, Jackson's Confederate troops completed their encirclement of Harpers Ferry. Surrounded on all sides and shelled by artillery, the garrison surrendered the next morning. Jackson left a division of troops at Harpers Ferry and rushed the remainder of his command to Sharpsburg, where Lee was concentrating his forces.

Situated between the Potomac River and Antietam Creek, Sharpsburg lay seventeen miles north of Harpers Ferry. As Jackson's troops arrived piecemeal, they were placed in battle line to await the Union advance. Lee took a defensive position on the west of the creek with his right flank in the woods north of Sharpsburg and his left one on bluffs overlooking the creek below the town.

At dawn on September 17, McClellan ordered his Union troops to attack Lee's left flank. Lee had approximately 35,000 men to McClellan's 71,500. Fighting swung back and forth, each side sustaining severe casualties. By midmorning, the fighting had shifted toward the middle of the Confederate line. Entrenched along an eroded farm road—called the Sunken Road—Lee's forces held off assaults from various Union divisions. When the Confederates were finally forced to withdraw from their position, dead defenders filled the road, earning the area the name the Bloody Lane.

The battle shifted to the southern end of the field, where Union General Ambrose E. Burnside attempted to cross Antietam Creek and assault Lee's right flank. Burnside sent his soldiers across a narrow stone bridge protected by Confederate defenders along a high bluff. Persevering soldiers suffered heavy casualties but finally took control of "Burnside's Bridge." By midafternoon, McClellan's troops were poised to drive toward Sharpsburg and cut off Lee's retreat when the last remnant of Confederate troops from Harpers Ferry under A. P. Hill arrived and clashed with Burnside's advancing command, forcing a Union withdrawal.

The battle concluded with Lee's army intact. By the end of the day almost all the buildings in the surrounding countryside had been turned into makeshift hospitals, with civilians and doctors doing their best to comfort the wounded. In the midst of the battle, having followed the sound of gunfire,

Clara Barton had arrived on the scene and worked to aid the wounded. She put herself in harm's way, working to help the wounded even before the fighting had ended. As she nursed the troops, Barton braved and eluded flying projectiles and, in an especially close call, a bullet that clipped her sleeve.

During the fighting, Sarah Emma Edmonds (Frank Thompson) fought along with at least three other women. Like other female soldiers, their battlefront experiences typically went unnoticed until either years later or until tragedy occurred. The latter was the case for Mary Galloway, whose sexual identity was discovered when Barton tried to treat the dying soldier's wounds.

President Abraham Lincoln claimed victory after Lee crossed back into Virginia during the night of September 18, and he used the victory as the occasion to issue the preliminary Emancipation Proclamation.

*Kanisorn Wongsrichanalai*

***See also*** Barton, Clara (1821–1912); Bull Run/Manassas, Second Battle of (August 29–30, 1862); Emancipation Proclamation (January 1, 1863).

**References and Further Reading**

Gallagher, Gary W., ed. 1999. *The Antietam Campaign.* Chapel Hill: University of North Carolina Press.

McPherson, James M. 2002. *Crossroads of Freedom: Antietam.* New York: Oxford University Press.

Sears, Stephen W. 1983. *Landscape Turned Red: The Battle of Antietam.* New Haven, CT: Ticknor and Fields.

## Antislavery Societies

Abolitionists formed antislavery societies because they believed collective action to be the most effective method of ending slavery. These societies brought abolitionists together to coordinate activities like fundraising events, petition drives, and public awareness campaigns. Eighteenth-century societies emphasized legislative action, gradual emancipation, and abolition of the slave trade. Those formed in the nineteenth century, the era most commonly associated with organized antislavery activity, varied in their goals and methods of emancipation, but all agreed that slavery needed to end. During the 1830s, large numbers of associations formed on local, state, and national levels. The antebellum abolitionist movement included women, black and white, as organizers of antislavery societies and fundraisers for the cause.

Early societies like the Pennsylvania Abolition Society (PAS), formed in 1775, and the New York Manumission Society (NYMS), organized in 1774, emphasized legislative action, gradual emancipation, and the abolition of the international slave trade. Their members were elite, white men who were often Quakers. Compared to the second-generation societies of the 1830s, the activities of these prominent organizations appear strikingly conservative. The NYMS and the PAS argued for the gradual abolition of slavery and fought to end the international slave trade, two issues abolitionists believed were intimately connected. Additionally, the societies established schools for free blacks and provided legal assistance to blacks in the courts.

In contrast with their antecedents, antebellum antislavery societies, recruited members across broad lines of race, class, and gender. Nineteenth-century antislavery societies differed in their methods and desired results of emancipation. Some pushed for gradual emancipation, and others stressed the need for immediate emancipation. In addition, some moderate abolitionists believed that the colonization of freed slaves was the only option. As a result, several prominent men met in December 1816 and founded the American Colonization Society (ACS) to establish an American colony in Africa for free blacks. These moderate abolitionists hoped that slaveholders would be encouraged to emancipate their slaves if the freed slaves left the United States for an African colony. This colonization plan would reduce the population of free blacks in the United States, thus addressing a fear held not only by Southerners, but also by many Northerners. The movement gained popularity with reformers, who hoped to end slavery but who did not necessarily support racial equality.

Colonization never gained the support of African American activists, who feared that blacks would be forced to emigrate. In addition, many antislavery activists—black and white—believed the ACS was antiblack, not antislavery. During the 1820s, black abolitionists were the primary opponents of the colonization movement, whose popularity forced them to organize into anticolonization groups. This organizational activity had a significant impact on the antislavery societies that formed in the 1830s. When the New England Anti-Slavery Society (NEASS), the first of the second-generation antislavery societies, organized in 1832, 25 percent of the initial signers were black.

Radical abolitionist William Lloyd Garrison condemned the ACS for its failure to condemn slaveholding as a sin. The racist spirit of the ACS, Garrison argued, assumed that whites and blacks could not live together. As evidence, Garrison quoted the society's own statements of horror at the prospect of a large black population resulting from abolition without colonization. In 1831, with the inaugural issue of his abolitionist newspaper, *The Liberator*, Garrison called for an immediate end to slavery. Influenced by the religious revivals of the 1820s, Garrison and other radical abolitionists called for the immediate and uncompromising end to the sin of slavery.

To these ends Garrison helped form the New England Anti-Slavery Society in 1832, the first of many antislavery organizations to take an uncompromising stand against slavery. In 1833, Garrison, Arthur and Lewis Tappan, and other abolitionists met in Philadelphia to organize the American Anti-Slavery Society (AASS). The AASS adopted a constitution and a Declaration of Sentiments written by Garrison, who would soon become the primary spokesperson for the organization. Like the NEASS, the AASS counted black abolitionists and women among its members; however, the role of women in the AASS as well as in the state societies would become a critical question as the 1830s drew to a close.

Women's involvement in the nineteenth-century antislavery movement built on established forms of female activism. White upper-class women had been involved in benevolent associations since the 1790s, performing community service for the benefit of women and children in particular. For example, women helped establish schools for the lower classes, and they supported the free produce movement, a boycott of slave-produced products, thus using their domestic role to strike an economic blow against slavery. From the beginning, Garrison and others actively recruited women into antislavery societies, employing gender-based tactics to invoke the sympathy of female abolitionists for female slaves. In 1832, Garrison established a women's department within the pages of *The Liberator* to encourage and recruit women for the antislavery movement. Garrison and other male abolitionists used images of female slaves beaten with whips and held in chains to gain the sympathy and support of women.

In addition to their participation in state and national societies, women often formed female antislavery societies as auxiliaries to the larger male-dominated societies. For example, women founded the Boston Female Anti-Slavery Society in 1833 as an auxiliary to the Massachusetts Anti-Slavery Society. Prominent members included Helen Garrison, Maria Weston Chapman, Louisa Sewell, and Lydia Maria Child. The society's work followed the traditional pattern of women's antislavery societies: organizing antislavery fairs to raise funds for the state society, circulating petitions to collect the signatures that the male societies presented to Congress, aiding in the creation and distribution of antislavery literature, and establishing organizations like the Samaritan Asylum for indigent black children. Women, like their male counterparts, joined antislavery societies for a variety of reasons, including a sense of upper-class noblesse oblige, religious conviction, hatred of racism and slavery, or following the lead of friends and families who had joined similar organizations. Similarly, the membership of women's organizations might be biracial, segregated, or integrated. Antislavery societies, regardless of gender, varied in membership and convictions reflecting the diverse interests drawing people to the antislavery cause. Many women's antislavery societies, as the Boston Female Anti-Slavery Society did in 1835, joined male societies to fight the American Colonization Society. But differences in tactics and

views, especially as the tactics related to women's involvement in antislavery societies, led to deep divisions in the American antislavery movement.

Many people saw women's participation in the abolitionist movement as an extension of feminine domestic roles. Although initially women served supporting roles in organizations, they assumed a more active role in antislavery societies, lecturing to mixed gender audiences and holding leadership positions in the state and national organizations. Eventually, debates about the role of women and their tactics in general caused fractures in the movement.

In 1836, Garrison hired Angelina and Sarah Grimké as lecturers for the AASS. As members of a well-known South Carolina slaveholding family, the Grimké sisters were powerful spokespersons for the antislavery cause. Their lectures had an authenticity that made the pair favorites on the antislavery lecture circuit. Within a short time, the women attracted large "mixed" audiences, along with a rebuke from the Congregational clergy of Massachusetts for their "unladylike" behavior. The sisters, who believed they were doing God's work, refused to stop lecturing. However, the clerical denunciations brought the "woman question" into sharp relief, as other women joined the Grimké sisters in stepping beyond the boundaries of conventional female behavior through work in antislavery societies.

The Anti-Slavery Conventions of Women held in 1837, 1838, and 1839 signaled the growing involvement of women in the movement. The convention speeches encouraged traditional antislavery activism, and delegates passed resolutions to abolish slavery in Washington, D.C., and in the territories. Delegates also passed a resolution calling on women to play a more public role in the movement. The first convention, held in 1837, drew two hundred women. A year later, more than three hundred women attended the second convention; however, the success of the event was marred by mob violence. In an attempt to quell the controversy over the Grimké sisters' lectures, convention organizers had encouraged men to attend a public but not officially sponsored session. Historians attribute the riots at the second convention to protests over the Grimké sisters, the public role antislavery women were assuming, and the presence of proslavery apologists. The violence at the second convention made locating the third convention difficult, and a much smaller crowd attended in 1839. Splits in the American antislavery movement contributed to the demise of the women's conventions.

In May 1840 conservative members of the AASS left to form the American and Foreign Anti-Slavery Society (AFASS). The AASS, under the leadership of Garrison continued to recruit all abolitionists, regardless of their religious, social, and political views. Membership in the AASS required only a desire to abolish slavery. As a result, the society attracted not only antislavery activists, but also women's rights and peace activists, among others. The conservative AFASS, under the leadership of Lewis Tappan, argued that other reform movements threatened the antislavery cause and stressed that the antislavery movement needed to remain orthodox and compatible with traditional views of issues. Embracing causes like women's rights, they asserted, might alienate the general Northern public. The AFASS also emphasized political action and formed the first antislavery party, the Liberty Party.

In 1840, events in the worldwide abolition movement also proved pivotal to the "woman question." As early as 1839, members of the newly formed British and Foreign Anti-Slavery Society (BFASS) discussed the possibility of hosting a World's Anti-Slavery Convention for the purpose of strengthening the international movement against slavery. The BFASS, particularly British abolitionist Joseph Sturge, organized the world gathering. Dubbed the London Committee, the organizers gathered information and statistics about slavery and the slave trade from throughout the world. Additionally, the London Committee provided tickets only to recognized members of antislavery organizations and made it clear that only male delegates would be seated. The AASS selected a pro-woman's rights delegation, including Lucretia Mott, Wendell Phillips, and Garrison. However, Garrison and many of his close associates delayed their departure for the convention because of the mid-May meeting of the AASS, which ultimately gave the more radical Garrison control of the society. Garrison arrived on

the fifth day of the convention to find that the London Committee had refused to seat his organization's female delegates. In protest, Garrison sat in the balcony with the ladies rather than enter the convention and be seated with the other delegates.

The first World's Anti-Slavery Convention included discussions of free labor as a means of combating slavery. In addition, delegates decried the role of the churches in supporting slavery in the United States. Delegates issued admonitions, memorials, and addresses to the people of Great Britain and the United States, but ultimately the convention could do little more than continue the moral and political campaign against slavery where it existed. A second World's Anti-Slavery Convention was held in London in 1843, and Garrison and his followers were not invited. The American delegation, led by Tappan representing the AFASS, discussed the possible annexation of Texas by the United States and the ongoing failure of American churches to take a stand against slavery and slaveholders. However, by 1843, the heyday of antislavery societies had clearly waned. Despite the weakening of the movement in the 1840s as a result of the schism in the American antislavery movement, antislavery societies remained active throughout the Civil War, keeping the abolition of slavery ever present in civic and political debates.

*Julie Holcomb*

**See also** Abolitionism and Northern Reformers; African American Women; Child, Lydia Maria Francis (1802–1880); Garrison, William Lloyd (1805–1879); Grimké (Weld), Angelina (1805–1879); Grimké, Sarah Moore (1792–1873); Mott, Lucretia Coffin (1793–1880); Northern Women.

**References and Further Reading**

Fladeland, Betty. 1972. *Men and Brothers: Anglo-American Antislavery Cooperation.* Urbana: University of Illinois Press.

Hansen, Debra Gold. 1993. *Strained Sisterhood: Gender and Class in the Boston Female Anti-Slavery Society.* Amherst: University of Massachusetts Press.

Jeffrey, Julie Roy. 1998. *The Great Silent Army of Abolitionism: Ordinary Women in the Antislavery Movement.* Chapel Hill: University of North Carolina Press.

Kraditor, Alison. 1967. *Means and Ends in American Abolitionism: Garrison and His Critics on*

*Strategy and Tactics, 1834–1850.* New York: Random House.

Newman, Richard S. 2002. *The Transformation of American Abolitionism: Fighting Slavery in the Early Republic.* Chapel Hill: University of North Carolina Press.

## Atlanta, Evacuation of
## (Special Field Orders Number 67)

On September 8, 1864, United States Major General William T. Sherman issued Special Field Orders Number 67, evacuating the civilian population of Atlanta, Georgia. This evacuation order was one of several cases in which a military officer attempted to extend his control through the forced evacuation of an occupied area's civilian population.

On September 1, 1864, Confederate General John Bell Hood and his Army of Tennessee evacuated Atlanta, Georgia, after a long four-month campaign to defend the city and its valuable rail lines.

As the Southern troops retreated, Mayor James M. Calhoun rode out beyond the battered entrenchments to find the nearest Federal unit. When he encountered a Union skirmish line belonging to the Twentieth Army Corps, he immediately surrendered the city. By nightfall, Union soldiers were in control of the Gate City of the South.

The city of Atlanta was an important rail center with the confluence of four railroads: the Georgia, Atlantic & West Point, Macon & Western, and Western & Atlantic. The war having turned the city into a major supply center for the Confederacy, Atlanta was home to an arsenal and to numerous businesses that catered both to the Confederate military and to a growing population. The city's population had grown from ten thousand in 1860 to nearly twenty-two thousand during the war.

Despite support for Unionist candidates in 1860, the city and county contributed approximately 2,660 soldiers to the Confederacy. The city also

Illustration from October 29, 1864 issue of *Frank Leslie's Illustrated Newspaper* of Atlanta citizens gathering to get travel passes after Sherman's order to clear the city. (Library of Congress)

contained a strong Unionist base that provided information to Federal forces and comfort to Federal prisoners held in the city. By the time of the Federal occupation, approximately thirty-five hundred men, women, and children and their slaves lived within the confines of Atlanta.

Sherman was notified of the surrender of the city on September 2, 1864. He quickly ordered his three armies to consolidate around Atlanta. Sherman first proposed the removal of Atlanta's civilian population to Major General Henry Halleck in a letter dated September 4. Sherman wanted to use the city to regroup after the arduous military campaign to capture Atlanta. He also saw the possibility of turning the battered city into a giant fortified base, where supplies could be transported by rail from Chattanooga, Tennessee. These supplies would be gathered in the city and protected by a strong garrison. In effect, Sherman wanted to build a fortified railhead from which he could draw supplies for a possible fall campaign against Hood's Confederate Army of Tennessee.

Sherman saw the city's mostly female residents as a stumbling block to his military plans. He did not want the complications of dealing with and supporting a hostile civilian population while he concentrated his energies on his next military campaign. Sherman also worried that the flow of supplies could be hindered by civilians using the city's rail lines. As a result, Sherman sought the removal of the remaining families from the city so that his forces would have unfettered use of the rail line back to Tennessee. He remained so concerned about the flow of supplies that he ordered army sutlers not to clog up the military railroads with their goods, threatening them with automatic conscription into his regiments if they disobeyed. In addition, Sherman wanted his chief engineer to reinforce the battered entrenchments surrounding the city with materials from abandoned houses and businesses, and he did not want civilians to interfere.

Before he issued the evacuation order, Sherman sent a letter to Hood informing him of his plans and asking the Confederate general's assistance in the transportation of refugees to the South. In his dispatch, Sherman explained the evacuation to Hood and offered a method to move the civilians into Confederate lines. Sherman offered to transport the families either north or south according to their preference. For those wanting to go north, he would provide rail service to Tennessee or Northern cities. To civilians who wanted to return to the Confederacy, he offered transportation by wagon to a rail station known as Rough and Ready. In addition, these families would be allowed to take any slaves who desired to remain in servitude. At Rough and Ready, Sherman would establish a two-mile neutral zone policed by two one-hundred-man detachments from both armies. In this area, civilians could cross over into Confederate control and responsibility. The next day, Sherman issued Special Field Orders Number 67 to take effect in the now designated post of Atlanta, Department of the Cumberland, United States Army.

The evacuation order came as a surprise to Hood, Mayor Calhoun, and the residents of Atlanta. Mayor Calhoun posted notices throughout the city explaining the evacuation and the procedures necessary to obtain transportation. Many of the households consisted of groups of women, some who had been widowed and others who had husbands fighting in the army. Other families were members of the mercantile class in the city, who had to find a way to evacuate their businesses and property. Unfortunately, because much of the city's population had already fled south in advance of the Federal armies, there was no housing or transportation south of the front lines. The mayor explained these problems to Sherman, who responded with a long letter explaining that the evacuation was part of a war that the Confederates themselves had started. Sherman also stressed that Atlanta's hostile civilians, regardless of sex, deserved punishment for their role in the war.

In addition to his correspondence with Atlanta's mayor, Sherman found himself in a long correspondence with Hood over the legality of the evacuation. Like two lawyers, the generals traded points and counterpoints over the evacuation, the reasons for war, and the brutality of Union actions. In the end, Hood had no choice but to assist in the removal of the largely female civilian population. To counter any negative publicity generated by Northern newspapers for his evacuation of women and children, Sherman enclosed the letters written by the Mayor and Hood in a dispatch to General Halleck.

By September 10, the two armies were trading dispatches regarding the neutral area for the transfer of Confederate refugees. The truce was set to last from daylight on September 12 to daylight on September 22. A detachment of the Ninety-seventh Indiana and the Eighth Tennessee would monitor the two-mile zone, which was marked by a large white flag. Sherman ordered all of his brigades and divisions to provide wagons and ambulances to assist in the transportation of the families. Most evacuated families were forced to choose which items of their property could be transported with them. In several cases, women traded items with Union soldiers, so that they could bring valuable goods with them in the wagons. They hoped that they could later sell these valuables for hard currency, which would be used to purchase food and medicine.

A number of Atlanta's Unionists found ways to remain with their homes and businesses. Several Unionist families approached three Union army surgeons, who had been imprisoned in the city. They asked these surgeons to write Sherman to get an exception to their expulsion, as thanks for their provision of food and medicine to Union prisoners. Based on the testimony of the former prisoners, Sherman granted an exception for fifty families to stay in Atlanta, but he warned the families that their homes might still be destroyed as the Union army built new entrenchments. About fifteen hundred Unionists left Atlanta. The majority of these families traveled northward to states such as Connecticut, Iowa, New Jersey, New York, and Pennsylvania. Some traveled to Washington, D.C., to join with other exiled Georgia families.

Sherman reported that 705 adults, 867 children, and 79 servants, with 1,651 pieces of baggage and furniture traveled southward to Rough and Ready. The Confederate officer in charge reported that roughly 1,600 persons with 8,842 parcels of baggage went through the neutral zone into the Confederacy. The Confederate truce officer complained about the delay in receiving the refugees at Rough and Ready. He believed that Union soldiers were robbing the refugees as they left the city. It was discovered that these delays occurred due to the shortage of wagons in Sherman's three field armies. The state of Georgia attempted to construct refugee camps for the southbound refugees. One camp was established on 47 acres in Terrell County, Georgia, and consisted of temporary tents. Another camp, named Fosterville after the state quartermaster general, was built to house three hundred refugees.

Sherman's evacuation of Atlanta's civilian population provoked criticism from men and women across the South. They lambasted the general for his callous treatment of the women and children of Atlanta. Sherman's actions met with approval from Northern soldiers and civilians, who applauded the general's willingness to deal sternly with the enemy population.

*William H. Brown*

***See also*** Destruction of Homes; Refugees; Sherman's Campaign (1864–1865); Sherman, William Tecumseh (1820–1891); Southern Unionists; Southern Women; Urban Women, Southern.

**References and Further Reading**

Carter III, Samuel. 1973. *The Siege of Atlanta, 1864.* New York: St. Martin's Press.

Castel, Albert. 1992. *Decision in the West: The Atlanta Campaign of 1864.* Lawrence: University Press of Kansas.

Dyer, Thomas G. 1999. *Secret Yankees: The Union Circle in Confederate Atlanta.* Baltimore, MD: Johns Hopkins University Press.

Garrison, Webb. 1995. *Atlanta and the War.* Nashville, TN: Rutledge Hill Press.

Grimsley, Mark. 1995. *The Hard Hand of War: Union Military Policy toward Southern Civilians, 1861–1865.* New York: Cambridge University Press.

Marszalek, John F. 1993. *Sherman: A Soldier's Passion for Order.* New York: Free Press.

McMurry, Richard M. 2000. *Atlanta 1864: Last Chance for the Confederacy.* Lincoln: University of Nebraska Press.

Russell, James M. 1988. *Atlanta, 1847–1890: Citybuilding in the Old South and the New.* Baton Rouge: Louisiana State University Press.

# B

## Bacot, Ada W. (1832–1911)

A wealthy South Carolina widow, Ada Bacot served as a nurse during the Civil War. Her diary of those years sheds light on the experiences and attitudes of upper-class Southern women of the time.

By the time the Civil War began, Bacot had lost her husband and both of her children. As a secessionist, Bacot longed to devote herself to the South's cause. Perhaps because there was no one at home depending on her, she felt useless remaining at home when she saw great need for her services elsewhere. Bacot saw nursing as an appropriate medium for expressing her patriotism.

In December 1861 Bacot answered Reverend Robert Woodward Barnwell's plea for nurses. Bacot traveled with Barnwell, the head of the South Carolina Hospital Aid Association, and several other female volunteers to Charlottesville, Virginia, where hospitals for South Carolinian soldiers had been set up. By the following year, hospitals were no longer state-based, and the Confederacy had taken upon itself the running of its hospitals.

As soon as Bacot began work in the Virginia hospitals, she felt imbued with purpose, serving her nation and her state. Initially, she and the other female nurses did not tend the wounded directly. Instead, she and others supervised meals for the patients and laundered the hospital's linens. They also visited with the men, wrote letters, and urged them to seek comfort in the Bible and Christianity. Yet it was impossible not to be aware of the terrible conditions under which the wounded sometimes arrived at the hospitals. At times the soldiers had lain outside for days without tents, beds, or food. Bacot felt great sympathy for the soldiers at times, but she also expressed her exhaustion with the endless job of caring for them.

Bacot embraced slavery, and, in her diary, she often discussed the relationships between owners and their slaves, as well as her own attitudes about the institution. Once, upon hearing how one owner was smothered by her servants, Bacot expressed the fear that the same thing could happen to her. When a neighbor's house caught fire, Bacot was certain that the slaves were responsible. When a teenage slave refused to clear the table at the house where Bacot and other medical staff boarded, Bacot hit the boy; when his mother defended him verbally, Bacot called in the white doctors, who whipped both mother and child.

Bacot's diary also provides insight into the relationship between the sexes in upper-class Southern society. Bacot had entered a profession that some saw as below her class and not suitable for women. At the beginning of the war, her family opposed her decision to become a nurse as a position not befitting a woman. After she had volunteered in Charlottesville for a year, Bacot was offered the matronship of Midway Hospital. She consulted a physician who had become her friend; he advised against her taking the position because it was below her station and she was unaccustomed to such labor. In addition, he thought it was unladylike to hold a paid position. Bacot took her friend's advice and turned down the offer, revealing her awareness of the patriarchal structure of Southern society.

Bacot embraced the male-dominated structure and operated within it, yet she also found opportunities to expand her life beyond its boundaries. Leaving home to volunteer as a nurse had opened new horizons for Bacot, and the war transformed her life in both positive and negative ways. She formed many lasting relationships with other staff members in the Virginia hospitals. She also found inner strengths and capabilities that had not been tested in her narrow existence before the war.

Bacot kept her diary until January 1863 and left the nursing profession shortly thereafter. It is not known why she relinquished either activity. By November 1863 she had returned to South Carolina, where she married Thomas A. G. Clarke, a fellow South Carolinian and a first lieutenant in the Confederate army.

*Ellen H. Todras*

**See also** Diaries and Journals; Nurses.
**References and Further Reading**

Berlin, Jean V. 1994. *A Confederate Nurse: The Diary of Ada W. Bacot, 1860–1863.* Columbia: University of South Carolina Press.

Campbell, Edward Jr., and Kym S. Rice. 1996. *A Woman's War: Southern Women, Civil War, and the Confederate Legacy.* Richmond, VA: The Museum of the Confederacy.

Faust, Drew Gilpin. 1996. *Mothers of Invention: Women of the Slaveholding South in the American Civil War.* Chapel Hill: University of North Carolina Press.

Rable, George C. 1989. *Civil Wars: Women and the Crisis of Southern Nationalism.* Urbana: University of Illinois Press.

## Baker, Mrs. E. H. (n.d.–n.d.)

Very little is known about the life of Mrs. E. H. Baker. As an agent of Union detective Allan Pinkerton, Baker spied on Confederate submarine technology and delivered critical intelligence to Union officials.

Baker was employed by Pinkerton's Chicago detective agency prior to the war. During the war, Pinkerton served as secret service chief to General George McClellan, and he used his agency's resources accordingly. In the fall of 1861, Pinkerton learned that Confederates were developing torpedoes and submarine vessels to break the Union blockade, and he believed that Richmond's Tredegar Iron Works, which provided the iron plating for the CSS *Virginia* (also called the *Merrimack*), was the leading producer of this technology. He dispatched Baker to Richmond to investigate.

Baker had once lived in Richmond and was acquainted with Captain Atwater of the Confederate navy. Under the pretense of a friendly visit, Baker traveled to Richmond in November 1861 and stayed with Atwater and his wife. Baker discussed the war with Atwater and expressed her curiosity about the preparations under way in Richmond. When a prototype submarine vessel was to be tested on the James River, Atwater took both Baker and his wife to the demonstration.

The vessel being tested was intended to destroy Union ships blocking the mouth of the James River. Baker used Atwater's binoculars to watch from shore as the small submarine vessel approached a barge anchored midriver. A diver swam out from the submarine to attach a floating magazine to the side of the barge. The submarine then backed away and detonated the charge, sinking the barge in a large explosion. Later that day she made detailed notes of her observations and she secured them in her clothing.

Atwater gave Baker a tour of Tredegar Iron Works the next day, where she saw under production a larger version of the submarine used in the demonstration. Baker immediately traveled to Washington and handed over her notes to Pinkerton. Baker also made a sketch of the vessel, showing its position under the surface of the water and its operation. Pinkerton reported these findings to General McClellan and the Secretary of the Navy.

Pinkerton claimed that Baker's findings thwarted an attack on the USS *Minnesota*, which captured a Confederate submarine using grappling hooks in Hampton Roads. This took place in October 1861, one month prior to the time Pinkerton reported Baker as being in Richmond. It is possible that Pinkerton recorded the date of Baker's visit incorrectly. The submarine that Baker observed was most likely that designed by William Cheeney. The race to develop submarine technology was an important component of naval warfare, and Baker's intelligence came at a crucial moment early in the war.

*Kristen L. Rouse*

***See also*** Female Spies.
**References and Further Reading**
Coski, John M. 1996. *Capital Navy: The Men, Ships, and Operations of the James River Squadron.* Campbell, CA: Savas Woodbury.
Pinkerton, Allan. 1883. *The Spy of the Rebellion; Being a True History of the Spy System of the United States Army during the Late Rebellion.* New York: G.W. Carleton.

## Banks, Nathaniel Prentiss (1816–1894)

A Civil War general and congressman, Nathaniel Prentiss Bank's career spanned much of the nineteenth century.

Born in Waltham, Massachusetts, on January 30, 1816, Banks grew up in a working-class family. He served as a representative to both the Massachusetts Legislature and the United States Congress, becoming Speaker of the House in both bodies. After being elected to three terms as governor of Massachusetts, Banks was appointed major general of volunteers during the Civil War. During the war, his lack of military skill marked him as a poor soldier. He accepted the surrender of the Confederate stronghold of Port Hudson and bungled the poorly conceived Red River Campaign in 1864. Following the war, Banks served again in Congress. During his political career, he had been a Democrat, a Know-Nothing, a Republican, and an Independent.

As a young man, Banks edited a small newspaper, clerked at the Boston Customs House, and gained acceptance to the bar. An effective public speaker, Banks soon became interested in politics. He joined the Democratic Party and successfully ran for the state legislature, serving from 1849 until 1852. As a moderate on the issue of slavery, Banks served in the U.S. House of Representatives from 1853 until 1857. His opposition to the Kansas-Nebraska Act led Banks to leave the Democrats and join the Republican Party. As a Republican, he became Speaker of the House, and then, in 1858, he became governor of Massachusetts. He ran for the Republican presidential nomination in 1860. Losing to Abraham Lin-

Gen. Nathaniel Banks of the Union army during the Civil War. Prior to the war Banks served as speaker of the House (1851–1852), and governor of Massachusetts (1858–1860). (National Archives and Records Administration)

coln, Banks accepted a position as a railroad director. After the sectional tension escalated into war, Banks accepted a commission as a major general in the Union army.

Banks had no military knowledge or experience. As a political general, he would constantly incur the resentment of the professional soldiers he commanded. Given command of Union forces in western Maryland, Banks's orders in early 1862 were to clear the Shenandoah Valley of Confederate troops and to prevent Confederates in western Virginia from reinforcing Richmond. Confederate General Thomas J. "Stonewall" Jackson had a much smaller force than Banks had, but he outmaneuvered the Union general during the 1862 Shenandoah Valley campaign, driving the Union forces back across the Potomac.

Despite his poor showing as a battlefield commander, Banks retained considerable political power and was ordered to New Orleans. There, he faced a host of challenges, including an unruly civilian population displeased with the Union occupation. Local citizens, especially women, had harassed Union troops and Banks' predecessor, General Benjamin F. Butler, had earned the Confederacy's hatred by treating them harshly. Banks tried a different technique, hosting balls and concerts for locals. This effort worked to a certain extent, but he eventually had to use force to control unruly female citizens who flaunted their Confederate loyalties and threatened order in New Orleans. Banks also needed to deal with the increasing number of black refugees from the surrounding area and to implement President Lincoln's experimental reconstruction plan. Finally, he was ordered to help General Ulysses S. Grant open the Mississippi River to Union traffic. As Grant's army advanced toward Vicksburg, Banks was to move north to capture the smaller Confederate stronghold of Port Hudson.

Banks twice failed to capture Port Hudson. Not until the Confederate defenders learned of Vicksburg's fall did they surrender on July 9, 1863. At Port Hudson, Banks had overseen one of the first assaults by black troops in the war. Despite their courageous showing, Banks reduced the number of black officers, demoralizing his African American troops. In March 1864, Banks set out to occupy eastern Texas and to capture Southern cotton for the cotton-starved mills in the North. He led a combined force of army troops and naval vessels up the Red River, but the campaign failed due to a lack of coordination and poor leadership.

After the war, Banks returned to politics and served again in Congress. He opposed President Andrew Johnson's lenient policies for former Confederates and voted to impeach the chief executive. Banks served as chairman of the Committee on Foreign Affairs where he championed the purchase of Alaska. Bribery and corruption charges against Banks provoked him to distance himself from President Grant's administration and led to the loss of his congressional seat in 1872. Banks spoke in support of women's suffrage and helped draft a Massa-

chusetts state law limiting the number of hours in the workday. Banks died in Massachusetts on September 1, 1894, at the age of 78.

*Kanisorn Wongsrichanalai*

***See also*** Butler, Benjamin F.; Politics; Reconstruction.

**References and Further Reading**

Harrington, Fred Harvey. 1948. *Fighting Politician: Major General N. P. Banks.* Philadelphia: University of Pennsylvania Press.

Hollandsworth, James G. 1998. *Pretense of Glory: The Life of Nathaniel P. Banks.* Baton Rouge: Louisiana State University Press.

## Bannister, Christiana Babcock Carteaux (ca. 1820–1902)

Businesswoman and activist Christiana Babcock Carteaux Bannister was president of the Boston Colored Ladies' Sanitary Committee that supported members of the Massachusetts Fifty-fourth Infantry Regiment.

Born in Rhode Island in 1820, Christiana Babcock was of African American and Narragansett Indian parentage. She moved to Boston, probably in the 1840s, and, after an unsuccessful first marriage, she married Canadian-born artist Edward Bannister in 1857. By this time she was a hairdresser with a city center salon catering mainly to white clients. She advertised frequently in William Lloyd Garrison's abolitionist newspaper, *The Liberator.*

The Bannisters were part of Boston's black middle class, active in cultural and abolitionist activities. They lodged in the home of Lewis Hayden, one of the most militant leaders of the Underground Railroad.

In January 1863, Massachusetts Governor John A. Andrew began recruiting for the Fifty-fourth Massachusetts Infantry Regiment, which he hoped would be a model for future black regiments. In May of that year, Christiana Bannister, president of the Colored Ladies' Relief Committee, traveled to Readville, south of Boston, to present the Fifty-fourth with its colors.

Members of the Fifty-fourth enlisted assuming they would receive the same pay as white soldiers, namely $13 a month plus a clothing allowance, but they were told in July 1863 that they would be paid only $10 a month with a clothing deduction. They refused to accept any pay. The order was reversed thirteen months later. In the meantime, the Fifty-fourth fought bravely at Fort Wagner, South Carolina. Led by Colonel Robert Gould Shaw, twenty-five-year-old son of a Boston Brahmin abolitionist family, they were heavily outnumbered and one-third of the officers, including Shaw, and almost half of the enlisted men were either killed or wounded.

Back in Boston, the Colored Ladies' Relief Organization had become the Colored Ladies' Sanitary Committee with Christiana Bannister as president. In October 1864, Bannister organized a five-day fundraising fair to aid disabled veterans and their families. In addition to the usual cake stalls and needlework, some valuable items were raffled, notably a piano, an organ, and a full-length portrait of Colonel Shaw painted by Edward Bannister. When abolitionist author Lydia Maria Child visited the fair, she was moved by the sign stretched across Summer Street advertising the Colored Soldiers' Fair and the inscription over the portrait of Shaw that read "our martyr."

After the Civil War, the Bannisters moved to Providence, Rhode Island, where he became a well-known painter, and she continued her hairdressing business. In 1890 she founded the Providence Shelter for Aged Colored Women. Christiana died in December 1902 and is buried in the North Burial Ground, Providence.

*Jane Lancaster*

**See also** African American Women; Aid Societies; Child, Lydia Maria Francis (1802–1880); Fairs and Bazaars; Native American Women; Northern Women.

**References and Further Reading**

Lancaster, Jane. 2001. "'I Would Have Made Out Very Poorly Had It Not Been for Her': The Life and Work of Christiana Bannister, Hair Doctress and Philanthropist." *Rhode Island History* 59 (4): 103–122.

O'Connor, Thomas H. 1997. *Civil War Boston: Home Front and Battlefield.* Boston: Northeastern University Press.

## Baptist Women

The slavery controversy permanently divided Baptists into Northern and Southern conventions in 1845. This split was triggered by the opposition of Northern Baptists to slavery and in particular by the 1844 statement of the Home Mission Society declaring that a person could not be a missionary and still keep slaves as property. This action led churches in the South, who a generation before had decried slavery, to bring into existence the Southern Baptist Convention. Northern Baptists at first did not recognize the separation, but the Civil War effectively sealed the division.

Northern female Baptists played a vital role during the Civil War. Many Baptist women worked through organized philanthropy, such as the United States Sanitary Commission and the United States Christian Commission, to aid Union soldiers. These women also formed church aid societies that provided soldiers and freed people with necessary articles of clothing and food. In 1862 female auxiliaries of the American Baptist Home Mission Society (ABHMS) pledged to provide education for the emancipated slaves, especially the training of black men for the ministry.

After the war, the ABHMS broadened its goal to include the collegiate training of black women. In 1881, the Women's Baptist Home Missionary Society of New England founded the Atlanta Baptist Female Seminary, later Spelman College, in the basement of Friendship Baptist Church in Atlanta, Georgia. By 1880, white Northern Baptists owned and supported eight schools for African Americans: Atlanta Baptist College, Benedict Institute, Leland University, Nashville Institute, Natchez Seminary, Richmond Institute, Shaw University, and Wayland Seminary. All but Richmond Institute and Atlanta Baptist College were open to black women as well as men.

In the South, the Baptist church served as a focal point for Southern women's wartime activities. The women of First Baptist Church in LaGrange, Georgia, for example, formed a Soldier's Relief and Sewing Society in 1862. The women also organized a home guard called the Nancy Harts in honor of a

Georgia Revolutionary heroine. When Union troops arrived, the group prepared for action but surrendered when they were assured the town would not be destroyed. The next year, the church became a temporary Confederate hospital.

The war intruded into church life in the South, often leaving women to carry on the church activities while their men were off at the battlefront. In Nashville, Tennessee, the pastor of the First Baptist Church was arrested and imprisoned with several other ministers when they refused to take an oath of loyalty to the United States government. Consequently, the women of the community carried on much of the work of the church in his absence.

The church could also serve as a meeting place for women to organize dissent. In April 1863 in Richmond, Virginia, approximately three hundred women met at Belvidere Baptist Church to demand food from the governor and to plan a protest to secure food for their families. The following day, April 2, approximately one thousand women, some carrying weapons, broke into stores and shops, taking food and clothing. They had to be subdued by local officials.

The end of the Civil War did not end the schism between white Baptists. After the war, the Southern Baptist Convention became one of the major institutional expressions of the South's cultural identity and emerged as the largest Protestant denomination in the reunited nation.

The end of the Civil War provided African American Baptists the opportunity to forge a religious identity of their own. During slavery, the independent polity and absence of formalism among Baptists had appealed to African Americans. Slave churches had appeared on Southern plantations as early as the mid-eighteenth century, and the first black Baptist church was organized near Augusta, Georgia, in 1773. In 1821, members of the Richmond African Baptist Missionary Society went to Liberia as missionaries. By the end of the Civil War, there were perhaps one million black Baptists in the South.

After the Civil War, black Baptists left white-dominated churches and formed the National Baptist Convention U.S.A. in 1895. The National Baptist Convention constituted the largest and most representative sample of African American church membership. In 1906 it had over 2 million members constituting more than 61 percent of all black church members in the United States. By 1916, the National Baptist Convention ranked as the third-largest religious body in the United States and as the largest denomination, black or white, in Atlanta, Memphis, Richmond, Birmingham, and Nashville.

*Karen Fisher Younger*

**See also** African American Women; Aid Societies; Bread Riots; Confederate Homefront; Education, Northern; Education, Southern; Hospitals; Northern Women; Religion; Sewing Bees; Southern Women; Union Homefront; United States Christian Commission; United States Sanitary Commission.

**References and Further Reading**

Ahlstrom, Sydney. 1972. *A Religious History of the American People.* New Haven, CT: Yale University Press.

Higginbotham, Evelyn Brooks. 1994. *Righteous Discontent: The Women's Movement in the Black Baptist Church, 1880–1920.* Cambridge, MA: Harvard University Press.

Jackson, Roswell F., and Rosalyn M. Patterson. 1989. "A Brief History of Selected Black Churches in Atlanta, Georgia." *Journal of Negro History* 74 (Winter): 31–59.

Massey, Mary Elizabeth. 1994. *Women in the Civil War.* Lincoln: University of Nebraska Press.

Miller, Randall M., Harry S. Stout, and Charles Reagan Wilson, eds. 1998. *Religion and the American Civil War.* New York: Oxford University Press.

Rikard, Marlene Hunt, and Elizabeth Wells. 1997. "'From It Begins a New Era': Women and the Civil War." *Baptist History and Heritage* 32 (3): 59–73.

## Barton, Clara (1821–1912)

Civil War nurse Clara Barton treated Union soldiers on the battlefields and continued her dedication to soldiers in the postwar era. She helped find missing soldiers, locate the graves of soldiers killed in battle and in prison camps, and founded the American Red Cross.

Born Clarissa Harlowe Barton in North Oxford, Massachusetts, on December 25, 1821, Clara was the last of five children of Stephen and Sarah Stone Barton. Captain Barton, a prosperous farmer and sawmill operator, had served under General "Mad" Anthony Wayne in the Indian wars that were part of the settlement of the Northwest Territory. His stories of his wartime experiences enthralled his daughter and prompted her later interest in the military.

A bright child who pursued Latin, chemistry, and philosophy, Barton began teaching school in May 1839 at the age of eighteen. At a time when women were expected to be timid and dependent, she was strong-minded and self-reliant, although always sensitive to perceived offense. Quickly becoming a much sought-after teacher for her ability to maintain discipline, Barton eventually became bored with the classroom. Seeking new challenges and hoping to snap out of a depression, she attended Clinton Liberal Institute in New York in 1850. In 1851, she organized and briefly headed one of the first free schools in New Jersey, in Bordentown. The success of the school prompted the town fathers to demote Barton in favor of a male administrator. Offended and infuriated, Barton left after a year to become a clerk-copyist in the United States Patent Office in Washington, D.C. She may have been the first regularly appointed female civil servant.

At the outset of the Civil War, Barton provided both nursing care and supplies for men in the Sixth Massachusetts Regiment who were wounded during the Baltimore riot in April 1861. She also organized a parcel post service for soldiers, which was maintained throughout the war. Along with many others in Washington, D.C., Barton witnessed the almost total lack of first aid facilities at the first Battle of Bull Run in Manassas, Virginia in 1861. She responded by using her own money to place advertisements in Massachusetts' *The Worcester Spy* for provisions for the wounded.

Barton determined to serve the soldiers in the field, because, in her mind, it enabled her to become close to being a soldier herself, fulfilling her soldier father's expectations. In early June 1862, she approached Colonel Daniel Rucker of the Quartermaster Corps. She had been gathering items for months and had filled a warehouse with a variety of goods that the army could use, including

Universally hailed as the "Angel of the Battlefield," Clara Barton spent a lifetime injecting a measure of humanity into the scourge of war by bringing medical supplies and comfort to soldiers on the battlefield. She also founded the American Chapter of the Red Cross. (National Archives and Records Administration)

food and medicine. Unable to persuade authorities to allow her to make deliveries, she had better luck with Rucker, who provided Barton with wagons and drivers as well as the necessary clearances from Washington, D.C.

As she moved throughout Virginia and Maryland, Barton and her supplies aided the wounded and dying at Cedar Mountain, Second Bull Run, Chantilly, South Mountain, Antietam, and Charleston, as well as in the Wilderness campaign. The Peninsula campaign was fully under way when Barton appeared at Fredericksburg, Virginia, in August 1862. Convention dictated that she wait until the wounded came to the rear to be treated. Refusing to wait for authorization, something that she was unlikely to receive, Barton moved onto the battlefield four days after the fighting had subsided. Accompanied by two civilian helpers, she saw men in the throes of death. The soldiers, lying helpless, were suffering from sunstroke, dehydration, and shock. Over the next two days, Barton cooked meals, washed wounds, applied dressings, assisted the surgeons in their gruesome tasks, distributed medicine, and offered kind words to the frightened soldiers. Her ministrations led to the nickname Angel of the Battlefield.

The 1862 Battle of Antietam may have been Barton's finest hour. It was certainly one of her most terrifying experiences. More men were killed, wounded, or declared missing on this day than on any other day in the Civil War, with total casualties of over twenty-five thousand. Ranging along the battlefield, Barton used a pocketknife to extract a bullet from the jaw of a young soldier, the procedure done without chloroform and with some trepidation on Barton's part. Shortly thereafter, as she gave a wounded man a drink of water, a bullet passed through the sleeve of her dress and struck the soldier dead. Barton continued to provide aid to the other wounded. At the Battle of Fort Wagner during the siege of Charleston, South Carolina, Barton waded ashore despite the danger of flying bullets and ministered to the men as they lay bleeding. To many soldiers, it seemed as if Barton's courage had no limits.

Barton increasingly won the respect and admiration of commanding officers and surgeons. However, she did not hesitate to voice complaints about army inefficiency. Her willingness to publicly berate army authorities for neglect of the wounded and her requests to draw stores from the quartermaster earned resentment. The army did not appreciate a freewheeling civilian—and a woman—in their midst.

As the press publicized Barton's actions and as soldiers wrote to their families about her, she received more fame and supplies. Yet Barton saw herself as one of hundreds of women providing aid to the wounded. In addition, she never hesitated to spend her own money to get materials for the soldiers. In June 1864, she became superintendent of nurses in General Benjamin Butler's Army of the James. No longer able to devote herself solely to providing succor on the battlefield, Barton cheerfully accepted her new duties as nurse, cook, and administrator at various corps hospitals in Virginia.

In March 1865, Barton received permission from President Abraham Lincoln and the limited cooperation from the War Department to search for missing prisoners of war, a difficult task in an era without dog tags or comprehensive prison camp records and when fellow soldiers typically identified the dead. Annapolis, Maryland, filled with many disoriented soldiers who needed advice and direction, had become an unofficial center for war refugees, and Barton took up her station there at the Office of Correspondence. Barton recruited a band of helpers to assist with both the missing and the disoriented soldiers.

When Barton received an inquiry about a missing man, the name of the soldier was listed by state. Lists were then circulated to local newspapers, displayed in post offices, and reviewed by various fraternal organizations. The hope was that veterans, seeing a particular name, might recall the fate of one or more of those cited and communicate the information to Barton, who would in turn write to the person making the initial inquiry. The army offered stationery, free postage, a tent, and some chairs. Barton covered most of the expenses herself, with later reimbursement by Congress. The Office of Correspondence reported on about fifteen thousand men, a fraction of the total number of the missing. With the aid of a man imprisoned at the notorious Confederate prison camp at Andersonville, Georgia, Barton traveled there to help mark graves on the site of the former camp and succeeded in identifying 90 percent of the graves.

From 1866 to 1868, while continuing her missing persons work on a reduced scale, Barton described her war experiences in about three hundred lectures throughout the North and West. The lecture tour substantially added to her fame and later helped her to persuade Congress to embrace American membership in the International Red Cross. In large part, Barton brought home to her listeners the reality of war. Of all the famous lecturers of the day, only she had seen action in the Civil War. Her accounts were definitely partisan, partly because the Southern side of the struggle was of little interest to her audience. When her voice gave out in 1868, she traveled to Europe to recover on the advice of a physician.

In Switzerland, Barton learned for the first time of the International Committee of the Red Cross, formed in 1863 at a convention in Geneva. The new organization aimed to reduce the horrors of war by bettering the wholly inadequate medical service typically provided to soldiers in the field. Learning that the U.S. State Department had refused to recommend ratification of the Red Cross agreement, Barton determined to get American backing.

In the meantime, Barton remained in Europe. Under the auspices of the International Red Cross, she served in military hospitals and distributed supplies during the 1870–1871 Franco-Prussian War. She also set up work systems in which needy French women war refugees could sew, producing necessary clothing in exchange for food.

In 1873, following another breakdown, Barton returned to the United States to live in semiretirement while recovering her health. With the outbreak of the Russo-Turkish War in 1877, her interest in the Red Cross movement revived, and Barton began a five-year campaign to develop an American Red Cross. President Rutherford B. Hayes opposed American involvement with the Red Cross because he believed that the signing of the Geneva Treaty was an involvement in foreign affairs that violated the spirit of the Monroe Doctrine. However, Hayes was a one-term president, and Barton had both good political connections and an excellent reputation as a humanitarian. In 1882, Congress approved the Geneva Convention and joined the International Red Cross movement.

Not waiting for the government to act, Barton founded the American Red Cross in 1881. Three years later, in 1884, as American delegate to the Red Cross conference in Geneva, Barton secured the adoption of an amendment that authorized the provision of Red Cross relief during peacetime emergencies. As president of the American Red Cross from 1882 to 1904, she often led relief expeditions to areas devastated by natural disasters. She helped the people of Charleston, South Carolina, after an 1882 earthquake and traveled to Galveston, Texas, in 1900 after a hurricane nearly destroyed the city.

Though the Red Cross typically provided clothing, food, medicine, and emergency shelter, it gave Galveston farmers a million and a half strawberry plants to enable them to resume their livelihoods.

When the United States entered the Spanish-American War in 1898, the Angel of the Battlefield leaped into action. Barton, now in her late seventies, rode mule wagons over primitive roads under a tropical sun to deliver provisions to Cuban civilians and American soldiers. Many in the Red Cross believed that she should have remained in Washington, D.C., to lead the organization. Although the organization had grown, communication between national headquarters and the branches was so poor that much of the local work was completely independent of the national Red Cross. Local chapters typically trained nurses without any national guidance.

Barton was indefatigable in promoting the Red Cross, seeing it as her child. Her domination of the organization also proved a weakness, because it led to methods of administration that alienated important people whose support would have bolstered its reputation and allowed it to better carry out its mission. Dealing with others, men or women, in any capacity but one of an authority did not come easily to Barton. Too often she took suggestions for criticism as threats and the critics themselves as enemies. Absolutely vital to its early successes of the Red Cross, Barton, with her singular proprietary style, stood in the path of continued growth. In December 1902, confronted by an open rebellion among the Red Cross board of directors, Barton had declared herself lifetime president of the American Red Cross. Nevertheless, she was eased out in 1904.

After resigning from the Red Cross, Barton spent her final years in Glen Echo, Maryland. In 1906, Barton founded the National First Aid Association and served as its president until her death. A feminist, she also supported efforts to get women the vote and to obtain equal pay for equal work. An advocate of Christian Science and a believer in spiritualism, she remained physically active and mentally alert to the end.

Clara Barton died on April 12, 1912, and is buried in North Oxford, Massachusetts.

*Caryn E. Neumann*

*See also* Aid Societies; Antietam/Sharpsburg, Battle of (September 17, 1862); Bull Run/Manassas, First Battle of (July 21, 1861); Bull Run/Manassas, Second Battle of (August 29–30, 1862); Domesticity; Education, Northern; Fredericksburg, Battle of (December 13, 1862); Hospitals; Northern Women; Nurses; Politics; Separate Spheres; Teachers, Northern; Wartime Employment.

**References and Further Reading**

Burton, David H. 1995. *Clara Barton: In the Service of Humanity.* Westport, CT: Greenwood Press.

Dulles, Foster Rhea. 1950. *The American Red Cross, a History.* New York: Harper & Row.

Gilbo, Patrick F. 1981. *The American Red Cross: The First Century.* New York: Harper & Row.

Hutchinson, John F. 1996. *Champions of Charity: War and the Rise of the Red Cross.* Boulder, CO: Westview Press.

Oates, Stephen B. 1994. *A Woman of Valor: Clara Barton and the Civil War.* New York: Free Press.

Pryor, Elizabeth Brown. 1987. *Clara Barton: Professional Angel.* Philadelphia: University of Pennsylvania Press.

## Battle, Mary Frances "Fanny" ("Fannie") (1842–1924)

A Nashville, Tennessee spy and smuggler for the Confederacy, who funneled goods and information to General Braxton Bragg's Coleman Scouts, Battle occasionally dressed as a boy when she ventured into Union-occupied Nashville, viewing fortifications and drawing maps from memory. Because she left no known diaries and refused to discuss her experiences, details of her espionage role remain murky. When taken into custody on April 7, 1863, she was carrying letters and messages for Confederates. Charged with spying, smuggling, and obtaining a forged pass, she was sent to Camp Chase in Ohio, moved to Old Capitol Prison in Washington, D.C., and later, in May, exchanged for several Federal officers held at City Point, Virginia. Exiled to the Deep South, Battle spent the remainder of the war near Atlanta with other Nashville expatriates.

Born to Joel A. Battle, Sr. and his second wife, Adeline Mosely, Fanny was one of Joel's nine children. She attended Nashville Female Academy, a finishing school offering ornamental courses but emphasizing academic studies. In April 1861, her father raised Company B, Twentieth Tennessee Volunteer Infantry (C.S.A.). Two of his sons, William and Allen, were killed at the Battle of Shiloh, where he was wounded, captured, and imprisoned at Johnson's Island, Ohio. His son Frank was captured and imprisoned multiple times. Meanwhile, Union soldiers burned the family home near Cane Ridge, and Fanny moved the family into their barn. As the men of the family fought on the battlefields, Fanny and her sisters did their part on the homefront as spies and supporters.

In 1870, Battle began a sixteen-year teaching career in Nashville's public school system. Because existing benevolent groups were not meeting needs, she launched a nonsectarian food drive for the poor during the 1881 Thanksgiving season. When December floods left more than a thousand Nashvillians homeless, Battle rallied civic leaders to assist victims, becoming treasurer of the resulting organization known as the Nashville Relief Society (NRS). In 1886, she quit teaching to manage NRS. The group reorganized as United Charities (UC), a diverse, private, nonsectarian charitable organization that created permanent facilities and offered ongoing services. They opened the Old Woman's Home in 1890, followed in 1891 by the Flower Mission Day Nursery to care for working women's children, the first such facility in the state. The UC also opened the John W. Thomas Fresh Air Camp, Addison Avenue Day Home, Watkins Settlement Home, A. B. Ransom Kindergarten, and Bertha Fensterwald Kindergarten. Battle belonged to McKendree Methodist Church, United Daughters of the Confederacy, the Woman's Christian Temperance Union, and the Centennial Club.

Fanny Battle never married. She is buried in Mt. Olivet Cemetery in Tennessee.

*Nancy L. Adgent*

*See also* Education, Southern; Female Spies.

**References and Further Reading**

Bakeless, John. 1970. *Spies of the Confederacy.* Philadelphia, PA: J. B. Lippincott Co.

Greene, Elna C., ed. 1999. *Before the New Deal: Social Welfare in the South, 1830–1930.* Athens: University of Georgia Press.

Morrow, Sara S. 1980. *The Legacy of Fannie Battle.* Nashville, TN: Fannie Battle Social Workers.

## Beecher, Catharine (1800–1878)

Many people consider Catharine Beecher to be the mother of home economics in America. She helped shape American middle-class female culture during the antebellum years by lobbying for higher education for women as well as for the advancement of female teachers in public education. More importantly, Beecher intellectually reconciled the status quo of female subordination to the values of American democracy by developing new ways of promoting the role of women within the nationalistic rhetoric. Beecher wrote prolifically on education and women's place in society, leading an American domestic science movement that was in tune with the demands of industrial capitalism of the late nineteenth century.

Born into a prominent family on September 6, 1800, Catharine was the daughter of Lyman Beecher and sister of Harriet Beecher Stowe and Henry Ward Beecher. The most conservative of the Beecher family, Catharine focused her life on educational reform and women's rights.

Her time as a student and an assistant teacher at Sarah Pierce's Litchfield Female Academy—from 1810 to 1816—influenced Beecher's way of thinking and her career as an educator. The Litchfield Academy inculcated, and Beecher embraced, the philosophy of Republican Motherhood, a concept of gender roles that emerged during the Early Republic era and stressed the importance of women's roles in an emerging nation. When Miss Pierce's nephew, Charles Brace, came to teach at the academy, he introduced a curriculum for boys along with Addisonian values of domestic gentility to female students. In this model, women and men shared intellectual equality in separate spheres: Men conducted business and social activities in the public sphere, and women managed the home and social obligations in the private sphere. The curriculum of the Litchfield Academy included reading, writing, composition, and English grammar; geography; ancient and modern history; philosophy and logic; spelling; and simple needlework.

Raised in a Calvinist household, Beecher studied music and drawing. Breaking with the Calvinist teachings of her father, which advocated strict separate spheres, she settled into what many members of her society saw as an acceptable occupation for a single woman: teaching. She planned to marry a mariner, which meant that she would need an occupation while he was at sea. Beecher's first teaching opportunity came in 1821 when she was hired to teach music and drawing in New London, Connecticut. After the death of her fiancé, Alexander Metcalf Fisher, at sea in 1823, Catharine inherited a small fortune from his estate. She and her sister Mary Foote Beecher used this money to establish a school for girls in Hartford, Connecticut, that evolved into the Hartford Female Seminary. Mary did the bulk of the basic teaching, leaving Catharine time to develop her own teaching philosophy, one in which academic excellence was fostered.

The Hartford Female Seminary differed from other schools that prepared girls for refined lifestyles because at the Seminary the students performed calisthenics. Beecher, like Lydia Maria Child who authored *The Girl's Own Book* (1828), focused on reforming the standards of diet, exercise, and restrictive clothing for women. Exercise played an important role in the education of young women at the Hartford Seminary. Beecher, in *Suggestions Respecting Improvements in Education* (1829), proposed that mothers and female teachers could fulfill the role traditionally held by ministers in educating the mind as well as nurturing a healthy soul.

When the Beecher family relocated to Cincinnati, Ohio, in 1831, Beecher continued in her chosen profession and continued writing. She and sister Harriet established the Western Female Institute. In 1832 Catharine and Harriet joined the Semi-Colon Club, an early literary discussion group for men and women. During the 1830s, Winthrop B. Smith of Truman & Smith, a Cincinnati publishing company, approached Catharine to compile a series of readers that would contain didactic literature from the best authors of the day, but she declined the offer. Young Calvinist schoolmaster William Holmes McGuffey accepted the challenge and developed the successful *McGuffey Eclectic Readers*. Beecher assisted him with the *Fourth Eclectic Reader* published in 1837. That year's financial panic forced Beecher's Western Female

A proponent of women's education and the author of the widely read *Treatise on Domestic Economy*, Catharine Beecher served as a self-appointed counselor to women of the United States in the nineteenth century. (Cirker, Hayward and Blanche Cirker, eds., *Dictionary of American Portraits*, 1967)

Institute to file for bankruptcy, but the setback did not slow Beecher down. She ignited a strenuous public debate through her much publicized correspondence with Southern abolitionists, Angelina and Sarah Grimké, in response to her *Essay on Slavery and Abolition* (1837).

Beecher's *A Treatise on Domestic Economy for the Use of Young Ladies at Home and at School* (1843) opened with a chapter describing the distinct characteristics of American women in contrast to Englishwomen. Beecher proposed that American women should be trained in domestic economy to gain the logical and practical skills needed to manage a household. Beecher felt that this pedagogy could be imparted when girls were between the ages of ten and fourteen years and that it could be best taught institutionally when girls were fifteen years of age. Instruction offered in Beecher's

book allowed girls at the age of sixteen to fulfill their prescribed roles in the household, whether for family, for hire, or for their own households. Reflecting her background in the ideals of Republican Motherhood, Beecher argued that this curriculum for women was central to the moral and political foundations of the nation.

Beecher was concerned that American women were being trained haphazardly to expound on frivolous and esoteric subjects, while the practical skills needed to build successful and healthy lives were neglected. She observed with irony that girls could easily construct and explain a geometric diagram "with far more skill" than they could a garment using the same geometric principles. Beecher argued that women in nineteenth-century America needed to master skills that would make their families self-sufficient in rural settings or that would have value-added benefits to families in urban environments. Beecher wanted to standardize American domestic practices, providing women with the values of self-reliance, hard work, egalitarianism, and independence within the home and family. As a result, she included sections in her book on preparing healthy food, maintaining cleanliness, systematically managing home and children, propagating plants, and basic animal husbandry. She developed a curriculum in home economy with a specific sensibility that the work of women should be valued in antebellum society.

In 1846, *Miss Beecher's Domestic Receipt-Book* was published as a supplementary manual on cooking. This work departed from other cookbooks printed in America that were simply reprints of British cookbooks because Beecher felt American women needed more practical advice. Accordingly, she included an entire chapter on preparing hashes, gravies, and sauces, suggesting that she valued hashes—dishes that combined chopped-up meat leftovers and potatoes—as a way to avoid waste. Her *Treatise on Domestic Economy* and her *Domestic Receipt-Book* were sold door-to-door throughout the country.

Throughout her career, Beecher worked for education reform as well as for women's rights. In 1852, she helped form the American Women's Educational Association to expand educational opportunities for women by sending teachers to Western frontier towns. She authored dozens of articles and books on female education that challenged patriarchy. Concerned with the health of American women, Beecher asked women she met on her travels to provide impressions on the health of ten women in their acquaintance. She compiled these responses in *Letters to People on Health and Happiness* (1855). Later, in her *An Appeal to the People on Behalf of their Rights as Authorized Interpreters of the Bible* (1860), Beecher challenged Calvinist doctrines and the authority of the ministry.

In the years leading up to the Civil War, Beecher's influence was eclipsed by sister Harriet's *Uncle Tom's Cabin,* a novel that invigorated the abolitionist movement and brought slavery to the forefront of people's minds. In 1869, the sisters collaborated on combining *Treatise on Domestic Economy* and *Domestic Receipt-Book* into the *American Woman's Home.*

Catharine Beecher's legacy was established in her argument that women's roles in the domestic and educational sphere were the foundations for social advancement and the cornerstone of American democracy. Beecher used Christian rhetoric to show women a new schema for creating professional domestic work, hoping to illustrate how rationalism and utilitarianism could give women the opportunity to turn ordinary female activities into a means to achieve success.

Catharine Beecher died in Elmira, New York, on May 12, 1878.

*Meredith Eliassen*

**See also** Domesticity; Fiction Writers, Northern; Grimké (Weld), Angelina (1805–1879); Grimké, Sarah Moore (1792–1873); Stowe, Harriet Elizabeth Beecher (1811–1896); Teachers, Northern.

**References and Further Reading**
Beecher, Catharine. 1850. *Miss Beecher's Domestic Receipt-Book: Designed as a Supplement to Her Treatise on Domestic Economy.* New York: Harper.
Kelley, Mary. 1984. *Private Women, Public Stage: Literary Domesticity in Nineteenth-Century America.* New York: Oxford University Press.
Lerner, Gerda. 1998. *The Grimké Sisters from South Carolina: Pioneers for Women's Rights and Abolition.* New York: Oxford University Press.
Fields, Catherine Keene, and Lisa C. Kightlinger, eds. 1993. *To Ornament Their Minds: Sarah Pierce's Litchfield Female Academy, 1792–1833.* Litchfield, CT: Litchfield Historical Society.
White, Barbara A. 2003. *The Beecher Sisters.* New Haven, CT: Yale University Press.
Sklar, Katherine Kish. 1973. *Catharine Beecher: A Study in American Domesticity.* New Haven, CT: Yale University Press.

## Bickerdyke, Mary Ann Ball "Mother" (1817–1901)

Mary Ann Ball "Mother" Bickerdyke nursed soldiers during the Civil War as part of a private effort to relieve the suffering of the troops.

She was born on a pioneer farm in Knox County, Ohio, on July 19, 1817, to Hiram and Annie Rodgers Ball. When Mary Ann was seventeen months old, her mother died, and the child went to live with her maternal grandparents in Richland County, Ohio. She remained with them until her father remarried a few years later. She returned to her grandparents at the age of twelve, before joining an uncle in Cincinnati.

In 1833, when she was sixteen, Ball went to Oberlin, Ohio, with the apparent intention of enrolling at newly opened Oberlin College. She likely found work in the household of a faculty member and audited classes, accounting for her later claim that she attended Oberlin. At some point, she may have attended classes at the Physio-Botanic Medical College, a school that was part of a medical reform movement that, unlike the established medical system, welcomed women. Ball's activities from 1837 to 1847 are unknown, but she may have worked as a botanic physician. On April 27, 1847, Ball married musician and housepainter Robert Bickerdyke, a Cincinnati widower with three young children. The couple had three children, but their only daughter died in early childhood.

Cincinnati, located just across the river from slaveholding Kentucky, was an important stop on the Underground Railroad. Bickerdyke received fugitive slaves into her house, hid them for as long as necessary, and helped them move on to a Quaker group in nearby Hamilton, the next stage on the road to Canada. Often, she drove them to Hamilton herself, using her husband's wagon and team. A move to Galesburg, Illinois, in 1856 presumably halted Bickerdyke's work with fugitive slaves.

In March 1859, Robert Bickerdyke suddenly died. Left penniless with two young sons to support, Bickerdyke opened a practice as a botanic physician. Much like a visiting nurse, Bickerdyke went into homes, bathed the patient, kept a sharp eye on the diet, opened the windows, and lectured the family on the need for cleanliness and fresh air. As a Civil War nurse, she would employ the same therapeutic practices, much to the outrage of army doctors. Bickerdyke's experience as a botanic physician gave her the confidence with which she later challenged army surgeons.

When the Civil War began, military and political authorities occupied themselves with raising and equipping armed forces. They gave almost no attention to the care of the sick and wounded. Field hospitals consisted of a few sheds or barns, a cabin, or a church containing no beds and almost no surgical supplies. Following a battle, wounded soldiers were carried in and laid on the bare floors to wait until transport could be arranged. Three or four army surgeons moved from one station to another, contriving bandages from the patient's own shirt if he seemed likely to bleed to death. Army doctors paid little attention to soldiers with civilian diseases such as typhoid or pneumonia. Such men were typically cared for by other convalescent patients.

The members of the Brick Congregational Church in Galesburg, Illinois, received a letter in 1861 from a local physician who had volunteered for the Union with five hundred other Galesburg men at the war's start. The physician reported that Galesburg soldiers were dying in filthy, ill equipped hospital tents of diseases that would not have killed them if they had received proper care. Anxious to protect their own sons, the parishioners sent supplies and Bickerdyke to the army hospital at Cairo, Illinois. Bickerdyke had medical knowledge, and, as her neighbors knew, she was a plainspoken, energetic woman who would not be intimidated by army authorities resentful of civilian interference. Essentially a stand-in for Galesburg parents, she was

Mary Ann Ball "Mother" Bickerdyke, a Civil War nurse known for her motherly treatment of wounded troops. (Library of Congress)

expected to judge whether the supplies sent were suitable, to advise of future supply needs, and to demand proper treatment for soldiers.

Reaching Cairo on June 9, 1861, Bickerdyke found that conditions in the regimental hospital tents were even worse than she had been led to expect. Without asking permission from anyone, she immediately set to work cleaning, nursing, and feeding the sick men. Bickerdyke moved about with a decisive air and gave directions in such decided, clarion tones as to ensure prompt obedience. The wounded called her Mother because she reminded them of their own mothers. She would continue in this work, both at the general hospital behind the front lines and at field hospitals, for the remainder of the war. In recognition of her success at saving men, she became the matron of the general hospital at Cairo in November 1861.

After helping evacuate the wounded from the Battle of Fort Donelson in February 1862, Bickerdyke decided that the most pressing need for nursing assistance was at the front. She joined General Ulysses S. Grant's army as it moved to control of the Mississippi River. For seven months, Bickerdyke worked at Union field hospitals in Memphis, Tennessee, at Iuka, Mississippi, and at Corinth, Mississippi. She laundered soiled clothing, negotiated with Confederate farmers to obtain food for the wounded, prepared vast quantities of food, and distributed tons of supplies.

Until this time, Bickerdyke had no commission from anyone in authority, although some military leaders such as Grant tolerated her presence. When challenged by an army surgeon who asked under whose authority she fed the wounded men, Bickerdyke once famously replied that she received her authority from the Lord God Almighty. In April 1862, Bickerdyke gained some authority when Chicago's Northwestern Sanitary Commission, whose food and medical supplies she had been unofficially distributing since her days in Cairo, appointed her an agent in the field.

Bickerdyke had gained some national renown at Fort Donelson by using a lantern to search the battlefield for wounded men at midnight before they froze to death. Newspaper reporters, having spotted a colorful character, publicized her activities and made Bickerdyke one of the best-known Civil War nurses. The Sanitary Commission took advantage of Bickerdyke's fame and sent her on a speaking tour in 1862 to raise funds to purchase more supplies. Convinced by her botanic training and by her own experience that wounded men did better if they were fed at once, Bickerdyke also obtained donated cows and chickens to give the men fresh milk and eggs.

Bickerdyke counseled the Sanitary Commission on the need for female nurses. In her opinion, the men who came to the battle sites with the Sanitary Commission knew little about caring for the sick, whereas a mother learned to give such care as her children grew up. Unfortunately, few women volunteers had Bickerdyke's energy or stomach for the horrors of war. Most of the women who joined Bickerdyke, with the exceptions of Mary Jane Safford and Eliza Chappell Porter, did not remain for long. Both Safford and Porter collapsed from overwork. At the Battles of Lookout Mountain and Missionary

Ridge in 1863, Bickerdyke was the only woman caring for seventeen hundred Union wounded at the field hospital of the Fifteenth Army Corps.

Bickerdyke accompanied General William T. Sherman's army as it marched toward Atlanta. After accompanying hospital trains as they moved north with wounded, she spent a couple of months on a Sanitary Commission speaking tour and had planned to rejoin Sherman's army. On the way to Savannah with supplies, Bickerdyke encountered emaciated Union soldiers making their way home from the Confederate prison camp at Andersonville, Georgia. She nursed some of the Andersonville survivors and was with Sherman when the war ended. Proceeding to Washington, D.C., with Sherman's forces, she had an honored place in the victory parade. In March 1866, Bickerdyke resigned her Sanitary Commission position after helping in the demobilization of Illinois soldiers.

Bickerdyke never stopped trying to aid Union soldiers. In 1867, she surrendered her job as assistant superintendent of Chicago's Home for the Friendless, a charity for indigent women and children. She joined a short-lived project that provided farms in Kansas to unemployed Union veterans. Bickerdyke made periodic trips to Washington, D.C., to press the pension claims of men she had known at the front, and she frequently visited veterans in soldiers' homes. Having moved to San Francisco in 1876 because of failing health, she helped organize the California branch of the Woman's Relief Corps, an auxiliary of the Grand Army of the Republic veteran's organization. In 1886, Congress recognized Bickerdyke with a monthly pension of $25.

Mary Ann Ball Bickerdyke died in Kansas on November 8, 1901, and is buried in Galesburg, Illinois.

*Caryn E. Neumann*

***See also*** Abolitionism and Northern Reformers; African American Women; Aid Societies; Disease; Education, Northern; Fundraising; Hospitals; Hospital Ships; Military Invasion and Occupation; Northern Women; Nurses; Politics; Safford [Stafford], Mary Jane (ca. 1831/1834–1891); Sherman, William Tecumseh (1820–1891); Union Homefront; United States Sanitary Commission; Wartime Employment.

**References and Further Reading**

Baker, Nina Brown. 1952. *Cyclone in Calico: The Story of Mary Ann Bickerdyke.* Boston: Little, Brown and Company.

Denney, Robert E. 1994. *Civil War Medicine: Care and Comfort of the Wounded.* New York: Sterling Publishing Co.

Freemon, Frank R. 2001. *Gangrene and Glory: Medical Care During the American Civil War.* Urbana: University of Illinois Press.

Livermore, Mary. 1978. *My Story of the War: A Woman's Narrative of Four Years Personal Experience as a Nurse in the Union Army.* Williamstown, MA: Corner House. (Orig. pub. 1887.)

Reverby, Susan M. 1987. *Ordered to Care: The Dilemma of American Nursing, 1850–1945.* New York: Cambridge University Press.

## Blackwell, Elizabeth (1821–1910)

Famous for her pioneering work on behalf of women entering the profession of medicine, Dr. Elizabeth Blackwell was the founder, in the 1850s, of the New York Infirmary for Women and Children (NYIWC). At the outset of the Civil War, she spearheaded New York meetings that led to the formation of the Woman's Central Association of Relief (WCAR), a centralized agency that organized volunteer efforts to meet the emerging needs of ill and wounded Union soldiers. Blackwell's activism contributed to the establishment of the United States Sanitary Commission (USSC) by the Department of War in June 1861. As a leader in the Ladies' Sanitary Aid Association, she helped coordinate work through the NYIWC and the Cooper Institute for the rest of the war. With her sister Dr. Emily Blackwell, Elizabeth coordinated the selection of volunteers for the training of wartime nurses through Bellevue Hospital. The new nurses were sent on to Dorothea Dix, who, as the Union's superintendent for nurses, placed them in military hospitals, battlefields, and wards. Blackwell viewed the war as a rebellion to preserve slavery and described her own actions as doing what she could for "freedom and justice" (Blackwell 1895, 235).

Elizabeth Blackwell was born near Bristol, England and immigrated with her reformist family to the United States at the age of eleven. Family

Elizabeth Blackwell was the first woman to receive a medical degree in the United States. (Library of Congress)

friends included William Lloyd Garrison, Harriet Beecher Stowe, and other prominent abolitionists. Blackwell was strongly influenced by Transcendentalism and Unitarianism and later by Christian Socialist thought. The death of her father, Samuel Blackwell, in Ohio in 1838 led her into work as a schoolteacher.

After studying medicine privately in the South and being turned away by major medical schools of the East, she gained admittance at Geneva Medical College in western New York. When she graduated in 1849, she became the first woman to earn a professional medical degree in the United States. She emphasized in her work the importance of sanitation and hygiene in public health. After further study and hospital experience in the United States and England, she opened a dispensary in lower Manhattan and treated impoverished residents of the nearby tenements. This service evolved, in 1857, into the Bleeker Street NYIWC. There Blackwell worked side by side with her sister Emily and with Dr. Marie E. Zakrzewska, who later founded the New England Hospital for Women and Children in Boston.

Blackwell's friendship with Florence Nightingale and her knowledge of Nightingale's work in the Crimea encouraged her to do relief work and deepened her resolve to develop a nursing school and eventually a medical school for women through the NYIWC. The immediate need for trained nurses in the war made Blackwell postpone plans for the medical school until after the war's end. The school for women physicians she had envisioned was established in 1868 and operated until 1899. Soon after it was established, however, Blackwell left the United States. Leaving the operation of the NYIWC to Emily, she moved to Britain in 1869 and maintained her residence and her medical career there for the rest of her life.

*Barbara Bair*

*See also* Abolitionism and Northern Reformers; Disease; Dix, Dorothea Lynde (1802–1887); Garrison, William Lloyd (1805–1879); Hospitals; Northern Women; Nurses; Stowe, Harriet Elizabeth Beecher (1811–1896); Union Homefront; United States Sanitary Commission; Women's Central Association of Relief; Zakrzewska, Maria [Marie Elizabeth] (1829–1902).

**References and Further Reading**

Blackwell, Elizabeth. 1895. *Pioneer Work in Opening the Medical Profession to Women.* London and New York: Longmans, Green & Company.

Ross, Ishbel. 1949. *Child of Destiny.* London: Gollancz.

Sanchez, Regina Morantz. 2000 [1985]. *Sympathy and Science: Women Physicians in American Medicine.* Chapel Hill: University of North Carolina Press. Reprint with new preface.

## Blair, Lorinda Ann [Annie Etheridge Hooks] (ca. 1840–1913)

Annie Etheridge Hooks, born Lorinda Anna Blair, is best-known for her bravery as a nurse in the Civil War, tending to wounded soldiers on the front lines of battle.

Lorinda Anna Blair was born in Detroit, Michigan, around 1840, with sources placing her year of birth anywhere between 1832 and 1844. After her mother died when Annie was young, she moved with her father, a merchant, to Milwaukee.

In 1860, Annie married James Etheridge. She returned to Detroit, where she enlisted as a regimental nurse when her husband joined the Second Michigan Infantry in 1861. After training for six weeks, the regiment left for Washington, D.C. By this point, Annie was the only woman left out of the twenty women who had enlisted with her.

Named the Daughter of the Regiment, Annie served with the Second Michigan Infantry for three years. On July 18, 1861, her regiment first engaged in war at Blackburn's Ford, with the Union troops losing seventy-eight men and the Confederates, sixty-eight. A few days later, on July 21, 1861, at the First Battle of Bull Run (Manassas), Annie's regiment was ordered to guard an escape route to Washington. Shortly after this battle, her husband deserted, but Annie stayed on with the regiment.

In the spring of 1862, Annie left the Second Michigan Infantry to work on hospital ships, transporting wounded soldiers to hospitals in New York, Washington, and Baltimore. In August 1862, she returned to regiment work, this time with the Third Michigan Infantry Regiment. That month, her regiment was involved in the Second Battle of Bull Run (Manassas), and Annie was on the front lines tending to the injured.

Throughout the war, Annie aided the wounded, serving in thirty-two battles, including the Battle of Antietam, the Battle of Fredericksburg, the Battle of Gettysburg, and the Battle of Chancellorsville. Besides providing medical care, there are accounts of her cooking and serving food to the soldiers. Even though she bravely served on the front lines of many of the war's bloodiest battles, the only wound she ever received was a shot to the hand.

In June 1864, the veterans of the Third Michigan Infantry, including Annie, were transferred to the Fifth Michigan Infantry Regiment, with which she served from 1864 to July 5, 1865, when it was mustered out of service. During this time, she also worked in a Union military hospital in City Point, Virginia, during the winter.

After the war, Annie worked as a clerk in the U.S. Pension Office in Washington. In 1870, she married Charles E. Hooks, a Civil War veteran of the Seventh Connecticut Infantry. In 1886, Congress authorized

Blair to receive a $25-a-month pension acknowledging her military service. She died in 1913 and was buried with honors in Arlington National Cemetery.

*Sigrid Kelsey*

**See also** Antietam/Sharpsburg, Battle of (September 17, 1862); Chancellorsville, Battle of (April 29–May 6, 1863); Fredericksburg, Battle of (December 13, 1862); Gettysburg, Battle of (July 1–3, 1863); Hospital Ships; Nurses; Vivandieres.
**References and Further Reading**
Eggleston, Larry G. 2003. *Women in the Civil War: Extraordinary Stories of Soldiers, Spies, Nurses, Doctors, Crusaders, and Others.* Jefferson, NC: McFarland.
Leonard, Elizabeth D. 1999. *All the Daring of the Soldier: Women of the Civil War Armies.* New York: W. W. Norton.
Schultz, Jane E. 2004. *Women at the Front: Hospital Workers in Civil War America.* Chapel Hill: University of North Carolina Press.

## Blalock, Malinda [Sam Blalock]
## (ca. 1840–1901)

Malinda Blalock is thought to be the only woman to fight on both sides of the Civil War, and she is the only woman known to have fought as a man from North Carolina.

Born Sarah Malinda Pritchard in about 1840 in Caldwell County, North Carolina, to Alfred and Elizabeth Pritchard, Malinda married William McKesson "Keith" Blalock in April 1861, at a small church near Grandfather Mountain in Watauga County. The two were Unionists.

Keith decided to join the Confederate army, desert as soon as possible, and join the Union army. Malinda cut her hair short and enlisted with Keith on March 20, 1862 as Sam Blalock in Company F, Twenty-sixth Regiment, North Carolina Troops. Malinda had assumed the name of Keith's half brother, and she claimed she was his brother. The Blalocks shared the same tent and drilled side by side until April 20, 1862, when Keith deceitfully obtained a discharge. Having realized that deserting to join the Union would not be easy, Keith rubbed himself with poison sumac and was subsequently discharged. Malinda then disclosed her identity as a woman and she was discharged as well.

Keith's deception was soon discovered and he was charged with desertion. He lived on Grandfather Mountain with several other deserters before fleeing for a short time to Tennessee, where he became a recruiter for a Michigan regiment.

Unionists at heart, Malinda and Keith went back to the North Carolina mountains and played an active role in the guerrilla raids and personal vendettas that characterized the war in that part of the state in 1864. The Blalocks joined George W. Kirk's partisan unit in North Carolina. Keith also served as a guide for Confederate deserters and for Unionists who were trying to make their way through the mountains to Federal lines in Tennessee.

In 1864, Malinda was wounded in a skirmish, and in another engagement Keith was blinded in one eye. In 1865 Keith shot and killed a man whom he believed had killed his stepfather Austin Coffey. Keith was apprehended, but, before he was brought to trial, he was pardoned by Governor William W. Holden.

After the war, the Blalocks became farmers in Mitchell County, North Carolina, and had at least four children: Columbus, John, Willie, and Samuel. Malinda died on March 9, 1901. She and her husband, who died August 11, 1913, are buried in the Montezuma Cemetery in Avery County, North Carolina.

*Gwen Thomas Mays*

**See also** Female Combatants.
**References and Further Reading**
Jordan, Waymouth T. Jr. 1979. *North Carolina Troops 1861–1865: A Roster.* Raleigh, NC: Division of Archives and History.
Leonard, Elizabeth D. 1999. *All the Daring of the Soldier: Women of the Civil War Armies.* New York: W. W. Norton.
McCrumb, Sharyn. 2003. *Ghost Riders.* New York: Dutton.
Stevens, Peter F. 2000. *Rebels in Blue: The Story of Keith and Malinda Blalock.* Dallas, TX: Taylor Publishing Company.

## Blockade Running

Eluding the Union naval blockade of Confederate seaports contributed to the very survival of the Confederacy. Beginning in 1861, the United States Navy stationed warships at the entrances to Southern ports, preventing the export of Southern cotton and the import of manufactured goods from Europe. Blockade runners—fast ships that sneaked past the Union Navy—transported cotton to Europe and the Caribbean while importing needed manufactured goods, weaponry, food, and luxury items to the South.

On April 19, 1861, President Abraham Lincoln issued an order to begin a naval blockade of Confederate seaports. In what would eventually become part of the Anaconda Plan, the Federal navy attempted to choke off the supply of goods entering and leaving the South. Because of the South's

reliance on agriculture—cotton and tobacco provided the majority of revenue for Southerners—few manufacturing centers were located in the South at the outbreak of the Civil War. Most manufactured goods, raw materials, and luxury items came from the North or from Europe. Union military strategists hoped that a blockade would force the Confederacy to its knees, leaving it unable to fight without supplies.

Even as the flow of manufactured goods slowed to a trickle, Southern factories shifted to war production. The Confederate government asked civilians to become self-sufficient to weather the crisis. Women absorbed the brunt of the shortages, especially in regard to cloth. With the decline of

Group of people on the deck of the USS *Hendrick Hudson.* Originally known as the CSS *Florida.* the ship was a Confederate blockade runner, later captured by Union forces and renamed. Southern women depended on runners such as the *Florida* to provide them with supplies like cloth, newspapers, books, foodstuffs, and luxuries during the Civil War. (National Archives and Records Administration)

domestic cloth manufacturing after the Revolution, most households purchased their clothing. Jefferson Davis and other Confederate officials urged women to make their own clothing as a patriotic gesture. However, elite women initially scoffed at the thought of wearing "Negro cloth" and therefore continued to buy clothing, imported by blockade runners from Bermuda, Nassau, or Havana. Clothing remained a staple cargo for import, since Southern women demanded it in such large quantities.

Refraining from mandating what the blockade runners could bring into the South, the Confederate government opted to allow ships to operate privately with little government oversight. For that reason, blockade running became extremely profitable. Those who could finance a ship and take the risk of running the blockade could reap incredible profits by providing wealthy Southerners with items that allowed them to continue their luxurious lifestyles. Ship captains favored highly profitable and easily transportable goods, such as clothing, medicine, and liquor, over bulkier products like foodstuffs.

Because the privatization of blockade running led to favoring luxury items over necessities such as sugar, flour, and meat, poor women had to deal with the loss of necessities more than their wealthy counterparts did. By 1865, prices for certain foodstuffs rose by more than one hundred times their 1861 level, with the inland areas suffering more than the port cities. Women, responsible for the family food supply, had to increase their household's production or find alternative sources of food for the family to survive. One alternative source in which women found food was the very institution that caused the shortages: the blockade runners. Both Georgia and North Carolina hired ships to run the Union blockade to export state-owned cotton and to bring back much needed foodstuffs and cotton cards.

Blockade runners also participated in the Confederacy's clandestine operations. At least two female spies, Rose O'Neal Greenhow and Belle Boyd, traveled by blockade runner to either collect or return information about Union forces to Confederate officials. The information these women gathered and delivered through the blockade helped plan military maneuvers.

Finally, blockade runners also linked women to the outside world. Each time they returned, ships brought mail, newspapers, and books from the North and Europe. For women in the South with relatives elsewhere, blockade runners provided an invaluable communication service. The importation of books and newspapers brought joy to educated elite women because the majority of book publishers resided in the North. Newspapers also helped to inform elite women of the political, economic, and social situation in both Europe and the North.

*James Gigantino*

**See also** Female Spies; Greenhow, Rose O'Neal (ca. 1814–1864); Homespun.

### References and Further Reading

Cochran, Hamilton. 1973. *Blockade Runners of the Confederacy.* Westport, CT: Greenwood Press.

Massey, Mary Elizabeth. 1952. *Ersatz in the Confederacy: Shortages and Substitutes on the Southern Homefront.* Columbia: University of South Carolina Press.

Wise, Stephen. 1988. *Lifeline of the Confederacy: Blockade Running during the Civil War.* Columbia: University of South Carolina Press.

## Border States

Women in the Border States, traditionally considered Missouri, Kentucky, Maryland, and Delaware, experienced the Civil War somewhat differently than either their Northern or Southern counterparts. Although they offered their men up to the cause, supplied and supported them, and faced their enemies with as much bravery as their Union and Confederate sisters, the status of the Border States during the war created unique circumstances for their female residents. The Border States played a pivotal role in the war: Their economies were tied to both sections, their men fought and died for both sides, and both governments and their armies competed for control of the region throughout the war.

The Union military held official control of the states by the early years of the conflict, but Confederate sentiment remained a powerful force, competing for civilian loyalties throughout the war. Slavery remained entrenched in these states' economies, and Abraham Lincoln's Emancipation Proclamation (and its nonapplication to these states) was designed specifically to secure Border State loyalty. The divided nature of the war experience in these states naturally affected the women. They faced family, friends, and neighbors with opposite sympathies to their own; endured political, social, and economic consequences for their devotions; withstood the seemingly constant presence of invading and occupying armies; and attempted to sustain themselves and their families in the midst of it all. The homefront in the Border States was truly contested terrain, with women playing out the political tensions within their families and communities on a daily basis.

Socially, women in the Border States faced pressures that their counterparts in the North or South did not deal with every day. Throughout all the Border States, loyalties were divided. Families turned against each other, and once friendly neighbors now looked on each other with suspicion. Perhaps more than in other regions, the Civil War divided families in the Border States. While the typical description of a civil war is a brothers' war, women, as wives, mothers, and sisters, were also often caught up in family feuds resulting from the conflict. If fathers and sons argued over loyalties or decided to fight for opposing sides, women tried to relieve the tension through mediation or by maintaining communication between the estranged members. Open dialogue may have existed between brothers and sisters with differing views, but tension over wartime matters could tear families apart.

In the patriarchal society of the mid-nineteenth century, loyalty disputes between husband and wife were frowned on, but they existed during the war. With wartime politics at the forefront of debate, a woman's political disagreement with her husband might be acceptable only if it remained confined to private discussion. Public demonstrations of loyalty opposite that of a spouse carried shame and fueled tension within many Border State families. The bonds between women, as friends and within families, were also strained as a result of the war.

Friends with opposite sympathies would often limit their discussion of war topics to avoid breaking the relationship. Some tensions reached a point when relatives or friends halted all communication with one another.

Women's interaction with troops was high in the Border States as the governments competed for control over the population. Soldiers continuously passed through these states on their way to the front, and women from both sides met them with provisions and emotional support. Women also offered to care for sick and wounded men; even if the wounded soldier was in an enemy uniform, women often took pity on the individual, overlooking political loyalties for humanity's sake. Personal relations between women and enemy soldiers developed, but society generally discouraged flowering romances between partners of opposite loyalties. Not only would family and friends express their disapproval, but also newspaper editors frequently warned against the possible ulterior motives the participants might bring to such a relationship during a time of war.

Union efforts to suppress Confederate influence in the Border States resulted in military policy that directly affected the women there. In 1863 in Kentucky, General Ambrose Burnside's General Order Number 66, issued in an effort to quell ongoing domestic resistance in that state, required Kentucky women who were married to Confederate soldiers either to swear loyalty to the Union or to face exile to the South. Even if the women were not married to a Confederate, once the state was under Union control in 1862, any support or association with the enemy warranted punishment. For instance, throughout the war, Confederate Cavalry General John Hunt Morgan made frequent raids in the state, and Union commanders sent any woman who publicly displayed support for the rebels to prison and further threatened her with exile from the state.

Similarly, in 1863 Missouri, Brigadier General Thomas Ewing issued General Order Number 11, calling for the evacuation of the civilian population from the western counties of Missouri, whose wartime experience was rife with guerrilla raids rather than organized military engagements. The women in the state, often out of fear of retribution as much as Confederate sympathy, frequently supplied the bands with food, shelter, and other provisions. In an effort to quell such civilian support and in direct response to repeated and increasingly violent guerrilla raids by William Quantrill, Ewing issued his order. If citizens in the region could establish loyalty to the Union, they would be permitted to return home; otherwise, all men, women, and children remaining devoted to the Confederacy would be forced to leave the state. The order produced widespread outrage; the public perceived it as cruelly affecting innocent women and children while not succeeding in eliminating the guerrilla threat.

Economically, socially, and politically, Maryland held strong ties to the Confederacy as war tensions grew. However, despite strong pro-Southern leanings, Maryland earned quick attention from the Union forces especially because of its geographic proximity to the Union capital, Washington, D.C. As a result, once war was declared, Maryland found herself flooded with Union troops and its citizens' abilities to express Confederate sympathies severely restricted. Interactions with soldiers from both sides became common for women in the state, especially when large battles like the one fought at Antietam broke out within the state's borders.

Women in Delaware had similar experiences. Despite its leading politicians' sympathies for the Confederacy, the civilian population proved more loyal to the Union than to the Confederacy. The state's slave population was not large, and its industrial potential proved valuable to the Union.

All four Border States' strongest tie to the Confederacy was the presence of slavery within their borders. While the slave population was not as great in these states as it was in those of the Deep South, the assertion of the right to own slaves and the corresponding racial attitudes provided a strong connection to the seceded states. Slave women in these areas frequently faced harsher treatment, including sexual assault, by invading military or guerrilla forces. These women also saw their men impressed into military service by both sides, putting added strain on their circumstances. Hope for freedom under the Emancipation Proclamation was dashed when the Border States were exempted from the policy.

*Kristen L. Streater*

***See also*** African American Women; Antietam/Sharpsburg, Battle of (September 17, 1862); Civilian Life; Confederate Homefront; Emancipation Proclamation (January 1, 1863); Family Life, Confederate; Family Life, Union; Foraging, Effects on Women; Guerrilla Warfare; Impressment; Loyalty Oaths; Military Invasion and Occupation; Northern Women; Politics; Quantrill, William Clarke (1837–1865); Rape; Refugees; Shortages; Slaveholding Women; Southern Women; Union Homefront.

## References and Further Reading

Cottom, Robert I., and Mary Ellen Hayward. 1994. *Maryland and the Civil War: A House Divided.* Baltimore: Maryland Historical Society.

Denton, Lawrence M. 1995. *A Southern Star for Maryland: Maryland and the Secession Crisis, 1860–1861.* Baltimore, MD: Publishing Concepts.

Gilmore, Donald L. 2006. *Civil War on the Missouri-Kansas Border.* Gretna, LA: Pelican Publishing Company.

Harrison, Lowell H. 1975. *The Civil War in Kentucky.* Lexington: University Press of Kentucky.

McKnight, Brian D. 2006. *Contested Borderland: The Civil War in Appalachian Kentucky and Virginia.* Lexington: University Press of Kentucky.

Taylor, Amy Murrell. 2005. *The Divided Family in Civil War America.* Chapel Hill: University of North Carolina Press.

## Bowser, Mary Elizabeth (ca. 1839–n.d.)

Little is known of Union spy Mary Elizabeth Bowser's life before or after the Civil War. During the war, she worked with Elizabeth Van Lew in Richmond to get information on Confederate war operations.

She was born a slave on the Richmond, Virginia plantation of John Van Lew. Upon his death, probably in 1851, his wife and daughter freed their slaves and purchased and manumitted a number of their former slaves' relatives. The daughter, Elizabeth Van Lew, became well-known as an abolitionist in Richmond during the 1850s. She arranged for Mary to be educated at the Quaker School for Negroes in Philadelphia. Mary returned to Richmond in 1861, and at the outbreak of the Civil War she married Wilson Bowser, a free black man.

During the Civil War, Mary's former owner, Elizabeth Van Lew, operated a Union spy ring in Richmond. Van Lew was able to allay suspicion by affecting an attitude of eccentric behavior, coming to be called Crazy Bet. Van Lew arranged for Bowser's employment as a servant in the household of Confederate President Jefferson Davis. There Bowser posed as a dull but hardworking slave and gained access to both conversations and documents concerning the most sensitive activities of the Confederate government and military. Bowser would repeat what she learned to Van Lew or to Thomas McNiven, the Union's Richmond spymaster, who operated a bakery that became a major information clearinghouse. McNiven credited Bowser with being one of his best sources of wartime intelligence because of her photographic memory.

It became obvious to Confederate authorities that there was a leak in the Davis household, but suspicion did not fall on Bowser until January 1865 when she chose to flee from Richmond to the North. Some reports indicate that her last act as a Union spy and sympathizer was an unsuccessful attempt to burn down the Confederate White House.

The specific details of Bowser's activities and the exact information she passed to the Union will never be known. After the war, the Federal government destroyed its records on McNiven, Van Lew, and their agents to protect them from retaliation by Confederate sympathizers.

Mary Elizabeth Bowser dropped out of sight after the Civil War. Nothing is known about where she went or what she did, and the date and place of her death are unknown. Papers believed to have been Bowser's diaries were apparently discarded by family members in the 1950s. Her descendants rarely talked about Bowser's work out of the same fear of retaliation that prompted the government to destroy the records of her activities.

The American government honored Mary Elizabeth Bowser's contributions in 1995 by inducting her into the Military Intelligence Corps Hall of Fame at Fort Huachuca, Arizona.

*Robert D. Bohanan*

**See also** African American Women; Female Spies; Van Lew, Elizabeth (1818–1900).

**References and Further Reading**

Coleman, Penny. 1992. *Spies!: Women in the Civil War.* White Hall, VA: Shoe Tree Press.
Ryan, David D. 1996. *A Yankee Spy in Richmond: the Civil War Diary of "Crazy Bet" Van Lew.* Mechanicsburg, PA: Stackpole Books.

## Boyd, Belle (1844–1900)

Confederate spy Marie Isabella "Belle" Boyd was born in 1844 in Martinsburg, Virginia (now West Virginia). Her father, Benjamin Reed Boyd, provided well for his family through the direction of a general store and a tobacco plantation. His success allowed the Boyd family to live a comfortable life, surrounded by household slaves, and provided Belle with an education appropriate for a Southern girl of her status.

Just weeks before Belle's seventeenth birthday, Virginia seceded from the Union and her father enlisted to serve under Confederate General Thomas "Stonewall" Jackson. Belle and her family found themselves in the midst of the Civil War as the Shenandoah Valley remained a key front throughout the conflict, experiencing over one hundred military engagements. A young and adventurous Belle found several opportunities to serve the Southern war effort in an area that was constantly exchanged between Confederate and Union troops.

In July 1861, Union troops occupied Martinsburg, and a fateful encounter with a Yankee soldier began Belle's service as a Confederate spy. During a July Fourth celebration, drunken Yankee soldiers entered the Boyd home demanding that Belle remove the Confederate flags rumored to decorate her room. The soldiers then threatened to hang a Union flag over the rebel house. When Mrs. Boyd protested the soldiers' actions, a soldier stepped forward to silence her and Belle shot him to protect her mother. Union authorities dismissed Belle's actions as self-defense. She realized the opportunities that her femininity provided in gathering information from unsuspecting Union soldiers, and this experience encouraged Belle to further defend the Southern cause. She willingly risked her reputation by openly associating and flirting with enemy soldiers to gain vital intelligence. Though eager to serve as a spy, Belle was naïve in the art of espionage. She passed on messages written verbatim and in her own handwriting. Only a week after the shooting of the Yankee soldier, Union forces intercepted one of her messages and easily identified her as the culprit. Nonetheless, she escaped formal punishment with a stern warning.

Belle continued to dabble in espionage after she was sent south to Front Royal, Virginia, to stay with her aunt and uncle. There she nursed wounded soldiers and pilfered weapons and other supplies from Union troops. By the fall of 1861, Belle became an official courier for the Confederate army. She risked her life to carry messages between Generals Pierre G. T. Beauregard and Jackson, using Federal passes she secured from Union officers and her horse, Fleeter, who allegedly could kneel on command to avoid enemy patrols. Once, while still in Front Royal, she hid for hours in an upstairs closet of her aunt and uncle's hotel to listen through a knothole and record the discussion of Union officers in the room below. She then traveled 15 miles to pass on the information undetected.

Belle's most famous exploit was her role in the Battle of Front Royal. Confederate forces under the command of General Jackson initiated a frontal attack on Union troops in the Shenandoah Valley on May 21, 1862. The Confederate army met the Union troops stationed in Front Royal two days later. Through a message passed on to her by another courier and information personally gathered from careless Union soldiers, Belle knew the position of five different Union divisions in the Shenandoah Valley and the potential for the forces to unite and surround Confederate troops. Belle perceived the importance of capturing Front Royal before retreating Union troops burned vital supplies and infrastructure. Desperate to inform Jackson's troops, Belle ran to meet the approaching army. Artillery exploded around her and bullets pierced her dress, but Belle successfully reached the Confederate troops, passed along the information, and waved her white sunbonnet to signal them to

Maria Isabella "Belle" Boyd, a Confederate spy, provided critical information about Union troop movements during the Civil War, most notably during the Shenandoah Valley Campaign in 1862. (Library of Congress)

advance into Front Royal. The Battle of Front Royal made Belle a legend in the both the North and the South. Jackson rewarded Belle's bravery in the fall of 1862 with an honorary commission as a captain and aide-de-camp. Meanwhile, stories of her espionage and character were also exaggerated and discredited in Northern newspapers. Accounts described an armed Belle leading the Confederate charge on Front Royal herself or reduced Belle's credibility by labeling her a prostitute.

Belle's legendary status made covert activities difficult, and the Federal Department of War imprisoned her in Washington, D.C., on two separate occasions. Shortly after the Battle of Front Royal, she mistakenly gave a secret message to a Union spy disguised as a rebel soldier. Secretary of War Edwin Stanton ordered her imprisonment in Old Capital Prison in July of 1862, but the Union released her a month later. In the summer of 1863, Union forces arrested Belle once more when she refused to leave

Martinsburg and her ailing mother. They transferred her to Carroll Prison in Washington, D.C. She was released the following winter. During both prison terms, Belle experienced limited hardships besides the loss of her freedom and a brief illness while in Carroll Prison. Belle found ways to communicate with fellow prisoners and was credited with increasing the morale of captive rebel soldiers. Southern sympathizers also secretly communicated or visited Belle and paid for supplies and luxuries to supplement the prison rations. On both occasions, Belle was never formally charged with a crime and specific reasons for her releases are unknown.

When released from prison the second time, Belle resumed her role as a Confederate spy. She volunteered to serve as a Confederate courier to Europe. Armed with secret dispatches from the Confederate secretary of state, Belle boarded the British steamer, the *Greyhound*, in May 1864. The Union navy apprehended the steamer on suspicion of blockade running within days of its departure and arrested Belle. While awaiting her fate as a prisoner for the third time, Belle developed a romance with Union navy Lieutenant Samuel Harding. Belle first used Lieutenant Harding as she did the romantic interests of previous Yankee soldiers, leveraging her influence with him to help the Southern captain of the *Greyhound* escape. However, Belle accepted when Harding proposed marriage. The Union ultimately exiled Belle to Canada and dishonorably dismissed Harding from service. The two lovers reunited in England and married in August 1864.

Despite the publicity surrounding their marriage, Samuel Harding risked returning to the United States, where Union forces arrested him on suspicion of carrying Confederate dispatches. Alone in England, Belle began writing her memoirs. Legend contends that Belle wrote a letter to President Abraham Lincoln, threatening to reveal damaging Union secrets in her memoirs unless her husband was released from prison. The specific reasons for Harding's release are unknown, as are the circumstances of his death. He mysteriously died after reuniting with Belle in England. To support herself and her daughter, Belle published her memoirs, *Belle Boyd in Camp and Prison*, in 1865 and began a career as an actress.

Belle returned to the United States in 1866. She continued her career as an actress until she married former Union officer and businessman John Swainston Hammond in 1869. Belle divorced Hammond in 1884 and maintained custody of her four surviving children. Less than six months after her divorce, she married Nat High, an actor seventeen years her junior, and resumed her career as an actress. For the next fifteen years, Belle toured with her family and gained notoriety for dramatic recitals of her years as a Confederate spy. She died of a heart attack in 1900 while in Kilbourn, Wisconsin, preparing for another performance. She is buried there.

Belle Boyd remains a controversial figure. Since the publication of her memoirs, historians have debated the historical integrity of her accounts. Belle wrote her memoirs in the melodramatic style of the literary genre and was admittedly hesitant to reveal the intimate details of her espionage work. However, historians have substantiated the important episodes discussed in her writings through the use of several contemporary sources. Historians also continue to examine the importance of Belle's legend and her ability to reinvent herself throughout her life.

*Katharine Lane Antolini*

***See also*** Blockade Running; Female Spies; Imprisonment of Women; Southern Women.

**References and Further Reading**

Bakeless, John. 1970. *Spies of the Confederacy*. Philadelphia, PA: J. B. Lippincott Co.

Boyd, Belle. 1998. *Belle Boyd in Camp and Prison*, with Foreword by Drew Gilpin Faust and Introduction by Sharon Kennedy-Nolle. Baton Rouge: Louisiana State University Press.

Faust, Drew Gilpin. 1996. *Mothers of Invention: Women of the Slaveholding South in the American Civil War*. Chapel Hill: University of North Carolina Press.

Scarborough, Ruth. 1983. *Belle Boyd: Siren of the South*. Macon, GA: Mercer University Press.

Siguad, Louis. 1944. *Belle Boyd: Confederate Spy*. Petersburg, VA: Dietz Press.

## Bread Riots

During the American Civil War, Southern women planned and executed urban food riots in a number of Southern states, including Georgia, Louisiana, Virginia, Tennessee, Alabama, and North Carolina. Most disturbances were well-planned reactions focused on the dramatic escalation in the prices, combined with a growing scarcity in the markets, of household commodities such as flour, sugar, coffee, butter, and bacon. In many cases, these food shortages resulted from the activities of Confederate impressment agents who, under the provisions of the Impressment Act of March 1862, traveled throughout the South, negotiating agreements with local farmers to sell their produce to the Confederate army at fixed prices. In anticipation of the impressment agents' arrival, farmers frequently withheld their goods from market, thus increasing scarcity and driving up the prices of the commodities available for sale to private citizens.

Common occurrences in seventeenth-, eighteenth-, and nineteenth-century Europe, bread or food riots are extralegal socioeconomic protests, usually aimed at eradicating or ameliorating unjust market practices related to the sale of household commodities such as bread, meat, flour, coffee, and tea. Such market practices are often the result of public policy decisions at either the local or national level.

The largest Civil War food riot, which took place in Richmond, Virginia, on April 2, 1863, typified most wartime Southern food riots. In this riot in the Confederacy's capital, a crowd estimated at nearly five hundred women, accompanied by adolescent boys and a few men, broke open the doors of Richmond's Main Street and Cary Street merchants. They seized coffee, candles, shoes, flour, bacon, and sides of beef. Although a number of the women were armed with guns or axes, which they apparently brandished in the faces of resisting merchants, no fatalities occurred. The riot ended after a short time when the city's Public Guard, which had been summoned at the request of Virginia Governor John Letcher, trained loaded rifles on the rioters. The crowd dispersed quickly, with many women carrying their seized bacon and flour home to share with family and neighbors. More than two-thirds of the sixty-eight people arrested in the riot were women. During the next few months, Richmond's municipal courts were filled with trials resulting from the arrests of female rioters. Many of those found guilty of misdemeanor charges for their role in the bread riot were required to pay fines. A few women who were identified as the leaders of the Richmond bread riot were convicted of felonies and sentenced to prison terms of five years or more.

Most Richmond newspaper accounts characterized the rioting women as prostitutes or vagrants. However, many involved in the Richmond disturbance, as well as in the bread riots occurring elsewhere in the Confederacy, were working-class women with husbands and sons in the Confederate army. Other participants worked in the ammunition laboratories and in sewing factories manufacturing percussion caps and uniforms for Confederate soldiers. These working-class women experienced more acutely the personal and economic privations of the Civil War than did their more affluent Southern sisters. Consequently, through the bread riots, they demanded that their government fulfill its responsibility to protect and feed them.

Food riots by Southern women contributed to a growing sense of Confederate dissatisfaction with or disaffection for the war. The riots also drew attention to serious problems of want and privation in many Southern communities. As Southern armies racked up discouraging battlefield losses and homefront shortages became more acute, the desertion rates among Confederate soldiers escalated, as men who were anxious about their families' well-being returned home.

Southern politicians attempted to respond to this dilemma by developing social welfare initiatives aimed at assisting needy Confederate families. In urban communities, they created free markets, which appear to be prototypes for twentieth-century food banks. Farmers contributed their excess produce, which was then sold at reduced prices to families meeting specific criteria. To qualify as free market recipients, women had to be the mothers or legally married wives of soldiers, either conscripts or volunteers, who were currently serving in the Confederate army. The families of substitute soldiers were excluded because these men typically received financial compensation for their military service from the families of the wealthy men they replaced. Common law wives and the children born of these unions were also not entitled to relief because these relationships did not meet the criteria for respectability. In North Carolina, eligible recipients received coupons that could be redeemed for food, a precursor to food stamps and Independence cards. In rural areas, county relief agents worked with home visitors, who were often married middle- and upper-class women from the community and who interviewed the families in their homes to determine their eligibility. The most ambitious statewide relief programs, which can be accurately characterized as precursors to the social welfare initiatives of the Progressive Era and perhaps even the New Deal, were implemented in Georgia and North Carolina.

*E. Susan Barber*

**See also** Confederate Homefront; Factory Workers, Southern; Food; Foraging, Effects on Women; Morale; Nationalism, Confederate; Rural Women; Shortages; Southern Women; Urban Women, Southern.

### References and Further Reading

Barber, E. Susan. 2000. "Cartridge Makers and Myrmidon Viragos: White Working-Class Women in Confederate Richmond." In *Dealing with the Powers That Be: Negotiating the Boundaries of Southern Womanhood,* edited by Janet Coryell. Columbia: University of Missouri Press.

Chesson, Michael B. 1984. "Harlots or Heroines? A New Look at the Richmond Bread Riot." *Virginia Magazine of History and Biography* 92: 131–175.

Escott, Paul D. 1977. "'The Cry of the Sufferers': The Problem of Welfare in the Confederacy." *Civil War History* 23: 228–240.

Faust, Drew Gilpin. 1990. "Altars of Sacrifice: Confederate Women and the Narratives of War." *Journal of American History* 76 (4): 1200–1228.

Fisher, Clyde Olin. 1971. "The Relief of Soldiers' Families in North Caroline during the Civil War." *South Atlantic Quarterly* 16: 60–72.

Owsley, Frank L. 1926. "Defeatism in the Confederacy." *North Carolina Historical Review* 3: 446–456.

Thompson, E. P. 1971. "The Moral Economy of the Crowd in the Eighteenth Century." *Past and Present* 50: 76–136.

## Breckenridge, Lucy Gilmer (1843–1865)

Virginia diarist Lucy Gilmer Breckenridge closely observed Southern culture, the effects of the Civil War, and her own family's dynamics before her untimely death in 1865.

Born February 1, 1843, into a prominent family of planters—her father owned one hundred thirty-one slaves in 1850, the largest number held by any individual in the county—Lucy grew to maturity in the home built by her grandfather. Grove Hill, a Federal estate built around the turn of the nineteenth century, became the setting of her intimate wartime diary.

Lucy's diary began as an attempt to lift the boredom of wartime life. With her sisters and her mother, Lucy spent her days at Grove Hill reading, welcoming guests, and discussing life and the war with her family. Later, she sewed, made bandages, and nursed the sick. Throughout the war she worried about her five brothers fighting for the Confederacy.

The diary's themes included the politics of the war, Lucy's own personal life, and the many comings and goings of her extended family and friends. She noted, for example, her disgust with Union General John Pope's 1862 order that his men should live off the land. Throughout the diary, Lucy made pointed statements about the subordination of women in marriage. Later, Lucy's ambivalence about her own engagement to Lieutenant Thomas Jefferson Bassett reflected many of the same ideas. In 1864 she wrote that a bad marriage was never the wife's fault because women were better than men.

Worry for absent members of her family occupied much of the diary. The first Breckinridge to fall was Lucy's brother Johnny, who died in 1862 at the Battle of Seven Pines. Lucy mourned him throughout the war. In May 1864, the family was horrified to hear that her brothers Major Cary Breckinridge and Peachy Gilmer Breckinridge had been killed at Kennon's Landing. Reports soon indicated that Cary was safe but confirmed Gilmer's death in combat. Gilmer's death crushed his wife Julia. Lucy herself began to believe that the war would never end, and she poured the bitterness of grief into her diary.

Lucy's diary ended at Christmas 1864. Despite their many ups and downs, she and Thomas Jefferson Bassett were married on January 28 of the new year. Their marriage was a brief one, ending with Lucy's death from typhus on June 16. Her diary, written on the pages of an account book, was found by a descendant many years after her death. It provides an invaluable glimpse into the emotional world of a young witness to the Civil War.

*Fiona Deans Halloran*

**See also** Civilian Life; Confederate Homefront; Courtship and Marriage; Diaries and Journals; Domesticity; Mourning; Separate Spheres; Slaveholding Women; Southern Women.

**References and Further Reading**

Breckenridge, Lucy. 1979. *Lucy Breckenridge of Grove Hill: The Diary of a Virginia Girl, 1862–1864*, edited by Mary D. Robertson. Kent, OH: Kent State University Press.

## Brevard, Keziah Goodwyn Hopkins (1803–1886)

Wealthy widow Keziah Goodwyn Hopkins Brevard kept a diary of events from July 1860 to April 1861. With all its contradictions, Brevard's diary captures the troubled view of a wealthy plantation mistress during a vital ten-month period at the onset of the Civil War.

Born in 1803, Brevard lived in the Richland District outside of Columbia, South Carolina. She had a troubled fifteen-year marriage, which ended in 1842 with the death of her husband. Two years later, her father perished, and Keziah inherited the family's extensive land and slaveholdings. A very successful plantation mistress, Brevard did not merely maintain this estate but doubled its size in the decade prior to the Civil War. Her secession-era diary records both routine items—the weather, the names of visitors, and the amount of jelly she made—and her opinions on weighty topics such as slavery, Lincoln's election, and South Carolina's secession.

Despite owning 209 slaves in 1860, Brevard expressed misgivings about the South's peculiar institution. She saw slavery as a burden to slave owners, wished it had never existed in the United States, and claimed that she would support its end if freed slaves would be forced to leave the country. Nevertheless, she had no sympathy for abolitionists, whom she considered to be evil, self-righteous fanatics who wanted to murder all white Southerners. Brevard also articulated contradictory attitudes regarding slaves. Slaves were her only daily companions, and she took a personal interest in their health. Yet she labeled them brutes and repeatedly chastised their impudence. Claiming that slaves with good owners, such as herself, were blessed, she nonetheless feared arson and poisoning. Though a paternalist, she possessed no misconceptions regarding where slaves' loyalty would lie in the upcoming war.

Brevard expressed her opinion on important political developments. She decried Lincoln's election and even wished for his death. She had mixed feelings regarding secession, expressing the belief both that Northern abolitionists should be happy that the South had left the Union and that South Carolina acted too hastily in seceding alone. Even while pledging money for guns, she echoed the arguments of cooperationists. Brevard opined that, if all the slave states had voted together in the 1860 presidential election, Stephen A. Douglas would have defeated Lincoln and that, if they had seceded together, they would present a much stronger deterrence to Northern invaders.

Though seemingly unaware of her unique situation, Brevard's actions challenged gender roles in the Civil War–era South. Not only did she run a plantation, but she did so very successfully. From 1844 to her death in 1886, she tripled her landholdings. With her overseer living on a separate plantation, Brevard lived as the only white person surrounded daily by at least twenty of her slaves. Living apart from other whites, she found comfort in her religion. She considered herself a religious person and repeatedly requested that God intervene in worldly affairs, yet she recorded her own infrequent attendance at church services.

*John M. Sacher*

*See also* Confederate Homefront; Diaries and Journals; Religion; Southern Women; Widows, Confederate.
**References and Further Reading**
Brevard, Keziah Goodwyn Hopkins. 1993. *A Plantation Mistress on the Eve of the Civil War: The Diary of Keziah Goodwyn Hopkins Brevard, 1860–1861*, edited by John Hammond Moore. Columbia: University of South Carolina Press.

## Brown, Addie (1841–1870)

Addie Brown worked as a domestic servant in the wealthy African American Primus household in Hartford, Connecticut. A series of letters surviving from her friendship with Rebecca Primus provides insight into black female relationships and the difficulties of life for Northern blacks during the Civil War.

Brown was born on December 21, 1841. Her father died when she was very young, and her mother remarried against her wishes. Her brother Ally served in the Civil War. Brown worked as a domestic servant in the households of various employers in Hartford, Farmington, and Waterbury, Connecticut, and in New York.

Brown wrote more than a hundred letters to her close friend, Rebecca Primus, who traveled south to Maryland to teach newly freed blacks after the Civil War. These letters reveal an intimate female friendship during the Civil War period. Exactly how and when the two met is unknown, but Brown's letters to Primus begin in 1859. Between 1859 and 1868, Brown's letters came from Hartford, Farmington, and Waterbury, Connecticut, and from New York City. The letters paint a vivid portrait of a flirtatious and sexual friendship. Several letters from Brown to Primus indicate that, when visiting, they shared a bed along with hugs, embraces, and kisses. Brown even discusses Primus's kisses.

Because she was not formally educated, Brown wrote as she would speak. Throughout the course of her correspondence with Primus, her confidence and literacy grew. Her letters tell the story of a bright, intelligent woman who struggled to make a living under difficult financial circumstances. Her writing also reveals a political awareness. Brown expressed an open dislike for President Andrew Johnson, and she discussed her refusal to attend a minstrel show that included a blackface performance.

In April 1868, while in her late twenties, Addie Brown married Joseph Tines. Brown's letters to Primus, who was also married, often discussed her courtship with Tines. The discussion of her relationship with her future husband suggests that both women kept their various relationships separate. None of Primus's letters to Brown have been discovered. Addie's death was recorded on the back of an envelope to Brown from Primus, who wrote, "Addie died at home, January 11, 1870."

*Eloise E. Scroggins*

*See also* African American Women; Primus, Rebecca (1836–1929); Northern Women.
**References and Further Reading**
Griffin, Farah Jasmine, ed. 1999. *Beloved Sisters and Loving Friends: Letters from Rebecca Primus of Royal Oak, Maryland, and Addie Brown of Hartford, Connecticut, 1854–1868*. New York: Alfred A. Knopf.
Hansen, Karen. 1995. "'No Kisses Is Like Youres': An Erotic Friendship between Two African American Women during the Mid-Nineteenth Century." *Gender and History* 7 (2): 151–182.

## Brown, Clara (1800–1885)

Born a slave in 1800, Clara Brown became an early Western pioneer. Brown settled in the Colorado Territory and owned several parcels of land, mining claims, and approximately $10,000 in savings. Never forgetting her past, Brown helped freed slaves settle in Colorado and fought to find the family from whom slavery had separated her.

Virginia's slave system split Clara and her mother from the remainder of their family in 1803. The two lived near Fredericksburg with their master, Ambrose Smith, until 1809 when Smith moved his family and slaves to Kentucky. Upon Smith's death in 1835, George Brown purchased Clara, while others bought her husband Richard, her son Richard Jr., and two daughters Margaret and Liza Jane. At George Brown's death, his children granted Clara her freedom in 1856. Under Kentucky law, she had to leave the state within one year of her manumission.

Clara traveled to St. Louis where she worked as a domestic servant for Jacob and Sarah Brunner. She moved with the Brunners to Leavenworth, Kansas, in 1858 in the middle of the violence that earned the territory the nickname Bloody Kansas. When the Brunners later moved to California, Clara stayed behind. She opened her own laundry business but soon decided to take her domestic services to Colorado.

Brown left Kansas in April 1859 and settled in Denver. She worked in Henry Reitze's bakery before reopening her laundry business. Her bakery contacts ensured her success in the city. Even so, she realized that the mining camps northwest of Denver could provide more profit than did the city. Brown moved to a two-room cabin in Mountain City, Colorado, in 1860. During the next five years, her business generated enough profit for her to leave Colorado in search of the family she had lost at the 1835 auction block. Before his death, George Brown had given her information on her family's whereabouts. Clara learned that Margaret had died from a respiratory disease and that in 1850 Liza Jane worked on a farm in Logan County, Kentucky. Because Clara's husband and son had been sold several times, George Brown could not locate them. In 1860, Clara set off in search of Liza Jane. She returned a year later without any information on her daughter, but with sixteen freed slaves. For the next ten years, she helped these ex-slaves by providing financial and moral assistance.

In 1882, Brown's longtime friend from Kansas, Becky Johnson, sent word from Iowa that she had located Liza Jane. Brown traveled east to meet her long-lost daughter as well as her granddaughter, Cindy. Cindy returned with Clara to Colorado. Clara died on October 23, 1885, and was buried with a funeral orchestrated by the Society of Colorado Pioneers.

*James Gigantino*

***See also*** African American Women; Slave Families.
**References and Further Reading**
Berwanger, Eugene. 1975. "Reconstruction on the Frontier: The Equal Rights Struggle in Colorado, 1865–1867." *Pacific Historical Review* 44 (3): 313–329.

Bruyn, Kathleen. 1970. *"Aunt Clara Brown:" Story of a Black Pioneer.* Boulder, CO: Pruett Publishing Company.

## Brownell, Kady (1842–1915)

A markswoman with the First Rhode Island Infantry volunteer unit during the Civil War, Kady Brownell proudly carried her unit's colors and fought openly as a woman in several battles alongside her husband Robert.

Born in 1842 in an army camp along the African coast, this daughter of a Scottish soldier in the British army grew up in the military life. Kady was nineteen years old, living in Rhode Island, and recently married when Fort Sumter was surrendered to Confederate forces in May 1861. The following day, Kady and her husband Robert signed up for a three-month enlistment with the Rhode Island Infantry, one of the earliest regiments to respond to the call for volunteers.

While in camp, Kady became known as the Daughter of the Regiment. She also gained skills as a sharpshooter and a sword handler, items she carried as a symbol of her position as sergeant and color bearer. In the middle of July, when her regiment moved south of the Potomac River and headed toward Richmond, Kady carried the flag. Her company came under fire, and she was separated from her husband, but she maintained the colors throughout the skirmish. As her regiment retreated and Kady found herself in the woods, she found a horse and rode to nearby Centreville to learn of Robert's fate.

After Kady found Robert unhurt, the pair returned to Providence, where they were discharged following the completion of their three-month term. They immediately joined the Fifth Rhode Island Infantry and participated in the January 1862 campaign for Roanoke Island. Kady became the regiment's acting nurse and Daughter of the Regiment. Soon thereafter she again carried the flag. During a friendly fire incident with Union soldiers, Kady ran to the front and waved the flag to stop it.

Another battle flared up soon after at New Bern, North Carolina, during which Robert sustained

Kady Brownell served in the Union army beside her husband with the Rhode Island Volunteers. (Library of Congress)

injuries. Kady tended to him and the other wounded soldiers on the field. She even helped a badly wounded Confederate soldier who insulted her after regaining consciousness, which prompted Kady to grab a bayonet and plunge it at his chest. She was stopped by a Union soldier nearby.

Kady spent the next six weeks nursing her husband and other Union soldiers back to health in New Bern. She continued to help a nearby Confederate hospital by bringing coffee and soup to the doctors, nurses, and patients. By late April, the Brownells were transferred by steamship to New York, where Robert spent several months recuperating in the Soldier's Relief Hospital. They were both discharged in the winter of 1863.

Robert's wounds prevented him from enlisting again, so the Brownells adopted a civilian life. Kady

kept her colors, which had been signed by General Ambrose Burnside. Beginning in 1884, Kady received a veteran's pension of $8 per month.

Kady Brownell died in a Women's Relief Corps Home in Oxford, New York, in January 1915.

*Eloise Scroggins*

***See also*** Nurses; Vivandieres; Northern Women.
**References and Further Reading**
Leonard, Elizabeth D. 1999. *All the Daring of the Soldier: Women of the Civil War Armies.* New York: W. W. Norton.
Moore, Frank. 1866. *Women of the War; Their Heroism and Self-Sacrifice.* Hartford, CT: S. S. Scranton & Company.

## Buck, Lucy Rebecca (1842–1918)

Civil War diarist Lucy Rebecca Buck was born near Front Royal, Virginia, on September 25, 1842.

Her father, William Mason Buck, was a planter and storeowner. Lucy was one of thirteen children and grew up on the family's plantation, named Bel Air. She attended school in Front Royal and, during the Civil War, tutored her younger siblings at home.

Buck commenced her Civil War diary on December 25, 1861. At this time her brothers, Alvin and Irving, had already joined the Confederate army. Lucy's diary chronicled her domestic and social life at Bel Air, as well as political and military news. Front Royal was strategically valuable to both Union and Confederate forces, and it changed hands over a dozen times during the war. Buck recorded regular visits from both armies, which, she noted on May 3, 1862, kept the family "in a state of continual ebullition." Union troops set up headquarters in May 1862, raiding the property of food and provisions. After their departure, Buck was forced to take on additional domestic duties as the family struggled to provide for themselves as well as for the hundreds of passing Confederate soldiers requesting food and lodgings. "I wish I had a great big larder at their disposal," she remarked on November 4, 1862.

Like most Confederate women, Lucy sewed for the soldiers and participated in fundraising activities. In January 1863, Buck took up a collection for the destitute citizens of Fredericksburg and raised $259 for the cause. She personally knew Confederate spy Belle Boyd and met General Robert E. Lee when he visited Bel Air on his way home from the Battle of Gettysburg. Lucy and her sister sang for Lee and obtained his autograph. While both her brothers survived the war, Lucy's cousin, Walter Buck, died in June 1863. Lucy's diary ended abruptly with the news of Lee's surrender at Appomattox in April 1865, but she resumed writing a new volume soon after and kept a diary until her death. Lucy and her four sisters never married. In 1897, financial circumstances forced the Buck family to sell Bel Air, and in 1905 Lucy moved into a house on Chester Street in Front Royal named Cozy Corner, which was designed by her and her sister. She died on August 20, 1918, at the age of seventy-five, and was buried in Prospect Hill Cemetery in Front Royal.

*Giselle Roberts*

**See also** Diaries and Journals; Southern Women.
**References and Further Reading**

Baer, Elizabeth R. 1997. *Shadows on My Heart: The Civil War Diary of Lucy Rebecca Buck of Virginia* Athens: University of Georgia Press.

## Bucklin, Sophronia E. (n.d.–1902)

Union army nurse Sophronia E. Bucklin made her greatest contribution to the war effort through her willingness to defend the soldiers in her care, her fellow nurses, and herself—an amazing feat for anyone, but especially for a woman who was technically too young to be an army nurse.

Bucklin was a seamstress in Auburn, New York, when the war began. She became a nurse out of patriotic fervor following the attack on Fort Sumter, although she had to delay her work due to societal and political resistance. Many believed that it was immoral for young, single, and attractive women to serve. Beyond the social and political impediments, she also had to meet the requirements of the Superintendent of Women Nurses for the Union army, Dorothea Dix. Bucklin did not meet the age requirement to serve, but the screening board forgot to ask her age. In September 1862 she began her work at the Judiciary Square Hospital in Washington. Following that assignment, she worked at hospitals in Virginia and Maryland, and she was at Gettysburg, Pennsylvania. Her duties included feeding and grooming the patients, dressing wounds, and doing laundry.

In 1869 Bucklin published an account of her experiences, *In Hospital and Camp: A Woman's Record of Thrilling Incidents among the Wounded in the Late War.* Her memoir detailed the hostility that she encountered from some male doctors, nurses, administrators, and officers. Bucklin often confronted these men, challenging their authority. She was dismissed from several hospitals when she refused to remain quiet about behavior she deemed inappropriate, unethical, and immoral. She found some hospitals were inadequately supplied and staffed, or they were staffed by poorly trained or uncaring personnel. Bucklin grew frustrated that her reports were often ignored. However, in the spring 1864 at Camp Stoneman, she managed to have a surgeon dismissed following her complaint that he was sexually harassing women at the hospital.

Bucklin never married, and after the war returned to her work as a seamstress. She joined the Woman's Relief Corps of the Grand Army of the Republic, a national organization for women who were Civil War veterans. She died in Ithaca, New York, in 1902.

*Paula Katherine Hinton*

**See also** Dix, Dorothea Lynde (1802–1887); Fort Sumter (April 12–14, 1861); Gettysburg, Battle of (July 1–3, 1863); Hospitals; Northern Women; Nurses; Separate Spheres; Wartime Employment.
**References and Further Reading**

Bucklin, Sophronia E. 1869. *In Hospital and Camp: A Woman's Record of Thrilling Incidents among the Wounded in the Late War.* Philadelphia, PA: John E. Potter and Co.
Clinton, Catherine, and Nina Silber, eds.1992. *Divided Houses: Gender and the Civil War.* New York: Oxford University Press.
Leonard, Elizabeth D. 1994. *Yankee Women: Gender Battles in the Civil War.* New York: W. W. Norton.

## Bull Run/Manassas, First Battle of
## (July 21, 1861)

The first major battle of the American Civil War occurred on July 21, 1861, about thirty miles south of Washington, D.C., near a creek called Bull Run. Expecting a spectacle of parades and drills, civilians gathered around the battlefield with their picnic baskets to watch the engagement and they were shocked by the realities of battle. Although at the time it was the largest battle in North America, the Battle of Bull Run (Manassas) would later be judged a relatively small clash by Civil War standards. Women played key roles as spies, soldiers, and medical personnel during the battle. Furthermore, the first civilian casualty of the war was a woman.

Newly enlisted Union forces under General Irvin McDowell were not well trained, but political pressure and the belief that the war would be a short-lived one led the West Point graduate to march on Virginia from Washington, D.C. On July 21, 1861, Federal forces charged the Confederate lines several times with minimal success. Confederate leader Thomas J. Jackson earned the nickname Stonewall as a response to his and his troops' firm stance despite heavy enemy fire. The arrival of General Joseph Johnston's reinforcements enabled the Confederates to mount a charge that ultimately broke the Union lines. The failure of the Union to break Jackson's line and the arrival of Confederate reinforcements led to a near rout. The Union's defeat at Bull Run ended notions among politicians and citizens in the North that the war would come to a quick end. On the other hand, after Bull Run, Southerners believed they had a chance for a quick victory to gain independence for the Confederacy.

Defeated Union forces retreated in disarray. Troops fled back to the capital over roads congested with Unionist politicians, newspaper reporters, and picnickers who had come to watch the battle. The civilians had expected a great event, having never seen the horrors of war for themselves. Some women sold foodstuffs to the spectators, and others took excitement in artillery bursts. The situation worsened for civilians and soldiers alike when a cannon shot struck a wagon crossing and subsequently blocked the Cub Run Bridge. The obstruction and rumors of approaching rebel cavalry made a bad situation worse; women were left to fend for themselves as the soldiers took their horses and carriages to make a faster retreat.

Despite the large numbers of civilian onlookers, the only civilian casualty was a Southern woman in her eighties. Bedridden Judith Carter Henry refused to leave her upstairs bedroom as the battle commenced on a hill named for the patriarch of her family, Henry Hill. At first, Confederate snipers used her home to ward off numerous Yankees. Eventually Henry decided to flee her home temporarily. Soon after her return, she was unable to escape an incoming cannon shot and died in her bed, the first civilian killed in the Civil War.

Refusing to stand on the sidelines, other women took part directly in the Battle of First Bull Run as they would in other Civil War battles. Confederate spy Rose O'Neal Greenhow sent two messages to General Pierre G. T. Beauregard, alerting him of Union movements, numbers, and bivouacs. Another Southern spy, Belle Boyd, shot and killed a Union soldier prior to the Battle of Bull Run. Before the battle commenced, several drunken Union soldiers arrived at the Boyd home near the battle site, and they harangued Boyd's mother when she refused to raise the Union flag over her home. The indignant Belle shot one of the soldiers but was not punished.

Women also disguised themselves as men to fight for their nation. Louisianan Loreta Janeta Velazquez dressed as a man, called herself Harry T. Buford, and joined General Barnard Bee's command to fight for the Confederacy. Velazquez served in at least four major engagements, including First Bull Run, and later became a spy for the Confederacy.

At least four women combatants served in the Union army during the Battle of Bull Run. Sarah Emma Edmonds, working as Private Franklin Thompson of the Second Michigan Infantry, shuttled back and forth from the nearby town of Centerville to the battlefield with supplies for field hospitals, including lint and brandy. She also filled canteens to quench the soldiers' thirst and comforted wounded and dying soldiers. Later in the war, Edmonds worked as a Union spy and mail carrier. Similarly, Annie Etheridge Hooks fought in a Michigan unit at Bull Run and for the duration of the war. Another woman, Louisa Thompson, served in the Union cavalry at the battle. Finally, after marching through the heat at her husband's side, Rhode Island's Kady Brownell guarded her regiment's flag during the melee and retreat until a Pennsylvania soldier dragged her to the rear.

Women also offered much needed medical services to the soldiers at the Battle of Manassas. Twenty-eight-year-old Dr. Mary Edwards Walker served as the only female doctor in the Union army. The valuable medical services she performed not only at Bull Run, but also at other battles throughout the war, eventually earned her the Congressional Medal of Honor. Furthermore, medical reformer Dorothea Dix, along with many other women, worked at the hospital in Georgetown that housed the Union wounded.

As with most other battles of the Civil War, women played key roles on and off the battlefield. They fought, served others, died, and fled in the Civil War's first major engagement.

*Scott L. Stabler*

**See also** Blair, Lorinda Ann [Annie Etheridge Hooks] (ca. 1840–1913); Boyd, Belle (1844–1900); Brownell, Kady (1842–n.d.); Civilian Life; Confederate Homefront; Dix, Dorothea Lynde (1802–1887); Edmonds, Sarah Emma [Franklin Thompson] (1841–1898); Female Combatants; Female Spies; Greenhow, Rose O'Neal (ca. 1814–1864); Northern Women; Southern Women; Velazquez, Loreta Janeta [Harry T. Buford] (1842–1897); Walker, Mary Edwards (1832–1919).

**References and Further Reading**

Blanton, Deanne, and Lauren M. Cook. 2002. *They Fought Like Demons: Women Soldiers in the American Civil War.* Baton Rouge: Louisiana State University Press.

Detzer, David. 2004. *Donnybrook: The Battle of Bull Run, 1861.* Orlando: Harcourt.

MacDonald, Joanna M. 1999. *"We Shall Meet Again": The First Battle of Manassas (Bull Run), July 18–21, 1861.* Shippensburg, PA: White Mane Publishing Co.

Rafuse, Ethan S. 2002. *A Single Grand Victory: The First Campaign and Battle of Manassas.* Wilmington, DE: SR Books.

Velazquez, Loreta Janeta. 2003. *The Woman in Battle: The Civil War Narrative of Loreta Velazquez, Cuban Woman and Confederate Soldier,* with introduction by Jesse Aleman. Madison: University of Wisconsin Press.

## Bull Run/Manassas, Second Battle of (August 29–30, 1862)

The Second Battle of Bull Run (Manassas) resulted from the Union threat to the Confederate capital of Richmond, Virginia. Unlike the 1861 battle on the same soil, Second Bull Run lacked the expectations of a relatively bloodless fight, and women came to the battle as nurses and soldiers, not observers.

In late June and early July 1862, Union General John Pope marched the Army of Virginia into enemy territory. To facilitate the campaign on Virginia, Pope issued a number of general orders to deal with the ongoing problems of operating in enemy territory. These orders covered a variety of problems, including foraging in the countryside, burning houses to control Confederate guerrillas, forcing civilians to repair damaged railroad lines, and authorizing Union officers to arrest any male civilian who would not take an oath of allegiance. The foraging and razing of homes had a particular effect on Confederate women, as the hardships of war became apparent.

By mid-July 1862, Pope's movement of his army south to Culpepper, Virginia pushed Lee to take the offensive. Starting with General Thomas "Stonewall" Jackson's force of two divisions, Lee began moving portions of the Army of Northern Virginia away from George McClellan's retreating Union troops and toward Pope's three corps. In mid-August, Pope continued to pull his army back to the Rappahannock River, as Lee continued to transfer his Confederate army from Richmond into Central Virginia. The fighting proved bloody, overwhelming those who tried to tend to the wounded. Union nurse Clara Barton, who had attached herself to the hospital trains of Pope's Army, quickly discovered that her small kit of supplies were no match for the massive influx of casualities. Barton was joined by several other female nurses in Manassas, including Charlotte Elizabeth Johnson McKay of Maine.

Pope pulled his army back to northern Virginia and soon discovered that the Rappahannock River was deep enough to block the Confederate advance. Pope continually shifted his forces along the river to prevent Lee and his army from crossing it. On August 22, Lee's cavalry found the Union right flank uncovered and with no support. While Pope and his army were pinned by inactivity along the river, Lee and Jackson planned to swing around Pope's exposed flank and cut him off from reinforcements.

On August 25, Jackson and three infantry divisions marched north toward Pope's right flank. The Confederates masked their march by hiding behind the Bull Run Mountains. After a one-day march, Jackson had possession of Pope's Manassas Rail Junction supply depot. On August 27, Pope's army pulled back from the Rappahannock River line as the first of McClellan's troops began arriving north of Jackson's Confederate forces. Jackson pulled his forces back from Manassas Junction and waited for the rest of Lee's army along an abandoned railroad cut near the old Manassas battlefield.

On the next day, Pope's units concentrated on Manassas Junction in an attempt to close in on Jackson's divisions. Near Groveton, Jackson decided to attack one of the Federal columns and quickly found his Stonewall brigade in a stand-up fight with the Iron brigade. Nightfall brought this severe fight to an end, but it alerted Pope to the location of Jackson's brigades. Pope did not realize that General James Longstreet's Confederate divisions were approaching, ready to join Jackson's forces.

Pope's corps began their attacks against Jackson's men on August 29. Reinforcements from the Army of the Potomac had arrived. In one of the corps, the Second Michigan Volunteer Infantry, Sara Emma Edmonds fought as a man under the name of Franklin Thompson. She and her regiment found itself in heavy fighting for the next two days. The Union's numerous, uncoordinated attacks against Jackson failed to push the Confederates back from the railroad cut.

Pope launched a massive assault the next day, using all of Porter's corps against both Jackson's and Longstreet's positions. This assault also failed. Lee then ordered Longstreet to counterattack against the Federal left flank. Longstreet's five divisions rolled forward and swung left to unhinge General Pope's lines. Toward nightfall on August 30, Pope's combined forces retreated toward Centerville, Virginia, and Washington, D.C. The Confederate pursuit ended with an indecisive battle at Chantilly, Virginia, where Pope finally withdrew into the defenses of Washington.

*William H. Brown*

**See also** Barton, Clara (1821–1912); Edmonds, Sara Emma [Franklin Thompson] (1841–1889); Female Combatants; McKay, Charlotte Elizabeth Johnson (1818–1894); Nurses.

**References and Further Reading**

Blanton, DeAnne, and Laura M. Cook. 2002. *They Fought Like Demons: Women Soldiers in the American Civil War.* Baton Rouge: Louisiana State University Press.

Grimsley, Mark. 1995. *The Hard Hand of War: Union Military Policy toward Southern Civilians, 1861–1865.* New York: Cambridge University Press.

Hennessy, John J. 1993. *Return to Bull Run: The Campaign and Battle of Second Manassas.* New York: Simon & Schuster.

Oates, Stephen. 1994. *A Woman of Valor: Clara Barton and the Civil War.* New York: Free Press.

Stackpole, Edward J. 1959. *From Cedar Mountain to Antietam: August–September, 1862.* Harrisburg, PA: Stackpole Books.

## Burge, Dolly Sumner Lunt (1817–1891)

Widowed plantation owner and slaveholder Dolly Lunt Burge kept a journal during the Civil War. During the war, her plantation near Covington, Georgia, suffered from Union General William Tecumseh Sherman's March to the Sea.

Born on September 29, 1817, in Bowdoinham, Maine, Burge was a relative of abolitionist and Massachusetts Senator Charles Sumner. She married Samuel H. B. Lewis in 1838. In 1842, the couple moved to Zebulon, Georgia, where her older sister had moved earlier. In Georgia, Dolly's husband trained and then began to work as a physician. He died in September 1843.

A widow and the mother of a daughter at the age of twenty-six, Dolly found employment as a teacher. Her daughter Susan died in 1844, and in 1850 Dolly remarried. Her second husband, Thomas Burge, came to the marriage with four children and an active plantation with several hundred acres under cultivation and more than thirty African American slaves. Dolly and Thomas had a daughter together, Sadai, in 1855. Dolly lived as a planter's wife and a mother until Thomas died in 1858. A widow once again, she maintained her control over the plantation and assumed all the duties of her late husband. Although she lost the assistance and guidance of her husband, the plantation continued to earn similar profits as it had under his governance. As an independent landholding widow, Dolly faced many legal and social hurdles in the years preceding the war.

When the secession crisis emerged, Dolly, despite her Northern upbringing, sided with her Southern neighbors. She expressed her support for the morality and necessity of slavery. While dealing with the shortages and uncertainty of the war, she faced a series of personal tragedies with the deaths of one of her young stepchildren and her parents. Her diary is one of the most insightful looks at the difficulties women and especially widows faced in running plantations during the Civil War.

The war literally came home for her in 1864, when Sherman's army marched through her plantation in Newton County, Georgia. They damaged her home and property, tearing clothes, stealing food and money, and liberating her slaves. In her diary, she discussed the uncertainty that Sherman's army brought to the region as well as her estimate that Sherman's men caused her personally $30,000 in damage.

When the war ended, Dolly turned to sharecropping to keep her plantation afloat. In 1866, she married Reverend William J. Parks, a longtime acquaintance and fellow Methodist. Parks apparently respected Dolly's independent spirit. The couple agreed to a prenuptial agreement, ensuring that Dolly would be able to pass her property to her own children when she died. In addition, they agreed to live initially at Burge's plantation home. When Parks died in 1872, Burge was coexecutor of his will.

Burge lived on her Georgia farm until she died on October 26, 1891.

*Andrew K. Frank*

***See also*** Destruction of Personal Property; Diaries and Journals; Education, Southern; Sherman's Campaign (1864–1865); Slaveholders Women; Southern Women; Teachers, Southern.

**References and Further Reading**

Carter, Christine Jacobson, ed. 1997. *The Diary of Dolly Lunt Burge, 1848–1879.* Athens: University of Georgia Press.

Wood, Kirsten. 2004. *Masterful Women: Slaveholding Widows from the American Revolution through the Civil War.* Chapel Hill: University of North Carolina Press.

## Butler, Benjamin F. (1818–1893)

Despite his many other accomplishments, Union General Benjamin Franklin Butler gained and has retained his historical notoriety as a result of the controversies generated during his occupation of New Orleans, especially General Order Number 28, also called the Woman Order.

Benjamin Franklin Butler, who had varied careers as a respected and prosperous litigator, a successful state and national politician, and an ambitious but deeply controversial Union general in the Civil War, was born in Deerfield, New Hampshire, on November 5, 1818. As a young man, Butler aspired to attend West Point but, failing to achieve that goal, opted to study law and began his practice in Lowell, Massachusetts, where he gained a reputation as a formidable criminal attorney and reformer who championed workers' rights. He also rose to leadership positions in state politics and the Massachusetts militia.

At the commencement of the Civil War, Butler used his influence to gain an appointment in the Union army, where he excelled at administrative duties but failed miserably on the few occasions when he led troops into battle. In 1862 Butler was ordered to accompany Admiral David Farragut on his mission to take control of the mouth of the Mississippi and New Orleans. Farragut was successful and turned the city over to Butler and his troops, effective May 1, 1862. The city's residents, in shock at their swift and unexpected occupation and furious at Confederate forces who failed to defend the city, vented their rage against the Union occupiers. Butler successfully subdued the male population but was troubled by the treatment he and his men received from the city's women, especially the ladies of the upper class. To bring their behavior under control, Butler authored an order that took advantage of the gender and class politics of the day. His infamous General Order Number 28, issued on May 15, 1862, promised that any woman, especially those "calling themselves ladies," who continued to taunt or insult his troops through "word, gesture, or movement" would be "liable to be treated as a woman of the town plying her avocation." Confederate politicians and newspaper editors decried the implicit sexual threat that they suggested would allow occupying troops to treat ladies as if they were prostitutes. Journalists and politicians in both England and France echoed these complaints. Some foreign leaders demanded that Butler be punished, but he was never formally censured or asked to withdraw the order.

Butler later claimed that the Woman Order had worked well because it was constructed in such a way that it would execute itself. As with many other issues related to Butler's tenure in New Orleans, the truth is more complicated. In fact, Butler incarcerated at least two women in the months that followed the order, most notably outspoken Confederate sympathizer Eugenia Levy Phillips, whom he prosecuted for laughing as the funeral procession of a Federal officer passed in front of her house.

Despite the venom directed at Butler, his administration had some positive effect in New Orleans, including his successful campaign to clean the infamously dirty city to discourage yellow fever outbreaks, as well as his establishment of free markets that made food available to the city's poor and hungry, among them Southern-sympathizing refugees and the wives and children of Confederate soldiers. Some were surely grateful to the man dubbed Beast Butler, but his imperiousness, combined with

Benjamin Butler's long and controversial political and military career spanned more than 30 years, including the tumultuous years of the Civil War and Reconstruction. His issuance of the "Woman Order" during his tenure as commander of occupied New Orleans led many to call him "Beast" Butler. In addition to serving as general in the U.S. Army, Butler was an antislavery leader, U.S. representative, and candidate for president in 1884. (Library of Congress)

extensive property seizures, angered foreign consuls, bankers, and business owners who accused him of using his authority to line his own pockets. These accusations, though never proven, bore fruit, and Nathaniel Banks relieved Butler of his command in December 1862.

Although Confederate President Jefferson Davis placed a bounty on Butler's head and Confederates almost universally reviled him, Butler was wildly popular in the Union and was mentioned as a presidential candidate in 1863. After the war he was elected to Congress from Massachusetts, served three terms (1867–1875), and advocated a wide variety of reforms, including civil rights and woman suffrage. He was elected governor of Massachusetts in 1882 and died a wealthy and respected elder statesman in 1893. Butler remains a controversial figure in the South and is still regarded in popular lore as a brute and spoiler. Although recent biographers have offered a more balanced view, Butler continues to serve as the quintessential example of the invading Yankee who lacked couth, chivalry, and the appropriate respect for Southern ladies.

*Alecia P. Long*

*See also* Civilian Life; Confederate Homefront; Phillips, Eugenia Levy (1819–1901); Southern Women; Urban Women, Southern; Woman Order (General Order Number 28).

**References and Further Reading**

Faust, Drew Gilpin. 1996. *Mothers of Invention: Women of the Slaveholding South in the American Civil War.* Chapel Hill: University of North Carolina Press.

Hearn, Chester. 1997. *When the Devil Came Down to Dixie: Ben Butler in New Orleans.* Baton Rouge: Louisiana State University Press.

Rable, George. 1992. "'Missing in Action': Women of the Confederacy." In *Divided Houses: Gender and the Civil War,* edited by Catherine Clinton and Nina Silber, 134–146. New York: Oxford University Press.

Ryan, Mary. 1990. *Women in Public: Between Banners and Ballots, 1825–1880.* Baltimore, MD: Johns Hopkins University Press.

# C

## Camp Followers

"Camp follower" was a general term describing people who traveled with the armies of the Civil War in unofficial, semiofficial, or official capacities. Some were the families of military personnel who visited the army camps, especially during the winter months, and who provided a touch of the typical home life of nineteenth-century Americans. Others provided essential services such as laundering, cooking, and nursing. Still others served as prostitutes.

Female camp followers traditionally were found in the vicinity of armies because they provided services that military organizations could not offer. During the Civil War, leaders on both sides continued to modernize the military. As they did so, they attempted to reduce the number of people among the camp followers by converting unofficial positions into official military positions. For instance, many medical tasks were transferred to army doctors and nurses.

Members of the families of military personnel, in particular of the officers, constituted one group of camp followers. The wives and children of the officers set up households in rented rooms or in the tents and cabins occupied by the men during the winter. The visits allowed the men to recreate the domestic lives they had left behind and to interrupt the boredom of the cold months. The women continued the practices they adopted in their regular lives, rising in the morning to answer cards and notes and holding afternoon teas at which they entertained the wives of other officers. In the evenings, the women attended serenades by military bands and ensembles of soldiers, or they participated in balls sponsored by various officers. They added a note of gaiety and home to the somber work the men were carrying out.

The presence of the officers' families created difficulties for the military. In some cases, they put a burden on an already overworked medical staff. The histories of military nurses report that they sometimes clashed with officers when they were asked to treat children who were visiting their fathers. William Tecumseh Sherman felt it necessary to post orders to keep women from traveling with the army. The orders had limited effect, and he had to repeatedly issue such injunctions. The wives of officers generally understood such commands to apply to those below them, but, as the war continued, women visited the armies less frequently.

Other family members visited the camps to care for husbands, sons, or brothers who were wounded or who became ill. They traveled to the vicinity of the armies and searched until they found the soldier in question. Although their presence sometimes relieved the workload of those charged with nursing, the family members required food, housing, and sometimes medical care of their own. Such people traveled as far toward the last location of the soldier as possible. Then they sought out an officer or some other official, who would provide them with a pass that allowed them through the military lines. Many of these people become physically and emotionally overcome by hospital conditions, requiring care themselves. Several nurses who penned memoirs following the war reported that women who came to the front looking for their husbands stayed long enough to give birth, again needing additional care themselves. Many of the family members who became camp followers for short periods of time located their relatives among the dead and took the bodies home for burial.

The military could not provide the soldiers with laundry facilities or meals during the Civil War. Traditionally, the wives of enlisted men filled these roles. During the Revolutionary War, the military attempted to determine a formula for the number of laundresses and cooks who would be supported by each unit, and that practice continued during the Civil War. The men were encouraged to form

messes. Officers pooled their financial resources to hire cooks for their messes. In most men units, these cooks were free blacks or contrabands, slaves who had been freed by the conflict. Contrabands also supported laundries. Soldiers who could not reach food-preparation and laundering facilities, or who could not afford to use them, learned to care for themselves. As a result, soldiers succumbed to disease that bred in poorly prepared food and filthy clothing.

Some women took on the responsibility of caring for groups of men. Vivandieres, or daughters of the regiment, received a charge from the commander of a particular unit or a mayor or governor. This semiofficial appointment was very important to some women who accompanied the men to the front, caring for them along the way. Most of the

The camp of the 31st Pennsylvania Infantry near Washington, D.C., in 1862, included women and children. (Library of Congress)

women were related to a man in the unit, usually a noncommissioned officer, and many of them had lived with the military their entire lives. The women also reminded the men of life at home and served to lift their spirits just by their presence.

The most problematical camp followers were the women who worked as prostitutes. The pairing of armies and prostitutes is as old as time. The pervasive presence of such women gave the term "camp follower" a negative connotation that it did not have in earlier years. The prostitutes, given the name "hookers" because of the numbers of them who followed the command of Joseph Hooker, indicated a basic conflict in social paradigms in the nineteenth century. Men were not supposed to live in an all-male environment. They needed the virtue of the domestic sphere, a sphere dominated by women. But virtuous wives could not maintain their domestic virtue in an army tent. Therefore, prostitutes provided a female presence in that all-male world. Unfortunately, prostitution did not provide the virtue that was the bedrock of the image of the middle-class family, and military officials worked to remove the women from the vicinity of the camps. In one memorable case, a boatload of "soiled doves" was sailed up and down Western rivers. In town after town, community officials refused to allow the women to land.

*Karen A. Kehoe*

**See also** Civilian Life; Contrabands; Domesticity; Family Life, Northern; Family Life, Southern; Northern Women; Nurses; Prostitution; Separate Spheres; Southern Women; Vivandieres.

**References and Further Reading**

Blumenthal, Walter Hart. 1974. *Women Camp Followers of the American Revolution.* New York: Arno Press.

Moore, Frank. 1866. *Women of the War: Their Heroism and Self–Sacrifice.* Hartford, CT: S. S. Scranton & Co.

Massey, Mary Elizabeth. 1966. *Bonnet Brigades.* New York: Alfred A. Knopf.

## Carroll, Anna Ella (1815–1894)

Political pamphleteer and military strategist Anna Ella Carroll, the daughter of Maryland Governor Thomas King Carroll, is best-known for her claim to have devised the so-called Tennessee Plan for the Union army's invasion in February 1862. Carroll wrote a series of pamphlets that laid out the legal rationale for using the army to enforce Federal laws in the Southern states.

Carroll wrote a number of pamphlets in support of the Union in 1861 and 1862. The most important of these, *Reply to Breckinridge* (1861), detailed the arguments that President Abraham Lincoln and Attorney General Edward Bates made that, as commander-in-chief, Lincoln could use the armed forces to perform his duties as chief enforcement officer of the United States. In other words, he could call for volunteers, suspend the writ of habeas corpus, institute a naval blockade, and use the army to put down a domestic rebellion. Lincoln employed this legal tactic throughout the course of the war.

Carroll's pamphlet was so clearly written that Secretary of State William Henry Seward ordered it distributed to Congress. The legal rationale Carroll described was later delineated by notable lawyer Horace Binney and published more widely, but Carroll provided the earliest explication of the legal basis for Lincoln's actions in the first months of the war.

Later pamphlets by Carroll criticized the president's actions, particularly regarding the Union's confiscation of slaves as contraband of war, arguing the Border States would rebel. She also promoted colonization efforts by Aaron Columbus Burr to settle exslaves in Central America in what he named the Lincoln Colony.

Carroll's claim to fame rests not on her writings but on her claim that she created the Tennessee Campaign. She approached the War Department in 1861 after she met riverboat Captain Charles Scott in St. Louis, Missouri. As Carroll wrote to the Washington, D.C. *National Intelligencer* shortly after the Confederate surrender in 1865, Scott pointed out the strategic value of using the Tennessee and Cumberland Rivers, which flowed north, instead of the Mississippi River, to invade the Confederacy via Tennessee. Neither river was strongly fortified and controlling them would relieve Union loyalists, particularly in eastern Tennessee. Any gunboats damaged by Confederate fire would float northward, back into Union territory, and the Tennessee was navigable clear to Alabama, providing excellent ingress to the heart of the Confederacy.

Carroll presented Scott's information to Assistant Secretary of War Thomas Scott in November 1861. Her plan duplicated others, including the overall strategy of the Union army under General Ulysses S. Grant, who had captured towns at the mouths of the rivers and was waiting for Union gunboats before venturing farther inland. In February 1862, the Union invaded Tennessee up the rivers, taking Forts Henry and Donelson.

Shortly after the war, Carroll began petitioning Congress to pay her as a strategist. Her claim was adopted by the suffragists Susan B. Anthony, Sarah Ellen Blackwell, and Elizabeth Cady Stanton, for whom Carroll became a symbol of the military's disregard for women when it came to the work of the war. Her role as a symbol endures in her continuing appearances in Civil War historiography as an unsung female hero. Her legal acumen, while widely respected by politicians, including Lincoln, has drawn less attention than her legendary status as military strategist.

*Janet L. Coryell*

**See also** Anthony, Susan B. (1820–1906); Border States; Civilian Life; Contrabands; Lincoln, Abraham (1809–1865); Northern Women; Stanton, Elizabeth Cady (1815–1902); Union Homefront.

**References and Further Reading**

Carroll, Anna Ella. 1861. *Reply to the Speech of Hon. J. C. Breckinridge*. Washington, DC: Henry Polkinhorn.

Carroll, Anna Ella. 1861. *The War Powers of the General Government*. Washington, DC: Henry Polkinhorn.

Coryell, Janet L. 1990. *Neither Heroine Nor Fool: Anna Ella Carroll of Maryland*. Kent, OH: Kent State University Press.

Williams, Kenneth P. 1950. "The Tennessee River Campaign and Anna Ella Carroll." *Indiana Magazine of History* 46: 221–248.

## Cary, Mary Ann Shadd (1823–1893)

The activist daughter of free black parents, Mary Ann Shadd Cary worked as a recruiting officer of black troops for the Union army from 1863 to 1864. Cary was a paid organizer of the Twenty-ninth Regiment Connecticut Volunteers and later of the Twenty-eighth Colored Infantry (Indiana). Working from a base in New Albany, Indiana, she used her considerable ties among networks of abolitionists and her skill at public speaking to muster in both enslaved and free African Americans. She also organized aid to contraband families. In her lifetime, Cary was an antislavery lecturer, a proponent of black nationalism, a participant in black emigration to Canada, an opinionated editor, teacher, writer, lawyer, and a women's rights advocate.

Mary Ann Shadd was born in Wilmington, Delaware. Her father, Abraham Shadd, worked with the Underground Railroad and was an agent for abolitionist William Lloyd Garrison's *The Liberator*. Mary Ann attended a Quaker school in Pennsylvania and soon became a teacher of free black children. With the 1850 passage of the Fugitive Slave Law, she joined other family members as they immigrated to Canada. She established an integrated school there through the auspices of the American Missionary Association. She also began publishing accounts that encouraged black migration to Canada West and was the strongly opinionated editor of the *Provincial Freeman* newspaper (ca. 1854–1860).

Mary Ann was attracted to the African colonization ideas of Martin Delany, but criticized James Redpath and Haitian emigration schemes. She married Thomas F. Cary of Toronto in 1856 but was widowed in 1860. Thwarted in her bid to become a missionary in Africa, she left her two young children with family and returned to the United States to work as Delany's agent, traveling across the Midwest, speaking in churches and other venues and canvassing possible recruits. The work was dangerous in states with black codes and in those where conservative Democrats feared an influx of African Americans as a result of the Emancipation Proclamation. Cary made her base in New Albany, a steamboat building center on the Ohio River with a proportionately high population of black residents and at the Kentucky state line—a good spot not only to recruit but also to aid runaways in their journey to Canada.

Cary's recruitment of African American soldiers for the Union army bore fruit in 1864. The Twenty-ninth Colored Infantry was mustered in Connecticut in March 1864 and sent to the Department of the South for active duty. Cary continued working as a recruiter for Connecticut and Indiana. She was also an agent for the Chicago-based Colored Ladies' Freedmen's Aid Society (CLFAS), which gathered and sent supplies to former slaves living on the front lines. She also raised funds for her Mission School in Chatham, Canada. She returned to Chatham in the last months of the war.

Cary later moved to Washington, D.C., where she attended Howard University Law School and earned her law degree in 1870, becoming the first black female lawyer in the United States. She was a strong advocate of women's rights, including the right to vote. She organized the Colored Women's Progressive Franchise Association in 1880.

*Barbara Bair*

***See also*** Abolitionism and Northern Reformers; African American Women; Aid Societies; Antislavery Societies; Garrison, William Lloyd (1805–1879); Northern Women; Teachers, Northern; Union Homefront.

**References and Further Reading**

Bearden, Jim, and Linda Jean Butler. 1977. *Shadd: The Life and Times of Mary Shadd Cary.* Toronto: N. C. Press.

Rhodes, Jane. 1998. *Mary Ann Shadd Cary: The Black Press and Protest in the Nineteenth Century.* Bloomington: Indiana University Press.

## Catholic Women

Lay and religious Catholic women offered their services to both the Union and Confederate armies during the American Civil War. Like their Protestant counterparts, lay Catholic women prepared bandages, sewed, and raised money. Religious Catholic women—women who entered a religious community and professed vows of poverty, chastity, and obedience—made the most significant contribution through their work as nurses.

At the beginning of the war, approximately five thousand Catholic sisters resided in the United States, of whom over six hundred assisted in the

Sister M.M. Joseph of the Sisters of Mercy. She and others of her order served in a military hospital at Beaufort, North Carolina, during the Civil War. (National Archives and Records Administration)

medical needs of the war. The women came from twenty-one communities and twelve different religious orders. These religious communities included the Daughters of Charity (Emmitsburg, Maryland), the Holy Cross (South Bend, Indiana), Sisters of Mercy (Baltimore, Maryland; Chicago, Illinois; Little Rock, Arkansas; Pittsburgh, Pennsylvania; Vicksburg, Mississippi), Sisters of Charity (Cincinnati, Ohio; Nazareth, Kentucky; New York, New York), the Sisters of St. Joseph (Philadelphia, Pennsylvania; Wheeling, West Virginia), Dominican Sisters (Memphis, Tennessee; Perrysville, Kentucky), Our Lady of Mt. Carmel Sisters (New Orleans, Louisiana), and the Ursuline Sisters (Galveston, Texas). The women who constituted these religious communities were primarily of working-class background and mainly of Irish, German, or French ancestry.

Sisters brought to the war both their religious vows and a Catholic tradition of caring for the sick. Professing religious vows ensured that the sisters acted out of compassion and charity, that they did not relate to soldiers in a sexual manner, and that they obeyed orders. The Catholic tradition of caring for the sick spanned first-century sick-rooms and the Crusades of the eleventh through the thirteenth centuries. Florence Nightingale, coordinator and administer of nurses for the British army during the Crimean War in the midnineteenth century, relied on the assistance of Catholic sisters. In the United States, women's religious communities founded and worked in hospitals, responded to citywide epidemics and diseases, and visited the sick.

Throughout the war, political leaders, medical authorities, and bishops requested the services of the sisters. Wartime demands and the course of battle meant that the sisters did not have time to seek the proper permission from their local ecclesiastical authority. The sisters worked in a variety of medical facilities and locations, including the battlefield, field tent hospitals, prison camps, transport ships, and other makeshift hospitals. Most sisters also traveled extensively outside the geographical boundaries of their religious communities. The Daughters of Charity, stationed in Emmitsburg, Maryland, worked in Washington, D.C., Richmond, Virginia, and New Orleans, Louisiana.

Sisters provided the armies with nursing, hospital management, and religious needs. Antebellum America looked down on women who cared for the sick outside of the family or home. Catholic sisters, however, responded quickly to the demands of war. Sisters performed a variety of jobs, often in poor and disorganized conditions, that placed significant demands on their time and physical well-being. They worked with doctors in the wards, dressed wounds, assisted with surgeries, prepared corpses for burial, and attended to soldiers with contagious diseases. The women also focused on the preparation of meals, the upkeep of the medical facilities, the administration of the hospital, and the acquisition of food and medical supplies. Finally, the sisters addressed the religious needs of the soldiers by performing baptisms, attending to the dying, and encouraging the repentance of sins.

Some religious communities required the fulfillment of spiritual and material needs, and a proper

work atmosphere. First, sisters and their ecclesiastical authority sought the presence of a Catholic chaplain who could say Mass. Due to the scarcity of Catholic chaplains, this request could not always be met. Second, religious communities required that they exercise control over the hospitals in which they served, that the government pay for the expenses of travel, food, board, and clothing, and that they need not associate with other female volunteers who might hinder their work.

Sisters maintained professional relationships with doctors and other female volunteers, and they gained the respect of the soldiers they served. Doctors generally did not care for the presence of female volunteer nurses, who often believed they knew better how to care for the sick and wounded. In working with sisters, the doctors, including U.S. Surgeon General William A. Hammond, commented positively on the skills and commitment of the sisters. Soldiers initially viewed the sisters with suspicion and perplexity because of a general prejudice toward Catholics and the clothing of the sisters. With time, the soldiers came to respect the sisters for their commitment, sacrifices, and impartiality. Some women also respected the work of the sisters, but other female nurses and Dorothea Dix, Superintendent of the United States Army Nurses, often discriminated against the sisters because of their religion, the question of control, and the perceived lack of warmth on the part of the sisters.

In 1918, a monument was erected in Washington, D.C., to the Catholic sisters in honor of their service during the Civil War.

*Sarah K. Nytroe*

***See also*** Hospitals; Nurses; Religion.

**References and Further Reading**

Barton, George. 1898. *Angels of the Battlefield: A History of the Labors of the Catholic Sisterhoods in the Late Civil War*. Philadelphia, PA: Catholic Art Publishing Company.

Ellefson, Cheryl. 1996. "Servants of God and Man: The Sisters of Charity." In *Valor and Lace: The Roles of Confederate Women, 1861–1865*, edited by Mauriel Phillips Joslyn, 175–184. Murfreesboro, TN: Southern Heritage Press.

Jolly, Ellen Ryan. 1927. *Nuns of the Battlefield*. Providence, RI: Providence Visitor Press.

Leonard, Ann. 1991. "Red Rover, The Civil War, and the Nuns." *Lincoln Herald* 93 (4): 136–140.

Leonard, Ann. 2000. "Catholic Sisters and Nursing in the Civil War." *Lincoln Herald* 102 (2): 65–81.

Maher, Sister Mary Denis. 1989. *To Bind up the Wounds: Catholic Sister Nurses in the U.S. Civil War.* Westport, CT: Greenwood Press.

Oakes, Sister Mary Paullina, ed. 1998. *Angels of Mercy: An Eyewitness Account of the Civil War and Yellow Fever; A Primary Resource by Sister Ignatius Sumner.* Baltimore, MD: Cathedral Foundation.

Wall, Barbra Mann. 1998. "Called to a Mission of Charity: The Sisters of St. Joseph in the Civil War." *Nursing History Review* 80 (1): 36–57.

## Cazneau, Jane McManus Storm [Cora Montgomery] (1807–1878)

Jane McManus Storm Cazneau, known best as Cora Montgomery, was a journalist who promoted United States territorial and commercial expansion before, during, and after the Civil War.

Cazneau was a native of New York and promoted gradual emancipation throughout her career. Educated at Emma Willard's Female Seminary, in the 1830s she speculated in land in Mexican Texas on which to settle freed blacks. In the 1840s she promoted Manifest Destiny in *The United States Magazine and Democratic Review* and *The New York Sun.* Cazneau worked with businessmen who sought to expand trade and commerce, convert sailing ships to steam and iron vessels, and establish coaling stations in the tropics. In editorials and journal articles in *The New York Sun, Tribune,* and *Herald,* she promoted revolutionaries friendly to the United States government in Mexico, Cuba, Nicaragua, and the Dominican Republic. Her most famous adventure was traveling to Mexico City during the Mexican War and reporting her exploits from behind enemy lines.

As Cazneau traveled in the tropics, she became an authority on the affairs of Mexico, Central America, and the Caribbean. Editors, diplomats, political leaders, and foreign dignitaries sought her advice. She advised presidents from James K. Polk through Ulysses S. Grant, in addition to the cabinet members in those administrations.

In the late 1850s, in anticipation of a migration of freed slaves financed by the Federal government, Jane and her husband William invested in land and port facilities in the Dominican Republic. When secession came, Secretary of State William Seward sent for her and paid her expenses at *The New York Sun,* where she wrote patriotic editorials and rallied support for President Abraham Lincoln's administration.

In August 1862, New Yorkers mobbed blacks, and President Lincoln proposed financial assistance to those who would emigrate. Congress abolished slavery in Washington, D.C., and appropriated $100,000 to aid in colonization. Cazneau published *Life in the Tropics* as a guide for the emigrants. In response to the Emancipation Proclamation, Cazneau helped New York investors organize the American West Indies Company to transport and settle emigrants on company land. Spain had reclaimed its colony and welcomed the former slaves, who would grow cotton, then in high demand because of the Union blockade of Confederate ports. Few exslaves migrated to Santo Domingo, but those who did helped oust the Spanish and restore the Dominican Republic. After the Civil War, Cazneau became involved in the Grant administration scandals involving the annexation of the Dominican Republic and Samana Bay for use by United States Navy and merchant ships.

During her thirty-year career, Cazneau published more than one hundred newspaper columns in six metropolitan newspapers, more than twenty journal articles in three national journals, and fifteen or more books and pamphlets, and she edited five or more newspapers and journals. Blind in her last years, she lived a quiet life in Jamaica at Keith Hall, a restored plantation she converted into a winter resort for tourists, where she established a vocational school for freed slaves. She died in a storm at sea.

*Linda S. Hudson*

***See also*** Lincoln, Abraham (1809–1865); Northern Women; Union Homefront.

### References and Further Reading

Hodgson, Godfrey. 2005. "Storm over Mexico." *History Today* 55: 34–39.

Hudson, Linda S. 2001. *Mistress of Manifest Destiny; A Biography of Jane McManus Storm Cazneau, 1807–1878*. Austin: Texas State Historical Association.

Reilly, Tom. 1981. "Jane McManus Storms, Letters from the Mexican War, 1846–1848." *Southwestern Historical Quarterly* 85: 21–44.

## Chamberlain, Frances Caroline "Fannie" Adams (1825–1905)

Wife of Civil War General Joshua Lawrence Chamberlain, Fannie Chamberlain was a skilled musician, aspiring artist, and dedicated teacher prior to her marriage in 1855. Raised by a Congregationalist minister and educated by some of the most famed musicians of the era, Fannie taught in both Maine and Georgia. During the Civil War, she aided her husband's recovery from wounds and ailments, sometimes traveling south to be by his side. The Chamberlains had a sometimes turbulent marriage, but they remained together, raising two children, until she passed away in 1905.

Born Caroline Frances Adams in 1825, Fannie, as she was called by family and friends, was a distant cousin of John Quincy Adams. Her parents, Ashur and Amelia Wyllys Adams, had six other children to care for, and at an early age they sent Fannie to live with their cousin, Reverend George E. Adams, and his wife Sarah. As the well respected minister of the Congregationalist First Parish Church in Brunswick, Maine, Reverend Adams had the resources to provide Fannie with a good education. As she grew older, Fannie was taught to appreciate music, literature, and art. Her music teachers included Frederick Crouch and George Frederick Root. Fannie also participated in the literary society in Brunswick, further sharpening her intellectual skills.

Fannie demonstrated her restraint in her courtship by a young scholar from neighboring Bowdoin College, Joshua Lawrence Chamberlain. As their relationship developed, Lawrence, as he was known, and Fannie parted ways in 1852. She headed south to a teaching position at a female academy in Milledgeville, Georgia, and he went on to pursue a degree at the Bangor Theological Seminary. Eventually, the two married in December 1855. Perhaps reluctantly, Fannie gave up her career and settled down to be a wife and mother. The couple had two children who survived infancy. The family made their home in Brunswick, Maine, where Lawrence had accepted a position at his alma mater.

During the Civil War, Fannie supported Lawrence, traveled with him to Washington, D.C., and spent time with him in camp. On more than one occasion, she nursed him back to health and comforted him during the conflict's bleakest months. The war would have a lasting impact on their relationship. Emerging as one of the Union's most popular heroes as a result of his actions at Gettysburg, Lawrence became governor of Maine for four consecutive terms. Fannie felt slightly neglected as a result of his constant absences from home, and she contemplated divorce in 1868 but the couple reconciled. Family life became more stable after Lawrence became Bowdoin's president in 1871.

Fannie's health deteriorated near the end of her life. Totally blind by 1900 and dependent on family members and helpers, she died at the age of 80. She was buried in Brunswick.

*Kanisorn Wongsrichanalai*

*See also* Teachers, Northern.

**References and Further Reading**

Smith, Diane Monroe. 1999. *Fanny and Joshua: The Enigmatic Lives of Francis Caroline Adams and Joshua Lawrence Chamberlain*. Gettysburg, PA: Thomas Publications.

Trulock, Alice Rains. 1992. *In the Hands of Providence: Joshua L. Chamberlain and the American Civil War*. Chapel Hill: University of North Carolina Press.

Smith, Jennifer Lund. "The Reconstruction of 'Home': The Civil War and the Marriage of Lawrence and Fannie Chamberlain." In *Intimate Strategies of the Civil War: Military Commanders and their Wives*, edited by Carol K. Bleser and Lesley J. Gordon, 157–177. New York: Oxford University Press.

## Chancellorsville, Battle of (April 29–May 6, 1863)

The Battle of Chancellorsville was a stunning Confederate victory, but it also resulted in the death of Confederate General Thomas "Stonewall" Jackson.

The battle, which took place primarily around the home of the Chancellor family, proved to be a harrowing event for the area's women and children.

After the Union defeat at the Battle of Fredericksburg (December 11–15, 1862) and the subsequent stalemate along the Rappahannock River, the Federal government replaced General Ambrose Burnside with General Joseph Hooker. In the spring of 1863, Hooker chose a more daring campaign than those of his predecessors. On the evening of April 30, Hooker divided the one hundred-thirty-thousand-soldier army of the Potomac, sending approximately seventy thousand troops to converge at Chancellorsville. The rest of the Army of the Potomac remained at Fredericksburg to threaten the Confederate front. Confederate General Robert E. Lee suspected Hooker's intentions and immediately realigned his troops to meet this threat. Vastly outnumbered with only sixty thousand troops, Lee risked leaving ten thousand soldiers under General Jubal Early at Fredericksburg and moved the rest of his forces toward Chancellorsville.

During the midday hours of May 1, Confederates moved into position through the Wilderness with the assistance of local citizens. Meanwhile, Hooker realigned his position so that the left was on the Rappahannock River and its center was on the high ground outside Chancellorsville.

On the morning of May 2, Jackson's thirty thousand troops performed an extremely risky flank movement across the front of the Union army, while Lee remained with approximately fifteen thousand soldiers to face Hooker's main force. These movements caused Lee, Jackson, and Early to be severely outnumbered and vulnerable to Union attack. Yet they believed that Hooker would not take the offensive, and they were correct. That evening, while General Oliver O. Howard's men were eating dinner, Jackson's troops burst out of the woods, causing the entire Union right eventually to crumble in chaos. Jackson pushed up the Union flank for two miles until the Federals were finally able to secure a defensive position. Meanwhile, Lee utilized two Confederate divisions to attack Hooker's front. When night enveloped the battlefield and created confusion, Jackson was accidentally shot in his left arm by friendly fire. His arm had to be amputated and Jackson succumbed to pneumonia eight days later.

Throughout May 3, the fighting continued on two fronts. Under Hooker's orders, General John Sedgwick's VI Corps broke the Confederates, while General Daniel Sickles retreated from his position on the high ground one mile west of Chancellorsville. Lee's troops immediately took advantage of this withdrawal by massing artillery in the vacated high ground and renewed the offensive. In the evening hours, Lee received notice of Sedgwick's breakthrough at Fredericksburg and sent troops to meet them. Although Sedgwick defeated the Confederates at Salem Church on May 4, he was forced to withdraw back across the Rappahannock River because of Hooker's failure to support his advances. During the evening hours of May 4, the Union leadership held a council of war and voted to counterattack Lee. The following day, despite the desire of many to launch a counterattack against Lee, Hooker refrained from attacking and ordered a retreat that night.

Trapped in the midst of the fighting armies were the women and children who lived in the nearby area. At the time of the battle, Chancellorsville was not a town; instead, it was named after the Chancellor family who owned a house on the property. In 1860, the widowed Mrs. Chancellor lived there with her six unmarried daughters and one son. Upon hearing that the Union army was heading in their direction, the family put on multiple layers of clothing and tied silverware and tea sets under their hoop skirts to protect them. When the Chancellor house was requisitioned for Hooker's headquarters, the family was forced to move into a back room. Eventually, sixteen other women and children joined the Chancellor family to seek refuge. By May 2, the house overflowed with wounded soldiers, and the family's piano served as the surgeon's operating table. Unable to do anything other than watch the battle preparations from the front window, one of the Chancellor girls, Sue, recalled feeling helpless as the sounds of battle grew louder. Finally, the women and children were moved to the cellar, where they saw amputated limbs being piled up in the yard. During the intense battle, the house caught fire, forcing the women and children to flee from the home among the confusion and chaos of the battle. Even in her old age, Sue was unable to forget the scenes of terror as she watched her childhood home burn to ashes among the dead and dying soldiers.

Although the Southerners suffered approximately thirteen thousand casualties (22 percent), the Battle of Chancellorsville ended as a decisive Confederate victory, and it led Lee to decide to take the offensive into Pennsylvania. With Union casualties numbering around seventeen thousand (15 percent) and in the face of another terrible morale collapse, President Abraham Lincoln replaced Hooker with General George Gordon Meade.

*Kristina K. Dunn*

**See also** Civilian Life; Confederate Homefront; Southern Women.
**References and Further Reading**
Gallagher, Gary, ed. 1996. *Chancellorsville: The Battle and Its Aftermath.* Chapel Hill: University of North Carolina Press.
Sears, Stephen. 1996. *Chancellorsville.* Boston: Houghton-Mifflin.
Waugh, Charles, and Martin Greenburg, eds. 1999. *The Women's War in the South: Recollections and Reflections of the American Civil War.* Nashville, TN: Cumberland House.

## Chesnut, Mary Boykin (1823–1886)

Prominent South Carolinian Mary Boykin Chesnut kept an extensive diary during the Civil War, recording her views on politics, people, and the momentous events around her. Chesnut carefully revised, reworked, and expanded the journals that she had begun compiling in early 1861 for future publication.

Mary Boykin Miller was born on March 31, 1823, near Camden, South Carolina. She was the first of the four children of Mary Boykin and Stephen Decatur Miller, an early proponent of states' rights who was elected to the governorship in 1828 and later to the United States Senate. Her father owned three plantations and hundreds of slaves in Mississippi, and in 1835 he resettled his family there.

Mary was taught at home, then sent to school in Camden until she was twelve. When her family left South Carolina, Mary entered Madame Talvande's French School for Young Ladies in Charleston, where she learned to speak French fluently and studied literature, natural sciences, German, and history with the daughters of South Carolina's plantation elite. When rumors that recent Princeton graduate James Chesnut Jr. was courting her reached her father, he took her to Mississippi. In 1837 she returned to Madame Talvande's, but her education ended with the 1838 death of her father. Mary and James Chesnut married on April 23, 1840, and went to live at Mulberry, the Chesnut plantation near Camden.

Although she had married the heir to a great fortune, Mary found that her father-in-law controlled the family assets. James's mother and two spinster sisters managed the household, which had more slaves than they could usefully employ. James was busy with his law practice and service in the state legislature. Mary's only responsibility was to produce children, but, to their sorrow and frustration, the couple remained childless. Bored with the elegant but dull life at Mulberry, Mary longed for clever companions.

James Chesnut was elected to the United States Senate in 1858. In Washington, Mary was at last surrounded by influential people who shared her interest in literature and politics and who admired her as a conversationalist and hostess. She was acutely aware that a woman's status depended on the success of her husband. In those two years she formed lasting friendships with Southern politicians and their wives—most notably Jefferson and Varina Davis. On November 10, 1860, to his wife's dismay, James Chesnut became the first Southern Senator to resign his Senate seat following Abraham Lincoln's election.

James helped draft South Carolina's ordinance of secession. Mary accompanied him to Montgomery, Alabama, for the first Confederate Congress and then to Charleston when he became an aide to General Pierre G. T. Beauregard in the weeks before the bombardment of Fort Sumter. The Chesnuts next went to the new Confederate capital, Richmond, for

Prominent South Carolinian Mary Boykin Chesnut kept a diary of her experience during the Civil War which was published posthumously (1823–1886). (Chesnut, Mary, *A Diary from Dixie*, 1905)

a few months. Mary reestablished her friendship with Varina Davis and worked briefly in a Confederate hospital. She chafed at her husband's aristocratic refusal to actively seek office or political appointment. When James was not elected to the Confederate Senate, President Davis sent him back to Columbia as a member of the powerful Council of Five to oversee South Carolina's defenses. Mary convalesced at her sister's home in Flat Rock, North Carolina, for much of this period, recovering from "hospital fever" contracted in Richmond.

James's commission as a colonel on President Davis's staff took the Chesnuts back to Richmond. They lived in rented rooms near the White House of the Confederacy and saw the Davises almost every day. This period of the war was the most interesting for Mary. Her parlor was an oasis of what she called "the old life," a distraction from the

Confederacy's shortages, dimming prospects, and mourning. The flirtations of her houseguests, the Preston sisters of Columbia, provided the romantic interest in *Mary Chesnut's Civil War*. She also chronicled political infighting in the Confederate government and military.

In April 1864, James was promoted to brigadier general and sent back to Columbia. As General William Tecumseh Sherman's forces approached South Carolina, James sent Mary to safety in Lincolnton, North Carolina, and then in Chester, South Carolina, where in her threadbare quarters she continued to provide a gracious welcome to old friends.

The Chesnuts returned penniless to Mulberry. The family fortune, chiefly slaves and Confederate bonds, was gone. They would struggle financially for the rest of their lives. While her husband involved himself in postwar conservative politics, Mary oversaw daily life at Mulberry and ran a small butter and egg business with her maid. In 1873, Mary and James moved into Sarsfield, a new home in Camden built with bricks salvaged from outbuildings at Mulberry. Mary wrote drafts of two novels, one about the war and another recounting her student days. Neither was ever finished or published. In the 1880s, using techniques she had learned writing fiction, she began rewriting her journals. The task was largely completed when James died in February 1885 and her mother a few days later. Exhausted and grieving, she lost everything but Sarsfield and a few cows in the settlement of her husband's debts. Mary turned her attention to putting her husband's papers in order and died of heart disease on November 22, 1886. Her rewritten journal, given to a close friend, was first published in 1905.

Mary's views on Southern society come through in her journals. She hated slavery, chiefly because of the sexual license it gave to men and the suffering this caused their wives and daughters, but she was dependent on slaves. She enjoyed flattery and deference, but disapproved of men's legal power over their wives' assets and activities, as well as of men who thought their sex conferred superior intelligence and wisdom.

*Nancy Gray Schoonmaker*

*See also* Confederate Homefront; Davis, Jefferson (1808–1889); Davis, Varina Banks Howell (1826–1906); Diaries and Journals; Hospitals; Plantation Life; Politics; Secession; Slaveholding Women; Southern Women.

**References and Further Reading**

Chesnut, Mary Boykin Miller. 1984. *The Private Mary Chesnut: The Unpublished Civil War Diaries,* edited by C. Vann Woodward and Elisabeth Muhlenfeld. New York: Oxford University Press.

Chesnut, Mary Boykin Miller. 2002. *Two Novels by Mary Chesnut,* edited by Elisabeth Muhlenfeld with an introduction by Elizabeth Hanson. Charlottesville: University Press of Virginia.

Kurant, Wendy. 2002. "The Education of a Domestic Woman in Mary Boykin Chesnut's *Two Years.*" *The Southern Literary Journal* 34 (2): 14–29.

Muhlenfeld, Elisabeth. 1981. *Mary Boykin Chesnut: A Biography.* Baton Rouge: Louisiana State University Press.

Wilson, Edmund. 1962 [1984]. *Patriotic Gore: Studies in the Literature of the American Civil War,* with a foreword by C. Vann Woodward. Boston: Northeastern University Press.

Woodward, C. Vann and Elisabeth Muhlenfeld, eds. 1981. *Mary Chesnut's Civil War.* New Haven, CT: Yale University Press.

## Chickamauga, Battle of (September 19–20, 1863)

The Battle of Chickamauga, Georgia, was one of several pivotal engagements in 1863. The battle pitted the Union Army of the Cumberland against the Confederate Army of Tennessee, the two primary adversaries in Tennessee throughout the conflict. Although militarily a Confederate victory, it prompted the Union to unite three of its armies. This consolidation ultimately led to a decisive Union victory at Chattanooga, Tennessee, in November 1863. Women took part in the Battle of Chickamauga, as they did in many Civil War battles, participating as soldiers and medical personnel. In addition, many women and their families witnessed and were displaced by the fighting because much of it literally took place on their farms.

By late summer 1863, Major General William S. Rosecrans's Army of the Cumberland occupied a front facing General Braxton Bragg's Army of Tennessee. Their positions had remained roughly the same since their winter engagement at Murfreesboro, Tennessee. On the heels of victories at Vicksburg, Mississippi, and Gettysburg, Pennsylvania, President Abraham Lincoln and the Union high command began to pressure Rosecrans to attack the Confederates in eastern Tennessee. In August 1863, Rosecrans and his men threatened the Confederate supply center at Chattanooga. Bragg retreated, allowing Chattanooga to fall on September 6, 1863. Simultaneously, Union Major General Ambrose Burnside's Army of the Ohio moved south from Kentucky and took control of Knoxville, Tennessee.

The loss of these two rail centers prompted Confederate President Jefferson Davis to pressure Bragg to attack Rosecrans. As Rosecrans prepared to move into Georgia, Bragg advanced to monitor both him and Burnside. Reinforcements were ordered to assist Bragg, who began to look for a way to destroy Rosecrans's army.

After taking Chattanooga, Rosecrans marched his men toward the Georgia mountains to flank Bragg again. This time, Bragg maintained his position and looked for an opportunity to strike at the Union flank. The Confederates missed two opportunities to attack Rosecrans as his troops advanced through the mountains, and an alerted Rosecrans pulled his corps back to Chattanooga. By September 18, Bragg's Confederates were on the eastern side of Chickamauga Creek, while Rosecrans marched his army to Chattanooga on the west side.

On September 19, a Union division probing toward Chickamauga Creek ran into Confederate cavalry and forced their retreat. The fighting soon escalated, and by nightfall every unit of Rosecrans's army was involved in the fighting, as well as all but two of Bragg's. That evening, Bragg received additional reinforcements from Virginia. After a few hours' delay the following morning, the Confederates pitched into the Union divisions and started to work their way around the Union left flank. In the midst of fierce fighting, a confused Rosecrans mistakenly ordered Brigadier General Thomas Wood's division to shift to the left and cover Thomas's right. Wood disengaged his division, which had been skirmishing with the Confederate infantry, and shifted his brigades to the Union left. This decision led Wood's men to the only farms that provided cleared terrain for troop deployments. The farms' families—the Brocks, Brothertons, Kellys, and Poes—evacuated the farms during the heavy fighting. The postwar writer Ambrose Bierce served with the Ninth Indiana Volunteers in the same area, and his short story *Chickamauga* featured a child who discovered his mother's dead body.

The following morning, Longstreet pushed his wing toward the Brothertons' field near the now vacant center of the Union line. Longstreet's brigades pushed aside the smaller Union brigades that tried to fill the gap and split the Union line in two. Rosecrans and the Union right flank were rolled up to the south, and they were forced to flee over the mountains into Chattanooga. Thomas and the Union left flank were pushed back to Horseshoe Ridge. After pulling his forces back to Chattanooga, Thomas became known as the Rock of Chickamauga. The Confederates were left in possession of the field, and they quickly pushed toward the high ground surrounding Chattanooga.

As they did at many Civil War battles, women witnessed and participated in the Battle of Chickamauga firsthand. Among the soldiers who fought at Chickamauga, Margaret Catherine Murphy served with her father in the Ninety-Eighth Ohio Volunteers. After his death at the battle, she continued to serve for an additional two and half years. Along Horseshoe Ridge, Hiram Vittatoe, his wife, and their three daughters rode out the fierce fighting in a hole below their kitchen floor. After the Confederates pushed the Union forces from their family homestead, they were finally able to emerge from the cellar.

As a result of two days of combat, the Union suffered 16,170 casualties to the Confederacy's 18,454. One of the Union casualties was Frances Hook, a woman who fought disguised as Frank Miller. Confederates captured Hook and later shot her as she tried to escape. When her sex was discovered, she was returned to Federal lines. Dr. Mary Edwards Walker operated as a regimental assistant surgeon and later treated Hook for her wounds. Walker arrived with the many women nurses who arrived to treat the wounded at Chickamauga and Chattanooga.

*William H. Brown*

***See also*** Female Combatants; Nurses; Walker, Mary Edwards (1832–1919).

**References and Further Reading**

Blanton, DeAnne, and Laura M. Cook. 2002. *They Fought Like Demons: Women Soldiers in the American Civil War.* Baton Rouge: Louisiana State University Press.

Connelly, Thomas. 1971. *Autumn of Glory: The Army of Tennessee, 1862–1865.* Baton Rouge: Louisiana State University Press.

Cozzens, Peter. 1992. *This Terrible Sound: The Battle of Chickamauga.* Urbana: University of Illinois Press.

Daniel, Larry J. 2004. *Days of Glory: The Army of the Cumberland, 1861–1865.* Baton Rouge: Louisiana State University Press.

Horn, Stanley. 1952. *The Army of Tennessee.* Norman: University of Oklahoma Press.

Schultz, Jane E. 2004. *Women at the Front: Hospital Workers in Civil War America.* Chapel Hill: University of North Carolina Press.

## Child, Lydia Maria Francis (1802–1880)

Writer, editor, abolitionist, and social reformer, Lydia Maria Child is one of the nation's premier nineteenth-century literary figures whose political and social activism helped to shape Northern antebellum politics and to establish women's rightful role in public discourse.

Born in Medford, Massachusetts, on February 11, 1802, to Susannah Rand and David Convers Francis, Lydia exhibited an early brilliance. As was typical of the period, she was sent to a preparatory school that prepared young girls for domestic life. Her older brother Convers, however, shared his books and lessons with her, nurturing her desire for intellectual advancement. Upon the death of her mother in 1814, Lydia was sent to live with her older sister, Mary Francis Preston, then living in Norridgewock, Maine. Lydia would later serve as a teacher in a local school in Gardiner, Maine, allowing her to earn her own income and pursue her passion for education.

Returning to Massachusetts in 1822, Child joined Convers Francis's Watertown household. A

Unitarian minister, Convers participated in Transcendentalism, a highly intellectual and literary movement. It was through Transcendentalist meetings in the Francis home that Lydia met American literary, philosophical, and political figures and theorists such as John Greenleaf Whittier, Theodore Parker, and Ralph Waldo Emerson. Her own literary ambitions emerged with the publication of her first novel, *Hobomok.* Its highly controversial plot involving the marriage of a white woman to a Native American man challenged racial assumptions and called for racial tolerance. The boldness of her work earned her considerable attention, launching her into Boston's highly elite literary circle. With her confidence bolstered by the success of *Hobomok,* Child began a prolific writing career that would last five more decades. Another novel, *The Rebels,* quickly followed a collection of short stories about New England. By 1826, she was editing and publishing a bimonthly educational magazine for children called *Juvenile Miscellany,* the first of its kind in the country.

In 1828, Lydia met and married David Lee Child, a lawyer, writer, and antislavery activist. Following her marriage, Lydia's work focused almost exclusively on women's lives and domestic concerns. In 1828, she published *The Frugal Housewife,* a guidebook on domestic duties. It was reprinted over thirty times, including several foreign editions, becoming one of the most enduring and popular books on household economy during the mid-nineteenth century. The book celebrated women's contributions to the home, but it did so within the gendered conventions of the day. Child followed this achievement with *The Mother's Book* and *The Little Girl's Own Book,* both successful works that rode the wave of popularity of female advice literature and the growing commodification of a separate female sphere. With no children of her own, she continued to pursue writing on a full-time basis. Writing almost exclusively for women, she published a series of compositions called "The Ladies' Family Library" and then broadened her work into three volumes of biographical sketches, published between 1832 and 1833, which earned her accolades from the prestigious *North American Review.* It would be her next book, however, that

Author Lydia Maria Child wrote *An Appeal in Favor of That Class of Americans Called Africans* (1833), an early and important antislavery book. (Library of Congress)

would create not only uproar among the nation's literary, political, and cultural elite, but also launch Child into a political career that would help shape and define public discourse on the subject of slavery and abolition for the next three decades.

Published in 1833, *An Appeal in Favor of That Class of Americans Called Africans* demanded immediate emancipation of the country's slaves, a shocking and daring call for action seen as radical and dangerous, particularly coming from a woman. Child interwove the history of slavery and the slave trade with arguments against the colonization of free blacks back to Africa, demands for racial equality, and an exposé of racial discrimination in the North. *An Appeal* was the product of Child's own expanding consciousness and years of research and correspondence with William Lloyd Garrison, Boston's foremost abolitionist and editor of *The Liberator.* In spite of heavy criticism, the book became standard reading for abolitionists throughout the North. Child wrote several more books on the subject, though none had as great an influence as *An Appeal.* She joined the Boston Female Anti-Slavery Society in 1834, beginning years of cooperative activism with other women abolitionists from New England, New York, and Pennsylvania.

Lydia and her husband David remained committed to abolition and to living lives dedicated to destroying the slave system. They moved to an experimental community in Northampton, Massachusetts, in 1838, where they farmed sugar beets. Lydia continued to write, becoming a regular contributor to the abolitionist annual, *The Liberty Bell.* In 1841, after a divisive controversy over the appointment of women as officers in the American Anti-Slavery Society split that organization, Child became editor of its publication, the *National Anti-Slavery Standard,* launching her into a publishing and political world dominated by men.

Her years at the *Standard* were challenging ones for Child. A difficult marriage, complicated by Lydia's living in New York with abolitionist Isaac Hopper while David fruitlessly tried to keep the farm going in Massachusetts, was only part of Lydia's problems. Trying to maintain a moderate editorial position in a highly fractured national abolition movement, Child struggled to remain inclusive of different points of view. Criticized from all factions of the movement for being either too radical or not radical enough, Child ultimately abandoned participation in any antislavery society. Her weekly personal ruminations—called "Letters from New York," reflections on daily life in New York City that she used to critique the worst of American culture and to suggest paths to greater spiritual awareness—were immensely popular, helping to push readership to new highs.

Frustrated and embattled, Child stepped down as editor of the *Standard* in 1843. Still estranged from her husband, who by now was deeply in debt and facing bankruptcy, Child concentrated on her "Letters from New York," publishing them as an edited collection, as well as a collection of children's stories. In 1849, she left New York, reunited with her husband, and settled in Wayland, Massachusetts to care for her aging father.

The rising tensions over the issue of slavery during the 1850s drew Child back into the public discourse over abolition. John Brown's raid and his subsequent trial brought Child back into the public view when she began a vigorous correspondence with Virginia Governor Henry Wise and his wife over their denouncement of the antislavery movement. Published by *The New York Tribune,* the letters were reprinted in pamphlet form by the American Anti-Slavery Society, selling over three hundred thousand copies and sparking renewed interest in the movement. Taking advantage of this momentum, Child published more antislavery essays during 1860 as the nation prepared for sectional conflict. The following year, Child wrote the introduction to and helped publish Harriet Ann Jacobs' autobiography, *Incidents in the Life of a Slave Girl,* a highly significant slave narrative that highlighted the particular plight of enslaved women. Critical of President Abraham Lincoln's early stance on emancipation and his refusal to allow the recruitment of black soldiers, Child continued to use her influence to promote the cause of the newly liberated slave, including education and the redistribution of confiscated Southern lands. She used her own funds to publish and distribute *The Freedman's Book,* an educational reader for newly freed blacks featuring historical and contemporary essays for and by African Americans.

After the war, she was highly critical of President Andrew Johnson's Reconstruction policies. In the postwar years Child continued writing articles advocating a variety of reform movements, including equal rights, African American suffrage, Indian rights, land redistribution, labor reform, and civil service reform. An advocate of woman suffrage, Child shied away from any associations with national or local suffrage organizations.

Her husband David died in 1874. Lydia remained close to William Lloyd Garrison, Wendell Phillips, Thomas Wentworth Higginson, Lucretia Mott, and other activists from her antislavery days. She died October 20, 1880.

*Kate Clifford Larson*

*See also* Abolitionism and Northern Reformers;
Antislavery Societies; Domesticity; Garrison, William
Lloyd (1805–1879); Jacobs, Harriet Ann [Linda
Brent] (1813–1897); Lincoln, Abraham (1809–1865);
Mott, Lucretia Coffin (1793–1880); Northern
Women; Reconstruction; Separate Spheres; Union
Homefront; Wartime Literature.

**References and Further Reading**

Clifford, Deborah Pickman. 1992. *Crusader for
    Freedom: A Life of Lydia Maria Child.* Boston:
    Beacon Press.

Karcher, Carolyn L. 1994. *The First Woman in the
    Republic: A Cultural Biography of Lydia Maria
    Child.* Durham, NC: Duke University Press.

Karcher, Carolyn L., ed. 1996. *An Appeal in Favor
    of That Class of Americans Called Africans.*
    Amherst: University of Massachusetts Press.

Sizer, Lyde Cullen, editor. 2000. *The Political Works
    of Northern Women Writers and the Civil War,
    1850–1872.* Chapel Hill: University of North
    Carolina Press.

## Churches

Churches, themselves struggling in the sectional crisis, occupied important places in the lives of American women during the difficult Civil War years. Churches offered women a place of solace and comfort as well as reassurance in the justness of their cause and the importance of their sacrifices. Churches also gave women a place in which they could take action and be useful, whether in prayer, in sustaining the life of the church, or in working to supply the troops and rebuild a war-shattered society.

In many ways, the national Protestant denominations mirrored events in the nation as a whole. As sectionalism grew in both the North and the South during the 1840s and 1850s, tensions also increased in many churches, especially the large evangelical denominations. In 1837, the Presbyterian Church broke apart into the Old School and New School wings, in part over the issue of slavery. Slavery was also the root cause for the 1844 split of the Methodist Episcopal Church and the 1845 schism of Baptist congregations. Other denominations, including the Catholic, Episcopal, and Lutheran churches, remained whole during the sectional conflicts of the 1840s and 1850s. Even they, however, could not withstand the pressures of secession

and war, splitting into northern and southern branches with the onset of hostilities.

Many ministers, both North and South, preached about the national crisis. At religious services throughout the war, women heard sermons asserting the rightness of their cause and asking for God's blessing and help. While some women recorded disapproval at the involvement of ministers in political matters, most were comforted to find that on Sunday they heard the same pro-Union or pro-Confederate arguments they were reading and discussing the other six days of the week.

In the first months of the war, as companies organized and began leaving for the front, American churches took the lead in sending them off. Across the Union and Confederacy, churches held special ceremonies to bless the troops and consecrate their cause. The work of women behind the scenes was vital; they prepared banners that would decorate the churches and accompany the soldiers into battle and prayed with their sons, brothers, husbands, and sweethearts for a swift victory and safe return.

By the end of the war, the message Southern women received in church had changed. In the face of mounting Confederate losses and increased hardship on the homefront, ministers could no longer claim with any authority that God blessed the Southern endeavor. Instead, they preached on a related, but very different theme: While the cause of Southern independence and the institution of slavery were noble, the Confederate population was corrupt and had not lived up to the goals of the South. Military defeat was therefore a sign of God's displeasure at the failings of Southerners, not their institutions. Northern churches could be more exultant, and many ministers preached that Union victories were proof of God's approval of their society and the need to remake the South in their image.

During the war, churches played numerous significant roles in the lives of women in both the North and the South. Church was a place for women to ask for forgiveness and support for their cause, to mourn their dead, to celebrate victories, and to receive solace, especially in the face of the tremendous suffering and death wrought by the war. Days of fasting and prayer, appointed in each nation by their respective presidents, were also commemorated in church as women abstained from food and prayed that their sacrifices would help win God's favor.

For slave women, churches played a similar but distinct function. Clandestine services in plantation churches served as venues to relay information they may have gleaned about the progress of the war and to pray for freedom. For black women living in territories occupied by Union forces, churches offered another important benefit: They were finally able to celebrate and record their marriages.

In addition to the psychological benefits that churches offered to women during the war years, women also had many opportunities for church-sponsored service. The shortage of men, especially in the South, opened up a number of spheres of activity to American church women. In many antebellum churches, women had made up the bulk of the congregations. That imbalance became more pronounced as men joined the armed forces, especially in the Confederacy where almost all able-bodied men entered the service. Not only did women find themselves surrounded by other women in the pews, but the traditionally male governing structure of the church disintegrated as well. Offices that men had often filled, like that of Sunday school teacher, became the province of female members, many of whom delighted in their new-found responsibility and took seriously their new task of helping the church continue to function.

A number of Southern churches, however, could not survive the enlistment of so many of their male members—and in many cases their ministers—in the army and therefore ceased operations. When a church closed, women felt that they had lost a vital part of their lives, and they often tried to make up for that loss through home-based devotions.

For women in both the North and the South, service in churches created opportunities for public works. While they continued to sustain the life of the church whenever possible, they also looked outward, building on their existing skills to help their societies. Church-sponsored wartime activities grew out of the antebellum benevolent work that

many women had undertaken on behalf of their churches. Women who had participated in the church sewing circle or fundraising bazaar before the war turned their talents to aiding the troops.

Through these benevolent activities, many Northern women became involved in more wide-spread and organized relief efforts, including the United States Christian Commission and the United States Sanitary Commission. While men primarily ran both groups, women played important roles in their daily operations. The Sanitary Commission, though founded by Unitarian minister Henry Bellows and connected to influential liberal denominations like the Episcopal and Unitarian Churches, remained the more secular of the two organizations, focusing on meeting the physical needs of Union soldiers. Women were extremely active in the collection of supplies, and many women also served as nurses in the army and in convalescent homes.

The Christian Commission—founded by the Young Men's Christian Association and connected with Northern evangelical churches, especially the Baptist and Methodist denominations—retained a religious focus in its ministries to Union troops. Like the Sanitary Commission, women connected to the Christian Commission gathered supplies and served as nurses to the troops. In addition, the Christian Commission distributed religious literature and Bibles to the soldiers and sent missionaries to the army.

Both the Sanitary Commission and the Christian Commission were the largest and most recognized of the relief societies in the Union and Confederacy, and they received extensive support from the Federal government. However, there were countless small, church-based groups that enabled women to aid the war effort and minister to the troops.

Some Northern women traveled south as church-sponsored missionaries, part of the Northern churches' attempts to reform and remake Southern society. The Baptist and Methodist denominations were especially active in this activity. The African Methodist Episcopal Church and African Methodist Episcopal Church Zion also sent male and female missionaries to help former slaves build churches. While male missionaries came to occupied territories as ministers and chaplains, female missionaries often worked as teachers, especially in schools and Sunday schools for freed people. While missions to white Southerners found little success, freedmen and freedwomen were often more receptive than their white counterparts.

Southern women generally lacked structured opportunities for activity. The Confederate churches created no large organizations like the Christian or Sanitary Commission to regulate the supply and care of its soldiers. At the local level, however, women could use their church and community networks to collect supplies, sew uniforms, and hold fundraising drives for the troops.

The end of the war brought changes in how churches functioned in the lives of American women. For several denominations, reconciliation came slowly. While the Episcopal, Catholic, and Lutheran Churches reunited at the end of hostilities, the major evangelical denominations did not reconcile until the twentieth century, if it can be said that they did at all. For many women, postwar churches became a place to commemorate their cause, whether Confederate or Union. Many Northern women also continued the church-sponsored missionary work that they had begun during the war.

*Julia Huston Nguyen*

**See also** Aid Societies; Enlistment; Religion; United States Christian Commission; United States Sanitary Commission.

### References and Further Reading

Faust, Drew Gilpin. 1996. *Mothers of Invention: Women of the Slaveholding States in the American Civil War.* Chapel Hill: University of North Carolina Press.

Goen, C. C. 1985. *Broken Churches, Broken Nation: Denominational Schisms and the Coming of the American Civil War.* Macon, GA: Mercer University Press.

Leonard, Elizabeth. 1994. *Yankee Women: Gender Battles in the Civil War.* New York: W. W. Norton.

Rable, George. 1991. *Civil Wars: Women and the Crisis of Southern Nationalism.* Urbana: University of Illinois Press.

Shattuck, Gardiner. 1987. *A Shield and Hiding Place: The Religious Life of the Civil War Armies.* Macon, GA: Mercer University Press.

Stowell, Daniel. 1998. *Rebuilding Zion: The Religious Reconstruction of the South, 1863–1877.* New York: Oxford University Press.

## Civilian Life

The civilian woman's experience during the Civil War depended on a series of factors. The geographic region in which she lived, proximity to the battling armies, socioeconomic class, and the support of family, friends, and the government were all factors in how the average women in the Union or Confederacy survived the conflict. However, certain experiences were universal for women regardless of class, race, or region. In most situations, women North and South, black and white, rich and poor all made contributions to the war effort while facing economic hardships, changing responsibilities at home, encounters with hostile populations, and the loss of loved ones. The Civil War demonstrated that the line separating civilian life from the military action was often an illusion; the two affected each other dramatically throughout the conflict.

As the war began, civilians in both the Union and the Confederacy rallied their efforts in support of their cause. For men, this typically meant joining regiments to head to the battlefields or otherwise serving the state. Women's wartime contributions were more supportive in nature. Women participated in and attended patriotic celebrations and military parades, and they worked to ensure that their soldiers had the supplies, resources, and encouragement they needed to be successful. On both sides, women served as recruiters, urging their men to join the military ranks, and withholding their affections from the men who failed to do so. Throughout the war, women spent concentrated energies on sewing socks and uniforms, gathering and distributing food, fundraising, and providing emotional support for their troops. Ladies' aid societies organized much of this effort, with women in local communities or churches coming together to produce or gather supplies. Often, women in the Union sent the materials directly to the troops in need, but the United States Sanitary Commission also oversaw much of the collection and distribution of women's contributions. In the Confederacy, no such national organization existed, so most war supplies were provided at the local or individual level. African American women also worked in war relief; they not only assisted in providing supplies for white soldiers, but also focused their attention on supporting black troops and exslaves in particular. All of these efforts made significant contributions to the governments' ability to fight the war and gave women an outlet for their patriotism.

As war tension mounted, civilians looked for entertainment avenues to distract them. Lavish balls and banquets continued among the elite in cities. Often, women's fundraising activities would incorporate dances, tableaux, concerts, or dinners as part of the bid for contributions. The absence of eligible male companions on the homefront often made women turn to individual diversions, such as checkers, chess, and backgammon, as well as singing, music, and debate. Books and magazines remained popular, although Confederate women often bemoaned the decrease in available literature once the Northern blockade became effective. Theater performances and public lectures also drew civilian audiences throughout the war. In all of these activities, women found social outlets to combat their loneliness, creating and reinforcing community ties.

Despite the attempts to forget their troubles, the realities of the conflict invaded civilians' lives. Another significant activity for female civilians during the war was nursing. Prior to the war, society viewed nursing as inappropriate for women, given its dangerous, dirty, and morally questionable environment. However, as the military need for nurses grew and women sought more avenues to express their patriotic fervor, the practice became increasingly feminized. Nursing encompassed a variety of duties, including food preparation, laundry, letter writing, and cleaning, as well as working directly with the doctors and performing medical procedures. Women of all classes served, as did African American women, although duties were typically assigned according to race and class—poorer and black women often receiving laundry and cleaning duty, with wealthier whites claiming medical func-

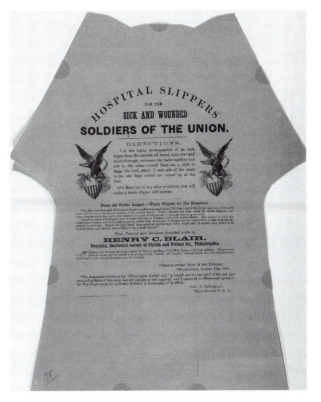

Women played a major role during the Civil War by supplying homemade garments and provisions for the soldiers. Ladies aid societies distributed over 1,000 pairs of slippers in addition to boxes of clothing, bedding, food, medicines, and books. This flyer, printed by a druggist in Pennsylvania, provides instructions for making slippers to assist the women's efforts. (Library of Congress)

tions. Doctors often resisted working with women in the hospitals, seeing them as bothersome and meddling or questioning their intentions. In trying to meet the demand for hospital workers, Union officials worked to combat the notion of nursing as a means to secure a husband, although such romantic relationships did exist. Under the leadership and demanding standards of Dorothea Dix, as well as the recruitment efforts and emphasis on medical training by Dr. Elizabeth Blackwell for the Women's Central Association of Relief and United States Sanitary Commission, a competent nursing corps emerged in the military hospitals throughout the Union. The Confederacy, on the other hand, had no such organized recruitment and, for most of their nursing needs, had to rely on their own military personnel, women camp followers, or local women wherever the battle took place. Regardless of the region, as the battlefields encroached on the homefront, many private civilians had nursing and hospital duty thrust upon them. If they did not travel to distant battlefields to care for their own wounded family members, women nursed those to whom they had access. Churches, schools, and private homes were frequently commandeered by the military as hospitals and their occupants were deputized into service.

Many of the activities women did during the conflict, including nursing, were unpaid, volunteer efforts done in the name of patriotism. However, with traditional male breadwinners absent, wartime circumstances in both the Union and Confederacy created difficult economic challenges that forced female civilians to find new ways to provide for themselves and their families. Daily, women faced the reality of managing the home economy in their men's absence, including paying bills, keeping track of accounts, and, in the case of some Confederate women, running large plantations. Women also kept family businesses and farms operating throughout the war. Soldiers often wrote home with advice on economic affairs, but women had to handle the increasingly challenging day-to-day affairs of living. In both sections, prices for common goods and services skyrocketed as inflation took hold of the economy. Middle- and upper-class women could typically take economizing steps to survive, but poorer classes struggled. Confederate civilians also felt the economic pinch more than their Union counterparts; Confederate money was increasingly worthless throughout the war, and meager supplies diminished as the blockade tightened. Typically, rural farming families could survive with less cash than urban civilians, being able to grow much of their own food. However, often that ability was not enough, and many rural residents fled to the cities where more employment opportunities and public charities existed.

Regardless of the status or region, women and their families needed cash to live. Those with men in the armies might receive a portion of the soldier's paycheck or pension, but those monies could not be consistently relied on. Many moved to live with relatives, sacrificing their own homes to economize.

Those women unwilling or unable to make such moves with private charitable funds rapidly dwindling, women had to find other ways to generate income. Domestic manufacturing increased, as women sold surplus home products such as fruits, vegetables, dairy products, and baked goods on the market. Women also took in sewing and laundry, or they provided space in their homes for boarders. If those options were not enough, many women entered the workforce beyond their homes. Both the Union and Confederate governments employed women as clerks in the Treasury Department, Post Office, and War Department. Other women took jobs in various war industries, working as seamstresses, in cotton mills, or even in arsenals manufacturing the weapons of war. Teaching was also acceptable employment, and the demand for instructors remained high, especially for the newly freed slaves. In most of these circumstances, women received lower pay than men, and African American women faced continuing prejudice. In their attempts to provision their families, women were frequently at the mercy of speculators or corrupt individuals looking to take advantage of women's misfortune and inexperience. Women were constantly looking for ways to budget, barter, and balance their economic lives while trying to survive the war.

Female civilians also faced new challenges when confronted by the enemy. Although women in the Confederacy had to handle this situation more often than their Union counterparts, both populations had to make adjustments when the enemy's troops arrived. For Confederate civilians, threats to person and property were foremost on their minds when the Union armies marched into town. Rumors of cruelties arrived ahead of the military, but the reality of the confrontation varied greatly depending on location. Some armies did burn homes, steal livestock and crops from farms, and attack women; troops associated with Generals Benjamin Butler in Louisiana and William T. Sherman in Georgia perhaps held the most notorious reputations among Confederate women. However, other Union soldiers offered payment for impressed supplies, were courteous toward female inhabitants of homes, and provided protection from marauders. Women's reactions, too, were diverse, ranging from avoidance to aggressive confrontation. Some chose to leave their homes, becoming refugees, while others, particularly in the economically struggling Confederacy, recognized that cooperation with the enemy could bring much needed provisions and relief for their families. For Union civilians, particularly in the border regions, enemy encounters usually took the form of confrontation with guerrilla raiders, military scouting and scavenging parties, or the occasional battle.

African American civilians also faced new situations as the war progressed. Again, their experiences varied depending on where they were during the war. For those living in the Union, opportunities to support the war effort existed, and many women volunteered their time and talents to the cause, often organizing their own aid societies and volunteering as nurses. Much of their attention was paid to the plight of the slave or to the needs of black troops. Northern racial prejudices limited many African American women's abilities to fully participate in the war effort or to seek employment to provide for their families. Aid societies were segregated, and jobs for blacks often brought lower pay. If confronted by the Confederate army, many black women feared being sent south into slavery. Most African American women in the Confederacy were slaves, much of whose attention was focused on attaining freedom. As the Union armies advanced and word of emancipation spread, slaves fled to Union military camps in droves. Women provided the needed domestic labor for the camps, serving as cooks and laundresses for the armies. However, their presence, often accompanied by children, placed a heavy burden on military supplies and rations, adding to the resentment and fueling prejudices.

Finally, civilians of all races, classes, and regions had to confront the daily emotional challenges of the war. Patriotism and self-sacrifice often conflicted with the desire to keep one's family out of harm's way. With the hundreds of thousands of men killed or wounded on both sides, few families remained untouched by the conflict. Grief was ever present. Political loyalties sparked tensions, often within individual families, and women civilians became more embroiled in politics than ever before. For African Americans, the hope of more freedom was often tainted by the presence of racial prejudice. The war provided waves of joy and sorrow for the civilians who daily struggled with the conflict.

*Kristen L. Streater*

***See also*** African American Women; Aid Societies; Blackwell, Elizabeth (1821–1910); Butler, Benjamin F. (1818–1893); Camp Followers; Confederate Homefront; Contrabands; Destruction of Homes; Destruction of Personal Property; Dix, Dorothea Lynde (1802–1887); Domesticity; Enlistment; Factory Workers, Northern; Factory Workers, Southern; Fairs and Bazaars; Family Life, Confederate; Family Life, Union; Farm Work; Food; Foraging, Effects on Women; Free Blacks; Fundraising; Government Girls; Guerrilla Warfare; Gunboat Societies; Homespun; Hospitals; Impressment; Letter Writing; Loyalty Oaths; Military Invasion and Occupation; Morale; Mourning; Nationalism, Confederacy; Nationalism, United States; Nonslaveholding Southerners; Northern Women; Nurses; Pensions, Confederate Widows; Pensions, Union Widows; Plantation Life; Politics; Prostitution; Rape; Refugees; Religion; Rural Women; Separate Spheres; Sewing Bees; Sheridan's Shenandoah Valley Campaign (1864); Sherman, William Tecumseh (1820–1891); Sherman's Campaign (1864–1865); Shortages; Slave Families; Slaveholding Women; Southern Women; Teachers, Northern; Teachers, Southern; Union Homefront; United States Sanitary Commission; Urban Women, Northern; Urban Women, Southern; Wartime Employment; Wartime Literature; Women's Central Association of Relief.

**References and Further Reading**

Cashin, Joan E., ed. 2002. *The War Was You and Me: Civilians in the American Civil War.* Princeton, NJ: Princeton University Press.

Clinton, Catherine, ed. 2000. *Southern Families at War: Loyalty and Conflict in the Civil War South.* New York: Oxford University Press.

Faust, Drew Gilpin. 1996. *Mothers of Invention: Women of the Slaveholding South in the American Civil War.* Chapel Hill: University of North Carolina Press.

Massey, Mary Elizabeth. 1994. *Women in the Civil War.* Lincoln: University of Nebraska Press.

Silber, Nina. 2005. *Daughters of the Union: Northern Women Fight the Civil War.* Cambridge, MA: Harvard University Press.

Vinovskis, Maris A. 1990. *Toward a Social History of the American Civil War.* Cambridge, UK: Cambridge University Press.

## Clalin, Frances Louisa [Francis Clayton] (n.d.–n.d.)

Frances Louisa Clalin disguised herself as a man to serve as a Union soldier. One of approximately four hundred women soldiers who served in the Civil War, Frances Clalin left behind photographs showing her as herself and disguised as Francis Clayton, Civil War soldier.

Little is known about her life outside the Civil War, and there is also uncertainty about her name, which is sometimes spelled Clalin, Clatin, Claytin, or Clayton. The first known accounts of her life place her in Minnesota, living with her husband John in 1861. When the war began, John enlisted in the Minnesota State Militia Cavalry. Frances enlisted alongside him, disguised as a man, possibly by the name of Francis Clayton. There is doubt surrounding not only her name and pseudonym, but also her military service. What little is known about Clalin is from the accounts about her published in the papers at the time and from an interview she gave after her military service ended.

Shortly after enlisting, Frances and John moved on to another regiment, most likely because the cavalry enlistment expired. Frances continued to act the part of a man, keeping her hair short, drinking, chewing tobacco, swearing, smoking cigars, and even gambling. A tall and masculine-looking woman, Frances was considered a good soldier by her comrades. There are varying reports of her military service after the cavalry enlistment, some placing her with Missouri regiments and others presuming she stayed with Minnesota units. Altogether, Frances and her husband fought side by side in eighteen battles. When her husband John was killed at the Battle of Stone's River, just a few feet in front of Frances, accounts record that she bravely stepped over his body and continued to fight. Because the only Minnesota military unit at Stone's Rives was the Second Minnesota Battery, this may have been her regiment.

Some sources record that she was shot in the hip at Stone's River and that it was while being treated for her injury that her gender was discovered. A *Fincher's Trades' Review* reporter who talked with Frances in November 1863 gave another account, claiming that Frances was not discovered while she was in the service, nor was she wounded at Stone's River. Instead, this reporter wrote, she was wounded at Fort Donelson.

On January 3, 1863, Clalin was discharged from the regiment, and she returned to Minnesota to recover from her injury. Upon recovering, Frances tried to return to the army, ostensibly to get money in back pay and bounty money that she and John had earned, but perhaps to seek another position in the army. In Louisville, the provost marshal intercepted her, ordering her to return home. Clalin was last reported going to Washington, D.C., but there are no records of what happened to her thereafter. Some sources speculate that she may have continued her masquerade in another section of the military.

*Sigrid Kelsey*

**See also** Female Combatants; Northern Women.
**References and Further Reading**

Eggleston, Larry G. 2003. *Women in the Civil War: Extraordinary Stories of Soldiers, Spies, Nurses, Doctors, Crusaders, and Others.* Jefferson, NC: McFarland.

Leonard, Elizabeth D. 1999. *All the Daring of the Soldier: Women of the Civil War Armies.* New York: W. W. Norton & Company.

## Clayton, Sarah "Sallie" Conley (1845–1922)

Sarah "Sallie" Conley Clayton's Civil War memoirs recount her experiences in the Confederacy, providing descriptions of the events from the point of view of a young woman in Atlanta. She offers detailed descriptions of the changes in daily life during the war for an upper-class white Atlanta woman.

Sallie Clayton was born April 9, 1845, in Athens, Georgia, the fourth of ten children. Her father, William Wirt, held various professional positions; he was a dry goods merchant, a member of the Georgia legislature, and a planter. In 1859 he moved his family to Atlanta, their home throughout the Civil War until the city's evacuation in September 1864. The family held a prominent place in Atlanta society.

Clayton was first educated at Spring Bank School, near Kingston, where she likely acquired her strong Southern loyalty. In 1862 she and her sister Caro began attending the Atlanta Female Institute. Sallie's memoirs include colorful portrayals of the faculty, hours, rules, and walk to school. She also describes fashions worn by the students, as well as events that include a visit by a military company and a May celebration at the school. Details include lists of students as well as the lyrics to the songs they sang.

Clayton's writings highlight how daily life for women changed dramatically during the war and provide details and a specific point of view. For example, she discusses several aspects of homespun material, the use of which the war had made necessary when other dress material was difficult to get. Clayton describes how acquaintances learned to spin, the different patterns available, and how wearing homespun dresses showed support for the Confederate cause. She also records her memories of a fair held in the City Hall to raise funds for the war, presentations of flags by the women of the town to departing soldiers, the formation of the Ladies Sewing Society, which sewed and rolled bandages for the military, and the younger girls' formation of a society to knit socks.

Clayton's accounts are not limited to social life. She also describes the horrors of the war, like the hanging of bridge burners and the attack and evacuation of Atlanta. A particularly affecting passage records the death of her sister Gussie from typhoid fever during the attack on Atlanta. Because a burial in the cemetery would have been dangerous, the family buried her in the garden with shells falling nearby. The family evacuated Atlanta, returning after the war with little left except their house.

In 1867, Sallie married Benjamin Elliot Crane, a wealthy wholesale grocer and former Confederate officer. Crane died in 1885, and Clayton spent her last years living with their daughter. After a sudden illness, Sallie Clayton died on February 5, 1922.

*Sigrid Kelsey*

*See also* Aid Societies; Atlanta, Evacuation of (Special Field Orders Number 67); Civilian Life; Confederate Homefront; Fairs and Bazaars; Girlhood and Adolescence; Homespun; Flags, Regimental; Military Invasion and Occupation; Mourning; Sherman's Campaign (1864 –1865); Southern Women.

**References and Further Reading**

Clayton, Sara "Sallie" Conley. 1999. *Requiem for a Lost City: A Memoir of Civil War Atlanta and the Old South,* edited by Robert Scott Davis Jr. Macon, GA: Mercer University Press.

## Clemson, Elizabeth Floride (1842–1871)

Wealthy poet and diarist, Elizabeth Floride Clemson experienced the Civil War from a privileged point of view. Through her diary and writings, she revealed the ability of a few white women to endure the war without tremendous sacrifice.

Called Floride or Floy by family and friends, Clemson was born into a prominent family. She was the granddaughter of John C. Calhoun, and her father ran a gold mine in Dahlonega, Georgia, as well as several plantations. When he experienced financial troubles, her father used his political connections to become chargé d'affaires to Belgium. Floride and her father took up residence in Prince Georges County, Maryland in 1853, where they lived on a 100-acre homestead they called The Home. From there, he edited his father's political writings, imported furniture and other fine goods from Belgium, and otherwise lived the life of a leisured gentleman. He also tried to obtain schooling for Floride and her brother Calhoun. Although she would become known for her writing, she had only two years of formal education.

When the Civil War began, Clemson continued to live a life of leisure that only the most privileged could afford. She traveled to visit loved ones, and she paid very close attention to fashion, her physical appearance, and her social position. She followed the political currents of the times and repeatedly expressed support for the Confederacy. Both her brother and father survived their service in the Confederate army. Floride's wealth did not make her immune from wartime tragedies, but it did ameliorate them. She experienced some food shortages, but for much of the war she noted that she was able to maintain or even gain weight. At the same time, she watched the sufferings of many other white Southerners, leading her to make small donations of clothing to the poor. Near the end of the war, her family was forced to sell many personal items.

Her grandmother, Mrs. John C. Calhoun, died as the Confederacy failed. Floride saw her nation's defeat as both financially and psychologically damaging. She estimated that she lost $20,000. In 1866, she inherited a small part of Fort Hill House, which is now part of Clemson University.

Much of what we know about Floride Clemson comes from her wartime diary, which she began in January 1, 1863, and ended October 24, 1866. She also wrote poetry, including "That 'Blessed' Sewing Machine" and "Strong-Minded Women," which revealed an aristocractic view of white womanhood in the nineteenth-century South.

After the war, Clemson married Gideon Lee, a New Yorker eighteen years her senior. The couple moved to New York and had one daughter, Folide Isabella, in 1870. A year later, Floride Clemson Lee died on July 23, 1871.

*Andrew K. Frank*

**See also** Civilian Life; Confederate Homefront; Diaries and Journals; Poets, Southern; Southern Women.

### References and Further Reading

Holman, Harriet R. 1965. *The Verse of Floride Clemson*. Columbia: University of South Carolina Press.

McGee, Charles M. Jr., and Ernest M. Landers, Jr., eds. 1989. *A Rebel Came Home: The Diary and Letters of Floride Clemson, 1863–1866*. Columbia: University of South Carolina Press.

## Columbia Bazaar (January 17–21, 1865)

Elite Southern women organized the Columbia Bazaar as a fundraiser for sick and wounded Confederate soldiers. The Columbia Bazaar was the largest of the Confederate fundraising affairs that took place during the Civil War.

The fair took place in South Carolina's Old State House and offered for sale patriotic goods—both homemade and imported. Although originally intended to last two weeks, the fear of Union advancement into the state resulted in a shorter, five-day event. Fairgoers purchased advance tickets for $1 at local hotels and bookstores or bought tickets at the door. The Bazaar opened at seven o'clock each night and from noon until four o'clock during its last four days. The event was highly popular and raised anywhere from $150,000 to $350,000.

Women spent months planning the Confederate bazaar in Columbia. The women who organized the bazaar, most of whom came from established South Carolina families, were active in various war relief projects, especially in hospital associations. For example, Mary Boykin Chesnut, the famous Southern diarist and wife of a Confederate politician, participated in numerous relief projects and presided at one of the bazaar booths. One of the event's main organizers, Mary Amarinthia Snowden, also from a prominent Carolina family, spent the war coordinating soldiers' aid societies and distributing goods to Confederate troops.

In May 1864, Columbia's white women began initial plans for a Confederate fundraising bazaar. Women in the city and throughout South Carolina sought cooperation from women and groups around the Confederacy to supply goods for the bazaar. They sent letters to friends, newspapers, and organizations across the Confederacy and abroad to get support and donations for the event. The Bazaar's organizers arranged for the railroads and the Southern Express Company to deliver these goods free of charge from as many Confederate states as possible. However, the difficulties of communicating and maneuvering in the wartime South resulted in fewer donations than the women had expected. The women also raised money for the Bazaar and the soldiers in the weeks leading up to the event by organizing smaller events, such as vocal concerts and dance recitals. The day before the Bazaar opened, the organizers requested donations of cooked provisions from anyone who could help.

Although women were the event's main organizers and workers, they created five all-male committees: notices and advertisements, correspondence and transportation, arrangement of halls and buildings, door committee, and general police. Prominent citizens of the community, such as Columbia Mayor Thomas Jefferson Goodwyn, sat on these committees.

At the Bazaar, booths or tables represented each Confederate state as well as two border states, Kentucky and Missouri, which shared a booth. The House of Representatives chamber in the old State House contained booths for South Carolina, Texas, Tennessee, Kentucky and Missouri, Louisiana, Mississippi, and Virginia. The Senate chamber housed booths for North Carolina, Florida, Arkansas, Georgia, and Alabama. The women decorated these booths to resemble military encampment tents, using red and white cloth to drape the tent sides and hanging the state shield in front of each "tent" for added decoration. White damask cloth, lace, and evergreens covered many tables. Flags and painted banners displaying patriotic slogans hung overhead.

Entertainments included a post office where fairgoers could pass love letters to one another, a bower of fate or fortune telling booth, as well as raffles and grab bags. The Texas, Louisiana, Virginia, and Arkansas booths offered restaurants that had an assortment of foods including roast turkey, salmon, lobster, duck, venison, soups, gumbo, plum pudding, ladyfingers, cakes, donuts, coffee, and tea. Articles for sale ranged from dolls, tobacco pouches, clothing and accessories for all sexes and ages, fancy goods, jewelry, cutlery, and livestock.

Confederates flocked to the Bazaar and enthusiastically purchased the goods available. The imminent approach of William T. Sherman's Union troops prompted organizers to close the Bazaar early, but they considered it a success.

*Sarah Wooton*

***See also*** Aid Societies; Blockade Running; Chesnut, Mary Boykin (1823–1886); Civilian Life; Confederate Homefront; Domesticity; Fairs and Bazaars; Fundraising; Gunboat Societies; Hospitals; LeConte, Emma Florence (1847–1932); Separate Spheres; Sherman's Campaign (1864–1865); Southern Women; United Daughters of the Confederacy; Wounded, Visits to.

**References and Further Reading**
Gordon, Beverly. 1998. *Bazaars and Fair Ladies: The History of the American Fundraising Fair.* Knoxville: University of Tennessee Press.
Hennig, Helen Kohn, ed. 1936. *Columbia, Capital City of South Carolina, 1786–1936.* Columbia, SC: Columbia Sesquicentennial Commission, R. L. Bryan Co.
Moore, John Hammond. 1993. *Columbia and Richland County: A South Carolina Community, 1740–1990.* Columbia: University of South Carolina Press.

## Confederate Soldiers, Motives

Southern men most commonly cited the defense of their homes as the reason they enlisted in the Confederate army, but they also evinced loyalty to their newly created nation. Indeed, protection of the home signaled a much broader rationale of male honor, white supremacy, and individual liberty. Many Southern soldiers hated the North, or at least the demonized version of it they had heard about. Many others enlisted due to peer pressure or a desire for adventure. Finally, Southern soldiers fought for the preservation of their military unit, as well as for self-preservation.

Southern soldiers created a composite view of their enemy that fueled a lasting animosity and repeatedly highlighted new reasons to fight. At the outset of the war, they expressed their hatred of Northern soldiers predominantly on racial grounds, citing fears that the Yankee invasion brought with it the twin specters of slave insurrection and racial equality. With a similar preoccupation with race, Confederate soldiers emphasized the polyglot nature of Northern society, noting that Irish and German immigrants composed the majority of the Union army and thus suggesting the cowardice of most Northerners. As the war progressed, Confederate soldiers described the Yankees as vandals who burned the homes of innocent civilians. All of these definitions of the enemy revealed that Confederate soldiers placed great importance on protecting the safety and stability—and particularly the racial order—of their homes and that they placed these ideas at the very center of their rationale for remaining in the army.

The soldiers' desire to protect their homes and families increasingly conflicted with the Confederacy's need to maintain armies in the field. Some soldiers were prompted to leave the ranks by evidence of deprivation and despondency on the homefront. Yet, despite entreaties from their families, substantial numbers of Confederate soldiers continued to see independent nationhood as a goal worth immense sacrifice until the very end of the conflict. They also viewed the Yankee destruction of Southern homes and communities as ample reasons for continuing to fight, thus adding vengeance to their list of motivations.

Protection of the home also invoked Confederate soldiers' desire to enlist as proof of their manliness. The rhetoric of manhood inflamed the desire of most volunteers to see battle as quickly as possible. After the first experience with battle, duty and honor compelled these men to continue fighting; Confederate soldiers explicitly fought to protect white Southern women. Their sense of duty and honor extended beyond their families to the defense of their comrades.

Confederate soldiers also maintained a devotion to the political ideologies that underlay their new nation. In particular, Southerners spoke of the American Revolution, drawing explicit connections between the Founding Fathers' revolt against British tyranny and their own bid for independence. Southern soldiers eagerly participated in the political development of the Confederacy, maintaining frequent contact with the homefront through letters and newspapers. They viewed political participation as a means for maintaining their civilian identities, thus reaffirming the ideal of the citizen-soldier and disgust for mercenaries, be they Hessians or Yankees. Devotion to the ideal of the citizen-soldier did not wane with the Confederate draft of 1862 or the involuntary reenlistment of all Confederate soldiers in 1864.

In addition to patriotism and an interest in politics, most Confederate soldiers shared a common belief in the providence of God, whatever their theological differences. Confederate clergy and citizens alike expressed the belief that God would bring them peace and independence as soon as they had adequately proven their faith. Victory signaled the favor of God, whereas defeat was a chastisement for unchristian behavior but not ultimately a sign of God's disfavor. Convinced that God favored the Confederacy, Southern soldiers had every reason to continue fighting.

*Jaime Amanda Martinez*

**See also** Confederate Homefront; Conscription; Desertion; Destruction of Homes; Destruction of Personal Property; Domesticity; Enlistment; Family Life, Confederate; Honor; Politics; Religion; Shortages; Southern Women.

**References and Further Reading**
Frank, Joseph Allan. 1998. *With Ballot and Bayonet: The Political Socialization of American Civil War Soldiers.* Athens: University of Georgia Press.
McPherson, James M. 1997. *For Cause and Comrades: Why Men Fought in the Civil War.* New York: Oxford University Press.
Mitchell, Reid. 1988. *Civil War Soldiers.* New York: Viking.
Power, J. Tracy. 1998. *Lee's Miserables: Life in the Army of Northern Virginia from the Wilderness to Appomattox.* Chapel Hill: University of North Carolina Press.
Wiley, Bell Irvin. 1943. *The Life of Johnny Reb: The Common Soldier of the Confederacy.* Indianapolis, IN: Bobbs-Merrill Company.
Woodworth, Steven E. 2001. *While God Is Marching On: The Religious World of Civil War Soldiers.* Lawrence: University Press of Kansas.

## Confederate Surrender (1865)

The surrender of the military forces of the Confederacy took place over a two-month period in 1865. The first, and most famous, capitulation took place at Appomattox Court House, Virginia when General Robert E. Lee surrendered the remnant of his once powerful Army of Northern Virginia to Union forces. Lee met with United States General Ulysses S. Grant on April 9 at the McLean house in Appomattox. There, Grant offered very generous terms to the defeated rebels. In a few days the Confederates were paroled and on their way home.

On April 18, Union commander William T. Sherman conferred with his Confederate opponent Joseph E. Johnston at the Bennett house near Durham, North Carolina. The two generals came up with an agreement that not only surrendered the troops under Johnston's immediate command but also dealt with political questions beyond the scope of strictly military operations. New President Andrew Johnson repudiated the so-called Sherman-Johnston Memorandum, and the rebel forces eventually laid down their weapons on terms very similar to those offered at Appomattox.

Two additional surrenders took place in 1865. On May 4, General Richard Taylor capitulated the Southern troops in Alabama, Mississippi, and eastern Louisiana after a conference with Federal authorities at Citronelle, Alabama. Others still serving under General Edmund Kirby Smith in the Trans-Mississippi Department received their parole papers after arrangements were finalized at a meeting held in New Orleans on May 26. Various units, including warships like the CSS *Shenandoah*, as well as individual Confederates, gave up in the weeks and months to come.

The end of armed resistance inevitably led to the collapse of the Confederate civilian government. The United States took Confederate President Jefferson Davis prisoner by the end of May, despite his attempts to avoid capture. Other high-ranking rebel leaders were also imprisoned. Others, like Judah P. Benjamin and John C. Breckinridge, made good their escape and found exile in foreign countries.

White Southern women mourned the passing of the cause, and many felt that male relatives and friends who died during the war had perished for nothing. Many expressed shock and disbelief that Lee had given up the fight. Surrender made it seem that the sacrifices that they had made and the discomforts they had endured on the Confederate homefront had all been in vain. On the other hand, some Southern women were happy, realizing that the end of the Confederate armies meant that their surviving loved ones would soon be returning home. After the official end of the military conflict, white women continued their struggle to survive on neglected farms or in battered cities like Richmond, Atlanta, and Columbia, South Carolina. Many white Southern women organized groups like the United Daughters of the Confederacy to commemorate the Confederate dead and to uphold the ideals of the Lost Cause.

Northern women also mourned the losses they had suffered during the four bloody war years, but the fact that they had emerged victorious helped them cope with the deaths. Much of their euphoria dissipated with the assassination of President Abraham Lincoln and the hard adjustments to a postwar society. Many women who had been active in organizations like the United States Sanitary Commission and the Christian Commission and whose horizons were broadened by working outside the home now chafed at the thought of returning to prewar social roles.

The Confederate surrender, of course, held special meaning for African American women in the North and South. The end of the Confederacy guaranteed that the institution of slavery would indeed end in the re-United States. However, questions remained about what social relationships would now exist, as well as what types of economic opportunities there would be for the freedpeople in the postwar South and in the Northern states. The fact that black troops in Union blue helped to make these surrenders a reality heartened those waiting to see what life would bring for them as the nation began Reconstruction in earnest.

*Robert A. Taylor*

**See also** Reconstruction (1865–1877); Sherman's Campaign (1864–1865).

**References and Further Reading**

Bradley, Mark L. 2000. *This Astounding Close: The Road to Bennett Place*. Chapel Hill: University of North Carolina Press.

Faust, Drew Gilpin. 1996. *Mothers of Invention: Women of the Slaveholding South in the American Civil War*. Chapel Hill: University of North Carolina Press.

Women in black walk by ruins in Richmond, Virginia, April 1865. (Library of Congress)

Gallman, J. Matthew. 1994. *The North Fights the Civil War: The Home Front.* Chicago: Ivan R. Dee.

Grimsley, Mark, and Brooks D. Simpson, eds. 2001. *The Collapse of the Confederacy.* Lincoln: University of Nebraska Press.

Marvel, William. 2000. *A Place Called Appomattox.* Chapel Hill: University of North Carolina Press.

Parrish, T. Michael. 1992. *Richard Taylor: Soldier Prince of Dixie.* Chapel Hill: University of North Carolina Press.

## Confederate Sympathizers, Northern

A broad spectrum of Northern women might be considered Confederate sympathizers. Some women, most of whom came from the border regions of the North, overtly supported the rebel war effort. Toward the middle of the spectrum were women from politically active Democratic families. Although they probably did not consider themselves pro-Confederate, these women were often castigated as such because of their political principles. At the other end of the spectrum were war-wearied women who probably did not support the rebels at all but who ardently wished to see their menfolk return home from the battlefield. Only those who actively sought to aid the rebels can unequivocally be regarded as Confederate sympathizers. However, because most Republicans believed most Democrats were Copperheads—a name Republicans used to denote Northerners who they believed were Southern sympathizers—it is helpful to consider the various types of women who might have been branded pro-Confederate in the Civil War North.

In the Border States and southern regions of the North, many women and girls worked as spies, saboteurs, and suppliers for the rebels. Some, like Nancy Hart of (West) Virginia, joined guerrilla outfits and worked as rebel spies. Others, like Olivia Floyd of Maryland, sent money, clothes, letters, arms, and Northern military secrets to the South. Charlotte "Lottie" Moon of southern Ohio carried messages to Confederate officers in Kentucky and Virginia, as well as to and from rebel agents in Canada. Virginia "Ginnie" Moon, Lottie's teenage sister, defiantly shot the stars out of an American flag and scratched "Hurrah for Jeff Davis" with her diamond ring into an Ohio storefront window. She, too, became a notorious Confederate spy. In some border regions, women convinced their husbands to join the Confederate army; other women harassed the Union forces by slicing telegraph lines or by treating Union soldiers disrespectfully; and in war-ravaged Missouri, women often sustained Confederate guerrillas by feeding, clothing, arming, housing, and hiding them.

Toward the middle of the spectrum were Peace Democrats. These women were sympathetic to slavery and to the grievances claimed by the South, and they probably came from families with similar political proclivities. When one small town editor in upstate New York was jailed for publishing the sentiment that Southern secession was justified, his wife, Louisa Flanders, took over his newspaper and wrote several letters to the Federal government to secure his release. She professed loyalty to the Union but, like her husband, believed that war could not reunite the nation. Both she and her husband believed that Lincoln's policies were destroying the Union, and she wondered why her husband had been deprived of the constitutional right to say so. She also insisted on her own right to do the same. Though claiming to be "a weak woman," Louisa asserted herself politically; she maintained her incarcerated husband's business and eventually secured his release from prison, all the while publishing a newspaper that explicitly justified a war for Southern independence.

More typical of Northern Democrats were anti-emancipation and anti-Lincoln women. These women fell within the mainstream of the Democratic party and remained fully loyal to the Union, but their political ideas often made their neighbors believe they were traitors to the Northern cause. For example, Maria Lydig Daly, the wife of a Democratic judge in New York City, was active in charitable work for Union soldiers, yet she confided strong anti-Lincoln thoughts to her diary. She castigated "Uncle Ape" for his seeming lack of manners and intelligence, and she believed the Emancipation Proclamation was the illegitimate act of a despot. Women who held views like these were often castigated as Copperheads and traitors. Some were also given insulting appellations, like Miss Secesh, even though they professed loyalty to the Union and showed little, if any, actual sympathy for Southern secessionists.

At the other end of the spectrum of those seen as Confederate sympathizers were Northern women who may not have had any disloyalty at all and whose feelings about the war were not necessarily influenced by partisan politics or sympathies for the South. Women suffered in many ways when their male relatives went off to fight. Many women begged their husbands, sons, brothers, or sweethearts to leave the battlefield and come home. Although most of these women did not intend to support the Confederate war effort, their correspondence was deemed subversive enough to be confiscated by Union military authorities. General George Cadwalader, for example, seized about one hundred letters in July 1861 because the female authors begged their menfolk not to re-enlist but to return home as soon as possible.

Identifying and categorizing the Copperhead women who did not intentionally support the rebel cause is a complicated task. First, Peace Democrats did not necessarily support secession. Indeed, most of them claimed to be more loyal to the Constitution and the Union than the abolitionists and Republicans. Women like Louisa Flanders believed it was impossible for war to restore the Union, but they still wished to see the states reunited. Second, nearly all Democratic women were sympathetic to slavery, but proslavery convictions did not necessarily mean that one favored Southern victory. Third, and most importantly, being a Confederate sympathizer was more often an ascribed characteristic than a term of self-identification. While most Northern Democrats had certain sympathies with the South, few were actual advocates for a separate Southern nation.

*Jonathan W. White*

**See also** Border States; Daly, Maria Lydig (1824–1894); Female Spies; Guerrilla Warfare; Hart, Nancy (ca. 1843–1902); Moon, Charlotte (Lottie) (1829–1895); Moon, Virginia (Ginnie) (1844–1925); Northern Women; Politics; Union Homefront.

**References and Further Reading**

Daly, Maria Lydig. 2000 [1962]. *Diary of a Union Lady, 1861–1865*, edited by Harold Earl Hammond. Lincoln: University of Nebraska Press.

Fellman, Michael. 1989. *Inside War: The Guerrilla Conflict in Missouri during the American Civil War.* New York: Oxford University Press.

Kane, Harnett T. 1954. *Spies for the Blue and Gray.* New York: Hanover House.

## Congregationalist Women

The Congregational Church escaped the division that characterized most churches before and during the Civil War. Congregationalists avoided division primarily because, unlike the three largest denominations—Presbyterians, Baptists, Methodists, which suffered serious division into northern and southern denominations before the Civil War—they did not have adherents in both regions. The Lutheran, Episcopal, and Roman Catholic churches remained officially undivided, but with large constituencies in both regions, each contributed vigorous polemicists on the slavery controversy.

The Congregational Church, however, did not escape the disruptive impact of the moral issue of slavery. Initially, most Congregationalists favored a conservative, gradual approach to ending slavery. At the same time, Congregationalists developed a strong abolitionist minority represented by leaders like Reverend David Thurston, the founder of the American Antislavery Society, and Reverend Moses Thacher, a founder and vice president of the New England Anti-Slavery Society and close friend of William Lloyd Garrison. By the time of the Civil War, Congregationalists had become increasingly unified in their call for an immediate end to slavery.

Once disunion was a reality, whatever disagreement individuals and Congregational churches may have had over slavery was transformed into support of the Union. Congregational churches throughout the North and Northwest actively participated in the war effort. Thousands of individuals volunteered as soldiers and as relief workers for the United States Christian Commission and the United States Sanitary Commission. Congregational ministers joined the army as chaplains. On occasion, church buildings served as way stations for soldiers as they headed to the front.

Congregational women played a vital role in the war effort by forming hundreds of aid societies. Most formed sewing circles for the express purpose of supplying Union hospitals and soldiers with necessary clothing and food. Some groups also looked to assist African Americans and made clothes for the freedpeople. The women of Park Street Church in Boston, Massachusetts, the flagship of Congregational churches, formed a Soldier's Circle to assist the already established Park Street Benevolent Sewing Circle. The groups contributed large amounts of homemade shirts, socks, linens, and edibles. The wife of Reverend Andrew Stone, the minister of Park Street Church, served as the group's president. In 1863, she visited Stone who had enlisted as a chaplain to the Forty-Fifth Massachusetts Regiment, during his stay in New Berne, North Carolina. During her four-week stay, she opened a day school for African American children in a local church. Enrollment reached five hundred students and continued throughout the regiment's term of service in New Berne. Most often the women's groups depended on the Christian Commission or the Sanitary Commission to deliver their goods safely. For example, Reverend William Horace Marble, a congregational minister appointed by the Christian Commission, delivered the many boxes of supplies and goods made by the ladies of the Congregational Church in Oshkosh, Wisconsin.

Congregational women also participated in aid societies outside the confines of the local church. Elizabeth Smith Abbey served as president of Akron's Soldiers Aid Society, an affiliate of Cleveland's Sanitary Commission, which donated thousands of dollars worth of food and clothing to the hospitalized soldiers. Abbey also served as the secretary of the Ladies National Covenant, an organization opposed to the import of goods during the Civil War, and after the war she collected clothes for freedmen.

Congregational women in Connecticut helped form the Stamford Ladies Soldiers' Aid Society, an interdenominational group that also included Baptist, Presbyterian, and Episcopalian women. Formed in July 1861 as an auxiliary to the Sanitary Commission, the group collected money and food, as well as bought and made clothing for the soldiers at the David's Island hospital off the coast of Long Island. When they discovered their contributions were not always arriving safely at the hospital, they hand delivered baskets of food and boxes of clothing. When visiting the hospital, women passed out the items and visited patients. They often served as unofficial mail couriers as well, delivering letters between patients and families.

Congregationalist Mary Ann Bickerdyke became a well respected wartime nurse. After the minister of the Brick Congregational Church of Galesburg, Illinois, Reverend Edward Beecher, read to his congregation a letter describing the suffering in the hospitals of Cairo, Illinois, the church discussed the best way to help. The congregation sent Bickerdyke, a widow and well-respected nurse to Dr. Woodward with medical supplies. Rather than return home after delivering the supplies, Bickerdyke devoted the next four years to the needs of the wounded in battles across the South. She earned the respect of generals and soldiers who gave her the nickname Mother Bickerdyke.

A number of prominent female writers were raised in Congregational churches. For example, Mary Abigail Dodge, also known as Gail Hamilton, authored numerous works including the essay, "A Call to My Country-Woman." Her works called for high patriotic fervor among Northern women. Congregationalist authors also included Elizabeth Stuart Phelps, author of *The Gates Ajar* (1868), and abolitionist novelist Harriet Beecher Stowe, who penned the 1852 best seller *Uncle Tom's Cabin*. As adults, these women rejected the Calvinist theology of Congregationalism and, as in the case of Stowe, left the denomination altogether.

The Civil War opened up new opportunities for women as teachers and missionaries at home and abroad. Congregational women made themselves essential to Reconstruction efforts as teachers for the American Missionary Association (AMA). The AMA was the most prominent of the Northern religious agencies that worked among African Americans during the Civil War and Reconstruction. Founded in Albany in 1846 by Congregationalists who shared a commitment to African Americans and antislavery, by 1860 the AMA had 112 missionaries in the South, and at the war's end it had 528 missionaries and teachers at work there. Most of the educators were women. The war also expanded women's role in the Congregational Church. Many of the sewing circles became permanent ministries that aided the poor, frontier missionaries in Western America, and overseas missionary efforts.

*Karen Fisher Younger*

**See also** Bickerdyke, Mary Ann Ball "Mother" (1817–1901); Dodge, Mary Abigail [Gail Hamilton] (1833–1896); Phelps, Elizabeth Stuart (Ward) [Mary Gray Phelps] (1844–1911); Religion; Stowe, Harriett Beecher (1811–1896); United States Christian Commission; United States Sanitary Commission.

**References and Further Reading**

Ahlstrom, Sydney. 1972. *A Religious History of the American People.* New Haven, CT: Yale University Press.

Baker, Nina Brown. 1952. *Cyclone in Calico.* Boston: Little, Brown and Company.

Englizian, H. Crosby. 1968. *Brimstone Corner: Park Street Church, Boston.* Chicago: Moody Press.

Massey, Mary Elizabeth. 1994. *Women in the Civil War.* Lincoln: University of Nebraska Press.

Miller, Randall M., Harry S. Stout, and Charles Reagan Wilson, eds. 1998. *Religion and the American Civil War.* New York: Oxford University Press.

## Conscription

Designed to increase the size of their armies, the Northern and Southern drafts also represented an unprecedented governmental intrusion into family life, forcing women to balance the needs of their nation against those of their families.

At the beginning of the Civil War, neither the Union nor the Confederacy foresaw the conflict's length or scope. As early as 1862, the initial enthusiasm that had sparked widespread enlistments in the prior year had worn off. In April 1862, the Confederacy passed a conscription law and the Union soon followed suit. The enactment of a draft law greatly affected the women of both sides, though Southern women faced more formidable challenges. The Southern conscript net snared both a larger number and a higher percentage of military-aged men, and thus, more than their Union counterparts, white women in the South found themselves living on a homefront denuded of male relatives. Additionally, Southern women likely felt more vulnerable with a potentially hostile slave population in their midst and the possibility of invading Union forces threatening their communities.

In issuing draft calls, politicians urged loyal women to serve as a conscript guard to bring in draftees, and some women, particularly those with relatives in the service, used honor and shame to prod shirkers into the service. More likely, however, women's actions and words led men to resist the draft. Service in the army meant putting one's country ahead of one's family, and for women, especially those who had already contributed a husband and several sons, the drafting of one more relative was a sacrifice that they were unwilling to make. Both Union and Confederate leaders contended that the war helped protect soldiers' wives and children, yet the draft often undermined this promise and belied the concept of paternalism. It also contributed to the notion that the government was indifferent to the sufferings of its people who, as civilians already weary of food shortages and inflation and perhaps fearful of the opposing army, had to relinquish some of the few men who remained to help defend and feed their communities.

The perceived inequities in the draft laws, especially those that made the war appear to be a "rich man's war and a poor man's fight," most angered women. In both the Union and the Confederacy, drafted soldiers could provide substitutes in their place. In the North, conscripts could also avoid service by paying a $300 fee, while in the South, the ownership of twenty slaves made men exempt. Women objected to being forced to sacrifice their loved ones while other healthy, capable men remained at home. Some sent pleas to military and political officials requesting exemptions for their relatives, with the missives often stressing the family's destitution and vulnerability. Other women not only encouraged their conscripted relatives to dodge the draft, but also denounced conscript hunters, hid draft dodgers, participated in draft riots, or helped provide for prospective conscripts hiding in the woods.

*John M. Sacher*

***See also*** Confederate Homefront; Draft Riots and Resistance; Honor; Non-slaveholding Southerners; Northern Women; Politics; Slaveholding Women; Southern Women; Union Homefront.

### References and Further Reading

Blair, William. 1998. *Virginia's Private War: Feeding Body and Soul in the Confederacy, 1861–1865.* New York: Oxford University Press.

Cashin, Joan E., ed. 2002. *The War Was You and Me: Civilians in the American Civil War.* Princeton, NJ: Princeton University Press.

Rable, George C. 1989. *Civil Wars: Women and the Crisis of Southern Nationalism.* Urbana: University of Illinois Press.

## Contraband Relief Association

The Contraband Relief Association (CRA), organized by free black women of Washington, D.C., in 1862, assisted ex-slaves during the Civil War. Founding member Elizabeth Keckley's connections to both white and black philanthropists helped to win support for the organization. Although not as financially successful as other freedmen's aid societies, the CRA is a commendable example of mid-nineteenth-century African American private charity and self-help.

Keckley, seamstress and confidant to Mary Todd Lincoln, understood the freedmen's problems. She had been a slave until 1855, when she purchased her freedom and that of her only child. After becoming a successful businesswoman in the District of Columbia, Keckley often used her experience and means to assist other blacks adjusting to freedom. The Civil War provided Keckley with an unprecedented opportunity to use her skills and humanitarianism to aid the growing number of impoverished contrabands entering the nation's capital.

Fugitive slaves first sought protection behind Union lines after the Confiscation Act of August 6, 1861. Congress declared that any property used in insurrection against the United States could be taken as contraband of war. Northern forces were ordered to free slaves captured as contrabands. Sometimes the army employed the contrabands. Most of the exslaves, camping near Northern troops for protection, lived in destitute conditions. After April 1862, when Congress abolished slavery in the District of Columbia, thousands of contrabands entered the city in search of protection and work. As a result, the migrant population surged from four hundred to almost forty thousand by 1865. Despite seemingly high wages, wartime inflation and the influx of additional workers restricted opportunities. Most continued to live in camps, with conditions similar to those they had just escaped. Hunger, disease, and insufficient housing led to misery and even death for the men, women, and children running from war and enslavement.

When abolitionists learned of the conditions in the contraband camps, they formed relief societies modeled on antebellum benevolent associations. Northern blacks formed their own associations but also worked with white groups. Later in the war, Southern blacks also organized. In August 1862, Keckley called on members of the Union Bethel Church to organize on behalf of the refugees. Forty women created the CRA and elected Keckley president. Soon they began distributing food and clothing to the freedmen in the D.C. area.

The CRA benefited from Keckley's relationship with the Lincolns. Mary Lincoln donated $200 from a fund originally established for Union soldiers. She visited camps receiving aid from the CRA, and on at least one occasion she was accompanied by President Abraham Lincoln. In September 1862, Keckley accompanied the first lady to New York and Boston. Seeking donations, Keckley spoke with the pastors' wives of the Twelfth Street Baptist Church in Boston. These women organized their own aid society through which they collected over eighty boxes of supplies for the CRA. Keckley also met with prominent abolitionists Wendell Phillips and Frederick Douglass. After donating $200, Douglass used his connections in Europe to procure over $350 in assistance from antislavery societies in Great Britain and Scotland. More contributions came from a group of Bostonians who held dramatic readings in support of the organization. In New York City, the black activist Reverend Henry Highland Garnett welcomed Keckley to the Shiloh Presbyterian Church. Black waiters at the Metropolitan Hotel collected money for the CRA, and a group of black women held a charity ball to add to its treasury. Supporters in other cities sent contributions. After Keckley returned home, Philadelphia's Mother Bethel Church organized a contraband committee to raise money for the CRA.

Despite widespread support, the CRA struggled financially, collecting only $838 the first year. In 1863, Keckley called attention to the group's need for more funds in a plea to readers of the *Christian Recorder*, the African Methodist Episcopal Church newspaper. Keckley's "Appeal in Behalf of Our People" reminded readers of their Christian duty to help those in need. She explained the CRA's mission to supply the contrabands with food, clothing, medical care, and housing. Volunteers also provided guidance and encouragement, as well as education and employment assistance so that exslaves could become self-sufficient. By the end of the second year, the group had collected an additional $1,228 and a total of 5,250 articles of clothing.

After the Emancipation Proclamation of 1863 allowed the Union army to accept freedmen for military service, the women expanded their interests to include black soldiers. These men often suffered from the army's discriminatory policies. Black soldiers initially received less pay than white volunteers, and they often received inferior supplies. Hardship also affected the soldiers' families. In 1864, as a result of their additional mission and to recognize that freedpeople were no longer considered property, the women changed the organization's name to the Freedmen and Soldier's Relief Association.

*Kelly D. Selby*

***See also*** African American Women; Aid Societies; Antislavery Societies; Baptist Women; Camp Followers; Contrabands; Douglass, Frederick (ca. 1818–1895); Food; Fundraising; Keckley, Elizabeth Hobbs (ca. 1818–1907); Lincoln, Abraham (1809–1865); Lincoln, Mary Todd (1818–1882); Northern Women; Politics; Religion; Shortages; Union Homefront.

### References and Further Reading

Berlin, Ira, Barbara J. Fields, Steven F. Miller, Joseph P. Reidy, and Leslie S. Rowland. 1992. *Slaves No More: Three Essays on Emancipation and the Civil War.* New York: Cambridge University Press.

Eggleston, G. K. 1929. "The Work of Relief Societies during the Civil War." *Journal of Negro History* 14 (3): 272–299.

Keckley, Elizabeth. 1868. *Behind the Scenes, or Thirty Years a Slave, and Four Years in the White House.* New York: G. W. Carleton & Co.

Quarles, Benjamin. 1953. *The Negro in the Civil War.* Boston: Little, Brown and Company. (Reprinted 1989. New York: DeCapo Press.)

Sterling, Dorothy, ed. 1984. *We Are Your Sisters: Black Women in the Nineteenth Century.* New York and London: W. W. Norton.

## Contrabands

In 1861, Union General Benjamin F. Butler characterized as "contraband of war" three male slaves who had left their posts working on Confederate fortifications and escaped to Union-held Fortress Monroe on the Virginia coast. While this standard of international law usually referred to goods used in the prosecution of war, Butler applied the term to the slave men when he refused to hand them over to the Confederate officer who requested their return. Butler's decision prompted numerous other slaves to flee to Fortress Monroe, and soon all former slaves were called contrabands by Federal officials, soldiers, journalists, and missionaries. As the first slaves to make the transition to freedom, contrabands planted the seeds of postwar black communities in Union-occupied areas of the South. As their families' primary caregivers and as individuals who were not recruited as soldiers, female contrabands played a significant role in defining wartime freedom.

Some of the first contraband women lived on the Sea Islands off the South Carolina and Georgia coasts. These former slaves gained their freedom when their owners fled as Union troops arrived late in 1861. As would happen to black women throughout the Confederacy, they effectively became free simply by staying put when their masters abandoned their homes before a Union advance. Others who lived nearby soon joined these contrabands, using their feet to demonstrate their determination to be free. Women who escaped to Union lines were not just rejecting slavery but also seeking respite from specific wartime concerns, including raids by scavenging troops and the threat of being involuntarily separated from family members as owners moved slaves away from the front lines.

As the war progressed, slave women also left home to escape hunger as conditions in the Confederacy deteriorated. Others hoped to avoid mistreatment by owners disgruntled by the departure of the women's male relatives to join the Union army. Women were especially attracted to Union-occupied towns, which offered the best possibility of gainful employment. Female contrabands usually brought along any tools and provisions they could, including clothing, blankets, bedding, livestock, and fowl, as well as tubs, pots, or boilers—carried on their heads.

Contraband women suffered considerably during their transition from slavery to freedom. Many received an unwelcome reception from Union military authorities who were willing to put men to work or, beginning in 1863, to sign them up as soldiers, but who were unprepared for the influx of women and children that accompanied Union occupation. Many commanders simply forbade women and children from entering army camps; others expelled women and children after they had

Fugitive slaves ford the Rappahannock River in Virginia in August 1862, as the Second Battle of Bull Run gets underway. (Library of Congress)

become settled, as in the notorious example of Camp Nelson, Kentucky. Some commanders returned women and children to their Unionist slave owners. When these tactics did little to stem the outpouring of escaped slaves, Union authorities set up contraband camps and regimental villages as temporary way stations.

While many former slaves found their own shelter in occupied towns and cities, others took up residence in hastily erected contraband camps in such locations as Beaufort, South Carolina; Craney Island, Virginia; Grand Junction, Tennessee; and Corinth, Mississippi. Because the Union army used many able-bodied former slave men as laborers at the front and as soldiers, contraband camp populations tended to contain mostly women, children, and elderly men. Camp residents lived in various types of shelter, including abandoned houses, former barracks, lean-tos, shanties, cabins, and tents. While the food supply was generally adequate in most camps, there was

rarely enough warm clothing during the winter. Poor sanitation, little protection from the elements, and overcrowding led to high rates of mortality. Many residents died from smallpox, consumption, and pneumonia, although government vaccination programs provided some relief. Women and girls in the camps ran a significant risk of being raped. Officers and soldiers could be brutally abusive to contraband women, whom some viewed as prostitutes and vagrants. Another constant danger was the threat of military action, as when the contraband camp at Fort Pillow, Tennessee was destroyed during a Confederate attack on the fort.

Daily camp life included roll calls each morning, work assignments, and the distribution of rations. Within the camps, women recreated aspects of the slave communities that had sustained them through the years. Contraband women and children almost always cultivated small garden plots. In the evenings, residents gathered to sew, sing, dance, play games, hold prayer meetings, and gossip. Women drew on this communal ethos when they protested the conscription of contraband men or spoke out against the sale of abandoned lands. Contraband women started orphanages and participated in Emancipation Day celebrations. With men, they sought to establish their independence and keep their families intact.

Contraband women worked as field hands, laundresses, seamstresses, hospital attendants, personal servants, cooks, and maids. Women who worked for the Federal government routinely received lower wages than men, except in agricultural work in some locales. Contract labor systems had been established in most areas under Union occupation by early 1864. Some women rejected wage labor and supported their families by marketing fruits and vegetables, dairy products, and prepared foods. Others operated their own businesses, selling groceries or running hotels and brothels. Contraband women could not always find enough work, and military officials and private groups relocated former slave women, many of whom were farm hands or housewives, from some camps to Northern employers.

Contraband women interacted frequently with Northern missionaries and teachers. Clashes of values and priorities resulted, as when some missionaries on the Sea Islands encouraged women to leave the fields permanently to become housewives. Marriage ceremonies were conducted in many contraband camps. Contrabands consistently demonstrated their eagerness for education, initiating the establishment of schools in many areas and gathering to learn in barns, kitchens, churches, tents, and schoolhouses. Some contraband women trained to become teachers themselves. The records kept and reminiscences shared by women who worked among the contrabands—including Harriet Tubman, Charlotte Forten, Laura Towne, Lucy and Sarah Chase, Elizabeth Botume, and Susie King Taylor—have proved invaluable to recreating the contraband experience.

*Antoinette G. van Zelm*

**See also** Abolitionism and Northern Reformers; African American Women; Contraband Relief Association; Education, Southern; Emancipation Proclamation (January 1, 1863); Forten (Grimké),

Charlotte L. (1837–1914); Freedmen's Bureau; Port Royal; Rape; Refugees; Slave Families; Taylor, Susie Baker King (1848–1912); Towne, Laura Matilda (1825–1901); Tubman, Harriet [Araminta Ross] (1822–1913); Urban Women, Southern; Wartime Employment.

**References and Further Reading**

Berlin, Ira, et al., eds. 1982–present. *Freedom: A Documentary History of Emancipation, 1861–1867.* New York: Cambridge University Press.

Botume, Elizabeth Hyde. 1968. *First Days Amongst the Contrabands.* New York: Arno Press and the New York Times.

Cimprich, John. 1985. *Slavery's End in Tennessee, 1861–1865.* Tuscaloosa: University of Alabama Press.

Schwalm, Leslie A. 1997. *A Hard Fight for We: Women's Transition from Slavery to Freedom in South Carolina.* Urbana: University of Illinois Press.

Swint, Henry L., ed. 1966. *Dear Ones at Home: Letters from Contraband Camps.* Nashville, TN: Vanderbilt University Press.

## Coppin, Fanny Jackson (1837–1913)

African American feminist, educator, journalist, and missionary Fanny Marion Jackson was born a slave in Washington, D.C., in 1837. She taught freed slaves during the Civil War.

After an aunt purchased Fanny's freedom, she moved to New Bedford, Massachusetts, then to Newport, Rhode Island, working as a domestic servant in both places. Her Newport employers, the wealthy and aristocratic author George H. Calvert and his wife, encouraged her efforts to get an education. After years of private lessons and attendance at the local public (colored) school, she attended the Rhode Island Normal School, where she decided she wanted to be a teacher. Accordingly, with financial help from her family, Fanny attended Oberlin College in northern Ohio, one of the few American colleges that admitted African Americans.

Fanny attended Oberlin from 1860 to 1865. After a year in the preparatory course, she transferred to the "gentleman's." She did well, and in her junior year she, with forty classmates, was assigned to teach students in the Preparatory Department.

The faculty was nervous about this experiment and said they would remove her if the students rebelled. They did not, and her classes were large and successful. During her senior year, she organized an evening class for some of the former slaves who had settled in Oberlin township, where she taught them to read and write.

The year before she graduated, Fanny was offered a job at the Institute for Colored Youth, a Quaker school in Philadelphia. She went there as a teacher of classics and mathematics after her graduation (when she was elected class poet), and within four years she became head principal: the first African American woman in such a high position in the country. Over her thirty-seven-year tenure, she introduced several reforms, including a teacher training section in 1871 and, after a ten-year crusade, an industrial training division in 1888. Her advocacy of industrial training predated Booker T. Washington's, and unlike him she wanted to combine it with classical training.

Starting in 1878 she wrote a women's column in the *Christian Reporter,* the newspaper of the African Methodist Episcopal (AME) Church. In 1888 she opened a shelter for homeless women, and in 1894 she opened a Women's Exchange, a kind of settlement house for women and girls of color.

Fanny married AME minister Eli Jenkins Coppin in 1881 and continued teaching. She had no children. As president of the Women's Home and Foreign Missionary Society of the AME, she traveled to London and throughout the United States discussing the role of African American women.

Fanny Coppin retired from teaching in 1902 and almost immediately accompanied her husband, now a bishop, to South Africa, where she spent the next ten years working as a missionary. She returned to Philadelphia where she died in January 1913.

*Jane Lancaster*

**See also** African American Women; Education, Northern; Methodist Women; Teachers, Northern.
**References and Further Reading**
Jackson-Coppin, Fanny. [1913] 1995. *Reminiscences of School Life and Hints on Teaching.*
Introduction by Shelley P. Haley. Boston: G. K. Hall & Co.

Fanny Jackson Coppin, African American teacher, journalist and missionary (1837–1913). (Library of Congress)

## Courtship and Marriage

The Civil War disrupted traditional courtship expectations and rituals and transformed existing marriages. The service of nearly 3 million men in the military reshaped the relationships between men and women. The influx of military troops or government workers into communities created new courtship opportunities for some women, and those women in areas where the number of potential suitors had declined relied on correspondence with soldiers to fill the void. These disruptions to the homefront relaxed traditional rules governing courtships, providing more freedom in the choices and behavior of men and women. Weddings continued throughout the conflict, but wartime conditions drastically altered their tone and style. Many women rushed to the altar to accommodate their soldier husband's schedule, and economic hardships on the homefront precluded extravagant ceremonies. Those married before or during the war endured long periods of separation that tested their relationships. Tensions emerged as women assumed their husbands' responsibilities in running the home as well as the farm, plantation, or business during their absence. The wives of soldiers serving on the military front also expressed concerns over their husband's moral and physical well-being. While some wives followed their husbands to the battlefront, most relied on correspondence as a source of comfort and continuity. The Federal presence in the South also reshaped existing slave marriages and provided opportunities for new unions among African American men and women.

Courtships underwent a dramatic transformation during the four years of war. In the North, the departure of men created a dearth of courtship prospects for women in small communities, whereas those in cities and towns with a larger male population experienced little change. Brief sojourns home allowed Union soldiers to pursue romantic relationships, but geographic distance often limited such opportunities. Couples who pursued a long-distance relationship depended on letters as the only source of contact. Northern soldiers sought relationships while on the battlefront, but their prospects were often limited to women they deemed undesirable, namely prostitutes, matronly nurses, and Confederate women. The paucity of "proper" Northern women led soldiers to place advertisements in newspapers and periodicals back home seeking women who would write to them. The relationships forged in correspondence served primarily as a source of comfort and connection to home as well as the means to finding a potential mate.

Southern women's prospects for courtships also varied according to geographic location. Those in rural areas witnessed a sharp decline in the number of potential suitors due to their isolation on the plantation or farm. Only with military units passing through or occupying their communities did single women see an increase in the number of potential suitors. The uncertainty of finding a mate in the rural South forced some women to ponder a life without men, and others turned to female friendships to fill the emotional void. Conversely, single women in areas with a large population of government or military personnel, such as the Confederate capital of Richmond, enjoyed a constant stream of potential suitors. Constance Cary, for example, met her future husband while working in a military hospital in Richmond; he served as an aide to Jefferson Davis.

Single men and women pursued a number of activities that eventually led to courtships. Social activities—ranging from church functions and war-related events to festive parties and dances—became the primary means for young men and women to meet and mingle. In Richmond, soldiers marching through the city engaged in flirtations with young women who greeted them with flowers and blew kisses. Single women also came out to greet soldiers on the trains, bringing them small gifts and mementos. Women who had opportunities to meet soldiers often promised to maintain a correspondence. Throughout the conflict, many Southern men and women engaged in letter writing as the sole means of pursuing a relationship.

Wartime conditions eased the restrictions governing courtship behavior. Although class biases often guided the interaction of young women with soldiers, many women abandoned class prejudices when interacting with troops, the romantic image of the soldier in uniform being powerful enough to relax class prescriptions. Letters also permitted courting couples to loosen the standards of proper courtship behavior. The privacy of correspondence allowed men and women to offer romantic expressions of devotion and love. Letter writing allowed courting couples to keep engagements a secret until they could ensure parental consent. Parents grew increasingly concerned with this relaxation of courtship behavior and standards, fearing the potential for inappropriate marriages and sexual impropriety.

Economic hardships on the homefront and geographic distance also changed the structure of weddings for couples who chose to marry during the war. Women from more economically well-to-do families traditionally enjoyed lavish weddings. In the South, shortages of supplies resulting from the blockade and high inflation by 1863 kept couples from holding such elaborate celebrations. The scarcity of goods on the Southern homefront forced brides to be resourceful in outfitting a wedding, and many borrowed a wedding dress. The separation of soldier and betrothed likewise shaped the type and length of wedding. Some soldiers, with limited time on a furlough, rushed home to marry and then returned to the battlefield. LaSalle Corbell, for example, planned her wedding to Union general George Pickett in the months following his charge at Gettysburg. They chose to marry quickly in Petersburg, Virginia, allowing George to return to his post after a short celebration.

The Civil War also reshaped the roles and relationships of husbands and wives. Some men, mainly from the upper and middle socioeconomic classes, remained with their wives throughout the course of the war by using exemption clauses, paying a fee, or hiring a substitute to avoid military service. The vast majority of couples, however, spent a portion of the conflict apart, as the result of either military duty or government work. Concerned about the physical safety of their spouses, wives endured long periods of emotional stress. Many women attempted to assuage their anxieties by volunteering for the war effort or by staying busy in the home. The primary source of comfort for many married couples, however, was the letters that they exchanged. Correspondences allowed men and women to express their romantic affections as well as discuss the mundane activities of the home and family. Most women relied on letters from the front as their only source of news on the war and their husbands' safety. The uncertainty of the mail service, nevertheless, created long periods of silence between spouses that exacerbated women's anxieties.

Wives also had the option of following their husbands to the military front. Some women remained with their husbands by finding employment as nurses, laundresses, and cooks in the camps. Their presence brought a sense of continuity and comfort for soldiers enduring the physical and emotional hardships of service. Wives of high-ranking officers had the financial means to accompany their husbands on their campaigns. Union General Ulysses S. Grant, for example, invited his wife, Julia, to set up housekeeping during his occupation of West Tennessee and Vicksburg, respectively, and to follow him to Virginia during his 1864 Overland Campaign.

A husband's absence from the home often strained relationships. Wives worried about possible marital infidelity as their husbands encountered other women—including nurses, prostitutes, and Southern women in occupied communities. Sexual transgressions were also a concern of men whose wives had greater opportunities to engage in affairs with men on the homefront. The accompanying dangers of childbearing for women of the nineteenth century caused some wives to temper their physical contact with husbands who returned home or to refuse to visit their spouses on the battlefield, which fueled tensions.

Conflicts also emerged as a wife assumed her husband's economic and familial duties in his absence. Many women had trouble adapting to their new roles. Some Southern women, for example, wrote to their husbands for advice, attempting to reaffirm traditional lines of authority. The tenuous nature of the South's social system also made the task of managing slaves unreliable and difficult. In spite of these hardships, wives proved adept at managing the plantation, farm, or business in their husbands' absence while maintaining their own maternal and domestic responsibilities. Women also found some relief from the burdens of work by relying on older children or extended kin to perform domestic tasks. Men were often reluctant to accept this reorganization of gender roles. In the marriage of Kate and William McLure of South Carolina, for example, William was unwilling to recognize his wife's abilities in running the plantation and supervising the slaves. He placed overseers and male relatives in charge and sent detailed letters to Kate on how to manage daily tasks. This situation created a competition for authority on the McLure plantation as well as tensions within the marriage. Most men, however, had little choice but to entrust their wives with the management of the household economy.

Slave marriages underwent drastic changes resulting from Union occupation of Southern territory. Fearing disruptions in their labor force, masters relocated slaves into the interior of the South, often separating married couples in the process. Slave men and women in locations that were farther removed from military presence managed to remain together on the same plantation or farm throughout the course of the war. Couples in areas under Union occupation, however, discovered that the Federal presence offered a means to secure existing marriages as well as to form new ones. Since slaves lacked legal recognition of their marriages under Southern state laws, they turned to the Federal government to sanction their marriages legally, and they traveled to military camps to have chaplains officiate their weddings. Many husbands fled the plantation to Union lines, leaving behind their wives and family in the hopes of returning under Federal protection to reclaim them. Wartime conditions likewise allowed couples to dissolve involuntary unions demanded by the master. Some spouses left the plantation or farm, never to return to the marriage. The presence of African American troops in the South also led to relationships between soldiers and slave women. Wives in the Union army camps, whose husbands served in the Union army as soldiers or laborers, experienced the same separation anxieties as those of white soldiers' wives as they watched their husbands leave for the battlefield. The only alternative for a wife was to follow her husband to the front, finding employment as a camp cook or laundress.

By the final year of the war, conditions on the homefront tempered women's enthusiasm for their husbands' service. While they continued to vocalize their support for the Union or Confederacy, many women increasingly wrote letters describing their difficulties in maintaining family finances. Wives on the Southern homefront, where privation threatened the livelihood and physical well-being of families, wrote letters to their husbands requesting that they return home for a short period to stabilize the home. Yet such a decision required a husband to desert his post. By the end of the war, nearly 620,000 men had lost their lives while serving in the military, leaving behind a population of war widows, many of whom would rely on the Federal government for financial assistance. Husbands who survived the war reunited with their wives and attempted to return to a normal life.

*Victoria E. Ott*

*See also* African American Women; Camp Followers; Confederate Homefront; Heyward, Pauline DeCaradeuc (1843–1914); Letter Writing; Northern Women; Pickett, LaSalle Corbell (ca. 1843–1931); Slave Families; Slaveholding Women; Southern Women; Union Homefront; Widows, Confederate; Widows, Union.

**References and Further Reading**

Bleser, Carol, and Lesley J. Gordon, eds. 2001. *Intimate Strategies of the Civil War: Military Commanders and Their Wives.* New York: Oxford University Press.

Cimbala, Paul A., and Randall M. Miller, eds. 2002. *Union Soldiers and the Northern Home Front: Wartime Experiences, Postwar Adjustments.* New York: Fordham University Press.

Clinton, Catherine, and Nina Silber, eds. 1992. *Divided Houses: Gender and the Civil War.* New York: Oxford University Press.

Clinton, Catherine, ed. 2000. *Southern Families at War: Loyalty and Conflict in the Civil War South.* New York: Oxford University Press.

Faust, Drew Gilpin. 1996. *Mothers of Invention: Women of the Slaveholding South in the American Civil War.* Chapel Hill: University of North Carolina Press.

Lystra, Karen. 1989. *Searching the Heart: Women, Men, and Romantic Love in Nineteenth-Century America.* New York: Oxford University Press.

Mitchell, Reid. 1993. *The Vacant Chair: The Northern Soldier Leaves Home.* New York: Oxford University Press.

## Crosby, Frances Jane "Fanny" (1820–1915)

Hymnist, poet, and writer of Civil War ballads, staunch abolitionist Fanny Crosby composed the text to over nine thousand hymns and had several Civil War ballads for the Union published in newspapers and newsletters.

The only child of John and Mercy Crosby, Frances Jane Crosby was born March 24, 1820, in the town of Southeast, New York, about sixty miles from New York City. She became blind during infancy. With the death of her father in 1825 and her mother's subsequent need to take on an occupation, Fanny went to live with her grandmother. In 1835, she was admitted to the New York Institution for the Blind, where she met many dignitaries, including Grover Cleveland, Henry Clay, and James K. Polk.

In 1858 she married Alexander Van Alstyne, a blind teacher at the institution.

During the 1850s, Fanny collaborated with George F. Root, music instructor at the institution. Politically, she leaned toward the Whigs, for whom she wrote the poem "Carry Me On" in 1852; she later became a Republican in support of Abraham Lincoln. Before she composed the texts to over nine thousand hymns, Crosby wrote Civil War ballads, which often went unattributed at the time.

Some of Crosby's ballads were distributed to public schools in the Union. One, "Dixie for the Union," was published as a colored song sheet and urged readers to "Go meet those Southern traitors/With iron will." Another edition, set to the tune of Daniel Decatur Emmet's "I Wish I Was in Dixie," was arranged by famous European composer Sigismond. Similarly, "The Dixie of Our Union" encouraged the Northern troops. Although other songs had different themes, they all took the side of the Union and hoped to spur Northern soldiers on to victory. Crosby's poem "Song to Jeff Davis" was directed at the Confederate president. "Good-By, Old Arm," a tribute to wounded soldiers, was a song sheet with music by Philip Phillips. After the Civil War, Crosby took an interest in philanthropy to the freedmen, reflected in her poem, "Our Call."

Crosby also proved versatile in applying her poetic skills. William Bradbury's "There is a Sound Among the Forest Trees" had been popular during the Civil War. Crosby wrote sacred lyrics to the melody, and it was retitled "There's a Cry from Macedonia." Other poems included "Our Country" and "A Tribute (to the memory of dead horses)."

During her lifetime, Crosby used over two hundred pseudonyms, including Mrs. Fanny Van Alstyne, Louis N. Tilden, Arthur J. Langdon, and initials, such as F.A.N., F.C., D.D., and even an asterisk (*).

Fanny Crosby suffered a massive stroke on February 12, 1915, the sixth anniversary of Abraham Lincoln's birthday as a Federal holiday. Her funeral was the largest ever held in Bridgeport, Connecticut.

*Ralph Hartsock*

Fanny Crosby wrote Civil War ballads for the Union, was a poet, hymnist, and abolitionist (1820–1915). (Cirker, Hayward and Blanche Cirker, eds., *Dictionary of American Portraits*, 1967)

***See also*** Education, Northern; Music, Northern; Northern Women; Religion; Union Homefront; Wartime Literature.

**References and Further Reading**

Blumhofer, Edith L. 2005. *Her Heart Can See: The Life and Hymns of Fanny J. Crosby.* Grand Rapids, MI: William B. Eerdmans Publishing Company.

## Cumming, Kate (ca. 1835–1909)

Confederate nurse Kate Cumming kept a detailed journal of her wartime experiences. Her journal, published in 1866, provides insight into gender roles, social mores, and medical practice. Her writings also record the names of other hospital workers and many of the soldiers she tended.

Born in Edinburgh, Scotland, Kate and her family moved first to Montreal, Canada when she was a child, and, a few years later, settled in Mobile, Alabama. When the war started, Kate was living in

Confederate nurse Kate Cumming published a journal of her wartime experience in 1866. (Library of Congress)

Mobile with her father, David Cumming, and her brother. Her mother and sisters had traveled to England in early 1861 and remained there. After hearing that Reverend Benjamin M. Miller, while speaking at Saint John's Episcopal Church, had urged women to aid the Confederate military's battlefield medical corps, Kate felt compelled to assist. Bowing to family objections, she initially limited her efforts to collecting supplies locally. Citing Florence Nightingale as an example of a nurse who retained respectability despite her Crimean War work, Kate later rejected family views and volunteered for nursing duty with the Army of the Mississippi (later renamed the Army of Tennessee). She began her hospital duties in 1862.

Most of Kate's hospital responsibilities consisted of controlling access to liquor and supervising the work of soldiers and slaves who performed more onerous hospital tasks, such as dressing wounds. However, she shouldered unpleasant tasks when necessary, particularly toward the end of the war. At Corinth, Mississippi, she rolled bandages, dispensed food and drink, and attended to the needs of wounded Confederates and prisoners of war from the Battle of Shiloh. After the Battle of Chickamauga, she served in the Chattanooga, Tennessee area, moving with the military as it retreated through Georgia.

Kate kept a detailed journal of her experiences as a wartime nurse. The combination of her British heritage and Southern upbringing contributed to Kate's unique perspective on women's wartime roles. While she was loyal to the Confederate cause, she vociferously criticized the prevailing Southern attitude that a hospital environment was not a proper place for ladies.

When the war ended, Kate returned to Mobile. In 1874 she and her father moved to Birmingham, Alabama, where she taught school and music and was active in the United Daughters of the Confederacy. She never married. Kate died on June 5, 1909, and her funeral was held at Saint John's Episcopal Church. She was buried in Magnolia Cemetery, Mobile.

*Nancy L. Adgent*

***See also*** Domesticity; Hospitals; Nurses; Separate Spheres; Southern Women; United Daughters of the Confederacy.

**References and Further Reading**

Clinton, Catherine. 1995. *Tara Revisited: Women, War, and the Plantation Legend.* New York: Abbeville Press.

Cumming, Kate. 1998 [1959]. *Kate: The Journal of a Confederate Nurse,* edited by Richard Barksdale Harwell. Baton Rouge: Louisiana State University Press.

Faust, Drew Gilpin. 1996. *Mothers of Invention: Women of the Slaveholding South in the American Civil War.* Chapel Hill: University of North Carolina.

## Cushman, Pauline [Harriet Wood] (1833–1893)

A Union spy during the American Civil War, Pauline Cushman was born Harriet Wood on June 10, 1833. Although born in New Orleans, Louisiana, she was raised in Grand Rapids, Michigan.

At eighteen, Wood changed her name to Pauline Cushman and embarked on a career as theatrical performer in Thomas Placide's Varieties. In 1853 she married musician Charles Dickinson, who later served as a member of the regimental band of the Forty-first Ohio Infantry. After his death in 1862, Cushman returned to the stage in a production of *Seven Sisters* at Woods Theatre in Louisville, Kentucky. According to her memoir, it was during this time that paroled Southern soldiers offered her money to toast Confederate President Jefferson Davis during a performance. After informing the provost marshal of her intentions, Cushman took to the stage and proclaimed her loyalty to Davis and the honor of the Southern Confederacy. She was promptly fired from the production and began her career as a spy for the Union army. Posing as a Confederate sympathizer, she was employed to seek out information on Southern spies in Louisville and their methods of smuggling medical supplies through Federal lines.

Cushman later secured a theatrical job in Nashville, Tennessee, where she obtained information on thefts from government stores, the trade in contraband, and the movements of Confederate troops and guerrillas. In May 1863 Cushman was captured during an assignment to ascertain the strength of Confederate fortifications in Shelbyville, Kentucky. She was court-martialed and sentenced to be hanged by General Braxton Bragg. Cushman escaped to the safety of Union lines during the Army of Tennessee's evacuation from Shelbyville in June 1863.

President Abraham Lincoln acknowledged Cushman's valuable work as "spy of the Cumberland" by granting her an honorary commission as a brevet major. She enjoyed a brief period of notoriety, completing a lecture tour on her adventures as a spy and posing in her soldier's uniform for photographer Mathew Brady. After the publication of her biography in 1865, Cushman moved to California, where she resumed her career as an actress. She married August Fictner in 1872 and was widowed less than a year later. Cushman spent the next five years working in the redwood logging camps near Santa Cruz, California, where she met Jere Fryer in 1879, married, and moved to Casa Grande, Arizona Territory, to operate a hotel and livery stable. When the couple separated in 1890, Cushman returned to San Francisco, finally overdosing on opium in 1893. She was buried by the Grand Army of the Republic with full military honors.

*Giselle Roberts*

**See also** Female Spies.
**References and Further Reading**
Sarmiento, Ferdinand L. 1865. *Life of Pauline Cushman, The Celebrated Union Spy and Scout.* Philadelphia, PA: John E. Potter and Company.

## Custer, Elizabeth "Libbie" Bacon (1842–1933)

The wife of United States General George Armstrong Custer, Elizabeth "Libbie" Bacon Custer touted her husband's accomplishments and vigorously defended his reputation after his death. She became an author and lecturer in the postwar era.

Elizabeth "Libbie" Bacon was born April 8, 1842, in Monroe, Michigan, the only surviving child of Judge Daniel Stanton Bacon and Eleanor Sophia Bacon. Her upbringing was sternly Presbyterian with an emphasis on academics and deportment. She was educated at Boyd's Seminary in Monroe, which was considered one of the most prestigious "young ladies" academies in the Midwest and drew upper-class girls from several states. She attended a year at the Auburn Institute in New York, where she was able to gain experience with travel and larger urban settings. Excelling in French, art, and composition, Libbie graduated valedictorian, and her graduation paper won accolades from the *Detroit Free Press*.

Libbie was a sophisticated young woman when she married George Armstrong Custer on February 9, 1864. They visited West Point and Washington, D.C., and then joined the Michigan Cavalry Brigade in winter quarters near Brandy Station, Virginia. There were few women with the Army of the Potomac in February 1864 and fewer officers' wives. The Custers lived in the headquarters, entertained the staff officers, and rode out with the troops. When General Hugh Judson Kilpatrick ordered a raid on Richmond, Libbie found herself virtually alone in a semi-deserted cavalry camp. She moved to Washington, D.C., until the troops returned, then rejoined them in Virginia.

Elizabeth Bacon Custer, writer and wife of George Armstrong Custer (1844–1933). (Courtesy New York Historical Society)

Libbie remained in the field with her husband; General Philip Sheridan, who usually opposed women in camp, allowed her the privilege because he felt she improved the officers' behavior. They were close to enemy lines, so she always went out with a cavalry escort, and she had the opportunity to observe pickets on duty, small emergency deployments, and prisoners being brought in. When the battle campaigns began in the spring, Libbie divided her time between a solitary apartment in Washington, D.C., and accompanying her husband into the field. In Washington, she visited the hospitals, comforting Michigan soldiers and cavalrymen from General Custer's command.

Libbie socialized with politicians, military officers, and other personages, and her intelligence,

good nature, and polished demeanor won her much admiration. Her ability to win favor in the capitol was an asset, because she was able to promote her husband's talents, improving his career prospects. Her friendship with Congressman F. W. Kellogg of Michigan proved particularly helpful; the senator helped assure her Democrat husband's promotions in a Republican-inclined political landscape.

During the Civil War, Libbie learned to negotiate army life both in the field and in garrison, lessons she would utilize as she followed the cavalry west during the Indian Wars. After George Armstrong Custer's death at the Battle of the Little Bighorn in 1876, Libbie remained in mourning until her own death in at age ninety-two in 1933. She used her position as a lady and an officer's widow, effectively staunching public criticism of her husband for the duration of her life. Her books and lectures contributed to myths of Little Bighorn, and she kept the memories of the Civil War's great Boy General in the forefront of American imagination.

*Dawn Ottevaere Nickeson*

***See also*** Education, Northern; Hospitals; Northern Women; Union Homefront; Wounded, Visits to.

**References and Further Reading**

Leckie, Shirley A. 1993. *Elizabeth Bacon Custer and the Making of a Myth.* Norman: University of Oklahoma Press.

Leckie, Shirley A. 2001. "The Civil War Partnership of Elizabeth and George A. Custer." In *Intimate Strategies of the Civil War: Civil War Commanders and their Wives,* edited by Carol K. Bleser and Lesley J. Gordon, 178–198. New York: Oxford University Press.

Merington, Marguerite, ed. 1950. *The Custer Story: The Life and Intimate Letters of General George Armstrong Custer and His Wife Elizabeth.* New York: Devon-Adair.

Reynold, Arlene. 1994. *The Civil War Memories of Elizabeth Bacon Custer.* Austin: University of Texas Press.

# D

## Daly, Maria Lydig (1824–1894)

Wartime diarist and wife of a New York Copperhead, Maria Lydig Daly grew up in a wealthy Dutch-German family and married Charles Patrick Daly, a self-made Irish American. Her diary recorded her struggle to maintain her household as well as her observations about class, ethnicity, politics, and the war. Her journal provides rare insights into the complexities of Victorian womanhood and life in a Northern city during the war.

Daly enjoyed a comfortable childhood with a good education and interaction with leading political and literary figures. Her choice of husband was unusual. Although he was a rising star in the judicial world, appointed to New York's Court of Common Pleas by age twenty, Daly was beneath the Lydigs socially. Maria waged a yearlong battle with her father for approval of the match and suggested the possibility of eloping. She maintained a fierce loyalty to the judge and helped maintain their household budget by "turning" her wardrobe and creating her own bonnets. Throughout their marriage, Maria worked with the judge's economic advisors to stabilize their income in spite of inflation. She also joined local women to discuss the causes of economic difficulties and to suggest a nonconsumption movement to boycott Southern goods. She dabbled in land speculation and in gold and silver investments, and she read extensively about economics. Careful study led her to suggest that the government fix prices and supervise the quality of food being sold in the city.

Daly shared her husband's enthusiasm for Copperhead politics. She deplored the actions of abolitionists and Republican politicians, and she blamed the two groups for the war. She sympathized with President Abraham Lincoln, a man she saw as well-meaning but incompetent. However, by the end of the war her sympathy gave way to disgust, and she openly supported her husband's work to remove Lincoln from office by supporting George B. McClellan in 1864. Her politics were tinged by racism, and she observed that the violence of the 1863 Draft Riots might help dispel the insolence she detected in the city's African Americans.

Despite her political beliefs, Daly worked to support the men of the Union army by collecting hospital supplies and sewing for the Sixty-ninth New York. She investigated the possibility of nursing but stopped when she encountered women who were as opinionated as she was about what was most needed for the men. She made a flag for an Irish regiment that she thought was being overlooked.

Daly's observations add to the complex interpretation of the effects of the Civil War on American society. She retained a lively interest in politics, society, and economics until her death in 1894.

*Karen A. Kehoe*

***See also*** Diaries and Journals; Northern Women.

**References and Further Reading**

Daly, Maria Lydig. 1962. *Diary of a Union Lady 1861–1865*, edited by Harold Earl Hammond. New York: Funk & Wagnalls.

Klement, Frank L. 1999. *Lincoln's Critics: The Copperheads of the North*, edited by Steven K. Rogstad. Shippensburg, PA: White Mane Publishing Co.

Massey, Mary Elizabeth. [1966] 1994. *Women in the Civil War*. Lincoln: University of Nebraska Press.

## Davis, Jefferson (1808–1889)

President of the Confederacy Jefferson Davis served as a United States Congressman and fought in the Mexican War before he was chosen to lead the seceded Southern states.

Kentucky-born on June 3, 1808, Jefferson was the tenth and last child of Samuel Emory Davis, a Revolutionary War veteran, and Jane Cook Davis, who together followed a traditional pattern of migration from Georgia through Kentucky to Mississippi. The Davises settled finally on a modest cotton plantation named Rosemont near Woodville. Jefferson Davis secured the best education of all his siblings, attending local schools, St. Thomas College near Bardstown, Kentucky, Transylvania University in Lexington, and finally, from 1824 to 1828, the United States Military Academy. There he formed lifelong friendships and developed an affinity for all things military.

After a series of postings on the frontier as a junior officer, he resigned his commission in 1835 to establish a cotton plantation near Vicksburg, Mississippi, adjoining that of his much older brother and father figure, Joseph E. Davis. That year he married Sarah Knox, daughter of Zachary Taylor, one of his former commanding officers; she died of fever three months later. Grief stricken and recovering from the same illness, Jefferson threw himself into farming and was a virtual recluse until he met Varina Howell of Natchez, the vivacious daughter of one of Joseph's longtime friends from Natchez. They married in 1845 and were eventually the parents of four sons and two daughters, only two of whom survived their father.

Davis began his political career in the Democratic Party during his courtship of Varina and was elected to Congress in 1845. The following summer he was chosen colonel of a Mexican War regiment that he led with distinction in the Battles of Monterrey and Buena Vista. Returning from the war a wounded hero, he was sent to the Senate in 1847, serving there until 1851 and again from 1857 to 1861. Between terms, he ran unsuccessfully for governor and was an exceptionally well qualified and able secretary of war, supervising many Washington building projects, including the expansion of the Capitol and the construction of the Washington Aqueduct. He was also responsible for real gains in the pay and size of the army, revamping the curriculum of West Point, surveying routes for a railroad to the Pacific, pushing westward the "chain of forts" for the protection of settlers, and overseeing hundreds of river and harbor projects in many states. Meanwhile, he was one of President Franklin Pierce's closest confidants, kept his eye on national and state politics, and, after leaving the War Department, was a powerful voice for the South in the years before secession.

A moderate during the secession crisis, Davis left the Union reluctantly and was more sobered than elated by his election to the presidency of the Confederacy, foreseeing "troubles and thorns innumerable" (Davis 1971–present, 7: 53–54). Balancing his own states' rights views with the need for a national effort against a common enemy, Davis strove continually for Confederate independence, often running afoul of Congress and the governors. In May 1865, Federal forces captured Davis in Georgia as he fled to reestablish the government in the West. Imprisoned for two years while his captors endeavored to try him for treason, he was eventually freed when the charges were dropped in 1868. By then he was traveling in Europe, investigating various job possibilities to support his young family.

Beginning in late 1869, he was president of a Memphis life insurance company that failed in the Panic of 1873. A few years later he accepted the offer of Sarah Ellis Dorsey to write his memoirs in a rented cottage on the grounds of Beauvoir, her estate near Biloxi, Mississippi. She died soon after, leaving him Beauvoir in her will. His *Rise and Fall of the Confederate Government* did not bring financial rewards, but in the late 1870s he was able to regain possession of Brierfield, which had been sold

Jefferson Davis had served as a war hero, U.S. representative, senator, and U.S. secretary of war before he accepted the presidency of the Confederate States of America in 1861. Despite his considerable military and political experience, Davis was unable to lead the Confederacy to victory during the Civil War. (National Archives and Records Administration)

by Joseph Davis in 1866 and subsequently became the focus of bitter family litigation. During the 1880s he continued to reside at Beauvoir and took part in various Confederate commemorations before dying of pneumonia in New Orleans on December 6, 1889. He was reinterred in Richmond in 1893.

*Lynda L. Crist*

**See also** Davis, Varina Banks Howell (1826–1906); Politics.

### References and Further Reading

Cooper, William J. 2000. *Jefferson Davis, American.* New York: Alfred A. Knopf.

Davis, Jefferson. 1971–present. *The Papers of Jefferson Davis.* 11 volumes to date. Baton Rouge: Louisiana State University Press.

Davis, Jefferson. 1881. *Rise and Fall of the Confederate Government.* 2 volumes. New York: D. Appleton & Co.

Davis, Varina Howell. 1890. *Jefferson Davis, A Memoir.* 2 volumes. New York: Belford.

Davis, William C. 1991. *Jefferson Davis: The Man and His Hour.* New York: HarperCollins.

## Davis, Rebecca Harding (1831–1910)

Author Rebecca Harding Davis published over a dozen novels, her autobiography, and more than five hundred short stories, juvenile stories, and essays. Her work included discussions of interracial sexuality, the horrors of slavery, and the Civil War.

Rebecca Blaine Harding was born June 24, 1831, in Washington, Pennsylvania, to Rachel Leet Wilson and Richard W. Harding. The family soon moved back home to Big Spring (now Huntsville), Alabama, and then to Wheeling, Virginia (now West Virginia). Her mother's love of literature and history influenced Rebecca's intellectual development. Rebecca attended Washington Female Seminary from 1845 to 1848 and graduated valedictorian. She married abolitionist lawyer Lemuel Clarke Davis on March 5, 1863. They had three children including famed journalist and war correspondent Richard Harding Davis.

Davis's writing career started in earnest in 1861 when *Life in the Iron Mills* came out serially in *The Atlantic Monthly.* A story about the dehumanization of industrial capitalism, *Life* met critical acclaim and launched Davis's career. In 1862 she published three short stories exploring interracial sexuality and the degradation of plantation slavery. In 1867 she published *Waiting for the Verdict*, a novel portraying the war and its aftermath from both regional perspectives. Her critique from the viewpoints of both regions grew out of Davis's life in Wheeling, a border town where ambiguity governed many people's attitudes about the war. She was ahead of her time as a parlor radical, exposing the evils of plantation slavery in the South and wage slavery elsewhere; however, notions of racial hierarchy common in the proslavery rhetoric of antebellum Virginia continued to inform her understanding of race. Davis's chief legacy to literature of the

Civil War era is an innovative literary form that links sentimentalism, realism, and naturalism, in a critique of power relations, slavery, racial identity, gender conventions, industrialism, individualism, and other cultural mainstays in the late nineteenth century.

Davis believed that the activism of the pen was more effective than the tactics used by other abolitionists and women's rights activists. In any case, Davis believed women were innately suited to write about the human condition because of their experience with conventional gender constraints. Her fiction deals with how race and gender circumscribe freedom and limit access to power. Davis integrated the personal and the political and used conventions of sentimental fiction to express historically rooted circumstance. Her characters challenge the traditional constraints. Her endings are rarely happy. Female characters who exploit possibilities to realize intellectual or artistic fulfillment generally become loners who are either punished socially or are haunted by self-doubt.

Rebecca Harding Davis died September 29, 1910.

*Catherine Oglesby*

**See also** Abolitionism and Northern Reformers; Fiction Writers, Southern.

### References and Further Reading

Davis, Rebecca Harding. 1995. *A Rebecca Harding Davis Reader: "Life in the Iron Mills," Selected Fiction, and Essays,* edited, with a Critical Introduction, by Jean Pfaelzer. Pittsburgh, PA: University of Pittsburgh Press.

Harris, Sharon M. 1991. *Rebecca Harding Davis and American Realism.* Philadelphia: University of Pennsylvania Press.

Henwood, Dawn. 1999. "Slaveries 'In the Borders': Rebecca Harding Davis's 'Life in the Iron Mills' in its Southern Context." *Mississippi Quarterly* 52 (4): 567–596.

Pfaelzer, Jean. 1996. *Parlor Radical: Rebecca Harding Davis and the Origins of American Social Realism.* Pittsburgh, PA: University of Pittsburgh Press.

## Davis, Varina Anne "Winnie" (1864–1898)

The youngest child of Confederate President Jefferson Davis, Varina Anne Davis, The Daughter of the Confederacy, became a living symbol of the Lost Cause. During her lifetime, she frequently served as the official Davis family representative at Confederate veterans' gatherings. Winnie was a talented writer who achieved a measure of literary success with the publication of several books and as a correspondent for the *New York World.* Her last years were filled with sadness: Varina experienced the death of her father, a failed romance, and ill health before her own premature death.

Varina was born on June 27, 1864, at the Confederate Executive Mansion in Richmond, Virginia. Nicknamed Winnie, the baby was the sixth child of Jefferson and Varina Davis. After the fall of the Confederate government, Varina and her infant daughter eventually joined Jefferson Davis at Fort Monroe. Their company was his sole source of comfort during his incarceration as a war criminal.

After her father's release in 1867, Winnie traveled extensively with her parents. In 1876, she entered the Friedlander School in Karlsruhe, Germany. She thrived academically, excelling in French, German, literature, and fine arts. Winnie joined her parents at their Mississippi home, Beauvoir, following the completion of her education. She served as her father's intellectual companion, sharing his interests in politics, poetry, literature, and travel.

As a young woman, Winnie attended Confederate veterans' assemblies. In 1886, she accompanied her father on a Southern tour. When her father was too exhausted to attend a ceremony in Atlanta, Winnie stood in for him. Introduced as The Daughter of the Confederacy, she carried the sobriquet for the rest of her life. Veterans demonstrated a special affection for Winnie, whom they viewed as a symbol of the Old South. She demonstrated her sympathy for the Lost Cause in an essay, "The Ante-Bellum Southern Woman."

Her status as a Confederate icon became burdensome when Winnie fell in love with Alfred Wilkinson, the grandson of a prominent abolitionist. The two became engaged after the Davises overcame their initial opposition. When the engagement became public, the South erupted with criticism. Devastated by the controversy, Winnie fell into a depression and her relationship eventually dissolved.

After Jefferson Davis's death, Varina and Winnie moved to New York in search of financial stability. Winnie continued her writing career. Her publications included a biography of the Irish patriot Robert Emmet and two novels: *A Romance of Summer Seas* and *The Veiled Doctor.* In 1898, Winnie attended the Confederate veterans' reunion during which she grew seriously ill. On September 18, 1898, Varina Anne Davis died of "malarial gastritis." The Daughter of the Confederacy was buried with full military honors beside her father at Hollywood Cemetery in Richmond, Virginia.

*Karen Kinzey*

**See also** Davis, Jefferson (1808–1889); Davis, Varina Banks Howell (1826–1906); Fiction Writers, Southern; Southern Women.

**References and Further Reading**

Cook, Cita. 2003. "Winnie Davis: The Challenges of Daughterhood." In *Mississippi Women: Their History, Their Lives,* edited by Martha Swift et al. Athens: University of Georgia Press, 21–38.

Ross, Ishbel. 1973. *First Lady of the South.* Westport, CT: Greenwood Press.

## Davis, Varina Banks Howell (1826–1906)

As the wife of a politician and the first lady of the Confederacy, Varina Howell Davis lived much of her life in the public eye. She helped husband Jefferson Davis complete his memoirs and, after his death, published her own.

Born May 7, 1826, at Marengo plantation, her maternal grandparents' home in Concordia Parish, Louisiana, Varina Banks Howell was the second child and eldest daughter of Margaret Louisa Kempe, whose father was an Irish nationalist, and of William Burr Howell, the son of a New Jersey governor and a relative of Aaron Burr. Varina was brought up at The Briars, an unpretentious house in Natchez, Mississippi. She attended a finishing school in Philadelphia and was tutored at home by Judge George Winchester.

In 1843 she met Jefferson Davis, a widower some eighteen years her senior, at the home of his older brother, a longtime friend of the Howell family. They were married on February 26, 1845, at The Briars and settled for a few months on his Brierfield

plantation near Vicksburg. After Jefferson was elected to Congress, the newlyweds lived in Washington until July 1846, when he assumed command of a Mississippi regiment in the Mexican War. Afterward, he was sent to the Senate, resigning in late 1851 to undertake a losing gubernatorial campaign. In 1853, not long after the birth of Samuel Emory Davis, their first child, the Davises returned to Washington, a city Varina Davis relished. A striking and intelligent women and a popular hostess prized for her social and conversational skills, she was a particular favorite of President James Buchanan.

Although the couple's firstborn Samuel died in 1854, the family continued to grow with the birth of Margaret Howell the next year, then Jefferson Jr., in 1857, Joseph Evan in 1859, William Howell in 1861, and Varina Anne in 1864. When her husband was elected president of the Confederacy in 1861, Varina Davis was for four years the nation's first lady in Montgomery and in Richmond, finding herself constantly in the public eye and continuing to act as her husband's helpmate. Because of his ill health and particularly after his eye surgery, she was often his amanuensis and was clearly his confidant on political and military matters. In Richmond she enjoyed a well-known circle of friends, notably the diarist Mary Boykin Chesnut, but also concentrated on managing a busy household and her lively young children. Tragedy struck in April 1864 when five-year-old Joseph was killed in an accidental fall at the Confederate White House. A year later, the Confederacy in shambles, she left Richmond with the young ones, fleeing southward until captured with her husband in May 1865.

While Jefferson was imprisoned at Fort Monroe, Virginia, Varina lived for a time in Savannah, sending Margaret, Jeff Jr., and William to Canada for education and safekeeping in the care of her mother and sister. Davis's last year of confinement was cheered by the presence of Varina and their youngest daughter, who were permitted to live at the fort with him. His release in May 1867 brought little stability. As he searched for a means of livelihood, Varina Davis lived abroad, then in Memphis with him (1870–1876), abroad again, and finally

President of the Confederacy Jefferson Davis and his wife Varina Howell Davis. (Miller, Francis Trevelyan and Robert Sampson Lanier, *The Photographic History of the Civil War," vol 9, 1911)*

(1878–1889) together at Beauvoir, their retirement home on the Mississippi Gulf Coast.

She assisted in the preparation of his memoirs and after his death in December 1889, wrote her own, two well-written and colorful volumes of reminiscences and documents, but not the financial success she wished. To have a regular income, she moved to New York City in 1892 and took a job writing for the *New York World*. A decade later she sold Beauvoir, never to return. Varina Anne's death in 1898 was another devastating loss, particularly since daughter Margaret had married in 1876 and lived in Colorado. On October 16, 1906, at the age of eighty, Varina Davis died of pneumonia and heart disease in New York; she was given a military funeral and interred with her husband in Hollywood Cemetery, Richmond.

*Lynda L. Crist*

**See also** Davis, Jefferson (1808–1889); Davis, Varina Anne "Winnie" (1864–1898).

**References and Further Reading**

Davis, Varina Howell. 1890. *Jefferson Davis, A Memoir.* 2 volumes. New York: Belford.

Dolensky, Suzanne T. 1985 "Varina Howell Davis, 1889 to 1906." *Journal of Mississippi History* 47 (May): 90–109.

Randall, Ruth Painter. 1962. *I, Varina.* Boston: Little, Brown and Company.

Ross, Ishbel. 1958. *First Lady of the South.* New York: Harper and Brothers.

Van der Heuvel, Gerry. 1988. *Crowns of Thorns and Glory: Mary Todd Lincoln and Varina Howell Davis.* New York: Dutton.

## Desertion

Both Confederate and Union women played key roles in soldiers' decisions to desert or not, and, once soldiers decided to desert, women frequently supplied them with vital aid or, less likely, turned them in to authorities. Partially because of the urging of soldiers' female relatives, both Northern and Southern armies suffered from the pernicious effects of desertion. While the exact numbers of deserters will never be known, estimates exceed two hundred thousand for the Union and one hundred thousand for the Confederacy. Though some men headed for Canada, the West, or enemy lines, the most probable destination for deserters was their home community. And some evidence indicates that men were most likely to desert if they were connected to a household in which all adult males had entered the army and only women and children remained behind.

Encouragement by civilians was perhaps the most important factor in the decision to desert. While some women begged husbands and sons to come home, more commonly, accurate descriptions of the family's privation, such as starvation, lack of money, exploitation by speculators, and crops dying in the field, made a persuasive implicit argument for abandoning the army. Most often, deserters decided that the government had broken an unspoken agreement to care for their families. With the nation failing to hold up its end of the bargain, these men felt that they no longer owed service to the army. Enlisting in the army had meant putting the needs of a man's country ahead of the needs of his family. Now, torn between competing notions of honor—a call to nation and a call to family—deserting meant reversing these priorities and putting family first. Though deserters could face execution if caught, they often believed that their family faced death if they did not leave their units. Officers and other fellow soldiers recognized that not all deserters were equal, and they generally expressed sym-

pathy for and leniency to those who had deserted to help their families, reserving their wrath for bounty jumpers or those who ran to enemy lines.

Desertion was inextricably bound with society's views of gender and paternalism. Men escaped the ranks to provide for their hungry families, and some soldiers feared that, if they did not desert, their spouses might leave them for a man who could take care of them. Simultaneously, women used their gender to either encourage or discourage desertion and to shield themselves from the wrath of soldiers hunting deserters. Both governments recognized that mothers had an especially powerful voice in their sons' decisions regarding desertion. Ironically, once they left the army, these men, rather than providing for their female relatives, instead often relied on these women for protection and provisions, thus reversing the main tenet of paternalism. In taking charge of deserters' welfare, women stepped out of their traditional family role of dependence and into a role of family leadership.

Some deserters simply returned to their communities and resumed their prewar lives. More likely, however, they hid near their homes. Deserters "lying out" in woods, swamps, or caves relied on women, most frequently their female relatives, for their survival. Women supplied them with food, blankets, clothing, and information. Additionally, when soldiers hunting for deserters swept through an area, these women might provide advanced warning in the form of clanging cowbells, blowing whistles, or hanging blankets outside their house as a coded message to those in hiding. Women might also give misinformation or false leads to those searching for deserters. Some women traded with deserter bands who had stolen goods from wealthier neighbors. With the aid of women, some deserters succeeded in evading capture for months or even years.

In effect, the women who abetted men in hiding had deserted the war themselves. In both the Union and the Confederacy, aiding deserters was a crime. In assisting deserters, women relied on society's gender norms to allow them to break these laws with impunity, but this strategy did not always work. Expressing their frustration at women's cavalier disregard for the law and their own failure to bring soldiers back into the ranks, some army officers treated women in a manner that they would not have used during peacetime. They burned women's out buildings and homes and imprisoned recalcitrant families. Soldiers also threatened women shielding deserters with bodily harm or rape, slapped or pushed them to the ground, and, in rare instances, tortured them in an effort to gain information about the location of bands of deserters. These soldiers flagrantly violated society's prescribed gender relations, thus demonstrating the extensive, though often unintended, impact of war on behavioral norms.

Not all women aided deserters. Some letters from home instructed husbands that their wives would rather hear of their death than the shame of their desertion. Southern newspapers printed appeals from The Women of the South, urging men to remain in the army, not to heap disgrace on the heads of their family's next several generations. Politicians echoed this sentiment and exhorted women to call for the husbands to remain in the army. In Georgia, state legislators, reminding their constituents of the opprobrium attached to desertion, passed legislation that would allow women whose husbands had deserted to be granted divorces. Some women did not abet deserters but instead provided information leading to their arrests. Women, especially those whose male relatives remained in the army, felt no need to harbor fugitives but instead urged that deserters be punished severely. Also, while some deserters relied on community support, others preyed on unprotected homes and communities, and women felt no need to hide these desperados. In some areas, female relatives of deserters suffered community ostracism with millers refusing to take their grain and with county relief agencies rejecting their applications for aid. In the North, the army captured eighty thousand deserters and in the South, the Confederate army nabbed twenty-one thousand. Without the aid of women, these numbers would have been lower.

*John M. Sacher*

**See also** Civilian Life; Confederate Homefront; Confederate Soldiers, Motives; Conscription; Family Life, Northern; Family Life, Southern; Foraging, Effects on Women; Honor; Impressment; Letter Writing; Military Invasion and Occupation; Morale; Northern Women; Rape; Shortages; Southern Women; Union Homefront; Union Soldiers, Motives.

**References and Further Reading**
Bynum, Victoria. 1992. *Unruly Women: The Politics of Social and Sexual Control in the Old South.* Chapel Hill: University of North Carolina Press.
Cashin, Joan E., ed. 2002. *The War Was You and Me: Civilians in the American Civil War.* Princeton, NJ: Princeton University Press.
Lonn, Ella. 1928. *Desertion during the Civil War.* New York: American Historical Association.
Weitz, Mark A. 2000. *A Higher Duty: Desertion among Georgia Troops during the Civil War.* Lincoln: University of Nebraska Press.

## Destruction of Homes

The devastation of homes during the Civil War resulted from a number of causes, including stray artillery shells, fire, or abandonment. Empty homes were often destroyed by military or civilian populations. Due to frequent invasions by Union forces and the high number of battles fought on Southern soil, the bulk of the devastation lay in Confederate territory. However, Confederates damaged homes on Northern soil during invasions led by General Robert E. Lee in 1862 and 1863.

The precise number of homes destroyed during the war remains unknown, largely because of the indiscriminate patterns of demolition and flawed record keeping by the Confederate government. Socioeconomic status did not protect homeowners; farmhouses and plantation homes alike were ruined. While the destruction of homes by battle munitions is believed to have been largely accidental, Union forces forthrightly occupied or burned Southern homes during invasions to erode the morale of the Confederate homefront. In any case, women suffered the brunt of wartime deprivation because they and their families often became refugees. Some sought shelter with neighbors or with extended family, paid inflated costs for rented quarters, or, if neither option was available, lived in tents, under bridges, or at public dwellings that offered protection from the elements. Along with the logistical hardships women suffered, the destruction of homes symbolized their persecution by Federal forces and the failure of Southern white men to provide protection from enemy hostility.

Homes destroyed by munitions were more often examples of collateral damage than targets of enemy forces, simply because they were located near battlefields or in cities under siege. The level of damage from military exchange varied considerably. In some cases, houses remained standing despite the stray bullets that chipped away the exteriors and the pieces of shells lodged in roofs or in walls. However, stray shells also demolished roofs, collapsed porticos, shattered windows, and destroyed homes altogether. By May 1865, entire districts near Manassas Junction, Virginia, had been completely destroyed, with only a cement foundation or a chimney among a pile of rubble as any indication that houses once existed. Advancing or retreating armies also damaged houses near battle sites. In Antietam, owners who temporarily abandoned their homes returned after the battle to find them stripped of furniture, wallpaper, rugs, and fixtures by the troops.

Most often fire consumed houses near battle sites and along routes of enemy invasion. In 1863 and 1864, Confederate forces burned homes in Chambersburg, Pennsylvania. In 1865, Confederates prepared for the arrival of Union troops in Richmond by burning public buildings to keep things out of Federal hands; many private homes also caught fire. That same year, artillery shells detonated in Charleston and started fires in parts of the city. Most fires, though, were started by Union troops during invasions in Southern territory. While the majority of Union commanders avoided torching occupied private homes, they frequently ordered the burning of public dwellings, such as mills, factories, and armories. Often these planned fires quickly spread to houses. Along their march through Georgia and the Carolinas in 1864 and 1865, troops under General William T. Sherman reportedly burned both occupied and unoccupied homes. In September 1864, fires from the war industries that Sherman's men burned in Atlanta quickly engulfed houses. In February 1865, Columbia lost a third of its buildings to fire. Private homes

were not spared. After the war, Sherman was exonerated from charges that his men started the fires, yet questions surrounding the responsibility for the Columbia burning remained. Nevertheless, Southern homes were indisputably lost to Sherman's scorched-earth ideology.

The threat of military hostility and invasion spurred citizens to abandon their homes. Estimates of Confederate refugees range as high as a quarter of a million. Abandoned houses were often stripped of any valuables or burned either by soldiers or by thieves. Unoccupied houses were also seized by the military for barracks or officers' quarters. If refugees were able to return to their homes, they might find their houses occupied by squatters, either poor Southern whites, former slaves, or Northerners who relocated in the South immediately after the war.

For women, the destruction of homes was both a physiological and psychological blow. The immediate need to provide food and shelter for dependents was a duty utterly foreign to most antebellum women. However, it became a harsh reality during wartime. In addition, although prior to the war some women had never left their communities, they were forced to leave familiar surroundings to find shelter and provisions elsewhere in the face of sure destitution. Wealthy women sometimes had additional property in other regions of the Confederacy, or they could rent or buy new, if temporary, housing. Yeomen and poor women had fewer options and found shelter wherever possible. Homelessness was a strange, daunting, and immediate plight for women to manage.

The wartime demolition of homes had far-reaching consequences. From a strategic standpoint, the military tactic successfully debilitated women's morale, yet it also exacerbated the resentment of Southern women toward the Union. This resentment reverberated in the postwar years. With the destruction of their houses and the deaths of their men, women believed they had literally lost everything and saw themselves as suffering immeasurably from the consequences of a war. Homeless and refugee women became symbols of Confederate failure. After Union forces inflicted devastation on

Southern populations and private property, women viewed Federal forces as barbaric, a sentiment that did not end with the 1865 surrender of Lee's forces. When Union armies turned women and children into homeless refugees, the psychological devastation became associated with the North, assuring that women's resentment of the Union would bleed into the Reconstruction years.

*Sara Marie Eye*

**See also** Confederate Homefront; Destruction of Personal Property; Military Invasion and Occupation; Morale; Refugees; Sheridan's Shenandoah Valley Campaign (1864); Sherman's Campaign (1864–1865); Southern Women, Union Homefront.

**References and Further Reading**
Ash, Stephen V. 1995. *When the Yankees Came: Conflict and Chaos in the Occupied South, 1861–1865.* Chapel Hill: University of North Carolina Press.
Faust, Drew Gilpin. 1996. *Mothers of Invention: Women of the Slaveholding South in the American Civil War.* Chapel Hill: University of North Carolina Press.
Rable, George C. 1989. *Civil Wars: Women and the Crisis of Southern Nationalism.* Urbana: University of Illinois Press.
Trowbridge, John Townsend. 1956. *The Desolate South, 1865–1866; A Picture of the Battlefields and of the Devastated Confederacy,* edited by Gordon Carroll. New York: Duell, Sloan and Pearce.

## Destruction of Personal Property

Concentrated almost wholly in the South, property destruction delivered a significant blow to the Confederacy's economy; yet it was equally devastating as a psychological weapon against the Southern populace. A Federal tactic of total warfare—making war on the enemy's will to fight—the extensive destruction of private property unnerved Southerners and hastened the sharp decline in the morale on the Confederate homefront.

Although Union troops inflicted the most damage in the South, Confederate troops also destroyed Southern private property through impressment. The total value of wartime property damage remains unknown, due to the unrestrained and haphazard patterns of destruction, the infinite variety of private property consumed, as well as to poor record keeping by the Confederate government. Historians' estimations of lost Southern property range from a monetary figure of $1,487,241,000 in decline of physical capital to broader estimates of a loss of one-third to two-thirds of total Confederate wealth.

The forms of destruction ranged widely, from fixed structures such as houses and barns, to personal effects of no military value, including women's clothing, silverware, and children's toys. Plantation owners, yeomen, and the poor alike were susceptible to property loss, as the misery of destruction crossed class lines. Furthermore, slave cabins were not excluded from looting, and slaves themselves were taken as impressed Confederate property after the Emancipation Proclamation in 1863. Items of monetary value were often shipped northward by Union soldiers, as gifts to Northern friends and relatives. Other personal objects, such as pianos and trunks, were chopped with axes or burned. For women, the destruction of personal property exacerbated their material deprivation while simultaneously shocking, frightening, and humiliating them. It shattered women's self-perception of being immune from military hostility. The long-term effects of this form of warfare would surface in the ideologies of women in the postwar decades.

The first military body to claim responsibility for Confederate citizens' lost property might have been the Confederates themselves. As inflation rose and perishable supplies rotted in Southern warehouses because of poor transportation systems, the 1863 defeats at Gettysburg and Vicksburg further strained Confederate resources. Consequently, Confederate troops sought to supplement their dwindling supplies with resources found in private homes as they marched across the South. In addition to livestock, Rebel soldiers took stores of dry goods, which placed additional pressure on women to provide for themselves and their families. Confederate soldiers left receipts for governmental reimbursement, and by May 1865 outstanding receipts held by the Confederate Treasury department for impressed goods stood at $500 million. Rebel soldiers also destroyed property, ruining farms and fields and removing fences as they traveled across private land. While some Southern women's resolve stayed firm, others who witnessed such impressments expressed resentment and despair over their newfound deprivation.

The amount of property destroyed by Union forces far outweighed that of Confederate impressments. In 1864, Federal strategy evolved from one of military victory alone to that of civilian and military subjugation. General William T. Sherman's March to the Sea in 1864 and through the Carolinas in 1865 encapsulated the total war ideology. The official position of the Union command on the destruction of personal property was paradoxical. Union generals officially condemned the destruction of the private property of peaceful Southern citizens and condoned only the confiscation of necessary supplies for the army, but they turned a blind eye to excessive looting and believed that, to defeat the Confederacy, the Union military had to secure the moral defeat of its citizenry. As such, the level of destruction by Union forces varied, due in part to the commander and in part to the region and its history. Parts of North Carolina that showed a high level of Union support were spared the burning that Sherman inflicted on Atlanta and Columbia. Conversely, Sherman intended to thoroughly ruin Confederate property in the Carolinas and Georgia. In Atlanta, Union troops burned thousands of bales of cotton. They confiscated pitchforks as well as flour, silverware, and watches. In South Carolina, soldiers destroyed floorboards of carriages with axes, trampled corn and grain under horses' hooves, emptied inkwells, and confiscated or killed livestock.

Southern women tried to protect what valuables they could from advancing enemy forces. Women were subjected to searches and seizures, regardless of race or class. In diaries and letters, women reported how they ripped mattresses open to fill them with clothing and blankets and save these valuable items from occupying forces. Others hid their valuables on their land in wells or cellars, or they buried them in gardens and fields. Union forces soon learned of the more common means of hiding valuables, and they used the points of bayonets to search fields for treasures. Soldiers also interrogated slaves and neighbors to find women's hiding places. Some women hid valuables on their bodies, hoping that they would not be molested by soldiers searching for treasures tucked in petticoats.

Some women were stripped of all their possessions, became homeless, and, along with their families, were reduced to beggars. With the majority of able-bodied Southern men away at battle, women were ill prepared to defend themselves or their property, and the burden of loss fell most heavily on them. Beyond the material loss of goods, the destruction of personal property demolished women's self-perception of being exempt from the abuse of enemy forces. The destruction of sentimental items and objects of family identity heightened women's sense of being wronged by Federal forces and exacerbated their resentment for the North.

*Sara Marie Eye*

**See also** Confederate Homefront; Destruction of Homes; Impressment; Military Invasion and Occupation; Morale; Sheridan's Shenandoah Valley Campaign (1864); Sherman's Campaign (1864–1865); Southern Women.

**References and Further Reading**

Ash, Stephen V. 1995. *When the Yankees Came: Conflict and Chaos in the Occupied South, 1861–1865.* Chapel Hill: University of North Carolina Press.

Goldin, Claudia D., and Frank D. Lewis. 1975. "The Economic Cost of the American Civil War: Estimates and Implications." *Journal of Economic History* 35 (2): 299–326.

McPherson, James M. 1988. *Battle Cry of Freedom.* New York: Ballantine Books.

Rable, George C. 1989. *Civil Wars: Women and the Crisis of Southern Nationalism.* Urbana: University of Illinois Press.

Sutherland, Daniel. 1995. *Seasons of War: The Ordeal of a Confederate Community, 1861–1865.* New York: Free Press.

Trowbridge, John Townsend. 1956. *The Desolate South, 1865–1866; A Picture of the Battlefields and of the Devastated Confederacy,* edited by Gordon Carroll. New York: Duell, Sloan and Pearce.

## Diaries and Journals

If soldiers' diaries reveal the ugly face of war, women's diaries and journals show war's battered soul. Relating much more than daily accomplishments such as sewing and feeding wounded soldiers, they reveal candid opinions about the causes of the war, slavery, gender roles, class divisions, relationships with slaves, difficulties of surviving in contested territory, and encounters with military personnel and civilians on both sides of the conflict.

Diaries and journals often replaced open discourse in an era when publicly verbalizing political or slavery views could easily lead to arrest, and conversing about activities of one's friends and family might arouse suspicion. Fervent patriotism and religious beliefs pervade most Civil War–era diaries, with many women wishing they had been born male so that they could fight in the war. Both Yankee and Rebel women relied on God not only for personal strength and protection, but also for military victory. Secessionist women often interpreted Southern battlefield defeat as God's punishment for arrogance, whereas Northern women perceived it as punishment for slaveholding. Women on both sides of the issue typically viewed African Americans as inferior to whites, yet they record teaching certain slaves to read and write. Southerners expressed anger and sorrow when slaves left to go north, despite these same women's previous recording of physical abuse that they or their acquaintances inflicted on slaves.

Women diarists during the Civil War were overwhelmingly white, young, unmarried, Southern, and wealthy. Generally older, black, and lower-class women lacked the leisure time and literacy required to chronicle their activities. Even before the Civil War, educated young women recorded daily events in diaries and, less frequently, more philosophical thoughts in journals. Teachers encouraged girls to practice penmanship and to reflect on their required readings through journal writing. In school as in wartime, the contemplative process served the dual purpose of providing a release for youthful energy and an outlet for fluctuating emotions in a society that placed high value on proper behavior and that considered physical exercise unbecoming for young ladies.

Leaf from Mary Boykin Chesnut's Civil War diary. (Chesnut, Mary, *A Diary from Dixie,* 1905)

After the war began, women understood that they were living in a momentous period and realized that future generations might value their annals. They often noted their self-conscious recognition of the importance of events occurring around them in their journals. One of the most famous Civil War diarists, Mary Boykin Chesnut, grasped the significance of the insights she could relate from her position as a Confederate congressman's wife.

With war came opportunities and danger. Confederate smuggler and spy Belle Edmondson's diary outlines her clandestine methods as she risked arrest and courted a damaged reputation, conduct generally alien to women's antebellum lives. The few women who joined the military typically did not keep diaries and were more likely than were diarists to be uneducated and unconcerned about societal mores. Because Southern women lived in the territory that troops traversed and in which battles raged, their lives were more perilous than Northern women's lives. Stark homefront pictures emerge from diaries: fear for safety, worry, hunger, cold, absence of social order, living in reduced circumstances, living with relatives or behind Confederate lines, providing supplies for soldiers, being subjected to bodily violence and property seizure, managing increasingly insolent slaves or coping without them, and relating the harm friends and neighbors suffered from soldiers or marauders impersonating soldiers. Massachusetts-born teacher, Caroline Seabury, annotated her journey from Mississippi to safety within Union lines in Memphis, giving a rare and vivid account of war's human and financial toll on poor whites and blacks she met along the way.

Others record a semblance of prewar routine in the midst of the Civil War: attending church regularly, reading popular literature, and living comfortably in the family home. From Alice Ready's diary, readers learn that civilians maintained social ties with military officers, exchanging visits when troops were camped near town. In addition, women often severed communication with family members and friends who joined the opposing side, or they merely confided their suspicions and criticism to their diaries.

Diarists rarely wrote with the thought of publishing, and most accounts remained private for decades after the war ended. More immediately afterward, women published memoirs, usually more sensational than diaries or journals. Rebel spy Belle Boyd sought the exposure to promote her acting career and lecture tours. Union soldier and spy Emma Edmonds only wanted to illuminate her unconventional wartime activities, giving the proceeds to soldiers' aid societies. Postwar publication of both men's and women's narratives proliferated, primarily as part of the reunification process encouraged by Union and Confederate leaders. Women who became proponents of the United Daughters of the Confederacy's mission to promote the war's "true history" perpetuated the happy, well treated slave portrait, pointing to journals and memoirs as evidence of their glorious past. The accumulation of women's narratives document the evolution of a new woman, a latent feminist, determined to find acceptable public outlets for the strength, autonomy, and self-confidence gained during war. Civil War journals hint of the changes that surfaced in the Progressive Era when women came to dominate teaching and social work, to form and join clubs for intellectual and political development, and to wage their own war for voting rights.

*Nancy L. Adgent*

***See also*** Chesnut, Mary Boykin (1823–1886); Edmondson, Belle (1840–1873); Solomon, Clara (ca. 1845–1907); Northern Women; Southern Women.

**References and Further Reading**

Bacot, Ada W. 1994. *A Confederate Nurse: The Diary of Ada W. Bacot, 1860–1863*, edited by Jean V. Berlin. Columbia: University of South Carolina Press.

Harrison, Kimberly. 2003. "Rhetorical Rehearsals: The Construction of Ethos in Confederate Women's Civil War Diaries." *Rhetoric Review* 22 (3): 243–263.

Kadzis, Peter, ed. 2000. *Blood: Stories of Life and Death from the Civil War.* New York: Thunder's Mouth Press.

Muhlenfeld, Elisabeth. 1981. *Mary Boykin Chesnut: A Biography.* Baton Rouge: Louisiana State University Press.

Cox, Karen L. 2003. *Dixie's Daughters: The United Daughters of the Confederacy and the Preservation of Confederate Culture.* Gainesville: University Press of Florida.

Faust, Drew Gilpin. 1996. *Mothers of Invention: Women of the Slaveholding South in the American Civil War.* Chapel Hill: University of North Carolina Press.

## Dickey, Sarah Ann (1838–1904)

Founder of Mount Hermon Female Seminary, Sarah Ann Dickey transformed a powerful will and deep Christian faith into a lifelong mission to educate freedwomen.

Dickey was born on April 25, 1838, near Dayton, Ohio. She was only six years old when her mother died, leaving Sarah in the care of relatives. Isolated on their farm, she received almost no education and at sixteen was illiterate. Dickey was determined, however, to become a teacher. Over the next ten years, she convinced a neighbor to help her obtain a primary education, earned a teaching degree, and taught in local schools. Obeying the dictates of a profound Christian faith, Dickey sought opportunities to use her teaching skills as a missionary. Eventually, in 1863, the American Missionary Association accepted her as a teacher in its Vicksburg, Mississippi school for freedmen. The assignment was harrowing, but it cemented Dickey's commitment to educating the newly freed slaves.

After the Vicksburg school closed, Dickey entered Mount Holyoke Seminary in Massachusetts as a working student. Graduating in 1869, she returned to teaching freedpeople. First in Raymond and then in Clinton, Mississippi, she taught in freedmen's schools. In Clinton, Dickey confronted harassment, threats, and even gunfire but became ever more determined that she would stay and teach.

Dickey's ultimate goal was to establish her own school for freedwomen. By 1873 she had enough funding to buy land and obtain a charter. Despite race riots in September, her school opened on October 4, 1875. It was called the Mount Hermon Female Seminary. Like Mount Holyoke, Dickey's school stressed domestic work, cleanliness, punctuality, and other community and personal qualities. Mount Hermon offered various levels of instruction, ranging from teacher preparation to a classically based curriculum including Latin. Most students sought teaching positions, for which the excellent reputation of Mount Hermon was an asset.

Although at first controversial, over time Mount Hermon won a measure of respect in Clinton. Dickey undertook a variety of additional missionary activities. When the local schools closed, the seminary taught local children. Dickey sometimes took in orphans and often aided needy students and their families. In 1890, she purchased one hundred and twenty acres of land and offered it on credit to freedmen for farming. Eight years before her death, Dickey attained an official title to correspond to her deep faith, becoming a minister of the United Brethren in Christ. She died in 1904 in Clinton.

Mount Hermon passed to the American Missionary Association but survived only until 1924.

*Fiona Deans Halloran*

**See also** African American Women; Education, Northern; Freedmen's Bureau; Northern Women; Religion; Teachers, Northern; Wartime Employment.

**References and Further Reading**

Griffith, Helen. 1966. *Dauntless in Mississippi: The Life of Sarah A. Dickey.* South Hadley, MA: Dinosaur Press.

## Dickinson, Anna Elizabeth (1842–1932)

Political and abolitionist orator Anna Elizabeth Dickinson gained fame during the Civil War for her fiery speeches. She highlighted injustices facing women, African Americans, and workers. In the postwar era, Dickinson also became a successful author, actress, and political campaigner.

Born in Philadelphia on October 28, 1842, Anna Elizabeth Dickinson was the youngest of five children of Quaker abolitionists John and Mary Edmundson Dickinson. John Dickinson died two years later, leaving his wife behind with two daughters, three sons, and little savings. Dickinson grew up in a modest home surrounded by newspapers, books, and political debate. For a time Mary ran a small school out of the home, and on occasion she took in boarders to make ends meet. Until she was fifteen, Anna enjoyed limited access to formal education, thanks largely to her own talents and modest assistance from benevolent Philadelphia Quakers. But clearly her greatest education came in the Dickinson parlor, where occasional guests included African American leaders Frederick Douglass and Robert Purvis, and various Quaker abolitionists.

Dickinson first entered the public arena in 1856, when she read a newspaper story about a Kentucky schoolteacher who had been tarred and feathered for publishing an antislavery letter. The irate thirteen-year-old fired off a letter to William Lloyd Garrison's abolitionist newspaper, *The Liberator,* protesting this affront to free speech. Four years later Dickinson joined a friend at a local meeting on women's rights. Upon hearing a male speaker declare that his daughters would never have professional careers, Dickinson rose to offer an impassioned rebuttal. Her impromptu eloquence created quite a stir. Over the next several months, the diminutive teenager received invitations to speak at meetings around the Philadelphia region. In October 1860 she spoke at the annual meeting of the Pennsylvania Anti-Slavery Association at Kennett Square, where she shared a platform with Lucretia and James Mott, Oliver Johnson, and Robert Purvis. Within a few weeks Republican Abraham Lincoln would be elected president, dramatically changing the political landscape and Anna Dickinson's professional future.

Dickinson's extraordinary Civil War career unfolded in three overlapping stages. At the outset she was a young, charismatic, darling of the abolitionist movement. In early 1862, anxious to build a career as an orator, Dickinson wrote to Garrison for advice. The antislavery patriarch took her under his wing, arranging a New England tour culminating in a celebrated appearance in Boston before Theodore Parker's old congregation. Soon she was a rising star, traveling from town to town, attracting enthusiastic audiences, earning handsome fees, and rubbing shoulders with the likes of Garrison, Wendell Phillips, and Lucretia Mott.

Dickinson's oratory combined personal charisma, radical sensibilities, patriotic passion, and a biting wit. Before long, savvy Republican operatives recognized Dickinson's great potential as a partisan orator, ushering in a new stage in her career. She spent much of 1863 on the campaign trail, earning modest fees stumping for state Republican candidates—and lambasting Copperhead Democrats—in New Hampshire, Pennsylvania, New York, and Connecticut. As her reputation spread, more than one party pundit credited Dickinson with helping to ensure crucial Republican successes.

By the war's final year, Dickinson was a true celebrity. Photographers vied to take her picture, fans clamored for autographs, young girls wrote seeking counsel, and politicians recognized that she was a woman to be reckoned with. The high point came in December 1863 when Dickinson received an invitation—signed by the vice president, twenty-

Anna Elizabeth Dickinson, orator known for her fiery speeches highlighting the injustices against women, African Americans, and workers (1842–1932). (Library of Congress)

three senators, and seventy-eight congressmen—to visit the nation's capital. On January 16, a huge crowd of officeholders, journalists, and celebrities, including Abraham and Mary Todd Lincoln, crowded the halls of the House of Representatives to hear the twenty-one-year-old orator. The feisty Dickinson spoke on "The Perils of the Hour," calling for continued support for the war while leveling some harsh criticism at the bemused president for his seemingly conciliatory approach to Reconstruction. In the presidential campaign to come, Dickinson would grudgingly endorse Lincoln while devoting most of her energies to attacking Democrats. Behind the scenes, a long list of prominent men and women—including Susan B. Anthony, Whitelaw Reid, Samuel Pomeroy, and Theodore Tilton—tried to influence her thinking and behavior, offering strong testimony to her political influence.

By the close of the Civil War, Anna Dickinson had risen to a unique position among America's public women. Although she was not the nation's first female public speaker, most of the handful who had come before had been reformers who spoke to kindred spirits. Dickinson, in contrast, had crossed over to the traditional male domain of partisan political campaigning. And, though her success produced a few female imitators, none approached her fame, success, or political influence.

As is often the case for people who rise to fame in their youth, the subsequent acts in Dickinson's life were always measured by the standard of her wartime fame, and in many senses her enduring fame reflected the significance of the Civil War in American memory. But although she would forever remain known as America's Joan of Arc for her youthful patriotism, Dickinson's public career was far from over. For a decade after Appomattox she was one of the nation's most active and highly compensated lyceum speakers. Dickinson generally selected political themes, often addressing the status of women, blacks, and workers. Meanwhile, her old allies in the women's movement and the abolitionist movement struggled to find an organizational identity and a strategic path in the postwar world. Dickinson supported woman suffrage, but she declined to take on a substantial institutional role. And she alienated Anthony and Elizabeth Cady Stanton by backing the Fifteenth Amendment, casting her lot with black male suffrage even at the expense of woman suffrage.

In 1868 Dickinson published a controversial novel, *What Answer?*, that featured an interracial marriage between a white soldier and a biracial woman. She also wrote two other books: one an amusing collection of anecdotes about life on the road, the other a high-minded treatise on the need for education reform. In 1872 she returned to the stump to campaign for Liberal Republican Horace Greeley. A few years later, when the lyceum circuit collapsed, Dickinson turned to the stage as both an actress and playwright. Several of her plays earned money and some modest critical acclaim, and her acting attracted substantial attention, particularly when she dressed as a man to play *Hamlet*, but her career on the stage never matched her earlier successes on the platform. In 1888 Dickinson once again returned to the campaign trail, stumping for successful Republican Benjamin Harrison.

Dickinson's highly celebrated public life was lived against a backdrop of personal illness, recurring family tensions, a series of failed relationships with various men and women, and a long list of private conflicts. At one point or another she battled vigorously with Reid, Anthony, Benjamin Butler, Frances Willard, actress Fanny Davenport, and the Republican National Committee. In 1891, as Dickinson was preparing to go to court to seek back payments from the GOP, her sister Susan arranged for her to be committed to a state hospital for the insane. After several weeks of incarceration, Dickinson managed to win her freedom, and she soon embarked on a complex series of lawsuits against those responsible for her commitment, the New York newspapers that had called her insane, and her old Republican adversaries. Her multiple suits won her modest vindication but limited financial gains. Dickinson eventually moved to Goshen, New York, where she lived with her close friend Sallie Ackley and Ackley's husband George. She died there in 1932, shortly before her ninetieth birthday.

*J. Matthew Gallman*

*See also* Abolitionism and Northern Reformers; Anthony, Susan B. (1820–1906); Antislavery Societies; Butler, Benjamin F. (1818–1893); Douglass, Frederick (ca. 1818–1895); Fifteenth Amendment; Lincoln, Abraham (1809–1865); Mott, Lucretia Coffin (1793–1880); Northern Women; Quaker Women; Stanton, Elizabeth Cady (1815–1902); Union Homefront Politics.

**References and Further Reading**

Dickinson, Anna Elizabeth. [1868] 2003. *What Answer?* New York: Humanity Books.

Gallman, J. Matthew. 2006. *America's Joan of Arc: The Life of Anna Elizabeth Dickinson.* New York: Oxford University Press.

## Dickinson, Emily (1830–1886)

Reclusive poet Emily Dickinson wrote some of her most powerful works in response to the American Civil War.

Emily Dickinson was born in 1830, in Amherst, Massachusetts, to Edward and Emily Dickinson. She was the second of three children, with an older brother Austin and a younger sister Lavinia. The Dickinson family was conservative orthodox Calvinist; her religious upbringing strongly influenced Dickinson's writing. An enigmatic figure, Dickinson wrote the bulk of her poetry unbeknownst to her parents and younger sister with whom she lived. Although she wrote 1,775 poems, only eleven were published during her lifetime. It was only after Emily's death, in 1886, that Lavinia discovered the treasure trove of Emily's works. Due to the efforts of family and friends, Emily's poems were published posthumously, beginning in 1890 and continuing into the twentieth century.

Born and raised in Amherst, Emily never married and lived with her family until her death. Her father was a prominent citizen and provided his daughter with an education suitable for girls of the time. She attended Amherst Academy and later Mount Holyoke Female Seminary. Known for her hermetic nature and desire for seclusion, she rarely left the comfort of her Amherst home. Although she spent her time in isolation, she maintained friendships through correspondence. It was through her poems and letters that Dickinson conveyed her thoughts on the society around her. Among those with whom Emily corresponded was Samuel Bowles, the editor of the *Springfield Republican,* and abolitionist Thomas Wentworth Higginson, who became a colonel in the Massachusetts Fifty-fourth, the Union army's first black regiment.

Emily's father dedicated his life to civil service; he was elected to the general court of Massachusetts, served twice as Massachusetts senator, and was also elected to Congress. Due to his political position, Edward Dickinson was directly involved with decisions leading to the Civil War. Her father and brother also recruited soldiers from Amherst to fight in the Union army. Additionally, the Dickinsons suffered the loss of a close family friend who was killed in battle, Lieutenant Frazer Stearns.

Perhaps it was the involvement of her family and close friends that made Emily so passionate about the Civil War. More than half of her poems were written during the Civil War. Some of them appeared in Union publications in an effort to raise money for the United States Sanitary Commission. Of the few poems published during her lifetime, six appeared in the *Springfield Republican.* Dickinson's Civil War poems express sorrow over the national conflict. Her imagery conveys battles between good and evil and questions that God would allow such evil and suffering. The interpretation of her works reveals the political, economic, social, and cultural representations of the period.

*Dawn M. Sherman*

**See also** Northern Women; Poets, Northern; Politics; Union Homefront; Wartime Literature.

**References and Further Reading**

Lease, Benjamin. 1990. *Emily Dickinson's Readings of Men and Books: Sacred Soundings.* New York: St. Martin's Press.

Pollak, Vivian R., ed. 2004. *A Historical Guide to Emily Dickinson.* New York: Oxford University Press.

Wolff, Cynthia Griffin. 1987. *Emily Dickinson.* New York: Alfred A. Knopf.

## Disease

During the Civil War, outbreaks of epidemic diseases among civilians created fear, a sense of helplessness, and often death. During the antebellum era, maladies such as smallpox, yellow fever, and malaria ran rampant in several cities. Yet between 1861 and 1865, the majority of epidemic outbreaks affecting civilians occurred in the South.

Yellow fever was perhaps the most feared disease among civilians during the Civil War. Spread by mosquitoes, yellow fever was a form of viral hepatitis. Yellow fever caused severe jaundice, or yellowing of the skin, and bleeding from the mouth, nose, and eyes. The most feared complication of this disease was for the kidneys to shut down, which usually led to death. During the time of the Civil War, no effective treatment for yellow fever existed.

Aside from yellow fever's ghastly symptoms, the disease also created panic among civilian populations. When news of a yellow fever epidemic reached a city's residents, many people fled, leaving behind few healthy civilians to care for the sick or bury the dead. Those who fled, however, faced an uncertain future. Residents of nearby towns frequently denied admission to fleeing refugees because they were afraid of contracting yellow fever themselves.

The residents of New Orleans, occupied by Union troops by the summer of 1862, attempted to use the specter of a yellow fever epidemic to scare Federal forces out of the city. Because they had survived numerous outbreaks of the disease during the antebellum years, many New Orleanians believed that they had acquired immunity; locals argued that their occupiers were more susceptible to yellow fever than they were. The native population did their best to keep Yankee soldiers in constant fear of the dreaded disease. While children taunted the troops with chants describing the devastating effect that yellow fever would have on them, adults spoke of previous epidemics and hinted that Union General Benjamin F. Butler had secured a contract for ten thousand coffins in which to bury the disease's Federal victims. Yet despite the residents' dire predictions, no cases of yellow fever appeared in New Orleans during the war.

Yellow fever did occasionally break out in some Southern port cities occupied by Union forces, including Galveston, Pensacola, and Key West. The most serious outbreaks occurred in Wilmington, North Carolina, in the fall of 1862 and in New Bern, North Carolina, in the fall of 1864. Although a few dozen civilians eventually succumbed to the disease, the mortality rate among Federal occupiers was much higher. In New Bern, for example, 571 Union soldiers contracted yellow fever and 228 (or 48.7 percent) of them died.

Epidemic diseases also claimed African American victims. In contraband camps, freedwomen confronted the devastating effects of various diseases. Unsanitary encampments, poor food rations, and crowded living conditions caused periodic outbreaks of diseases such as dysentery, malaria, and yellow fever. Moreover, sexual contact between black women and Union soldiers led to the spread of venereal diseases. The mortality rate in contraband camps, which consisted mostly of women and children because the Union army impressed all able-bodied freedmen, was approximately 25 percent during the Civil War.

*Nancy Schurr*

***See also*** Civilian Life; Confederate Homefront; Contrabands; Hospitals; Military Invasion and Occupation; Northern Women; Nurses; Rape; Refugees; Southern Women; Union Homefront; Urban Women, Southern.

**References and Further Reading**

Bollet, Alfred J. 2002. *Civil War Medicine: Challenges and Triumphs.* Tucson, AZ: Galen Press.

Capers, Gerald M. Jr. 1964. "Confederates and Yankees in Occupied New Orleans, 1862–1865." *Journal of Southern History* 30: 405–426.

Farnham, Thomas J., and Francis P. King. 1996. "'The March of the Destroyer': The New Bern Yellow Fever Epidemic of 1864." *North Carolina Historical Review* 73: 435–483.

Humphreys, Margaret. 1992. *Yellow Fever and the South.* Piscataway, NJ: Rutgers University Press.

## Divers, Bridget (ca. 1840–n.d.)

An Irish immigrant from a working-class background, Bridget Divers—also known as Bridget Deavers, Devens, or Devins—was likely in her early twenties when she joined the First Michigan Cavalry with her husband and perhaps her child. Most details of Divers's life remain a mystery, though it is clear that she served as a daughter of the regiment, part of a female support staff of the volunteer regiments. Daughters of the regiment served a variety of roles including ornamental mascot during parades and military reviews, cook, laundress, sutler, and nurse. Some of these women also undertook military roles on the battlefield.

Known to her comrades as Irish Biddy or Michigan Bridget, Divers earned a reputation for her willingness to remain with her regiment no matter what the dangers. Among the most famous moments of her military career came at the June 1862 Battle of Fair Oaks, Virginia, when Confederate forces surprised Union troops with a sudden attack. While many responded immediately, others panicked and resisted officers' attempts to rally them to fight. According to soldiers' accounts of the battle, the order to advance was all but ignored until Bridget Divers waved her cap in the air, urging them to fight to revenge her husband's death. The men rallied and drove the Confederates back.

Divers's wartime reputation also resulted from the nurturing stance she took toward the "boys" of her regiment. Several accounts detail her unwavering devotion late in the war. After a raid in which the regiment's colonel was wounded and its captain killed, Divers cared for the wounded and escorted the colonel by train to a hospital. Upon her arrival at the hospital, she discovered that the body of the captain had been left on the field. Unwilling to leave him behind, Divers reportedly rode her horse 15 miles into Confederate lines, recovered the captain's body, and brought him to the hospital. She then obtained a coffin and saw that his body was sent back home.

Divers performed another important service for the men of her regiment: coordination of their movements. She kept an unofficial directory detailing the whereabouts of the men and tracking their needs for supplies and armaments. Regimental commanders often directed inquiries about men in the regiment to Divers. Her heroism on the field, skills as a coordinator, and concern for the men of the First Michigan gained her the respect not only of the regiment but also of Sanitary Commission officials and other female army nurses.

Little is known about Divers's antebellum or postwar life. However, sources agree that. after the war. Divers, who had become accustomed to military life, joined a regiment and traveled west for duty on the frontier.

*Lisa M. Smith*

***See also*** Female Combatants; Immigrant Women; Northern Women; Nurses; United States Sanitary Commission; Vivandieres.

**References and Further Reading**

Leonard, Elizabeth. 1999. *All the Daring of the Soldier: Women of the Civil War Armies*. New York: W. W. Norton & Company.

Moore, Frank. 1866. *Women of the War: Their Heroism and Self-Sacrifice*. Chicago: R. C. Treat.

## Dix, Dorothea Lynde (1802–1887)

The Superintendent of the United States Army Nurses, Dorothea Lynde Dix played many promi-

nent roles in her lifetime. Her colorful career ranged from jobs as a teacher to that of a psychiatric advocate in an era when it was not popular to be proactive for the needs of the mentally ill.

Born on April 4, 1802, Dorothea was the eldest of three children born to Joseph and Mary Dix. She grew up under the stern hand of her father, a book dealer, a manufacturer, and a distributor of religious tracts, who sometimes called himself a minister though he was not ordained. The family moved often, and Dolly, as she was called, was forced to put together the booklets, stitch binding and gluing them until late at night. Her father was the dominant force in the family; her mother was weak and ineffective. Dorothea deeply resented her father's abusiveness and alcoholism, eventually running away from home at twelve to live with her paternal grandmother in Boston, Massachusetts. Her grandmother later sent Dolly to her aunt's home in Worcester for a more ladylike upbringing.

In Worcester, Dix decided to teach, opening a private school that drew many eager students. When she moved back to Boston in 1821, she opened another school, this one exclusively for

Dorothea Dix was world-renowned for her work on behalf of the mentally ill and for her services as a nurse during the Civil War. (Library of Congress)

young girls. Dix was one of the first educators in the nation to provide a free education for poor children, which she did at night when her paying students went home. Dix also found the time to write four books: *Conversations on Common Things* (1824), *Meditations for Private Hours* (1828), *The Garland of Flora* (1829), *and American Moral Tales for Young Persons* (1832). She was well read and well traveled and became an expert on many subjects. Rejecting her father's Methodist fire and brimstone approach to religion, she joined the Unitarian Church and became an active advocate for the homeless and hungry.

In 1836, Dix contracted tuberculosis and had to take a break from teaching. She moved to Liverpool, England, for a year and then returned to the United States when her grandmother passed away. She continued to travel, however, and over the next four years regained the strength to return to teaching. Her first job after returning was as a teacher at East Cambridge Jail in 1841.

Appalled by the conditions in which prisoners were housed, she began a lifelong crusade against the treatment she had witnessed. She was outraged over the housing of felons and the mentally ill together, and in 1843 wrote a memorial presented to the Massachusetts Legislature by Dr. Samuel Gridley Howe, Director of the Perkins School for the Blind. Although first rejected, her claims were soon proven to be true, and the legislature allocated funds for a large expansion of the State Mental Hospital at Worcester. She went on to write other memorials as well and established thirteen hospitals in eleven states, including St. Elizabeth's Hospital in Washington, D.C.

Dix spent another two years in Europe in an effort to reform hospitals there. She returned to America in 1856, discouraged by her lack of success overseas and glad to be back in the United States.

As the Civil War began in 1861, she turned her attentions to the deplorable conditions at field hospitals set up to provide services to the soldiers. She was distressed to see the lack of concern for cleanliness and the behavior of the doctors and nurses who treated the operating room more like a bordello than a surgical theater. Drinking and flirting

seemed to be more prevalent than saving lives. Dix could not stand by; at age fifty-nine, she volunteered her services to the Union and quickly thereafter was named the Superintendent of the United States Army Nurses. Among the first items that Dix had to address were the directives to organize first aid stations, purchase supplies, set up training facilities, and recruit nurses. Performing her duties unpaid, she put together a volunteer female nursing corps that was the first in the nation and eventually included over three thousand nurses in its ranks. Dix was criticized by the army but enthusiastically received by the civilian authorities, and she soon earned a reputation for enforcing tough, unyielding standards that some nurses and doctors resented but that were effective and long lasting.

Until Dix took over, nurses had few requirements to meet and were often untrained and unskilled. Besides requiring the nurses to have extensive training, Dix also enforced a standard of dress and appearance that many protested. She wanted the nurses to be "plain-looking" because she believed it was more appropriate and professional than to have attractive young women tending to the needs of the soldiers. She also insisted that nurses wear modest clothing in black or brown and that they not wear any jewelry or hoops under their skirts. Some of the nurses started calling her Dragon Dix for her hard-nosed attitude, but her methods proved effective. The reputation of the nurses for their attentiveness and skill rose even as dissent stirred among the rest of the medical staff.

In addition, Dix made it her mission to prosecute the many doctors who operated on patients while drunk. They resented her bringing this to the public's attention. Dix clashed often with the prevailing bureaucracies, but nonetheless managed to accomplish her goals of better sanitation, better treatment for soldiers, and more attention to good surgical outcomes.

After the Civil War, Dix resumed her tireless work advocating for the poor, displaced, and mentally ill. She became overwhelmed and discouraged by the lack of progress in hospitals, and in her later years she did not like to talk about her work, her life, or her career. She did not put her name on most of her publications and refused efforts to have hospitals named after her.

Dorothea Dix was autonomous to the end, dying as she had lived—alone—on July 17, 1887. Dix was buried in Mt. Auburn Cemetery in Cambridge, Massachusetts.

*Jay Warner*

***See also*** Abolitionism and Northern Reformers; Domesticity; Education, Northern; Hospitals; Northern Women; Nurses; Religion; Separate Spheres; Teachers, Northern; Unitarian Women; Wartime Employment.

**References and Further Reading**

Brown, Thomas J. 1997. *Dorothea Dix: New England Reformer.* Cambridge, MA: Belknap/Harvard University Press.

Dix, Dorothea L. 1999. *Asylum, Prison, and Poorhouse: The Writings and Reform Work of Dorothea Dix in Illinois,* edited by David L. Lightener. Carbondale: Southern Illinois University Press.

Dix, Dorothea L. 1975. *On Behalf of the Insane Poor: Selected Reports 1842–1862.* North Stratford, NH: Ayer Company.

Marshall, H.E. 1937. *Dorothea Dix, Forgotten Samaritan.* Chapel Hill: University of North Carolina Press.

Wilson, Dorothy C. 1975. *Stranger and Traveler.* Boston: Little, Brown and Company.

## Dodge, Mary Abigail [Gail Hamilton] (1833–1896)

Mary Abigail Dodge was one of the earliest American women to find success as a writer and critic. Under the pen name Gail Hamilton, Dodge became a popular and controversial writer of her time. Her works include countless newspaper articles, essays, more than twenty-five books, a poetry collection, children's books, and one novel. She wrote about issues including religion, education, country life, authorship, contemporary politics, and women's issues.

Mary Abigail Dodge was born in Hamilton, Massachusetts, on March 31, 1833, the daughter of Hannah Stanwood and James Brown Dodge. Her father was a farmer, and her mother was a former schoolteacher. Though a shy child, Dodge showed an early interest in education and learning. Dodge's parents sent her to a boarding school in Cambridge, Massachusetts, when she was twelve. By the time she was thirteen, she was accepted into Ipswich Female Seminary, an academically challenging school that stressed self-reliance. Dodge graduated in 1850.

Upon graduating, Dodge taught at Ipswich before taking positions at Hartford Female Seminary and, from 1855 to 1858, at Hartford High School. Although Dodge was a gifted teacher, she still hoped to make a career as a writer. In 1856, Dodge sent samples of her poetry to the *National Era,* an antislavery publication, and the *Independent,* a Protestant paper.

Gamaliel Bailey, the editor of *National Era,* was impressed with Dodge's writing style and invited her to move to Washington to work as governess for his children. She took the position, viewing it as an opportunity to spend more time writing. In Washington, Dodge became more familiar with political circles and began writing commentaries, book reviews, and opinion pieces for publications such as the *Congregationalist, National Era,* and the *Independent.*

As she began publishing more work, Dodge developed two pen names: Cunctare and Gail Hamilton. Dodge maintained that her use of a pen name was to ensure that her personal life was private and separate from her career. Eventually she dropped Cunctare and was known for the rest of her career as Gail Hamilton.

In 1860, Dodge returned to her childhood home to care for her mother. In the country, she continued to write and steadily gained notoriety. By the early 1870s Dodge had published numerous works, including a collection of essays about rural New England life, *Country Living and Country Thinking;* two books about women's suffrage and related issues, *Woman's Wrongs: A Counter Irritant* and *Woman's Worth and Worthlessness;* and a controversial book about the publishing industry, *Battle of the Books.*

Dodge was known for the divisive opinions that she expressed in her works. Most notably, her opinion that women should focus on becoming the spiritual leaders of society did not parallel the mainstream women's suffrage movement. Furthermore, Dodge's critiques of the publishing industry initiated debate among writers.

In 1895, Dodge was working on a biography of former Speaker of the House James Blain when she suffered a stroke. Although she recovered enough to return to her home in Hamilton, Dodge died a year later on August 17, 1896.

*Jessie Wilkerson*

**See also** Education, Northern; Fiction Writers, Northern; Northern Women; Politics; Religion; Teachers, Northern; Union Homefront; Wartime Literature.

**References and Further Reading**
Coultrap-McQuin, Susan, ed. 1992. *Gail Hamilton: Selected Writings.* Piscataway, NJ: Rutgers University Press.
Sizer, Lyde Cullen. 2000. *The Political Work of Northern Women Writers and the Civil War, 1850–1872.* Chapel Hill: University of North Carolina Press.

## Domesticity

In the antebellum world, domesticity played an important role in the changing American family. Regardless of race, class, or religion, virtually all women were touched in some way by the cult of domesticity and the middle-class ideal of "true womanhood." But no women would feel the effects of domesticity more than women in the growing urban North.

Significant economic changes took place during the first half of the nineteenth century. These developments changed the American family and made a newly emerging middle class the transmitter of society's values. The new middle class no longer had to personally manufacture what it needed for the family to survive. Husbands began to work away from the home in factories or offices, and their wives stayed at home, engaged in domestic pursuits. As men began working outside the home, they helped create a view that men should support their families while women stayed behind in a world where they were protected from the cold realities of politics and capitalism. Work became increasingly associated with men, and the home became identified as female.

The cult of domesticity grew as the urban Northern family lost its function as an economic unit and as the emergence of the market economy devalued women's work at home. The home became self-contained; families became smaller and children became what the family produced.

Middle-class women gained power through their association with the home. Most of the prescriptive literature of the time extolled the virtues of this "cult of domesticity" through stories, pictures, and editorials. Advice books, periodicals, religious journals, fiction, and popular culture all provided the new view of women's duty and explaining women's special virtues as the keepers of the family. Women were instructed to actively pursue the virtues of piety, purity, submissiveness, and domesticity and to exercise their power in the home. They were protected from the outside world, a rough place, full of temptations, violence, trouble, and wickedness. The prescriptive literature gave women the tools to make the home quiet and peaceful. Women were instructed to identify with their roles not only as daughters and sisters, but especially as wives and mothers. Consequently, domesticity became the most prized of women's virtues.

According to the prescriptive literature, a wife should comfort her husband by creating a cheerful home. This haven would bring him closer to God and less likely to drink, gamble, or look for his sustenance in other places. Catharine Beecher, in her 1841 *Treatise on Domestic Economy,* argued that women's subordinate place in American society was the ultimate fulfillment of democratic and Christian principles. A woman knew her place as the keeper of Christian values and cherished that place, protected by her husband or father.

Middle-class women were also responsible for busying themselves with morally uplifting domestic tasks. Books extolled housework as especially rewarding because it required good judgment and energy. Making beds not only served as good exercise, but its repetitiveness gave a woman patience and perseverance. Needlework was also considered morally uplifting, and women practiced to be the most skilled at lacework, knitting, and painting on fabrics. The advice manuals held that reading novels could interfere with a woman's piety, but morally uplifting novels were acceptable, as were magazines such as *Godey's Lady's Book.*

One of middle-class women's most important functions as a comforter of her family was her role as nurse. Maintaining the sickroom called for women to exercise patience, mercy, and gentleness, as well as to apply their housewifely arts. Cookbooks of the time, in addition to recipes, offered remedies for all sorts of ailments from cough to gout to women's complaints.

To fulfill her role in the home, a woman needed an adequate education that included the art of homemaking. The new public schools and higher education for young women offered housewifery courses alongside the more traditional reading, writing, and mathematics, with the idea that better educated women would make better mothers.

The cult of true womanhood stressed the fulfillment that women gained through motherhood. Religious sermons, reinforced by prescriptive literature, emphasized that there was no higher calling in the eyes of God than to be a mother. The reduced middle-class family size allowed mothers more time to devote to each child. Rearing good and faithful children, especially sons, was seen as the highest responsibility of a woman to God and to the nation.

As these ideas of domesticity for women became institutionalized, they had serious consequences for those who could not meet their rigid prescriptions. By defining the role at home as the measure of respectability, the domestic code indirectly sharpened class differences, excluding most women who had to work in the paid labor force. Southern women living on plantations may have come close to the domestic ideal, but in reality domesticity was an ideal that few women could engage in full-time during their adult lives. Women of the working classes were too busy with scraping together a living to worry too much about proper domesticity, but they were among the biggest consumers of ladies' periodicals and probably thought about middle-class life with some sort of longing. Black women, whether enslaved or free, occupied the lowest rungs of the socioeconomic scale, working outside the ideal of domesticity most of or all of their lives. Women on America's frontiers were still working at the subsistence level and were little touched by the cult of domesticity except for the occasional popular account that came into their possession.

In the cult of domesticity, a woman's place was in the home. She may have been a cultural hostage, but in urban centers of the North, she was dusting off her own pedestal.

*Jill M. Nussel*

***See also*** Beecher, Catharine (1800–1878); Northern Women; Separate Spheres; Southern Women.

**References and Further Reading**

Matthews, Glenna. 1997. *"Just a Housewife": The Rise and Fall of Domesticity in America.* New York: Oxford University Press.

Romero, Laura. 1997. *Home Fronts: Domesticity and Its Critics in the Antebellum United States.* Durham, NC: Duke University Press.

Ryan, Mary P. 1982. *The Empire of the Mother: American Writing about Domesticity, 1830–1860.* New York: Institute for Research in History and Haworth Press.

Welter, Barbara. 1966. "The Cult of True Womanhood: 1820–1860." *American Quarterly* 18 (Summer): 151–174.

Woloch, Nancy. 2000. *Women and the American Experience.* 3rd ed. New York: McGraw-Hill.

## Douglass, Frederick (ca. 1818–1895)

Runaway slave Frederick Douglass became an instrumental part of the abolitionist movement. He became an agent and lecturer for the American Anti-Slavery Society in 1841 and later published his autobiography to aid in the fight against slavery.

The son of Harriet, a black slave, and an unknown white father, he was born Frederick Augustus Washington Bailey (or Baily) at Holme Hill Farm in Talbot County, Maryland. Separated from his mother at an early age, he lived with his grandmother Betsey on a plantation until the age of eight, when he was sent to work for the Hugh Auld family in Baltimore. Defying state law, Auld's wife, Sophia, acquiesced to Douglass's request and taught him to read. From 1836 to 1838, Douglass worked in the Baltimore shipyards as a caulker, where he met Anna Murray, a free woman of color, who worked as a domestic. He and Murray married after he escaped to New York City in 1838. After hearing him speak

Frederick Douglass, former slave and leader in the abolitionist movement (1818–1895). (Library of Congress)

at a meeting of the Bristol Anti-Slavery Society in 1841, William Lloyd Garrison arranged for Douglass to become an agent and lecturer for the American Anti-Slavery Society.

Unlike other women, such as Sarah Remond who worked with her brother Charles, Susan Paul of the Massachusetts Female Antislavery Society, and Sarah Mapps Douglass of the Philadelphia Female Antislavery Society, Anna Douglass did not participate in the lecture circuit. Instead, she supported her husband's travels and their five children by working in a shoe factory.

In addition to the abolitionist lecture tour, Frederick Douglass was also a familiar figure at Conventions of Free People of Color. In 1845, the Anti-Slavery Society assisted in the publication of the first of Douglass's three autobiographies: *The Narrative of the Life of Frederick Douglass: An American Slave.* The book's popularity forced Douglass to spend the next two years in England to avoid recapture. In the interim, American abolitionists raised money for his eventual emancipation.

Although abolitionists generally agreed on the principal goal of ending the practice of slavery, the movement exhibited deep philosophical divisions. Primary among them was the issue of gender equality. While both Garrison and Douglass believed that women's voices should be heard, the exclusion of women from decision making by the Anti-Slavery Society leadership precipitated the growth of same-sex antislavery societies. Douglass, however, became well-known for his outspoken stance on women's rights. Drawn in part by his friendship with abolitionist Amy Post, Frederick and Anna Douglass moved their family to Rochester, New York, in 1847. Already known as a haven for abolitionism, the women of Rochester were active in antislavery societies. Douglass was in close proximity to the leaders in the fight for women's rights, including Susan B. Anthony, Lucretia Mott, and Elizabeth Cady Stanton.

Although he and Garrison were in agreement on the role of women in the abolitionist movement, they parted ways in December 1847 when Douglass decided to publish his own antislavery newspaper, *The North Star,* along with Martin R. Delany and black Boston historian William C. Nell. After 1851, the newspaper became known as *Frederick Douglass' Paper.*

Douglass's personal relationships with white women, however, raised the ire of both white and black communities. One of his financial supporters was Julia Griffiths, whom he had met in England. Griffiths was one of six founders of the Rochester Ladies' Anti-Slavery and Sewing Society, which held annual festivals or bazaars that raised money for the movement through the sale of items and sponsorship of lectures by activities. The efforts not only kept *The North Star* afloat, but they also supported individual fugitives and a school for freedmen in Kansas. In 1848, Douglass brought Griffiths to Rochester as a live-in tutor for his children and wife. Citizens of Rochester objected vociferously when Griffiths began to serve as his office and business manager and personal companion.

Consistent with the egalitarian impulse of abolitionism, Douglass advocated for the rights of women throughout his life. He participated in the first Women's Rights Convention in Seneca Falls in 1848 and signed the Declaration of Sentiments. Elizabeth Cady Stanton afterward credited Douglass's efforts for the passage of the resolution calling for women's suffrage by the Convention. In the July 1848 issue of *The North Star,* Douglass published an editorial entitled "The Rights of Women." In 1853, Douglass endorsed "The Just And Equal Rights of Women," a call and resolutions for the Women's Rights State Convention held in Rochester, and he was a featured speaker at the meeting.

During the antebellum period, Douglass was a close friend of Susan B. Anthony and her family. Between 1865 and 1870, however, Douglass split from many women's rights activists over the issue of the passage of the Fourteenth and Fifteenth Amendments. Douglass aligned himself with abolitionists who believed that it was more important to gain the rights of African American males than the rights of women. As an advisor to President Abraham Lincoln, Douglass protested the discrimination against black enlisted troops and fought for the adoption of constitutional amendments that guaranteed voting rights and other civil liberties for blacks. In 1866, he clashed with women's rights leaders at the convention of the Equal Rights Association over their insistence that the vote not be extended to black men unless it was also given to all women. For their part, Anthony and Stanton refused to support the Fifteenth Amendment because it excluded women. After the amendment passed in 1870, Douglass immediately called for an amendment giving women the right to vote, writing an editorial supporting women's suffrage entitled "Women and The Ballot." In 1878, he attended the thirtieth anniversary celebration of the first Women's Rights Convention, held by the National Woman Suffrage Association (NWSA) in Rochester. He also attended the 1881 NWSA meeting held in Washington, D.C. In 1888, Anthony introduced Douglass to the audience of the International Council of Women as a women's rights pioneer.

Douglass continued to form personal attachments to white women throughout his life. After the pressure of an interracial relationship with Douglass caused Julia Griffiths to return to England, Douglass met Ottilie Assing, a German journalist, when she traveled to Rochester in 1856 to interview him. An abolitionist herself, Assing entered into a liaison with Douglass that lasted for twenty-six years. In 1884, two years after the death of his wife Anna, Douglass married Helen Pitts, a white woman from New York who was his secretary. Pitts was a graduate of Mount Holyoke Seminary and the daughter of Gideon Pitts Jr., an abolitionist colleague and friend of Douglass. Prior to her marriage, Helen had worked on a radical feminist publication called the *Alpha.* Stanton defended Douglass, who was stung by the general criticism, and Pitts against their detractors.

Relocating to Washington, D.C., during the 1870s, Douglass not only worked with his sons to publish the weekly *New National Era,* but also entered government service. The newspaper chronicled the political progress of the Republican Party and its new black constituency. In 1872, the Equal Rights Party, on a ticket headed by Victoria Woodhull, nominated him for the vice presidency of the United States. Douglass became District of Columbia Recorder of Deeds (1881–1886) and then director of United States diplomatic relations with Haiti (1889–1891). In Washington, Douglass, John Mercer Langston, and others contributed to the growth of a cadre of black intellectuals that included literate women such as Frances Ellen Watkins Harper, Maria Stewart, and Charlotte Forten.

In 1893, articulating a vision of America as a "composite" nation of many peoples and cultures, Douglass assisted Ida B. Wells in her sustained campaign against lynching. Douglass seems to have valued Wells's focus on women's rights and social justice during the 1880s and 1890s. In reaction to the exclusion of blacks from the 1893 Chicago World's Fair, Wells and Douglass collaborated on a pamphlet entitled "Reasons Why the Colored American is Not in the World's Colombian Exposition," which documented the progress of blacks since their arrival in America. He encouraged Wells to hire detectives to investigate a lynching in Paris, Texas, and to subsequently share her findings on a European speaking tour. He also wrote an introduction to *A Red Record,* her 1895 statistical report on lynching since the passage of the Emancipation Proclamation.

The day of Douglass's death, February 20, 1895, he had attended a meeting of the National Council of Women in Washington, D.C. During that meeting, he was recognized for his lifelong commitment to women's rights and given a standing ovation by the audience. At his funeral, Susan B. Anthony delivered a eulogy written by Elizabeth Cady Stanton.

*Jayne R. Beilke*

**See also** Abolitionism and Northern Reformers; Anthony, Susan B. (1820–1906); Antislavery Societies; Fairs and Bazaars; Fifteenth Amendment; Forten (Grimké), Charlotte L. (1837–1914); Fourteenth Amendment; Free Blacks; Freedmen's Bureau; Garrison, William Lloyd (1805–1879); Lincoln, Abraham (1809–1865); Politics; Remond, Sarah Parker (1826–1894); Stanton, Elizabeth Cady (1815–1902).

**References and Further Reading**

Diedrich, Maria. 1999. *Love Across Color Lines: Ottilie Assing and Frederick Douglass.* New York: Hill and Wang.

Douglass, Frederick. 1962. *Life and Times of Frederick Douglass: His Early Life as a Slave, His Escape From Bondage, and His Complete History Written by Himself.* New York: Collier Books.

Douglass, Frederick. 1976. *Frederick Douglass on Women's Rights*, edited by Philip S. Foner. Westport, CT: Greenwood Press.

Douglass, Frederick. 1997. *Narrative of the Life of Frederick Douglass, an American Slave, Written by Himself: Authoritative Text, Context, Criticism*, edited by William L. Andrews and William S. McFeely. New York: W. W. Norton & Company.

## Draft Riots and Resistance

Wherever any kind of resistance to the draft occurred, including rioting, women could be found as active participants. So common was draft dodging and desertion, North and South, that men trying to keep out of the army could usually count on help from sympathetic neighbors, especially female relatives.

All across the North, women often took whatever steps were necessary to protect their men. In Indiana, they pelted enrollment officials with eggs. Others had more deadly intentions. In Illinois, two women fired on troopers coming to take their father and brother. Because of female opposition, officials in Milwaukee, Wisconsin, found it impossible to carry out the draft without a large detachment of armed guards. Milwaukee's provost marshal wrote that the city was controlled by mobs of draft opponents. He hastened to add that almost all the trouble was brought on by women and children, the former threatening to make use of hot water and the latter throwing rocks.

Pennsylvania's *Easton Argus* wrote that conscription was as unpopular as a plague of smallpox and conscript officers as welcome as a pack of mad dogs. Mad dogs could not have been treated much worse. When an armed conscript company rode into Archbald, a mob of angry women drove them out. In another town, twenty-five women stoned two conscript officers. A Berks County woman threw boiling water on an enrolling officer attempting to arrest her half-blind husband. Union County women rushed to the aid of a local deserter attending his sister's funeral. During the service, an army detachment arrived to arrest him. The deserter wounded one soldier before being fatally shot himself. Enraged women in the congregation attacked the injured arresting soldier and forced him to flee. The women's action reflected not only their anger at soldiers invading a church but also their view of enrollment officials.

Enrolling officers throughout the North faced violence from the civilian population. On conscription day at the courthouse in Port Washington, Wisconsin, women led one thousand antidraft protesters. When the local draft commissioner tried to turn the protesters back, some of the men and several women attacked him—pushing, kicking, and knocking him in the head. He ran to safety in the post office basement when the protesters turned their energies to breaking up the draft box. Women in Chicago formed part of a mob numbering several hundred that attacked enrolling officers who had arrested two men for protesting conscription. After being pummeled with stones, bricks, and any other missiles the crowd found convenient, the officers released their prisoners and made a hasty retreat.

Women also took an active role in the 1863 New York City draft riots. Angered at the government's efforts to take their husbands, sons, and fathers away from what little employment they had and leave the women to fend for themselves, women became especially violent in the factory districts where their families labored at menial jobs for dismal pay. Local women vowed vengeance against all enrolling officers and provost marshals. Some assaulted the police by grabbing stones and using their stockings as slingshots.

Boston's draft riot began when a conscript officer tried to arrest a woman who had slapped him. Her screams for help quickly brought neighbors to her aid. Soon hundreds of citizens rampaged through the city, attacking enrollment officers. When police tried to intervene, the crowds attacked them as well. A pack of enraged women reportedly trampled a lieutenant trying to report for duty. Soldiers rushed out to rescue the man, firing into the air as they dragged him back into their armory. The gunfire sent the mob of men, women, and children into a violent rage. They tore up sidewalk bricks and hurled them at the armory.

On the other side of the Mason-Dixon line, many Southern women prepared to kill anyone who tried to take their men. A Missouri woman stared down Confederates with a gun when they tried to enlist her husband. A group of Florida women behaved similarly when Confederate officials came after their deserter husbands. The women came out with hoes and axes, unhorsed one of the riders, and kept the rest occupied as their husbands escaped.

Popular support and plenty of hiding places made it almost impossible for Confederate authorities to find deserters. When patrols were nearby, women had various ways of calling for help or warning their men—blowing horns or whistles, ringing bells, or hanging out quilts of different colors or patterns to signal danger. One deserter band set up camp on an island in the Chattahoochee River just north of Columbus, Georgia. Family and friends kept them supplied until the end of the war. In North Carolina's Montgomery County, two sisters took food and supplies to their draft-dodging husbands hiding in the surrounding woods.

Draft resistance could be dangerous or even deadly. A North Carolina woman complained to Governor Zebulon Vance about the treatment state militia troops meted out to women suspected of helping their men avoid service. She wrote of officials rounding up women and violently beating them in an effort to force confessions from them and to get information on their men's whereabouts. Two women had their hands held under a fence rail while a soldier sat with his full weight on it. The wife of William Owen, leader of a North Carolina deserter band, experienced similar torture. When she refused to tell a Rebel home guard where her husband was, its commander slapped her. His men then tied her thumbs together behind her back and suspended her from a limb with her toes just touching the ground.

In spite of the danger, many Southern women continued to stand up for deserters. Two North Carolina women threatened to torch the residence of a captain who held two of their menfolk. He brushed their warning aside as an idle threat and did not release the men; his barn was torched that night.

Women played a part in draft resistance throughout the war in both the Union and the Confederacy, and their efforts affected the war in numerous ways.

*David Williams*

***See also*** Civilian Life; Confederate Homefront; Conscription; Desertion; Enlistment; Northern Women; Southern Women; Union Homefront.

**References and Further Reading**

Bynum, Victoria E. 1992. *Unruly Women: The Politics of Social and Sexual Control in the Old South.* Chapel Hill: University of North Carolina Press.

Edwards, Laura F. 2000. *Scarlett Doesn't Live Here Anymore: Southern Women in the Civil War Era.* Urbana: University of Illinois Press.

Hanna, William F. 1990. "The Boston Draft Riot." *Civil War History* 36: 262–273.

Larsen, Lawrence H. 1961. "Draft Riot in Wisconsin, 1862." *Civil War History* 7: 421–427.

Murdock, Eugene C. 1971. *One Million Men: The Civil War Draft in the North.* Madison: State Historical Society of Wisconsin.

O'Sullivan, John, and Alan M. Meckler, eds. 1974. *The Draft and Its Enemies: A Documentary History.* Urbana: University of Illinois Press.

Shankman, Arnold. 1980. *The Pennsylvania Antiwar Movement, 1861–1865.* Madison, NJ: Fairleigh Dickinson University Press.

Williams, David. 2005. *A People's History of the Civil War: Struggles for the Meaning of Freedom.* New York: New Press.

# E

## Edmonds, Amanda Virginia (1839–1921)

Twenty years old when she began her journal, Amanda Edmonds chronicled her life during the tumultuous years from 1857 to 1867. It records her daily life during the Civil War and is a valuable source of information about her feelings and experiences on the homefront.

Amanda Edmonds was born in 1839, the seventh of ten children of Lewis and Elizabeth Settle Edmonds. Called Tee by friends and family, Edmonds lived at Belle Grove, a plantation of about one thousand acres in Fauquier County, Virginia. Before the war, her life was filled with social activities like balls, sewing parties, and visits from family. This happy time was interrupted by the death of Lewis Edmonds in 1857. Debts against the estate required that the family sell seven slaves, and the financial stability of Belle Grove was precarious for many years thereafter.

Events in the world intruded into life at Belle Grove as the war approached. John Brown's raid, for example, excited both comment and fear in Edmonds. She railed against Brown and rejoiced on the day of his hanging. Fears that his raid would induce a slave revolt at Belle Grove quieted over time, but Edmonds recorded the tense nights her brothers spent watching over the house.

By 1861, Virginia had seceded and was among the Confederate States of America, and Edmonds was busily sewing uniforms and watching men enlist. She noted the powerful emotions felt by a crowd of men and women when the Confederate flag was presented to a local rifle unit. While romantic, Edmonds recognized that the war would result in death, and she watched the young men around her with her mind on the future.

The great strength of Edmonds' diary is its ability to convey the tone and pace of the war for those at home. Edmonds describes the many visits from Confederate soldiers, friends, and family. Over the course of the war, she comments on the death of acquaintances, rumors, and occasionally the incursions of Union troops into Belle Grove. Her staunch loyalty to the Confederacy emerges at various points, including her satisfaction at Mosby's refusal to surrender after Appomattox. Later, she rejoices at the assassination of Abraham Lincoln.

Edmonds' diary is full of references to romance and young men, but none of her relationships lasted long. Finally, in 1870, Edmonds married Armistead Chappelear, who saved Belle Grove by paying Lewis Edmonds' debts. The couple had five children.

Amanda Edmonds died in 1921, leaving her diary as a testament to her life on a Virginia plantation during the Civil War.

*Fiona Deans Halloran*

***See also*** Aid Societies; Confederate Homefront; Diaries and Journals; Enlistment; Family Life, Confederacy; Flags, Regimental; Nationalism, Confederate; Plantation Life; Sewing Bees; Slaveholding Women; Southern Women.

**References and Further Reading**

Edmonds, Amanda Virginia. 1984. *Journals of Amanda Virginia Edmonds: Lass of the Mosby*

*Confederacy, 1857–1867*, edited by Nancy Chappelear Baird. Stephens City, VA: Commercial Press.

Selby, John G. 2002. *Virginians at War: The Civil War Experiences of Seven Young Confederates*. Wilmington, DE: Scholarly Resources.

## Edmonds, Sarah Emma [Franklin Thompson] (1841–1898)

Few expected New Brunswicker Sarah Emma Edmonds to emerge as the Civil War's most famous female soldier, spy, and nurse.

Born in 1841 as the fifth daughter of Isaac and Elisabeth Edmonds, Sarah's disapproving father compounded the rural drudgery, isolation, and severity that characterized her early life. Despite her ability to hunt, fish, and work as hard as a boy, her father continued to punish Sarah for not being a boy. Sarah hoped that the birth of her brother would soften her father's emotions toward her and make her life easier. Relief turned to despair when her brother displayed signs of epilepsy and her father's anger toward her intensified. In 1856, Isaac betrothed Sarah to a much older and, in her opinion, unacceptable man. Rather than marry him, Sarah fled to a family friend in Moncton, New Brunswick, and worked as a salesgirl in a hat shop before making her way to Flint, Michigan, where she survived by posing as a man—Franklin Thompson—and working as a door-to-door bible salesman.

With the outbreak of the Civil War in 1861, Sarah volunteered for service as Franklin Thompson and was mustered into the Second Michigan Volunteer Regiment as a nurse. She served in the hospitals and on the battlefields of Bull Run and Antietam, among others, and several times she donned the disguise of a slave to spy behind Confederate lines. Disguised as a slave, Sarah could listen to and observe Confederate plans unnoticed. In March 1862, she discovered that the Confederates planned to bluff the Union at Yorktown, Virginia. Instead of cannons, the Confederates crafted Quaker guns, that is, logs painted to look like cannons and designed to exaggerate the size of the force the Union would meet. Sarah relayed the information to the Union command, perhaps contributing to the Union victory in April 1862.

Sarah Emma Edmonds disguised herself as a man and enlisted with the Second Michigan regiment during the American Civil War. She served as a nurse and mail carrier and participated in major battles. After her true identity was revealed, she received a full veteran's pension for her war service. (Courtesy Archives of Michigan)

In the spring of 1863, Sarah contracted malaria and chose to abandon the Second Michigan Volunteer Regiment rather than seek medical help that might reveal her identity as a woman. Sarah planned to recover in Cairo, Illinois, and return to service, but she discovered that the Union army had listed Frank Thompson as a deserter. Instead of returning to her regiment, she published a highly fictionalized version of her life in 1864. *Nurse and Spy in the Union Army* details Sarah's adventures during the war, but excludes the details relating to her time disguised as Franklin Thompson. Sarah donated all the proceeds from the book to various charities, including the United States Sanitation Commission. For the remainder of the Civil War, Sarah worked for the Commission as a nurse and Franklin Thompson remained, in the eyes of his comrades and the United States government, a deserter.

Sarah returned to Canada after the Civil War and married fellow Canadian Linus Seeyle in 1867. The two raised a family while frequently moving between Illinois, Michigan, Ohio, and Kansas. Over the course of these years, Franklin Thompson's status as a deserter bothered Sarah. In 1884, she revealed the truth to her military comrades at a reunion. Although surprised by the revelation, they supported her quest to clear Franklin's name. Many veterans offered Sarah affidavits that she used to petition the Federal government for an honorable discharge and a pension. On July 7, 1886, President Grover Cleveland granted both of her requests. Sarah received a $12-a-month veteran's pension for the rest of her life. She spent her remaining years in La Porte, Texas.

She died on September 5, 1898, of malaria, the very disease that led her to desert her military post during the Civil War. On Memorial Day in 1901, Sarah's military comrades reburied her with full military honors in the Grand Army of the Republic cemetery in Houston, making her the organization's only female member. In 1988, the United States Military Intelligence Hall of Fame inducted Sarah into their organization. Four years later, the Michigan Women's Hall of Fame followed suit. Both recognized Sarah's contributions to the United States generally and specifically to the Union military effort.

*Cheryl A. Wells*

**See also** Female Combatants; Female Spies; United States Sanitary Commission.

### References and Further Reading

Blanton, Deanna, and Lauren M. Cook. 2002. *They Fought Like Demons: Women Soldiers in the Civil War.* New York: Vintage.

Hoy, Claire. 2004. *Canadians in the Civil War.* Toronto: McArthur & Company.

Leonard, Elizabeth D. 1999. *All the Daring of the Soldier: Women of the Civil War Armies.* New York: W. W. Norton & Company.

Stevens, Bryna. 1992. *Frank Thompson: Her Civil War Story.* Toronto: Maxwell MacMillian Canada.

## Edmondson, Belle (1840–1873)

Born in Pontotoc, Mississippi, on November 17, 1840, Isabella Buchanan Edmondson was one of eight children. She became a spy and smuggler for the Confederacy in 1862, operating from her family farm near Memphis, Tennessee. Her diaries and correspondence, published one hundred and twenty-five years after the Civil War, reveal typical espionage activities. When returning from Memphis shopping trips, she shrouded hats, boots, and fabric for uniforms under her large hoop skirts; hid letters, money, and buttons in her dress bodice; and concealed morphine, chloroform, and whiskey in her wagon.

During her childhood, her parents, Mary Ann Howard and Andrew Jackson Edmondson, lived in Holly Springs, Mississippi, where her father was a surveyor, recorder of deeds, and chancery court clerk before he began farming in 1856. She excelled in music at Franklin Female College, a finishing school offering ornamental and academic courses. In 1860, the family moved to Elm Ridge, a farm just north of the state line. At the outbreak of war, Belle's brother, Jimmie, a Memphis merchant, organized Company B, One hundred fifty-fourth Tennessee Regiment, known as the Bluff City Grays, in May 1861, and he later operated a blockade runner. Another brother, Eddie, joined the Grays, subsequently becoming one of Nathan Bedford Forrest's scouts.

Ignoring Federal prohibitions against transporting Confederate correspondence and items such as quinine and newspapers, Edmondson helped individuals and the Confederate army get items across enemy lines. Edmondson received letters from areas like Kentucky and Missouri for Confederate soldiers on duty in the Deep South. Sorting them by commanding officer, she conveyed them to male accomplices for final delivery. When returning couriers brought letters from Dixie, she mailed them in Memphis to destinations in the North and West. Edmondson risked imprisonment by regularly furnishing goods and information to Captain Thomas H. Henderson of Henderson's Scouts and to Forrest. She personally presented boots she smuggled to Generals Sterling Price, Earl Van Dorn, and John Pemberton. She also designed a Confederate battle flag for General Price that featured stars inside a white Latin cross on a blue field bordered in red. Later, minus the stars, it became known as the Bowen pattern.

While in Memphis on April 21, 1864, Edmondson learned that Union General Stephen Hurlbut had issued an order to arrest her for smuggling. Although she returned home safely using a borrowed pass, her access to Memphis and thus her usefulness as a smuggler was over. Six weeks later, she left for Oxford, Mississippi, where her younger sister Helen married Major Brodie Crump on June 23. Edmondson stayed there until late September, visiting friends and assisting wounded soldiers. After returning home briefly in early October, she rejoined friends at Waverly Plantation in Clay County, Mississippi, where she apparently remained until the war ended.

Despite her covert operations, Edmondson maintained household and social routines, participating in the usual women's support efforts. She sewed clothing for soldiers, herself, and other family members; taught her servant basic literacy; and regularly visited friends and neighbors. When wounded soldiers from the Battle of Shiloh were brought to Overton Hospital in Memphis, she fed and attended to them.

Throughout the war, Edmondson's diaries recorded backaches so severe she needed morphine and laudanum. However, she likely used the medications as much to relieve her emotional pain as her physical ailments. From childhood, her family regarded her as headstrong and unruly, and her diaries and letters reinforce that opinion, reflecting her lifelong struggle against family and societal behavioral expectations and resulting ostracism. Perpetuating her depression were wartime shortages, safety concerns, travel restrictions, concern for her soldier brothers, as well as the added strain of her smuggling activities, her beloved mother's death on August 3, 1861, and two broken engagements.

Little is known of Edmondson's postwar life. After their father died in 1872, Eddie and his family lived with his spinster sisters, Belle and Joanna, at Elm Ridge. On July 1, 1873, Belle became engaged to a "Col. H." The cause of her sudden death two weeks later remains a mystery. She is buried in the family plot at Elmwood Cemetery, Memphis.

*Nancy L. Adgent*

*See also* Blockade Running; Female Spies.
**References and Further Reading**
Clinton, Catherine, and Nina Silber, eds. 1992. *Divided Houses: Gender and the Civil War.* New York: Oxford University Press.
Galbraith, William, and Loretta Galbraith, eds. 1990. *A Lost Heroine of the Confederacy: The Diaries and Letters of Belle Edmondson.* Jackson: University Press of Mississippi.
Stern, Philip Van Doren. 1959. *Secret Missions of the Civil War.* Chicago: Rand McNally and Company.

## Edmondston, Catherine Ann Devereux (1823–1875)

Wealthy slaveholder Catherine Ann Devereux Edmondston kept an extensive journal detailing her life during the Civil War.

Catherine Devereux was one of six daughters and one son born to a wealthy North Carolina planter family. In 1846 she married Patrick Muir Edmondston of Charleston, South Carolina, where she lived for a short time before returning to North Carolina. There the couple spent their time running Looking Glass Plantation, which adjoined her father's estate, and at Hascosea, their summer home. The lands were part of a $10,000 marriage settlement. At the outbreak of the Civil War, the Edmondstons owned approximately 2,000 acres of land and eighty-eight slaves.

The Edmondstons were an exceptionally close couple, perhaps because they never had children. Consequently Catherine was extremely reluctant to be separated from Patrick. Nevertheless, she saw the North as a threat to her privileged position and firmly maintained that the South should be left alone to manage its own domestic affairs, among which she regarded slavery as central. Her father, on the other hand, retained strong Unionist sympathies, and the consequent friction in the family was very troubling. Edmondston, however, remained steadfast in her opinions and was not hesitant to express her political views.

Despite her lofty rhetoric, Catherine always remained reluctant to make personal sacrifices. She was particularly averse to her husband's wartime absences, although these were relatively brief. Initially Patrick Edmondston remained at home in charge of the local Home Guard. He later obtained a certificate of disability exempting him from military service. Catherine always maintained that her husband was too delicate and aristocratic for military service.

Catherine's war efforts were largely supervisory; she simply put her slaves to work sewing uniforms and knitting socks. Because her plantation was relatively isolated, she had few disciplinary problems with her own slaves and suffered only minor hardships. During the final months of the war, she was horrified to learn that the Confederacy was considering arming slaves. She never deviated from her firm belief in the racial inferiority of African Americans.

In April 1865 Catherine feared that Union General William T. Sherman's troops would reach her plantation. Rather than have her personal papers fall into Yankee hands, she destroyed them all herself. She was especially distraught at burning all her husband's love letters and harbored a burning resentment toward Yankees all her life for forcing her to take such a preemptive measure. Although her home remained untouched, this did nothing to soften her sentiments.

In 1872 she published *Morte d'Arthur: Its Influence on the Spirit and Manner of the Nineteenth Century.* Here she praised the chivalry and honor of Southern behavior while hurling accusations against the Yankees especially for their alleged treatment of Southern women and children. Edmondston remained a staunch supporter of Southern independence and white supremacy until her death in 1875.

*Jacqueline Glass Campbell*

**See also** Diaries and Journals; Sherman's Campaign (1864–1865).

### References and Further Reading
Crabtree, Beth G., and James W. Patton, eds. 1979. *Journal of a Secesh Lady: The Diary of Catherine Ann Devereux Edmondston, 1860–1866.* Raleigh: North Carolina Division of Archives and History.

Faust, Drew Gilpin. 2000. "A Moment of Truth: A Woman of the Master Class in the Confederate South." In *Slavery, Secession and Southern History,* edited by Robert Louis Paquette and Louis A. Ferleger, 126–139. Charlottesville: University Press of Virginia.

## Education, Northern

During the Civil War, Northern women experienced not only deprivations but also new opportunities, particularly in employment and education. The expansion of professional opportunities for women was most prominent in education. During the war, women assumed places in the schools and colleges, both as teachers and as students. They not only attended school in greater numbers than ever, but they also became the backbone of the teaching force and the impetus for educational reform in both the North and the South.

During the antebellum period, educational opportunities for Northern women expanded along with the women's rights movement. The primary reason for this expansion was the popularization of schooling itself, which resulted in more girls and women going to school and the attendant growth of educational institutions such as common schools, high schools, academies, normal schools, and colleges. By 1860, private schools had become rarer and more elite. More children now went to tuition-free public schools, and the rise in school attendance created a need for teachers that could not be filled by men alone. The growing presence of women in the teaching force contributed not only to the feminization of teaching, but also to its professionalization.

At the same time, the women's rights movement and the growth of women's education spurred many women to become political actors. For example, due in part to their liberal classical education, which included the study of rhetoric, South Carolinians Sarah and Angelina Grimké began to speak out against slavery as early as 1837. While feminist women joined the ranks of the abolitionists, more conservative middle-class Northern women demonstrated a missionary zeal in their belief that education was liberating in itself. Northern free blacks, on the other hand, argued for a broadened abolitionist agenda that included the assurance of education, suffrage, equality, and civil rights for all

African Americans, in addition to the advocation of emancipation.

By 1860, the numbers of women teachers in some localities, particularly urban areas, surpassed those of men. New England, with its well-developed school system, was in the forefront of this trend. The region was also the first to institute a normal school for the training of teachers, the first being established in 1839 in Lexington, Massachusetts.

Despite the unquestionable need for additional teachers, the entrance of Northern women into the teaching profession was governed by several factors, including prevailing nineteenth-century gender prescriptions. Women were portrayed as superior moral beings who held the elevated status of motherhood. It was believed that women's domestic responsibilities transferred easily to teaching and that their innate nurturing ability made them ideally suited for working with young children. Conversely, opposition to female teachers was based on women's alleged lack of intellectual rigor to teach higher subjects and their lack of physical strength to control older male pupils in class. These presumptions led to a hierarchical practice of grouping female assistants under male principal teachers in antebellum common schools. It also established a pattern of economic discrimination whereby women taught for a fraction of the money paid to men. By midcentury, Northern school reformers had successfully argued for inexpensive female teachers. In Massachusetts, the salary differential remained around 40 percent throughout the period, while the proportion of females in the teaching force increased from 56 percent in 1834 to 78 percent in 1860.

By the onset of the Civil War, women also began to participate in higher education in greater numbers. Available to middle- and upper-class women were various collegiate institutions, many of which featured a classical curriculum—including courses in science, psychology, philosophy, and rhetoric—similar to that of men's institutions. Forms of higher educational institutions open to women included private women's colleges, religiously oriented coeducational colleges, public and private secular coeducational institutions, public single-sex vocational institutions, and normal or teacher preparation institutes.

In the North, coeducation became dominant in public and private universities. However, many female academies were established to give women educational opportunities. Emma Willard, Zilpah Grant, and others established female academies and seminaries in New England and New York. The Troy Female Seminary, Hartford Female Seminary, and Mount Holyoke Female Seminary became models for women's institutions not only in the North, but also in the Midwest and West. In 1862, the Federal passage of the Morrill Land Grant Act gave public funding for agricultural schools and bolstered the emphasis placed on public higher education.

With the issuance of the Emancipation Proclamation in 1863, Northern women educators directed their efforts southward. Capitalizing on society's view of women as nurturers and teachers, people like Josephine Griffing, an Ohio agent for the National Freedmen's Relief Association of Washington, D.C., petitioned Congress to give Northern and Western women responsibility for the care and education of recently freed slaves. Northern white and black women who linked the rights of emancipated slaves to women's rights devoted themselves to freedmen's relief during the Civil War and Reconstruction. To advance the rights of both disenfranchised groups, women lobbied the government, worked as agents of the Freedmen's Bureau, raised money for freedmen's aid, and started common and industrial schools for the freedpeople. Several thousand New England white women, most of whom were single, upper or middle class, unemployed, and New England educated, journeyed South to work and teach freedmen after the Civil War.

In addition, educated black women migrated or returned south after emancipation to aid in the transition of newly freed blacks from slavery to freedom. For example, noted lecturer Louise DeMontie, who had migrated from Virginia to Boston in the 1850s, moved to New Orleans in 1865 to open the city's first orphanage for black youth. Mary Ann Shadd Cary, who migrated to Canada in the 1850s, returned to the United States after the outbreak of the Civil War to serve as a scout for the Union army. Scores of other black women went south to engage in the massive effort to educate the newly emancipated blacks.

During Reconstruction, the most common, traditional, and available option open to women was teaching in freedmen's schools. In 1869, Sallie Holley, the daughter of abolitionist Myron Holley, joined Caroline Putnam in Virginia to teach at the Holley School for freedpeople. For Holley, as for other women, teaching was a natural continuation of her antislavery efforts. As Northern women remained in, or returned to, the South to teach and work for freedmen's rights, the schools they founded there planted the seeds of a school system based on the model of the Northern common school.

With the withdrawal of the Union army from the South, however, Northern women teachers were largely on their own. Although there was always a steady supply of Northern white women willing to teach in freedmen's schools, aid societies could no longer raise the funds to cover their salaries. Moreover, as the war concluded and Reconstruction ended, freedmen's aid societies turned their attention to normal schools and the training of African American teachers rather than to common schools, hoping the states would initiate efforts to develop a common school system where none had existed before the war. Typically, however, the burden fell on the freedpeople to provide their own schools and on whoever responded with money and in-kind gifts.

During Reconstruction, teaching continued to provide women of all backgrounds with important ways to serve and to support themselves. The crucial need for schoolteachers prior to and during the Civil War became exacerbated and more generalized. Hundreds of the black and thousands of the Northern white women who were initially drawn to the war effort later taught in the rural areas of the South. Due to immigration and westward expansion, urban and rural America required more teachers. Begun in the North, tested in the crucible of the Civil War, the common school and the feminization of teaching would be diffused throughout the South.

The end of the Civil War brought about the realization that the women's rights movement of the antebellum period had been supplanted by the push for African American rights. This was confirmed at the 1868 American Equal Rights Association annual meeting, where women who had devoted themselves to the causes occasioned by the war learned that the antebellum support for women's rights had been diverted, for political reasons, to the cause of black male suffrage. Despite this setback, women who entered colleges and universities in substantial numbers in the decades following the Civil War would eventually reinvigorate the women's rights movement.

*Jayne R. Beilke*

***See also*** Cary, Mary Ann Shadd (1823–1893); Education, Southern; Grimké (Weld), Angelina (1805–1879); Grimké, Sarah Moore (1792–1873); Northern Women; Teachers, Northern.

**References and Further Reading**

Cott, Nancy F., ed. 1993. *History of Women in the United States. Historical Articles on Women's Lives and Activities*. Vol. 12. *Education*. Munich: K. G. Saur Publishing.

Noble, Jeanne L. 1956. *The Negro Woman's College Education*. New York: Teachers College, Columbia University, Bureau of Publications.

Silber, Nina. 2002. "A Compound of Wonderful Potency: Women Teachers of the North in the Civil War South." In *The War Was You and Me: Civilians in the American Civil War*, edited by Joan E. Cashin, 35–59. Princeton, NJ: Princeton University Press.

Solomon, Barbara Miller. 1985. *In the Company of Educated Women: A History of Women and Higher Education in American*. New Haven, CT: Yale University Press.

Woody, Thomas. 1929. *A History of Women's Education in the United States*. 2 volumes. New York: Science Press.

## Education, Southern

During the antebellum period, the South had no system of common schools. By the end of the Civil War, however, women's efforts had been largely responsible for the establishment of a nascent system of public schools and the creation of a professional role for women in the field of teaching. In addition, the efforts of both Northern and Southern women on behalf of recently emancipated slaves also furthered the shared national cause of women's rights.

Within the Southern planter culture, women received an education consistent with their social status. Private tutors, generally male, traveled among plantations teaching elite children. During the antebellum period, girls and women of the planter class attended private schools and academies staffed largely by graduates of well-known Northern private schools. During the 1850s, numerous female colleges, which grew out of female academies and seminaries, were founded in the South. Southern schools were unique in that they offered women a classical liberal curriculum that included mandatory instruction in both Latin and Greek, for the purpose of understanding Western civilization.

Southern women also studied rhetoric, although they were not expected to engage in public oratory. Elite Southern women were expected to symbolize a gentility worthy of their elevated social class and culture, so they were also taught ornamental subjects such as fancy needlework, dancing, music, drawing, and painting. Since Southern women in general, however, were not expected to work outside the home for reasons other than economic necessity, Southern schools did not prepare them for the teaching profession. White lower- and middle-class Southern women received little or no education; their lack of education was considered consistent with their social class.

Educational opportunities for African American women in the South were not only limited, but forbidden by law. A few private academies for African American girls had been established in large cities

Students at Wesleyan Female Institute in North Carolina, 1854. (North Carolina Collection, University of North Carolina Library at Chapel Hill)

such as Washington, D.C., and Baltimore for the children of free persons of color. The education of slaves, however, was forbidden by the Slave Codes established by each Southern state (and some Border States) that restricted slaves' rights to assemble, bear witness against whites, travel without permission, and so forth. Slaves as well as owners were punished if the Codes were violated. Ironically, however, the slave system itself provided educational opportunity. Skilled workers were given relevant instruction in mathematics and reading in order to perform their work. In addition, social interaction with white children at a young age enabled some children of slaves to learn the alphabet. And house slaves who lived and worked in close proximity to educated whites learned informally.

The haphazard nature of Southern education was further disrupted by the Civil War. In Northern cities such as Boston, New York, and Philadelphia, benevolent societies were formed to promote the work of abolitionist missionaries. Sponsored by organizations such as the American Missionary Association, they raised funds, sent supplies south, and recruited and supported teachers. In 1865, these efforts were undertaken and coordinated by the Union army through the Bureau of Refugees, Freedmen, and Abandoned Lands (Freedmen's Bureau). The most numerous participants in this movement were Northern unmarried women called Yankee Schoolmarms, who taught in freedmen's schools. By 1870, the Freedmen's Bureau had placed about seven thousand teachers in the South, instructing some quarter of a million students. The curriculum not only included rudimentary literacy and numeracy, but also the inculcation of New England Puritan, or middle-class, values such as industriousness, self-reliance, and cleanliness.

The first schools for newly freed slaves were missionary efforts by the American Missionary Association and the Freedmen's Bureau. Local and Northern teachers taught in crowded night schools, Sunday schools, and common schools attended by emancipated blacks of all ages. Women constituted three-quarters of these teachers, and about one-eighth of the total number of teachers were African Americans. Charlotte Forten, the daughter of

James Forten, a prosperous free black Philadelphia sailmaker, was among the first contingent of Northern teachers to travel to the South Carolina Sea Islands as part of the Port Royal Experiment in early 1862. The Port Royal Experiment was a New England–based program designed to prove that freed persons could produce more cotton on government-managed and Northern-owned plantations than they had as slaves. The Port Royal education program instilled Northern values in its students, along with remedial instruction. An African American, Forten taught freed people on the South Carolina Sea Islands between 1862 and 1864. Hired by the Port Royal Relief Committee of Philadelphia, she taught rudimentary skills to children during the day and she taught adults at night. Threatened and harassed by local Southerners who resented the Northern women's interference, the teachers were often left to fend for themselves in a hostile environment. Exhausted by the work and inhospitable conditions, Forten left South Carolina after eighteen months and returned to the North.

The experience of serving the recently emancipated freedpersons was an education in itself. While women abolitionists were intellectually familiar with the rhetoric of antislavery and fugitive slave narratives, they came to know "the blasting effects of the system" (Slaughter 1869) only after they had arrived in the South. Hailing from Philadelphia, Laura Towne was a white woman who went south as part of the Port Royal Experiment and frequently disagreed with the men's oppressive supervision of the experiment. Although white women generally left the South to return home, Towne and her companion, Ellen Murray, stayed in South Carolina for the remainder of their lives.

Although advanced education for African Americans lagged behind that offered by white schools for several decades, the first black colleges and training institutions began during the Civil War era. Many African American teachers who had been trained at Oberlin College or elsewhere created their own institutions to help expand educational opportunities among black Americans. Anna Julia Cooper, Fanny Jackson Coppin, Nannie Helen Burroughs, and others joined Booker T. Washington and

W.E.B. DuBois as educational leaders of African Americans and eventually founded their own schools. Nannie Helen Burroughs, founder and longtime head of the National Training School for Women and Girls in Washington, D.C., was particularly interested in providing opportunities for black working-class women by professionalizing jobs in domestic service and manual training. While DuBois and Washington argued over what kind of education blacks should receive—classical liberal or vocational, respectively—women generally negotiated an educational practice that served both the vocational and professional needs of the African American population. Among the historically black colleges and universities founded between 1865 and 1870, Bethune-Cookman College, Spelman College, the Institute for Colored Youth, and Howard University all served African American women who pushed for a share of the educational opportunities for blacks that had opened up as a result of the Civil War and emancipation.

Having survived the Civil War, many white Southern women were faced with the reality of having to support themselves and their families economically. One-fourth of the Confederate army was dead, slaves were emancipated, and many plantations and towns were burned or otherwise destroyed. Southern women had to negotiate a new landscape. The need for employment led to the growth of normal (teacher training) schools and the addition of vocational and professional courses to the curriculum. Salem Female Academy in North Carolina remained open during the Civil War, and male institutions such as Trinity College, now Duke University, began to accept women. Out of necessity, white Southern women began to take their place in the teaching profession. North Carolina's Statesville Female College inaugurated a teaching department, and Hollins College in Virginia established scholarships for future teachers. Southern women founded schools, taught school, and gave music lessons at their homes.

Women's involvement in the South during the Civil War was educational in another way. Some women used the Freedmen's Bureau to advance women's rights. In addition to providing relief to contrabands, women in the Freedmen's Aid movement empowered themselves politically and socially; through their work with the movement, female abolitionists also furthered the realization of women's rights. In fact, the fractures within the Freedmen's Aid movement contributed to variants of feminism that came to fruition in the postbellum period. After Reconstruction, the dialogue associated with feminism was diffused in the North through the growth of women's organizations such as the New England Women's Club, the Philadelphia Society for Organizing Charity, and the Children's Aid Society. Likewise, black women who remained in the South developed similar organizations such as the National Association of Colored Black Women. But while white women in the North turned their attention to universal suffrage, black women in the South were confronted with the expectation of working to improve the conditions of their race as a whole.

*Jayne R. Beilke*

**See also** Coppin, Fanny Jackson (1837–1913); Forten (Grimké), Charlotte L. (1837–1914).

**References and Further Reading**

Farnham, Christie Anne. 1994. *The Education of the Southern Belle: Higher Education and Student Socialization in the Antebellum South.* New York: New York University Press.

Faulkner, Carol. 2004. *Women's Radical Reconstruction: The Freedmen's Aid Movement.* Philadelphia: University of Pennsylvania Press.

Hoffman, Nancy. 1981. *Woman's "True" Profession: Voices from the History of Teaching.* Old Westbury, NY: The Feminist Press / New York: McGraw-Hill.

Silber, Nina. 2002. "A Compound of Wonderful Potency: Women Teachers of the North in the Civil War South." In *The War Was You and Me: Civilians in the American Civil War,* edited by Joan E. Cashin. Princeton, NJ: Princeton University Press.

Slaughter, Linda Warfel, ed. 1869. *The Freedmen of the South.* Cincinnati, OH: Elm St. Printing Co.

## Election of 1860

The election of 1860 was the most anticipated presidential contest in American history. Even casual observers recognized that its outcome would probably determine whether the Union continued. Women and men of both regions watched the election carefully, frequently commenting on its implications to each other and in their journals and letters.

Throughout the 1850s, many Southerners threatened to secede if someone committed to free soil and pushing the idea of preventing the expansion of slavery into the Western territories was elected president. After 1855 the new, free soil Republican Party gained popularity across the North as it broadened its appeal among voters, emphasizing that free soil would break the political power of Southern planters and preserve the West for whites and farmers. By 1860, Republicans believed they could win the election because they needed no Southern votes to carry the electoral college, due to much greater population growth in the free states.

Before their Chicago convention, the leading Republican candidate was New York Senator William Seward, but many delegates considered him radical, especially on the issues of slavery and abolition, and feared he would cost the party Northern votes. Instead, Abraham Lincoln was nominated on the third ballot. A free soil moderate, Lincoln's rags-to-riches life story was perfect for American politics. A former Whig, he also came from a crucial swing state, Illinois, which Republicans needed to win. In their convention, the Democrats—the nation's only national party—divided over the selection of a presidential candidate and a policy for slavery in the territories. Most Northern Democrats supported Illinois Senator Stephen Douglas, who championed popular sovereignty—allowing residents in the territories to decide whether to have slavery. A majority of Southern Democrats, however, did not trust Douglas or popular sovereignty after the policy failed in Kansas Territory in the mid-1850s. A second convention failed to reunite the party, and two Democrats ran for president: Douglas from the North and Kentucky's John C. Breckinridge from the South. Finally, a new organization formed just for the election. The Constitutional Union Party hoped to attract moderates from both North and South who wanted to avoid disunion and a possible civil war. John Bell, a slave owner and senator from

Tennessee, was the Constitutional Union Party's nominee.

The presidential campaign was really two campaigns: Lincoln versus Douglas in the North; Breckinridge versus Bell in the South. Republicans emphasized free soil, a high tariff to promote American manufacturing, and policies intended to facilitate western settlement. Douglas stood by popular sovereignty and claimed to be the only national candidate capable of uniting the country, and he actually campaigned across the South despite numerous death threats. Breckinridge personally disavowed secession, but most Southern Democrats pledged to leave the Union if Lincoln was elected. They wanted Federal protection for slavery in all the territories. The Constitutional Unionists vaguely promised to support "the Constitution of the Country, the Union of the States, and the enforcement of the laws."

Lincoln won less than 40 percent of the popular vote, but nearly two-thirds of electors by carrying all the free states. He was only on the ballot in five slave states, finishing last in each. Douglas won only Missouri and three New Jersey electors, although he received the second-highest popular vote total. Bell and Breckinridge split the remaining slave states. In the wake of Lincoln's victory, Americans waited to see what the angered Southerners would do.

*Christopher J. Olsen*

**See also** Lincoln, Abraham (1809–1865); Politics; Secession.

**References and Further Reading**

Crenshaw, Ollinger. 1945. *The Slave States in the Presidential Election of 1860.* Baltimore, MD: Johns Hopkins University Press.

Donald, David Herbert. 1995. *Lincoln.* New York: Simon & Schuster.

Foner, Eric. 1970. *Free Soil, Free Labor, Free Men: The Ideology of the Republican Party before the Civil War.* New York: Oxford University Press.

Greeley, Horace, and John Cleveland. 1860. *A Political Text-Book for 1860.* New York: Tribune Association.

Luebke, Frederick C. 1971. *Ethnic Voters and the Election of Lincoln.* Lincoln: University of Nebraska Press.

Nevins, Allan. 1950. *The Emergence of Lincoln.* 2 volumes. New York: Scribner's.

Potter, David. 1976. *The Impending Crisis 1848–1861.* New York: Harper & Row.

## Election of 1864

United States President Abraham Lincoln insisted that the election of 1864 take place despite the Civil War. Lincoln reasoned that, if it were postponed, as many people thought it could or should be, the Southern effort to overthrow majority rule and deny the fair workings of American democracy, as Lincoln characterized the secession and the war, would succeed. Instead, Lincoln's reelection became the war's final turning point, ensuring a Union victory.

The progress of Union forces in 1864 as well as Lincoln's war leadership, especially the Emancipation Proclamation and the enrollment of African American troops, dominated the 1864 presidential campaign. Northern forces made painfully slow progress in Georgia and Virginia, suffering fearful losses. By September 1 the Union had suffered over one hundred thousand casualties, pushing war weariness to new depths in the North. Some Republicans schemed to replace Lincoln, believing he could not be re-elected, given the worsening military situation. Most Republicans, however, defended their war record. The platform included ringing endorsements of Lincoln, the Emancipation Proclamation as "a deathblow at this gigantic evil" of slavery, and the use of African American men in combat. Republicans made one fateful change to their ticket, replacing Hannibal Hamlin with Tennessee's Andrew Johnson as the vice president. This choice for vice president appealed to Unionist, prowar Democrats because Johnson was the only Confederate-state senator who had remained in his Federal office in 1861.

Democrats nominated former Union General George B. McClellan for president. Divided between Peace and War wings, the Democratic Party never quite constructed a harmonious campaign strategy. All Democrats criticized Lincoln's military leadership and blamed Republicans for Union losses, but they disagreed about how to proceed. McClellan favored winning the war first, then negotiating a peace. The party platform, however, called for peace first, Union second, if possible. Most controversial was a plank declaring the war a failure, something written by Peace wing leader Clement Vallandigham. Democrats agreed on matters of slavery and race, opposing emancipation, and they attacked Republicans as radical advocates of racial equality. Lincoln's occasional suspension of habeas corpus and the breakdown of prisoner exchange were other issues agitated by Democrats.

Republican prospects looked bleak in late August, but finally the Union armies made some progress. Most important was the successful capture and occupation of Atlanta by General William Tecumseh Sherman's forces on September 3, much to Lincoln's relief and gratitude. Not all states voted on the same day, and in October Lincoln carried Pennsylvania, Ohio, and Indiana, and the election ultimately delivered a huge Republican landslide. Lincoln won the electoral college 212 to 21; Republicans controlled the Senate 42 to 10 and the House of Representatives 145 to 40. Union soldiers voted overwhelmingly for Lincoln; the men who actually had to do the fighting wanted to see the war finished. Lincoln and Secretary of War Edwin Stanton furloughed home thousands of soldiers in closely contested states as well as those from states whose Democratic-controlled legislatures, such as Indiana's, did not allow absentee voting. Close analysis suggests that soldiers helped Republicans carry New York and Connecticut, and possibly Indiana and Maryland. In a supremely symbolic act, venerable abolitionist William Lloyd Garrison cast his first ever vote for president when he supported Lincoln. Almost certainly the election of 1864 represented the Confederacy's last real chance to win the war, through a Democratic victory and negotiated settlement. After the results became public, a stream of deserters left Confederate armies.

*Christopher J. Olsen*

***See also*** Politics; Lincoln, Abraham (1809–1865); Sherman's Campaign (1864–1865); Union Homefront.

**References and Further Reading**

Baker, Jean. 1983. *Affairs of Party: The Political Culture of Northern Democrats in Mid-*

*Nineteenth-Century America.* Ithaca, NY: Cornell University Press.

Donald, David Herbert. 1995. *Lincoln.* New York: Simon & Schuster.

Long, David. 1994. *Jewel of Liberty: Abraham Lincoln's Reelection and the End of Slavery.* Mechanicsburg, PA: Stackpole Books.

Paludan, Phillip Shaw. 1994. *The Presidency of Abraham Lincoln.* Lawrence: University Press of Kansas.

Paludan, Phillip Shaw. 1988. *A People's Contest: The Union and Civil War, 1861–1865.* New York: Harper & Row.

Silbey, Joel. 1977. *A Respectable Minority: The Democratic Party in the Civil-War Era.* New York: W. W. Norton & Company.

## Elmore, Grace Brown (1839–1912)

Diarist and ardent Confederate Grace Brown Elmore kept a detailed journal of life in South Carolina during the Civil War.

Elmore was born into a privileged Southern family. Her mother, Harriet Chesnut Elmore, was the daughter of Governor John Taylor of South Carolina, one of the founders of the city of Columbia; her father, Franklin Harper Elmore, began his career as a lawyer and later served in the United States House of Representatives. In 1840 Franklin Elmore was appointed president of the Bank of South Carolina and moved his family to Charleston. Grace was the fourth youngest of a family of twelve, eight of whom survived to adulthood. When her father died, Elmore's mother moved the family back to Columbia, where she spent most of her life. Although her late father's estate provided Elmore with financial independence, she was not autonomous. Elmore frequently expressed her frustrations over the limitations imposed by the patriarchal society in which she lived and expressed an aversion to marriage.

Elmore was well educated and deeply religious. She led a happy and privileged childhood, largely under the care of a slave woman whom she called Mauma Binah. There are few details of her life during the decade before the war, but five months after the outbreak of hostilities Elmore began her two-volume journal. Like other women of her race and class, Elmore was involved in fundraising for the Southern cause to which she remained deeply committed. Her diary contains many reflections on Southern men's duty and commitment to war and on the ironies that men, whom she felt had not fulfilled their roles, still depended on women on the homefront.

Elmore was deeply attached to her slaves, and never wavered in her commitment to slavery as an institution that served the needs of both blacks and whites. Despite her expressed gratitude to the loyalty of the slaves who remained with her, she firmly maintained that they were, and always would be, her property. In the final months of the war, her tone turned increasingly racist.

Elmore's diary gives a particularly detailed account of General William T. Sherman's attack on Columbia in February 1865. The consequent devastation of the city caused Elmore to become even more devout in her faith in God and the Confederate cause. When Elmore heard that Lee had surrendered, she was filled with grief for the South, with pity for newly freed African Americans, and with fear of Yankee vengeance. In the wake of war, Elmore briefly questioned but never rejected her faith. Instead she turned her acerbic tone to blame Yankees and blacks for all that she had lost.

In the postwar years, Elmore suffered financial hardships that forced her to live with her siblings, with whom she had always had strained relations. When her sister opened a school, Elmore took a position as a teacher. Although she had expressed a desire for independence, she resented having to work for pay and did not see it as liberating. Her life seemed increasingly burdensome, especially when compared with her privileged upbringing. In her later years, Elmore moved to Jacksonville, Florida, where she died in 1912.

*Jacqueline Glass Campbell*

**See also** Diaries and Journals; Sherman's Campaign (1864–1865); Southern Women.

**References and Further Reading**

Weiner, Marli F. 1997. *A Heritage of Woe: The Civil War Diary of Grace Brown Elmore, 1861–1868.* Athens: University of Georgia Press.

# Emancipation League

Formed in 1861 by Boston abolitionists, the Emancipation League urged President Abraham Lincoln to make freeing the slaves a primary war goal. This group also helped to promote the creation of African American military units, such as the Fifty-fourth Massachusetts.

The first meeting of what would initially be called the Boston Emancipation League took place on September 5, 1861. In attendance were a group of Boston's most famous abolitionists, including William Lloyd Garrison, Samuel Gridley Howe, Wendell Phillips, Frank Sanborn, George Stearns, Edmund Quincy, and Frank Bird. The nascent organization soon agreed on a primary objective and a set of short-term goals. The objective was to educate the public about the centrality of slavery to the successful prosecution of the war. To do this, the League intended to solicit articles and editorials from a variety of abolitionist writers and then distribute the material to Northern newspapers. The League's approach proved popular with abolitionists throughout the North. New leagues formed in Washington, D.C., New York City, and Rochester, New York. Like the Boston League, these groups sponsored lectures, produced editorials, and worked to disseminate the emancipation message.

In 1862, the Emancipation League began to push the Federal government to create an emancipation bureau. Arguing that a national bureau could help to create order in dealing with emancipated slaves and in ensuring employment for them, members of the League urged Lincoln and the Senate to address the looming problem of the freedmen. As it had done with public opinion, the League emphasized education in its campaign for an emancipation bureau. It sent out a questionnaire to men in charge of freedmen in the Union Army and Treasury Department, and then it compiled the data into articles highlighting the chaos of the present system. The results of this survey served not only to undergird the League's arguments, but also to provide valuable information on the status of the freedmen.

The Emancipation League never had an easy relationship with the president. It criticized Lincoln for not committing to emancipation soon enough or enthusiastically enough, and it flirted with John C. Frémont and alternate Republican candidates in the election of 1864. During the Johnson administration, it pressured the president to include suffrage for freedmen in his reconstruction plan. In every case, the League found presidential leadership disappointing on questions of abolition and civil rights for black Americans.

The League officially ceased to exist during the Johnson administration. Deeply committed to voting rights for black Americans, it decided that public opinion and official action could be moved with the same tactics the League used for emancipation. Changing the name of the organization to the Impartial Suffrage Organization underlined this new focus, but the organization's tactics remained the same. Under its new rubric, editorials, articles, and lectures supporting black civil rights poured forth. Thus, while the Emancipation League ceased to exist in 1866, its energy and personnel simply shifted toward new goals, much as the sentiment behind abolition began to shift after the war toward a variety of new issues.

*Fiona Deans Halloran*

***See also*** Abolitionism and Northern Reformers; Antislavery Societies; Civilian Life; Election of 1864; Emancipation Proclamation (January 1, 1863); Freedmen's Bureau; Garrison, William Lloyd (1805–1879); Lincoln, Abraham (1809–1865); Union Homefront.

**References and Further Reading**

McPherson, James. 1964. *The Struggle for Equality.* Princeton, NJ: Princeton University Press.

# Emancipation Proclamation (January 1, 1863)

This document, first announced on September 22, 1862, by President Abraham Lincoln, is commonly hailed as the instrument that initially freed the slaves in response to a series of events and developments, both political and military. It is an unusual document in that it freed the slaves only in territory behind Confederate lines in states that had seceded from the Union; it left the slaves behind Federal lines in bondage in the seceded states, as well as in slave states loyal to the Union such as Missouri and Kentucky. The Emancipation Proclamation did not free all of the slaves. It did not even declare slavery to be illegal, and it enjoined slaves to refrain from violent insurrection. The Federal government simultaneously enacted an endorsement enlisting black men into the army and navy.

Lincoln had been working on the document for some time, but he did not show it to his cabinet until midsummer 1862. There were mixed reactions, including Postmaster General Montgomery Blair's contention that it would make the Republicans lose the upcoming midterm Congressional elections. Secretary of State William Seward suggested that the president keep the proclamation quiet until the North had won a victory, lest it seem like a last shriek of desperation. When at last General George McClellan's army delivered the first serious check to Confederate General Robert E. Lee by ending his invasion of Maryland at the Battle of Antietam, Lincoln felt that this was victory enough. On September 22, 1862, five days after the battle, Lincoln preliminarily announced the proclamation, stating that it would become law on January 1, 1863, partly in the hopes that some Confederate states would give in and comply rather than suffer the consequences of forced emancipation.

Lincoln made changes in the preliminary proclamation and in the final Emancipation Proclamation that he signed into law on January 1, 1863. In the former, Lincoln mentioned his former pet projects of compensated emancipation and colonization, ideas he had promoted for years. As a member of the House of Representatives, in 1848, he had proposed a measure to end slavery in the District of Columbia, but it would have to be gradual, voluntary, and compensated. But the final draft of the Emancipation Proclamation made no mention of these proposals. The final document also authorized the use of African Americans in the armed forces, another item that did not appear in the preliminary announcement.

This proclamation has been an object of critical controversy since that time. In his own time, the Radical Republicans, with abolitionist fervor, continually protested Lincoln's lack of decisive action to free the slaves. Critics of Lincoln point to the Proclamation as a cynical political ploy from a president who was more interested in placating the Border States, conservative Republicans, and War Democrats than he was in freeing the slaves—that this was merely a military measure designed to keep the British out of the war by redefining it as a war against slavery. Others have called it an empty gesture, freeing only the slaves that the Federal Army had no power to free. On the other side, supporters, then and now, point out that the document thereafter defined every move of the Union army: Every time new Southern territory was occupied, emancipated slaves would be free in the practical sense. By defeating Confederate armies and occupying Southern territory, the Union armies necessarily freed slaves as a military by-product. Regardless of the Confederates' original war aims, their cause had been redefined into a war fought to keep their slaves in bondage, simply by resisting Federal invasion. The essential character of the war had been changed from a mere civil war to a struggle to free those in bondage. Sympathizers with the South, such as those in Great Britain, could no longer seriously entertain the possibility of helping the Confederacy. Aiding a new nation in a struggle for independence had some public relations appeal; aiding a nation in keeping its slaves in chains would never play well with British public opinion.

More recently, scholars have pointed out that Lincoln's Emancipation Proclamation was only one more step in a process that had been begun by the slaves themselves, the so-called contrabands who had been escaping to Union lines since the beginning of the war. The two Confiscation Bills in Congress gave the Union army the right to seize and liberate the property—including escaped slaves—of those in rebellion against the government. Lincoln defended the partial liberation defined by the proclamation by pointing out that he, as president, had no constitutional authority to free the slaves but that he could take measures as commander in chief to punish those in rebellion against the Federal government. Whether he did this because it gave him a legal excuse to abolish slavery, as he had always wanted, or he reluctantly executed this half measure only in response to abolitionist and Radical pressure remains a matter of debate.

*Randal Allred*

**See also** Abolitionism and Northern Reformers;
African American Women; Antietam/Sharpsburg,
Battle of (September 17, 1862); Border States;
Contrabands; Freedmen's Bureau; Lincoln,
Abraham (1809–1865); Politics; Slave Families.

**References and Further Reading**

Franklin, John Hope. 1963. *The Emancipation
Proclamation.* Garden City, NY: Doubleday.

Guelzo, Allen C. 2004. *The Emancipation
Proclamation: The End of Slavery in America.*
New York: Simon & Schuster.

Johnson, Michael P., ed. 2001. *Abraham Lincoln,
Slavery, and the Civil War: Selected Writings and
Speeches.* Boston: Bedford/St. Martin's.

Tackach, James. 2002. *Lincoln's Moral Vision: The
Second Inaugural Address.* Jackson: University
Press of Mississippi.

## Enlistment

In both the South and the North, women had a vital role to play in the enrollment process. After the firing on Fort Sumter in April 1861, both sides mobilized for war by calling for volunteers. Almost no one, regardless of gender, considered women enlisting in the army to be a viable option, though some women disguised themselves as men to serve. In forming their armies, the Union and Confederacy mobilized soldiers as members of community units, and the entire community, both men and women, participated in the enlisting process. During subsequent enlistment drives, community pride was at stake, with towns competing against one another to enroll more men into the army. For both women and men in the North and the South, the patriotic zeal of the summer of 1861 eclipsed any prior lukewarm feelings regarding the need for war. The excitement of community competition and the social activities surrounding enlistment also overshadowed the harsh reality that some of the enlistees would not return home.

Politicians, prospective recruits, and women themselves recognized that women had a key role to play in the enlistment process. Women aided the process both tangibly and intangibly. Extending their traditional domestic duties, they raised money, donated their own valuables, rolled bandages, made cartridge bags, collected supplies, and made quilts,

Civil War poster advertising for recruits: $100 Bounty, $13 Pay per month, $6 State pay for married men, $4 State pay for single men, $3 per month for clothes, board and rations. (ac03077 / Collection of The New York Historical Society)

blankets, and tents. They also sewed uniforms. In 1861, the standard Union blue and Confederate gray had not yet emerged, and communities improvised their own styles and designs with gray being the most common choice of both sides. Most significantly, at least from a symbolic point of view, women also sewed the flags that the male members of their community would carry into battle.

To accomplish traditionally domestic tasks on a widened scale, the women of some communities formed committees. Generally, the wife of a prominent politician or army officer presided over the organization, which might meet in a local church. At these meetings, women would work alongside each other in a public display of their domestic abilities. Thus, from the early days of the war, women's contributions moved from a private to a public sphere. Although not an intentional move from the domestic sphere, these committees demonstrate the unintentional transforming effects of war. Many of these committees stayed in existence after enlistment drives to become soldiers' aid societies or to help care for soldiers' families.

Although some female diarists lamented that they could not enlist and bemoaned their position as women, more commonly women realized that they had a vital role to play in encouraging men to join the army. Women could use the romantic sentiments of the period as a form of intimidation to encourage men to enlist. Some women proclaimed that they would marry only soldiers, not cowards; they would marry a soldier or be an old maid. According to one popular Confederate song, "None but the brave deserve the fair." Others postponed engagements until after enlistments. Married women declared similar sentiments, asserting that they would not keep a husband who did not join the army. In other cases, some of which are perhaps apocryphal, women sent petticoats, bonnets, and hoopskirts to men who declined to serve their nation.

Women recognized that the enlistment of a male relative challenged their family's way of life and its economic security. Some women chose to put their families ahead of their country and urged their male relatives to remain at home. Yet, more commonly, women who feared the possible death of a male relative or the disruption of their domestic life realized that the shame of a healthy male failing to enlist would be cast on the whole family. Additionally, women had long been expected to subordinate their needs to those of society and their husbands, and they recognized that manhood required fighting for one's country. Thus, many women who had reservations about their husband's or son's service kept these concerns to themselves. While perhaps privately fearing the death of a relative or the difficult circumstances that the family left behind would face, publicly they appeared resilient, attempting not to cry at the departure of their loved ones. Those women continued to epitomize the expected feminine values of self-sacrifice and patient suffering that put public duty ahead of private interest. A

Confederate poem, "I've Kissed Him & Let Him Go," demonstrated the sacrifices that women made for the army. While postwar speakers who spoke of mothers regretting not having more sons to provide to the army exaggerated, they probably did not miss the mark by much. Women from the Border States often faced an even more difficult balancing task than those of either the North or the South. In some cases, they found themselves attempting to mediate a family divided, with a son wishing to fight for one side and a husband supporting the other.

On the formal day of enlistment or departure, the community cemented its ties to its soldiers with a parade and a public gathering. Women crowded the parade route or the railroad station and cheered for, waved handkerchiefs at, and presented cards and flowers to the departing soldiers. A combination of excitement and sadness pervaded these events, with women trying to stifle tears, lest they unman the men they were sending forth.

The ceremonial presentation of a flag provided women their most public role in the enrolling of their sons, brothers, and husbands into the army. In this highly ritualized ceremony, the departing unit was given a flag sewn by the women of their community. In some cases, even the material symbolized the connection between soldiers and the women of the community, with the flag being made from a dress of the wife of one of the company's officers. The flags varied, some having political slogans such as "The Union as Our Fathers Made it," "Let Us Alone," or "The Rights of the South at All Hazards." Others contained local or regional symbols combined with national emblems. Though women remained publicly silent in most of these ceremonies, in others, an elite woman of the community gave a brief speech after unfurling and presenting the banner. They urged the enlisting soldiers to consider the flag, which was sewed as a labor of love, to be a reminder that the community's thoughts and prayers were with them and that the soldiers battled for their homes, their communities, and their country. Thus, the soldiers should protect the flag as they would protect their families, and, likewise, to dishonor it was to dishonor their entire community, including its women. The ceremony continued with a picnic or banquet with the women of the community cooking meals for the men they were sending forth to battle.

In the initial enlistment process in 1861, Northern and Southern women played similar roles, though evidence suggests that Southern women were given more credit for enlistments than their Northern counterparts. As the war continued, the roles of women in the two regions diverged, with Southern women coming to increasingly oppose the enlistment of their male relatives. This divergence stemmed from a combination of factors: the relative scarcity of men on the Southern homefront (whereas the North enlisted approximately half of its white, male, military age population, the South enlisted 75 to 85 percent of its eligible soldiers); the presence of the Union army in the South, which rendered Southern women more vulnerable to physical attack and to material privation than their Northern counterparts; and the increasing likelihood that the South could not win the war. As they had to do at the onset of the war, women continued to balance national and military needs with family and community needs, but, for Southern women more than Northern women, this balance shifted evermore to the family side of the ledger, leading more and more Southern women to oppose further enlistments. With the nation failing to protect their families, some Confederate women felt less and less inclined to hold up their end of the bargain.

*John M. Sacher*

**See also** Aid Societies; Border States; Confederate Homefront; Evans, Augusta Jane (1835–1909); Flags, Regimental; Fort Sumter (April 12–14, 1861); Honor; Music, Northern; Music, Southern; Nationalism, Confederate; Nationalism, Union; Nonslaveholding Southerners; Northern Women; Poets, Northern; Poets, Southern; Sewing Bees; Slaveholding Women; Southern Women; Union Homefront; Wartime Literature.

**References and Further Reading**

Attie, Jeanie. 1998. *Patriotic Toil: Northern Women and the American Civil War*. Ithaca, NY: Cornell University Press.

Clinton, Catherine, and Nina Silber, eds. 1992. *Divided Houses: Gender and the Civil War*. New York: Oxford University Press.

Faust, Drew Gilpin. 1996. *Mothers of Invention: Women of the Slaveholding South in the American Civil War*. Chapel Hill: University of North Carolina

Linderman, Gerald E. 1987. *Embattled Courage: The Experience of Combat in the American Civil War*. New York: Free Press.

Rable, George C. 1989. *Civil Wars: Women and the Crisis of Southern Nationalism*. Urbana: University of Illinois Press.

## Eppes, Susan Branch Bradford (1846–1942)

Floridian Susan Bradford Eppes recorded her Civil War era experiences in her memoir, *Through Some Eventful Years*.

Born on March 8, 1846, at Pine Hill Plantation, located north of Tallahassee, Florida, Susan Branch Bradford was the daughter of Dr. Edward and Martha Lewis Branch Bradford. Her maternal grandfather, John Branch, had served as governor and senator from North Carolina, as Secretary of the Navy, and finally as territorial governor of Florida. Susan's father worked as a physician before retiring from the medical profession to spend most of his time administering his several plantations in north Florida. By the time of the Civil War, Edward Bradford owned several thousand acres of land and one hundred and forty-two slaves.

Susan briefly attended a local female seminary, but she received her education primarily from a succession of tutors. As the member of a privileged social class, she spent the antebellum years enjoying social events and other luxuries. The secession crisis and Civil War altered the frivolity of her life. The Bradfords strongly supported the Confederacy. Susan and her family remained in the vicinity of Tallahassee throughout the war. Although north Florida was spared the worst of the fighting, the residents still suffered through the trials associated with life on the homefront.

Following the war, Susan married Nicholas Ware Eppes, an ex-Confederate officer. Together they had six children, five of whom survived to adulthood. The couple lived with Susan's parents after their marriage, and Eppes eventually took over the administration of the family plantation. He also served a number of terms as county Superintendent of Public Instruction. Eppes' brutal murder on September 3, 1904, provoked many rumors. Although three African American men stood trial for the crime, some believed that Nicholas was killed as a result of a conspiracy of corrupt state officials who feared Eppes might reveal their dealings.

Following her husband's death, Susan withdrew for a time from the public eye, though she eventually regained her position as one of Tallahassee's social elite. She became active in organizations like the United Daughters of the Confederacy and the Daughters of the American Revolution.

In her later years Eppes authored two books relating to her experiences in Florida during the antebellum and Civil War years: *The Negro of the Old South* and *Through Some Eventful Years.* In addition, she wrote a number of historical articles and a volume of poetry. Like many Southerners, Eppes romanticized the antebellum plantation South.

While Eppes devotes considerable attention to life among the plantation elite during the 1850s, a large portion of *Through Some Eventful Years* deals with Florida's secession and the Civil War. She offers a detailed account of the state's January 1861 Secession Convention, the organization of military units at the war's outbreak, the role of Florida's Confederate women in supporting the war effort, the frustrations of dealing with wartime shortages, her father's establishment of a makeshift military hospital at Pine Hill Plantation, her recollections of the battles of Olustee and Natural Bridge, and the collapse of the Confederacy and the Federal occupation of Tallahassee. Part of the volume is written in the form of a diary, although the location of the original is unknown, and it was likely written from memory decades after the events actually occurred. As a result a number of details and dates are incorrect. However, *Through Some Eventful Years* remains a valuable source on Civil War–era Florida.

Susan Bradford Eppes died in Tallahassee on July 2, 1942. She was buried in her family's plot at Pine Hill Plantation.

*David Coles*

**See also** Aid Societies; Confederate Homefront; Hospitals; Plantation Life; Secession; Shortages; Slaveholding Women; Southern Women.

## References and Further Reading

Eppes, Susan Bradford. 1968 [1926]. *Through Some Eventful Years.* Gainesville: University Press of Florida.

Revels, Tracy J. 2004. *Grander in Her Daughters: Florida's Women during the Civil War.* Columbia: University of South Carolina Press.

## Evans, Augusta Jane (1835–1909)

Augusta Jane Evans Wilson was one of the nineteenth-century South's most popular female authors.

Born in Columbus, Georgia, on May 8, 1835, Evans spent most of her childhood and preteen years in San Antonio, Texas, which provided her with the inspiration for her first novel, *Inez: A Tale of the Alamo.* In 1849 Evans moved with her family to Mobile, Alabama, where she lived until her death May 9, 1909. Her works with their dates of publication are as follows: *Inez: A Tale of the Alamo* (1856); *Beulah* (1859); *Macaria; or, Altars of Sacrifice* (1864); *St. Elmo. Or, Saved at Last* (1866); *Vashti; or, Until Death Us Do Part* (1869); *Infelice* (1875); *At the Mercy of Tiberius* (1887); *A Speckled Bird* (1902); and *Devota* (1907).

While many literary critics and reviewers panned her work along with that of many other domestic novelists, some, like O. J. Victor of the *Cosmopolitan Journal,* consistently praised Evans's work in reviews and editorials for her adherence to traditional sentimental values. More important, Evans's readers responded to her novels with enthusiasm. Though most of her works have been forgotten today, scholars consistently identify two of her books, *Beulah* and *St. Elmo,* as national best sellers for their periods of publication. Indeed, G. W. Carleton, Evans's publisher, was so sure of her popularity after the publication of *St. Elmo* that they sent her an advance of $25,000 for any novel she had to submit, sight unseen. Evans's works provoked loyal fans to name or rename homes, towns, steamboats, hotels, and pets as well as countless children in honor of her heroes and heroines. Eudora Welty may have even been one such loyal fan. In *The Ponder Heart,* Welty named the heroine who owned the Beulah Hotel Edna Earle Ponder.

Despite the best-selling status of *Beulah* and *St. Elmo* and the generally prolific nature of her authorship, Evans is best-known for her third novel, *Macaria*. She wrote the novel on scraps of paper while she kept watch over Confederate soldiers' bedsides at Camp Beulah, a makeshift Civil War hospital near her home. Because it was published during the war and appeared initially only in the South, *Macaria* did not sell enough copies to warrant best-seller status. Even so, this war-themed novel contributed significantly to Evans's reputation as one of the leading literary women of the nineteenth-century South. One of only several books published in the South during the war, *Macaria* was arguably the most popular book in the Confederacy. Published on crude brown wrapping paper in 1863 by the Richmond firm of West and Johnson, more than twenty thousand copies eventually circulated throughout the South during the war. Filled with celebrations of the Southern way of life, tributes to the heroism of Southerners, the glorification of Confederate politics and victories, and criticisms of the demagogic North, *Macaria* delighted Southern men and women. The novel was so popular that it generated several romantic war legends. One such tale was based on a passage of the novel in which the hero survived because an enemy bullet hit the ambrotype of his lady love that he carried in his pocket. Similarly, the legend holds that a volume of *Macaria* had saved a Confederate soldier's life when a Yankee bullet struck it as he carried it over his heart. *Macaria* remained a continual favorite among Southerners for many decades after the war, being reprinted in 1867, 1869, 1875, 1887, 1888, 1896, and 1903. Over the years, and especially in the later editions, *Macaria* was altered to remove the most vitriolic denunciations of the North and some of the more obscure analogies, gaining it greater acceptance among Northern readers.

Even during the war, *Macaria*'s publication and popularity were not limited solely to the South. A few months after its Southern debut, Michael Doolady obtained a copy of it through the blockade and promptly published and sold five thousand counterfeits to Evans's Northern fans. While many such fans lauded it for its typically sentimental

virtues, others did not receive *Macaria* as graciously. Northern General G. H. Thomas considered it so damaging to Northern morale that he banned it among his troops. Thereafter, if one of his soldiers was found with the novel, it was confiscated and immediately burned.

Although only the final hundred and twenty pages of the four-hundred-page novel dealt with the war, Evans clearly wrote the whole of *Macaria* in its context. In fact, it is the novel's treatment of the war that Southerners, male and female, probably found the most compelling. *Macaria* had a little something for everyone. For its male readers, it contained detailed descriptions of Southern heroism in the Confederate victory at first Manassas, the glowing account of which was provided to Evans by General Pierre G. T. Beauregard. The purely propagandistic elements decrying the North as the betrayer of the United States' heritage of democracy undoubtedly appealed to Southern politicians. Furthermore, the traditional sentimental trappings of the love story certainly pleased the female audience. Moreover, *Macaria* was a call to arms for Southern women. It gave them a portrait of exemplary feminine wartime behavior in the character of Irene Huntingdon, a beautiful and intelligent young woman born into a life of wealth and privilege, who gave everything up to serve the Confederacy when her beloved, Russell Aubrey, died in battle.

Although none of Evans's novels are purely autobiographical, *Macaria* perhaps comes closest with its nontraditional ending in which the heroine chooses to remain single because her true love dies in the war. In 1861, three years prior to the publication of *Macaria*, Evans had been engaged to James Reed Spaulding, a Northern journalist whom she had met several years earlier. She ended this engagement when the war erupted because she believed their opposing political positions—he was as pro-Northern as she was pro-Southern—would impede any chance for a happy marriage. While writing *Macaria* in the midst of the war and after the end of this engagement, Evans noted in letters to several friends that she had sacrificed love and her chance at matrimony for the Confederacy. As the war progressed well beyond the romantic notion of one decisive battle, the combination of the rising death toll among Southern men and her ever increasing age must have made her chances for true love and marriage seem increasingly slim. Despite all this, in 1868 Evans did marry, finding a spouse in Colonel Lorenzo Madison Wilson, a Confederate veteran several years her senior. They had been married over twenty years when he died in 1891.

A number of scholars have labeled *Macaria* a protofeminist novel, interpreting Evans's decision to keep her heroine Irene single as a feminist act. For these scholars, the nontraditional ending of an otherwise traditional domestic novel signals a significant transformation for Evans. Others disagree. They argue that such conclusions ignore important evidence. First, Evans's overall portrayal of women's proper place and duties in *Macaria* and in all her other works was consistently traditional. Never in any of her novels or in her own life did Evans advocate the overthrow of the traditional gender roles of the patriarchal system. Rather, she recognized the validity of nineteenth-century gender prescriptions. Second, any variation from this theme in *Macaria* was less a symptom of her own change in beliefs and more the result of the historical context of the war. In a region in which tens of thousands of young men would die before the war's end, these scholars argue, Evans empathized with the many Southern women who would face the dilemma of manlessness. For these scholars, Evans's *Macaria* is a traditional work of domestic fiction that recognized a grim future for the postwar South, asserting that, when marriage is impossible as it was for many Southern women during and after the war—and as it seemed for Evans herself—women can find happiness, fulfillment, usefulness, and perhaps even glory in their lives as single women. Her use of a heroine who chooses to remain unmarried was a reaction to the time in which she wrote and an attempt to deal with an emerging South in which many women would find themselves unable to attain the prescribed goal of marriage and domesticity.

*Jennifer Lynn Gross*

**See also** Confederate Homefront; Fiction Writers, Southern; Southern Women; Wartime Literature.

## References and Further Reading

Bakker, Jan. 1987. "Overlooked Progenitors: Independent Women and Southern Renaissance in Augusta Jane Evans Wilson's *Macaria; or, Altars of Sacrifice.*" *The Southern Quarterly* 25: 131–141.

Faust, Drew Gilpin. 1992. "Introduction: *Macaria*, A War Story for Confederate Women." In *Macaria; or, Altars of Sacrifice*, xiii–xxvi. Baton Rouge: Louisiana State University Press.

Fidler, William Perry. 1951. *Augusta Evans Wilson, 1835–1909*. Tuscaloosa: University of Alabama Press.

Jones, Ann Goodwyn. 1981. *Tomorrow Is Another Day: The Woman Writer in the South, 1859–1936*. Baton Rouge: Louisiana State University Press.

Muhlenfeld, Elisabeth. 1985. "The Civil War and Authorship." In *The History of Southern Literature*, edited by Louis Rubin. Baton Rouge: Louisiana State University Press.

## Ewell, Elizabeth "Lizinka" McKay Campbell Brown (1820–1872)

Wealthy, independent, and from a prominent Tennessee family, Lizinka Campbell married Confederate General Richard Stoddert Ewell in 1863 and frequently accompanied him at camp. Following the war, her land holdings were the key to the family's financial success in stock breeding.

Daughter of George Washington Campbell and Harriot Stoddert, Elizabeth McKay Campbell was born in Saint Petersburg while her father was serving as U.S. minister to Russia. Nicknamed in honor of Czar Alexander's wife, Lizinka grew up in Nashville, Tennessee, as the daughter of a prominent statesman.

Richard Stoddert Ewell was Lizinka's cousin, the son of her mother's sister. The two spent time together during Ewell's first term at West Point in 1837 and the couple corresponded in subsequent years. In 1839 Lizinka married slaveholder James Percy Brown, an attaché in the American Embassy in Paris. They were married for five years and had three children before Brown committed suicide in 1844. Lizinka returned to Nashville with her children and spent the next two decades as a wealthy widow, having inherited vast tracts of land in Tennessee, Mississippi, and Missouri from her deceased husband, father, and brother. She had endured great personal loss but was left one of the most wealthy and influential women in the nation.

When Union forces took Nashville in March 1862, Lizinka fled to Virginia. Tennessee's military governor, Andrew Johnson, took up residence in Lizinka's house. When Richard Ewell fell wounded and lost his leg at the Battle of Groveton that fall, Lizinka came to Ewell's side and nursed him during his months of recovery at their cousins' estate of Dunblane in Virginia. The couple then moved to Richmond, where they married at Richmond's St. Paul's Episcopal Church on May 25, 1863.

After Ewell resumed command, Lizinka traveled with him in Virginia and organized her husband's affairs in the field, garnering resentment from her husband's officers. Ewell and his men suffered a series of tactical losses, and he was captured after the fall of Richmond in April 1865. After his capture, Lizinka set about reclaiming the majority of her landholdings that had been seized by the Johnson government. She directly and successfully petitioned the president, who restored her land titles within six months. Following Richard's parole, the couple settled in Tennessee on what would become known as Ewell Farm.

In the postwar years, Ewell Farm became a prominent stockbreeding plantation, being the first to introduce Jersey cattle to the South and also to breed some of the first harness racing horses in the country. In 1872, both Richard and Lizinka Ewell contracted a respiratory infection and died within two days of each other.

*Kristen L. Rouse*

***See also*** Civilian Life; Confederate Homefront; Courtship and Marriage; Family Life, Confederate; Military Invasion and Occupation; Nurses; Southern Women.

**References and Further Reading**

Carmichael, Peter S. 2001. "'All Say They Are under Petticoat Government': Lizinka Brown and Richard Ewell." In *Intimate Strategies: Military Marriages of the Civil War*, edited by Carol Bleser and Lesley Gordon, 87–103. New York: Oxford University Press.

Pfanz, Donald C. 1998. *Richard S. Ewell: A Soldier's Life*. Chapel Hill: University of North Carolina Press.

# F

## Factory Workers, Northern

As the Civil War forced Northern industries to increase the production of war materials, factories expanded and adapted. As men joined the armies and inflation soared, many Northern women took manufacturing positions to support themselves and their families. The factories they entered were becoming increasingly demanding places to work. To meet wartime needs, operators sped up the production process, required lengthened hours and work weeks, adopted machinery that allowed them to cut some positions, and turned a blind eye to increasingly hazardous health and safety conditions.

By 1861, native and immigrant women were firmly established as industrial workers in Northern factories, comprising 50 percent of all industrial workers and a much higher percentage of those in some industries. In spite of such numerical dominance, employers strictly limited the positions available to women to the least skilled and lowest paying.

Northern women's presence in factory work increased throughout the war as employers recognized them as effective workers who could be paid less than men for the same work. Increasing industrial capacity to arm and outfit Union troops, the largest group of fighting men ever assembled by the United States government up to that point, required a rapid shift from peacetime to wartime production. Some areas of manufacture, such as the tent industry, adapted quickly and profitably to the challenge and hired additional women workers to carry out its work.

Factories that had turned out sailcloth prior to the war soon turned to tent making for the Union armies. Women, who had made up the majority of antebellum sailmaking workers, now found work in central production facilities sewing tents, by hand or with sewing machines. Some male tent makers feared the intrusion of women into the factories and complained when women performed what had been men's work.

Not all sewing took place in factories. Some was performed by women hired by subcontractors to assemble products in a shop or their own homes. Subcontractors made their profits by paying seamstresses little or nothing, and this practice effectively lowered wages. Across the North, needlework became some of the most poorly compensated work. Union widows and soldiers' wives flooded into the needle trades, and the oversupply of workers caused wages to plummet while wartime inflation soared. Many women worked through contractors, who pocketed profits while women starved.

The plight of Northern women in needle trades became an issue of public concern. Consequently, male trade unionists, philanthropists, and the women themselves organized in attempts to improve factory work wages and conditions. They created protective associations and trade unions in several cities. Such associations were occasionally able to achieve small improvements in wages and conditions in New York, Philadelphia, and Detroit. Although female protective associations and unions made minimal gains during the war, they laid the groundwork for postwar labor organizations that helped increase pay and improve labor conditions.

In some cases, struggling working women appealed directly to the Secretary of War and President Abraham Lincoln for help. They outlined their grievances, asked that government wages be increased to keep up with inflation, and requested that the government avoid the use of contractors and limit its profits. In Detroit, a protective association organized women and established a price scale and cooperative workrooms. Other associations trained women for new, higher-paying occupations such as operating a sewing machine. They also successfully pushed for protective legislation.

Northern women found more profitable work in other wartime industries, but these options presented greater threats to life and limb. In the summer of 1862, the Allegheny Arsenal hired young women to make cartridges in Lawrenceville, Pennsylvania, where the government did nothing in response to reports of hazardous conditions at the facility. On September 17, 1862, a spark from a wagon wheel ignited gun powder in the factory, causing an explosion in the ammunition room. Seventy young women, most between the ages of sixteen and twenty, were killed in the blast, the worst industrial disaster of the war.

War industries did well, but others languished. In some cases women who had worked in antebellum factories lost their positions during the war or saw their wages decline. Textile factories in Indiana found the war period to be one of decline rather than expansion. The blockade and restrictions on obtaining Southern cotton forced them to curtail production and the hours of workers, most of whom were women. Some factories even closed for short periods. Women workers, the first laid off and the last rehired, were forced to seek charity and relief services to survive.

African American women were some of the most distressed workers of the war. During the war they were generally excluded from factory work because employers feared racially motivated violence. White female factory workers, who feared competition, often physically assaulted Northern black women.

*Theresa R. McDevitt*

Filling cartridges at the United States Arsenal at Watertown, Massachusetts, *Harper's Weekly*, July 20, 1861. (Library of Congress)

*See also* Allegheny Arsenal, Explosion at (September 17, 1862); Civilian Life; Factory Workers, Southern; Free Blacks; Immigrant Women; Northern Women; Union Homefront; Urban Women, Northern; Wartime Employment.

**References and Further Reading**

Ashendel, Anita. 1997. "Fabricating Independence: Industrial Labor in Antebellum Indiana." *Michigan Historical Review* 23 (2): 1–24.

Foner, Philip Sheldon. 1980. *Women and the American Labor Movement: From Colonial Times to the Eve of World War I.* New York: Free Press.

Kessler-Harris, Alice. 2003. *Out to Work: A History of Wage-Earning Women in the United States.* New York: Oxford University Press.

Wertheimer, Barbara M. 1977. *We Were There: The Story of Working Women in America.* New York: Pantheon.

Wilson, Mark R. 2001. "The Extensive Side of Nineteenth-Century Military Economy: The Tent Industry in the Northern United States during the Civil War." *Enterprise and Society: The International Journal of Business History* 2: 297–337.

Wudarczyk, James. 1999. *Pittsburgh's Forgotten Allegheny Arsenal.* Apollo, PA: Closson Press.

## Factory Workers, Southern

During the Civil War, thousands of black and white women worked in Southern factories. The wartime need to clothe, house, and arm the Confederate forces fostered an expansion of old and the creation of new manufacturing establishments and opened more positions to potential laborers. Economic necessity pushed more and more white women into industrial work to provide for themselves and their families. As enslaved males were impressed to work nearer the front, enslaved women took their places in factories. As the war progressed, increasing numbers of women took up places in Southern factories.

The antebellum economy of the South was overwhelmingly agricultural, but by 1860 the region had twenty thousand manufacturing establishments employing one hundred and ten thousand workers. Enslaved and free women and children made up a significant percentage of factory operatives, but they were generally restricted to the least skilled occupations with the lowest compensation.

White women were particularly well represented in textile production. In the antebellum era, poor families in the rural South attempted to improve their economic condition by moving to mill towns for work in nearby textile mills. There, women and children made up the majority of the workforce but were restricted to the lowest-skilled positions. Frequent fires, epidemic levels of communicable diseases, noisy machines, choking fibers, as well as heat and poor ventilation made working hazardous as well as uncomfortable. In addition, the pay these workers received barely provided for basic necessities.

African American slave women labored in many industries, including the production of textiles, hemp, and tobacco, as well as the milling of sugar, grist, and rice. The gendered division of labor that governed white factory workers did not apply to black women. As a result, slave women were compelled to perform the same heavy work as men in iron working, lumbering, building levees, and railroads.

The war spawned new industries, and mills already employing women expanded production dramatically to produce war goods, such as uniforms, blankets, and tents. Needing a way to provide for their families, women and their children entered factory employment in greater numbers than they had during the antebellum period. Jobs available to women remained the lowest paying and least skilled. Enslaved women in factories found strict controls on their forced labor and a deterioration in their already poor housing, clothing, and food allowances.

Life as a Confederate factory worker proved exhausting and often dangerous for women. The drive to produce goods for civilian and military consumers quickly led factory operators to extend workdays and workweeks, speed up production, and turn a blind eye to the safety and health concerns of their workers, particularly in hazardous new wartime industries. As production quotas increased, operators extended the workday from twelve to eighteen hours and the workweek from five to six days. Work was also sped up, and workers were directed to tend more than one machine. Conditions were increasingly unhealthy and hazardous.

Furthermore, disruptions caused by enemy forces became added threats to workers in Southern factories. Invading troops commonly destroyed factories and the housing where operatives lived, and they sometimes forcefully removed female factory workers from their jobs and homes.

Munitions work was one of the most dangerous of the new wartime industries that employed women. An 1863 explosion in Richmond's Confederate States' Laboratory, where several hundred women worked making munitions, cost nearly fifty women and girls their lives. The casualties included girls as young as ten and young women in their early twenties. An investigation into the tragedy, the Confederacy's worst homefront disaster, discovered that the negligence of a young Irish female factory worker caused the explosion. However, it also revealed that poor safety conditions had increased the amount of damage caused—both to the factory and to the lives of its female workers.

Factory work in the Confederacy could also be dangerous as a result of the war itself. In some instances, wartime workers found themselves suddenly unemployed and without housing when invading troops reached them. In a dramatic episode in July 1864, hundreds of textile workers, many of them women, in the cotton and wool mills of Roswell and Sweetwater, Georgia, found their lives forever changed when General William T. Sherman's forces swept through the area. Invading Union troops destroyed the factories and the mill housing where textile employees lived. More surprising was Sherman's order to have the factory employees evacuated and sent north to Indiana. He considered these women traitors and wanted to prevent them from working in other factories to supply Confederate troops. Although the evacuation and transportation of factory workers was rare, women's loss of employment during the war was less so. By the end of the war, the destruction of textile mills by both retreating Confederates and invading Union soldiers was common.

Enslaved women found the war period offered even worse conditions for them than did the antebellum era. As male slaves were impressed for warfront work, African American women were sent to replace them in iron furnaces, in cotton and woolen mills, and in the production of war-related goods such as friction matches, army boots, shoes, hats, and saddles. With their work closely supervised and physical punishments common, black women were expected to do more than they had before, even as their already low housing, food, and clothing allowances were cut due to scarcity.

*Theresa R. McDevitt*

**See also** African American Women; Confederate Homefront; Factory Workers, Northern; Roswell Women; Southern Women; Urban Women, Southern.

**References and Further Reading**

Burton, David L. 1982. "Richmond's Great Homefront Disaster: Friday the 13th." *Civil War Times Illustrated* 21 (6): 36–41.

Delfino, Susanna, and Michele Gillespie, eds. 2002. *Neither Lady Nor Slave: Working Women of the Old South.* Chapel Hill: University of North Carolina Press.

Edwards, Stewart C. 2001. "'To Do the Manufacturing for the South.'" *Georgia Historical Quarterly* 85 (4): 538–554.

Foner, Philip Sheldon. 1979. *Women and the American Labor Movement: From Colonial Times to the Eve of World War I.* New York: Free Press.

Kessler-Harris, Alice. 2003. *Out to Work: A History of Wage-Earning Women in the United States.* New York: Oxford University Press.

Starobin, Robert S. 1970. *Industrial Slavery in the Old South.* New York: Oxford University Press.

Wertheimer, Barbara M. 1977. *We Were There: The Story of Working Women in America.* New York: Pantheon.

## Fairs and Bazaars

A popular method of raising money for charitable purposes, nineteenth-century fairs and bazaars were planned and carried out by charitable people, but they were dominated by women. They combined the opportunity for social interaction and using domestic skills with charitable work. Wartime fairs and bazaars generally raised money for soldiers or freedmen and allowed women to gain management skills.

Fundraising bazaars were often elaborate affairs in both regions. Planning began months before the occasion. At meetings, participants determined goals and elected general managers for the event. Representatives of as many charitable groups as possible attended the meetings, which provided opportunities to catch up with old friends and make new ones. Women planned their own participation carefully. Some agreed to staff booths to sell hand-made goods. Others served as hostesses for meals or entertainments, or they participated in concerts, plays, or tableaux. Planning committees recruited women to solicit and collect donations of money or materials or to invite dignitaries to attend. They chose the dates of the events and the location, and set entrance fees. All these activities reflected ante-bellum methods used to support charities.

In many ways the labor that Southern and North-ern women performed for fairs was an extension of their domestic responsibilities. Many fairs and bazaars were organized around food. Strawberry fes-tivals, oyster suppers, harvest meals, teas, and dessert tables formed the core of most fundraising efforts. Even the smallest event had some food or beverages for sale. Women collected, prepared, and sold food. The women added tables filled with hand-made articles for sale. These items showed off their sewing and artistic skills just as the foods highlighted their culinary skills. Women sold items that included embroidery-covered caps, pen wipers, cigar cases, slippers, feathered items, hair jewelry, and shell, wax, paper, or feathered flowers. In the South, women highlighted items that demonstrated their resource-fulness in the face of shortages. At many bazaars spe-cific groups of women sponsored themed tables. Planning the elaborate displays took many hours but often proved fun and satisfying for participants.

The planners of fairs called on the men of their towns to help. Men who had particular skills donated their talents for entertainment. If the com-munity had a brass band, the men were invited to perform. Businessmen were asked to display their most modern items and encouraged to donate things for auctions. Women also solicited farmers to donate produce for the food tables. Men were also expected to purchase entry tickets for themselves and their families as well as many items and as much food as their wallets allowed.

During the Civil War, the number of charities receiving the money made by Southern and North-ern women increased. Orphans, impoverished fam-ilies, and churches continued to be the beneficiar-ies of donations from the affairs, but most of the efforts raised funds to support the troops. Initially women held small events to raise money for shirts, blankets, food, or medicine for local men who went to war. Eventually, most local Northern groups real-ized that they could be more effective working for the national aid societies, like the United States Christian Commission (USCC) and the United States Sanitary Commission (USSC). Without an overarching organization like the USSC, Southern fairs were locally managed and money was usually distributed to individual Confederate regiments.

In early 1863, the women of Lowell, Massachu-setts, held a fair to support the USSC. They con-tacted every charitable group in the town for help. Each group agreed to sponsor some part of the

Abraham Lincoln to Ladies in Charge of North-Western Sanitary Fair, Monday, October 26, 1863. The Letter accompanied the original draft of the Emancipation Proclamation, which Lincoln donated for exhibit at the North-Western Sanitary Fair. (Library of Congress)

undertaking, and the successful effort provided almost $5,000 for the USSC. The fair in Lowell set off a wave of giant fairs across the Union.

The women of the Northwest Branch of the USSC at Chicago began planning their first fair in the fall of 1863. They invited representatives of patriotic and charitable groups throughout Illinois, Iowa, and Wisconsin to attend their two-day organizing meeting and mailed nearly twenty thousand flyers to members of the groups as well as to town halls, newspaper editors, and ministers. The managers of the fair hired six buildings for the two-week event and planned a dining hall with more than a dozen tables that would be set and restocked up to five times a day during the fair. The ladies solicited donations of artifacts from the war and received captured swords, battlefield mementoes, flags taken from Rebel units, as well as tattered and torn ensigns from highly decorated units. Even President Abraham Lincoln responded by donating a copy of the Emancipation Proclamation. Beginning on October 27, 1863, five thousand people a day poured into the fairgrounds. Each paid 75¢ to visit the curiosities gathered in the halls, taste the many delicacies donated, play games, view floral displays, and attend concerts and speeches. The women raised nearly $79,000 through the Chicago fair. For the remainder of the war, other large fairs were held throughout the North.

Fairs in both regions provided the funds to establish soldiers' homes and homes for the soldiers' orphans. The events tested the abilities of women and encouraged their creativity in many fields. Women wrote and published newspapers, ran post offices during the fairs, kept detailed records and accounts, and negotiated for the purchase or rental of halls. In addition, participating women published accounts of their events and handled the press, dignitaries, and crowds. Their efforts provided comfort for needy men, women, and children, and they helped make charitable organizations financially strong.

*Karen A. Kehoe*

**See also** Columbia Bazaar (January 17–21, 1865); Confederate Homefront; Fundraising; Northern Women; Southern Women; Union Homefront;

United States Christian Commission; United States Sanitary Commission

**References and Further Reading**
Attie, Jeanie. 1998. *Patriotic Toil: Northern Women and the American Civil War*. Ithaca, NY: Cornell University Press.
Gallman, James Mathew. 1994. *The North Fights the Civil War: The Home Front*. Chicago: Ivan R. Dee.
Gordon, Beverly. 1998. *Bazaars and Fair Ladies*. Knoxville: University of Tennessee Press.
Henshaw, Sarah Edwards. 1868. *Our Branch and Its Tributaries*. Chicago: A. L. Sewell.
Livermore, Mary Ashton Rice. 1888. *My Story of the War*. Hartford, CT: A. D. Worthington and Company.

## Family Life, Confederate

The American Civil War exacted as heavy a toll on the families of Confederates as it did on the buildings, farms, and factories on which those families depended. The material burdens created by supporting Confederate armies, the physical necessity of sustaining slavery without men to police the institution, and the hardships and deprivations caused by Union invasion, confiscation, and hard war challenged every family and destroyed many. The nature of the war, especially the Union occupation of parts of the South and the Confederacy's defeat, challenged the intellectual and social basis of the Southern family. Before the war, many Southerners thought in terms of households—an extended group of people joined by their common dependency on a single head. But the war forced Southerners to abandon the obligations that brought indirect blood and nonblood relations under their roofs and led most white Southerners to reconceptualize their domestic space in terms of their immediate families. Both femininity and masculinity underwent significant changes during the war, and both changed shape once again at the war's end. The contingencies of war forced women into new occupations and roles, and the defeat of Confederate armies undercut the central element of prewar masculinity: protection of one's dependents. The political, economic, and, above all, racial challenges provided by Reconstruction compelled white Southerners to rebel against the changes in family organization created by the war and to recreate a traditional, hierarchical model of family life.

The nearly total absence of adult-age white men on the homefront marked the most important social effect of the war. In communities all across the Confederacy, enlistment rates for the armies routinely ran to 60, 70, or even 80 percent of eligible men. Women thus bore the brunt of sustaining their families. In addition to the pre-existing duties of raising children and household management, women were obligated to assume more active roles as income earners or, for rural families, as full-time farmers. These new duties concerned many women who believed in the prewar division of paid and unpaid labor between men and women. Many elite women looked with scorn on white women who resorted to paid work. The sight of women walking through the streets of major towns on their way to work in the mornings at factories, offices, and shops unsettled many observers. Eventually, however, social conservatives reconciled themselves to the changes, arguing that, if victory required the transformation of gender roles, they would accept the new conditions.

Among the most problematic new domestic responsibilities that women faced was the management and control of slaves. In slaveholding families, women were now responsible for the oversight of all slaves. They had to enforce rules, including physical punishment, something that women did not formerly do and that most did not like. Women were not the only ones who noticed this problem. Slaves often exploited signs of weakness among female masters, as women knew all too well. Letters to soldier husbands from wives left alone to manage slaves reveal the women's awareness that they did not command the respect that men did.

The burden of new responsibilities weighed even heavier on women because their prewar duties became vastly more difficult during the war. By mid-1862, the most pressing issue was ensuring a steady supply of food. The demands of Confederate armies took precedence for the nation, and huge volumes of foodstuffs were transferred to camps and battlefields across the region. Previously com-monplace items, like coffee, sugar, and fresh fruit, became rare and eventually unobtainable in many places. Confederate women exercised significant creativity in inventing substitutes for daily items, but the absence of satisfying and nutritious food was felt by all families. Prices rose continually throughout the war, exacerbating the problems of scarcity. Despite the difficulties of securing food, clothing, and shelter, women struggled to maintain family connections by writing to distant relatives, by spreading news and stories of loved ones, and by convening with local friends and family to celebrate events whenever possible.

Location profoundly affected how Confederate families experienced the war. Unlike the soldiers, who moved around, most white families remained in their home communities. People who resided in the interior parts of the Confederacy, such as central and western North and South Carolina and central and southern Georgia, did not see Union troops until late in the war, if ever. Many of these communities suffered the same strains of scarcity and high prices as communities closer to the centers of military action, but they did not have to contend with the added problem of occupation. Families in northern and central Virginia, east and central Tennessee, and northern Alabama, by contrast, experienced persistent Union invasion and occupation from the early days of the war. Places that were permanently occupied, such as New Orleans, remained reasonably stable, and families could usually obtain food and news and mail. But places along the shifting borders between Union and Confederate territory saw the harshest conditions. Periodic raids from troops of either army kept civilian institutions perpetually suspended. As a result, churches, schools, and courts all discontinued their activities or held them irregularly. Raids likewise consumed most of the agricultural products of these regions, exacerbating the problem of scarcity. The solution to such problems in these areas required Confederates to adopt more flexible attitudes toward their relationships with Union soldiers than most of them would have preferred. In the lower Shenandoah Valley of Virginia, for instance, Confederate civilians traded with enemy soldiers to obtain the necessities of life, rejoicing in opportunities to gouge Yankees who were desperate for tobacco and ignoring the ethical problems raised by cooperating with their oppressors.

For families who felt the shock of invasion too often or suffered under the anxiety of what trauma such an event would bring, abandoning their homes became an alternative. The first refugees were the wealthy planters and their families who abandoned the South Carolina Sea Islands in the wake of the Union navy's capture of the region in November 1861. Unlike many other refugees, the Sea Islanders often had second homes at inland locations, so their movement was more of a relocation than a flight. For most refugees in the Confederacy, leaving one's home meant a leap into the void. The effort to hold together household possessions, slaves, and children in the confusion of movement often overwhelmed people. The reports of refugees vividly capture the chaos of flight, as slaves sought opportunities to escape and household goods spilled from overstuffed caravans. Many travelers lost their slaves in flight. Becoming refugees thus often precipitated the very event that Southerners anticipated the Yankees were planning to force upon them: the loss of their slaves, homes, and worldly possessions.

Surprisingly, the turmoil of war did not dim Southern notions of domesticity. Women labored to maintain regular household routines as much as possible, and both families and soldiers focused on the themes of domestic affection in their correspondence. If anything, soldiers developed more highly attuned romantic sensibilities. Long days in camp, surrounded by other lonesome men, led most correspondents to focus their attention on the glories and memories of their loving families. Soldiers lamented their missed families and homes. Few could think of anything beyond the return to normalcy that home promised, and soldiers filled letter after letter with plaintive reminiscences of times together and dreams of a reunited future.

The fact of asserting that their families were the center of their lives and that their identities as husbands and fathers were the most important to them personally had profound ramifications for how soldiers understood their military duties. The majority of soldiers conceptualized their families as the main reason for their sacrifice, but, as those families suffered hardships, soldiers differed in their responses. Some men, responding to pleas from their wives or children that they abandon the armies and return to protect them, deserted and assumed what they took to be their primary obligation: ensuring the survival of their family. The perceived need for desertion seems to have been more common for the men whose families were exposed to Northern armies late in the war, though it never affected a majority of men in uniform. Many North Carolina and Georgia soldiers received requests for help from home in late 1864 and early 1865, and some subsequently deserted.

Far more men, however, stayed in the army, and their decisions were, more often than not, based on supporting their families as well. These men believed that they could most effectively protect their loved ones by sticking with the armies and saw the preservation of the Confederacy as a crucial precondition for the success of their domestic lives. The more hardship families suffered, the more it strengthened the sense among some soldiers that they must not give up. Even as families might have preferred that their soldier husbands or fathers return home, soldiers understood a renewed obligation based on the sacrifices of loved ones at home. The shared sense of sacrifice, something that was hardly avoidable for most Confederates by 1863 given the scarcity of food, bonded civilians and soldiers together in a deep commitment to creating a truly independent Confederacy.

The unexpected situation in which men felt they could protect their starving families by remaining in the armies was not the only unpredictable outcome of the war and its effect on Confederate families. Women themselves had substantially reshaped the contours of Southern femininity through their willingness to adopt new duties traditionally reserved for men. Ultimate defeat in the war made clear that Southern white men had failed in their basic masculine duty of protecting their dependents. These two elements put the system of gender relations on which the Southern family rested under great strain. One possible outcome could have been the creation of a new system of gender duties, with public and private responsibilities balanced more evenly between men and women. Instead, in the postwar era many white Southerners embraced a return to an extreme version of prewar gender relations. The shock of defeat and the necessity of shoring up the idea of hierarchy in a suddenly emancipated society overwhelmed the movement toward shared duties that started during the war.

The conservative turn in gender relations could also be seen in the shape that Southern families assumed in the aftermath of the conflict. Throughout the conflict, enslaved African Americans had seized opportunities to find freedom—running away to the Union army or the North and actively aiding the Union army as it entered the South—and most Southern whites interpreted this behavior as a betrayal. Long conditioned to regard slaves as docile and obedient, whites were shocked and angered to find an effective enemy in their midst. As a result, most of them interpreted emancipation as absolving them of any future responsibilities toward African Americans. The effort to subjugate black Southerners in the postwar world required nearly unanimous participation by whites. This solidarity grew out of and strengthened the renewed commitment to a hierarchical form of gender relations.

The conservatism that dominated Southerners' postwar recreation of gender roles also influenced the size and shape that their families assumed. The violence and hardships of war burned away much of the Southern household. Confederate defeat, by repudiating the central value of Southern masculinity, compelled men to draw much narrower boundaries around their homes in the postwar era. The households that had characterized the antebellum period became the families of the postbellum period. The result was a fracturing of one of the antebellum South's most important social institutions. The new family included only whites, and the bonds among members were cemented by an affection strengthened by the absences and hardships caused by the war. It was this institution, a family born of war, that carried the white South through Reconstruction and into the era of Jim Crow.

*Aaron Sheehan-Dean*

*See also* African American Women; Civilian Life; Confederate Homefront; Destruction of Homes; Destruction of Personal Property; Domesticity; Food; Guerrilla Warfare; Military Invasion and Occupation; Nationalism, Confederate; Nonslaveholding Southerners; Shortages; Slaveholding Women; Southern Women.

**References and Further Reading**

Ash, Stephen. 1995. *When the Yankees Came: Conflict and Chaos in the Occupied South.* Chapel Hill: University of North Carolina Press.

Berry III, Stephen W. 2003. *All That Makes a Man: Love and Ambition in the Civil War South.* New York: Oxford University Press.

Bleser, Carol K., and Lesley J. Gordon, eds. 2001. *Intimate Strategies of the Civil War: Military Commanders and Their Wives.* New York: Oxford University Press.

Faust, Drew Gilpin. 1996. *Mothers of Invention: Women of the Slaveholding South in the American Civil War.* Chapel Hill: University of North Carolina Press.

Rable, George. 1991. *Civil Wars: Women and the Crisis of Southern Nationalism.* Urbana: University of Illinois Press.

Whites, LeeAnn. 1995. *The Civil War as a Crisis in Gender: Augusta, Georgia, 1860–1890.* Athens: University of Georgia Press.

## Family Life, Union

The initial impact of the war on the Northern family was the separation of family members from one another. Fathers, husbands, and brothers enlisted and prepared to leave for camp, and mothers, wives, and sisters assisted their new recruits in support of the cause. Victorian ideals about gender roles and the family shaped how Union soldiers and female civilians participated in and were affected by the war.

By the mid-nineteenth century, middle-class husbands and wives gradually viewed one another as partners in a companionate marriage. In addition, children were regarded as individuals who required love and nurture. As parents became increasingly conscientious about child rearing and child development, a new division of sex roles emerged within the family. The father assumed the position of sole breadwinner for the family and the wife reared the children. Men provided the economic support and protection for the home, while

Union Gen. Edward O. C. Ord with his wife and child at the residence of Jefferson Davis. In the doorway is the table on which the surrender of Gen. Robert E. Lee was signed, April 1865. Gen. Ord was a career officer. He and his wife, Mary Mercer Thompson, had thirteen children. (Library of Congress)

women emotionally nurtured, spiritually guided, and physically refreshed family members.

The antebellum North had many classes of people, however. The working-class family had much in common with the middle-class family. In these households, the two-parent, nuclear family was the norm; the wife seldom worked for wages outside the house; the division of labor was gender based; and family members treasured the sanctity of the home. Most of these similarities derived not from emulation, but rather from economic necessity.

Home ownership and a gendered division of labor allowed families autonomy within the household and gave them a place to reassert family and class obligations. The lifestyles of working-class families differed from middle-class families most in their use of the streets. Members of working-class families scavenged, hawked, sold goods, and socialized outside their homes.

Black families utilized similar techniques to ensure the family's survival. The two-parent, male-headed, nuclear family was the dominant household among free blacks. African American families, like their white counterparts, provided both emotional and physical support for their members. They recognized the sanctity of marriage and had a gender-based division of labor. Although similarities existed between working-class and African American families, racism and economics further defined the lives of African Americans. Racism in the North affected the type of employment blacks could get, where they lived, and their access to education and transportation. These factors in turn ultimately influenced a family's income, status, and survivability. The two greatest sources of support for black families came from the African American community and from the emotional strength and hope gained from religion.

Nuclear family, male-headed households responded to President Abraham Lincoln's call for troops on April 15, 1861. A whirlwind of activity began as Northern citizens gathered for local war meetings. Across the North, white and black, old and young, men, women, and children met to discuss the impending war. As the protectors of hearth and home, men enlisted in local regiments, and the women of their families helped them get ready for battle.

Women also took on their own tasks in preparation for war. Following the tradition of antebellum benevolence work, Northern women created soldiers' aid societies to send their men to war with supplies. Women also presented the men of their communities with a regimental flag at ritualized farewell celebrations attended by most of the town. Over the course of the Civil War, tens of thousands of women would work for soldiers' aid societies as their part in putting down the rebellion.

Children, too, felt the impact of the war and were perhaps its most innocent victims. They were inundated with war news and the patriotic fervor that swept through their towns. Boys and girls quickly took up the cause by scraping lint at their local aid society, participating in concerts to raise money for society supplies, and contributing their meager savings or clothes for runaway slaves or contrabands. Some also began their own juvenile societies. Children enjoyed dressing in military garb or wearing patriotic ribbons, visiting the local recruiting camps and watching the soldiers drill, and cheering local regiments as they marched off to war.

But families learned that the festivities ended as the last soldiers marched out of town. With their men gone, it fell to the women to maintain the family, household, farm, and business. These multiple duties put tremendous pressure on women during the war. Not only did many women become single parents overnight, but they also had to continue their own household chores while taking on the responsibility for their husbands' work. Some women reveled in the expanded responsibility and freedoms attached to male authority. Many became good farm and business managers, thereby relieving their husbands' concerns about the prosperity and security of home. Other women dreaded the public interaction with men that business required, as well as the anxiety created by dealing with business finances. In addition some were simply not suited to this work and willingly gave up the duties when their husbands returned home. Because farming and business had primarily been the purview of men, women generally relied on male relatives on the homefront to guide them in money matters and farming decisions. Women also wrote letters to their husbands seeking advice on plowing, planting, weeding, and harvesting crops, as well as on basic home maintenance. However, the unreliability of the mail and the inability of husbands to understand wartime circumstances on the homefront, eventually led women to trust their own opinions. The deaths of loved ones brought the greatest hardships, leaving permanent emotional and physical scars on families.

Wives, mothers, daughters, and sisters used letters to stay in contact with their soldiers. Letters represented not only communication with family and friends, but also an essential psychological link with loved ones. In their correspondence, soldiers treated relatives to a taste of military life, and civilians responded with domestic details. Letters connected the soldiers to their homes and families by allowing them an outlet through which they could reveal the woes of war and receive news of the world outside the army. In addition, soldiers' families felt connected to the cause through their volunteers. They followed the battles through reports in local newspapers and through letters from loved ones. Because mail could be slow and newspapers often printed faulty information, the war caused much stress for families at home. Too often newspapers reported men dead when in fact they had survived a battle. In other instances, the papers reported the reverse: that someone who had died had survived.

Along with these psychological difficulties, many soldiers' families suffered physical hardships. Many civilian families depended on their soldier's pay to sustain them. A private in the Union army earned $13 a month at the start of the war and saw an increase to $16 a month toward the end of the war. Because the paymaster averaged a six-month backlog on pay, by the time the soldier was paid, he and his family had often accrued debts that needed immediate attention. Likewise, some soldiers gambled and drank their money away, leaving their families destitute.

Wives tried to supplement the family income through paid work. However, because of household chores and child care duties, women were not always successful. Some soldiers' aid societies paid poor soldiers' wives and widows to sew shirts and knit socks for the soldiers. For example, the wives and daughters of soldiers in Chelsea, Massachusetts, received 11¢ per shirt. Each woman usually made four shirts a day, but still made hardly enough money to survive with inflated war prices. The most destitute soldiers' wives received food from sympathetic aid societies.

The desperate times faced by white families could not compare to the destitution experienced by black soldiers' families during the war. When Lincoln called for troops in 1861, Northern blacks, like their white counterparts, gathered in war meetings. However, when African Americans offered their services, they were turned away. They bided their time, and, after the passage of the Emancipation Proclamation and the Enrollment Act in 1863, black men were finally allowed to enlist in the Union army. As had white men and women, black families answered their country's call. African American men enlisted in colored regiments, and black women worked in soldiers' aid societies, joining existing societies or forming their own. As did white soldiers, black enlistees kept in contact with loved ones through the mail. Black families could also learn about their soldiers in the pages of African American–owned newspapers like Philadelphia's *Christian Recorder* or New York City's *Anglo-African.*

African American soldiers and their families faced a difficulty specific to their race. Pay became perhaps the most destructive issue for African American soldiers. Despite the fact that Northern black men had enlisted with the promise of receiving the same pay as their white counterparts, the soldiers soon discovered that this equality was not a reality. The paymaster offered black soldiers a salary of only $10 a month with $3 deducted for uniforms. White Union soldiers received a higher pay rate and had no uniform deduction. Out of principle, many black soldiers refused to accept the pay offered, believing that their refusal would serve the cause of freedom and equality. Unfortunately, the soldiers' gesture put pressures on their families, who were struggling to make ends meet. Families sent letters detailing their difficulties; some were starving and freezing, while others ended up in the poorhouse. Not until August 1864 did Congress rectify the situation, passing a bill that provided equal pay for black soldiers. In the meantime, black women, already at the bottom of the pay scale, had to turn to help from the black community.

In spite of the fact that African American men were risking their lives on the battlefield for the Union, blacks were routinely subjected to racism at home. The Enrollment Act allowed for the enlistment of black soldiers, but many Northern whites did not agree with the idea. Some civilian whites took out their frustrations with Lincoln's policies on black men and women. In addition, most Northern restaurants, hotels, schools, streetcars, and trains were segregated, and blacks were denied equal access to jobs and housing. Racism figured prominently in the July 1863 New York City draft riots when working-class Irish mobs targeted African Americans. In a violent backlash against Lincoln's

Emancipation Proclamation and the Enrollment Act, hundreds of black citizens were forced from the city, fearing for their lives. After four days of violence, the mobs had killed eleven blacks, destroyed and looted numerous black homes, and burned the Colored Orphan Asylum.

The exigencies of war shaped family life for all in the Union—white or black, middle or lower class. Women of all ages, classes, and races equipped and sent their men to war and then took on the additional work of the homefront household. They aided the war effort through work in soldiers' aid societies and by sending letters to remind soldiers of the goodness of home. They often endured psychological hardships brought on by having a loved one in harm's way. Many lower-class and black women suffered physical hardships when their husbands' pay was delayed. Overall, Northern women felt the sacrifices and hardships that war brought and worked to preserve their families throughout the conflict.

*Patricia Richard*

**See also** Aid Societies; Civilian Life; Domesticity; Draft Riots and Resistance; Free Blacks; Fundraising; Girlhood and Adolescence; Letter Writing; Northern Women; Shortages.

**References and Further Reading**
Coontz, Stephanie. 1999. "Working-Class Families, 1870–1890." In *American Families: A Multicultural Reader*, edited by Stephanie Coontz, Maya Parson, and Gabrielle Raley, 94–127. New York: Routledge.
Forbes, Ella. 1998. *African American Women during the Civil War*. New York: Garland Publishing.
Gallman, J. Matthew. 1994. *The North Fights the Civil War: The Home Front*. Chicago: Ivan R. Dee.
Horton, James Oliver, and Lois E. Horton. 1979. *Black Bostonians: Family Life and Community Struggle in the Antebellum North*. New York: Holmes and Meier Publishers.
Mitchell, Reid. 1993. *The Vacant Chair: The Northern Soldier Leaves Home*. New York: Oxford University Press.
Paludan, Phillip Shaw. 1998. *War and Home: The Civil War Encounter*. Milwaukee, WI: Marquette University Press.
Stevenson, Louise L. 1991. *The Victorian Homefront: American Thought and Culture, 1860–1880*. New York: Twayne Publishers.

## Farm Work

Farm families confronted a major problem during the Civil War. In particular, they had to determine who would raise the crops and livestock when the men were away. Women had always participated in farm work, although the extent to which they did so varied by ethnic group, socioeconomic status, and location. On many farms, women were responsible for some dairying, poultry care, and occasionally assisting with fieldwork during planting and harvest seasons when they could be spared from other household, family, or profit-making obligations.

With as many as one-third of Northern farm laborers and a smaller but still significant portion of owners and tenants in military service, it was inevitable that women would help fill the void. In 1863, a writer for the Illinois Agricultural Society urged women to put on thick-soled shoes, sunbonnets, and their "other dress" to take the place of men. Women informed their husbands of their willingness to take on all duties during the war, including raising crops, paying taxes, and otherwise supporting the war effort. As a result, during the Civil War, Northern food and fiber production soared even as many rural communities lost manpower. While mechanization played an important part of the solution to the labor problem, farm women were critical workers in the fields and farmyards and also important decision makers on Northern farms. The women who labored on Northern farms helped preserve the Union by doing more fieldwork or even adding new tasks to their already heavy burden of taking care of homes, raising children, producing and preserving food, and making clothes.

Contemporary observers noted the important role that women played in Northern agriculture. In 1863 Mary Livermore of the United States Sanitary Commission, traveling through Wisconsin and Iowa, commented on the prevalence of women in the fields, as well as their ability to bind sheaves with precision and their skill in using horses to thresh grain by treading. The *New England Farmer* reported in 1863 that women seldom worked in the fields before the war, but thousands took on the tasks necessary during wartime. Throughout the Northwest, women operated reapers, bound and shocked sheaves, and loaded grain during the summer small grain harvest. One Milwaukee correspondent reported, after a trip to Wisconsin's "northern counties" in 1864, that the fields were filled with women and children doing farm labor. That year an editor of a Green Bay paper noted that the work of immigrant farm women made up for the loss of male laborers to the armies. European-born women, unlike many native-born women, shared a tradition in which they regularly performed fieldwork. This work was stigmatized in peacetime but became an asset in wartime.

Correspondence between wives and their soldier husbands details the specific accommodations they made on the farm to meet the crisis. In New York, Rosella Benton and her children conducted tillage, planted field and garden crops, harvested, milked seven cows, and made good money selling butter and eggs. Benton hired men to help with the most physically demanding labor of haymaking, but she hired a girl to do housework while she did the barn chores and fieldwork. Similarly, Iowan Sarah Carr Lacey supported her family by milking nine cows and selling butter at high wartime prices after her husband enlisted in 1862. In addition to taking care of a garden and milk cow on her family's Iowa farm, Maria Sharp struggled to chop enough wood to warm her family, took in washing for other families, and stripped sorghum cane for molasses. The Roberts sisters of western New York conducted all the family harvesting, haying, dairying, and cheese manufacturing on their farm.

Not all women did as much farm work as Benton, Lacey, Sharp, or the Roberts women. Officers' wives or women who married men with large estates frequently engaged tenants to run the farm in their husbands' absence. Women sometimes made arrangements with tenants, although the men cautioned their wives not to rent to Copperheads. Mary Vermillion's husband, an infantry captain, stated that he would rather let their farm remain idle than rent to a Copperhead. Women frequently relied on their fathers or in-laws as farm labor.

There was more to farm work than simply tending crops and livestock. Managing the farm was also work, and women often assumed responsibility for this critical task, even instructing hired men and tenants. In most cases, the degree to which women managed the family farm varied with the degree of cooperation from the absent husband. Rosella Benton not only did much of the physical labor on the family's New York farm, but she also made important decisions about marketing products. The longer they were separated, the less her husband John made management suggestions, recognizing that he was not in the best position to understand the situation back home. Other women were passive about managing the farm, relying more on the absent husband or soliciting advice on marketing livestock and other issues from kin and neighbors.

The war was a time of increased production in the Northern states in spite of manpower losses due to military service. While historians have attributed much of these increases to the mechanization of farming, particularly the rapid spread of the mechanical reaper, it was still important to have people to sow, bind, and thresh the grain. Furthermore, most farm work was done by hand, most notably raising the corn crop, tending livestock, and growing truck crops. Immigration to the North continued during the war and provided some of the labor needed to meet domestic and foreign demand for Northern commodities, but women's contributions played a decisive role in keeping farms intact and productive during the war.

*Joe L. Anderson*

**See also** Immigrant Women; Northern Women; Plantation Life; Rural Women; Union Homefront; Wartime Employment.

### References and Further Reading
Elder, Donald C. III, ed. 2003. *Love amid the Turmoil: The Civil War Letters of William and Mary Vermillion.* Iowa City: University of Iowa Press.
McMurry, Sally. 1995. *Transforming Rural Life: Dairying Families and Agricultural Change, 1820–1885.* Baltimore, MD: Johns Hopkins University Press.
Paludan, Phillip S. 1988. *"A People's Contest": The Union and Civil War, 1861–1865.* New York: Harper & Row.
Riley, Glenda. 1981. *Frontierswomen: The Iowa Experience.* Ames: Iowa State University Press.

## Felton, Rebecca Ann Latimer (1835–1930)

Reformer, journalist, women's activist, temperance reformer, writer, orator, and teacher, Rebecca Ann Latimer Felton was the first woman to serve in the United States Senate. She and her family spent the war in Georgia, narrowly avoiding the devastation of Sherman's March through the state.

Born June 19, 1835, in De Kalb County, Georgia, Rebecca was the daughter of Charles Latimer, an area merchant and planter, and Eleanor Swift. In 1852 she graduated from Madison Female College, and the following year she married William Harrell Felton, a Methodist minister and physician who had already served in the state legislature.

They lived in Cartersville, Georgia. Of their five children, only one survived to adulthood. A daughter died in 1857, at the age of one. Two sons died during the Civil War—one from measles, the other from malaria. The Civil War and the lack of supplies and treatment available during the war may have contributed to both deaths.

Felton was very concerned about the issues of slavery and secession. Although William Felton favored the Confederacy, Rebecca was not a secessionist—she was dismayed when her son, John Latimer, appeared in Rebel garb. She claimed to own one of the few existing copies of the original proceedings of the Secession Convention of 1861, and she opined that Georgia was the crucial state in the formation of the Confederacy. After Georgia seceded, the Feltons assisted their community in the war effort; William served as a Confederate surgeon at a military camp, and Rebecca sewed shirts.

The Civil War complicated the Feltons' lives, just as it did those of other Southerners. They had to make do without everyday conveniences, including certain foods, cooking supplies, and materials for clothes. Due to the Federal blockade, Felton, like her fellow Southerners, had to substitute sweet potatoes and other foods for coffee. In the late summer of 1863, several soldiers wounded in the battles at Chickamauga arrived in Cartersville; Rebecca attended to the injured.

In March 1864, the Feltons moved to Macon in the hopes of avoiding more battles. However, during the summer they found themselves raided by

Rebecca Latimer Felton, the first woman to serve in the U.S. Senate (1835–1930). (Library of Congress)

those under the command of General George Stoneman. About this time, measles became an epidemic at the farm, causing seven deaths in two weeks, including that of the Feltons' son, William Jr. In the fall of 1864, Rebecca went to Crawfordsville, Georgia, to nurse her ill mother; she narrowly avoided William T. Sherman's army. As Sherman approached, she took her children to Quitman, Georgia, near the Florida border. On the way, Felton saw Federal prisoners being transferred from Andersonville to other prisons.

When Rebecca returned to Macon, a wounded Confederate soldier was in one of the beds. In the following months, several others visited the farm, including Confederate officers demanding food, deserters, and liberated slaves. When the Feltons returned to Cartersville, theirs was one of the few homes still standing.

In January 1866, the Feltons founded a school in the Methodist church, at which Rebecca taught three classes and gave piano lessons. Because education had virtually ceased during the Civil War, her students ranged from children to soldiers.

Following the Civil War, Felton served as the press secretary and campaign manager for her husband in his campaigns for the United States House of Representatives, where he served from 1875 to 1881. She also supported her husband in his final unsuccessful 1894 bid for a Senate seat. Both Feltons spoke out against convict labor and leasing, a practice that allowed women and children convicts to be housed with men; convicts worked at lumber mills, plantations, and railroads and they were housed in camps.

In 1885, the Feltons purchased the Cartersville *Courant,* a weekly newspaper that Rebecca edited. A dedicated feminist, Rebecca advocated female admission to state universities. She published her strong opinions via articles and editorials in the *Jackson Herald,* in the *People's Party Paper* (Atlanta), and later in a column in the *Atlanta Journal* (1899–1920s). At times her outspoken nature became a political liability to her husband.

Rebecca Felton also published a number of memoirs. In her first, *My Memoirs of Georgia Politics* (1911), she recounted the legislative history of Georgia, its 1861 Secession Convention, the politics of Reconstruction, as well as presidential and other elections from 1844 to the end of the nineteenth century. She also described the debates of the Confederate Congress, the early Confederacy in Montgomery and its move to Richmond, and the life of Alexander H. Stephens, vice president of the Confederacy. In *Country Life in Georgia* (1919), she detailed her childhood and early married life in Georgia. This volume included vivid descriptions of her escape from Sherman's March to the Sea, Southern women in the Civil War, and slavery in the South.

In November 1922, she became the first woman to serve in the United States Senate, appointed by Governor Thomas Hardwick upon the death of Thomas E. Watson. She filled the position for only twenty-four hours, until a successor was elected.

Although Rebecca was known for her reformism in convict labor and woman suffrage, she retained the traditional regional views on race issues. She blamed the freedmen for the demise of the Southern farm. During the 1890s, with the increased accusations of the rape of white women by black men, she applauded the subsequent lynchings, fearing the alleged rapists. She linked such rape with black voting, whiskey, and interracial lusts.

Rebecca Felton died January 24, 1930, in Atlanta.

*Ralph Hartsock*

***See also*** Confederate Homefront; Disease; Military Invasion and Occupation; Nurses; Secession; Sherman's Campaign (1864–1865); Shortages; Southern Women.

**References and Further Reading**

Felton, Rebecca Latimer. 1911. *Memoirs of Georgia Politics.* Atlanta, GA: Index Publishing Co.

Felton, Rebecca Latimer. 1919. *Country Life in Georgia in the Days of My Youth.* Atlanta, GA: Index Publishing Co.

Talmadge, John Erwin. 1960. *Rebecca Latimer Felton: Nine Stormy Decades.* Athens: University of Georgia Press.

Whites, LeeAnn. 2005. *Gender Matters: Civil War, Reconstruction, and the Making of the New South.* New York: Palgrave Macmillan.

## Fiction Writers, Northern

During the American Civil War, female authors in the North created a litany of writings for public consumption. Many of these authors used poems, short stories, and novels as explicit political commentaries on the state of public affairs; others created literary forms that seemed unconnected to the war.

Most Northern women writers during the Civil War came from urban, white, middle-class families. Like their prominent male counterparts, including Walt Whitman, Herman Melville, and Ambrose Bierce, female writers benefited from a public audience that was eager for written news and entertainment. Unlike their male counterparts, however, female authors were constrained by a society that typically expected women to refrain from expressing independent and political ideas in public. As a result, most female authors carefully balanced the content of their writing with the era's gender norms.

During the war, the literary marketplace expanded to include new venues, even as established venues expanded their circulations. *Frank Leslie's Illustrated Newspaper,* created out of the secessionist turmoil, was one of many outlets for war-related short stories. By the end of 1860, it boasted a circulation of one hundred sixty-four thousand. Other established periodicals had impressive circulations as well. *Harper's Weekly* printed and sold more than one hundred fifteen thousand copies in 1861, and *The Atlantic Monthly* circulation grew to thirty-two thousand copies by the middle of the war. Some local publications had even greater reach. The *New York Ledger,* for example, had a readership of about four hundred thousand at the start of the war. Traditional publishing houses also expanded to capitalize on the widespread interest in the war, which led to the publication of hundreds of volumes of poetry, anecdotes, incidents, documents, illustrations, and pamphlets. Northern women created many of them. In July 1861, for example, Mary J. Webber and Phebe Anne Coffin Hanaford published the patriotic poems of prominent antebellum writers in *Chimes of Freedom and Union.* In addition to including established male writers like Oliver Wendell Holmes and John Greenleaf Whittier, the volume also contained the poetry of several women, including Harriet Beecher Stowe, Lucy Larcom, Rose Terry, and Lydia Sigourney.

Sarah Josepha Hale's *Godey's Lady's Book* offered a unique venue for female authors. When the war began, it had a national circulation of one hundred fifty thousand, which gave it one of the nation's largest readerships. In addition to providing a forum for Hale to promote social causes through her own fictional and nonfictional accounts, *Godey's Lady's Book* served as a place for women to read the writings of other women. Although Hale published the writing of men as well, the magazine contained many songs, recipes, short stories, household hints, and other articles of interest to middle-class women. The wartime disruption of the mail limited the number of Southern readers, but the magazine did not become explicitly political. Even as it consistently published short stories about the war and was colored by sectional overtones, Hale insisted that the volume remain a national publication.

In contrast to Hale's experience, the expansion of the literary market rarely translated into economic security for female authors. Most women writers received significantly lower rates than their male counterparts, although Fanny Fern was the highest-paid newspaper columnist when the war began. Even accomplished female writers often discovered that publishing provided insufficient and unreliable wages. Louisa May Alcott, for example, could not translate her literary successes into a full-time occupation. Although she published several articles in magazines like *Atlantic Monthly,* became a playwright for a United States Sanitary Commission version of "Scenes from Dickens," and achieved fame for her fictionalized account of her wartime nursing experiences, she found it necessary to work as a governess to support her family. The financial limitations of fiction writing were further magnified by the inability of most writers, male or female, to find an outlet for their prose. Many authors submitted their writing to newspaper and magazine editors without any expectation of receiving payment, hoping that they could create a relationship that would eventually result in future payments. Most of these expectations never came to fruition.

Louisa May Alcott, U.S. novelist, short-story writer (1832–1888). (National Archives and Records Administration)

The marketplace did more than govern which writers got published or paid; it also often shaped what was written. Female writers who wanted to benefit from the maturity and growth of the Northern literary market often had to write their poetry, short stories, songs, and other fictional accounts to suit the tastes and expectations of the editors of the large periodicals and publishing houses. Presumed marketability, a desire to foster nationalism, and the era's Victorian sensibilities typically determined what was and what was not published. As a result, Northern women tended to publish literature that conformed to conventional gender norms and that was highly patriotic. Such catering to the marketplace was especially true at the start of the war, as otherwise ordinary women routinely published poems in their local newspapers to celebrate the forming of military companies, the departure of loved ones, and the values of national pride. Women also participated in the widespread and often maligned attempts to create new national hymns.

Most of the literature created by Northern women during the war can be categorized as domestic fiction, literature written by and for other middle-class women. These works rarely ventured far from the daily private lives of women, emphasizing romance and married life. Much of this literature drew heavily on the era's Victorian cult of true womanhood, even as the authors flaunted their own literary skills, educations, and intelligence. These sentimental novels, as they were called, often contained subtle indictments of the restrictions placed on women as well as the problems faced by strong-willed women in a society that demanded their submission.

During the Civil War, many Northern female authors increasingly prioritized public affairs in their fictional accounts. Following in the path of Harriet Beecher Stowe's antislavery *Uncle Tom's Cabin* (1852), these women used their fiction to pursue political ambitions. Rebecca Harding Davis, for example, published several wartime stories for *The Atlantic Monthly* that detailed the cruelties of slavery and the restrictions suffered by married women in American society. Through her writing, Davis also exposed the dangers of industrialization and the brutality of the war. Other writers offered social commentary through their published fictional accounts. Several magazine editors urged women to write stories that explicitly challenged men to do their duty. Some of these pieces, like many written by Fanny Fern, were considered nonfictional accounts. Others, like Kate Sutherland's "The Laggard Recruit" used the genre of fiction to urge action.

Much of the literature created for and by Northern women adhered to the cult of true womanhood even as it entered the political sphere. These works often emphasize the wartime importance of women on the homefront. Many female authors, following the framework of their male counterparts, emphasized the importance of women's domestic responsibilities during the war. Poems and short stories extolled the virtues of sewing uniforms, knitting socks, and supporting enlistment. They also penned hundreds of war romances, where young women typically struggle, come to embrace the enlistment of a loved one, and then eventually marry the sweetheart. In this way, female authors helped create and spread the prevailing wisdom that women had to sacrifice their needs and even their men on behalf of the nation.

The prejudice against the literary abilities of women and against women who would dare to voice their opinion led many women to write anonymously or to use masculine pennames. Literary critics routinely ignored the writing of women, especially works that could be characterized as Victorian sentimental novels. When critics assessed their merits of female fiction, these critics often chastised the authors for directly or indirectly engaging in the masculine world of politics, academics, and ideas in general. Even prominent authors chose to write under pen names when their topics ventured too far from accepted feminine literature. This was the case for Louisa May Alcott, who published short story thrillers and sensationalized newspaper accounts about personal vengeance. Consequently, Northern newspapers published hundreds of poems and short stories that were written by anonymous female authors.

A few female Northern writers offered critiques of the war through their fictional accounts. In "The

Volunteer's Wife," for example, Carry Stanley pointed to the difficulties that working-class women would face when their husbands left for the war. Others pointed to the suffering that women faced when wartime casualties mounted, frequently declaring that the death or suffering of soldier also literally killed or wounded a woman. Elizabeth Stuart Phelps's "A Sacrifice Consumed," published in *The Atlantic Monthly,* used a fictionalized and semi-autobiographical account of a woman who lost a husband at Antietam to force readers to recognize the heroism of common women who sacrificed their happiness for the war.

As casualties mounted, Northern women turned to writing for economic needs as well as to fulfill a psychological need. They published solemn tributes to defeat, rejoiced in victories, and lamented fallen soldiers as martyrs. Women contributed their poems to many periodicals, leading *Harper's Monthly* and others to create a poet's column to capitalize on the desire to consume these messages. One poem, "Kiss Me, Mother, and Let Me Go," by Nancy A. W. Priest was republished in several periodicals and published in poetry collections during the war.

Female authors also increasingly created stories that emphasized the active roles of women during the war and that often directly challenged the era's gender conventions. Rather than placing women on the sidelines, the fictional and semi-fictional accounts portray women as central characters in the war. Like many earlier literary works, these accounts frequently blurred the distinction between fact and fiction, allowing female authors to critique society through the words of a third party rather than through the first person. Northern newspapers routinely contained fictionalized stories about wartime experiences that drew on the experiences of cross-dressing spies, scouts, and soldiers. Sarah Emma Edmonds's *Unsexed; or, the Female Soldier* (1864) sensationally augmented the author's personal experiences in the Union army with fictional details and anecdotes. Other works drew on women's firsthand knowledge of the war, especially information gathered by female nurses. Even authors of newspaper accounts of female soldiers shaped their details to suit the literary and

social conventions of the era. Similarly, Louisa May Alcott's *Hospital Sketches,* published first in serial form and later as a book, relayed both firsthand and fictional accounts of female nurses and a dying soldier. In this work, like other semi-fictional accounts, fictional characters experience and discuss the experiences that female nurses like Alcott faced during the war.

Northern women writers continually shaped homefront views about the Civil War as they produced a widely circulated literature for the reading public. Throughout the war, these authors used their skills both to support the Union and to subtly criticize policies or society.

*Andrew K. Frank*

***See also*** Alcott, Louisa May (1832–1888); Davis, Rebecca Harding (1831–1910); Domesticity; Edmonds, Sarah Emma [Franklin Thompson] (1841–1898); Female Combatants; Female Spies; Fiction Writers, Southern; Hale, Sarah Josepha (1788–1879); Larcom, Lucy (1824–1893); Music, Northern; Northern Women; Nurses; Phelps, Elizabeth Stuart (Ward) [Mary Gray Phelps] (1844–1911); Poets, Northern; Politics; Separate Spheres; Stowe, Harriet Elizabeth Beecher (1811–1896); Union Homefront; United States Sanitary Commission; Wartime Literature; Willis, Sara Payson [Fanny Fern] (1811–1872).

**References and Further Reading**

Aaron, Daniel. 1987. *The Unwritten War: American Writers and the Civil War.* Madison: University of Wisconsin Press.

Coultrap-McQuin, Susan. 1990. *Doing Literary Business: American Women Writers in the Nineteenth Century.* Chapel Hill: University of North Carolina Press.

Fahs, Alice. 2001. *The Imagined Civil War: Popular Literature of the North and South, 1861–1865.* Chapel Hill: University of North Carolina Press.

Kelley, Mary. 1984. *Private Woman, Public Stage: Literary Domesticity in Nineteenth-Century America.* New York: Oxford University Press.

Sizer, Lyde Cullen. 2000. *The Political Work of Northern Women Writers and the Civil War, 1850–1872.* Chapel Hill: University of North Carolina Press.

Wilson, Edmund. 1972. *Patriotic Gore: Studies in the Literature of the American Civil War.* New York: W. W. Norton & Company.

## Fiction Writers, Southern

The Civil War presented Southern women fiction writers with a new topic and a new purpose for their writing. As Augusta Jane Evans wrote in *Macaria; or, Altars of Sacrifice* (1864), because Southern women could not take up arms and join the battle, they had to contribute to the Confederate cause in other ways. For Evans and a small group of her contemporaries, this call to action meant contributing to the war effort through writing patriotic stories that bolstered the cause by inspiring both men and women to rally behind the Confederacy in whatever way possible.

While Evans was arguably the most popular writer of the wartime South, the war did not make her popular. Like many other women wartime writers, Evans was already an established author in the antebellum era, having published a national best seller, *Beulah,* in 1859. Similarly, Maria McIntosh's

Augusta Jane Evans, nineteenth-century Southern novelist (1835–1909). (Cirker, Hayward and Blanche Cirker, eds., *Dictionary of American Portraits*, 1967)

wartime novel, *Two Pictures; or, What We Think of Ourselves, and What the World Thinks of Us* (1863), was, in fact, her ninth and final novel, following a series of popular works in the 1840s and 1850s. In the antebellum decades, Southern white women writers, like their Northern counterparts, had focused on sentimental or domestic storylines that upheld nineteenth-century notions of women finding happiness and meaning through marriage and family. Beyond just the home and nuclear family, antebellum Southern women writers romanticized the larger household of the plantation. But the Civil War brought an opportunity to move beyond the domestic scenes of the plantation household and engage larger, more political issues related to the Confederacy, the Federal government, and even military strategy, all from a Southern woman's point of view.

The war changed women's lives, and, although Confederate women writers supported the Southern cause, they also wanted to give a perspective on the war that acknowledged its devastation and its impact on the lives of women and families. The focus of most wartime fiction by Southern women dealt with the question of women's changing roles: their potential contribution to the Confederacy and consequently their changing roles within the family. McIntosh's *Two Pictures* was a direct response to the image of the South and, in particular, of Southern women put forth in Northern novels, such as Harriet Beecher Stowe's *Uncle Tom's Cabin* (1852). McIntosh dealt with the theme of marriage, but in a less traditional way. In her story, an elite Southern woman and a Yankee man marry, but rather than representing the happy union of the two cultures, their marriage emphasized the role of Southern women in bringing the North around to see the superiority of the Southern system. In the novel, the Yankee husband settles into his role as planter and master, and he ends up justifying slavery to his Northern colleagues. Such portrayals of Southern women counter the perception that white women of the slaveholding class saw slavery as a necessary evil. During wartime, with the future of their society on the line, these novelists argued that Southern women could be counted on to uphold the values of the Southern way of life with slavery at its center.

Unlike almost all antebellum novels by women, however, marriage was not necessarily at the center of Civil War stories of women's self-realization. The reality of war was that many women would inevitably be single or widowed, or that they would have disabled spouses due to the heavy human costs of the war on the Southern white male population. Approximately one-fourth of the South's young men were killed in the war and as much as another fourth returned wounded or disabled. Writers like Evans began with the assumption that women's energies would have to move from the family to the war, and she also explored the postwar implications of the South's dependence on its women. In Evans's *Macaria,* it is the single woman who is available to serve the Confederacy. The main character, Irene, is a woman who, by avoiding a "loveless marriage," is better able to serve the nation and the cause. Irene belongs to nobody; so she can dedicate herself to the Confederacy's soldiers. In her novel, Evans brought home the powerful message that the Confederacy depended not only on its soldiers, but also on its women. But if the single woman could be of more use to the cause, she also had the freedom now to search for a wider role in general. The war was an opportunity for women to prove their usefulness to the south, and also to seek self-realization. The characters in women's wartime fiction find different ways to be useful, just as the novelists themselves had done. Through the publication of novels, writers such as Evans found their own paths of "womanly usefulness" by producing literature. The novels served both as wartime service and artistic contribution to the South's new culture.

While novelists such as Evans and Florence O'Connor, author of *Heroine of the Confederacy; or, Truth and Justice* (1864), presented a Southern feminist vision of female independence and self-realization, envisioning new roles for women both within and outside the family, Southern writers were also careful to distance themselves from association with the image of the Northern woman writer as a woman's rights activist. Although many women writers in the North also downplayed their abilities and justified their writing in terms of social rather than individual benefit, O'Connor, for example, explicitly assured her readers that she was only writing to tell the correct history of the South and was not to be seen as a "female politician." And, though these Southern women writers went on to make arguments similar to those of Northern women's rights activists about a woman's duty to serve all of humanity and even about her individual right to do so, there were, of course, limits to their social reform vision, most notably that they were fighting for a cause that upheld racialized slavery. Evans may have drawn on the language of Northern liberal reformers in the years leading up to the Civil War, but she ultimately praised and fought to save a Southern vision of hierarchy and inequalities based on race and class as well as on gender. Besides having her strong-minded female character reject the idea of universal suffrage, the Southern cause that Evans and other writers fought to defend depended on the enslavement of other human beings.

Women wartime novelists such as Evans and Kentucky's Sallie Rochester Ford, author of *Raids and Romance of Morgan and His Men* (1864), addressed not only the wartime experience and unique perspective of Confederate women, but also ventured into commenting on Federal politics and military action itself, previously a topic for male writers. They told how the North had brought an unjust, cruel, and unconstitutional war to the South and detailed Northern attacks on the South, along with examples of Southern military strength, through accounts of specific battles. In the interest of accuracy as well as immediacy, Evans, for example, wrote in 1863 to General Pierre G. T. Beauregard regarding the earlier battle at Manassas, asking for him to proofread her account. Seeing the importance of her work in boosting Southern morale and inspiring hope in a Southern victory, Evans had no qualms about approaching a powerful general about her writing in the midst of war itself.

In *Raids and Romance,* Ford went even further in describing border battles that the Confederacy had lost. Ford's purpose was not only to accurately report on the battles, but also to comment on the particulars of Confederate strategy. Her accounts also emphasized the brutality of warfare. Florence O'Connor as well highlighted the human cost of war and, of course, the North's responsibility for the needless and continued bloodshed.

As promoters of the Confederacy, these writers were involved not only in winning a war, but in the project of building a nation. Even if the war had never come or if it ended soon enough, Southern writers emphasized that the social and cultural differences between the North and the South were too great to continue as one nation. They supported the creation of the Confederacy and the idea of escaping from the North altogether. Women writers linked the political and the cultural in arguing that the South had been too long held back by the North, who had now brought the war to a peace-loving South. Writing before the end of the war, these authors exhibited optimism about a Confederate victory and looked forward to the chance for the South to thrive on its own. Of course, predictions that the South would ultimately win the war were born not just of patriotic optimism. In addition, the novels served to encourage and justify those fighting and risking their lives for the cause in military service.

Popular women authors were immensely important in shaping the contemporary view of the war and in creating a Southern literary culture. Wartime Southern writers were not only telling a Southern story, but, in the process, they were also creating a Southern infrastructure for literature. On the eve of the Civil War, the center of publishing and printing activity was in the North, as was the Federal mail service. Southern newspapers were so desperate that they had to advertise their need of paper and ink. Southerners not only had to create their own stories, but they had to create the means to distribute them; and, without mail, they were also cut off from any Northern reading material. Southerners wanted to be independent of Northern writers and literary tastes, but, with the literary infrastructure concentrated in the North, it was difficult even to produce Southern writers. Some Southerners celebrated the separation from

the North in this regard and how it would spur Southern cultural and creative work.

Women wrote not only novels, but also poetry, songs, and stories for newspapers and journals. Of course, the work of many women in telling stories about the war and about the South remained hidden away in private rather than in public forums. Southern women's diaries, journals, and letters are filled with their first-person accounts of the war and its impact on families, as well as perspectives on slavery, on the Southern cause, and on national politics. But novelists were able to take those perspectives and those female insights to a larger public audience. Of course, fiction writing was popular from the 1820s onward, and many wartime novelists had published before the war, but the exigencies of war itself provided new material and new justification for women's cultural work.

Although the South would eventually lose the war, women novelists worked to tell a correct history of the South's involvement in the war and thus began a tradition, continued in the postwar years, of Southerners telling their own version of the story and celebrating what became a Lost Cause.

*Tiffany K. Wayne*

**See also** Civilian Life; Confederate Homefront; Courtship and Marriage; Diaries and Journals; Domesticity; Evans, Augusta Jane (1835–1909); Fiction Writers, Northern; Letter Writing; Nationalism, Confederate; Poets, Northern; Poets, Southern; Politics; Separate Spheres; Slaveholding Women; Southern Women; Stowe, Harriet Elizabeth Beecher (1811–1896); Widows, Confederate.

**References and Further Reading**

Fahs, Alice. 2001. *The Imagined Civil War: Popular Literature of the North and South, 1861–1865*. Chapel Hill: University of North Carolina Press.

Faust, Drew Gilpin. 1996. *Mothers of Invention: Women of the Slaveholding South in the American Civil War*. Chapel Hill: University of North Carolina Press.

Gardner, Sarah E. 2004. *Blood and Irony: Southern White Women's Narratives of the Civil War, 1861–1937*. Chapel Hill: University of North Carolina Press.

Young, Elizabeth. 1999. *Disarming the Nation: Women's Writing and the American Civil War*. Chicago: University of Chicago Press.

## Fifteenth Amendment

Conflicts over the Fifteenth Amendment resulted in a twenty-one-year split (1869–1890) in the woman suffrage movement.

After the 1868 presidential election, Congress continued to focus on several unfinished Reconstruction issues. The Fourteenth Amendment had granted black men citizenship, but not voting privileges. As a condition of readmission into the Union, former Confederate states gave black men the vote, but Congress feared they would eventually be disenfranchised by Southern states where Democrats had regained control. Thus, Congress began drafting an amendment to enfranchise black men. Seeing an opportunity to enfranchise women, Elizabeth Cady Stanton and Susan B. Anthony circulated woman suffrage petitions for an amendment that granted women voting rights.

Members of Congress introduced many versions of the Fifteenth Amendment. Some, like Congressmen George W. Julian and Samuel Pomeroy, were open to the idea of universal suffrage. Julian introduced an amendment to grant voting rights to all citizens without regard to race, color, or sex, and Pomeroy's bill enfranchised black men and women, but Congress did not debate these bills. Most opposed including woman suffrage in the amendment, fearing that the issue would jeopardize the enfranchisement of black men. Thus the amendment did not include woman suffrage.

To ensure that Congress and the states would vote in favor of the amendment, Senator Henry Wilson of Massachusetts asked abolitionist Abby Kelley Foster to campaign in favor of the Fifteenth Amendment. She agreed. She held fundraisers for the campaign and sent copies of the *Standard*, the journal of the American Anti-Slavery Society, to each member of Congress and state legislators. On February 26, 1869, Congress passed the Fifteenth Amendment, prohibiting states from denying voters the ballot on the grounds of race, color, or previous condition of servitude. Outraged, Stanton published several anti–Fifteenth Amendment articles in the *Revolution,* a feminist newspaper headed by Stanton and Anthony.

By contrast, members of the New England Woman Suffrage Association supported the Fifteenth Amendment. The association also favored woman suffrage but was willing to delay women's enfranchisement until black suffrage was achieved. Unlike Stanton and Anthony, the women of the New England association carefully avoided sparking any debates about black suffrage and the Fifteenth Amendment, choosing instead to petition state legislatures on the issue of women's enfranchisement and to lobby for legislation enfranchising women who lived in the District of Columbia and the territories of the United States.

The approach of the New England association did not sit well with Anthony and Stanton, who saw Reconstruction as a chance for change. Woman suffrage had its best chance of passage during Reconstruction, they believed. They feared that, once the debates over citizenship and voting for black men had been concluded, it would be years before the issue of woman suffrage would be revisited by Congress. The New England association viewed the passage of the Fifteenth Amendment as a progression in the securing of democratic rights for women, thus making it less difficult to pass woman suffrage. By contrast, Stanton believed that the inclusion of the Fifteenth Amendment in the Constitution would render women politically powerless, making it much more difficult to enfranchise women.

Working against the passage of the amendment, Stanton and Anthony used racist and elitist arguments. Stanton, for instance, suggested that it was unacceptable for Chinese immigrants and freedmen to make laws governing educated middle- and upper-class women. Anthony spoke in favor of limiting the franchise to those who were educated and intelligent.

In addition to their anti–Fifteenth Amendment campaign, Anthony and Stanton convinced Congressman Julian to draft a woman suffrage amendment to the Constitution. He introduced this amendment, the Sixteenth Amendment, on March 15, 1869. Recalling their success in the passage of the Thirteenth Amendment, Stanton and Anthony circulated petitions favoring the passage of the amendment. They also toured several Western states, organized new suffrage associations, and identified many new allies for the cause of woman suffrage.

These women were invited to the spring convention of the American Equal Rights Association.

At the May 1869 meeting of the American Equal Rights Association, the debates were fierce, and some of the delegates turned against Anthony and Stanton. Stephen S. Foster objected to Stanton's and Anthony's connection to George Train, a Democrat opposed to black suffrage, and he called for Stanton and Anthony to step down as officers of the association. Frederick Douglass chastised Anthony and Stanton for the use of racist arguments against the Fifteenth Amendment, and he introduced a resolution to support the Fifteenth Amendment. Anthony objected to Douglass's comments and introduced an anti–Fifteenth Amendment resolution and another favoring educated suffrage. Lucy Stone rose and objected to Anthony's anti–Fifteenth Amendment resolution, speaking in favor of the amendment. In the end, the association defeated Anthony's anti–Fifteenth Amendment resolution in favor of Douglass's resolution to support the Fifteenth Amendment.

Once the Equal Rights Association came out in favor of the amendment, Anthony and Stanton recognized that the association had overlooked women's enfranchisement in favor of black suffrage. They concluded that women needed a separate organization run entirely by women, and they formed the National Woman Suffrage Association. The association favored the passage of a Sixteenth Amendment to the Constitution to enfranchise women, and it opposed the Fifteenth Amendment.

Not all feminists supported the National Woman Suffrage Association. Lucy Stone and other female abolitionists opposed the formation of a new association. These women favored the Fifteenth Amendment and the enfranchisement of black men, and they were afraid that Stanton and Anthony's campaign against the Fifteenth Amendment would single-handedly defeat the amendment. In November 1869, this faction of the suffragist movement formed the American Woman Suffrage Association in Cleveland. Delegates elected Henry Ward Beecher president and Stone chair of the executive committee. Unlike the National Woman Suffrage Association, which hoped to secure women's enfranchisement through an amendment to the U.S. Constitution, the American Woman Suffrage Association chose to secure women's enfranchisement through state campaigns.

On March 30, 1870, the Fifteenth Amendment became part of the United States Constitution, and abolitionist reformers rejoiced because equal rights for the black men had been achieved.

*Jennifer Ross-Nazzal*

**See also** Abolitionism and Northern Reformers; Anthony, Susan B. (1820–1906); Douglass, Frederick (ca. 1818–1895); Fourteenth Amendment; Kelley, Abby (1811–1887); Stanton, Elizabeth Cady (1815–1902); Stone, Lucy (1818–1893); Thirteenth Amendment.

**References and Further Reading**
DuBois, Ellen Carol. 1978. *Feminism and Suffrage: The Emergence of an Independent Women's Movement in America 1848–1869.* Ithaca, NY: Cornell University Press.

Evans, Sara M. 1997. *Born for Liberty: A History of Women in America.* New York: Free Press.

Kerr, Andrea Moore. 1995. "White Women's Rights, Black Men's Wrongs, Free Love, Blackmail, and the Formation of the American Woman Suffrage Association." In *One Woman, One Vote: Rediscovering the Woman Suffrage Movement,* edited by Marjorie Spruill Wheeler, 61–80. Troutdale, OR: NewSage Press.

Lutz, Alama. 1940. *Created Equal: A Biography of Elizabeth Cady Stanton, 1815–1902.* New York: John Day Company.

Sterling, Dorothy. 1991. *Ahead of Her Time: Abby Kelley and the Politics of Antislavery.* New York: W. W. Norton & Company.

## Flags, Regimental

Regimental battle flags were some of the most visible evidences of women's involvement in the Civil War. For most regiments, a ladies' aid society or auxiliary was organized to make uniforms or other clothing items and to sew the regimental or company flags. The ladies often made the flag from silk from their own dresses if commercial fabric was scarce; the banners often portrayed slogans, devices, and emblems of local historical or patriotic significance. The attachment and devotion that each regiment felt toward its colors was symbolically linked to their devotion to the ladies at home and to the community: an iconic representation of a soldier's most sacred connections. Most often, there was an elaborate public ceremony when the flag was presented by the ladies to the regiment.

Regiments were raised locally, and the distinctive esprit de corps of each unit found representation in the regimental flag. Although United States regulations called for each regiment to carry a national flag along with a blue army flag carrying the seal of the United States, units on both sides of the Mason-Dixon line showed a high degree of individuality in their regimental colors. Some flags, such as the green banner of the famous Irish Brigade, became beacons on the battlefield.

Some flags were made by contract with private manufacturers, often drapers or sail-makers who adapted their businesses. Later in the war, most flags were manufactured at government depots. Northern regiments commonly used the national flag with the regiment's name stitched into a middle stripe. This was also common with Southern units

with the Stars and Bars, the first Confederate national flag. The battle flag, the more familiar Southern Cross, was also commonly used later in the war, with the regiment's name stitched across the middle. Some units used a state flag with regimental designation and battle names sewn in, such as the First Texas Infantry. Some Confederate armies had approved patterns. For instance, the Army of Northern Virginia used a square battle flag with white trim around the edge. In both armies, it became common to list on the flag the names of engagements fought. Wool and even cotton duck or canvas, being cheaper and more available than silk, became common fabrics for flags.

For many units, individual companies began the war with their own flags and retired them only when the regiment adopted its own colors. The Perote Guards of the First Alabama Infantry Regiment, for example, had their own flag sewn and presented by Miss Martha Crossley, Miss Queen Gamble, and unnamed others who officially presented it to the Guards on September 1860 at the

Photograph shows Major General G. K. Warren and staff posed in front of a tent and flag with "5" on it between 1861–1865. (Library of Congress)

entrance to the Methodist church in Perote. When the Guards were mustered into the First Alabama Infantry, the company flag was retired. The flag of Company C of the Fourth Alabama was a white field and a magnolia wreath with the words "Magnolia Cadets" painted on, and it was sewn and presented by two of Mary Todd Lincoln's half sisters, Elodie Todd and Martha Todd White (Alabama).

*Randal Allred*

**See also** Aid Societies; Northern Women; Southern Women.

**References and Further Reading**

Bonner, Robert E. 2002. *Colors and Blood: Flag Passions of the Confederate South.* Princeton, NJ: Princeton University Press.

Cannon, Devereux D. 1994. *Flags of the Confederacy: An Illustrated History.* Gretna, LA: Pelican Publishing Company.

Cannon, Devereux D. 1994. *Flags of the Union: An Illustrated History.* Gretna, LA: Pelican Publishing Company.

Katcher, Phillip, and Richard Scollins (illus.). 2000. *Flags of the Civil War.* Oxford: Osprey Publishing.

## Fogg, Isabella Morrison (1823–1873)

Isabella Fogg was a volunteer nurse during the Civil War, first for the Maine Camp and Hospital Association based in Portland, Maine, and later for the Maine Soldier's Relief Agency and the United States Sanitary Commission (USSC). Her letters to agency officials provide an informed, objective assessment of the desperate situation among wounded and displaced soldiers. Her writings describe the Union's failure to provide troops with the bare minimum of food, clothing, and medical attention, responsibilities that civilian relief organizations strained to accomplish.

In 1861, Fogg left her home in Calais, Maine, to visit her son Hugh, who was with the Sixth Maine Regiment in Washington, D.C. While there, she saw the need for hospital workers and volunteered for duty in the Capital's hospital through the Maine Camp and Hospital Association. After she rallied her hometown residents to conduct a letter writing campaign, Maine's governor appointed Colonel John Hathaway to manage the state's Soldier's Relief Agency, headquartered in Washington.

Learning that the wounded soldiers left behind on a battlefield when the Federal Army moved on were in more dire need than those in Washington's hospitals, Fogg and other volunteers persuaded Maine relief groups to allow the women to go to the field. Beginning in November 1862, Fogg traveled through the Maryland and West Virginia countryside searching abandoned buildings and tents for needy soldiers. She followed the Union army as it advanced toward Richmond, caring for Union and Confederate soldiers who were wounded or taken prisoner during the battles at Antietam, Chancellorsville, Gettysburg, and Fredericksburg. In addition to collecting food, clothing, and quilts from area residents, Fogg set up temporary stations where wounded were fed during stops on the way to hospitals.

In 1863 Fogg joined the USSC. When her son's wounded leg required amputation, she went to Baltimore to care for him. She returned to her duties and continued lobbying the Maine legislature for additional relief funds, which were allocated in the winter of 1864. The next year, while serving aboard the *Jacob Strader* hospital boat on the Ohio River near Louisville, Kentucky, she fell, permanently injuring her spine. Union officers, including Generals Ulysses S. Grant, Joshua Chamberlain, and George Meade petitioned Congress to give her a pension. In February 1866, they awarded her $8 per month, increasing it to $20 the next year.

*Nancy L. Adgent*

**See also** Aid Societies; Antietam/Sharpsburg, Battle of (September 17, 1862); Chancellorsville, Battle of (April 29–May 6, 1863); Food; Fredericksburg, Battle of (December 13, 1862); Gettysburg, Battle of (July 1–3, 1863); Hospitals; Hospital Ships; Letter Writing; Northern Women; Nurses; Politics; Union Homefront; United States Sanitary Commission; Wartime Employment.

**References and Further Reading**

Moore, Frank. 1866. *Women of the War: Their Heroism and Self-Sacrifice.* Hartford, CT: S. S. Scranton & Co.

Schultz, Jane E. 2004. *Women at the Front: Hospital Workers in Civil War America.* Chapel Hill: University of North Carolina Press.

Young, Agatha. 1959. *The Women and the Crisis: Women of the North in the Civil War.* New York: McDowell, Obolensky.

## Food

During the Civil War, women struggled to secure food to feed themselves and their dependents. With most able-bodied men enlisted in the armies, the planting, harvesting, and processing of agricultural products became women's responsibilities. Many women on both homefronts reduced their consumption of foodstuffs in order to supply soldiers with provisions to give them strength. Though women in both the North and the South experienced deprivations during the war's four years, food was not rationed in the North and the shortages were less severe. Class and geography played ultimate roles in who starved and who managed.

At the beginning of the Civil War, U.S. President Abraham Lincoln established blockades that prevented the importation of foodstuffs to the Confederate states. Initially, this meant that Southern women lacked luxury items like chocolate, tea, and coffee. However, as the war progressed, staples grew scarce. Upper- or plantation-class women suffered little, and many threw lavish parties, boasting coffee, pastries, and other items that were either not available to or beyond the means of the general populace. Evidence of economic difficulties or food shortages rarely appeared in the letters and diaries of urban and planter-class women. Planters pledged to feed the soldiers' wives and children, but they often broke those promises, instead selling food to speculators whose high prices made it impossible for the women of other classes to afford food.

Union farmers produced an abundance of grain during the war, and the North experienced no rationing, but women across the Southern states dealt with the scarcity of foodstuffs almost from the war's onset. Fertile land in the South was dominated by the cotton cultivation, and little land remained available for food production. In 1861, a massive crop failure in northwest Arkansas, which provided most of the state's grain, habituated women to hard times. The following year, wheat, oat, and corn crops failed, and a hog cholera epidemic diminished the meat supply. Prior to the war, Georgia faced similar agricultural and livestock disasters that caused it to be the worst affected of the states by food shortages and also the most dependent on imports from the North for its survival.

Tennessee women experienced the least wartime food shortages because their state was the South's main source for food. The state provided the Confederacy with half its pork supply and produced the most corn and second-largest amount of wheat in the region. New Orleans imported most of its foodstuffs from Tennessee and Kentucky, but grain and packed meat came from the Northern states.

Part of the Federal campaign to quell the rebellion meant the destruction of food crops in the South. Accordingly, Generals Ulysses S. Grant and Benjamin F. Butler destroyed or appropriated agricultural products bound for Richmond and Petersburg, Virginia. In 1864 and 1865, General William Tecumseh Sherman's troops destroyed foodstuffs all along their march through Georgia and the Carolinas.

Diets in the South varied based on area, class, and race. Staples of the slave diet were pork, corn, and molasses, which typified the poor white diet in the South as well. Seafood was plentiful in the coastal areas along the Carolinas, Georgia, Florida, and the Deep South. The scarcity of salt affected the preservation of meat. Corn was a commodity, and distilleries bought the majority of the corn crops for liquor production.

Throughout the war, inflated food prices and shortages forced women to be creative with their recipes and resourceful with their supplies. Substitutions became common. Women made teas from herbs, and they often used peanuts and acorns to replace coffee and chocolate. Demonstrating the importance of food substitutes, two of the few books published in the Confederacy were cookbooks. *The Confederate Receipt Book* (1863) offered inventive substitutions for items no longer available. *Resources of the Southern Fields and Forests* (1863) taught women to forage for nuts, berries, and other nutrient rich plants in their backyards. Women and their families subsisted on wild greens, poke sallet, dandelion, and lamb's quarter.

Women expended as much energy protecting their food supply as they did procuring it; they buried meat and hid it under landings so that something was left after scavenging soldiers took their fill. When hosting enemy soldiers in their homes, both Northern and Southern women introduced the men to alternate foodways. Northern soldiers were especially fond of Southern cookery, a blend of African, Native American, and English ingredients and techniques. Their devotion to the cuisine created opportunities in the North for newly freed slaves to become professional cooks.

In 1863 the Confederacy impressed a 10 percent confiscation levy on livestock, wheat, corn, oats, sugar, rye, buckwheat, sweet potatoes, Irish potatoes, tobacco, peas, bean, and peanuts. Women's scanty resources dwindled further because soldiers often impressed more than the 10 percent level. Additionally, women were angered by planters who hoarded food and whose stores were impressed at lower levels. Small landowning women could not retaliate, whereas those in planter class, given their political connections, were often unmolested by soldiers.

To help their families survive, women did whatever they could to procure food. Some left their children behind as they traveled from plantation to plantation pleading for provisions. Often, they stole to provide for their children when their pleas for assistance fell on deaf ears. In the spring, after exhausting their winter supplies, women in most Southern states took up arms to liberate staples located along rail lines where food was amassed. As early as July 1861, women rioted in New Orleans. In Georgia, women rioted for food in 1862 and 1863. Other food-related uprisings occurred in Mobile, Alabama, in Salisbury, North Carolina, and in Richmond, Virginia.

With supply lines cut and transportation routes halted, women in urban areas had few food options. Lack of land or experience with gardening prevented them from growing vegetables to meet their needs. Some women in urban areas consequently exchanged sex for food.

Though there were few reasons for celebrations during the war years, women saved what little ingredients they could to celebrate holidays. They served tea and ginger cakes, which otherwise were rare. Sorghum grown in their own fields also helped them provide cake for celebrations. Others saved what they could to pay exorbitant prices for holiday foods. For example, at Christmastime in Savannah in 1864, turkeys ranged in price from $50 to $100.

With the destruction of their homes, many rural women fled to the cities for the protection that populated areas offered them; this influx of refugees corresponded with critical food shortages. When Union forces captured a city, it became their responsibility to feed its inhabitants. Officials dipped into military supplies to assuage the shortages of the citizenry's foodstuffs. Likewise, refugees, mostly women and children, flocked to army posts where supplies were abundant.

Four years of biting hunger and malnutrition, coupled with their useless pleas to governors and local officials for relief, diminished some Confederate women's patriotism. Letters sent to husbands focused on the lack of food, causing some soldiers to desert so that they could attend to business at home. Food shortages on the homefront played a large role in reducing the Confederacy's manpower and thus contributed to the loss of the war.

*Rebecca Tolley-Stokes*

**See also** Aid Societies; Bread Riots; Confederate Homefront; Destruction of Personal Property; Domesticity; Fairs and Bazaars; Family Life, Confederate; Foraging, Effects on Women; Prostitution; Rural Women; Shortages; Southern Women; Southern Union Homefront; Urban Women.

**References and Further Reading**

Grivetti, Louis E., Jan L. Corlett, and Cassius T. Lockett. 2002. "Food in American History. Part 5: Pork: A Nation Divided: The American Civil War Era (1861–1865)." *Nutrition Today* 37 (3): 110–118.

Smith, Andrew F. 2005. "The Civil War and American Food, or How Nationalized, Industrialized American Cookery Got Its Start." *The Food Journal* 5 (Winter): 4–5.

Williams, Teresa Cusp, and David Williams. 2002. "'The Women Rising': Cotton, Class, and Confederate Georgia's Rioting Women." *Georgia Historical Quarterly* 86 (1): 49–83.

## Foraging, Effects on Women

Both the Union and Confederate armies used foraging to obtain supplies from the civilian population during active military campaigns. Because the majority of men were serving in the armies, women faced this military practice more than other civilians. Foraging soldiers sometimes took their official task too far, posing a sexual and physical threat to civilian women. Their exposure to foraging transformed many Southern women into stalwart defenders of their cause, and their nationalist passion reinforced their support for war.

The use of foraging by military forces was not a concept new to the American Civil War. The practice existed in military campaigns throughout history, and civilian populations became thereby intertwined with active combat. Soldiers obtained supplies from the countryside during the American Revolution as well as during other conflicts on the continent. However, Civil War foraging shocked nineteenth-century Americans, who had a romanticized notion that civilians were to be protected from the horrors of combat and that women in particular should not experience the dangers of military campaigns. Perhaps this belief stemmed from the concept that war was a gentleman's duel over a political idea, in which women had no place or voice.

Early in the conflict, many military men saw foraging as a drastic measure. Union soldiers' early foraging focused mainly on the issue of escaped slaves within their lines. Southern property owners requested, and often obtained, the return of their chattel. Many campaigns saw military officers take efforts to protect enemy civilians, especially women, from the effects of armies on the march. For example, in 1862 Confederate General Robert E. Lee issued orders to prevent his men from foraging in Maryland for humanitarian and political reasons. His actions were mirrored by Union officers such as Don Carlos Buell and George B. McClellan, who also pursued a genteel approach to civilians.

As the war continued, each side increasingly viewed and treated the other's civilian population as the enemy. Union columns, operating deep in the South, forced Confederate civilians to face the brunt of their foraging and other destruction. In 1862, Union General John Pope identified the Confederate civilian population as part of the active rebellion against the United States. By 1863, military foraging became an accepted means for obtaining supplies during a campaign. Union officers and soldiers also began using foraging to punish civilians for the actions of their political representatives and their roles in the Confederate war effort. The military campaigns of 1864–1865, especially those led by Generals Philip Sheridan and William T. Sherman, utilized foraging to reduce the enemy's desire to fight.

Foraging affected civilian women on both physical and emotional levels. Through these military actions, soldiers hoped to destroy their opponent's will to fight by placing their families in danger. As the heads of many wartime households, women had to make decisions to protect the physical safety of their families. They struggled with these decisions, knowing that no choice ensured their personal safety or that of their property. Women who moved their families to a safer location often ran the risk of returning to destroyed homes and of otherwise losing possessions. In most cases, foragers, or bummers, would not destroy occupied dwellings but would steal what they wanted from the family. Women who hid valuables, monetary or otherwise, often faced angry soldiers who took out their frustrations on the family's possessions or slaves.

Many women used their femininity to appeal for protection from invading troops. They played on their sex and their status as mothers to convince enemy soldiers and officers to protect them. In addition, although far from home, many soldiers advised their wives on the course of action needed to protect themselves, their families, and their property. For example, members of the Masonic order often instructed their wives to find a Union officer who belonged to the Masons and appeal to him for protection. Soldiers also urged their wives to hide valuable property and papers.

However, requests for help often fell on deaf ears. In many cases, women found themselves forced to find food for their family. Many became refugees, moving to a nearby town or city in the hopes of finding a safe haven and sustenance. In rare cases, invading soldiers posed a physical threat to Southern women and their families. The South's female slaves had no protection from invading troops, and they were subjected to physical violence and rape by both Union and Confederate soldiers throughout the conflict.

In many instances, foraging did not break civilians' will to fight. Instead, foraging parties often had an opposite effect, on an emotional level, than intended: the trauma of the destruction of their homes and possessions by foraging parties served to strengthen the resolve of many civilians.

White women prepared themselves emotionally for invasion. Through newspapers, personal correspondence, and gossip, they followed the progress of enemy armies and prepared their homes. When foraging parties arrived, many women protected their families and slaves, becoming verbally belligerent to the soldiers. In addition, once the invading armies moved on, women worked to restore their families' harmony, and provide for their children and relatives.

Instead of destroying the enemy's will, foragers' actions frequently served to personalize the war for civilians. Just as Union soldiers' destruction of Southern homes and property could reinforce Confederate nationalism, so the thievery of Southern soldiers reinforced the beliefs of Southern Unionists.

After the Civil War, Southern women who had experienced the effect of foraging parties on their homes became some of the most vocal proponents of the Lost Cause. Their experiences during invasion led many to see Yankees as inhuman, and reunion as impossible.

*William H. Brown*

**See also** African American Women; Civilian Life; Confederate Homefront; Destruction of Homes; Destruction of Personal Property; Family Life, Confederate; Honor; Military Invasion and Occupation; Morale; Nationalism, Confederate; Plantation Life; Rape; Refugees; Rural Women; Sheridan's Shenandoah Valley Campaign (1864); Sherman's Campaign (1864–1865); Shortages; Southern Unionists; Southern Women.

**References and Further Reading**

Campbell, Jacqueline Glass. 2003. *When Sherman Marched North from the Sea: Resistance on the Confederate Home Front*. Chapel Hill: University of North Carolina Press.

Grimsley, Mark. 1995. *The Hard Hand of War: Union Military Policy toward Southern Civilians, 1861–1865*. New York: Cambridge University Press.

Thomas, Emory. 1979. *The Confederate Nation, 1861–1865*. New York: Harper & Row.

Wiley, Bell I. 1970. *Confederate Women*. Westport, CT: Greenwood Press.

Whites, LeeAnn. 1995. *The Civil War as a Crisis in Gender, Augusta, Georgia, 1860–1890*. Athens: University of Georgia Press.

## Ford (Willard), Antonia (1838–1871)

Arrested and imprisoned as a Confederate spy, Antonia Ford was among the many women who served as clandestine agents or informants during the Civil War. Like other women, Ford used feminine wiles to further the Confederate cause.

Ford was born in Fairfax Court House, Virginia, the daughter of a prosperous merchant and slaveholder. Educated at Virginia's Buckingham Female Collegiate Institute, Ford graduated in 1857 with a degree in English Literature. The Ford home served as a social center for lawyers, military men, government officials, planters, and entrepreneurs who came into Fairfax to conduct business. Its location near Washington, D.C., made the area one of flux between secessionist and Union sentiments. The charming and well-bred Antonia Ford was pro-secession.

Fairfax changed hands frequently during the Civil War. During the Peninsular campaign, the Ford house was alternately used as a boardinghouse by Confederate and Union officers. Confederate General Pierre G. T. Beauregard used it to house officers for the Army of Northern Virginia before the First Battle of Bull Run. Ford also befriended J.E.B. Stuart.

When the Ford home shifted to Union control, Ford cultivated friendships with the men and passed along information she gained from casual conversations. Stuart trusted her surveillance and jokingly awarded her a commission as an aide-de-camp of his staff in October 1861. Ford also made herself useful to the Grey Ghost, John Singleton

Antonia Ford, Confederate spy (1838–1871). (Library of Congress)

Mosby, a Stuart scout who organized the Partisan Rangers in 1863 and who staged highly successful raids and strategic small strikes of guerrilla warfare, disrupting supply lines while harassing and distracting Union forces.

One night in early March 1863, almost certainly acting on Ford's information, Mosby's men raided Fairfax Courthouse, capturing Union Brigadier General Edwin Stoughton as he slept, as well as dozens of Union soldiers, a stable of excellent horses, and the unit's weapon supply. When captured, Stoughton was heavily intoxicated after an evening at the Ford home. Secretary of War Edwin Stanton sent a U.S. Secret Service chief detective to investigate. A female operative infiltrated the Ford household and gained Antonia's confidence. On the strength of the information she gathered, as well as physical evidence, Ford was arrested for espionage

and imprisoned without trial in Washington's Old Capitol Prison. After a brief release in May 1863, she was rearrested and returned to the prison, where she remained until September.

Ford's captor, Major Joseph C. Willard, was a successful businessman and, with brother Henry, proprietor of Washington's Willard Hotel before he entered wartime military service. The Willard Hotel, located two blocks from the White House, was the temporary home to many prominent American political and literary figures, as well as to visiting world dignitaries. Willard, who was eighteen years her senior, fell in love with Ford at their first meeting, and he worked feverishly for her release. After he escorted her home from prison, they began to court secretly. When Willard resigned his commission in March 1864, they eloped, marrying almost exactly a year after Mosby's raid on Fairfax Courthouse.

Their happy marriage was marred by Antonia's problems with childbirth. After successfully giving birth to a son in 1865, she lost two more boys at birth. In February 1871, at the age of thirty-two, Antonia died from complications from childbirth in Washington. Willard was devastated and never remarried.

*Barbara Bair*

***See also*** Bull Run/Manassas, First Battle of (July 21, 1861); Confederate Homefront; Female Spies; Southern Women.

**References and Further Reading**

Furguson, Ernest B. 2004. *Freedom Rising: Washington in the Civil War.* New York: Alfred A. Knopf.

Leonard, Elizabeth D. 1999. *All the Daring of the Soldier: Women of the Civil War Armies.* New York: W. W. Norton & Company.

## Fort Sumter (April 12–14, 1861)

Fort Sumter, in Charleston, South Carolina's harbor, heard the first shots of the Civil War in the early morning of April 12, 1861. After thirty-three hours of shelling, Major Robert Anderson, a Southerner himself, surrendered the Federal fort to Confederate General Pierre G. T. Beauregard on April 14. The attack on Fort Sumter exacerbated the already fragile sectional crisis and propelled Northerners and Southerners to arm themselves for what would become four years of bloody war.

After the secession of the lower South, the newly formed Confederate government seized Federal arsenals, forts, and outposts across the South. By March 1861, only four Southern military installations remained in Federal hands: two forts in the Florida Keys, Fort Pickens in Pensacola, and Fort Sumter. Nestled in a hotbed of secessionism, Sumter became the symbol of Federal oppression. The nation wondered whether President Abraham Lincoln would use force to defend Sumter and its eighty-man garrison.

Lincoln decided to reinforce Anderson even at the cost of provoking the South. On April 9, 1861, Confederate President Jefferson Davis ordered Confederate forces to surround and take control of the fort before Federal supplies arrived. At four-thirty in the morning of April 12, Confederate artillery opened fire. Major Anderson surrendered after suffering an intense artillery bombardment that destroyed portions of the fort and started fires in the interior. A one-hundred-gun salute by departing Federal forces produced the battle's only casualties: one dead and five wounded (one mortally).

Although women played no direct role in the battle, the women of Charleston actively participated in the controversy that surrounded the fall of Sumter. For days, women watched the harbor to catch a glimpse of the first shots of war, hoping to witness the moment the South began its fight for independence. After Sumter fell, Charleston's women participated in the victory celebrations and praised the virtues of the Confederacy.

The Confederate capture of Fort Sumter caused Lincoln to call for seventy-five thousand volunteers to suppress the Southern insurrection. Many in the North overwhelmingly supported war, and Lincoln's call for volunteers forced all to take sides. Teetering on the brink of secession since the beginning of 1861, Virginia seceded only three days after Sumter fell. North Carolina, Arkansas, and Tennessee soon followed, citing Lincoln's call to arms as their reason for finally abandoning the Union.

The women gazing over Charleston Harbor could not have known the changes that the events at Fort Sumter and the Civil War would bring. War brought women into new professions such as nursing, civil service, and teaching as well as expanded responsibility at home when the control of land, slaves, and money fell into their sphere. The four years of conflict, begun on that brisk April morning in 1861, also brought pain and heartache. Deaths and wounded veterans—husbands, sons, brothers, or loved ones—became daily reminders of the sacrifice of hundreds of thousands of women. Fort Sumter altered women's roles, propelling them into new situations and giving them power previously unimaginable.

*James Gigantino*

***See also*** Confederate Homefront; Secession; Southern Women.

**References and Further Reading**

Detzer, David. 2001. *Allegiance: Fort Sumter, Charleston, and the Beginnings of the Civil War.* New York: Harcourt Brace.

Klein, Maury. 1997. *Days of Defiance: Sumter, Secession, and the Coming of the Civil War.* New York: Alfred A. Knopf.

## Forten (Grimké), Charlotte L. (1837–1914)

Abolitionist, educator, civil rights activist, and poet, Charlotte Forten Grimké kept detailed journals of her time as a teacher to the freedpeople in Port Royal. Her attention to detail, her keen commentaries, and rare insights offer an important perspective of nineteenth-century African American life.

The daughter of Mary Woods and Robert Forten, prominent antislavery activists and a leading African American family of Philadelphia, Charlotte Forten was born on August 17, 1837. After her mother died in 1840, Forten became very close to three of her aunts: Sarah and Harriet Forten Purvis, and Margaretta Forten. Their antislavery politics would define her life. Precocious and bright, Charlotte received tutoring at home, and later, when she expressed a desire to become a teacher, was sent to Salem, Massachusetts, to study in integrated educational institutions, including Higginson Grammar School and Salem Normal School. She boarded with the renowned Remond family, which afforded her many opportunities to mingle with New England's abolitionist vanguard.

Continuing a long family tradition of antislavery and civil rights activism, Forten joined the Salem Female Anti-Slavery Society, one of the oldest in the country. In June 1854, the trial of Anthony Burns, a fugitive slave, was held in nearby Boston. His conviction and return to slavery sparked mass protest and mob action. This event deeply troubled Forten, and she dedicated herself more deeply to fighting for immediate emancipation and the cause of the enslaved.

During this time, she met William Lloyd Garrison, editor of *The Liberator*, and, with his encouragement, she published several works in his newspaper and, later, in the *National Anti-Slavery Standard* and the *Anglo-African* magazine. While poetry dominated much of her writing, she also wrote essays. Antislavery themes were common, but she also wrote on a variety of topics, including love, morality, religion, temperance, education, and politics.

Forten completed her studies, and in 1856 began teaching at the Epes Grammar School, becoming Salem's first African American public school teacher. Tuberculosis forced her to resign after two years, and she returned to Philadelphia. She continued to write, however, maintaining a strong presence in local and national abolition politics.

With the onset of the Civil War, Forten hoped to contribute her services to the Union cause. When the Boston Education Commission called for volunteers for its Port Royal Experiment in South Carolina in early 1862, Forten applied. They were slow to approve her application, however, so she turned to the newly forming Pennsylvania Freedmen's Relief Association, which was just beginning to organize and eager to send its own teachers to the war zone. Forten would be the first African American teacher assigned to the Port Royal district, and, for many of her students and their parents, she would be the first free, well educated African American they would meet.

Forten arrived in the late fall of 1862 and devoted two years to teaching the newly freed slaves of the local Sea Islands. With two friends, Laura Towne and Ellen Murray, Forten set up a school in a local Baptist church on St. Helena Island. She published several essays in *The Atlantic Monthly* about her work and observations of the local people. While many Northerners and some abolitionists doubted the abilities, both intellectually and physically, of the newly freed people of the South, Forten provided a convincing portrait of an eager and fully capable people, striving, through education and training initiatives, to make the transition into a free society.

She also recorded many of her thoughts and experiences in journals that reveal the daily joys and struggles Forten faced teaching her students, her keen interpretations of life in the community, and her observations of the bravery and deportment of the increasing number of black troops stationed in the district. She became quite close to several of their commanding officers, and she recorded both the excitement over their victories and the tremendous pain of their losses. She described with great excitement her meeting with Harriet Tubman, the famous Underground Railroad conductor who was then serving Union forces in the district as a spy and scout, nurse, and cook. Forten was also there at the reading of the Emancipation Proclamation on January 1, 1863, at Camp Saxton near Beaufort, South Carolina.

Her father, Robert, had become frustrated by the persistent racism in America and moved his family from Philadelphia to Ontario, Canada, in 1855, then to England. The Civil War and the Emancipation Proclamation brought him back to the United States, and, at the age of fifty-one, he joined the Forty-third United States Colored Troops. Promoted to sergeant, he had been assigned to recruit black soldiers in Maryland when he caught typhoid fever and died.

After the war, Charlotte recruited teachers for posts in the South under the auspices of Boston's Freedmen's Relief Association. She taught briefly at the Sumner High School in the nation's capitol, then served as a clerk in the United States Treasury Department during the 1870s.

On December 19, 1878, Charlotte married Francis Grimké, the son of a formerly enslaved woman, Nancy Weston, and her master, Henry Grimké, and nephew to Henry's famous abolitionist sisters, Sarah and Angelina Grimké. Frank, as he was known, earned an undergraduate degree at Lincoln University, and, though he also studied law there, he moved on to Princeton Theological Seminary and later took a position as pastor at the Fifteenth Street Presbyterian Church in Washington, D.C., in 1877. Charlotte and Frank had met in Boston just after the end of the Civil War, and they remained acquaintances. She joined his church in Washington when he arrived, and in spite of the significant age difference—she was forty-one and he was twenty-eight—they fell in love and married. Frank would become a prominent African American civil rights activist and a vocal critic of Booker T. Washington.

The death of their infant daughter, Theodora, in 1880, devastated Charlotte and Frank. They moved to Jacksonville, Florida, when Frank accepted a pastorship there. Charlotte published little after her marriage, but she remained an active and dedicated minister's wife and activist.

Persistent illness significantly restricted her activities the last twenty years of her life. She died on July 23, 1914.

*Kate Clifford Larson*

**See also** Abolitionism and Northern Reformers; African American Women; Antislavery Societies; Diaries and Journals; Education, Northern; Free Blacks; Garrison, William Lloyd (1805–1879); Grimké (Weld), Angelina (1805–1879); Grimké, Sarah Moore (1792–1873); Port Royal; Remond, Sarah Parker (1826–1894); Teachers, Northern; Towne, Laura Matilda (1825–1901); Tubman, Harriet [Araminta Ross] (1822–1913).

### References and Further Reading
Perry, Mark. 2001. *Lift Up Thy Voice: The Grimké Family's Journey from Slaveholders to Civil Rights Activists.* New York: Viking Penguin.
Rose, Willie Lee. 1999. *Rehearsal for Reconstruction. The Port Royal Experiment.* Indianapolis, IN: Bobbs-Merrill Company.
Stevenson, Brenda, ed. 1988. *The Journals of Charlotte Forten Grimké.* New York: Oxford University Press.

### Foster, Sarah Jane (1839–1868)
Sarah Jane Foster was one of many Northern women who taught freedmen in the South after the Civil War. Like many of them, she was deeply religious and considered herself as much a missionary as a teacher. She detailed her experiences in letters.

Some of her letters, published contemporaneously in a Baptist Missionary newspaper, *The Zion Advocate,* addressed topics that most Southern whites refused to acknowledge: miscegenation, blacks' intellectual aptitude, and whites' mistreatment of blacks. Foster also published poems and stories.

Originally from Gray, Maine, Foster lived in Portland during the war, working for railroad engineer Frederick Cobb's family. Her sister Emma also lived in the city, employed by her aunt who operated a millinery shop. In November 1865, Foster and other teachers traveled to West Virginia to join Reverend N. C. Brackett, Superintendent of the Free Baptists' Shenandoah Mission center. She taught first in Martinsburg and in April 1866 transferred to Harper's Ferry, conducting night as well as day classes. Foster boarded with a local white family and attended services at black churches.

Prevalent in New England, the antislavery Free Baptists established schools that often functioned as churches in four West Virginia towns during the next few years. The Bureau of Refugees, Freedmen and Abandoned Lands, as well as students and their families, supplied a portion of the expenses. Beginning as a missionary school in abandoned buildings previously occupied alternately by Union and Confederate troops, the Free Baptist school in Harper's Ferry became Storer College in 1867 when Maine philanthropist John Storer made an agreement with the denomination to expand their schools to higher levels. It was chartered to accept students regardless of race.

Foster's letters and diary provide ample evidence that former slaves were eager and able students and that they endured significant hardship in pursuit of education. Commenting on postwar strife between former Confederates and Unionists, as well as on the landscape's devastation, her letters reflect worsening economic conditions for the freedmen that led to declining school attendance between the fall of 1865 and the spring of 1866. Soon thereafter, when Storer College accepted money from the Peabody Fund, it agreed to require that its teachers have a normal school teaching certificate. This stipulation meant Foster would have to find teaching positions elsewhere, a situation she seemed to accept.

Sarah Jane Foster died from yellow fever in 1868 while teaching in South Carolina.

*Nancy L. Adgent*

**See also** Abolitionists and Northern Reformers; Diaries and Journals; Education, Southern; Freedmen's Bureau; Letter Writing; Northern Women; Poets, Northern; Reconstruction (1865–1877); Religion; Teachers, Northern; Wartime Literature.

### References and Further Reading
Foster, Sarah Jane. 2001. *Sarah Jane Foster: Teacher of the Freedman, The Diary and Letters of a Maine Woman in the South after the Civil War,* edited by Wayne E. Reilly. Rockland, ME: Picton Press.

## Fourteenth Amendment

Battles over the Fourteenth Amendment resulted in a break between suffragists and their abolitionist allies, leading to the creation of a woman's movement.

In 1865, Congress began drafting the Fourteenth Amendment. In one section, the draft granted citizenship rights to all men born and naturalized in the United States. If the amendment was ratified, it would be the first time the word "male" had been included in the Constitution, and its inclusion angered woman suffragists. Appealing to their abolitionist friends, feminists insisted that the amendment include women. Elizabeth Cady Stanton feared the amendment would severely limit women's political rights, making woman suffrage even more difficult to pass because a separate woman suffrage amendment would have to be drafted and ratified for women to be enfranchised.

Abolitionists refused to support the views of the woman suffragists, claiming that it was the "Negro's hour." Wendell Phillips, president of the American Anti-Slavery Society, expected women to support black male suffrage over woman suffrage until black men became citizens. He saw no reason to risk the enfranchisement of black men by pushing for universal suffrage—black and woman suffrage. Furthermore, the mere emancipation of slaves, abolitionists determined, had not changed Southern society, which began passing black codes as early as 1865. These codes limited the behavior of

the freedman, and abolitionists concluded that black men had to be protected by the Constitution.

Feminists disagreed with the abolitionists. They did not perceive Reconstruction as the "Negro's hour." Instead they saw a chance for change as the definition of citizenship was being debated on the floors of Congress.

In an attempt to prevent the passage of the amendment as written, Stanton and Susan B. Anthony began circulating woman suffrage petitions. Compared to the petitions gathered for the support of the Thirteenth Amendment, this drive was unsuccessful. Only ten thousand individuals signed the petitions, and, when the petitions were presented, the Republicans, many of whom who had previously

Petition for Universal Suffrage, signed by Elizabeth Cady Stanton, Susan B. Anthony, and others, 1866. (National Archives and Records Administration)

supported woman suffrage, refused to introduce them on the floor of Congress. By the spring of 1866, feminists recognized that the Fourteenth Amendment, as drafted, would pass Congress.

As a result, feminists decided to push for universal suffrage by merging the black and woman suffrage movements in one society. They approached their abolitionist friends in the American Anti-Slavery Society with their idea. Some supported the plan, but Phillips prevented the merger from taking place. He thought it was best to keep the society focused on a single issue: black suffrage.

Feminist leaders like Anthony, Stanton, and Lucy Stone disagreed with Phillips and held the first women's rights convention since the start of the Civil War. Delegates to the convention formed the American Equal Rights Association, a group that supported both black and woman suffrage. In June 1866, Congress passed the Fourteenth Amendment, submitting the amendment to the states for ratification, but the Equal Rights Association did not campaign against ratification. Instead, it began a campaign to remove the racial and sexual restrictions placed on voters in their state constitutions.

Members of the Equal Rights Association began to circulate petitions to delete the word "male" from the New York State Constitution and to eliminate property qualifications for black male voters. As feminists focused on these state campaigns, they also tried to persuade abolitionists to see Reconstruction through their eyes. Stone tried to convince Abby Kelley Foster, a member of the American Anti-Slavery Society and an early supporter of women's rights, to support equal rights, but she disagreed with Stone. Foster preferred to help the freedmen secure their citizenship before women received political rights.

In 1867, feminists headed to Kansas, where they battled to secure the passage of two amendments to the state constitution: one to enfranchise African Americans and another to enfranchise women. Members of the Equal Rights Association were confident that both issues would pass, and they actively campaigned in Kansas. Feminists were especially hopeful about the issue of woman suffrage because the state constitution, passed in 1861, included school suffrage for women. While the prospects for both issues seemed bright, feminist optimism quickly dimmed as editors of reform newspapers failed to endorse the equal rights campaign, urging voters instead to support black suffrage. Throughout the campaign, feminists appealed to abolitionists to work in the campaign, but they refused. Then the Kansas Republican Party began to verbally attack feminists.

Events in New York influenced the Kansas campaign. On June 25, 1867, Horace Greeley, chair of the suffrage committee for the New York constitutional convention and a supporter of women's rights, announced that the committee had rejected suffrage for women, stating that women's enfranchisement would be too revolutionary. This decision reaffirmed the anti-feminist campaign headed by the Kansas Republican Party.

In early fall, abolitionist leaders finally began to endorse the woman suffrage amendment. Even Greeley admitted that he would be willing to see Kansas pioneer woman suffrage. His endorsement had little impact on the Republican anti-feminist campaign, however. To counter the anti-feminist attacks, Anthony and Stanton turned to the Democrats. Their new ally became George Francis Train, a Democrat who favored woman suffrage but opposed black male suffrage. Although the black suffrage amendment had received support from the Republican Party, the issue failed at the polls. So did the woman suffrage amendment.

As a result of the campaign, Anthony, Stanton, and their followers began to break away from their abolitionist friends, who they believed had betrayed them by supporting black suffrage but not women's rights in Kansas. A rift also occurred in the leadership of the American Equal Rights Association. Stone and her husband Henry B. Blackwell criticized Anthony and Stanton for associating with Train, a man who used racist arguments to win support for woman suffrage. From this point on, Anthony, Stanton, and their followers began developing a women's movement that was independent of their abolitionist allies.

In spite of the work of women's rights leaders, the Fourteenth Amendment was ratified in July 1868, after Congress made approval of the amendment a requirement for the readmission of former Confederate states to the Union.

*Jennifer Ross-Nazzal*

***See also*** Abolitionism and Northern Reformers; Anthony, Susan B. (1820–1906); Fifteenth Amendment; Kelley, Abby (1811–1887); Stanton, Elizabeth Cady (1815–1902); Stone, Lucy (1818–1893); Thirteenth Amendment.

**References and Further Reading**

DuBois, Ellen Carol. 1978. *Feminism and Suffrage: The Emergence of an Independent Women's Movement in America 1848–1869.* Ithaca, NY: Cornell University Press.

Foner, Eric. 1988. *Reconstruction: America's Unfinished Revolution, 1863–1877.* New York: Harper & Row.

Griffith, Elisabeth. 1984. *In Her Own Right: The Life of Elizabeth Cady Stanton.* New York: Oxford University Press.

## Fox, Tryphena Blanche Holder (1834–1912)

Tryphena Blanche Holder Fox was a native of Massachusetts who chronicled her life as the wife of a Southern doctor in a series of letters to her mother and siblings. She recorded her views of Southern society as well as her experiences in Louisiana and Mississippi during the Civil War.

Born in 1834, Tryphena Blanche Holder grew up in a family struggling to maintain a middle-class existence in Pittsfield, Massachusetts. Educated at the Maplewood Young Ladies Institute, her comfortable lifestyle ended with the death of her father when she was in her teens. To help support her mother and siblings, Tryphena took up teaching. In 1852, she went to Mississippi to serve as a governess to the young children of George Messenger, who owned a plantation near Vicksburg. There she met and married Dr. David Raymond Fox, the son of a nearby plantation owner, in 1856.

Tryphena and Raymond Fox moved to Jesuit Bend, Louisiana, located in Plaquemines Parish 35 miles downriver from New Orleans. In Jesuit Bend, Dr. Fox made his living as a physician to the area's wealthy sugar planters. Tryphena embarked on the life of a Southern housewife and mother, and her letters to her mother recorded the growth of her family and her difficulties in managing household slaves. Her letters also revealed her concerns about her husband's business, observations on southeastern Louisiana society, and laments about her home's isolation. Although a native of Massachusetts, Tryphena embraced the loyalties and prejudices of her adopted region, protesting the depiction of the South in Northern newspapers and staunchly supporting the Confederate cause.

During the Civil War, Tryphena was confronted with a heartbreaking division in her family. While she and her husband continued to support the Confederacy, her brother joined the Union navy. The war also brought more immediate troubles when southeastern Louisiana fell to Union control in the spring of 1862, and Raymond moved his family to his father's plantation near Vicksburg, Mississippi, shortly before the surrender of New Orleans. Tryphena spent the remaining war years in Mississippi, coping with inflation, blockade-induced shortages, and the siege of Vicksburg while tending to her growing family. After the fall of Vicksburg, Raymond joined the Confederate army as a surgeon. His military service added to his wife's growing list of worries.

After the war, the Fox family returned to their home at Jesuit Bend to find that it had been looted during their years in Mississippi. Tryphena faced the loss of much of her household property, as well as an adjustment to life without slave labor. She also discovered that one of her outbuildings was being used as a school for freedpeople. Although she initially determined to close the school, she did not once she realized that the rent would provide much needed income for her family.

*Julia Huston Nguyen*

***See also*** Family Life, Southern; Letter Writing.

**References and Further Reading**

Fox, Tryphena Blanche Holder. 1993. *A Northern Woman in the Plantation South: Letters of Tryphena Blanche Holder Fox, 1856–1876,* edited by Wilma King. Columbia: University of South Carolina Press.

## Fredericksburg, Battle of
### (December 13, 1862)

Union troops had occupied the city of Fredericksburg, Virginia, prior to the December 1862 battle, but few Confederate civilians there expected the abrupt changes that the battle brought. The Union's conciliatory stance in the early occupation gave way to a harsher policy toward Southern civilians during the battle. When Union Major General Ambrose E. Burnside's one hundred thirty-four thousand troops gathered along the Rappahannock River to face Robert E. Lee's eighty thousand soldiers, few local civilians, most of them women, had personally experienced the horrors of war. The battle forced them, as well as Union army nurses, to witness its devastation.

In 1860, Fredericksburg's population of roughly fifty-two hundred included approximately four hundred free blacks and a large slave population that numbered about one-third of the total residents. Many of Fredericksburg's African Americans fled to Union lines or moved north during the Union occupation of the city in the spring and summer of 1862, leaving few black women in Fredericksburg for the battle.

The occupation resulted in a similar exodus of the town's white women. Most of the town's female inhabitants continued their lives as normally as possible during the uneasy peace of Federal occupation. Some complained of the presence of the enemy but did not leave. Women's motives for staying included a fear of fleeing for economic reasons, a commitment to waiting to see what would happen, or a hope that war would not come near their homes a second time. Many of these attitudes would change in late 1862.

Located between the capitals of Richmond and Washington, D.C, Fredericksburg stood in the path of war. The relative tranquility of Fredericksburg's early war experience ended with the arrival of Burnside's army at Falmouth in mid-November 1862. Fredericksburg lay undefended by the Confederates, but their burning of the bridges across the Rappahannock earlier that year kept the Federal Army out. The situation changed on November 21–22, when Confederate troops arrived to fortify Marye's Heights behind the town. Lee ordered Fredericksburg evacuated, and many women, children, slaves, and old men fled to Stafford, Spotsylvania, and Caroline Counties. Those who remained found themselves and their property vulnerable to Union attacks. In early December, when Burnside's men arrived at Stafford Heights across from town, Lee's army held a commanding position overlooking the city. Women arrived with both armies, as camp followers, vivandiéres, prostitutes, laundresses, or nurses. Others served in the ranks disguised as men.

Burnside, who had planned to march his army rapidly south, use pontoons to cross the Rappahannock River at Fredericksburg, and steal a march on Lee before he could stop their movement toward Richmond, was delayed by supply problems and poor communication. However, Burnside remained convinced that his plan could succeed.

As the two armies faced each other from opposite sides of the river in early December, many local women fled to the outlying areas around Fredericksburg. Others remained to see what the Union would do next. This first wave of evacuees included Fredericksburg Female Charity School students, who fled to a plantation south of town. By the second week of December, fewer than one thousand residents remained in Fredericksburg.

Lee and his troops worked to prevent the Union crossing of the Rappahannock River. On December 11, Confederate troops began sniping at Union engineers building a pontoon bridge across the river. Lee's decision to use Fredericksburg as a military position prompted Burnside's bombardment of the town. During the barrage, many townspeople fled in a second wave of evacuations; others, including local Confederate diarist and schoolteacher Jane Beale, used their basements as refuges. After a forced crossing by Union troops and street fighting in the town, Lee ordered his soldiers to evacuate.

Burnside spent December 12 crossing a large portion of his army into Fredericksburg, giving Lee more time to strengthen defenses behind the town. Most of Fredericksburg's remaining women, including Beale, fled to Salem Church, which overflowed with refugees. By the end of the day, Union soldiers had looted Fredericksburg, and only a small number of local women, hoping to protect their homes, remained in the city.

During the battle, Burnside's forces attempted to flank the enemy troops south of the town at Prospect Hill. Although they met with initial success, miscommunication led to seven futile and deadly Union assaults against the Sunken Road below Marye's Heights against what Burnside mistakenly believed was a break in the Southern lines. During the battle, local proprietor Martha Stephens, one of the few remaining women, allegedly gave aid under fire to wounded and thirsty soldiers in the Sunken Road area. After a devastating day, Burnside's subordinates convinced him of the pointlessness of another frontal assault against Lee's fortifications.

The battle altered the people and landscape of Fredericksburg. Virtually all buildings, including churches, became hospitals. During and after the battle, Clara Barton and other nurses tended the wounded in these makeshift hospitals. Other Union women, like Isabella Fogg, read the Bible, wrote letters, and took clothes, blankets, and food to needy soldiers. The bombardment and looting left approximately eighty structures in Fredericksburg destroyed and many others damaged. Upon their return, residents found more than five hundred dead bodies in the town.

It took decades for Fredericksburg to recover its antebellum population and grandeur. The Union suffered twelve thousand six hundred casualties during the battle—60 percent of them died in the charge against the stone wall at the base of Marye's Heights. By December 15, the Union army had retreated across the river. Suffering only fifty-four hundred casualties, Confederates rejoiced in their success. After the war, local women would become instrumental in the commemoration of Fredericksburg's Confederate dead and the battle as Lee's most lopsided victory.

*Barton A. Myers*

***See also*** African American Women; Barton, Clara (1821–1912); Camp Followers; Confederate Homefront; Destruction of Homes; Destruction of Personal Property; Female Combatants; Fogg, Isabella Morrison (1823–1873); Hospitals; Military Invasion and Occupation; Northern Women; Nurses; Refugees; Southern Women; Vivandiéres; Wounded, Visits to.

**References and Further Reading**
Hennessy, John. 2005. "For All Anguish, For Some Freedom: Fredericksburg in the War." *Blue and Gray Magazine* 22: 6–53.
O'Reilly, Francis Augustin. 2002. *The Fredericksburg Campaign: Winter War along the Rappahannock.* Baton Rouge: Louisiana State University Press.
Rable, George C. 2002. *Fredericksburg! Fredericksburg!* Chapel Hill: University of North Carolina Press.

## Free Blacks

When the Civil War began, members of the free black community attempted to shape the conflict to their own ends. As the war continued, the ranks of free African Americans swelled as runaways, contrabands, and then emancipated slaves left bondage.

When the Civil War began, the United States census listed approximately 488,070 free African Americans. This population was evenly divided between the free and slave states, with 226,152 free blacks living in the North and 261,918 living in the South. Although the free blacks lived restricted lives in segregated Northern towns, their lives were much more constricted in the South. Perceived as a threat to the natural order in the slave South, free blacks faced legal restrictions in many Southern states. These laws restricted African Americans' social and economic freedoms. Furthermore, well-paid occupations were often restricted to whites only, and African Americans' ability to travel was severely curtailed. These laws became increasingly difficult to enforce during the war, as free African Americans in the South worked to undermine the Confederacy and as white men left for the battlefields.

The war made the lives of free African Americans in the South even more precarious than they had been in the antebellum years. Aware of their perceived threat to the social order, many free African Americans migrated to the North to find temporary refuge. Others became refugees within the South, as soldiers threatened their homesteads. Most refugees moved to urban centers, where they lived with loved ones and friends and received aid from African American churches.

During the Civil War, many free male African Americans enlisted in the Union army when they had the opportunity. Their participation was initially limited, but as wartime policies concerning black soldiers changed, free blacks formed several units. By the end of the war, approximately one hundred eighty-six thousand African American soldiers served in the Union army. In this regard, the actions of free black women paralleled that of white society. They pushed their husbands, sons, and other male relatives and neighbors to fight for the Union, and they often provided clothing and supplies for black military units. Their motivations varied, but most free black women urged African American men to enlist with the belief that their participation would help emancipate family members and other African American slaves.

Like their white neighbors, African American women worried about their husbands and sons who served in the army. In addition to the general anxieties about the hardships that soldiers could face, African American women feared that their husbands would be enslaved if they were captured by Confederate troops. Southern military officials vocalized this intention. Furthermore, in several instances, Southern troops refused to accept the surrender of African American soldiers. After the massacre of black soldiers at Fort Pillow in 1864, the wives of African Americans who were killed in battle became eligible to receive pensions. In recognition of the legal constraints on slave marriage, the Federal government declared that cohabitation was enough to prove one's claim for a widow's pension.

African American women formed dozens of relief societies to send aid to those still in slavery and to assist black troops. Initially excluded from white aid societies, African American women in the North formed separate black-only organizations. In Philadelphia, for example, free black women formed the Colored Women's Sanitary Commission and the Ladies Sanitary Association of St. Thomas's African Episcopal Church. Free black women started organizations in other cities as well. The Colored Ladies' Freedmen's Aid Society formed in Chicago, and a Contraband Relief Association formed in Boston and in some other Northern cities. Elizabeth Keckley, First Lady Mary Todd Lincoln's seamstress, helped to found a contraband relief organization in Washington, D.C. Many of the organizations began as extensions of churches that directed their charitable energies toward the war. The Israel Bethel Church (African Methodist Episcopal) in Washington, D.C., formed a Union Relief Association in the fall of 1862, to alleviate the suffering of former slaves who were pouring into the city. With contributions from Frederick Douglass, President Abraham Lincoln, and other dignitaries, the association donated more than one hundred crates and barrels of goods to former slaves in the city. The organization's ambitions went beyond sending supplies to the African American troops; it explicitly made racial justice and the support of the quest for freedom equal to its desire to provide assistance to soldiers.

For many free black women, the Civil War provided new opportunities for work. While most remained working in the fields or doing domestic labor, many took jobs with the Federal government. In addition, many African American women from the North staffed the relief camps. Sojourner Truth and Harriet Jacobs, two renowned African American abolitionists and former slaves, both served these functions during the war. Other free black women served as nurses. As both African Americans and as women, these workers were expected to be especially obedient. Their responsibilities were also constrained because most black women were confined to the most menial tasks as cooks and laundresses. These women also tended to work under the oversight of either white men or women.

The entrance of African American men and women into the workplace did not occur smoothly in many American cities. In 1862, between two and three thousand white workers threatened to burn down two tobacco factories if black female workers were not evicted from the buildings. These tensions continued to shape animosities toward free black men and women. During the New York City Draft riots in 1863, African American women found them-

Nine soldiers and a female African American cook posed in front of the Fifth Army Corps Headquarters tent at Harrison's Landing, James River, Virginia, in 1862. (Library of Congress)

selves the recipient of much of the antiwar, antidraft sentiment in the city's Irish community. Although most of the violence was directed at African American men, women too faced violent assaults.

Other African American women became teachers during and after the war. Many free black Northern women traveled to the South to teach the freedmen and freedwomen. Mary Chase, a free black, established a school in Alexandria, Virginia, in 1861. In addition, Philadelphian Charlotte Forten, spent eighteen months teaching basic skills to former slave children and adults in Port Royal, one of the South Carolina's Sea Islands. The first African American teacher to work in the Sea Islands, Forten would not be the last. In subsequent years, free black women who went to the Sea Islands tended to be poorer than Forten and her white counterparts. African American teachers in the Sea Islands also tended to stay longer than white women and to emphasize racial pride along with literacy and other skills.

During Reconstruction, individuals who were free prior to the war held a disproportionate amount of representation in the Southern states. Half of the twenty-two African Americans who served in Congress between 1865 and 1900 were former free blacks, and a similar story occurred on the local level. Although restricted from governmental positions before the war, their literacy and financial resources helped this "free Negro caste" to rise to prominence. These political gains came to an abrupt halt as Reconstruction ended, but the black caste system endured into the late nineteenth century.

*Andrew K. Frank*

***See also*** African American Women; Camp Followers; Civilian Life; Contraband Relief Association; Contrabands; Douglass, Frederick (ca. 1818–1895); Draft Riots and Resistance; Education, Southern; Enlistment; Family Life, Confidence; Family Life, Union; Forten (Grimké), Charlotte L. (1837–1914); Freedmen's Bureau; Fundraising; Letter Writing; Lincoln, Abraham

(1809–1865); Lincoln, Mary Todd (1818–1882); Northern Women; Pensions, Union Widows; Politics; Port Royal; Reconstruction (1865–1877); Refugees; Religion; Teachers, Northern; Teachers, Southern; Truth, Sojourner [Isabella Baumfree] (1797–1883); Tubman, Harriet [Araminta Ross] (1822–1913); Union Homefront; Wartime Employment; Widows, Union.

### References and Further Reading

Berlin, Ira. 1974. *Slaves without Masters: The Free Negro in the American South.* New York: New Press.

McPherson, James M. 1965. *The Negro's Civil War: How American Blacks Felt and Acted during the War for the Union.* New York: Ballantine Books.

Silber, Nina. 2005. *Daughters of the Union: Northern Women Fight the Civil War.* Cambridge, MA: Belknap/Harvard University Press.

## Freedmen's Bureau

Established by Congress in March 1865, the Bureau of Refugees, Freedmen and Abandoned Lands, or Freedmen's Bureau, was intended to help formerly enslaved black men and women in their transition to freedom.

Charged with providing rations, distributing lands, mediating labor contracts, establishing schools, promoting education, and securing civil rights for freed blacks, the Bureau had an almost impossible task. Aside from its restricted resources and limited lifespan, the Freedmen's Bureau faced opposition from Southern whites, Democrats in Congress, and President Andrew Johnson. The Bureau also suffered from ideological limitations for, although it hoped to help freedmen, it did not wish for them to become too dependent on Federal aid. To this end, the Freedmen's Bureau relied heavily on the goodwill of Southerners to treat freedmen as their equals. By the time of its final disbandment in 1872 due to sustained opposition, the Bureau still left many of its goals unaccomplished.

As a branch of the War Department, the Freedmen's Bureau recruited its agents from the military ranks. Major General Oliver Otis Howard, a pious and dedicated soldier, served as the Bureau's commissioner for its entire existence. Howard was a graduate of Bowdoin College and the United States Military Academy at West Point. A veteran of many Civil War battles, he was also greatly concerned with the welfare of freedmen. Tirelessly working for freedmen's rights, Howard set a good example for his subordinates, many of whom also cared deeply about the plight of newly freed slaves. Other Bureau agents, however, had little concern for the freedmen and sought only to get blacks back to work in the ravaged South. With only approximately nine hundred agents working throughout the South at the height of its influence, the Freedmen's Bureau faced the daunting task of meeting the needs of liberated slaves.

At the close of the Civil War, thousands of refugees, blacks and whites, needed medicine, food, clothing, and aid. Freedmen's Bureau officers distributed needed supplies and helped many individuals find their way home. Bureau agents also offered temporary shelter for blacks who needed a place to rest while they tracked down their lost family members, scattered by the antebellum slave trade and the war. Providing aid for destitute black Southerners, however, was only an immediate task; the larger goal was to rebuild Southern society.

The Bureau's most crucial test involved the conflict between Southern whites and blacks over the issues of land and labor. More than anything, newly freed slaves wanted land. Many freedmen saw the ownership of their own farms as the pinnacle of true freedom. Following the war, the Freedmen's Bureau controlled vast amounts of land confiscated from rebellious Southerners. Despite the fact that many freedmen had already settled on some newly distributed lands, President Andrew Johnson, a staunch opponent of the Freedmen's Bureau, brought an end to the program by pardoning former Confederates, ordering that their seized lands be returned to them, and evicting freedmen. This reversal of one of its primary principles weakened the Bureau's standing in the eyes of the freedmen.

Even though freedmen did not have access to land, they were still expected to work for a living. Toward the goal of jump-starting the Southern economy, promoting the Northern Free Labor ideology, and putting workers back in the fields, the Freedmen's Bureau pressed black men and women to sign labor contracts with landowning whites. With slavery dead, victorious Northerners wished to implant their labor views on the defeated South. Their ideals of Free Labor required that all laborers work hard for their own advancement without depending on government handouts. Those who were able to work, it was believed, should be put to work and denied aid. Perhaps underestimating the level of animosity between the two races in the South, Bureau agents did not entirely recognize the fact that Southern whites resented having to pay their former slaves and that many freedmen did not wish to work in any capacity for their former masters. The Bureau was under great pressure to get African Americans working again because one of its main fears was that continued aid would create a class of dependent freedmen. Despite the fact that many blacks were forced into signing contracts to work on white-owned lands, freedmen were often given the chance to choose their employers and Bureau agents aided them in negotiating fair contracts.

Freedmen's Bureau agents concerned with implanting a Free Labor work ethic did not always respect the integrity of freedpeoples families and tried to get blacks of both sexes and all ages back to work. Many black husbands attempted to shield their wives and children from labor, saying that freedwomen should, like white women, tend to the home and that their children should attend school. Control over one's family was, after all, one of the freedoms that had been denied to slaves. For their part, freedwomen, some of whom were single parents, took whatever opportunities they could to provide for their children. In some instances, freedwomen and their children were forced into seasonal work to sustain themselves. Many black women found it difficult to gain employment not only because of their sex but also because they had to find a way to take care of their children. Bureau agents sometimes stepped in and attempted to get wayward husbands to take responsibility for their wives and families.

The Bureau's greatest achievement came in the realm of education. Even before the Bureau began to support freedmen's schools, many blacks had organized schools for themselves in churches and private homes. Freedmen of all ages understood the necessity of education and filled up classrooms all over the South. In conjunction with Northern aid societies such as the American Missionary Association (AMA), the Freedmen's Bureau helped acquire land and supply building materials for thousands of new schools. The AMA and organizations like it helped recruit Northern teachers to come south.

Many of those who answered the call were young, educated, middle-class white women from New England who brought with them a missionary zeal and a dedication to help freedmen's advancement. These Northern teachers, or Yankee schoolmarms as they came to be called, also used the opportunity to travel south to escape their domestic lives, seeking new opportunities and adventures. Northern teachers worked hard, rising early and getting to sleep late. They sacrificed not only their time, but also their comfort; the accommodations that awaited them in the South were far from ideal. While the Freedmen's Bureau donated funds for construction and resources, the AMA helped pay the salaries of these Northern teachers. Classes consisted of education in writing, math, and social norms. Teachers believed that slavery had degraded blacks and sought to instill the virtues of responsibility and discipline, corresponding with the Bureau's policy of getting freedmen to work on their own. Southern whites often shunned these schools, not allowing their own children to be educated alongside freed blacks. Other than local schools, the Bureau also helped create institutions of higher learning such as Howard University, the Hampton Institute, and Fisk University. When the Bureau was finally disbanded, it had established thousands of schools throughout the South. These institutions remained as the foundation of Southern education.

Freedmen's Bureau agents also served the vital function of being blacks' advocates in the Southern courts. Aside from helping with labor contract negotiations, the Bureau also advised freedmen on legal matters and defended blacks' civil rights. To the best of their ability, Bureau agents defended blacks from violence and also sought to ensure their

A classroom at the Freedmen's Bureau in Richmond, Virginia. (Library of Congress)

rights to impartial justice. The Bureau, perhaps naively, attempted to get Southern courts to recognize freedmen's rights and equality before the bar. The state statutes, therefore, were altered but the courts themselves remained prejudiced against blacks, and the use of military courts to guarantee an impartial verdict for freedmen was no longer an option once civil courts re-opened throughout the South. Freedmen's Bureau officers continued to monitor cases and stepped in when they saw a need to do so. Due to its limited resources and temporary mandate, however, the Bureau ultimately could not guarantee justice for freedmen in local courts.

Often the actions on behalf of newly freed blacks cost the agents the goodwill of the local population. While blacks saw the Bureau as their ally, Southern whites viewed it as a symbol of Northern oppression and learned to associate it with the Confederacy's

defeat. Black men and women understood that the Bureau was there to protect them and used its services accordingly. They came to the agents with personal and domestic problems but also lodged complaints against whites who defrauded or threatened them. Actions like these outraged white Southerners, who saw the Bureau agents as meddling in their affairs. Determined to halt black advancement and curb Bureau influence, Southerners used various means to thwart the agents' activities. On the local level, Southerners threatened Bureau agents, treated them with disdain, and offered little or no cooperation. Northern schoolteachers, also seen as representatives of a triumphant North, were harassed and terrorized by local whites. Paramilitary groups burned down black schools, caused chaos in some sections of the South, and interfered with the Bureau's operations. Due to the demobilization of the wartime army, Bureau officers had limited resources and could not always count on troop reinforcements in the South. Without troops to uphold Federal policy, it became very difficult to maintain Bureau operations in hostile communities. Many agents understood that they had to compromise with white Southerners to accomplish their tasks. To this end, they sometimes sided with local whites at the expense of the freedmen.

On the national level, Southerners had allies in Congress and the White House. Democrats and President Andrew Johnson warred against the Bureau from the very start of its operations. When former Confederates attempted to re-establish limits on black freedoms with the notorious black codes, the Republican-controlled Congress moved to extend the life of the Freedmen's Bureau for an additional year and also proposed the Civil Rights bill. President Johnson, arguing that the Bureau represented Federal patronage that favored one group of citizens over another and citing fiscal limitations, vetoed the two bills. Republicans passed the measures over Johnson's veto and also sought to guarantee freedmen's civil rights by successfully including the Fourteenth and Fifteenth Amendments to the Constitution.

By the late 1860s, support for the Freedmen's Bureau waned, many Northerners believing that the task of getting blacks back to work and securing blacks' civil rights had been accomplished. The Bureau remained partially functional after 1868 and permanently closed its offices in 1872. The Freedmen's Bureau succeeded in providing for refugees in the immediate wake of the Civil War and in building a new educational system for the South. In land distribution, labor negotiation, and civil rights, however, the Bureau's record was less than stellar. These failures, however, were caused mostly by Southern opposition, both on the grassroots and the governmental levels. The Bureau itself may have been too reliant on the goodwill of Southerners. Understanding that their mission was temporary, Bureau agents hoped that white Southerners would learn to treat blacks as fellow citizens, perhaps ignoring white resentment over Confederate military defeat and deep-seated prejudices

against former slaves. Overall, the Bureau had a mixed record that highlighted some of the ideological limitations and failures of Reconstruction.

*Kanisorn Wongsrichanalai*

**See also** African American Women; Education, Southern; Fifteenth Amendment; Fourteenth Amendment; Reconstruction (1865–1877); Sherman Land (Special Field Orders Number 15); Teachers, Northern; Thirteenth Amendment.

**References and Further Reading**

Cimbala, Paul A. 1997. *Under the Guardianship of the Nation: The Freedmen's Bureau and the Reconstruction of Georgia, 1865–1870.* Athens: University of Georgia Press.

Cimbala, Paul A., and Randall M. Miller, eds. 1999. *The Freedmen's Bureau and Reconstruction: Reconsiderations.* New York: Fordham University Press.

Finley, Randy. 1996. *From Slavery to Uncertain Freedom: The Freedmen's Bureau in Arkansas, 1865–1869.* Fayetteville: University of Arkansas Press.

Foner, Eric. 1988. *Reconstruction, 1863–1877.* New York: Harper & Row.

Jones, Jacqueline. 1980. *Soldiers of Light and Love: Northern Teachers and Georgia Blacks, 1865–1873.* Chapel Hill: University of North Carolina Press.

Richter, William L. 1991. *Overreached on All Sides: The Freedmen's Bureau Administration in Texas, 1865–1868.* College Station: Texas A&M University Press.

## Frémont, Jessie Benton (1824–1902)

Prolific writer and intellectual partisan of Republican and antislavery politics, Jessie Benton Frémont was the favored daughter of Missouri Senator Thomas Hart Benton. Living in an age when she was unable to enter politics on her own, she was the force behind the career of her husband, the controversial explorer, military leader, and politician John Charles Frémont. She was indispensable in shaping his 1856 campaign for the presidency on an antislavery platform. She also helped to frame the August 30, 1861 unauthorized emancipation proclamation he issued as major general in command of the Department of the West. The document claimed authority to confiscate property and

Jessie Benton Frémont (1824–1902), writer and wife of John Charles Frémont. (Cirker, Hayward and Blanche Cirker, eds., *Dictionary of American Portraits*, 1967)

freed slaves of Missouri rebels in the name of martial law.

Jessie Benton eloped with John Frémont at the age of seventeen. Her father used his considerable political connections to further his son-in-law's expeditions to survey large regions of the West in the 1840s. Appointed governor of the new civil government in California, John Frémont faced a court-martial but was pardoned by President James Polk after Jessie and others lobbied on his behalf. Jessie shaped the well-received published accounts of the Western expeditions, embellishing her husband's dictation. Prior to John Frémont's run for the presidency as the Republican candidate in 1856, the Frémonts made a fortune in gold mining and raised a family in California. Able and popular, Jessie served as a primary asset in her husband's unsuccessful bid for the presidency. Her high profile also made her a target of criticism for Democratic opponents, who castigated her, as a woman, for her public participation in politics.

When John was put in command of the Department of the West in St. Louis, Jessie continued as his unofficial chief aide. When, in the midst of controversy, Abraham Lincoln stripped Frémont of his post, Jessie came personally to Washington to confront the president. The interview was highly charged. Lincoln derided the charming but uncompromising Jessie for her unfeminine participation in politics. Jessie, meanwhile, criticized Lincoln's reluctance to act on emancipation. Jessie worked tirelessly to utilize her political and social networks behind the scenes while her husband served as standard bearer for the radical wing of the Republican Party.

When in postwar years the Frémonts were bankrupted by railroad speculation, Jessie Benton Frémont supported the family through her writing. *The Story of the Guard: A Chronicle of the War*, a defense of her husband's leadership in Missouri during the Civil War, was the first book she published under her own name. As her husband's star dimmed through scandal and bad business ventures in the 1870s, she did what she could to maintain his reputation. The Frémonts moved back to California in 1887. Jessie died in Los Angeles, philosophical about the difficulties of life for women.

*Barbara Bair*

**See also** Abolitionism and Northern Reformers; Lincoln, Abraham (1809–1865); Northern Women; Politics.

**References and Further Reading**

Herr, Pamela. 1988. *Jessie Benton Frémont: A Biography.* Norman: University of Oklahoma Press.

Herr, Pamela, and Mary Lee Spence, eds. 1993. *The Letters of Jessie Benton Frémont.* Urbana: University of Illinois Press.

## French, Mansfield (1810–1876)

Educator, abolitionist, and religious leader Reverend Mansfield French worked to improve the conditions for the freedmen in the Sea Islands by helping to establish schools, hospitals, and homesteads for the former slaves.

Born in Manchester, Vermont, on February 21, 1810, Mansfield French moved to Ohio as a young man, where he studied at the Kenyon College divinity school. French established or served as the principal of several schools, including the Granville Female Seminary and the Circleville Female College. He became a minister with the Methodist Episcopal Church and served for three years as president of the Xenia, Ohio Female Seminary during the late 1840s. He also worked as an agent for Wilberforce University, founded in Ohio in 1856 as the first African American–owned and–operated institution of higher learning in the United States.

By the late 1850s, French was living in New York City, where he published *The Beauty of Holiness*, a religious magazine with the aid of wife Austa. He frequented antislavery meetings and became friendly with Lewis Tappan and George Whipple of the American Missionary Association, as well as with other abolitionist leaders. During his days in Ohio, French had also become acquainted with Salmon Chase, ex-governor who would serve as treasury secretary in Abraham Lincoln's cabinet.

In 1862 French became involved in the efforts of the American Missionary Association and other groups to organize religious and educational programs for the newly free black population of the South Carolina Sea Islands. French traveled to Union-controlled Port Royal to examine firsthand conditions among freedmen. Upon his return north, French organized a meeting, held at New York's Cooper Institute, which led to the formation of the National Freedmen's Relief Association. French was elected the organization's general agent, and in March 1862 he returned to Port Royal with a group of missionaries and teachers. In a letter to Chase, French had asked for government cooperation in the transportation of missionaries, physicians, and teachers and their supplies, as well as the use of buildings to establish schools and hospitals.

In August 1862, French returned to Washington and met with Chase and Secretary of War Edwin Stanton. French received authorization to allow General Rufus Saxton to begin the recruitment up to five thousand black soldiers in the Sea Islands. This ultimately resulted in the formation of Thomas Wentworth Higginson's First South Carolina Volunteers.

In late 1863, French was again in Washington, this time attempting to settle the thorny question of land

ownership for freedmen. His mission at first appeared successful, with President Lincoln authorizing blacks to "preempt" a homestead of 20 or 40 acres with a small down payment. Unfortunately, the policy was reversed in early 1864, forcing blacks to compete for land at public auction or to apply for a small amount of land set aside for charitable purposes. Consequently, few black families ultimately obtained their own land, and French's efforts to establish the freedmen as farmers on abandoned Sea Island plantations met with only partial success. At one point, two of Chase's direct tax commissioners asked that French be removed from the Department of the South, and several fellow missionaries complained that he used his religious position to promote his political views, particularly on the land issue.

After the war, French remained in South Carolina. At one point he campaigned for a United States Senate seat, but charges concerning various real estate activities hurt his credibility. French eventually returned to New York in 1872. He became pastor of the St. James Methodist Episcopal Church in Pearsalls, on Long Island, where he died on March 15, 1876 of dysentery.

*David Coles*

***See also*** Abolitionism and Northern Reformers; Antislavery Societies; Freedmen's Bureau; Lincoln, Abraham (1809–1865); Politics; Port Royal; Religion.
**References and Further Reading**
Rose, Willie Lee. 1964. *Rehearsal for Reconstruction: The Port Royal Experiment.* Indianapolis, IN: Bobbs-Merrill Company.

## Fundraising

The need for Civil War supplies and funds far outweighed what women could produce on their own, so they turned to solicitation to make up the difference and meet wartime demands. In both the Union and Confederacy, individuals, local aid societies, and national organizations, such as the United States Sanitary Commission (USSC), solicited money and supplies to assist soldiers on the battlefield, sick and wounded soldiers, and soldiers' families. Efforts included fairs, concerts, raffles, picnics, and tableaux. All of these activities were principally organized, promoted, and performed by women. The amount of public interaction required for these activities challenged many traditional nineteenth-century gender expectations, but wartime necessity and women's successful efforts overcame issues of propriety.

Confederate women's fundraising efforts arose from a constant need to supply soldiers as well as an ongoing dependence of the Confederate government on private sources for supplies. When individual home manufacturing proved insufficient, individuals and local ladies' and societies organized activities to raise funds to purchase the needed goods. Individually, Confederate women would often stand on street corners or go door-to-door soliciting funds. On a much larger scale, local ladies' aid societies organized, advertised, supplied products for, and performed in benefit concerts, theatricals, raffles, and suppers to raise money for the Confederate cause.

Many fairs featured the sale of women's donated and handmade products. Items for sale ranged from homemade baked goods and clothing to jewelry, fine china, and furniture. While admission to the fairs was minimal, averaging between 25¢ and a dollar, the cost of the items reflected the increasing wartime inflation. For instance, a small cake might sell for $75, while a doll might fetch $1,000. Consequently, most fundraising fairs, and indeed most other activities, raised only a couple of hundred dollars, with a very few gathering thousands.

Another popular activity was the *tableaux vivant*. These were popular public performances where women posed in a still life as background music played. The subjects of the performances included literature, history, and current events, with interpretations of the works of Shakespeare or representations of war issues (with young ladies dressing as states) proving the most frequent.

Beginning in 1862, Confederate women also began forming gunboat societies, local groups that sought funds for the construction of military gunboats to serve as homeland defense for the Confederacy. Recognizing the inability of the Confederate government to provide complete security for the homefront, women in coastal cities, such as Charleston, Mobile, Savannah, and New Orleans, collected money to finance their own waterfront defense.

Some debate and criticism took place over the appropriateness of these public activities by women. Traditional gender boundaries limited women to private avenues of support; the expectation was that women would not be the public face of the war effort. With the creation of gunboat societies, the gender transgression appeared severe. Women were encroaching on the male military realm and should not be directing or financing the Confederacy's military needs. However, most women in these organizations were trying to fill a need left vacant by their government rather than criticizing specific military policy. Indeed, throughout the war, material need overshadowed gender conventions, and Confederate women largely gained favorable public recognition for their wartime fundraising efforts.

Women in the Union also made significant contributions to the war effort through fundraising. Like their Confederate counterparts, Union women, both individually and as part of local church or aid societies, hosted and performed in benefit concerts, tableaux, suppers, theatricals, and raffles to raise money for their cause. Both cash and supplies in-kind were accepted as admission fees; the purpose of Union women's efforts was to provide whatever material assistance they could to their troops.

Unlike the Confederacy's mostly local efforts, Union women were able to organize their fundraising on a national scale. Estimates suggest between ten thousand and twelve thousand local aid societies were gathering money and supplies for the Union during the war. In an effort to streamline and centralize these disparate efforts, in 1861, a group of women met in New York City to create the Women's Central Association of Relief. Recognizing the need for cooperation with and support from the Federal government, the ladies presented their ideas to President Abraham Lincoln and won his approval for the establishment of the United States Sanitary Commission (USSC). The goals of the organization were threefold: to supplement government aid to soldiers, to coordinate the fundraising efforts of smaller aid societies, and to gather information on the conditions in and the needs of military camps and hospitals. To achieve these aims, the USSC established ten regional headquarters that would serve as collection and distribution centers.

Although gathering the contributions from small local fairs occupied much of the early work of the USSC, war needs demanded larger-scale efforts. In October 1863, the Northwestern branch of the USSC held a two-week fundraising fair in Chicago. As with the smaller fairs, women were the driving organizational and promotional force. In addition to door-to-door solicitations, women traveled throughout the region to gain support and sent countless letters and pamphlets to advertise the fair. Admission to the Chicago fair was 25¢, or $1 for a season pass, with soldiers and sailors given free admission. On the fairgrounds, attendees could buy products, view war memorabilia, or attend tableaux, concerts, or other theatrical performances. At the end of the two-week run, proceeds amounted to over $100,000 for the Northwestern Sanitary Commission.

The success of the Chicago fair led to others in Cleveland, Boston, Pittsburgh, St. Louis, and California. One of the largest and most financially successful events was the New York City Metropolitan Fair, held in April 1864. Again, women led the organizational efforts. Fairgoers paid between 25¢ and $1 entry fee for the opportunity to purchase goods ranging from furniture and sewing machines to dry goods and lingerie. Special events also drew interest, including a gallery of Mathew Brady pho-

tographs, as well as musical and theatrical performances with patriotic themes; these events charged an additional 25¢. The women organizers' work was richly rewarded: the fair was open for three weeks, and, in May 1864, organizers sent the USSC a check for $1 million. Throughout the war, the time, talents, and determination of Union women's fundraising activities, whether at the local, regional, or national level, contributed between $15 and $50 million dollars in goods procured or money raised for the Union cause.

*Kristen L. Streater*

***See also*** Aid Societies; Columbia Bazaar (January 17–21, 1865); Confederate Homefront; Domesticity; Fairs and Bazaars; Gunboat Societies; Northern Women; Separate Spheres; Southern Women; Union Homefront; United States Sanitary Commission; Women's Central Association of Relief.

**References and Further Reading**

Attie, Jeanie. 1998. *Patriotic Toil: Northern Women and the American Civil War*. Ithaca, NY: Cornell University Press.

Culpepper, Marilyn Mayer. 1991. *Trials and Triumphs: The Women of the American Civil War*. East Lansing: Michigan State University Press.

Faust, Drew Gilpin. 1996. *Mothers of Invention: Women of the Slaveholding South in the American Civil War*. Chapel Hill: University of North Carolina Press.

Massey, Mary Elizabeth. 1994. *Women in the Civil War*. Lincoln: University of Nebraska Press.

Rable, George C. 1989. *Civil Wars: Women and the Crisis of Southern Nationalism*. Urbana: University of Illinois Press.

Whites, LeeAnn. 1995. *The Civil War as a Crisis in Gender: Augusta, Georgia, 1860–1890*. Athens: University of Georgia Press.

# G

## Garrison, William Lloyd (1805–1879)

Radical abolitionist William Lloyd Garrison published the antislavery paper *The Liberator*. He supported the necessity of immediate emancipation of slaves and equality for African Americans.

William Lloyd Garrison was born in 1805 in Newburyport, Massachusetts. In 1808, his father, who had struggled with unemployment and alcoholism, abandoned the family. William attended school infrequently, often working odd jobs to help his mother support the family, especially after his older brother James left the family to go to sea. After serving short stints as an apprentice first to a shoemaker and then to a cabinetmaker, William found his true calling as an apprentice to Ephraim W. Allen, owner and editor of the *Newburyport Herald*.

In the 1820s, Garrison joined the leading antislavery organization of the time, the American Colonization Society (ACS). He met abolitionist Benjamin Lundy who traveled the antislavery lecture circuit calling for the gradual emancipation of slaves. Garrison helped Lundy revive his antislavery newspaper, the *Genius of Universal Emancipation*. By 1830, however, Garrison had converted to what was then called immediatism and left the ACS. Lundy and Garrison dissolved their partnership.

Garrison published the first issue of his antislavery newspaper *The Liberator* on January 1, 1831. In his newspaper Garrison wrote that slavery was a sin against God and that all slaveholders were sinners. The abolition of slavery had to begin without delay. *The Liberator* became the antislavery movement's pre-eminent publication and served as the main instrument for Garrison's views. In 1832, Garrison helped found the New England Anti-Slavery Society and a year later took a prominent role in the founding of the American Anti-Slavery Society (AASS). Garrison authored the AASS's Declaration of Sentiments, which combined religious and human rights arguments against slavery. Under Garrison's leadership, the AASS emphasized moral suasion by promoting the abolition of slavery through an appeal to the religious conscience of Americans, particularly slaveholders.

As his involvement in the antislavery movement grew, Garrison developed close ties with the abolitionist movement in England, supporting visits by British abolitionists like George Thompson to the United States and in turn visiting abolitionists in England. In the midst of the postal campaign of 1835, Garrison was mistaken for Thompson, attacked in Boston, dragged through the streets to be lynched, and was saved only through the quick action of the city mayor and police who fought off the mob. In the South, Garrison was burned in effigy. Throughout the 1830s, Garrison developed a reputation as a harsh and unrelenting critic of slavery.

Garrison shared much in common with the reformers of his time. Slavery was but one battle against the social inequities and moral depravity that reformers saw everywhere in American society in the antebellum period. Like other reformers, Garrison was involved in many movements to remake American society. Because of his broad interests in

With the help of abolitionist philanthropist Arthur Tappan, radical abolitionist William Lloyd Garrison started an antislavery paper, *The Liberator*, on January 1, 1831. (National Archives and Records Administration)

reform and his sharp, uncompromising style, Garrison had trouble with his supporters and opponents in the AASS. Garrison supported women's rights and, unlike many abolitionists of the time, equal rights for African Americans. He further believed in nonresistance, the rejection of government politics, and Christian perfectionism. The tensions in the AASS reached a flash point in 1840 when Garrison's opponents, led by Lewis and Arthur Tappan, broke away from the organization and founded the American and Foreign Anti-Slavery Society. Garrison was left with full control of the AASS, which left the American antislavery movement forever split between Garrisonians and Tappanites.

In the 1850s Garrison's belief that a slave power conspiracy dominated Congress deepened, and on July 4, 1854, after fugitive slave Anthony Burns was returned to his owner under the newly adopted Fugitive Slave Law, Garrison staged a public burning of the Constitution, calling the document a covenant with death. In 1859 Garrison expressed his admiration of John Brown as a martyr to the slaves' cause. Garrison did not support Lincoln's soft stand on slavery, but he did support the Union during the Civil War. In 1863, he rejoiced at the issuance of the Emancipation Proclamation, which he believed transformed the war for the Union to a war to free the slaves. With the successful passage of the Thirteenth Amendment, Garrison believed his mission was finished. In May 1865, he abandoned the AASS, leaving its leadership to Wendell Phillips who continued the organization until 1870. In December 1865, Garrison ceased publication of *The Liberator*. After the war, Garrison supported the Radical Republicans' plans for Reconstruction.

William Lloyd Garrison died at his daughter's home in 1879.

*Julie Holcomb*

**See also** Abolitionism and Northern Reformers; African American Women; Antislavery Societies; Free Blacks; Politics; Thirteenth Amendment; Union Homefront.

### References and Further Reading

Kraditor, Aileen S. 1969. *Means and Ends in American Abolitionism: Garrison and His Critics on Strategy and Tactics, 1864–1850.* New York: Random House.

Mayer, Henry. 1998. *All on Fire: William Lloyd Garrison and the Abolition of Slavery.* New York: St. Martin's Griffin.

Stewart, James Brewer. 1997. *Holy Warriors: The Abolitionists and American Slavery.* New York: Hill and Wang.

### Gay, Mary Ann Harris (1829–1918)

A native of Decatur, Georgia, Mary Ann Harris Gay witnessed General William T. Sherman's conquest of Atlanta as a young woman and published her memoir, *Life in Dixie during the War*, in 1892.

Born in Milledgeville, Georgia, Mary Gay was raised in Decatur as the daughter of an upper-class slaveholding family. Her family staunchly supported the Confederacy and invested heavily in Confederate war bonds. In addition, her only brother served under General John Bell Hood. Gay remained in Decatur for the duration of the war years and worked diligently to support the Confederate effort. On several occasions, she hid clothing and contraband for Confederate troops, conveyed information and even people across battle lines, and spoke unapologetically in favor of the Confederate cause both during and after the war.

During the siege of Atlanta, Union troops overtook her home and utilized it as a headquarters office. Gay unrelentingly spoke in favor of Confederate troops and communicated what she learned from Union officers to officers in the camp of General Hood. After Sherman's evacuation of the city, Gay worked to help those who remained in Atlanta by collecting minié balls from the battlefields and exchanging them for bread. In the final months of the war, Gay was devastated by news of her brother's death at the Battle of Franklin.

Mary Gay had been a published author before the war, and during the Reconstruction years she used her writing talents as a means to support her family. She had her 1858 collection of poems and essays, *Prose and Poetry by a Southern Lady*, reprinted and marketed it aggressively, even selling it door-to-door. She gained national attention with her work: Mark Twain lampooned her florid and highly dramatic style of writing in *Tom Sawyer*, but the book went through eleven editions.

Gay's postwar activities included advocating for the preservation of battlefields and the construction of Confederate memorials, fundraising for the Baptist Church, and the organization of a local chapter of the United Daughters of the Confederacy. Her 1892 memoir, based on her brother's wartime letters, her sister's journal, and her own memories, quickly became a favorite of Confederate veterans and a staple of Atlanta's wartime lore. It also provided some inspiration for Margaret Mitchell's best-selling *Gone with the Wind*.

*Kristen L. Rouse*

**See also** Atlanta, Evacuation of (Special Field Orders Number 67); Sherman's Campaign (1864–1865); United Daughters of the Confederacy.

**References and Further Reading**
Gay, Mary A. H. [1892] 2001. *Life in Dixie during the War*, edited by J. H. Segars. Macon, GA: Mercer University Press.

## Gettysburg, Battle of (July 1–3, 1863)

One of the few battles that directly engaged Northern civilians, the Battle of Gettysburg was the bloodiest battle of the Civil War. Fought in and around the town of Gettysburg, Pennsylvania, on July 1–3, 1863, this military engagement resulted in approximately fifty thousand combined casualties. During the battle, hundreds of female civilians were trapped in their homes. They successfully endured the contest and afterward aided the hundreds of doctors, nurses, and other volunteers who flooded the town to help the wounded.

Confederate General Robert E. Lee began his second invasion of the North in June 1863 with the intention of drawing the Union army of the Potomac into a decisive battle. The Union army, ordered to repel Lee's troops and prevent an advance by Confederate columns on key cities such as Washington, D.C., and Baltimore, pursued the Confederates with approximately ninety thousand men. By the end of June, Lee's forces were scattered in Pennsylvania. Upon learning that General George Meade was pursuing him, Lee ordered a concentration of his men at the nearest crossroads town: Gettysburg, a town of about twenty-four hundred citizens.

On June 30, Federal cavalry arrived in Gettysburg. On the next day, supported by infantry, Union soldiers attempted to hold off attacks by two of Lee's corps. Eventually, the Confederates got the upper hand and flanked the Union line. Withdrawing through Gettysburg in confusion, Union troops rallied on a ridge to the south of the town. Many soldiers got lost during the retreat and were captured in the streets. Unionist women and other civilians, unable or unwilling to leave their homes before the battle began, did their best to shelter hiding Union troops as they settled in to prepare for the Confederate occupation of the town.

On July 2 when both armies had brought up a majority of their units, Meade's line was in the shape of a fishhook, anchored by two hills and curved around Cemetery Ridge. Lee, whose forces continued to hold the town, took the initiative and ordered an attack on both Union flanks. Meeting with initial success on their right, rebel troops shattered one Union corps. However, after meeting stiff resistance on a hill named Little Round Top and along the center of the Union line, the attack failed to achieve its goal of crushing the Federal army. On the Confederate left the fighting yielded equally disappointing results.

Lee decided to stake the entire battle on one final assault against the center of the Union line on the next day. At about one in the afternoon on July 3, Confederate artillery opened up a concentrated fire on the Union front. After the bombardment, approximately fifteen thousand Confederate infantrymen advanced across a mile of open ground against Cemetery Ridge. Afterward known as Pickett's Charge, the assault failed due to well-aimed Union artillery and determined defenders along Cemetery Ridge.

Following this repulse, Lee ordered a retreat. Columns of worn-out Confederate troops crowded the roads south, marching along with wagon trains filled with the wounded and dying. Thousands of other wounded men were left behind, in the care of Union doctors and medical volunteers who descended on the town after the battle ended. A Union field hospital was created on the outskirts of town to better handle the vast numbers of wounded. Members of the United States Sanitary Commission and the United States Christian Commission offered their services to the Union medical authorities, who were overburdened in the immediate aftermath of the conflict.

In Gettysburg, civilians emerged from their hiding places into a town that had been battered and fought over for three days. A stray bullet had killed one of their own, a young woman named Jenny Wade, as she baked bread for the soldiers during the battle. The civilians, both those who had lived through the battle and those who were returning to town, had little time to mourn the near destruction of their community. Whether enthusiastically or reluctantly, they opened their doors to the wounded, serving as nurses and improvising makeshift hospitals out of barns, houses, public buildings, and churches. For the next few weeks, the cleanup of the town consumed their time and energy as they comforted the wounded and dug graves for the dead.

Lee's second invasion of the North failed to bring the decisive victory he sought. However, the Confederate defeat at Gettysburg did not ensure a Union victory. Bitter combat would continue for two more years. In November 1863, President Abraham Lincoln dedicated a national cemetery at Gettysburg to commemorate the fifty thousand casualties of the battle.

*Kanisorn Wongsrichanalai*

**See also** African American Women; Civilian Life; Foraging, Effects on Women; Impressment; Hospitals; Lee, Robert Edward (1807–1870); Military Invasion and Occupation; Northern Women; Nurses; Union Homefront; United States Christian Commission; United States Sanitary Commission.

**References and Further Reading**

Boritt, Gabor S., ed. 1999. *The Gettysburg Nobody Knows.* New York: Oxford University Press.

Creighton, Margaret S. 2005. *The Colors of Courage: Gettysburg's Forgotten History: Immigrants, Women, and African Americans in the Civil War's Defining Battle.* New York: Basic Books.

Sears, Stephen W. 2003. *Gettysburg.* Boston: Houghton Mifflin Company.

Trudeau, Noah Andre. 2002. *Gettysburg: A Testing of Courage.* New York: HarperCollins.

## Gibbons, Abigail "Abby" Hopper (1801–1893)

Quaker abolitionist and prison reformer Abigail "Abby" Hopper Gibbons spent the Civil War nursing sick and wounded soldiers in battlefield areas as well as in hospitals. She dedicated herself before and after the war to improve prison conditions for women, to rehabilitate released women, and to aid needy and outcast women and children.

Both the Hopper and Gibbons families were accustomed to activism and its attendant censure. Born in Philadelphia, Pennsylvania, to Quakers, Isaac T. and Sarah Hopper, Abby grew up knowing that her father was not only a tailor who assisted needy prisoners and prostitutes, but also an underground railroad operative. Abby was educated in a Quaker school taught by Lucretia Mott and later started her own school. In the late 1820s, she went to New York to be close to her widowed father, who had moved there with his second wife. Abby continued to teach. In February 1833, she married James Sloan Gibbons, a Quaker from Delaware and a partner in her brother-in-law's mercantile business. Between 1834 and 1843, Abby had six children, four of whom lived to adulthood: Sarah, Julia, Lucy, and Willie. The latter died as the result of an accident while attending Harvard.

After their marriage, Abby opened a school for blacks in her home, and her husband worked for a bank. Abby joined the Manhattan Anti-Slavery Society, a group with a majority black membership, while her husband represented the American Anti-Slavery Society. In 1841 their local Society of Friends disowned the Hopper and Gibbons families because they persisted in actively working to end slavery and to achieve other social reforms and because Hopper continued to serve on the committee that published the *National Anti-Slavery Standard*, which criticized an influential Quaker minister.

After seeing the unsanitary and dangerous conditions that female prisoners experienced in New York prisons, Abby established the Female Department of the New York Prison Association in 1845, an organization that became the Women's Prison Association. She also pushed for mandates requiring separate quarters and matrons for female prisoners. Working with prostitutes and women inmates led her also to become concerned about children's welfare. She started a school for German immigrants and sought better conditions for New York orphans and mentally impaired children.

Initially, Gibbons joined countless other women in sending supplies to soldiers. On winter visits in 1861 to hospitals that received her food and bandages, she realized she could be more useful as a nurse. She and her daughter, Sarah, volunteered to assist sick and wounded soldiers, preparing special food, bathing, comforting, and writing letters. Their

mission took them to Washington, D.C., Winchester, Virginia, and Point Lookout, Maryland; Abby was in charge of nursing for a time in Point Lookout.

Throughout her service, Gibbons was an advocate for contrabands, facing criticism and ostracism. When mobs rioted in New York against the military draft, they expressed their anger at the family's abolitionist and Unionist activities by burning the Gibbons house. Undaunted, Abby returned to nursing duty. Daughter Lucy, who with her father and sister had been forwarding supplies and tending to veterans from their home, accompanied Abby.

After the war, Abby organized several charities in her home state: the Labor and Aid Society to provide work for returning veterans, a dining hall offering nutritious meals for hospital patients, and an orphanage. During the 1870s and 1880s, in collaboration with the Women's Prison Association and as a national leader for the Moral Reform Movement, she championed several reforms to improve women's lives. She successfully petitioned the New York governor to place women on school, hospital, prison, and other social institution boards. She lobbied New York State and Federal legislators to oppose the regulation of prostitution and urged them instead to support rehabilitation of prostitutes as well as criminalizing their solicitation.

Shortly after obtaining legislative approval for a women's rehabilitation center in a country setting with residential cottages and gardens, Gibbons died in January 1893. She is buried in Greenwood Cemetery, Brooklyn, New York.

*Nancy L. Adgent*

***See also*** Abolitionism and Northern Reformers; Aid Societies; Contrabands; Draft Riots and Resistance; Education, Northern; Hospitals; Mott, Lucretia Coffin (1793–1880); Northern Women; Nurses; Prostitution; Quaker Women; Religion; Teachers, Northern; Union Homefront; Wartime Employment.

**References and Further Reading**

Bacon, Margaret Hope. 2000. *Abby Hopper Gibbons: Prison Reformer and Social Activist.* Albany: State University of New York Press.

Emerson, Sarah Hopper, ed. 1986. *The Life of Abby Hopper Gibbons, Told Chiefly through Her Correspondence.* New York: G.P. Putnam's Sons.

### Gilman, Caroline Howard (1794–1888)

Perhaps the most popular Southern female writer of her time, Caroline Howard Gilman is best recognized for her domestic novels representing women and children as the moral basis of society. Gilman is also known as a poet, children's author, and editor of and writer for one of the first American children's journals.

Gilman was born in Boston on October 8, 1794, to a prosperous family, the fifth of six children. Her father Samuel Howard, a shipwright, died when she was a toddler, and her mother, Anna Lillie Howard, died in 1804. After her mother's death, Caroline's older sister raised her, and she was moved around the Boston suburbs without receiving regular formal education. She began writing poetry at a young age, and in 1810 a newspaper published her poem "Jephthah's Rash Vow" without permission. Gilman later wrote that the poem's unauthorized publication had caused her great embarrassment. In her early twenties, she allowed a story to be published in the *North American Review.*

Caroline met Samuel Gilman, a Harvard graduate and clergyman, in 1810. They wed on September 25, 1819, and moved to Charleston, South Carolina, where Samuel was a minister. The couple had seven children, four of whom survived. Perhaps grief at the loss of their sixth child in 1831 caused Caroline to plunge into her editing and writing career.

On August 11, 1832, the first issue of *Rose-Bud, or Youth's Gazette,* was published. Gilman's literary magazine for youth underwent a number of name changes, including *The Rose Bud* (August 11, 1832–August 24, 1833), *The Southern Rose Bud* (August 31, 1833–August 22, 1835), and *The Southern Rose* with the September 5, 1835 issue. A format change accompanied the last name change, transforming the magazine from a weekly to an eight-page bimonthly, printed on a higher-quality paper, with a higher subscription rate. Additionally, the intended audience widened to include adults. Gilman wrote a number of the magazine's items, including most of the poetry, fiction, travel accounts, and book and magazine reviews. She had the privilege of publishing Hawthorne's poem, "Lily's Quest," which he submitted in appreciation

Caroline Howard Gilman, the nineteenth-century Southern writer known for her novels of domestic life which centered around women and children (1794–1888). (Duyckinck, E. A. and G. L. Duyckink, *Cyclopaedia of American literature,* 1866)

of a favorable review of his work. Later issues of the journal published fewer original works, and the last issue was published August 17, 1839.

Gilman endeavored to bring the North and South together through her writing, but she strongly favored the South. A Southern writer brought up in the North, she was generally supportive of the South, but did not firmly establish her Southern allegiance until the attack on Fort Sumter. The Gilmans kept house slaves, and Caroline believed that slaves were better off than the freed workers in the North. Nonetheless, there are accounts of the couple buying slaves for the purpose of giving them an education and freeing them to pursue a trade. Gilman's writings in her magazine reflected her views regarding slavery, including sketches of Negro life around Charleston that depicted slaves as part of a happy and idle community. This belief, which isolated her from some of her Northern readers, may have been what led to her strong support of the Confederacy during the Civil War.

Three of her serialized novels that she published in her magazine were also published separately.

*Recollections of a Housekeeper* (1834), written under the pseudonym Mrs. Clarissa Packard, is a narrative of a middle-class woman who trains young women as domestic workers. *Recollections of a Southern Matron* (1838) depicts life on a plantation. Her third novel, *Love's Progress,* was published in 1840.

In 1858, Samuel died, and Caroline stayed in Charleston. In March 1862, her house was shelled, and she moved to Greenville, South Carolina, to help Confederate soldiers by supplying them with food and medical aid. Gilman returned to Charleston after the war to discover that most of her possessions and papers had been destroyed.

In 1870, she returned to Cambridge, Massachusetts. During the 1870s, she published four books, two with her daughter, but she never regained the popularity she had enjoyed before the war. She lived in Washington, D.C., with her daughter Eliza, where she died September 15, 1888.

*Sigrid Kelsey*

*See also* Fiction Writers, Southern.
**References and Further Reading**

Moss, Elizabeth. 1992. *Domestic Novelists in the Old South: Defenders of Southern Culture.* Baton Rouge: Louisiana State University Press.

Saint-Amand, Mary Scott. 1941. *A Balcony in Charleston.* Richmond, VA: Garrett & Massie.

## Girlhood and Adolescence

Whether girls were raised in the North or the South, their fortunes were set by the priorities of fathers and male relatives during the Civil War era. Brothers were first to get educations, so girls trained at an early age to accommodate acceptable female gender roles. Girls provided labor on farms, in households, and in factories, but their educations were subordinate to brothers, who would be wage earners. Some girls kept journals to record the momentous events occurring around them.

The agricultural and urban settings in which girls were raised often determined the opportunities that they would have in adult life. As soon as girls could walk and move about independently, they entered long-term apprenticeships with their mothers or other older women in the household. Although in England many girls during the 1860s entered domestic service to earn extra income for their fathers' households, in America mostly orphaned girls went into domestic apprenticeships. Many girls living in antebellum America longed for better opportunities outside the household. Once they completed their educations, the extent of which depended on their families' financial situations, they helped their mothers care for younger children in the household or went to live with another family to help with domestic duties.

During the early months of the Civil War, boys and girls traveled to battle sites and viewed skirmishes. However, children did not always have to travel to see action; as the war progressed, women and children often got caught in riots or battles that flared up in the countryside. Girls in the South became firsthand witnesses to battles and sometimes helped care for wounded soldiers. They also helped their mothers create and deliver items to needy soldiers.

Girls did their part to aid the soldiers of their nation. Many girls became active fundraisers for specific units, hospitals, and soldiers' aid societies for both sides of the war. In Philadelphia there was a flurry of children's fairs during 1862 to raise cash and supplies for local companies and army hospitals. Schools gathered wagons of food and linens. Institutions such as asylums for the disabled, industrial and missionary schools, orphanages, houses of refuge, the so-called colored homes, and schools all donated handmade items that could be sold at the fairs to benefit the war effort. In addition, children held their own sanitary fairs in backyards, on front porches, and in homes, where they sold lemonade and baked goods. School girls gathered on Saturdays to sew and knit and to do fancy needlework projects to sell. Many sanitary fairs in Northern cities featured girls dressed like the "old woman who lived in the shoe" who sold dolls to raise money; other girls sold baked goods, handicrafts, and kisses.

For female slaves, childhood was an indoctrination into a highly stratified plantation structure. The most important familial relationship in the slave community was between mother and child. Since slave women were not allowed to fulfill the traditional domestic roles for their own families, they created order in their own communities. Elder slaves, including pregnant women, women with nursing infants, and children, initiated slave girls into their roles on the plantation. By adolescence, slave girls had already learned brutal life lessons from elders. Sex role differentiation for girls in field labor was not guaranteed. Slave women had little control over their work, but in some instances they could cultivate food for their own children or develop gray market industries. Slave girls were trained to do domestic chores, but in rare cases they could move into certain less menial occupations including work as forewomen, cooks, or medical care providers, where they could develop connections to white populations. For example, elite plantation women relied on slave midwifes to bring children into the world, and the slave women provided early child care. Older slave women and adolescent girls provided surrogate mothering to white children, often at the expense of their own children.

In literature, new concepts of girlhood and female adolescence emerged out of the Civil War. In antebellum America, few women authors could expect to earn a living by writing for children. However, changes in the publishing and reading market during the war allowed the success of a new type of author. The war put a halt to publishing while supplies were scarce, especially in the South. Northern publishers concentrated on lucrative family markets. In addition, American literature achieved an economic boost after the war. The phenomenon of girl and family stories, or domestic novels, written by female authors, reflected the development of a middle-class domestic audience that would become pivotal to American literary history.

The financial and emotional stability of many families was shattered during and after the Civil War. Women were left to support families when husbands, brothers, or fathers were killed or disabled. This challenge opened the door for female authors and stories for girls, many of which offered wartime roles for girls to emulate. The most popular girls' stories were written by women describing aspects of

A portrait of a young girl near the end of the Civil War, 1865. (Library of Congress)

their own domestic lives and reflecting important social issues for women and girls. Many authors projected their own desire for social change into their juvenile female characters. Early female authors of girls' stories included Sophie May, the pseudonym for Rebecca Sophia Clarke, who was known for her Little Prudy series, first published in 1863. She developed her lively and natural girl characters within familial environments and lightly conveyed moral lessons. Elizabeth Stuart Phelps Ward created books about twelve-year-old tomboy Gypsy Breynton, including *Gypsy's Cousin Joy* (1866), *Gypsy's Sowing and Reaping* (1866), and *Gypsy's Year at the Golden Crescent* (1867). Louisa May Alcott's *Little Women* (1868), set during the Civil War, established the standard for adolescent girlhood by tracing the struggles of the March girls to endure adversities while their father was at the front.

The Civil War affected how girls saw and interpreted the world around them. It created a new landscape, both physical and literary. Girls that came of age in the Civil War era found their lives forever shaped by their experiences as workers, aid providers, writers, and readers.

*Meredith Eliassen*

**See also** Alcott, Louisa May (1832–1888); Diaries and Journals; Fairs and Bazaars; Family Life, Confederate; Family Life, Union; Slave Families.

**References and Further Reading**

Nelson, Claudia, and Lynne Vallone, eds. 1994. *The Girl's Own: Cultural Histories of the Anglo-American Girl, 1830–1915.* Athens: University of Georgia Press.

Horn, Pamela. 1985. *The Victorian Country Child.* Wolfeboro Falls, NH: Alan Sutton.

Marten, James. 1998. *The Children's Civil War.* Chapel Hill: University of North Carolina Press.

## Gorgas, Amelia Gayle (1826–1913)

The entries in Amelia Gayle Gorgas's Civil War journal reveal much of the daily labors, fears, and challenges faced by women on the Southern homefront. After the war, Gorgas remained an unreconstructed Rebel and supported the creation of the Museum of the Confederacy.

Born June 1, 1826, in Greensboro, Alabama, Amelia was the third child of Sarah Haynesworth and John Gayle. Her mother died of lockjaw when Amelia was eight. As a judge, lawyer, United States congressman, and two-term governor of Alabama, John Gayle played a prominent part in society. Her family's prominence opened many doors for Amelia. She attended schools in Greensboro and Tuscaloosa before being sent, in 1841, to the Columbia Female Institute in Tennessee. When her father was elected to Congress in 1846, she accompanied him to Washington, D.C. In 1853, when her family moved to Mount Vernon, Alabama, she met Josiah Gorgas, a career army officer. The two married later that year and had six children: four girls and two boys.

When the South seceded, Josiah resigned his army commission and joined the Confederate army. The family lived briefly in Charleston until Josiah became chief of the Confederate Ordnance Department. After giving birth to her fifth child in Charleston, Amelia and her children joined Josiah in Richmond. Amelia reconnected with family and friends living in the state and focused much of her energy on the Confederate cause. Amelia helped raise money for the troops, nursed the wounded soldiers in Richmond's hospitals, sewed items for the soldiers, and fed hungry soldiers. She often sent her children to deliver baskets of provisions. Despite frequent food shortages across the Confederacy, the Gorgases led an active social life in Richmond. When Amelia and her children traveled briefly to Greensboro, North Carolina, in mid-1862, they experienced the food shortages that plagued the South.

During the evacuation and occupation of Richmond in April 1865 Amelia stayed at her sister's home, comforting her children while looters and arsonists roamed the streets. When the cost of living increased beyond the family's means, she took her children to Baltimore, where they remained until April 1866 when the family moved back to Alabama. After Josiah suffered a massive stroke in 1879, the University of Alabama gave him the position of university librarian, which Amelia fulfilled. After his 1883 death, she officially became the university librarian. She became the second woman to receive a pension from the Carnegie Foundations. Amelia died January 3, 1913. In 1925, the University of Alabama named the library in her honor.

*Rebecca Tolley-Stokes*

**See also** Confederate Homefront; Diaries and Journals; Domesticity; Family Life, Confederate; Southern Women.

**References and Further Reading**

Johnston, Mary Tabb, with Elizabeth Johnston Lipscomb. 1978. *Amelia Gayle Gorgas: A Biography.* Tuscaloosa: University of Alabama Press.

Wiggins, Sarah Woolfolk. 1998. "Amelia Gayle Gorgas and the Civil War." *Alabama Review* 51 (2): 83–95.

Wiggins, Sarah Woolfolk. 2001. "The Marriage of Amelia Gayle and Josiah Gorgas." In *Intimate Strategies of the Civil War: Military Commanders and their Wives*, 104–119. New York: Oxford University Press, 2001.

## Government Girls

During the Civil War, many Northern women took jobs as clerks and office workers in the expanding Federal bureaucracy. Often called government girls, these women filled positions previously held by men in peacetime as well as new positions made necessary by the war. Government girls worked in the Treasury and War Departments, as well as in the post office and Quartermaster General's Office. As they did in many jobs, female government workers received lower pay than their male counterparts. However, the pay for government girls was higher than women could make in other wartime jobs.

The Civil War did not mark women's first entry into government jobs. Before the war, for example, Union nurse Clara Barton worked in the United States Patent Office alongside other women. Still other women held jobs at the United States Mint. The expansion of the Federal government and its departments during the lengthy Civil War required the creation of a new workforce. With so many men fighting on the battlefront or involved in the military aspects of the Union war effort, the United States government turned to its women to fill the new posts. Many women welcomed the opportunity to aid their nation and earn much needed money. The government's wartime hiring practices often prioritized the applications of wives and widows of Union soldiers.

In 1862, United States Treasurer Francis Elias Spinner authorized the hiring of women in his department. The new female employees, who worked as currency trimmers, copyists, and currency counters, received $600 a year—half the salary of men—for their five-and-a-half-hour workdays. Other government girls worked in the War Department and the Quartermaster General's Office as copyists and clerks. By the end of the war, hundreds of women had worked in United States government.

Nineteenth-century gender ideals led many Americans to publicly question the morals of female workers, whether in government jobs or otherwise. Criticism centered on the propriety of women working in the public sphere alongside men. In response to these concerns, many administrators established separate workspaces for their female employees. The quartermaster general even posted a guard at the female clerks' workroom door. In 1864, playing on societal fears, newspapers publicized various allegations of immorality in the Treasury Department. A Congressional investigation proved the accusations false, but many female workers never escaped the suspicion of impropriety.

In 1864, Federal legislation capped the salaries of female clerks in Federal offices at $600, though it was raised to $720 by 1865. It was not until 1870 that Congress passed legislation allowing female government clerks equal pay to men. However, women were kept at an effectively lower rate of pay because they were rarely assigned the high-paying jobs given to men, but were instead given low-paying menial jobs.

*Lisa Tendrich Frank*

**See also** Barton, Clara (1821–1912); Domesticity; Factory Workers, Northern; Northern Women; Separate Spheres; Treasury Girls; Union Homefront; Wartime Employment.

**References and Further Reading**

Massey, Mary Elizabeth. 1994. *Women in the Civil War.* Lincoln: University of Nebraska Press.

Silber, Nina. 2005. *Daughters of the Union: Northern Women Fight the Civil War.* Cambridge, MA: Harvard University Press.

## Grant, Julia Dent (1826–1902)

The pampered daughter of a prosperous Missouri planter, Julia Dent Grant was the wife of Ulysses S. Grant, the lieutenant general of the Union's armed forces and president of the United States from 1869 to 1877.

Despite her marriage to a man who would instigate so much carnage toward ending the institution of slavery and preserving the Union, Julia Dent was an unrepentant slaveholder who retained idyllic memories of her privileged youth in slave-owning society. Her engagement to Grant, the handsome young army officer who had been her brother's roommate at West Point, was frowned on by both families. The Dents feared Grant's apparent lack of economic prospects; the Grants disapproved of the slaveholding status of the Dents. The couple never-

Julia Dent Grant, wife of Ulysses S. Grant (1826–1902). (Library of Congress)

but also that she monitored his alcoholism, helping to ensure that his ability to exercise good judgment in military command remained uncompromised by liquor. Julia staunchly denied her husband had problems with drink or depression, and she attributed this version of events to his detractors. She did, however, accept that he expected her support and her focus on family life. Their long affectionate relationship was one of the great love affairs of nineteenth-century public life, and there is little question that she was a personal mainstay during Ulysses Grant's stressful military command.

After Ulysses's scandal-ridden two terms as president, the couple toured the world from 1877 to 1879, feted by heads of state and royalty. Business failure and financial ruin dominated the postpresidential years, capped with Ulysses's painful death from cancer. Written at the end of this life, his *Personal Memoirs of U.S. Grant* was tremendously successful. Julia's memoirs were not published in her lifetime. However, the royalties from his book allowed Julia to live comfortably after her husband's July 1885 death.

Julia died in 1902 and was buried in New York in Grant's Tomb with her husband.

*Barbara Bair*

**See also** Northern Women; Politics; Slaveholding Women; Southern Women; Union Homefront.
**References and Further Reading**
Ross, Ishbel. 1959. *The General's Wife: The Life of Mrs. Ulysses S. Grant.* New York: Dodd, Mead and Company.
Simon, John Y., ed. 1975. *The Personal Memoirs of Julia Dent Grant.* New York: G.P. Putnam's Sons.
Simon, John Y. 2001. "A Marriage Tested by War: Ulysses and Julia Grant." In *Intimate Strategies of the Civil War: Military Commanders and their Wives,* edited by Carol K. Bleser and Lesley J. Gordon, 123–137. New York: Oxford University Press.

theless married in St. Louis in 1848. They began their family while Ulysses pursued his early, and greatly dissatisfying, military career, and then a highly unsuccessful stint in the civilian world. With the Civil War came his re-entry into military life, and an upsurge in his direction and spirits, as he rose to become commander of the Union forces. Julia, meanwhile, achieved celebrity status in the press, and, during the war and in the presidential years, she enjoyed the public spotlight. Although a novice to the Washington social scene in the Lincoln era, during her husband's administration, she became known for the lavish entertainments held at the White House.

Rumors about the Grants circulated throughout their marriage. Stories about Julia stressed that she functioned as an important steadying presence for her complex, shy, brilliantly decisive and daring, but inconsistent and easily corrupted husband. The two delighted in one another's company and she visited him in the field during many of the key campaigns of the Civil War. Rumors had it not only that she bolstered and focused her husband's energies,

## Greenhow, Rose O'Neal (ca. 1814–1864)
An outspoken proponent of Southern rights, Rose O'Neal Greenhow actively participated in the Civil War by supplying military information to Confederate leaders. She traveled to Europe in 1863 on what

some speculate was official business and, upon her return to the Confederacy, tragically died.

Rose O'Neal likely was born around 1814 in Port Tobacco, Maryland, the middle of five daughters born to John O'Neal and Elizabeth Hamilton. Her father was killed by a servant in 1817, and her mother probably died before 1830. Rose and some of her sisters went to live with an aunt and uncle at the Old Capital Boardinghouse in Washington, D.C. Rose was greatly influenced by the congressmen, especially Southern fire-eater John C. Calhoun, who lived at the boardinghouse when Congress was in session.

Rose married Virginian Robert Greenhow, a lawyer, linguist, and historian in 1835 in Washington, D.C. During the 1830s and 1840s, the Greenhows had three of their daughters, Florence, Leila, and Gertrude, as well as a son, Morgan, who died as an infant. Robert traveled often during this time, and Rose helped him with his research and writing. During the late 1840s and early 1850s, the Greenhows worked in Mexico City and San Francisco, where Robert opened a law office. In late 1852 a pregnant Rose returned to Washington, D.C. Daughter Rose was born in the winter of 1853.

Robert was injured in February 1854 in San Francisco and died in March. Rose traveled to California to handle her husband's affairs and sued the city for his injuries. She won a settlement of $10,000 and went back to Washington.

During the late 1840s and 1850s, Rose Greenhow became one of the most influential women in Washington. She corresponded with many people, knew everyone of consequence, and entertained prominent people of various political persuasions. By 1860 the Greenhow home was a well-known meeting place for Southern sympathizers.

Captain Thomas Jordan, a member of General Winfield Scott's staff, made Rose Greenhow the center of a Washington spy ring. Jordan, who intended to join the Confederate army, stayed with Scott for about a month before resigning. During this time, he studied Scott's plans for conducting the war and established a Rebel spy ring. By the time he joined the Confederate army as a member of General Pierre G. T. Beauregard's staff, Jordan's spy ring was well organized. Jordan gave Rose a cipher with which to encode messages, and she provided news about troop movements. With the help of Greenhow's timely information, Beauregard won a significant victory at Bull Run in July 1861.

In August 1861, the Union Secret Service arrested Rose O'Neal Greenhow at her home and searched the premises for several days. Rose tore up many important documents before they put a guard on her, but the bits of paper found in her grate were pasted back together to provide the detectives with enough information to charge Greenhow. She and her youngest daughter became prisoners in their home. Other prisoners soon joined them there.

Indignant articles about the imprisonment of women appeared in newspapers, some contributed by Rose. The publicity was damaging, and, worse, United States officials could not keep Greenhow from continuing to channel valuable information south. Greenhow became a liability to the War Department, and the government decided to take a firmer stand with her. In January 1862 they moved her and her daughter to the Old Capitol Prison. In March Greenhow was brought before the United States Commissioners. On June 2, 1862, she signed a statement pledging not to cross north of the Potomac River during the war without permission from the United States Secretary of War, and she was sent south.

Greenhow arrived in Richmond, Virginia, two days later. To her delight, when she met with President Jefferson Davis, he praised her for her role in the first battle of Bull Run. Greenhow, probably in conference with Davis, decided to go to England to publish the book she had written about her imprisonment. Greenhow may have also hoped to gain support for the Confederacy from the officials of England and France.

Greenhow and Little Rose embarked for England from Wilmington, North Carolina, on a blockade runner in August 1863. She published her diary, *My Imprisonment and the First Year of Abolition Rule in Washington* (1863). In England, to gain support for the Confederacy, Greenhow visited with dignitaries, including Lords Russell and

Palmerston, and she traveled to France, where she had an audience with Emperor Napoleon III. In the early fall of 1864, after unsuccessful meetings with British and French officials, Greenhow decided to return home with the information she had gathered. On her trip home, she may have carried important dispatches for Confederate officials in Richmond.

Greenhow left Scotland in August 1864 on the blockade runner, the *Condor.* In the early morning hours of October 1, 1864, the *Condor* ran aground while attempting to run the blockade into Wilmington. Evidently in fear that she might be imprisoned by Federal authorities again, Greenhow demanded to be put ashore in a small boat. It capsized and she drowned.

The ladies of Wilmington cared for Greenhow's body and the Soldiers' Aid Society arranged for the funeral. Greenhow's body lay in their chapel on a bier draped with a Confederate flag, as hundreds of people paid their last respects. She was buried in Oakdale Cemetery in Wilmington.

*Debra A. Blake*

**See also** Blockade Running; Bull Run/Manassas, First Battle of (July 21, 1861); Female Spies; Southern Women.

### References and Further Reading
Greenhow, Rose O'Neal. 1863. *My Imprisonment and the First Year of Abolition Rule in Washington.* London: Richard Bentley.
Ross, Ishbel. 1954. *Rebel Rose: Life of Rose O'Neal Greenhow, Confederate Spy.* New York: Harper & Brothers, Publishers. (Reprinted 1989. Ballantine.)
Tidwell, William A., with James O. Hall and David Winfred Gaddy. 1988. *Come Retribution: The Confederate Secret Service and the Assassination of Lincoln.* Jackson: University Press of Mississippi.

## Griffing, Josephine Sophia White (1814–1872)

Abolitionist, lecturer, women's rights activist, and freedmen's aid reformer, Josephine Sophia White Griffing participated in the Western Anti-Slavery Society, the Loyal League, and the National Freedmen's Relief Association of Washington, D.C.

Born on December 18, 1814, in Hebron, Connecticut, Josephine was the daughter of farmer Joseph White and Sophia Waldo. Her father had also served in the state legislature. Little is documented of her childhood. She married Charles Stockman Spooner Griffing on September 16, 1835; they soon moved to Litchfield, Ohio, and became active in the Western Anti-Slavery Society, affiliated with the Garrisonian wing of abolitionism. Josephine gave birth to five children, although two died in childhood.

During the 1850s she offered her home to slaves using the Underground Railroad. As a paid agent for the Western Anti-Slavery Society, she lectured and sang abolition songs at several antislavery meetings and contributed to the *Anti-Slavery Bugle,* published in Salem, Ohio. Griffing also used this newspaper to present her views on women's rights, joining and later serving as president of the Ohio Woman's Rights Association.

Griffing's efforts increased with the commencement of the Civil War. She joined the Loyal National League in 1863 and spearheaded an antislavery petition drive. As a paid lecturing agent, she traveled to Ohio, Indiana, Illinois, Michigan, and Wisconsin to secure signatures for petitions.

In September 1864, in a letter to President Abraham Lincoln, she addressed issues of newly emancipated freedmen, whose loss of bondage meant that they needed training and employment for sustenance. She also recommended unlimited asylum for freedmen, and cooperation between the churches and other relief organizations.

Having foresight not exhibited by other abolitionists, Griffing went to Washington, D.C., in 1864 to become the general agent of the National Freedmen's Relief Association of the District of Columbia. Here she managed a vocational school for seamstresses.

She promoted creation of the Bureau of Refugees, Freedmen, and Abandoned Lands, commonly known as the Freedmen's Bureau, and was hired in 1865 as the assistant to the Assistant Commissioner for Washington, D.C. She made many public appeals, much to the chagrin of the Bureau and was dismissed later that year. Even after her departure, she worked to secure free transportation of former slaves to the North by contacting the presidents of the Baltimore and Ohio and Pennsylvania Railroads.

Rehired by the Bureau as an employment agent in 1867, Griffing located jobs for former slaves. In 1868 she convinced the Bureau to adapt the Sanitary Commission building as a tenement for the poor. When the Bureau ceased in 1869, Griffing continued her work with the National Freedmen's Relief Association, helping especially the elderly and disabled. She was credited with assisting seven thousand freedmen in their quest for new jobs and homes in the North. During her final years, Griffing was elected a vice president of the American Equal Rights Association in 1866, and addressed the Senate Judiciary Committee in 1871.

Griffing died on February 18, 1872, likely of tuberculosis.

*Ralph Hartsock*

**See also** Abolitionism and Northern Reformers; Antislavery Societies; Freedmen's Bureau; Garrison, William Lloyd (1805–1879); National Women's Loyal League [Women's National Loyal League]; Northern Women; Union Homefront.

### References and Further Reading

Melder, Keith E. 1963–1965. "Angel of Mercy in Washington: Josephine Griffing and the Freedmen, 1864–1872." *Records of the Columbia Historical Society of Washington, DC.*

Stanton, Elizabeth, Susan B. Anthony, and Matilda Joslyn Gage. 1970. *History of Woman Suffrage.* Vol. 2. New York: Source Book Press.

### Grimké (Weld), Angelina (1805–1879)

South Carolina–born Angelina Grimké became a leading abolitionist and women's rights activist. She spoke publicly against slavery and published antislavery tracts at a time when women were not allowed to speak in public forums. As a highly charismatic debater, she penned one of the earliest documents by an American woman supporting the abolition of slavery with her controversial work, *An Appeal to the Christian Women of the South.* She worked with her sister Sarah, as well as with other prominent abolitionists, to make Northerners aware of the conditions of Southern slaves.

Angelina Emily Grimké was the youngest daughter of Mary Smith and prominent Charleston judge John Faucheraud Grimké. Angelina was very close to her older sister, Sarah, who treated her like a goddaughter. The girls had a relatively easy childhood, and Angelina was more capricious and forceful than her sister. Angelina first demonstrated her independent mind when she refused to be confirmed in the Episcopal Church at the age of thirteen, instead converting to the Presbyterian Church.

Frustrated with her family's determination to hold slaves, Angelina convinced church members to speak out against slavery. She organized an interfaith female prayer meeting—a move that seemed unorthodox to Charleston society. Although she suffered with bouts of agonizing self-doubt, Angelina found her vocation in her determination to abolish slavery. During the winter of 1827, sister Sarah, a member of the Society of Friends, visited Angelina and introduced her to Quaker beliefs. Once she moved to Pennsylvania, Angelina's strong rhetoric brought her to the attention of leading abolitionists, who tapped her speaking abilities to attract audiences.

Angelina began keeping a journal in January 1828, and she continued to make regular entries in it for five years. Her journal detailed the horrors of slavery and chronicled her growing displeasure at the injustice of the institution. During the autumn of 1829, alienated from her South Carolina family, Angelina left Charleston to join her sister in Philadelphia. She wrote a letter to an abolitionist newspaper supporting the antislavery work of William Lloyd Garrison and giving her personal accounts of experiences in a South Carolina slave-owning family. Her letter was published in Garrison's *The Liberator,* publicly linking Angelina to the abolitionist movement.

Angelina and Sarah worked for charity organizations in Philadelphia. During 1831, Angelina became a member of the Fourth and Arch Street Meeting of Quakers, and she contacted Catharine Beecher to enroll in her Hartford Female Seminary to train to be a teacher at an infant school. Angelina attended an antislavery meeting in early 1835, and then was the first Grimké sister to join the Philadel-

South Carolinian Angelina Grimké and her sister, Sarah Grimké, played important roles in the U.S. abolition and women's rights movements. (Library of Congress)

phia Female Anti-Slavery Society. In 1836 Angelina wrote *An Appeal to the Christian Women of the South,* published by the American Anti-Slavery Society. In the *Appeal,* Angelina asserted that slavery harmed white Southern women by fostering sexual misconduct among slaveholding men. This radical essay offended the sensibilities of many white Southerners by pointing out that many slave children resembled their white fathers. Postmasters in Southern states were ordered to confiscate copies sent through the mail, and Angelina was advised not to return to Charleston.

Angelina accepted an appointment by the American Anti-Slavery Society and moved to New York City, where she organized meetings for women interested in the abolitionist cause. A more eloquent and easy speaker then her sister Sarah, Angelina's meetings soon outgrew the private parlors of female abolitionists. After a few ministers opened their churches to her speeches, Angelina drew mixed crowds of men and women. In 1837,

she wrote a second pamphlet, *Appeal to the Women of Nominally Free States.* A year later, she became the first woman ever to testify before a Massachusetts legislative committee on the subject of antislavery petitions. The Grimké sisters saw war over slavery as inevitable and saw no other way to abolish the South's "peculiar institution."

Angelina married antislavery activist Theodore Weld in 1838. Two days later, she delivered a lecture to an antislavery convention in Philadelphia. Her rhetoric so impassioned the mob outside the convention hall that they torched the building, burning it to the ground. As early articulators of abolition and women's rights, the Grimké sisters received far more censure than their Northern female counterparts. During lecture tours, they drew men and women to their events, raising the ire of the Massachusetts Association of Congregational Ministers, which issued a publication entitled "Pastoral Letter," condemning their behavior as unwomanly. The letter further denounced the sisters' public speaking as antibiblical.

The Grimké sisters found themselves in a two-way battle for the abolition of slavery and for the defense of the rights of women. They were at the forefront of an unprecedented movement by women in the United States to address moral and social reform, as well as married women's property rights, which went beyond the issue of slavery. The sisters went against the wishes of some powerful male abolitionists when they spoke and participated in national discourses. Angelina believed adamantly that women needed to be recognized as moral, intelligent, and responsible members of society.

Angelina and Theodore Weld had three children: Charles Stuart, Theodore Grimké, and Sarah Grimké Weld. For the couple, the Civil War came at a time of familial loss. Their younger son, Theodore, became ill with an affliction known as Sody. In 1863, they closed their school in Eagleswood, New Jersey, resettling in West Newton, Massachusetts, and then in Hyde Park, a community south of Boston, where the Welds and Sarah taught at a progressive school for young ladies until after the Civil War.

Angelina Grimké died October 26, 1879.

*Meredith Eliassen*

*See also* Abolitionism and Northern Reformers; Garrison, William Lloyd (1805–1879); Grimké, Sarah Moore (1792–1873); Quaker Women.

**References and Further Reading**

Birney, Catherine H. 1969. *The Grimké Sisters: Sarah and Angelina Grimké: The first American Women Advocates of Abolition and Women's Rights.* Westport, CT: Greenwood Press. (Orig. pub. 1885.)

Browne, Stephen Howard. 1999. *Angelina Grimké: Rhetoric, Identity, and the Radical Imagination.* East Lansing: Michigan State University Press.

Ceplair, Larry, ed. 1989. *The Public Years of Sarah and Angelina Grimké, Selected Writings, 1835–1839.* New York: Columbia University Press.

Lerner, Gerda. 1998. *The Grimké Sisters from South Carolina: Pioneers for Women's Rights and Abolition.* New York: Oxford University Press.

## Grimké, Sarah Moore (1792–1873)

The daughter of Mary Smith and prominent Charleston judge John Faucheraud Grimké, Sarah Moore Grimké became an important abolitionist who shaped the rhetoric of feminism during the antebellum era. Born and raised on a slaveholding plantation, Sarah witnessed contradictions of the ruling elite in South Carolina. Throughout her adult life, Sarah challenged women to develop intellectually rather than relying solely on physical appearance and superficial charm to gain social recognition.

Sarah, known as a woman of great force and directness, was a highly intelligent girl who excelled in all the branches of polite education for ladies. Based on her sex, she was denied access to subjects that her brothers could study. Although Judge Grimké refused to allow his daughter to study Latin with her brother Thomas, he did not object to her debating with her brothers around the house. In this forum, Sarah honed her ability to argue with razor sharp logic. She later used this skill to argue effectively for the abolition of slavery and for women's rights.

During her twenties, Sarah began to have mystical experiences. While traveling in Pennsylvania and New Jersey with her ailing father, Sarah was impressed with the simplicity of the Quaker lifestyle. This experience presented a way of life that contradicted Sarah's Southern sensibilities, because she perceived that women in the Quaker community shared authority with men. Sarah was motivated to exert her moral authority at home. When she returned to Charleston, Sarah used her position as a Sunday school teacher to defy laws against teaching black children to read. At the time, this was a radical move, and the community took notice.

After their father's death in 1819, Sarah and her younger sister Angelina convinced their mother to give them slaves as their share of the family estate. Then, to their mother's displeasure, the sisters freed their slaves. In 1821, Sarah relocated to Philadelphia and joined the Society of Friends. The Quakers allowed women to become ministers, but Grimké was discouraged from taking this course. She became involved in the abolitionist movement when she clashed with Quaker elders over their treatment of African Americans and her inability to speak on their behalf. She wrote the *Epistle to Clergy of the Southern States* (1828) containing a rhetorical refutation of any biblical justification of slavery.

Sarah maintained an on-again, off-again relationship with widower Israel Morris, a Quaker merchant who proposed marriage to her twice; each time Sarah refused him—and she never married. After Angelina married the ardent abolitionist Theodore D. Weld, Sarah joined their household when the Welds settled in Belleville, New Jersey. Sarah taught at Weld's school, and the sisters gathered articles containing proof culled from Southern newspapers of the harsh realities of slavery. This collection provided the material for *American Slavery as It Is: Testimony of a Thousand Witnesses* (1839), by Sarah and her brother-in-law. This book inspired a plotline utilizing a fugitive slave character Lucy that appeared in Harriet Beecher Stowe's *Uncle Tom's Cabin* (1852).

In response to a "Pastoral Letter" by the Massachusetts Association of Congregational Ministers, which condemned the sisters' public speaking, Sarah and Angelina agreed that they could not move forward in the abolitionist movement until they had dealt with women's rights. Sarah's *Letters on the Equality of the Sexes and the Condition of Women* (1838), first published in Boston newspapers and then bound as a book a year later, became

With her sister, Angelina Grimké, South Carolinian Sarah Grimké was active in the U.S. abolition and women's rights movements. (Library of Congress)

the first American feminist treatise on women's rights. Sarah chronicled the legal and economic disabilities of women around the world, creating an innovative argument about the theological and ethical rationale for women's rights and rejecting the two-sphere schema that asserted men and women had radically different natures and roles in the world. Antebellum sensibilities, in line with the common law practice of coverture in marriage, asserted that a woman held power in "her dependence." This was based on the belief that husbands would act in the best interests of family stability. Sarah undermined this notion when she argued that women had far greater influence over the minds and character of children of both sexes and therefore should have access to education.

Sarah and the Welds faced financial hardship during the late 1840s, and opened a boarding school in 1851. In 1854 they opened the Eagleswood School in connection with Raritan Bay Union, a communal settlement established by Marcus Spring in Perth Amboy, New Jersey. While the utopian settlement soon failed, Eagleswood lasted until 1862. The sisters never severed ties with their family in Charleston. Their brother Charles died in 1857, and, during the Civil War, they contributed support for their invalid brother John until his death in 1864.

Sarah hoped that slavery would be abolished without going to war, and she criticized Lincoln for fighting the war to save the Union rather than for emancipation. She wanted the South to work out the problem of slavery, but she recognized that it would happen only out of dire necessity. Sarah felt the South incorrectly focused its fight to maintain the Southern lifestyle, culture, and economy, to the point that it was going to die "a coward's death." Sarah felt that the North, with an ambiguous agenda, was ambivalent in its rhetoric to end slavery. Therefore, the inevitable abolition of slavery was likely to bring a mired period of reconstruction, during which any dignity in the Southern lifestyle would be lost.

In 1868, Sarah and Angelina Grimké discovered that two young black men studying in Pennsylvania were their nephews. The sisters acknowledged the young men, welcoming them into their household. Archibald Henry Grimké, a Harvard Law School graduate, became a prominent writer and civil rights leader in the National Association for the Advancement of Colored People, while Freeman Jones Grimké, a Princeton Theological Seminary graduate, became a minister and spokeperson for the African American community.

Sarah Grimké died on December 23, 1873.

*Meredith Eliassen*

***See also*** Abolitionism and Northern Reformers; Garrison, William Lloyd (1805–1879); Grimké (Weld), Angelina (1805–1879); Quaker Women.

**References and Further Reading**

Birney, Catherine H. 1969. *The Grimké Sisters: Sarah and Angelina Grimké: The First American Women Advocates of Abolition and Women's Rights.* Westport, CT: Greenwood Press. (Orig. pub. 1885.)

Ceplair, Larry, ed. 1989. *The Public Years of Sarah and Angelina Grimké, Selected Writings, 1835–1839.* New York: Columbia University Press.

Lerner, Gerda. 1998. *The Grimké Sisters from South Carolina: Pioneers for Women's Rights and Abolition.* New York: Oxford University Press.

## Guerrilla Warfare

Civil War guerrillas were self-identified groups who did not belong to, or receive pay from, the regular army; they seldom took prisoners, and they engaged their enemy through raids, demolition, executions, and other forms of violence outside set battlefields. "Guerrilla warfare" is a term often used to describe all irregular actions, but it is only one component of unconventional warfare and differs from both partisanship and organized army raids. Civil War partisans were regulated units of the conventional army that provided reconnaissance, scouting, ambushes, stealth operations, and harassment of conventional enemy forces; they were also used as counterirregular forces against guerrillas. Uniformed partisans could be made prisoners of war, but guerrillas were often hanged as outlaws. This type of nineteenth-century combat differs from twentieth-century guerrilla warfare and insurgencies, both ideologically and doctrinally, and it must be understood as historically distinct.

The term "guerrilla" was widely applied by Civil War veterans to describe unconventional actions. Most guerrilla and partisan operations took place in the South and Trans-Mississippi West, with significantly more Confederate than Union participation. The Confederacy passed the Partisan Ranger Act in 1862, legitimizing the role of certain independent unconventional units. In contrast, the Union did not distinguish between the regular and irregular tactics of their cavalry and never formalized a doctrine defining different roles. During the Civil War, participants acknowledged a hierarchy of unconventional and conventional warfare, ranging from disorganized criminals to organized armies. From the least organized to the most, the hierarchy moved from irregular factions to regular troops: brigands and criminals, bushwackers, guerrillas, partisan rangers, Mosby's rangers, Morgan and Forrest's raiders, and, for example, the Army of Northern Virginia. Conventional forces typically had little regard for irregulars, and the name "guerrilla" was often applied as a pejorative, particularly to diminish the contributions of Confederate partisan leaders.

Women were supporters, participants, resisters, and victims of guerrilla warfare. Regular soldiers might become guerrillas after finding their homes destroyed and their families starving or killed. Anti-guerrilla strategies often focused on destroying the irregular forces, regardless of civilian casualties. Counterinsurgency operations were initiated throughout the war to undermine grassroots support of guerrilla units in occupied areas. Guerrilla and partisan operations often had severe and detrimental effects on civilian women, exposing them to torture, sexual assault, forced migration, and displacement.

As supporters and participants in guerrilla warfare, women experienced many roles. Some adhered to gender conventions, acting in their positions as wives, lovers, mothers, and sisters, while others acted outside the prescribed norms of female behavior. Kate King Quantrill, the wife of guerrilla leader William Clarke Quantrill, accompanied his raiders into the field against pro-Union jayhawkers. She often wore men's clothing and became indistinguishable from the other guerrillas. A West Virginia woman using the name Nancy Hart led mounted patrols against Union troops, becoming so successful that a reward was offered for her arrest. She was captured, but she was able to shoot and kill her guard and escape. Malinda Blalock dressed as a man to enlist in the Twenty-sixth North Carolina Infantry with her husband Keith, but the couple was soon discharged and became Unionist guerrillas, responsible for several bloody skirmishes.

Women supplied male guerrillas with food, shelter, and information, often jeopardizing themselves. If caught, they were subject to arrest and jail. In November 1862, Brigadier General John McNeil arrested Margaret Creath and Mildred Elizabeth "Lizzie" Powell for smuggling munitions, and accused them of using their beauty to make honest men into guerrillas. Under similar circumstances, Federal troops arrested Sallie and Jennie Mayfield in Missouri, eventually incarcerating them in the female military prison in St. Louis. Detainment was the most benign consequence of guerrilla involvement, and the possibility of torture, assault, and murder was constant. During the winter of 1863, the Sixty-fourth North Carolina Infantry beat and hanged the wives, mothers, and grandmothers of

Attack led by Confederate guerrilla leader William Clarke Quantrill against the abolitionist stronghold of Lawrence, Kansas, on August 21, 1863. During this raid, 150 unarmed men and boys were murdered and most of the town was burned. (Library of Congress)

suspected Unionist guerrillas in Shelton Laurel, North Carolina, before rounding up and killing thirteen men. In a different raid, one woman was tied to a tree with her baby left crying several feet away; the guerrillas threatened to leave her there, unable to tend her infant, unless she confessed her husband's whereabouts.

As resisters and victims of guerrilla warfare, women struggled to defend their homes and children. Women in the South and the Trans-Mississippi region were in the path of both regular and irregular armies. The constant danger and deprivation forced them to develop different tactics of survival. One group of educated middle- and upper-class women from LaGrange, Georgia, responded to their vulnerable position by forming a militia unit they named the Nancy Harts, after a Revolutionary War heroine. They learned to drill and use firearms, but maintained their positions as elite ladies by

focusing solely on the defense of their homes. They supported the homefront cause while their husbands fought with the regular army, and after the war they spoke about their actions as respected members of the Daughters of the Confederacy.

Female civilians were targets of unconventional warfare for many reasons and from both sides of the conflict. Guerrillas sought to drive opposition from their territory through terror, or they stole food and livestock, leaving families without resources; anti-guerrilla operations deprived the enemy of supplies by burning crops and homes. Refugees fled to avoid persecution, only to find themselves more vulnerable to guerrilla attacks. Escaping Arkansas guerrillas, for example, Bethy Toney and her children were robbed of their wagon and oxen by bushwackers and left alone in the wilderness with nothing but their clothes. The Toneys were not the only refugees from Arkansas; guerrillas in the region so viciously terrorized the citizenry that a mass forced migration resulted. Similar forced migrations occurred throughout Kansas, Missouri, and the South. Refugee women faced starvation and exposure, and, when they were relocated, they often found overcrowded accommodations with poor sanitation and high rates of disease. Without male support or resources, they had difficulties feeding and caring for themselves and their children.

Guerrilla warfare is a people's war, with no front lines. During the American Civil War, women were both willing participants and innocent victims of irregular operations throughout the South and Trans-Mississippi West. They became refugees, militia members, and guerrillas in an effort to survive and sustain their loyalties.

*Dawn Ottevaere Nickeson*

**See also** Blalock, Malinda [Sam Blalock] (ca. 1842–1901); Civilian Life; Confederate Homefront; Destruction of Homes; Destruction of Personal Property; Disease; Domesticity; Family Life, Confederate; Female Combatants; Female Spies; Hart, Nancy (ca. 1843–1902); Imprisonment of Women; Military Invasion and Occupation; Mosby's Rangers; Quantrill, William Clarke (1837–1865); Refugees; Southern Women.

**References and Further Reading**

Fellman, Michael. 1989. *Inside War: The Guerrilla Conflict in Missouri during the American Civil War.* New York: Oxford University Press.

Goodrich, Thomas. 1995. *Black Flag: Guerrilla Warfare on the Western Border, 1861–1865.* Bloomington: Indiana University Press.

Joslyn, Muriel Phillips, ed. 1996. *Confederate Women.* Gretna, LA: Pelican Publishing Company.

Leonard, Elizabeth D. 1999. *All the Daring of a Soldier: Women of the Civil War Armies.* New York: W. W. Norton & Company.

Mackey, Robert R. 2004. *The Uncivil War: Irregular Warfare in the Upper South, 1861–1865.* Norman: University of Oklahoma Press.

O'Brien, Sean Michael. 1999. *Mountain Partisans: Guerrilla Warfare in the Southern Appalachians, 1861–1865.* Westport, CT: Praeger.

Schultz, Duane. 1996. *Quantrill's War: The Life and Times of William Clarke Quantrill.* New York: St. Martin's Press.

## Gunboat Societies

Gunboat Societies offered women a unique way of providing homefront support to their husbands, sons, and fathers serving in the Confederate military. Based on the antebellum practice of female fundraising activities for benevolent associations, Gunboat Societies served as a vehicle for women to raise money that would be used to build ironclad boats. These vessels, called Ladies Gunboats or Petticoat Gunboats by some, were needed to protect Southern coasts and rivers from Union advances during the first years of the Civil War.

Women in New Orleans held the first gunboat fair in November 1861. By February, the idea had spread to Mobile, Alabama. During the spring and summer of 1862, women across the South started their own associations, including the Charleston Ladies Gunboat Association, the Ladies Defense Association of Richmond, the Augusta Gunboat Society, and the Alabama Women's Gunboat Fund. In addition to fairs, women held concerts, bazaars, auctions, and dinners to raise money. Society members collected whatever they could from supporters, including everything from common household items to fancy needlework. Newspapers published the names of contributors, large and small, creating friendly rivalries between cities and more important, publicly announcing who supported the Confederacy. Society members also made donations. Many gave personal objects such as jewelry to be melted down by the Tredegar Ironworks to make necessary items to outfit the ships. In addition to fundraising, some women toured the finished gunboats with Confederate dignitaries.

The most active members of the Gunboat Societies were from wealthy Southern families, but women from all economic groups, both black and white, supported them. Some Southerners questioned the appropriateness of such public actions, while others encouraged and assigned women this role as a necessity of war. *The Montgomery Advertiser* called on its female citizens to do more than their noble deeds of rolling bandages and caring for the wounded. They wanted women to contribute to the war effort by raising funds for a new military vessel.

The women of these societies often found themselves competing against more powerful male organizations devoted to raising money for gunboats. Therefore, the success of female activities depended on the public support of civic and business leaders. Some made significant contributions such as the $20,000 gift from Augusta city officials to the Georgia Ladies' Gunboat Fund. Men also collected pledges and took care of the women's growing treasuries.

Gunboat Societies remained active until 1863, when Southerners no longer supported the public boatbuilding efforts due to disappointing Confederate naval losses in 1862 and the effectiveness of the Union blockade. As gunboat donations waned, women shifted their attention to raising funds for more immediate needs. Local authorities often requested this redirection of purpose. For example, officials in Petersburg and Mobile asked the women to delay or cease their gunboat campaigns and instead purchase hospital supplies. By this time, duty-bound Southern women had raised over $60,000 to finance the construction of three gunboats: the *Charleston*, the *Fredericksburg*, and the *Georgia*. Female collections also paid in part for the ironclad *Palmetto State*.

*Kelly D. Selby*

***See also*** Confederate Homefront; Domesticity; Fairs and Bazaars; Fundraising; Separate Spheres; Southern Women.

**References and Further Reading**

Campbell, Edward D. C. Jr., and Kym S. Rice, eds. 1996. *A Woman's War: Southern Women, Civil War, and the Confederate Legacy.* Richmond, VA: Museum of the Confederacy/Charlottesville: University Press of Virginia.

Faust, Drew Gilpin. 1990. "Altars of Sacrifice: Confederate Women and the Narratives of War." *Journal of American History* 76 (4): 1200–1228.

Joslyn, Mauriel Phillips, ed. 2004. *Confederate Women.* Gretna, LA: Pelican Publishing Company.

Still, William N. Jr. 1971. *Iron Afloat: The Story of the Confederate Armorclads.* Nashville, TN: Vanderbilt University Press.

# Bibliography

Aaron, Daniel. 1987. *The Unwritten War: American Writers and the Civil War.* Madison: University of Wisconsin Press.

Abel, E. Lawrence. 2000. *Singing the New Nation: How Music Shaped the Confederacy, 1861–1865.* Mechanicsburg, PA: Stackpole Books.

Abel, Emily K. 2000. *Hearts of Wisdom: American Women Caring for Kin, 1850–1940.* Cambridge, MA: Harvard University Press.

Ahlstrom, Sydney. 1972. *A Religious History of the American People.* New Haven, CT: Yale University Press.

Albers, Henry, ed. 2001. *Maria Mitchell: A Life in Journals and Letters.* Clinton Corners, NY: College Avenue Press.

Alcott, Louisa May. 1960. *Hospital Sketches*, edited by Bessie Z. Jones. Cambridge, MA: Harvard University Press. (Reprint of Boston: James Redpath, 1863.)

Aleman, Jesse, ed. 2003. *The Woman in Battle: The Civil War Narrative of Loreta Velazquez, Cuban Woman and Confederate Soldier*, with introduction by Jesse Aleman. Madison: University of Wisconsin Press.

Alleman, Tillie Pierce. 1994. *At Gettysburg or What a Girl Saw and Heard of Battle.* Baltimore, MD: Butternut & Blue.

An Act for Enrolling and Calling Out the National Forces, and for Other Purposes. 1863. HR 125, 37th Congress, 3rd Session. *Statutes at Large of the United States.* Vol. 12. Boston: Little, Brown and Company.

Anderson, John Q., ed. 1955. *Brokenburn: The Journal of Kate Stone, 1861–1868.* Baton Rouge: Louisiana State University Press. (Reprinted 1995 with Introduction by Drew Gilpin Faust.)

Andrews, Eliza Frances. 1908. *The War-Time Journal of a Georgia Girl, 1864–1865.* New York: D. Appleton & Co.

Andrews, Eliza Frances. 2002. *Journal of a Georgia Woman 1870–1872*, edited with an introduction by S. Kittrell Rushing. Knoxville: University of Tennessee Press.

Andrews, Melodie. 1990. "'What the Girls Can Do': The Debate over the Employment of Women in the Early American Telegraph Industry." *Essays in Economic and Business History* 8: 109–120.

Andrews, William L., and William S. McFeely. 1997. *Narrative of the Life of Frederick Douglass, an American Slave, Written by Himself: Authoritative Text, Context, Criticism.* New York: W. W. Norton & Company.

Ash, Stephen V. 1988. *Middle Tennessee Society Transformed, 1860–1870: War and Peace in the Upper South.* Baton Rouge: Louisiana State University Press.

Ash, Stephen V. 1990. "White Virginians under Federal Occupation, 1861–1865." *Virginia Magazine of History and Biography* 98: 169–192.

Ash, Stephen V. 1995. *When the Yankees Came: Conflict and Chaos in the Occupied South, 1861–1865.* Chapel Hill: University of North Carolina Press.

Ashdown, Paul. 2002. *The Mosby Myth: A Confederate Hero in Life and Legend.* Wilmington, DE: Scholarly Resources.

Ashendel, Anita. 1997. "Fabricating Independence: Industrial Labor in Antebellum Indiana." *Michigan Historical Review* 23 (2): 1–24.

Atkinson, Maxine P., and Jacqueline Boles. 1985. "The Shaky Pedestal: Southern Ladies Yesterday and Today." *Southern Studies* 24: 398–406.

Attie, Jeanie. 1998. *Patriotic Toil: Northern Women and the American Civil War.* Ithaca, NY: Cornell University Press.

Austin, Anne. 1971. *The Woolsey Sisters of New York: A Family's Involvement in the Civil War and a New*

*Profession (1860–1900)*. Philadelphia, PA: American Philosophical Society.

Bacon, Margaret Hope. 1896. *Mothers of Feminism: The Story of Quaker Women in America*. New York: Harper & Row.

Bacon, Margaret Hope. 1980. *Valiant Friend: The Life of Lucretia Mott*. New York: Walker & Company.

Bacon, Margaret Hope. 2000. *Abby Hopper Gibbons: Prison Reformer and Social Activist*. Albany: State University of New York Press.

Baer, Elizabeth R., ed. 1997. *Shadows on My Heart: The Civil War Diary of Lucy Rebecca Buck of Virginia*. Athens: University of Georgia Press.

Bailey, Anne J. 2000. *The Chessboard of War: Sherman and Hood in the Autumn Campaigns of 1864*. Lincoln: University of Nebraska Press.

Baird, Nancy Chappelear, ed. 1984. *Journals of Amanda Virginia Edmonds: Lass of the Mosby Confederacy, 1857–1867*. Stephens City, VA: Commercial Press.

Bakeless, John. 1970. *Spies of the Confederacy*. Philadelphia, PA: J. B. Lippincott Co.

Baker, Jean. 1983. *Affairs of Party: The Political Culture of Northern Democrats in Mid-Nineteenth-Century America*. Ithaca, NY: Cornell University Press.

Baker, Jean H. 1987. *Mary Todd Lincoln: A Biography*. New York: W. W. Norton.

Baker, Nina Brown. 1952. *Cyclone in Calico: The Story of Mary Ann Bickerdyke*. Boston: Little, Brown and Company.

Baker, Paula. 1984. "The Domestication of Politics: Women and American Political Society, 1780–1900." *American Historical Review* 89 (June): 620–647.

Bakker, Jan. 1987. "Overlooked Progenitors: Independent Women and Southern Renaissance in Augusta Jane Evans Wilson's *Macaria; or, Altars of Sacrifice*." *The Southern Quarterly* 25: 131–141.

Banner, Lois W. 1980. *Elizabeth Cady Stanton: A Radical for Woman's Rights*. Boston: Little, Brown and Company.

Barber, E. Susan. 2000. "Cartridge Makers and Myrmidon Viragos: White Working-Class Women in Confederate Richmond." In *Negotiating the Boundaries of Southern Womanhood: Dealing with the Powers That Be*, edited by Janet Coryell, 199–214. Columbia: University of Missouri Press.

Barber, E. Susan. 2002. "'Depraved and Abandoned Women': Prostitution in Richmond, Virginia, across the Civil War." In *Neither Lady Nor Slave: Working Women of the Old South*, edited by Susanna Delfino and Michele Gillespie, 155–173. Chapel Hill: University of North Carolina Press.

Bardaglio, Peter. 1995. *Reconstructing the Household: Families, Sex, and the Law in the Nineteenth-Century South*. Chapel Hill: University of North Carolina Press.

Barney, William. 1974. *The Secessionist Impulse: Alabama and Mississippi in 1860*. Princeton, NJ: Princeton University Press.

Barry, Kathleen. 1988. *Susan B. Anthony: A Biography of a Singular Feminist*. New York: New York University Press.

Barton, George. 1898. *Angels of the Battlefield: A History of the Labors of the Catholic Sisterhoods in the Late Civil War*. Philadelphia, PA: Catholic Art Publishing Company.

Baym, Nina. 2000. "Introduction." In *Three Spiritualist Novels*, by Elizabeth Stuart Phelps, vii–xxiii. Urbana: University of Illinois Press.

Bearden, Jim, and Linda Jean Butler. 1977. *Shadd: The Life and Times of Mary Shadd Cary*. Toronto: N. C. Press.

Beecher, Catharine. 1850. *Miss Beecher's Domestic Receipt-Book: Designed as a Supplement to Her Treatise on Domestic Economy*. New York: Harper.

Bennett, Paula Bernat. 2003. *Poets in the Public Sphere: The Emancipatory Project of American Women's Poetry, 1800–1900*. Princeton, NJ: Princeton University Press.

Bercaw, Nancy. 2003. *Gendered Freedoms: Race, Rights, and the Politics of Household in the Delta, 1861–1875*. Gainesville: University Press of Florida.

Berlin, Ira. 1974. *Slaves without Masters: The Free Negro in the American South*. New York: New Press.

Berlin, Ira. 2003. *Generations of Captivity: A History of African-American Slaves*. Cambridge, MA: Harvard University Press.

Berlin, Ira, Steven F. Miller, Joseph P. Reidy, and Leslie S. Rowland, eds. 1982–present. *Freedom: A Documentary History of Emancipation, 1861–1867*. New York: Cambridge University Press.

Berlin, Ira, Barbara J. Fields, Steven F. Miller, Joseph P. Reidy, and Leslie S. Rowland. 1992. *Slaves No More: Three Essays on Emancipation and the Civil War*. Cambridge, UK, and New York: Cambridge University Press.

Berlin, Ira, and Leslie Rowland, eds. 1997. *Families and Freedom: A Documentary History of African-American Kinship in the Civil War Era*. New York: New Press.

Berlin, Jean V., ed. 1994. *A Confederate Nurse: The Diary of Ada W. Bacot, 1860–1863*. Columbia: University of South Carolina Press.

Berlin, Jean V. 2001. "Did Confederate Women Lose the War? Deprivation, Destruction, and Despair on the Homefront." In *The Collapse of the Confederacy*, edited by Mark Grimsley and Brooks D. Simpson, 168–193. Lincoln: University of Nebraska Press.

Bernard, Jacqueline, with Introduction by Nell Irvin Painter. [1967] 1990. *Journey toward Freedom: The Story of Sojourner Truth.* New York: Feminist Press at The City University of New York.

Berry III, Stephen W. 2003. *All That Makes a Man: Love and Ambition in the Civil War South.* New York: Oxford University Press.

Berwanger, Eugene. 1975. "Reconstruction on the Frontier: The Equal Rights Struggle in Colorado, 1865–1867." *Pacific Historical Review* 44 (3): 313–329.

Birney, Catherine H. [1885] 1969. *The Grimké Sisters: Sarah and Angelina Grimké: The First American Women Advocates of Abolition and Women's Rights.* Westport, CT: Greenwood Press.

Black, Linda. 1994. "A Wife's Devotion: The Story of James and Fanny Ricketts." *Blue and Gray Magazine* 11: 22–28.

Black, Linda. 1994. "Three Heroines of Gettysburg." *Gettysburg Magazine* 11:119–125.

Blackwell, Elizabeth. 1895. *Pioneer Work in Opening the Medical Profession to Women.* London and New York: Longmans, Green & Company.

Blainey, Ann. 2001. *Fanny and Adelaide.* Chicago: Ivan R. Dee.

Blair, William A. 1998. *Virginia's Private War: Feeding Body and Soul in the Confederacy, 1861–1865.* New York: Oxford University Press.

Blair, William. 2004. *Cities of the Dead: Contesting the Memory of the Civil War in the South, 1865–1914.* Chapel Hill: University of North Carolina Press.

Blakey, Arch Fredric, Ann Smith Lainhart, and Winston Bryan Stephens Jr., eds. 1998. *Rose Cottage Chronicles: Civil War Letters of the Bryant-Stephens Families of North Florida.* Gainesville: University Press of Florida.

Blanton, DeAnne, and Laura M. Cook. 2002. *They Fought Like Demons: Women Soldiers in the American Civil War.* Baton Rouge: Louisiana State University Press.

Bleser, Carol, ed. 1991. *In Joy and in Sorrow: Women, Family, and Marriage in the Victorian South.* New York: Oxford University Press.

Bleser, Carol K., and Lesley J. Gordon, eds. 2001. *Intimate Strategies of the Civil War: Military Commanders and Their Wives.* New York: Oxford University Press.

Blight, David. 2001. *Race and Reunion: The Civil War in American Memory.* Cambridge, MA: Harvard University Press.

Blom, Ida. 1991. "The History of Widowhood: A Bibliographic Overview." *Journal of Family History* 16 (2): 191–210.

Blumenthal, Walter Hart. 1974. *Women Camp Followers of the American Revolution.* New York: Arno Press.

Blumhofer, Edith L. 2005. *Her Heart Can See: The Life and Hymns of Fanny J. Crosby.* Grand Rapids, MI: William B. Eerdmans Publishing Company.

Bollet, Alfred J. 2002. *Civil War Medicine: Challenges and Triumphs.* Tucson, AZ: Galen Press.

Bonner, Robert E. 2002. *Colors and Blood: Flag Passions of the Confederate South.* Princeton, NJ: Princeton University Press.

Boritt, Gabor S., ed. 1999. *The Gettysburg Nobody Knows.* New York: Oxford University Press.

Botume, Elizabeth Hyde. 1968. *First Days Amongst the Contrabands.* New York: Arno Press and the New York Times.

Boyd, Belle. 1998. *Belle Boyd in Camp and Prison,* with Foreword by Drew Gilpin Faust and Introduction by Sharon Kennedy-Nolle. Baton Rouge: Louisiana State University Press.

Boyd, Melba Joyce. 1994. *Discarded Legacy: Politics and Poetics in the Life of Frances E.W. Harper, 1825–1911.* Detroit, MI: Wayne State University Press.

Bradford, Sarah H. 1869. *Scenes in the Life of Harriet Tubman.* Auburn, NY: W. J. Moses.

Bradford, Sarah H. 1886. *Harriet, The Moses of Her People.* New York: Geo. R. Lockwood & Son.

Bradley, Mark L. 2000. *This Astounding Close: The Road to Bennett Place.* Chapel Hill: University of North Carolina Press.

Breckenridge, Lucy. 1979. *Lucy Breckinridge of Grove Hill: The Diary of a Virginia Girl, 1862–1864,* edited by Mary D. Robertson. Kent, OH: Kent State University Press.

Bremner, Robert Hamlett. 1890. *The Public Good: Philanthropy and Welfare in the Civil War Era.* New York: Alfred A. Knopf.

Brevard, Keziah Goodwyn Hopkins. 1993. *A Plantation Mistress on the Eve of the Civil War: The Diary of Keziah Goodwyn Hopkins Brevard, 1860–1861,* edited by John Hammond Moore. Columbia: University of South Carolina Press.

Broadwater, Robert P. 1993. *Daughters of the Cause: Women in the "Civil War."* Santa Clarita, CA: Daisy Publishing Company.

Brockett, L. P., and Mary C. Vaughn. 1867. *Women's Work in the Civil War: A Record of Heroism, Patriotism and Patience.* Philadelphia, PA: Zeigler, McCurdy & Co./Boston: R. H. Curran.

Brown, Alexis Girardin. 2000. "The Women Left Behind: The Transformation of the Southern Belle, 1840–1880." *The Historian* 62: 759–778.

Brown, Elizabeth Potts, and Susan Mosher Stuard, eds. 1989. *Witnesses for Change: Quaker Women over Three Centuries.* Piscataway, NJ: Rutgers University Press.

Brown, Thomas. 1998. *Dorothea Dix: New England Reformer.* Cambridge, MA: Harvard University Press.

Browne, Stephen Howard. 1999. *Angelina Grimké: Rhetoric, Identity, and the Radical Imagination.* East Lansing: Michigan State University Press.

Brumgardt, John R., ed. 1980. *Civil War Nurse: The Diary and Letters of Hannah Ropes.* Knoxville: University of Tennessee Press.

Bruyn, Kathleen. 1970. *"Aunt Clara Brown:" Story of a Black Pioneer.* Boulder, CO: Pruett Publishing Company.

Bucklin, Sophronia E. 1869. *In Hospital and Camp: A Woman's Record of Thrilling Incidents among the Wounded in the Late War.* Philadelphia, PA: John E. Potter and Co.

Bulloch, Joseph Gaston Baillie. 1901. *A history and genealogy of the Habersham family: in connection with the history, genealogy, and mention of the families of Clay, Stiles, Cumming, King, Elliott, Milledge, Maxwell, Adams, Houstoun, Screvens, Owens, Demere, Footman, Ellis, Washington, Newell, deTreville, Davis, Barrington, Lewis, Warner, Cobb, Flournoy, Pratt, Nephew, Bolton, Bowers, Cuthbert, and many many other names.* Columbia, SC: R.L. Bryan Company.

Bunch, Jack A. 2000. *Military Justice in the Confederate States Armies.* Shippensburg, PA: White Mane Publishing Co.

Burgess, Lauren Cook, ed. 1994. *An Uncommon Soldier: The Civil War Letters of Sarah Rosetta Wakeman, alias Pvt. Lyons Wakeman, 153rd Regiment, New York State Volunteers, 1862–1864.* New York: Oxford University Press.

Burlingame, Michael. 1994. *The Inner World of Abraham Lincoln.* Urbana: University of Illinois Press.

Burnham, John C. 1971. "Medical Inspection of Prostitutes in America in the Nineteenth Century: The St. Louis Experiment and Its Sequel." *Bulletin of the History of Medicine* 45: 203–218.

Burton, David H. 1995. *Clara Barton: In the Service of Humanity.* Westport, CT: Greenwood Press.

Burton, David L. 1982. "Richmond's Great Homefront Disaster: Friday the 13th." *Civil War Times Illustrated* 21 (6): 36–41.

Burton, Georganne B., and Orville Vernon Burton, eds. 2002. *The Free Flag of Cuba, The Lost Novel of Lucy Holcombe Pickens.* Baton Rouge: Louisiana State University Press.

Burton, Orville Vernon. 1985. *In My Father's House Are Many Mansions: Family and Community in Edgefield, South Carolina.* Chapel Hill: University of North Carolina Press.

Butchart, Ronald E. 1980. *Northern Schools, Southern Blacks, and Reconstruction: Freedmen's Education, 1862–1875.* Westport, CT: Greenwood Press.

Butler, Anne M. 1985. *Daughters of Joy, Sisters of Misery: Prostitutes in the American West, 1865–90.* Chicago: University of Chicago Press.

Butler, Benjamin F. 1892. *Autobiography and Personal Reminiscences of Major-General Benjamin F. Butler.* Boston: A. M. Thayer & Co.

Bynum, Hartwell T. 1970. "Sherman's Expulsion of the Roswell Women in 1864." *Georgia Historical Quarterly* 54: 169–182.

Bynum, Victoria E. 1992. *Unruly Women: The Politics of Social and Sexual Control in the Old South.* Chapel Hill: University of North Carolina Press.

Bynum, Victoria. 2001. *The Free State of Jones: Mississippi's Longest Civil War.* Chapel Hill: University of North Carolina Press.

Campbell, Edward D. C. Jr., and Kym S. Rice, eds. 1996. *A Woman's War: Southern Women, Civil War, and the Confederate Legacy.* Richmond, VA: Museum of the Confederacy/Charlottesville: University Press of Virginia.

Campbell, Jacqueline Glass. 2003. *When Sherman Marched North from the Sea: Resistance on the Confederate Home Front.* Chapel Hill: University of North Carolina Press.

Campbell, James. 1998. *Songs of Zion: The African Methodist Episcopal Church in the United States and South Africa.* New York: Oxford University Press.

Cannon, Devereux D. 1994. *Flags of the Confederacy: An Illustrated History.* Gretna, LA: Pelican Publishing Company.

Cannon, Devereux D. 1994. *Flags of the Union: An Illustrated History.* Gretna, LA: Pelican Publishing Company.

Capers, Gerald M. Jr. 1964. "Confederates and Yankees in Occupied New Orleans, 1862–1865." *Journal of Southern History* 30: 405–426.

Capers, Gerald M. 1965. *Occupied City: New Orleans under the Federals, 1862–1865.* Lexington: University of Kentucky Press.

Carmichael, Peter S. 2001. "'All Say They Are under Petticoat Government': Lizinka Brown and Richard Ewell." In *Intimate Strategies: Military Marriages of the Civil War,* edited by Carol Bleser and Lesley Gordon, 87–103. New York: Oxford University Press.

Carroll, Anna Ella. 1861. *Reply to the Speech of Hon. J. C. Breckinridge.* Washington, DC: Henry Polkinhorn.

Carroll, Anna Ella. 1861. *The War Powers of the General Government.* Washington, DC: Henry Polkinhorn.

Carter, Christine Jacobson, ed. 1997. *The Diary of Dolly Lunt Burge, 1848–1879.* Athens: University of Georgia Press.

Carter III, Samuel. 1973. *The Siege of Atlanta, 1864.* New York: St. Martin's Press.

Cashin, Joan E. 1990. "The Structure of Antebellum Families: 'The Ties That Bound Us Was Strong.'" *Journal of Southern History* 56: 55–70.

Cashin, Joan E. 1992 "'Since the War Broke Out': The Marriage of Kate and William McLure." In *Divided Houses: Gender and the Civil War,* edited by Catherine Clinton and Nina Silber, 200–212. New York: Oxford University Press.

Cashin, Joan E. 1996. *Our Common Affairs.* Baltimore, MD: Johns Hopkins University Press.

Cashin, Joan E. 2002. "Deserters, Civilians, and Draft Resistance in the North." In *The War Was You and Me: Civilians in the American Civil War,* edited by Joan E. Cashin, 262–285. Princeton, NJ: Princeton University Press.

Cashin, Joan E., ed. 2002. *The War Was You and Me: Civilians in the American Civil War.* Princeton, NJ: Princeton University Press.

Caskie, Jacquelin Ambler. 1928. *The Life and Letters of Matthew Fontaine Maury.* Richmond, VA: Richmond Press, Inc.

Cassedy, James H. 1992. "Numbering the North's Medical Events: Humanitarianism and Science in Civil War Statistics." *Bulletin of the History of Medicine* 66 (2): 210–233.

Castel, Albert. 1992. *Decision in the West: The Atlanta Campaign of 1864.* Lawrence: University Press of Kansas.

Castel, Albert. 1999. *William Clarke Quantrill: His Life and Times.* Norman: University of Oklahoma Press.

Catton, Bruce, and James McPherson, eds. 1996. *The American Heritage New History of the Civil War.* New York: MetroBooks.

Cazalet, Sylvain. 1866. *History of the New York Medical College and Hospital for Women.* New York: University of the State of New York.

Censer, Jane Turner, ed. 1986. *The Papers of Frederick Law Olmsted,* vol. IV: *Defending the Union.* Baltimore, MD: Johns Hopkins University Press.

Censer, Jane Turner. 1987. *North Carolina Planters and Their Children, 1800–1860.* Baton Rouge: Louisiana State University Press.

Censer, Jane Turner. 2003. *The Reconstruction of White Southern Womanhood, 1865–1895.* Baton Rouge: Louisiana State University Press.

Ceplair, Larry, ed. 1989. *The Public Years of Sarah and Angelina Grimké, Selected Writings, 1835–1839.* New York: Columbia University Press.

Channing, Steven. 1970. *A Crisis of Fear: Secession in South Carolina.* New York: Simon & Schuster.

Chartrand, René. 1996. *Napoleonic Wars, Napoleon's Army.* Washington, DC: Brassey's.

Chesson, Michael B. 1984. "Harlots or Heroines? A New Look at the Richmond Bread Riot." *Virginia Magazine of History and Biography* 92: 131–175.

Cimbala, Paul A. 1997. *Under the Guardianship of the Nation: The Freedmen's Bureau and the Reconstruction of Georgia, 1865–1870.* Athens: University of Georgia Press.

Cimbala, Paul A., and Randall M. Miller, eds. 1999. *The Freedmen's Bureau and Reconstruction: Reconsiderations.* New York: Fordham University Press.

Cimbala, Paul A., and Randall M. Miller, eds. 2002. *Union Soldiers and the Northern Home Front: Wartime Experiences, Postwar Adjustments.* New York: Fordham University Press.

Cimbala, Paul, and Randall Miller, eds. 2002. *An Uncommon Time: The Civil War and the Northern Home Front.* New York: Fordham University Press.

Cimprich, John. 1985. *Slavery's End in Tennessee, 1861–1865.* Tuscaloosa: University of Alabama Press.

Clayton, Sara "Sallie" Conley. 1999. *Requiem for a Lost City: A Memoir of Civil War Atlanta and the Old South,* edited by Robert Scott Davis Jr. Macon, GA: Mercer University Press.

Cliff, Michelle. 1993. *Free Enterprise: A Novel of Mary Ellen Pleasant.* New York: Dutton.

Clifford, Deborah Pickman. 1978. *Mine Eyes Have Seen the Glory: A Biography of Julia Ward Howe.* Boston: Little, Brown and Company.

Clifford, Deborah Pickman. 1992. *Crusader for Freedom: A Life of Lydia Maria Child.* Boston: Beacon Press.

Clinton, Catherine. 1982. *The Plantation Mistress: Woman's World in the Old South.* New York: Pantheon Books.

Clinton, Catherine. 1984. *The Other Civil War: American Women in the Nineteenth Century.* New York: Hill and Wang.

Clinton, Catherine. 1991. "'Southern Dishonor': Flesh, Blood, Race, and Bondage." In *In Joy and in Sorrow: Women, Family, and Marriage in the Victorian South,* edited by Carol Bleser, 52–68. New York: Oxford University Press.

Clinton, Catherine. 1995. *Tara Revisited: Women, War, and the Plantation Legend.* New York: Abbeville Press.

Clinton, Catherine. 1998. *Civil War Stories.* Athens: University of Georgia Press.

Clinton, Catherine. 2000. *Fanny Kemble's Civil Wars.* New York: Simon & Schuster.

Clinton, Catherine, ed. 2000. *Southern Families at War: Loyalty and Conflict in the Civil War South.* New York: Oxford University Press.

Clinton, Catherine, and Nina Silber, eds. 1992. *Divided Houses: Gender and the Civil War,* with Introduction by James M. McPherson. Oxford: Oxford University Press.

Cochran, Hamilton. 1973. *Blockade Runners of the Confederacy.* Westport, CT: Greenwood Press.

Coleman, Penny. 1992. *Spies! Women in the Civil War.* White Hall, VA: Shoe Tree Press.

Connelly, Thomas. 1971. *Autumn of Glory: The Army of Tennessee, 1862–1865.* Baton Rouge: Louisiana State University Press.

Connelly, Thomas L. 1977. *The Marble Man: Robert E. Lee and His Image in American Society.* New York: Alfred A. Knopf.

Cook, Cita. 2003. "Winnie Davis: The Challenges of Daughterhood." In *Mississippi Women: Their History, Their Lives,* edited by Martha Swift et al., 21–38. Athens: University of Georgia Press.

Coontz, Stephanie. 1999. "Working-Class Families, 1870–1890." In *American Families: A Multicultural Reader,* edited by Stephanie Coontz, Maya Parson, and Gabrielle Raley, 94–127. New York: Routledge.

Cooper, Edward S. 2004. *Vinnie Ream: An American Sculptor.* Chicago: Academy Chicago Publishers.

Cooper, William J. 2000. *Jefferson Davis, American.* New York: Alfred A. Knopf.

Corbin, D. T. 1866. *Digest of Opinions of the Judge Advocate General of the Army.* Washington, DC: U.S. Government Printing Office.

Coryell, Janet L. 1990. *Neither Heroine Nor Fool: Anna Ella Carroll of Maryland.* Kent, OH: Kent State University Press.

Coski, John M. 1996. *Capital Navy: The Men, Ships, and Operations of the James River Squadron.* Campbell, CA: Savas Woodbury.

Cott, Nancy F., ed. 1993. *History of Women in the United States. Historical Articles on Women's Lives and Activities,* vol. 12: *Education.* Munich: K. G. Saur Publishing.

Cottom, Robert I., and Mary Ellen Hayward. 1994. *Maryland and the Civil War: A House Divided.* Baltimore: Maryland Historical Society.

Coulling, Mary P. 1987. *The Lee Girls.* Winston-Salem, MA: John F. Blair.

Coulter, E. Merton. 1948. *Travels in the Confederate States: A Bibliography.* Norman: University of Oklahoma Press.

Coultrap-McQuin, Susan. 1990. *Doing Literary Business: American Women Writers in the Nineteenth Century.* Chapel Hill: University of North Carolina Press.

Coultrap-McQuin, Susan, ed. 1992. *Gail Hamilton: Selected Writings.* Piscataway, NJ: Rutgers University Press.

Cox, Karen L. 2003. *Dixie's Daughters: The United Daughters of the Confederacy and the Preservation of Confederate Culture.* Gainesville: University Press of Florida.

Cox, LaWanda. 1985. *Lincoln and Black Freedom: A Study in Presidential Leadership.* Urbana: University of Illinois Press.

Cozzens, Peter. 1992. *This Terrible Sound: The Battle of Chickamauga.* Urbana: University of Illinois Press.

Crabtree, Beth G., and James W. Patton, eds. 1979. *Journal of a Secesh Lady: The Diary of Catherine Ann Devereux Edmondston, 1860–1866.* Raleigh: North Carolina Division of Archives and History.

Crawford, Richard. 1977. *The Civil War Songbook.* New York: Dover Publications.

Creighton, Margaret S. 2005. *The Colors of Courage: Gettysburg's Forgotten History: Immigrants, Women, and African Americans in the Civil War's Defining Battle.* New York: Basic Books.

Crenshaw, Ollinger. 1945. *The Slave States in the Presidential Election of 1860.* Baltimore, MD: Johns Hopkins University Press.

Crofts, Daniel. 1989. *Reluctant Confederates: Upper South Unionists in the Secession Crisis.* Chapel Hill: University of North Carolina Press.

Cromwell, Otelia. 1958. *Lucretia Mott.* Cambridge, MA: Harvard University Press.

Cullen, Jim. 1995. *The Civil War in Popular Culture: A Reusable Past.* Washington, DC: Smithsonian Institution Press.

Culpepper, Marilyn Mayer. 1991. *Trials and Triumphs: The Women of the American Civil War.* East Lansing: Michigan State University Press.

Culpepper, Marilyn Mayer. 2002. *All Things Altered: Women in the Wake of Civil War and Reconstruction.* Jefferson, NC: McFarland.

Cushman, Stephen. 1999. *Bloody Promenade: Reflections on a Civil War Battle.* Charlottesville: University of Virginia Press.

Cutter, Barbara. 2003. *Domestic Devils, Battlefield Angels: The Radicalization of American Womanhood, 1830–1865.* DeKalb: Northern Illinois University Press.

Dale, Edward Everett, and Gaston Litton. 1939. *Cherokee Cavaliers.* Norman: University of Oklahoma Press.

Dall, Caroline, ed. 1860. *A Practical Illustration of "Woman's Right to Labor;" or, A Letter from Marie E. Zakrzewska.* Boston: Walker, Wise & Co.

Daly, Maria Lydig. 1962. *Diary of a Union Lady 1861–1865*, edited by Harold Earl Hammond. New York: Funk & Wagnalls.

Daniel, Larry J. 1997. *Shiloh: The Battle That Changed the Civil War.* New York: Simon & Schuster.

Daniel, Larry J. 2004. *Days of Glory: The Army of the Cumberland, 1861–1865.* Baton Rouge: Louisiana State University Press.

Dannett, Sylvia G. L. 1959. *Noble Women of the North.* New York: Thomas Yoseloff.

Dannett, Sylvia G. L. 1960. *She Rode with the Generals: The True and Incredible Story of Sarah Emma Seelye, Alias Franklin Thompson.* New York: Thomas Nelson & Sons.

Dargan, Elizabeth Paisley, ed. 1994. *The Civil War Diary of Martha Abernathy: Wife of Dr. Charles C. Abernathy of Pulaski, Tennessee.* Beltsville, MD: Professional Printing.

Davis, Jefferson. 1881. *Rise and Fall of the Confederate Government.* 2 vols. New York: D. Appleton & Co.

Davis, Jefferson. 1971–present. *The Papers of Jefferson Davis.* 11 vols. to date. Baton Rouge: Louisiana State University Press.

Davis, Varina Howell. 1890. *Jefferson Davis, A Memoir.* 2 vols. New York: Belford.

Davis, William C. 1991. *Jefferson Davis: The Man and His Hour.* New York: HarperCollins.

Davis, William C. 1999. *Lincoln's Men: How President Lincoln Became Father to an Army and a Nation.* New York: Free Press.

Decker, William Merrill. 1998. *Epistolary Practices: Letter Writing in America before Telecommunications.* Chapel Hill: University of North Carolina Press.

DeForest, John William. 1969. *Miss Ravenel's Conversion from Secession to Loyalty.* Columbus, OH: Charles E. Merrill Publishing Company. (Reprint of 1867 edition. New York: Harper & Brothers.)

Degler, Carl N. 1974. *The Other South: Southern Dissenters in the Nineteenth Century.* New York: Harper & Row.

Degler, Carl. 1980. *At Odds: Women and the Family from the Revolution to the Present.* New York: Oxford University Press.

Dehart, William C. 1869. *Observations on Military Law and the Constitution and Practice of Courts Martial.* New York: D. Appleton & Co.

Delauter Jr., Roger U. 1992. *Winchester in the Civil War.* Lynchburg, VA: H. E. Howard.

Delfino, Susanna, and Michelle Gillespie, eds. 2002 *Neither Lady Nor Slave: Working Women of the Old South.* Chapel Hill: University of North Carolina Press.

Denney, Robert E. 1994. *Civil War Medicine: Care and Comfort of the Wounded.* New York: Sterling Publishing Co.

Denton, Lawrence M. 1995. *A Southern Star for Maryland: Maryland and the Secession Crisis, 1860–1861.* Baltimore, MD: Publishing Concepts.

De Pauw, Linda Grant. 1998. *Battle Cries and Lullabies: Women in War from Prehistory to the Present.* Norman: University of Oklahoma Press.

Detzer, David. 2001. *Allegiance: Fort Sumter, Charleston, and the Beginnings of the Civil War.* New York: Harcourt Brace.

Detzer, David. 2004. *Donnybrook: The Battle of Bull Run, 1861.* Orlando: Harcourt.

Dickinson, Anna Elizabeth. [1868] 2003. *What Answer?* New York: Humanity Books.

Diedrich, Maria. 1999. *Love Across Color Lines: Ottilie Assing and Frederick Douglass.* New York: Hill and Wang.

Diffley, Kathleen. 2002. *To Live and Die.* Durham, NC: Duke University Press.

Diner, Hasia R. 1983. *Erin's Daughters in America: Irish Immigrant Women in the Nineteenth Century.* Baltimore, MD: Johns Hopkins University Press.

Dix, Dorothea L. 1975. *On Behalf of the Insane Poor: Selected Reports 1842–1862.* North Stratford, NH: Ayer Company.

Dobson, Joanne. 1986. "The Hidden Hand: Subversion of Cultural Ideology in Three Mid-nineteenth-century American Women's Novels." *American Quarterly* 38 (2): 223–242.

Dolensky, Suzanne T. 1985. "Varina Howell Davis, 1889 to 1906." *Journal of Mississippi History* 47 (May): 90–109.

Donald, David Herbert. 1995. *Lincoln.* New York: Simon & Schuster.

Dorr, Rheta Childe. 1970. *Susan B. Anthony: The Woman Who Changed the Mind of a Nation.* New York: AMS Press. Reprint.

Dorsey, Bruce. 2002. *Reforming Men and Women: Gender in the Antebellum City.* Ithaca, NY: Cornell University Press.

Douglas, Ann. 1974. "Heaven Our Home: Consolation Literature in the Northern United States, 1830–1880." *American Quarterly* 26 (5): 496–515.

Douglas, Ann. 1998. *The Feminization of American Culture.* New York: Farrar, Straus and Giroux. (Orig. pub. 1977.)

Douglass, Frederick. 1962. *Life and Times of Frederick Douglass: His Early Life as a Slave, His Escape From*

*Bondage, and His Complete History Written by Himself.* New York: Collier Books.

Douglass, Frederick. 1976. *Frederick Douglass on Women's Rights,* edited by Philip S. Foner. Westport, CT: Greenwood Press.

Dowdy, Clifford. 1964. *The Seven Days: The Emergence of Lee.* Boston: Little, Brown.

DuBois, Ellen Carol. 1978. *Feminism and Suffrage: The Emergence of an Independent Women's Movement in America 1848–1869.* Ithaca, NY: Cornell University Press.

Dulles, Foster Rhea. 1950. *The American Red Cross, a History.* New York: Harper & Row.

Durrill, Wayne K. 1990. *War of Another Kind: A Southern Community in the Great Rebellion.* New York: Oxford University Press.

Dyer, Thomas G. 1992. "Vermont Yankees in King Cotton's Court: The Case of Cyrena and Amherst Stone." *Vermont History* 60: 205–229.

Dyer, Thomas G. 1995. "Atlanta's Other Civil War Novel: Fictional Unionists in a Confederate City." *Georgia Historical Quarterly* 79: 147–168.

Dyer, Thomas G. 1999. *Secret Yankees: The Union Circle in Confederate Atlanta.* Baltimore, MD: Johns Hopkins University Press.

East, Charles, ed. 1991. *Sarah Morgan: The Civil War Diary of a Southern Woman.* New York: Simon & Schuster.

Edmonds, S. Emma. 1864. *Unsexed; or, The Female Soldier: The Thrilling Adventures, Experiences and Escapes of a Woman, as Nurse, Spy and Scout, in Hospitals, Camp and Battlefields.* Philadelphia, PA: Philadelphia Publishing.

Edmonds, S. Emma E. 1865. *Nurse and Spy in the Union Army.* Hartford, CT: W. S. Williams and Company.

Edmonds, Sarah Emma. 1999. *Memoirs of a Soldier, Nurse and Spy: A Woman's Adventures in the Union Army.* DeKalb: Northern Illinois University Press.

Edward, Laura F. 1997. *Gendered Strife and Confusion: The Political Culture of Reconstruction.* Urbana: University of Illinois Press.

Edwards, Laura F. 1999. "Law, Domestic Violence, and the Limits of Patriarchal Authority in the Antebellum South." *Journal of Southern History* 65: 733–770.

Edwards, Laura F. 2000. *Scarlett Doesn't Live Here Anymore: Southern Women in the Civil War Era.* Urbana: University of Illinois Press.

Edwards, Stewart C. 2001. "'To Do the Manufacturing for the South.'" *Georgia Historical Quarterly* 85 (4): 538–554.

Eggleston, G. K. 1929. "The Work of Relief Societies during the Civil War." *Journal of Negro History* 14 (3): 272–299.

Eggleston, Larry G. 2003. *Women in the Civil War: Extraordinary Stories of Soldiers, Spies, Nurses, Doctors, Crusaders, and Others.* Jefferson, NC: McFarland.

Eiselein, Gregory, and Anne K. Phillips, eds. 2001. *The Louisa May Alcott Encyclopedia.* Westport, CT: Greenwood Press.

Elder, Donald C. III, ed. 2003. *Love amid the Turmoil: The Civil War Letters of William and Mary Vermillion.* Iowa City: University of Iowa Press.

Ellefson, Cheryl. 1996. "Servants of God and Man: The Sisters of Charity." In *Valor and Lace: The Roles of Confederate Women, 1861–1865,* edited by Mauriel Phillips Joslyn, 175–184. Murfreesboro, TN: Southern Heritage Press.

Elmore, Grace Brown. 1997. *A Heritage of Woe: The Civil War Diary of Grace Brown Elmore, 1861–1868,* edited by Marli F. Weiner. Athens: University of Georgia Press.

Emerson, Sarah Hopper, ed. 1986. *The Life of Abby Hopper Gibbons, Told Chiefly through Her Correspondence.* New York: G.P. Putnam's Sons.

Englizian, H. Crosby. 1968. *Brimstone Corner: Park Street Church, Boston.* Chicago: Moody Press.

Eppes, Susan Bradford. [1926] 1968. *Through Some Eventful Years.* Gainesville: University Press of Florida.

Escott, Paul D. 1977. "'The Cry of the Sufferers': The Problem of Welfare in the Confederacy." *Civil War History* 23: 228–240.

Escott, Paul D. 1978. *After Secession: Jefferson Davis and the Failure of Confederate Nationalism.* Baton Rouge: Louisiana State University Press.

Evans, Augusta Jane. 1992. *Macaria; or, Altars of Sacrifice,* with Introduction by Drew Gilpin Faust. Baton Rouge: Louisiana State University Press. (Reprint of 1864 edition. Richmond: West & Johnston.)

Evans, Clark. 1994. "*Maum Guinea:* Beadle's Unusual Jewel." *Dime Novel Roundup* 63 (4): 77–80.

Evans, David. 1996. *Sherman's Horsemen: Union Cavalry Operations in the Atlanta Campaign.* Bloomington: Indiana University Press.

Evans, Sara M. 1997. *Born for Liberty: A History of Women in America.* New York: Free Press.

Everett, Robinson O. 1956. *Military Justice in the Armed Forces of the United States.* Harrisburg, PA: Military Service Publishing Company.

Fahs, Alice. 1999. "The Feminized Civil War: Gender, Northern Popular Literature and the Memory of the Civil War, 1861–1900." *Journal of American History* 85: 1461–1494.

Fahs, Alice. 2001. *The Imagined Civil War: Popular Literature of the North and South, 1861–1865.* Chapel Hill: University of North Carolina Press.

Farnham, Christie Anne. 1994. *The Education of the Southern Belle: Higher Education and Student Socialization in the Antebellum South.* New York: New York University Press.

Farnham, Thomas J., and Francis P. King. 1996. "'The March of the Destroyer': The New Bern Yellow Fever Epidemic of 1864." *North Carolina Historical Review* 73: 435–483.

Farrell, James J. 1980. *Inventing the American Way of Death, 1830–1920.* Philadelphia, PA: Temple University Press.

Faulkner, Carol. 2003. *Women's Radical Reconstruction: The Freedmen's Aid Movement.* Philadelphia: University of Pennsylvania Press.

Faust, Drew Gilpin. 1988. *The Creation of Confederate Nationalism: Ideology and Identity in the Civil War South.* Baton Rouge: Louisiana State University Press.

Faust, Drew Gilpin. 1989. "Race, Gender, and Confederate Nationalism: William D. Washington's *Burial of Latane.*" *Southern Review* 25: 297–307.

Faust, Drew Gilpin. 1990. "Altars of Sacrifice: Confederate Women and the Narratives of War." *Journal of American History* 76 (4): 1200–1228.

Faust, Drew Gilpin. 1992. "Introduction: *Macaria*, A War Story for Confederate Women." In *Macaria; or, Altars of Sacrifice*, by Augusta Jane Evans, xiii–xxvi. Baton Rouge: Louisiana State University Press.

Faust, Drew Gilpin. 1992. *Southern Stories: Slaveholders in Peace and War.* Columbia: University of Missouri Press.

Faust, Drew Gilpin. 1992. "'Trying to Do a Man's Business': Gender, Violence, and Slave Management in Civil War Texas." *Gender and History* 4: 197–214.

Faust, Drew Gilpin. 1996. *Mothers of Invention: Women of the Slaveholding South in the Civil War.* Chapel Hill: University of North Carolina Press.

Faust, Drew Gilpin. 1998. "'Ours as Well as That of the Men': Women and Gender in the Civil War." In *Writing the Civil War: The Quest to Understand*, edited by James M. McPherson and William J. Cooper Jr., 228–240. Columbia: University of South Carolina Press.

Faust, Drew Gilpin. 2000. "A Moment of Truth: A Woman of the Master Class in the Confederate South." In *Slavery, Secession and Southern History*, edited by Robert Louis Paquette and Louis A. Ferleger, 126–139. Charlottesville: University Press of Virginia.

Faust, Drew Gilpin. 2005. "'The Dread Void of Uncertainty': Naming the Dead in the American Civil War." *Southern Cultures* 11 (2): 7–32, 113.

Fellman, Michael. 1989. *Inside War: The Guerrilla Conflict in Missouri During the American Civil War.* New York: Oxford University Press.

Fellman, Michael. 1994. "Women and Guerrilla Warfare." In *Divided Houses*, edited by Catherine Clinton and Nina Silber, 147–165. New York: Oxford University Press.

Fellman, Michael. 1995. *Citizen Sherman: A Life of William Tecumseh Sherman.* New York: Random House.

Fellman, Michael. 2000. *The Making of Robert E. Lee.* New York: Random House.

Felton, Rebecca Latimer. 1911. *Memoirs of Georgia Politics.* Atlanta, GA: Index Publishing Co.

Felton, Rebecca Latimer. 1919. *Country Life in Georgia in the Days of My Youth.* Atlanta, GA: Index Publishing Co.

Fidler, William Perry. 1951. *Augusta Evans Wilson, 1835–1909.* Tuscaloosa: University of Alabama Press.

Fields, Catherine Keene, and Lisa C. Kightlinger, eds. 1993. *To Ornament Their Minds: Sarah Pierce's Litchfield Female Academy, 1792–1833.* Litchfield, CT: Litchfield Historical Society.

Finley, Randy. 1996. *From Slavery to Uncertain Freedom: The Freedmen's Bureau in Arkansas, 1865–1869.* Fayetteville: University of Arkansas Press.

Fishel, Edwin C. 1996. *The Secret War for the Union: The Untold Story of Military Intelligence in the Civil War.* Boston: Houghton-Mifflin.

Fisher, Clyde Olin. 1971. "The Relief of Soldiers' Families in North Carolina during the Civil War." *Southern Atlantic Quarterly* 16: 60–72.

Fladeland, Betty. 1972. *Men and Brothers: Anglo-American Antislavery Cooperation.* Urbana: University of Illinois Press.

Fleischner, Jennifer. 2003. *Mrs. Lincoln and Mrs. Keckly.* New York: Broadway Books.

Foner, Eric. 1970. *Free Soil, Free Labor, Free Men: The Ideology of the Republican Party before the Civil War.* New York: Oxford University Press.

Foner, Eric. 1988. *Reconstruction: America's Unfinished Revolution, 1863–1877.* New York: Harper & Row.

Foner, Philip Sheldon. 1979. *Women and the American Labor Movement: From Colonial Times to the Eve of World War I.* New York: Free Press.

Forbes, Ella. 1998. *African American Women during the Civil War.* New York: Garland Publishing.

Foster, Frances Smith. 2005. "Frances Ellen Watkins Harper." In *Black Women in America*, edited by Darlene Clark Hine, 2: 532-537. New York: Oxford University Press.

Foster, Gaines M. 1987. *Ghosts of the Confederacy: Defeat, the Lost Cause, and the Emergence of the New South.* New York: Oxford University Press.

Fought, Leigh. 2003. *Southern Womanhood and Slavery: A Biography of Louisa S. McCord, 1810–1879.* Columbia: University of Missouri Press.

Fox, Arthur B. 2002. *Pittsburgh during the American Civil War, 1860–1865.* Chicora, PA: Mechling Books.

Fox-Genovese, Elizabeth. 1988. *Within the Plantation Household: Black and White Women of the Old South.* Chapel Hill: University of North Carolina Press.

Frank, Joseph Allan. 1998. *With Ballot and Bayonet: The Political Socialization of American Civil War Soldiers.* Athens: University of Georgia Press.

Frank, Lisa Tendrich. 2001. "To 'Cure Her of Her Pride and Boasting': The Gendered Implications of Sherman's March." Ph.D. diss. University of Florida.

Frank, Lisa Tendrich. 2005. "War Comes Home: Confederate Women and Union Soldiers." In *Virginia's Civil War,* edited by Peter Wallenstein and Bertram Wyatt-Brown, 123-136. Charlottesville: University of Virginia Press.

Franklin, John Hope. 1963. *The Emancipation Proclamation.* Garden City, NY: Doubleday.

Frederickson, George M. 1965. *The Inner Civil War: Northern Intellectuals and the Crisis of the Union.* Urbana: University of Illinois Press.

Freehling, William W. 2001. *The South vs. the South: How Anti-Confederate Southerners Shaped the Course of the Civil War.* New York: Oxford University Press.

Freeman, Douglas Southall. 1942–1944. *Lee's Lieutenants: A Study in Command.* 3 vols. New York: Scribner's.

Freemon, Frank R. 2001. *Gangrene and Glory: Medical Care During the American Civil War.* Urbana: University of Illinois Press.

French, Stanley. 1974. "The Cemetery as Cultural Institution: The Establishment of Mount Auburn and the 'Rural Cemetery' Movement." *American Quarterly* 26 (1): 37–59.

Friedman, Jean E. 1985. *The Enclosed Garden: Women and Community in the Evangelical South, 1830–1900.* Chapel Hill: University of North Carolina Press.

Furgurson, Ernest B. 2004. *Freedom Rising: Washington in the Civil War.* New York: Alfred A. Knopf.

Furnas, J. C. 1982. *Fanny Kemble: Leading Lady of the Nineteenth-Century Stage.* New York: Dial Press.

Gabaccia, Donna. 1994. *From the Other Side: Immigrant Life in the U.S., 1820–1990.* Bloomington: Indiana University Press.

Gaines, W. Craig. 1989. *The Confederate Cherokees: John Drew's Regiment of Mounted Rifles.* Baton Rouge: Louisiana State University Press.

Galbraith, William, and Loretta Galbraith, eds. 1990. *A Lost Heroine of the Confederacy: The Diaries and Letters of Belle Edmondson.* Jackson: University Press of Mississippi.

Gallagher, Gary. 1986. "A Widow and Her Soldier: LaSalle Corbell Pickett as Author of the George E. Pickett Letters." *The Virginia Magazine of History and Biography* 94: 329–344.

Gallagher, Gary, ed. 1989. *Fighting for the Confederacy: The Personal Recollections of General Edward Porter Alexander.* Chapel Hill: University of North Carolina Press.

Gallagher, Gary, ed. 1996. *Chancellorsville: The Battle and Its Aftermath.* Chapel Hill: University of North Carolina Press.

Gallagher, Gary W. 1997. *The Confederate War: How Popular Will, Nationalism, and Military Strategy Could Not Stave Off Defeat.* Cambridge, MA: Harvard University Press.

Gallagher, Gary W., ed. 1997. *The Wilderness Campaign.* Chapel Hill: University of North Carolina Press.

Gallagher, Gary W., ed. 1999. *The Antietam Campaign.* Chapel Hill: University of North Carolina Press.

Gallagher, Gary W., ed. 2006. *The Shenandoah Valley Campaign of 1864.* Chapel Hill: University of North Carolina Press.

Gallman, J. Matthew. 1994. *The North Fights the Civil War: The Home Front.* Chicago: Ivan R. Dee.

Gallman, J. Matthew. 2006. *America's Joan of Arc: The Life of Anna Elizabeth Dickinson.* New York: Oxford University Press.

Gardner, Sarah E. 2001. "'A Sweet Solace to My Lonely Heart': 'Stonewall' and Mary Anna Jackson and the Civil War." In *Intimate Strategies of the Civil War: Military Commanders and their Wives,* edited by Carol K. Bleser and Lesley J. Gordon, 49–68. New York: Oxford University Press.

Gardner, Sarah E. 2004. *Blood and Irony: Southern White Women's Narratives of the Civil War, 1861–1937.* Chapel Hill: University of North Carolina Press.

Garfield, Deborah, and Rafia Zafar, eds. 1996. *Harriet Jacobs and 'Incidents in the Life of a Slave Girl': New Critical Essays.* New York: Cambridge University Press.

Garrison, Nancy S. 1999. *With Courage and Delicacy: Civil War on the Peninsula: Women and the U.S. Sanitary Commission.* Mason City, IA: Savas Publishing Company.

Garrison, Webb. 1995. *Atlanta and the War.* Nashville, TN: Rutledge Hill Press.

Gay, Mary A. H. [1892] 2001. *Life in Dixie during the War.* Edited by J. H. Segars. Macon, GA: Mercer University Press.

Geer, Emily Apt. 1984. *The First Lady, The Life of Lucy Webb Hayes.* Kent, OH: Kent State University Press.

Geisberg, Judith Ann. 2000. *Civil War Sisterhood: The U.S. Sanitary Commission and Women's Politics in Transition.* Boston: Northeastern University Press.

Genovese, Elizabeth Fox. 1988. *Within the Plantation Household: Black and White Women of the Old South.* Chapel Hill: University of North Carolina Press.

Genovese, Eugene D. 1991. "Toward a Kinder and Gentler America: The Southern Lady in the Greening of the Politics of the Old South." In *In Joy and in Sorrow: Women, Family, and Marriage in the Victorian South,* edited by Carol K. Bleser, 125–134. New York: Oxford University Press.

Gienapp, William. 1987. *The Origins of the Republican Party, 1852–1856.* New York: Oxford University Press.

Giesberg, Judith Ann. 1995. "In Service to the Fifth Wheel: Katharine Prescott Wormeley and Her Experiences in the United States Sanitary Commission." *Nursing History Review* 3: 43–53.

Giesberg, Judith Ann. 2000. *Civil War Sisterhood: The U.S. Sanitary Commission and Women's Politics in Transition.* Boston: Northeastern University Press.

Gilbert, Olive. [1878] 1968. *Narrative of Sojourner Truth: A Bondswoman of Olden Time.* New York: Arno Press.

Gilbo, Patrick F. 1981. *The American Red Cross: The First Century.* New York: Harper & Row.

Gilmore, Donald L. 2006. *Civil War on the Missouri-Kansas Border.* Gretna, LA: Pelican Publishing Company.

Ginzberg, Lori D. 1990. *Women and the Work of Benevolence: Morality, Politics, and Class in the Nineteenth-Century United States.* New Haven, CT: Yale University Press.

Glatthaar, Joseph T. [1985] 1995. *The March to the Sea and Beyond: Sherman's Troops in the Savannah and Carolinas Campaigns.* Baton Rouge: Louisiana State University Press.

Goen, C. C. 1985. *Broken Churches, Broken Nation: Denominational Schisms and the Coming of the American Civil War.* Macon, GA: Mercer University Press.

Goldin, Claudia D., and Frank D. Lewis. 1975. "The Economic Cost of the American Civil War: Estimates and Implications." *Journal of Economic History* 35 (2): 299–326.

Goodrich, Thomas. 1995. *Black Flag: Guerilla Warfare on the Western Border, 1861–1865.* Bloomington: Indiana University Press.

Gordon, Beverly. 1998. *Bazaars and Fair Ladies: The History of the American Fundraising Fair.* Knoxville: University of Tennessee Press.

Gordon, Lesley J. 1998. *General George E. Pickett in Life and Legend.* Chapel Hill: University of North Carolina Press.

Gordon, Lesley J. 2001. "'Cupid Does Not Readily Give Way to Mars': The Marriage of LaSalle Corbell and George E. Pickett." In *Intimate Strategies of the Civil War: Military Commanders and Their Wives,* edited by Carol K. Bleser and Lesley J. Gordon, 69–86. New York: Oxford University Press.

Gorman, Kathleen. 1999. "Confederate Pensions as Southern Social Welfare." In *Before the New Deal: Social Welfare in the South, 1830–1930,* edited by Elna C. Green, 24–39. Athens: University of Georgia Press.

Gould, Virginia Meacham. 1998. *Chained to the Rock of Adversity: To Be Free, Black, and Female in the Old South.* Athens: University of Georgia Press.

Graf, Mercedes. 2001. *A Woman of Honor: Dr. Mary E. Walker and the Civil War.* Gettysburg, PA: Thomas Publications.

Grant, Mary H. 1994. *Private Woman, Public Person: An Account of the Life of Julia Ward Howe from 1819 to 1868.* Brooklyn, NY: Carlson Publishing..

Greeley, Horace, and John Cleveland. 1860. *A Political Text-Book for 1860.* New York: Tribune Association.

Green, Carol C. 2004. *Chimborazo: The Confederacy's Largest Hospital.* Knoxville: University of Tennessee Press.

Greene, Dana, ed. 1980. *Lucretia Mott, Her Complete Speeches and Sermons.* Lewiston, NY: Edwin Mellen Press.

Greene, Elna C., ed. 1999. *Before the New Deal: Social Welfare in the South, 1830–1930.* Athens: University of Georgia Press.

Greenhow, Rose O'Neal. 1863. *My Imprisonment and the First Year of Abolition Rule in Washington.* London: Richard Bentley.

Greer, Jack. 1975. *Leaves from a Family Album.* Waco: Texian Press.

Griffin, Farah Jasmine, ed. 1999. *Beloved Sisters and Loving Friends: Letters from Rebecca Primus of Royal Oak, Maryland, and Addie Brown of Hartford, Connecticut, 1854–1868.* New York: Alfred A. Knopf.

Griffith, Elisabeth. 1984. *In Her Own Right: The Life of Elizabeth Cady Stanton.* New York: Oxford University Press.

Griffith, Helen. 1966. *Dauntless in Mississippi: The Life of Sarah A. Dickey.* South Hadley, MA: Dinosaur Press.

Griffith, Lucille. 1953. "Mrs. Juliet Opie Hopkins and Alabama Military Hospitals." *Alabama Review* 6: 99–120.

Grimsley, Mark. 1995. *The Hard Hand of War: Union Military Policy toward Southern Civilians, 1861–1865.* New York: Cambridge University Press.

Grimsley, Mark, and Brooks D. Simpson, eds. 2001. *The Collapse of the Confederacy.* Lincoln: University of Nebraska Press.

Grivetti, Louis E., Jan L. Corlett, and Cassius T. Lockett. 2002. "Food in American History. Part 5: Pork: A Nation Divided: The American Civil War Era (1861–1865)." *Nutrition Today* 37 (3): 110–118.

Groce, W. Todd. 1999. *Mountain Rebels: East Tennessee Confederates and the Civil War, 1860–1870.* Knoxville: University of Tennessee Press.

Gross, Jennifer Lynn. 2001. *"Good Angels": Confederate Widowhood and the Reassurance of Patriarchy in the Postbellum South.* Ph.D. diss., University of Georgia.

Guelzo, Allen C. 2004. *The Emancipation Proclamation: The End of Slavery in America.* New York: Simon & Schuster.

Guerin, Elsa Jane. 1968. *Mountain Charley, or the Adventures of Mrs. E. J. Guerin, Who Was Thirteen Years in Male Attire: An Autobiography Comprising a Period of Thirteen Years Life in the States, California, and Pike's Peak,* with Introduction by Fred W. Mazzulla and William Kostka. Norman: University of Oklahoma Press.

Guilfoyle, Timothy. 1992. *City of Eros: New York City Prostitution and the Commercialization of Sex, 1790–1920.* New York: W. W. Norton.

Guterman, Benjamin. 2000. "Doing 'Good Brave Work'. Harriet Tubman's Testimony at Beaufort, South Carolina." *Prologue* 42: 155–165

Gutman, Herbert G. 1977. *The Black Family in Slavery and Freedom, 1750–1925.* New York: Vintage.

Hague, Parthenia Antoinette. [1888] 1991. *A Blockaded Family: Life in Southern Alabama During the Civil War.* Lincoln: University of Nebraska Press.

Hall, Richard. 1993. *Patriots in Disguise: Women Warriors of the Civil War.* New York: Paragon House.

Halttunen, Karen. 1982. *Confidence Men and Painted Women: A Study of Middle-Class Culture in America, 1830–1870.* New Haven, CT: Yale University Press.

Hanna, William F. 1990. "The Boston Draft Riot." *Civil War History* 36: 262–273.

Hansen, Debra Gold. 1993. *Strained Sisterhood: Gender and Class in the Boston Female Anti-Slavery Society.* Amherst: University of Massachusetts Press.

Hansen, Karen. 1995. "'No Kisses Is Like Youres': An Erotic Friendship between Two African American Women during the Mid-Nineteenth Century." *Gender and History* 7 (2): 151–182.

Harker, Jaime. 2001. "'Pious Cant' and Blasphemy: Fanny Fern's Radicalized Sentiment." *Legacy* 18 (1): 52–64.

Harper, Ida Husted. 1898. *The Life and Work of Susan B. Anthony.* Vol. 1. Indianapolis, IN: Hollenbeck Press.

Harrington, Fred Harvey. 1948. *Fighting Politician: Major General N. P. Banks.* Philadelphia: University of Pennsylvania Press.

Harris, Sharon M. 1991. *Rebecca Harding Davis and American Realism.* Philadelphia: University of Pennsylvania Press.

Harrison, Kimberly. 2003. "Rhetorical Rehearsals: The Construction of Ethos in Confederate Women's Civil War Diaries." *Rhetoric Review* 22 (3): 243–263.

Harrison, Lowell H. 1975. *The Civil War in Kentucky.* Lexington: University Press of Kentucky.

Hart, John S. 1852. *The Female Prose Writers of America, with Portraits, Biographical Notices, and Specimens of their Writing.* Philadelphia, PA: E. H. Butler & Co.

Harwell, Richard Barsdale. 1950. *Confederate Music.* Chapel Hill: University of North Carolina Press.

Harwell, Richard Barsdale, ed. [1959] 1998. *Kate: The Journal of a Confederate Nurse.* Baton Rouge: Louisiana State University Press.

Hauptman, Laurence. 1993. *The Iroquois in the Civil War: From Battlefield to Reservation.* Syracuse, NY: Syracuse University Press.

Haviland, Laura Smith. 1881. *A Woman's Life Work: Labors and Experiences of Laura S. Haviland.* Cincinnati, OH: Walden and Stowe.

Headley, John W. 1906. *Confederate Operations in Canada and New York.* New York: Neale Publishing Company.

Heaps, Willard A., and Porter W. Heaps. 1960. *The Singing Sixties: The Spirit of Civil War Days Drawn from the Music of the Times.* Norman: University of Oklahoma Press.

Hearn, Chester. 1997. *When the Devil Came Down to Dixie: Ben Butler in New Orleans.* Baton Rouge: Louisiana State University Press.

Hennessy, John J. 1993. *Return to Bull Run: The Campaign and Battle of Second Manassas.* New York: Simon & Schuster.

Hennessy, John. 2005. "For All Anguish, For Some Freedom: Fredericksburg in the War." *Blue and Gray Magazine* 22: 6–53.

Hennig, Helen Kohn, ed. 1936. *Columbia, Capital City of South Carolina, 1786–1936.* Columbia, SC: Columbia Sesquicentennial Commission, R. L. Bryan Co.

Henshaw, Sarah Edwards. 1868. *Our Branch and Its Tributaries.* Chicago: Alfred L. Sewell & Co.

Henwood, Dawn. 1999. "Slaveries 'In the Borders': Rebecca Harding Davis's 'Life in the Iron Mills' in its Southern Context." *Mississippi Quarterly* 52 (4): 567–596.

Herr, Pamela. 1988. *Jessie Benton Frémont: A Biography.* Norman: University of Oklahoma Press.

Herr, Pamela, and Mary Lee Spence, eds. 1993. *The Letters of Jessie Benton Frémont.* Urbana: University of Illinois Press.

Herran, Kathy Neill. 1997. *They Married Confederate Officers: The Intimate Story of Anna Morrison, Wife of Stonewall Jackson and Her Five Sisters.* Davidson, NC: Warren Publishing.

Hess, Earl J. 1997. *The Union Soldier in Battle: Enduring the Ordeal of Combat.* Lawrence: University Press of Kansas.

Higginbotham, Evelyn Brooks. 1994. *Righteous Discontent: The Women's Movement in the Black Baptist Church, 1880–1920.* Cambridge, MA: Harvard University Press.

Higonnet, Margaret R. 1989. "Civil War and Sexual Territories." In *Arms and the Woman: War, Gender, and Literary Representation,* edited by Helen M. Cooper, Adrienne Auslander Munich, and Susan Merrill Squier, 80–96. Chapel Hill: University of North Carolina Press.

Hill, Marilyn Wood. 1993. *Their Sisters' Keepers: Prostitution in New York City, 1830–1870.* Berkeley: University of California Press.

Hodgson, Godfrey. 2005. "Storm over Mexico." *History Today* 55: 34–39.

Hoff, Joan. 1991. *Law, Gender, and Injustice: A Legal History of U.S. Women.* New York: New York University Press.

Hoffert, Sylvia D. 2004. *Jane Grey Swisshelm: An Unconventional Life, 1815–1884.* Chapel Hill: University of North Carolina Press.

Hoffman, Nancy, ed. 1981. *Woman's "True" Profession: Voices from the History of Teaching.* Old Westbury, NY: Feminist Press/New York: McGraw-Hill.

Hoffman, Nicole Tonkovich. 1990. "Legacy Profile: Sarah Josepha Hale." *Legacy* 7 (2): 47–55.

Hoge, Jane (Mrs. A. H.). 1867. *The Boys in Blue, or Heroes of the "Rank and File."* New York: E. B. Treat and Company.

Hoisington, Daniel John, ed. 2001. *My Heart toward Home: Letters of a Family during the Civil War.* Roseville, MN: Edinborough Press.

Holdredge, Helen. 1953. *Mammy Pleasant.* New York: G.P. Putnam's Sons.

Holland, Mary Gardner, with Introduction by Daniel John Hoisington. 1998. *Our Army Nurses: Stories from Women in the Civil War.* Roseville, MN: Edinborough Press.

Holland, Rupert Sargent, ed. 1969. *Letters and Diary of Laura M. Towne: Written from the Sea Islands of South Carolina, 1862–1884.* New York: Negro University Press.

Hollandsworth, James G. 1998. *Pretense of Glory: The Life of Nathaniel P. Banks.* Baton Rouge: Louisiana State University Press.

Holman, Harriet R. 1965. *The Verse of Floride Clemson.* Columbia: University of South Carolina Press.

Holmes, Amy. 1990. "'Such Is the Price We Pay': American Widows and the Civil War Pension System." In *Toward a Social History of the American Civil War: Exploratory Essays,* edited by Maris Vinovskis, 171–195. Cambridge University Press.

Holt, Thad, Jr., ed. 1964. *Miss Waring's Journal, 1863 and 1865: Being the Diary of Miss Mary Waring of Mobile, during the final days of the War Between the States.* Chicago: The Wyvern Press of S. F. E.

Holtzman, Robert S. 1959. "Sally Tompkins, Captain, Confederate Army." *American Mercury* 127–130.

Hoogenboom, Ari. 1995. *Rutherford B. Hayes.* Lawrence: University Press of Kansas.

Hopley, Catherine Cooper. 1863. *"Stonewall" Jackson, Late General of the Confederate States Army. A Biographical Sketch, and an Outline of His Virginia Campaigns.* London: Chapman and Hall.

Hopley, Catherine Cooper. 1971. *Life in the South from the Commencement of the War by a Blockaded British Subject. Being a Social History of Those Who Took Part in the Battles, from a Personal Acquaintance with Them in Their Own Homes.* 2 vols. New York: Augustus M. Kelley Publishers. (Reprint of 1863 edition.)

Horn, John. 1993. *The Petersburg Campaign: June 1864–April 1865.* Conshohocken, PA: Combined Books.

Horn, Pamela. 1985. *The Victorian Country Child.* Wolfeboro Falls, NH: Alan Sutton.

Horn, Stanley. 1952. *The Army of Tennessee.* Norman: University of Oklahoma Press.

Horton, James Oliver, and Lots E. Horton. 1979. *Black Bostonians: Family Life and Community Struggle in the Antebellum North.* New York: Holmes and Meier Publishers.

Hoy, Claire. 2004. *Canadians in the Civil War.* Toronto: McArthur & Company.

Hudson, Linda S. 2001. *Mistress of Manifest Destiny; A Biography of Jane McManus Storm Cazneau, 1807–1878.* Austin: Texas State Historical Association.

Hudson, Lynn M. 2003. *The Making of "Mammy" Pleasant: A Black Entrepreneur in Nineteenth-Century San Francisco.* Urbana: University of Illinois Press.

Humez, Jean M. 2003. *Harriet Tubman: The Life and the Life Stories.* Madison: University of Wisconsin Press.

Humphreys, Margaret. 1992. *Yellow Fever and the South.* Piscataway, NJ: Rutgers University Press.

Hunter, Tera W. 1997. *To 'Joy My Freedom: Southern Black Women's Lives and Labors After the Civil War.* Cambridge, MA: Harvard University Press.

Hurn, Ethel Alice. 1911. *Wisconsin Women in the War between the States.* Madison: Wisconsin History Commission.

Hutchinson, John F. 1996. *Champions of Charity: War and the Rise of the Red Cross.* Boulder, CO: Westview Press.

Hutton, Paul Andrew. 1985. *Phil Sheridan and His Army.* Lincoln: University of Nebraska Press.

Hyman, Harold M. 1954. *Era of the Oath: Northern Loyalty Tests during the Civil War and Reconstruction.* Philadelphia: University of Pennsylvania Press.

Hyman, Harold M. 1973. *"A More Perfect Union": The Impact of the Civil War and Reconstruction on the Constitution.* New York: Alfred A. Knopf.

Inscoe, John. 1992. "Coping in Confederate Appalachia: A Portrait of a Mountain Woman and Her Community at War." *North Carolina Historical Review* 69: 388–413.

Inscoe, John. 1996. "The Civil War's Empowerment of an Appalachian Woman: The 1864 Slave Purchases of Mary Bell." In *Discovering the Women in Slavery: Emancipating Perspectives of the American Past,* edited by Patricia Morton, 61–81. Athens: University of Georgia Press.

Inscoe, John C., and Robert C. Kenzer, eds. 2001. *Enemies of the Country: New Perspectives on Unionists in the Civil War South.* Athens: University of Georgia Press.

Jackson, Mary Anna. 1892. *Life and Letters of General Thomas J. Jackson.* New York: Harper and Brothers.

Jackson, Roswell F., and Rosalyn M. Patterson. 1989. "A Brief History of Selected Black Churches in Atlanta, Georgia." *Journal of Negro History* 74 (Winter): 31–59.

Jackson-Coppin, Fanny. [1913] 1995. *Reminiscences of School Life and Hints on Teaching.* Introduction by Shelley P. Haley. Boston: G. K. Hall & Co.

Jacob, Katherine Allamong. 2000. "Vinnie Ream: The 'Prairie Cinderella' Who Sculpted Lincoln and Farragut—And Set Tongues Wagging." *Smithsonian* 31 (5): 104–115.

Jacobs, Harriet A. [1861] 1987. *Incidents in the Life of a Slave Girl,* edited by Jean Fagan Yellin. Cambridge, MA: Harvard University Press.

Jacobs, Joanna. 1988. "Eugenia Levy Phillips vs. The United States of America." *Alabama Heritage* 50: 22–29.

Jaquette, Henrietta Stratton, ed. 1937. *South after Gettysburg: Letters of Cornelia Hancock, 1863–1865.* New York: Thomas Y. Crowell & Company.

Jeffrey, Julie Roy. 1998. *The Great Silent Army of Abolitionism: Ordinary Women in the Antislavery Movement.* Chapel Hill: University of North Carolina Press.

Jenkins, Wilbert L. 2002. *Climbing up to Glory: A Short History of African Americans during the Civil War and Reconstruction.* Wilmington, DE: Scholarly Resources.

Jepsen, Thomas. 2000. *My Sisters Telegraphic: Women in the Telegraph Office, 1846–1850.* Athens: Ohio University Press.

Johannsen, Albert. 1950. *The House of Beadle and Adams.* Norman: University of Oklahoma Press.

Johnson, Carolyn Ross. 2003. *Cherokee Women in Crisis: Trail of Tears, Civil War, and Allotment.* Tuscaloosa: University of Alabama Press.

Johnson, Michael P., ed. 2001. *Abraham Lincoln, Slavery, and the Civil War: Selected Writings and Speeches.* Boston: Bedford/St. Martin's.

Johnston, Mary Tabb, with Elizabeth Johnston Lipscomb. 1978. *Amelia Gayle Gorgas: A Biography.* Tuscaloosa: University of Alabama Press.

Jolly, Ellen Ryan. 1927. *Nuns of the Battlefield.* Providence, RI: Providence Visitor Press.

Jones, Ann Goodwyn. 1981. *Tomorrow Is Another Day: The Woman Writer in the South, 1859–1936.* Baton Rouge: Louisiana State University Press.

Jones, Jacqueline. 1980. *Soldiers of Light and Love: Northern Teachers and Georgia Blacks, 1865–1873.* Chapel Hill: University of North Carolina Press.

Jones, Jacqueline. 1985. *Labor of Love, Labor of Sorrow: Black Women, Work and the Family from Slavery to the Present.* New York: Vintage.

Jones, James Boyd. 1985. "A Tale of Two Cities: The Hidden Battle against Venereal Disease in Civil War Nashville and Memphis." *Civil War History* 31 (3): 270–276.

Jones, Katharine M., ed. 1962. *Ladies of Richmond, Confederate Capital.* Indianapolis, IN: Bobbs-Merrill.

Jones, Katherine M., ed. 1964. *When Sherman Came: Southern Women and the "Great March."* Indianapolis, IN: Bobbs-Merrill.

Jones, Mary Sharpe, and Mary Jones Mallard. 1959. *Yankees a'Coming: One Month's Experience during the Invasion of Liberty County, Georgia, 1864–1865,* edited by Haksell Monroe. Tuscaloosa, AL: Confederate Publishing Company.

Jones, Paul Christian. 2001. "'This Dainty Woman's Hand . . . Red with Blood': E. D. E. N. Southworth's *The Hidden Hand* as Abolitionist Narrative." *American Transcendental Quarterly* 15 (1): 59–80.

Jordan, Waymouth T. Jr. 1979. *North Carolina Troops 1861–1865: A Roster.* Raleigh, NC: Division of Archives and History.

Josephy, Alvin M. Jr. 1992. *The Civil War in the American West.* New York: Alfred A. Knopf.

Joslyn, Mauriel Phillips, ed. 2004. *Confederate Women.* Gretna, LA: Pelican Publishing Company.

Kadzis, Peter, ed. 2000. *Blood: Stories of Life and Death from the Civil War.* New York: Thunder's Mouth Press.

Kaestle, Carl. 1983. *Pillars of the Republic: Common Schools and American Society, 1780–1860.* New York: Hill and Wang.

Kampmeier, Rudolph H. 1982. "Venereal Disease in the United States Army, 1775–1900." *Sexually Transmitted Diseases* 9 (2): 100–108.

Kane, Harnett T. 1954. *Spies for the Blue and Gray.* New York: Hanover House.

Karcher, Carolyn L. 1994. *The First Woman in the Republic: A Cultural Biography of Lydia Maria Child.* Durham, NC: Duke University Press.

Karcher, Carolyn L., ed. 1996. *An Appeal in Favor of That Class of Americans Called Africans.* Amherst: University of Massachusetts Press.

Katcher, Phillip, and Richard Scollins (illus.). 2000. *Flags of the Civil War.* Oxford: Osprey Publishing.

Kaufmann, Janet E. 1984. "Under the Petticoat Flag: Women Soldiers in the Confederate Army." *Southern Studies* 23: 363–375.

Kaufman, Janet E. 1986. "Working Women of the South: 'Treasury Girls.'" *Civil War Times Illustrated* 25: 32–38.

Keckley, Elizabeth. [1868] 1988. *Behind the Scenes, or Thirty Years a Slave and Four Years in the White House.* New York: Oxford University Press.

Kelley, Mary. 1984. *Private Woman, Public Stage: Literary Domesticity in Nineteenth-Century America.* New York: Oxford University Press.

Kelly, Bruce C., and Mark A. Snell, eds. 2004. *Bugle Resounding: Music and Musicians of the Civil War Era.* Columbia: University of Missouri Press.

Kelly, Lori Duin. 1983. *The Life and Works of Elizabeth Stuart Phelps, Victorian Feminist Writer.* Albany, NY: Whitston Publishing Company.

Kemble, Frances Anne. 1961. *Journal of a Residence on a Georgian Plantation: 1838–1839,* with Introduction by John A. Scott. Athens: University of Georgia Press. (Reprint of 1863 edition.)

Kennett, Lee. 1995. *Marching through Georgia: The Story of Soldiers and Civilians during Sherman's Campaign.* New York: HarperPerennial.

Kenzer, Robert C. 1987. *Kinship and Neighborhood in a Southern Community: Orange County, North Carolina, 1849–1881.* Knoxville: University of Tennessee Press.

Kerr, Andrea Moore. 1992. *Lucy Stone: Speaking out for Equality.* Piscataway, NJ: Rutgers University Press.

Kerr, Andrea Moore. 1995. "White Women's Rights, Black Men's Wrongs, Free Love, Blackmail, and the Formation of the American Woman Suffrage Association." In *One Woman, One Vote: Rediscovering the Woman Suffrage Movement,* edited by Marjorie Spruill Wheeler, 61-80. Troutdale, OR: NewSage Press.

Kessler, Carol Farley. 1982. *Elizabeth Stuart Phelps.* New York: Twayne Publishers.

Kessler-Harris, Alice. 1982. *Out to Work: A History of Wage-Earning Women in the United States.* Oxford: Oxford University Press.

Kete, Mary Louise. 2000. *Sentimental Collaborations: Mourning and Middle-Class Identity in Nineteenth-Century America.* Durham, NC: Duke University Press.

Kinchen, Oscar A. 1972. *Women Who Spied for the Blue and the Gray.* Philadelphia, PA: Dorrance & Company.

King, Spencer Bidwell, Jr., ed. 1958. *Ebb Tide: As Seen through the Diary of Josephine Clay Habersham, 1863.* Athens: University of Georgia Press.

King, Wendy A. 1992. *Clad in Uniform: Women Soldiers of the Civil War.* Collingswood, NJ: C. W. Historicals.

King, Wilma, ed. 1993. *A Northern Woman in the Plantation South: Letters of Tryphena Blanche Holder Fox, 1856–1876.* Columbia: University of South Carolina Press.

Klein, Maury. 1997. *Days of Defiance: Sumter, Secession, and the Coming of the Civil War.* New York: Alfred A. Knopf.

Klement, Frank L. 1999. *Lincoln's Critics: The Copperheads of the North,* edited by Steven K. Rogstad. Shippensburg, PA: White Mane Publishing Co.

Kohlstedt, Sally Gregory. 1978. "Maria Mitchell and the Advancement of Women in Science." *New England Quarterly* 51: 39–63.

Kolchin, Peter. 2003. *American Slavery: 1619–1877.* New York: Hill and Wang.

Korn, Bertram W. 1961. *American Jewry and the Civil War,* with Introduction by Allan Nevins. Cleveland, OH, New York, and Philadelphia, PA: Meridian Books and Jewish Publication Society.

Kraditor, Aileen S. 1969. *Means and Ends in American Abolitionism: Garrison and His Critics on Strategy and Tactics, 1864–1850.* New York: Random House.

Kurant, Wendy. 2002. "The Education of a Domestic Woman in Mary Boykin Chesnut's *Two Years.*" *The Southern Literary Journal* 34 (2): 14–29.

Laas, Virginia Jeans, ed. 1991. *Wartime Washington: The Civil War Letters of Elizabeth Blair Lee.* Urbana: University of Illinois Press.

Laas, Virginia Jeans. 2001. "'A Good Wife, the Best Friend in the World': The Marriage of Elizabeth Blair and S. Phillips Lee." In *Intimate Strategies of the Civil War: Military Commanders and Their Wives,* edited by Carol K. Bleser and Lesley J. Gordon, 225–242. New York: Oxford University Press.

Ladies' Christian Commission. 1864. *Ladies' Christian Commissions: Auxiliary to the U.S. Christian Commission.* Philadelphia: C. Sherman.

Lancaster, Jane. 2001. "'I Would Have Made Out Very Poorly Had It Not Been for Her': The Life and Work of Christiana Bannister, Hair Doctress and Philanthropist." *Rhode Island History* 59 (4): 103–122.

Lane, Mills, ed. 1990. *"Dear Mother: Don't grieve about me. If I get killed, I'll only be dead": Letters from Georgia Soldiers in the Civil War.* Savannah, GA: Beehive Press. (Reprint of 1977 edition.)

Larsen, Arthur J., ed. 1934. *Crusader and Feminist: Letters of Jane Grey Swisshelm 1858–1865.* Saint Paul: Minnesota Historical Society Press.

Larsen, Lawrence H. 1961. "Draft Riot in Wisconsin, 1862." *Civil War History* 7: 421–427.

Larson, C. Kay. 1992. "Bonny Yank and Ginny Reb Revisited." *Minerva, Quarterly Report on Women and the Military* 10 (2): 33–48.

Larson, Kate Clifford. 2004. *Bound for the Promised Land: Harriet Tubman, Portrait of an American Hero.* New York: Ballantine Books.

Larson, Rebecca D. 1996. *Blue and Grey Roses of Intrigue.* Gettysburg, PA: Thomas Publications.

Lassen, Coralou Peel, ed. 1999. *"Dear Sarah:" Letters Home from a Soldier of the Iron Brigade.* Bloomington: Indiana University Press.

Lawson, Melinda. 2002. *Patriot Fires: Forging a New American Nationalism in the Civil War North.* Lawrence: University Press of Kansas.

Lease, Benjamin. 1990. *Emily Dickinson's Readings of Men and Books: Sacred Soundings.* New York: St. Martin's Press.

Lebsock, Suzanne. 1984. *The Free Women of Petersburg: Status and Culture in a Southern Town, 1784–1860.* New York: W. W. Norton & Company.

Leckie, Shirley A. 1993. *Elizabeth Bacon Custer and the Making of a Myth.* Norman: University of Oklahoma Press.

Leckie, Shirley A. 2001. "The Civil War Partnership of Elizabeth and George A. Custer." In *Intimate Strategies of the Civil War: Civil War Commanders and their Wives,* edited by Carol K. Bleser and Lesley J. Gordon, 178–198. New York: Oxford University Press.

LeConte, Emma. 1987. *When the World Ended: The Diary of Emma LeConte,* edited by Earl Schenck Meirs, with Foreword by Anne Firor Scott. Lincoln: University of Nebraska Press.

Leonard, Ann. 1991. "Red Rover, The Civil War, and the Nuns." *Lincoln Herald* 93 (4): 136–140.

Leonard, Ann. 2000. "Catholic Sisters and Nursing in the Civil War." *Lincoln Herald* 102 (2): 65–81.

Leonard, Elizabeth D. 1994. *Yankee Women: Gender Battles in the Civil War.* New York: W. W. Norton.

Leonard, Elizabeth D. 1995. "Civil War Nurse, Civil War Nursing: Rebecca Usher of Maine." *Civil War History* 41 (3): 190–208.

Leonard, Elizabeth D. 1999. *All the Daring of a Soldier: Women of the Civil War Armies.* New York: W. W. Norton & Company.

Leonard, Elizabeth D. 2004. *Lincoln's Avengers: Justice, Revenge, and Reunion after the Civil War.* New York: W. W. Norton & Company.

Lerner, Gerda. 1998. *The Grimké Sisters from South Carolina: Pioneers for Women's Rights and Abolition.* New York: Oxford University Press.

Leslie, Edward E. 1998. *The Devil Knows How to Ride: The True Story of William Clarke Quantrill and His Confederate Raiders.* New York: Da Capo Press.

Lewis, Charles Lee. 1927. *Matthew Fontaine Maury: The Pathfinder of the Seas.* Annapolis, MD: U.S. Naval Institute.

Lewis, Elizabeth Wittenmyer. 2002. *Queen of the Confederacy, the Innocent Deceits of Lucy Holcombe Pickens.* Denton: University of North Texas Press.

Lightener, David L., ed. 1999. *Asylum, Prison, and Poorhouse: The Writings and Reform Work of Dorothea Dix in Illinois.* Carbondale: Southern Illinois University Press.

Linderman, Gerald E. 1987. *Embattled Courage: The Experience of Combat in the American Civil War.* New York: Free Press.

Link, William. 2003. *Roots of Secession: Slavery and Politics in Antebellum Virginia.* Chapel Hill: University of North Carolina Press.

Lively, Robert A. 1957. *Fiction Fights the Civil War: An Unfinished Chapter in the Literary History of the American People.* Chapel Hill: University of North Carolina Press.

Livermore, Mary Ashton Rice. 1890. *My Story of the War: A Woman's Narrative of Four Years Personal Experience as a Nurse in the Union Army.* Hartford, CT: A. D. Worthington and Company. (Reprinted 1974 in Women in America, from Colonial Times to the Twentieth Century series. New York: Arno Press.)

Logan, Kate Virginia Cox. 1932. *My Confederate Girlhood: The Memoirs of Kate Virginia Cox Logan,* edited by Lily Logan Morrill. Richmond, VA: Garrett and Massie.

Long, David. 1994. *Jewel of Liberty: Abraham Lincoln's Reelection and the End of Slavery.* Mechanicsburg, PA: Stackpole Books.

Long, Ellen Call. [1882] 1962. *Florida Breezes; or, Florida, New and Old.* Gainesville: University Press of Florida.

Lonn, Ella. 1928. *Desertion during the Civil War.* New York: American Historical Association.

Lonn, Ella. 2002. *Foreigners in the Confederacy.* Chapel Hill: University of North Carolina Press.

Loughridge, Patricia R., and Edward D. C. Campbell Jr. 1985. *Women and Mourning.* Richmond, VA: Museum of the Confederacy.

Lowry, Thomas P. 1994. *The Story the Soldiers Wouldn't Tell: Sex in the Civil War.* Mechanicsburg, PA: Stackpole Books.

Luebke, Frederick C. 1971. *Ethnic Voters and the Election of Lincoln.* Lincoln: University of Nebraska Press.

Lutz, Alama. 1940. *Created Equal: A Biography of Elizabeth Cady Stanton, 1815–1902.* New York: John Day Company.

Lutz, Alma. 1959. *Susan B. Anthony: Rebel, Crusader, Humanitarian.* Boston: Beacon Press.

Lystra, Karen. 1989. *Searching the Heart: Women, Men, and Romantic Love in Nineteenth-Century America.* New York: Oxford University Press.

Mabee, Carleton, with Susan Mabee Newhouse. 1993. *Sojourner Truth: Slave, Prophet, Legend.* New York: New York University Press.

Macaulay, John Allen. 2001. *Unitarianism in the Antebellum South: The Other Invisible Institution.* Tuscaloosa: University of Alabama Press.

MacDonald, Joanna M. 1999. *"We Shall Meet Again": The First Battle of Manassas (Bull Run), July 18–21, 1861.* Shippensburg, PA: White Mane Publishing Co.

MacDonald, Rose. 1939. *Mrs. Robert E. Lee.* Boston: Ginn & Company.

MacKethan, Lucinda H., ed. 1998. *Recollections of a Southern Daughter: A Memoir by Cornelia Jones Pond of Liberty County.* Athens: University of Georgia Press.

Mackey, Robert R. 2004. *The Uncivil War: Irregular Warfare in the Upper South, 1861–1865.* Norman: University of Oklahoma Press.

Maher, Sister Mary Denis. 1989. *To Bind up the Wounds: Catholic Sister Nurses in the U.S. Civil War.* Westport, CT: Greenwood Press.

Mahin, Dean B. 2002. *The Blessed Place of Freedom: Europeans in Civil War America.* Washington, DC: Brassey's.

Marchalonis, Shirley. 1988. "Lucy Larcom." *Legacy: A Journal of American Women Writers* 5 (1): 45–52.

Marchalonis, Shirley. 1989. *Worlds of Lucy Larcom, 1842–1893.* Athens: University of Georgia Press.

Markle, Donald E. 2000. *Spies and Spymasters of the Civil War.* New York: Hippocrene Books. (Revised edition in 2004.)

Marsh, Thomas O., and Marlene Templin. 1988. "The Ballad of Lottie Moon." *Civil War: The Magazine of the Civil War Society* 21: 40–45.

Marshall, H. E. 1937. *Dorothea Dix, Forgotten Samaritan.* Chapel Hill: University of North Carolina Press.

Marshall, Megan. 2005. *The Peabody Sisters: Three Women Who Ignited American Romanticism.* Boston: Houghton Mifflin Company.

Marszalek, John F. 1993. *Sherman: A Soldier's Passion for Order.* New York: Free Press.

Marszalek. John F., ed. 1994. *The Diary of Miss Emma Holmes, 1861–1866.* Baton Rouge: Louisiana State University Press. (Reprint of 1979 edition.)

Marszalek, John F. 2001. "General and Mrs. William T. Sherman, A Contentious Union." In *Intimate Strategies of the Civil War, Military Commanders and Their Wives,* edited by Carol K. Bleser and Lesley J. Gordon, 138-156. New York: Oxford University Press.

Marszalek, John F. 2005. *Sherman's March to the Sea.* Civil War Campaigns and Commanders Series. Abilene, TX: McWhiney Foundation Press.

Marten, James. 1990. *Texas Divided: Loyalty and Dissent in the Lone Star State.* Lexington: University of Kentucky Press.

Marten, James. 1998. *The Children's Civil War.* Chapel Hill: University of North Carolina Press.

Marvel, William. 1991. *Burnside.* Chapel Hill: University of North Carolina Press.

Marvel, William. 2000. *A Place Called Appomattox.* Chapel Hill: University of North Carolina Press.

Massey, Mary Elizabeth. 1949. "The Food and Drink Shortage on the Confederate Homefront." *North Carolina Historical Review* 26: 306–334.

Massey, Mary Elizabeth. 1952. *Ersatz in the Confederacy: Shortages and Substitutes on the Southern Homefront.* Columbia: University of South Carolina Press.

Massey, Mary Elizabeth. 1964. *Refugee Life in the Confederacy.* Baton Rouge: Louisiana State University Press.

Massey, Mary Elizabeth. 1973. "The Making of a Feminist." *Journal of Southern History* 39 (1): 3–22.

Massey, Mary Elizabeth. 1994. *Women in the Civil War.* Lincoln: University of Nebraska Press. (Reprint of *Bonnet Brigades.* New York: Alfred A. Knopf, 1966.)

Matthews, Glenna. 1992. *The Rise of Public Woman: Woman's Power and Place in the United States, 1630–1970.* New York: Oxford University Press.

Matthews, Glenna. 1997. *"Just a Housewife": The Rise and Fall of Domesticity in America.* New York: Oxford University Press.

Maxwell, William Quentin. 1956. *Lincoln's Fifth Wheel: The Political History of the United States Sanitary Commission.* New York: Longmans, Green & Company.

Mayer, Henry. 1998. *All on Fire: William Lloyd Garrison and the Abolition of Slavery.* New York: St. Martin's Griffin.

McAllister, Anna. 1936. *Ellen Sherman, Wife of General Sherman.* New York: Benziger Brothers.

McClintock, Megan J. 1996. "Civil War Pensions and the Reconstruction of Union Families." *Journal of American History* 83: 456–479.

McCrumb, Sharyn. 2003. *Ghost Riders.* New York: Dutton.

McCurry, Stephanie. 1992. "The Politics of Yeoman Households in South Carolina." In *Divided Houses: Gender and the Civil War,* edited by Catherine Clinton and Nina Silber, 22–38. New York: Oxford University Press.

McCurry, Stephanie. 1992. "The Two Faces of Republicanism: Gender and Proslavery Politics in Antebellum South Carolina." *Journal of American History* 78: 1245–1264.

McCurry, Stephanie. 1995. *Masters of Small Worlds: Yeoman Households, Gender Relations and the Political Culture of the Antebellum South Carolina Low Country.* New York: Oxford University Press.

McDevitt, Theresa R. 2004. "'A Melody before Unknown': The Civil War Experiences of Mary and Amanda Shelton." *Annals of Iowa* 63 (2): 105–136.

McDonald, Cornelia Peake. 1992. *A Woman's Civil War: A Diary with Reminiscences of the War from March 1862,* edited by Minrose C. Gwin. Madison: University of Wisconsin Press.

McElligott, Mary Ellen, ed. 1977. "'A Monotony Full of Sadness': The Diary of Nadine Turchin, May, 1863–April 1864." *Journal of the Illinois State Historical Society* 70: 27–89.

McGee, Charles M. Jr., and Ernest M. Landers Jr., eds. 1989. *A Rebel Came Home: The Diary and Letters of Floride Clemson, 1863–1866.* Columbia: University of South Carolina Press.

McGuire, Judith W. 1995. *Diary of a Southern Refugee during the War, by a Lady of Virginia,* with Introduction by Jean V. Berlin. Lincoln: University of Nebraska Press.

McKay, Charlotte E. 1876. *Stories of Hospital and Camp.* Philadelphia, PA: Claxton, Remsen & Haffelfinger.

McKnight, Brian D. 2006. *Contested Borderland: The Civil War in Appalachian Kentucky and Virginia.* Lexington: University Press of Kentucky.

McMurry, Richard M. 2000. *Atlanta 1864: Last Chance for the Confederacy.* Lincoln: University of Nebraska Press.

McMurry, Sally. 1995. *Transforming Rural Life: Dairying Families and Agricultural Change, 1820–1885.* Baltimore, MD: Johns Hopkins University Press.

McPherson, James M. 1964. *The Struggle for Equality.* Princeton, NJ: Princeton University Press.

McPherson, James M. 1965. *The Negro's Civil War: How American Blacks Felt and Acted during the War for the Union.* New York: Ballantine Books.

McPherson, James M. 1982. *Ordeal by Fire: The Civil War and Reconstruction.* New York: Alfred A. Knopf.

McPherson, James M. 1996. *Drawn with the Sword: Reflections on the American Civil War.* New York: Oxford University Press.

McPherson, James M. 1997. *For Cause and Comrades: Why Men Fought in the Civil War.* New York: Oxford University Press.

McPherson, James M. 2002. *Crossroads of Freedom: Antietam.* New York: Oxford University Press.

McPherson, James M. 2003. *Battle Cry of Freedom: The Civil War Era.* New York: Oxford University Press. (Reprint of 1988 edition. New York: Ballantine Books.)

McPherson, James M., and William J. Cooper Jr., eds. 1998. *Writing the Civil War: The Quest to Understand.* Columbia: University of South Carolina Press.

Melder, Keith E. 1963–1965. "Angel of Mercy in Washington: Josephine Griffing and the Freedmen, 1864–1872." *Records of the Columbia Historical Society of Washington, DC.*

Menendez, Albert J. 1986. *Civil War Novels: An Annotated Bibliography 1986.* New York: Garland Publishing.

Merington, Marguerite, ed. 1950. *The Custer Story: The Life and Intimate Letters of General George Armstrong Custer and His Wife Elizabeth.* New York: Devon-Adair.

Meriwether, Elizabeth Avery. 1880. *The Master of Red Leaf.* New York: E. J. Hale & Son.

Meriwether, Elizabeth Avery. 1958. *Recollections of 92 Years.* Nashville: Tennessee Historical Commission.

Miller, Edward A. 1997. *Lincoln's Abolitionist General: The Biography of David Hunter.* Columbia: University of South Carolina Press.

Miller, Randall M., Harry S. Stout, and Charles Reagan Wilson, eds. 1998. *Religion and the American Civil War.* New York: Oxford University Press.

Mills, Cynthia, and Pamela H. Simpson, eds. 2003. *Monuments to the Lost Cause: Women, Art, and the Landscapes of Southern Memory.* Knoxville: University of Tennessee Press.

Mitchell, Reid. 1988. *Civil War Soldiers.* New York: Viking.

Mitchell, Reid. 1993. *The Vacant Chair: The Northern Soldier Leaves Home.* New York: Oxford University Press.

Mohr, Clarence L. 1986. *On the Threshold of Freedom: Masters and Slaves in Civil War Georgia.* Athens: University of Georgia Press.

Moon, Virginia B. No date. "Experiences of Virginia B. Moon, during the War between the States." Moon Collection. Oxford, OH: Smith Library of Regional History.

Moore, Frank. 1997. *Women of the War: Their Heroism and Self-Sacrifice.* Alexander, NC: Blue/Gray Books. (Reprint of 1866 edition. Hartford, CT: S. S. Scranton & Co.)

Moore, John Hammond. 1993. *Columbia and Richland County: A South Carolina Community, 1740–1990.* Columbia: University of South Carolina Press.

Morgan, David T. 1984. "Eugenia Levy Phillips: The Civil War Experiences of a Southern Jewish Woman." In *Jews of the South: Selected Essays from the Jewish Historical Society,* edited by Samuel Proctor and Louis Schmier with Malcolm Stern, 95–106. Macon, GA: Mercer University Press.

Morris, Roy. 1992. *Sheridan: The Life and Wars of General Phil Sheridan.* New York: Crown.

Morrow, Sara S. 1980. *The Legacy of Fannie Battle.* Nashville, TN: Fannie Battle Social Workers.

Morton, Patricia, ed. 1996. *Discovering the Women in Slavery: Emancipating Perspectives of the American Past.* Athens: University of Georgia Press.

Moss, Elizabeth. 1992. *Domestic Novelists in the Old South: Defenders of Southern Culture.* Baton Rouge: Louisiana State University Press.

Moss, Lemuel. 1868. *Annals of the United States Christian Commission.* Philadelphia, PA: J. B. Lippincott Co.

Moulton, Louise Chandler. 1909. *The Poems and Sonnets of Louise Chandler Moulton.* Boston: Little, Brown and Company.

"Mrs. Edmund Kirby Smith." 1907. *Confederate Veteran* 15: 563.

Muhlenfeld, Elisabeth. 1981. *Mary Boykin Chesnut: A Biography.* Baton Rouge: Louisiana State University Press.

Muhlenfeld, Elisabeth. 1985. "The Civil War and Authorship." In *The History of Southern Literature,* edited by Louis Rubin, 178–187. Baton Rouge: Louisiana State University Press.

Muhlenfeld, Elisabeth, ed. 2002. *Two Novels by Mary Chesnut,* with an introduction by Elizabeth Hanson. Charlottesville: University Press of Virginia.

Murdock, Eugene C. 1971. *One Million Men: The Civil War Draft in the North.* Madison: State Historical Society of Wisconsin.

Murrell, Amy E. 2000. "'Of Necessity and Public Benefit: Southern Families and Their Appeals for Protection." In *Southern Families at War: Loyalty and Conflict in the Civil War South,* edited by Catherine Clinton, 77–100. New York: Oxford University Press.

Neff, John R. 2005. *Honoring the Civil War Dead: Commemoration and the Problem of Reconciliation.* Lawrence: University Press of Kansas.

Nelson, Claudia, and Lynne Vallone, eds. 1994. *The Girl's Own: Cultural Histories of the Anglo-American Girl, 1830–1915.* Athens: University of Georgia Press.

Nelson, Michael C. 1997. "Writing during Wartime: Gender and Literacy in the American Civil War." *Journal of American Studies* 31 (1): 43–68.

Nevins, Allan. 1950. *The Emergence of Lincoln.* 2 vols. New York: Scribner's.

Newman, Richard S. 2002. *The Transformation of American Abolitionism: Fighting Slavery in the Early Republic.* Chapel Hill: University of North Carolina Press.

Noble, Jeanne L. 1956. *The Negro Woman's College Education.* New York: Teachers College, Columbia University, Bureau of Publications.

Oakes, Sister Mary Paullina, ed. 1998. *Angels of Mercy: An Eyewitness Account of the Civil War and Yellow Fever; A Primary Resource by Sister Ignatius Sumner.* Baltimore, MD: Cathedral Foundation.

Oates, Stephen B. 1977. *With Malice toward None: A Life of Abraham Lincoln.* New York: Harper & Row.

Oates, Stephen B. 1994. *A Woman of Valor: Clara Barton and the Civil War.* New York: Free Press.

O'Brien, Sean Michael. 1999. *Mountain Partisans: Guerrilla Warfare in the Southern Appalachians, 1861–1865.* Westport, CT: Praeger.

O'Connor, Thomas H. 1997. *Civil War Boston: Home Front and Battlefield.* Boston: Northeastern University Press.

Odendahl, Laura. 2003. "A History of Captivity and a History of Freedom." In *Searching for Their Places: Women in the South across Four Centuries,* edited by Thomas H. Appleton Jr. and Angela Boswell, 122–143. Columbia: University of Missouri Press.

O'Donnell-Rosales, John. 1997. *Hispanic Confederates.* Baltimore, MD: Clearfield Co.

Okker, Patricia. 1995. *Our Sister Editors: Sarah J. Hale and the Tradition of Nineteenth-Century American Women Editors.* Athens: University of Georgia Press.

Olsen, Christopher. 2000. *Political Culture and Secession in Mississippi: Masculinity, Honor, and the Antiparty Tradition, 1830–1860.* New York: Oxford University Press.

Olson, Kenneth E. 1981. *Music and Musket: Bands and Bandsmen of the American Civil War.* Westport, CT: Greenwood Press.

O'Reilly, Francis Augustin. 2002. *The Fredericksburg Campaign: Winter War along the Rappahannock.* Baton Rouge: Louisiana State University Press.

O'Sullivan, John, and Alan M. Meckler, eds. 1974. *The Draft and Its Enemies: A Documentary History.* Urbana: University of Illinois Press.

Oubre, Claude F. 1978. *Forty Acres and a Mule: The Freedman's Bureau and Black Landownership.* Baton Rouge: Louisiana State University Press.

Owsley, Frank Lawrence. 1926. "Defeatism in the Confederacy." *North Carolina Historical Review* 3: 446–456.

Owsley, Frank Lawrence. 1949. *Plain Folk of the Old South.* Baton Rouge: Louisiana State University Press.

Padilla, Genaro M. 1993. *My History, Not Yours: The Formation of Mexican American Autobiography.* Madison: University of Wisconsin Press.

Painter, Nell Irvin. 1990. "The Journal of Gertrude Clanton Thomas: An Educated White Woman in the Eras of Slavery, War, and Reconstruction." Introduction to *The Secret Eye: The Journal of Gertrude Clanton Thomas, 1848–1889*, edited by Virginia Ingraham Burr, 1–67. Chapel Hill: University of North Carolina Press.

Painter, Nell Irvin. 1996. *Sojourner Truth: A Life, A Symbol.* New York: W. W. Norton & Company.

Painter, Nell Irvin. 2002. *Southern History across the Color Line.* Chapel Hill: University of North Carolina Press.

Paludan, Phillip Shaw. 1975. *A Covenant with Death: The Constitution, Law and Equality in the Civil War Era.* Urbana: University of Illinois Press.

Paludan, Phillip Shaw. 1988. *"A People's Contest": The Union and Civil War, 1861–1865.* New York: Harper & Row.

Paludan, Phillip Shaw. 1994. *The Presidency of Abraham Lincoln.* Lawrence: University Press of Kansas.

Paludan, Phillip Shaw. 1998. *War and Home: The Civil War Encounter.* Milwaukee, WI: Marquette University Press.

Parks, Joseph H. 1982. *General Edmund Kirby Smith C.S.A.* Baton Rouge: Louisiana State University Press. (Reprint of 1954 edition.)

Parrish, T. Michael. 1992. *Richard Taylor: Soldier Prince of Dixie.* Chapel Hill: University of North Carolina Press.

Parsons, Theophilus. 1880. *Memoir of Emily Elizabeth Parsons.* Boston: Little, Brown and Company.

Pease, Jane H., and William H. Pease. 1999. *A Family of Women: The Carolina Petigrus in Peace and War.* Chapel Hill: University of North Carolina Press.

Peavy, Linda, and Ursula Smith. 1994. *Women in Waiting in the Westward Movement.* Norman: University of Oklahoma Press.

Pember, Phoebe Yates Levy. [1879] 2002. *A Southern Woman's Story,* with Introduction by George C. Rable. Columbia: University of South Carolina Press.

Penningroth, Dylan. 1997. "Slavery, Freedom, and Social Claims to Property among African Americans in Liberty Country, Georgia, 1850–1880." *Journal of American History* 84: 405–436.

Penny, Virginia. 1870. *How Women Can Make Money.* Springfield, MA: Fisk.

Perdue, Theda. 1999. *Cherokee Women: Gender and Culture Change, 1700–1835.* Lincoln: University of Nebraska Press.

Perry, Carolyn, and Mary Louise Weeks, eds. 2002. *The History of Southern Women's Literature.* Baton Rouge: Louisiana State University Press.

Perry, John. *The Lady of Arlington: The Life of Mrs. Robert E. Lee.* 2001. Sisters, OR: Multnomah Publishers.

Perry, Mark. 2001. *Lift Up Thy Voice: The Grimké Family's Journey from Slaveholders to Civil Rights Activists.* New York: Viking Penguin.

Peterson, Carla L. 1995. *"Doers of the Word": African-American Women Speakers and Writers in the North (1830–1880).* Piscataway, NJ: Rutgers University Press.

Pfaelzer, Jean, ed. 1995. *A Rebecca Harding Davis Reader: "Life in the Iron Mills," Selected Fiction, and Essays,* with a Critical Introduction, by Jean Pfaelzer. Pittsburgh, PA: University of Pittsburgh Press.

Pfaelzer, Jean. 1996. *Parlor Radical: Rebecca Harding Davis and the Origins of American Social Realism.* Pittsburgh, PA: University of Pittsburgh Press.

Pfanz, Donald C. 1998. *Richard S. Ewell: A Soldier's Life.* Chapel Hill: University of North Carolina Press.

Phipps, Sheila R. 2004. *Genteel Rebel: The Life of Mary Greenhow Lee.* Baton Rouge: Louisiana State University Press.

Piehler, G. Kurt. 1995. *Remembering War the American Way.* Washington DC: Smithsonian Institution.

Pike, Martha V., and Janice Gray Armstrong. 1980. *A Time to Mourn: Expressions of Grief in Nineteenth Century America.* Stony Brook, NY: Museums at Stony Brook.

Pinkerton, Allan. 1883. *The Spy of the Rebellion; Being a True History of the Spy System of the United States Army during the Late Rebellion.* New York: G.W. Carleton.

Pleck, Elizabeth. 1999. "The Making of the Domestic Occasion: The History of Thanksgiving in the United States." *Journal of Social History* 32 (4): 773–790.

Plum, William R. 1882. *The Military Telegraph during the Civil War in the United States.* 2 vols. Chicago: Jansen, McClurg & Company.

Pollak, Vivian R., ed. 2004. *A Historical Guide to Emily Dickinson.* New York: Oxford University Press.

Porter, Dorothy B. 1935. "Sarah Parker Remond, Abolitionist and Physician." *Journal of Negro History* 20 (3): 287–293.

Potter, David. 1976. *The Impending Crisis 1848–1861.* New York: Harper & Row.

Power, J. Tracy. 1998. *Lee's Miserables: Life in the Army of Northern Virginia from the Wilderness to Appomattox.* Chapel Hill: University of North Carolina Press.

Poynter, Lida. 1946. "Dr. Mary Walker, M.D. Pioneer Woman Physician." *Medical Woman's Journal* 53 (10): 43–51.

Prushankin, Jeffery S. 2005. *A Crisis in Confederate Command: General Edmund Kirby Smith, Richard Taylor, and the Army of the Trans-Mississippi.* Baton Rouge: Louisiana State University Press.

Pryor, Elizabeth Brown. 1987. *Clara Barton: Professional Angel.* Philadelphia: University of Pennsylvania Press.

Pryor, Sara Rice (Mrs. Roger A.). 1905. *Reminiscences of Peace and War.* New York: Grosset & Dunlap.

Putnam, Sallie Brock. 1996. *Richmond during the War: Four Years of Personal Observation,* with Introduction by Virginia Scharff. Lincoln: University of Nebraska Press.

Quarles, Benjamin. 1953. *The Negro in the Civil War.* Boston: Little, Brown and Company. (Reprinted 1989. New York: DeCapo Press.)

Rable, George C. 1989. *Civil Wars: Women and the Crisis of Southern Nationalism.* Urbana: University of Illinois Press.

Rable, George C. 1992. "'Missing in Action': Women of the Confederacy." In *Divided Houses: Gender and the Civil War,* edited by Catherine Clinton and Nina Silber, 134–146. New York: Oxford University Press.

Rable, George C. 1994. *The Confederate Republic: A Revolution against Politics.* Chapel Hill: University of North Carolina Press.

Rable, George C. 2002. *Fredericksburg! Fredericksburg!* Chapel Hill: University of North Carolina Press.

Raboteau, Albert J. 2004. *Slave Religion: The "Invisible Institution" in the Antebellum South.* New York: Oxford University Press.

Rafuse, Ethan S. 2002. *A Single Grand Victory: The First Campaign and Battle of Manassas.* Wilmington, DE: Scholarly Resources Books.

Ramage, James A. 1999. *Gray Ghost: The Life of Col. John Singleton Mosby.* Lexington: University Press of Kentucky.

Ramsdell, Charles W. 1943. *Behind the Lines in the Confederacy.* Baton Rouge: Louisiana State University Press.

Randall, Ruth Painter. 1962. *I, Varina.* Boston: Little, Brown and Company.

Ream, Debbie Williams. 1993. "Mine Eyes Have Seen the Glory." *American History Illustrated* 27: 60–64.

Regosin, Elizabeth. 2002. *Freedom's Promise: Ex-Slave Families and Citizenship in the Age of Emancipation.* Charlottesville: University Press of Virginia.

Reilly, Tom. 1981. "Jane McManus Storms, Letters from the Mexican War, 1846–1848." *Southwestern Historical Quarterly* 85: 21–44.

Reilly, Wayne E., ed. 2001. *Sarah Jane Foster: Teacher of the Freedman, The Diary and Letters of a Maine Woman in the South after the Civil War.* Rockland, ME: Picton Press.

Remond, Sarah P. 1942. "The Negroes in the United States of America." *Journal of Negro History* 27 (2): 216–218.

Reveley, Bryce. 1993. "The Black Trade in New Orleans: 1840–1880." *Southern Quarterly* 31 (2): 119–122.

Revels, Tracey J. 2004. *Grander in Her Daughters: Florida's Women during the Civil War.* Columbia: University of South Carolina Press.

Reverby, Susan M. 1987. *Ordered to Care: The Dilemma of American Nursing, 1850–1945.* New York: Cambridge University Press.

Reynold, Arlene. 1994. *The Civil War Memories of Elizabeth Bacon Custer.* Austin: University of Texas Press.

R.G. 153. No date. Records of the U.S. Army, Office of the Adjutant General. Washington, DC: National Archives and Records Service.

Rhea, Gordon C. 2004. *The Battle of the Wilderness May 5–6, 1864.* Baton Rouge: Louisiana State University Press.

Rhodes, Jane. 1998. *Mary Ann Shadd Cary: The Black Press and Protest in the Nineteenth Century.* Bloomington: Indiana University Press.

Richard, Patricia L. 2003. *Busy Hands: Images of the Family in the Northern Civil War Effort.* New York: Fordham University Press.

Richardson, Marilyn. 1995. "Edmonia Lewis's 'The Death of Cleopatra.'" *The International Review of African American Art* 12 (2): 36–52.

Richter, William L. 1991. *Overreached on All Sides: The Freedmen's Bureau Administration in Texas, 1865–1868.* College Station: Texas A&M University Press.

Rikard, Marlene Hunt, and Elizabeth Wells. 1997. "'From It Begins a New Era': Women and the Civil War." *Baptist History and Heritage* 32 (3): 59–73.

Riley, Glenda. 1981. *Frontierswomen: The Iowa Experience.* Ames: Iowa State University Press

Roark, James L. 1977. *Masters without Slaves: Southern Planters in the Civil War and Reconstruction.* New York: W. W. Norton.

Roark, James L. 1998. "Behind the Lines: Confederate Economy and Society." In *Writing the Civil War: The Quest to Understand,* edited by James M. McPherson and William J. Cooper Jr., 201–227. Columbia: University of South Carolina Press.

Roberts, Giselle. 2003. *The Confederate Belle.* Columbia, OH: University of Missouri Press.

Robertson, Mary D., ed. 1992. *A Confederate Lady Comes of Age: The Journal of Pauline DeCaradeuc Heyward.* Columbia: University of South Carolina Press.

Rodgers, Mark E. 1999. *Tracing the Civil War Veteran Pensions System in the State of Virginia: Entitlement or Privilege.* Lewiston, NY: Edwin Mellen Press.

Rogers, Sherbrooke. 1985. *Sarah Josepha Hale: A New England Pioneer 1788–1879.* Grantham, NH: Thompson and Rutter.

Romero, Laura. 1997. *Home Fronts: Domesticity and Its Critics in the Antebellum United States.* Durham, NC: Duke University Press.

Ronda, Bruce, ed. 1984. *Letters of Elizabeth Palmer Peabody, American Renaissance Woman.* Middletown, CT: Wesleyan University Press.

Ronda, Bruce. 1999. *Elizabeth Palmer Peabody: A Reformer on Her Own Terms.* Cambridge, MA: Harvard University Press.

Rose, Anne C. 1992. *Victorian America and the Civil War.* New York: Cambridge University Press.

Rose, Willie Lee. 1999. *Rehearsal for Reconstruction. The Port Royal Experiment.* Athens: University of Georgia Press. (Reprint of 1964 edition. Indianapolis, IN: Bobbs-Merrill Company.)

Ross, Ishbel. 1949. *Child of Destiny.* London: Gollancz.

Ross, Ishbel. 1954. *Rebel Rose: Life of Rose O'Neal Greenhow, Confederate Spy.* New York: Harper & Brothers, Publishers. (Reprinted 1989. New York: Ballantine Books.)

Ross, Ishbel. 1959. *The General's Wife: The Life of Mrs. Ulysses S. Grant.* New York: Dodd, Mead and Company.

Ross, Ishbel. 1973. *First Lady of the South.* Westport, CT: Greenwood Press. (Reprint of 1958 edition. New York: Harper & Brothers, Publishers.)

Ross, Kristie. 1992. "Arranging a Doll's House: Refined Women as Union Nurses." In *Divided Houses: Gender and the Civil War,* edited by Catherine Clinton and Nina Silber, 97–113. New York: Oxford University Press.

Royster, Charles. 1991. *The Destructive War: William Tecumseh Sherman, Stonewall Jackson, and the Americans.* New York: Vintage.

Rubin, Anne Sarah. 2005. *Shattered Nation: The Rise and Fall of the Confederacy.* Chapel Hill: University of North Carolina Press.

Rubin, Louis D. 1958. "The Image of an Army: Southern Novelists and the Civil War." *Texas Quarterly* 1: 17–34.

Rubin, Louis D. Jr., ed. 1985. *The History of Southern Literature.* Baton Rouge: Louisiana State University Press.

Ruiz De Burton, Maria Amparo. 1995. *Who Would Have Thought It?* Houston, TX: Arte Público Press.

Russell, James M. 1988. *Atlanta, 1847–1890: Citybuilding in the Old South and the New.* Baton Rouge: Louisiana State University Press.

Ryan, David D. 1996. *A Yankee Spy in Richmond: The Civil War Diary of "Crazy Bet" Van Lew.* Mechanicsburg, PA: Stackpole Books.

Ryan, Mary P. 1981. *Cradle of the Middle Class: The Family in Oneida County, New York, 1790–1865.* New York: Cambridge University Press.

Ryan, Mary P. 1982. *The Empire of the Mother: American Writing about Domesticity, 1830–1860.* New York: Institute for Research in History and Haworth Press.

Ryan, Mary. 1990. *Women in Public: Between Banners and Ballots, 1825–1880.* Baltimore, MD: Johns Hopkins University Press.

Rybczynski, Witold. 1999. *A Clearing in the Distance: Frederick Law Olmsted and America in the Nineteenth Century.* New York: Scribner's.

Saint-Amand, Mary Scott. 1941. *A Balcony in Charleston.* Richmond, VA: Garrett & Massie.

Sally Louisa Tompkins Papers. Eleanor S. Brockenbrough Library, Museum of the Confederacy, Richmond, VA.

Samuelson, Nancy. 1989. "Employment of Female Spies in the American Civil War." *Minerva* 7: 57–66.

Sanchez, Regina Morantz. [1985] 2000. *Sympathy and Science: Women Physicians in American Medicine.* Chapel Hill: University of North Carolina Press. Reprint with new preface.

Sarmiento, Ferdinand L. 1865. *Life of Pauline Cushman, The Celebrated Union Spy and Scout.* Philadelphia, PA: John E. Potter.

Saville, Julie. 1994. *The Work of Reconstruction: From Slave to Wage Laborer in South Carolina, 1860–1870.* New York: Cambridge University Press.

Saxon, Elizabeth Lyle. 1905. *A Southern Woman's War Time Reminiscences, by Elizabeth Lyle Saxon, for the Benefit of the Shiloh Monument Fund.* Memphis, TN: Press of the Pilcher Printing Co.

Scadron, Arlene, ed. 1988. *On Their Own: Widows and Widowhood in the American Southwest, 1848–1939.* Urbana: University of Illinois Press.

Scarborough, Ruth. 1983. *Belle Boyd: Siren of the South.* Macon, GA: Mercer University Press.

Schultz, Duane. 1996. *Quantrill's War: The Life and Times of William Clarke Quantrill.* New York: St. Martin's Press.

Schultz, Jane E. 1989. "Mute Fury: Southern Women's Diaries of Sherman's March to the Sea." In *Arms and the Woman: War, Gender, and Literary Representation,* edited by Helen M. Cooper, Adrienne Auslander Munich, and Susan Merrill Squier, 59–79. Chapel Hill: University of North Carolina Press.

Schultz, Jane E. 1992. "The Inhospitable Hospital: Gender and Professionalism in Civil War Medicine." *Signs* 17 (2): 363–392.

Schultz, Jane E. 1994. "Race, Gender and Bureaucracy: Civil War Army Nurses and the Pension Bureau." *Journal of Women's History* 6: 45–69.

Schultz, Jane E. 2004. *Women at the Front: Hospital Workers in Civil War America.* Chapel Hill: University of North Carolina Press.

Schulz, Karen. 1966. "Descendant of Woman Captain Remembers Heroine of Civil War." *Richmond News Leader,* July 21.

Schwalm, Leslie A. 1997. *A Hard Fight for We: Women's Transition from Slavery to Freedom in South Carolina.* Urbana: University of Illinois Press.

Schwartz, Gerald, ed. 1984. *A Woman Doctor's Civil War: Ester Hill Hawks' Diary.* Columbia: University of South Carolina Press.

Scott, Anne Firor. 1970. *The Southern Lady: From Pedestal to Politics, 1830–1930.* Charlottesville: University of Virginia Press.

Sears, Stephen W. 1983. *Landscape Turned Red: The Battle of Antietam.* New Haven, CT: Ticknor and Fields.

Sears, Stephen W. 1988. *George B. McClellan: The Young Napoleon.* New York: Ticknor & Fields.

Sears, Stephen W. 1992. *To The Gates of Richmond: The Peninsular Campaign.* New York: Ticknor & Fields.

Sears, Stephen W. 1996. *Chancellorsville.* Boston: Houghton-Mifflin.

Sears, Stephen W. 2003. *Gettysburg.* Boston: Houghton Mifflin Company.

Selby, John G. 2002. *Virginians at War: The Civil War Experiences of Seven Young Confederates.* Wilmington, DE: Scholarly Resources.

Selleck, Linda B. 1995. *Gentle Invaders: Quaker Women Educators and Racial Issues during the Civil War and Reconstruction.* Richmond, IN: Friends United Press.

Shaffer, Donald R. 2004. *After the Glory: The Struggles of Black Civil War Veterans.* Lawrence: University Press of Kansas.

Shammas, Carole, Marylynn Salmon, and Michel Dahlin. 1987. *Inheritance in America from Colonial Times to the Present.* Piscataway, NJ: Rutgers University Press.

Shankman, Arnold. 1980. *The Pennsylvania Antiwar Movement, 1861–1865.* Madison, NJ: Fairleigh Dickinson University Press.

Shattuck, Gardiner. 1987. *A Shield and Hiding Place: The Religious Life of the Civil War Armies.* Macon, GA: Mercer University Press.

Sherman, William T. 1875. *Memoirs of General William T. Sherman.* 2 vols. New York: D. Appleton & Co.

Siguad, Louis. 1944. *Belle Boyd: Confederate Spy.* Petersburg, VA: Dietz Press.

Silber, Nina. 1993. *The Romance of Reunion: Northerners and the South, 1865–1900.* Chapel Hill: University of North Carolina Press.

Silber, Nina. 2002. "A Compound of Wonderful Potency: Women Teachers of the North in the Civil War South." In *The War Was You and Me: Civilians in the American Civil War,* edited by Joan E. Cashin, 35–59. Princeton, NJ: Princeton University Press,.

Silber, Nina. 2005. *Daughters of the Union: Northern Women Fight the Civil War.* Cambridge, MA: Harvard University Press.

Silbey, Joel. 1977. *A Respectable Minority: The Democratic Party in the Civil-War Era.* New York: W. W. Norton & Company.

Simkins, Francis Butler, and James Welch Patton. 1936. *The Women of the Confederacy.* Richmond, VA: Garrett & Massie.

Simmons, James C. 2000. *Star Spangled Eden.* New York: Carroll and Graf Publishers.

Simmons, Michael K. 1976. "*Maum Guinea:* or, A Dime Novelist Looks at Abolition." *Journal of Popular Culture* 10 (1): 81-87.

Simon, John Y., ed. 1975. *The Personal Memoirs of Julia Dent Grant.* New York: G.P. Putnam's Sons.

Simon, John Y. 2001. "A Marriage Tested by War: Ulysses and Julia Grant." In *Intimate Strategies of the Civil War: Military Commanders and their Wives,* edited by Carol K. Bleser and Lesley J. Gordon, 123–137. New York: Oxford University Press.

Simonhoff, Harry. 1963. *Jewish Participants in the Civil War.* New York: Arco Publishing.

Sinha, Manisha. 2000. *The Counterrevolution of Slavery: Politics and Ideology in Antebellum South Carolina.* Chapel Hill: University of North Carolina Press.

Sizer, Lyde Cullen. 1992. "Acting Her Part: Narratives of Union Women Spies." In *Divided Houses: Gender and the Civil War,* edited by Catherine Clinton and Nina Silber, 114–133. New York: Oxford University Press.

Sizer, Lyde Cullen. 2000. *Political Work of Northern Women Writers and the Civil War, 1850–1872.* Chapel Hill: University of North Carolina Press.

Skaggs, Merrill Maguire. 1972. *The Folk of Southern Fiction.* Athens: University of Georgia Press.

Sklar, Katherine Kish. 1973. *Catharine Beecher: A Study in American Domesticity.* New Haven, CT: Yale University Press.

Skocpol, Theda. 1992. *Protecting Soldiers and Mothers: The Political Origins of Social Policy in the United States.* Cambridge, MA: Harvard University Press.

Slaughter, Linda Warfel, ed. 1869. *The Freedmen of the South.* Cincinnati, OH: Elm St. Printing Co.

Smith, Andrew F. 2005. "The Civil War and American Food, or How Nationalized, Industrialized American Cookery Got Its Start." *The Food Journal* 5 (Winter): 4–5.

Smith, Anna Habersham Wright, ed. 1999. *A Savannah Family, 1830–1901: Papers from the Clermont Huger Lee Collection.* Milledgeville, GA: Boyd Publishing Company.

Smith, Diane Monroe. 1999. *Fanny and Joshua: The Enigmatic Lives of Francis Caroline Adams and Joshua Lawrence Chamberlain.* Gettysburg, PA: Thomas Publications.

Smith, Jennifer Lund. "The Reconstruction of 'Home': The Civil War and the Marriage of Lawrence and Fannie Chamberlain." In *Intimate Strategies of the Civil War: Military Commanders and their Wives,* edited by Carol K. Bleser and Lesley J. Gordon, 157–177. New York: Oxford University Press.

Smith, Orphia. 1962. *Oxford Spy: Wed at Pistol Point.* Oxford, OH: Cullen Printing Co.

Smith, Timothy B. 2004. *This Great Battlefield of Shiloh: History, Memory, and the Establishment of a Civil War National Military Park.* Knoxville: University of Tennessee Press.

Snyder, Charles McCool. 1974. *Dr. Mary Walker: The Little Lady in Pants.* New York: Arno Press.

Solomon, Barbara Miller. 1985. *In the Company of Educated Women: A History of Women and Higher Education in American.* New Haven, CT: Yale University Press.

Solomon, Clara. 1995. *The Civil War Diary of Clara Solomon: Growing Up in New Orleans 1861–1862,* edited, with introduction, by Elliott Ashkenazi. Baton Rouge: Louisiana State University Press.

Sommerville, Diane M. 2004. *Rape and Race in the Nineteenth-Century South.* Chapel Hill: University of North Carolina Press.

Southworth, Emma Dorothy Eliza Nevitte. 1997. *The Hidden Hand,* with Introduction by Nina Baym. New York: Oxford University Press.

Speer, Lonnie R. 1997. *Portals to Hell: Military Prisons of the Civil War.* Mechanicsburg, PA: Stackpole Books.

Spiegel, Marcus. 1985. *Your True Marcus: The Civil War Letters of a Jewish Colonel,* edited by Frank L. Byrne and Jean Powers Soman. Kent, OH: Kent State University Press.

Stackpole, Edward J. 1959. *From Cedar Mountain to Antietam: August–September, 1862.* Harrisburg, PA: Stackpole Books.

Stansell, Christine. 1986. *City of Women: Sex and Class in New York, 1789–1860.* New York: Alfred A. Knopf.

Stanton, Elizabeth, Susan B. Anthony, and Matilda Joslyn Gage. 1970. *History of Woman Suffrage.* Vol. 2. New York: Source Book Press.

Stanton, Elizabeth, Susan B. Anthony, and Matilda Joslyn Gage. 1970. *History of Woman Suffrage.* Vol. 2. New York: Source Book Press.

Starobin, Robert S. 1970. *Industrial Slavery in the Old South.* New York: Oxford University Press.

Staudenraus, P. J. 1961. *The African Colonization Movement, 1816–1865.* New York: Columbia University Press.

Stearns, Amanda Akin. 1909. *Lady Nurse of Ward E.* New York: Baker & Taylor Company.

Steers, Edward. 2001. *Blood on the Moon: The Assassination of Abraham Lincoln.* Lexington: University Press of Kentucky.

Sterkx, H. E. 1970. *Partners in Rebellion: Alabama Women in the Civil War.* Madison, NJ: Fairleigh Dickinson University Press.

Sterling, Dorothy, ed. 1984. *We Are Your Sisters: Black Women in the Nineteenth Century.* New York and London: W. W. Norton.

Sterling, Dorothy. 1991 *Ahead of Her Time: Abby Kelley and the Politics of Antislavery.* New York: W. W. Norton & Company.

Stern, Philip Van Doren. 1959. *Secret Missions of the Civil War.* Chicago: Rand McNally.

Stevens, Bryna. 1992. *Frank Thompson: Her Civil War Story*. Toronto: Maxwell MacMillian Canada.

Stevens, Peter F. 2000. *Rebels in Blue: The Story of Keith and Malinda Blalock*. Dallas, TX: Taylor Publishing Company.

Stevenson, Brenda E., ed. 1988. *The Journals of Charlotte Forten Grimké*. New York: Oxford University Press.

Stevenson, Brenda E. 1996. *Life in Black and White: Family and Community in the Slave South*. New York: Oxford University Press.

Stevenson, Louise L. 1991. *The Victorian Homefront: American Thought and Culture, 1860–1880*. New York: Twayne Publishers.

Stewart, James Brewer. 1997. *Holy Warriors: The Abolitionists and American Slavery*. New York: Hill and Wang.

Still, William N. Jr. 1971. *Iron Afloat: The Story of the Confederate Armorclads*. Nashville, TN: Vanderbilt University Press.

Still, William. [1872] 1970. *The Underground Railroad: a record of facts, authentic narratives, letters, &c., narrating the hardships, hair-breadth escapes, and death struggles of the slaves in their efforts for freedom, as related by themselves and others or witnessed by the author: together with sketches of some of the largest stockholders and most liberal aiders and advisers of the road*. Chicago, IL: Johnson Publishing.

Stock, Mary Wright, ed. 1975. *Shinplasters and Homespun: The Diary of Laura Nisbet Boykin*. Rockville, MD: Printex.

Storey, Margaret M. 2004. *Loyalty and Loss: Alabama's Unionists in the Civil War and Reconstruction*. Baton Rouge: Louisiana State University Press.

Stowe, Harriet Beecher. [1852] 2001. *Uncle Tom's Cabin, or Life among the Lowly*, with Introduction by Jane Smiley. New York: Modern Library.

Stowell, Daniel. 1998. *Rebuilding Zion: The Religious Reconstruction of the South, 1863–1877*. New York: Oxford University Press.

Streeby, Shelley. 2002. *American Sensations: Class, Empire, and the Production of Popular Culture*. Berkeley: University of California Press.

Sullivan, Regina Diane. 2002. "Woman with a Mission: Remembering Lottie Moon and the Woman's Missionary Union." Ph.D. diss. University of North Carolina, Chapel Hill.

Sullivan, Walter. 1953. "Southern Novelists and the Civil War." In *Southern Renascence: The Literature of the Modern South*, edited by Louis D. Rubin Jr. and Robert D. Jacobs, 123–125. Baltimore, MD: Johns Hopkins University Press.

Sutherland, Daniel. 1995. *Seasons of War: The Ordeal of a Confederate Community, 1861–1865*. New York: Free Press.

Sutherland, Daniel E., ed. 1996. *A Very Violent Rebel: The Civil War Diary of Ellen Renshaw House*. Knoxville: University of Tennessee Press.

Swint, Henry L., ed. 1966. *Dear Ones at Home: Letters from Contraband Camps*. Nashville, TN: Vanderbilt University Press.

Swint, Henry L. 1967. *The Northern Teacher in the South, 1862–1870*. New York: Octagon Books.

Swisshelm, Jane Grey Cannon. [1880] 1970. *Half a Century*. New York: Source Book Press.

Tackach, James. 2002. *Lincoln's Moral Vision: The Second Inaugural Address*. Jackson: University Press of Mississippi.

Talmadge, John Erwin. 1960. *Rebecca Latimer Felton: Nine Stormy Decades*. Athens: University of Georgia Press.

Taylor, Amy Murrell. 2005. *The Divided Family in Civil War America*. Chapel Hill: University of North Carolina Press.

Taylor, Lou. 1983. *Mourning Dress: A Costume and Social History*. London: George Allen & Unwin.

Taylor, Susie King. 1988. *A Black Woman's Civil War Memoirs*, edited by Patricia W. Romero and Willie Lee Rose. Princeton, NJ: Markus Weiner Publisher. (Orig. pub.1902 as *Reminiscences of My Life in Camp: With the 33rd United States Colored Troops, late 1st S.C. Volunteers.*)

Taylor-Colbert, Alice. 1997. "Cherokee Women and Cultural Change." In *Women of the American South*, edited by Christie Anne Farnham, 43–55. New York: New York University Press.

Thomas, Ella Gertrude Clanton. 1990. *The Secret Eye: The Journal of Ella Gertrude Clanton Thomas, 1848–1889*, edited by Virginia Ingraham Burr. Chapel Hill: University of North Carolina Press.

Thomas, Emory M. 1979. *The Confederate Nation, 1861–1865*. New York: Harper & Row.

Thomas, Emory M. 1991. *The Confederacy as a Revolutionary Experience*. Columbia: University of South Carolina Press. (Reprint of 1971 edition. Englewood Cliffs, NJ: Prentice-Hall.)

Thomas, Emory M. 1995. *Robert E. Lee*. New York: Random House.

Thompson, E. P. 1971. "The Moral Economy of the Crowd in the Eighteenth Century." *Past and Present* 50: 76–136.

Thompson, Jerry D. 2000. *Vaqueros in Blue and Gray*. Austin, TX: State House Press.

Tidwell, William A., with James O. Hall and David Winfred Gaddy. 1988. *Come Retribution: The Confederate Secret Service and the Assassination of Lincoln.* Jackson: University Press of Mississippi.

Tinling, Marion. 1986. *Women Remembered: A Guide to Landmarks of Women's History in the United States.* Westport, CT: Greenwood Press.

Todras, Ellen. *Angelina Grimké: Voice of Abolition.* 1999. North Haven, CT: Linnet Books.

Tonkovich, Nicole. 1997. *Domesticity with a Difference: The Nonfiction of Catharine Beecher, Sarah J. Hale, Fanny Fern, and Margaret Fuller.* Jackson: University Press of Mississippi.

Trindal, Elizabeth Steger. 1996. *Mary Surratt: An American Tragedy.* Gretna, LA: Pelican Publishing Company.

Trowbridge, John Townsend. 1956. *The Desolate South, 1865–1866; A Picture of the Battlefields and of the Devastated Confederacy,* edited by Gordon Carroll. New York: Duell, Sloan and Pearce.

Trudeau, Noah Andre. 1989. *Bloody Roads South: The Wilderness to Cold Harbor May–June 1864.* Boston: Little, Brown and Company.

Trudeau, Noah Andre. 1995. *National Parks Civil War Series: The Siege of Petersburg.* Fort Washington, PA: Eastern National Park and Monument Association.

Trudeau, Noah Andre. 2002. *Gettysburg: A Testing of Courage.* New York: HarperCollins.

Trulock, Alice Rains. 1992. *In the Hands of Providence: Joshua L. Chamberlain and the American Civil War.* Chapel Hill: University of North Carolina Press.

Truth, Sojourner. 1997. *Narrative of Sojourner Truth.* New York: Dover Publications.

Tucker, St. George, ed. 1803. *Blackstone's Commentaries.* New York: Augustus M. Kelley Publishers. (Reprinted 1969. South Hackensack, NJ: Rothman Reprints.)

Turner, Justin G., and Linda Levitt Turner, eds. 1987. *Mary Todd Lincoln: Her Life and Letters.* New York: Fromm International Publishing Corporation.

United States Sanitary Commission. 1972. *The Sanitary Commission of the United States Army: A Succinct Narrative of Its Works and Purposes.* New York: Arno Press and New York Times. (Reprint of 1864 edition.)

U.S. War Department. 1880–1902. *The War of the Rebellion: A Compilation of the Official Records of the Union and Confederate Armies.* 130 vols. Records and Pension Office. Washington, DC: U.S. Government Printing Office.

Van der Heuvel, Gerry. 1988. *Crowns of Thorns and Glory: Mary Todd Lincoln and Varina Howell Davis.* New York: Dutton.

Varon, Elizabeth R. 2003. *Southern Lady, Yankee Spy: The True Story of Elizabeth Van Lew, A Union Agent in the Heart of the Confederacy.* New York: Oxford University Press.

Velazquez, Loreta Janeta. 1876. *The Woman in Battle: A Narrative of the Exploits, Adventures, and Travels of Madame Loreta Janeta Velazquez, Otherwise Known as Lieutenant Harry T. Buford, Confederate States Army,* edited by C. J. Worthington. Richmond, VA: Dustin, Gilman & Co.

Venet, Wendy Hamand. 1991. *Neither Ballots Nor Bullets: Women Abolitionists and the Civil War.* Charlottesville: University Press of Virginia.

Vietor, Agnes C., ed. [1924] 1972. *A Woman's Quest: The Life of Marie E. Zakrzewska, M.D.* New York: Arno Press.

Vinovskis, Maris A. 1990. *Toward a Social History of the American Civil War.* New York: Cambridge University Press.

Vorenberg, Michael. 2001. *Final Freedom: The Civil War, the Abolition of Slavery, and the Thirteenth Amendment.* New York: Cambridge University Press.

Walker, Nancy A. 1993. *Fanny Fern.* New York: Twayne Publishers.

Walkowitz, Judith R. 1980. *Prostitution in Victorian Society: Women, Class, and the State.* New York: Cambridge University Press.

Wall, Barbra Mann. 1998. "Called to a Mission of Charity: The Sisters of St. Joseph in the Civil War." *Nursing History Review* 80 (1): 36–57.

Warren, Edward. 1885. *A Doctor's Experiences in Three Continents.* Baltimore, MD: Cushings and Bailey.

Warren, Joyce W. 1992. *Fanny Fern: An Independent Woman.* Piscataway, NJ: Rutgers University Press.

Waugh, Charles, and Martin Greenburg, eds. 1999. *The Women's War in the South: Recollections and Reflections of the American Civil War.* Nashville, TN: Cumberland House.

Waugh, Joan. 1997. *Unsentimental Reformer: The Life of Josephine Shaw Lowell.* Cambridge, MA: Harvard University Press.

Weatherford, Doris. 1986. *Foreign and Female: Immigrant Women in America, 1840–1930.* New York: Schocken Books.

Weathers, Willie T. 1974. "Judith W. McGuire: A Lady of Virginia." *Virginia Magazine of History and Biography* 82 (1): 100–113.

Weiner, Marli F. 1997. *A Heritage of Woe: The Civil War Diary of Grace Brown Elmore, 1861–1868.* Athens: University of Georgia Press.

Weiner, Marli F. 1998. *Mistresses and Slaves: Plantation Women in South Carolina, 1830–80.* Urbana: University of Illinois Press.

Weitz, Mark A. 2000. *A Higher Duty: Desertion among Georgia Troops during the Civil War.* Lincoln: University of Nebraska Press.

Welter, Barbara. 1966. "The Cult of True Womanhood: 1820–1860." *American Quarterly* 18 (Summer): 151–174.

Wert, Jeffry D. 1990. *Mosby's Rangers.* New York: Simon & Schuster.

Wertheimer, Barbara M. 1977. *We Were There: The Story of Working Women in America.* New York: Pantheon.

Wheeler, Richard. 1986. *Sword Over Richmond: An Eyewitness History of McClellan's Peninsular Campaign.* New York: Harper.

White, Barbara A. 2003. *The Beecher Sisters.* New Haven, CT: Yale University Press.

White, Deborah Gray. 1985. *Ar'n't I a Woman? Female Slaves in the Plantation South.* New York: W. W. Norton.

Whites, LeeAnn. 1992. "The Civil War as a Crisis in Gender." In *Divided Houses: Gender and the Civil War,* edited by Catherine Clinton and Nina Silber, 3–21. New York: Oxford University Press.

Whites, LeeAnn. 1995. *The Civil War as a Crisis in Gender, Augusta, Georgia, 1860–1890.* Athens: University of Georgia Press.

Whites, LeeAnn. 2005. *Gender Matters: Civil War, Reconstruction, and the Making of the New South.* New York: Palgrave Macmillan.

Whiting, Lilian. 1910. *Louise Chandler Moulton: Poet and Friend.* Boston: Little, Brown and Company.

Whitney, Louisa M. 1903. *Goldie's Inheritance: A Story of the Siege of Atlanta.* Burlington, VT: Free Press Association.

Wiggins, Sarah Woolfolk. 1998. "Amelia Gayle Gorgas and the Civil War." *Alabama Review* 51 (2): 83–95.

Wiggins, Sarah Woolfolk. 2001. "The Marriage of Amelia Gayle and Josiah Gorgas." In *Intimate Strategies of the Civil War: Military Commanders and their Wives,* 104–119. New York: Oxford University Press, 2001.

Wiggins, William H., Jr. 1987. *O Freedom!: Afro-American Emancipation Celebrations.* Knoxville: University of Tennessee Press.

Wiley, Bell Irvin. 1943. *The Life of Johnny Reb: The Common Soldier of the Confederacy.* Indianapolis, IN: Bobbs-Merrill Company.

Wiley, Bell Irvin. 1952. *The Life of Billy Yank: The Common Soldier of the Union.* Indianapolis, IN: Bobbs-Merrill Company.

Wiley, Bell Irvin. 1970. *Confederate Women.* Westport, CT: Greenwood Press.

Williams, David. 2005. *A People's History of the Civil War: Struggles for the Meaning of Freedom.* New York: New Press.

Williams, Gary. 1999. *Hungry Heart: The Literary Emergence of Julia Ward Howe.* Amherst: University of Massachusetts Press.

Williams, Julieanna. 1996. "The Homefront: 'For Our Boys—The Ladies' Aid Societies.'" In *Valor and Lace: The Roles of Confederate Women 1861–1865,* edited by Mauriel Phillips Joslyn, 16–33. Murfreesboro, TN: Southern Heritage Press.

Williams, Kenneth P. 1950. "The Tennessee River Campaign and Anna Ella Carroll." *Indiana Magazine of History* 46: 221–248.

Williams, Teresa Cusp, and David Williams. 2002. "'The Women Rising:' Cotton, Class, and Confederate Georgia's Rioting Women." *Georgia Historical Quarterly* 86 (1): 49–83.

Willingham, Robert M., Jr. 1976. *No Jubilee: The Story of Confederate Wilkes.* Washington, GA: Wilkes Publishing.

Wilson, Charles Reagan. 1980. *Baptized in Blood: The Religion of the Lost Cause 1865–1920.* Athens: University of Georgia Press.

Wilson, Dorothy C. 1975. *Stranger and Traveler.* Boston: Little, Brown and Company.

Wilson, Edmund. 1984. *Patriotic Gore: Studies in the Literature of the American Civil War,* with a foreword by C. Vann Woodward. Boston: Northeastern University Press. (Also published: New York: Farrar, Straus and Giroux, 1962 and New York: W. W. Norton, 1972.)

Wilson, Mark R. 2001. "The Extensive Side of Nineteenth-Century Military Economy: The Tent Industry in the Northern United States during the Civil War." *Enterprise and Society: The International Journal of Business History* 2: 297–337.

Wise, Stephen. 1988. *Lifeline of the Confederacy: Blockade Running during the Civil War.* Columbia: University of South Carolina Press.

Wittenmyer, Annie Turner. 1895. *Under the Guns: A Woman's Reminiscences of the Civil War.* Boston: E. B. Stillings & Co.

Wolf, Simon. 1972. *The American Jew as Patriot, Soldier and Citizen,* with new Introduction and Preface by George Athan Billias. Boston: Gregg Press.

Wolff, Cynthia Griffin. 1987. *Emily Dickinson.* New York: Alfred A. Knopf.

Woloch, Nancy. 2000. *Women and the American Experience.* 3rd ed. New York: McGraw-Hill.

Wood, Ann Douglas. 1972. "The War Within a War: Women Nurses in the Union Army." *Civil War History* 18: 197–212.

Wood, Kirsten E. 2004. *Masterful Women: Slaveholding Widows from the American Revolution through the Civil War.* Chapel Hill: University of North Carolina Press.

Woodward, C. Vann, and Elisabeth Muhlenfeld, ed. 1981. *Mary Chesnut's Civil War.* New Haven, CT: Yale University Press.

Woodward, C. Vann, and Elisabeth Muhlenfeld, ed. 1984. *The Private Mary Chesnut: The Unpublished Civil War Diaries.* New York: Oxford University Press.

Woodworth, Steven E. 2001. *While God Is Marching On: The Religious World of Civil War Soldiers.* Lawrence: University Press of Kansas.

Woody, Thomas. 1929. *A History of Women's Education in the United States.* 2 vols. New York: Science Press.

Woolsey, Jane Stuart. 2001. *Hospital Days: Reminiscence of a Civil War Nurse.* Roseville, MN: Edinborough Press.

Wooster, Ralph. 1962. *The Secession Conventions of the South.* Princeton, NJ: Princeton University Press.

Wormeley, Katharine P. 1889. *The Other Side of War: With the Army of the Potomac.* Boston: Ticknor.

Wright, Helen. 1949. *Sweeper in the Sky: The Life of Maria Mitchell, First Woman Astronomer in America.* New York: Macmillan.

Wudarczyk, James. 1999. *Pittsburgh's Forgotten Allegheny Arsenal.* Apollo, PA: Closson Press.

Wyatt-Brown, Bertram. 1982. *Southern Honor: Ethics and Behavior in the Old South.* New York: Oxford University Press.

Wyatt-Brown, Bertram. 2001. *The Shaping of Southern Culture: Honor, Grace and War, 1760s–1880s.* Chapel Hill: University of North Carolina Press.

Yellin, Jean Fagan. 2004. *Harriet Jacobs: A Life.* New York: Basic Civitas Books.

Young, Agatha. 1959. *The Women and the Crisis: Women of the North in the Civil War.* New York: McDowell, Obolensky.

Young, Elizabeth. 1999. *Disarming the Nation: Women's Writing and the American Civil War.* Chicago: University of Chicago Press.

Young, James R. 1982. "Confederate Pensions in Georgia." *Georgia Historical Quarterly* 62: 47–52.

Young, Mel. 1991. *Where They Lie: The Story of the Jewish Soldiers of the North and South Whose Deaths—Killed, Morally Wounded or Died of Disease or Other Causes—Occurred During the Civil War, 1861–1865.* Lanham, MD: University Press of America.

# Index

New York State Charities Aid Association, 489
New York Women's Protective Union, 85
Nightingale, Florence, 48, 131, 158, 480
Nonslaveholding Southerners, **422–426**
*Notes on Nursing* (Nightingale), 480
*The North Star* [*Frederick Douglass' Paper*], 220
Northern women, **41–47**
*Northwood* (Hale), 321
*Nurse and Spy in the Union Army* (S. Edmonds), 226
Nursing, **47–54**, 115, 171–172, 216, 626
   African American women as nurses, 12
   Catholic sisters as nurses, 50, 157–158, 340, 343, 493
   on hospital ships, 428
   Northern women as nurses, 44, 79
   Southern women as nurses, 21, 22, 52–53, 71

O'Connor, Florence, 267, 268
Office of Correspondence, 125
*Old Washington* (Prescott), 456
*Old-town Folks* (H. Stowe), 531
Olmsted, Frederick Law, 342, **427–428**, 427 (illustration), 564, 597
*On Picket Duty* (Alcott), 98
Ord, O. C., 256 (photo)
Osterman, Rosanna Dyer, 358
Otey, Lucy Mina, 339
*The Other Side of War* (Wormeley), 597
*Our Charley, and, What to Do with Him* (H. Stowe), 529
Overall, Mary, 31

Page, Thomas Nelson, 88
Palmer, Benjamin, 61
Palmer, Phoebe, 389–390
Pardington, Sarah Knapp, 586–587
Parker, Theodore, 384
Parsons, Emily Elizabeth, **429–430**
Partisan Ranger Act, 314
"Pastoral Letter" (Massachusetts Association of
   Congregational Ministers), 311, 312
Patriotism, 33, 420
Patterson, Mary Jane, 539
Paul, Susan, 220
*Pauline of the Potomac* (Bradshaw), 99
Payne, Lewis, 533–534
Peabody, Elizabeth Palmer, **430–431**, 430 (illustration)
Peabody, Mary, 430
*The Pearl of Orr's Island* (H. Stowe), 530–531
Pember, Phoebe Yates Levy, 52, 359, 407, **431–432**
Pendleton, George, 59
Peninsular Campaign, **432–433**
Pennsylvania Abolition Society (PAS), 4–5, 104
Pennsylvania Peace Society, 403
Pensions
   and Confederate widows, **434–435,** 587
   and Union widows, **435–437,** 587
*Personal Memoirs of U.S. Grant,* 307
Personal property, destruction of, **206–207**
Petersburg Campaign, **437–438**

*Peterson's Magazine,* 404
Petticoat Gunboats, 316
Pettus, John Jones, 58
Phelps, Elizabeth Stuart (Ward) [Mary Gray Phelps], 183,
   265, **438–439,** 438 (illustration)
Philadelphia Female Anti-Slavery Society, 403
Philadelphia Ladies' Liberia Association, 101–102
Phillips, Eugenia Levy, 352, 358–359, 359 (photo), 431,
   **439–440**
Phillips, Philip, 439
Phillips, Wendell, 8, 9, 105, 110, 185, 236, 281, 282, 298,
   523–524
Pickens, Lucy Petway Holcombe [H. M. Hardimann],
   **440–441**
*The Picket Slayer* (Bradshaw), 99
Pickett, George, 441
Pickett, LaSalle Corbell, **441–442**
*Pickett and His Men* (L. Pickett), 441
Pinkerton, Allen, 30, 116
Pinkerton Agency, 45
Pitman, Mary Ann [Rawley Pitman], 506
Pitts, Helen, 221
*Pittsburgh Saturday Visitor,* 535
Plantation life, **442–446**
Pleasant, Mary Ellen ("Mammy Pleasant"), **446**
Pledge of Allegiance, 420
*Poems on Miscellaneous Subjects* (F. Harper), 323
Poets, Northern, **447–449**
   male poets, 447
   song lyrics, 447
   women poets, 447–448
Poets, Southern, **449–450**
Politics, **54–60,** 83
Pomeroy, Samuel, 211, 269
Pond, Cornelia "Nela" Jones, **450–451**
*The Ponder Heart* (Welty), 243
Pope, John, 141, 148, 149, 275
Poppenheim, Mary, 560–561
Port Royal, **451–454**
Port Royal Experiment, 233, 453, 554, 620
Porter, Eliza Chappell, 129
Post, Amy, 220, 356
Powell, Mildred Elizabeth "Lizzie," 314
Presbyterian Church, 168, 182, **454–455**
   Covenanter Church, 534
   Old School and New School groups of, 61, 454
   Presbyterian Church in the Confederate States of America
     (PCCSA) (Southern Presbyterian Church; Presbyterian
     Church of the United States), 454
   United Presbyterian Church in the United States of
     America (UPCUSA) (Northern Presbyterian Church),
     454
Prescott (Spofford), Harriet E., **455–456,** 456 (photo)
Preston, Margaret Junkin, 450
Priest, Nancy A. W., 265
Primus, Rebecca, 143, **456–457**
*Prince Hal; or; The Romance of a Rich Young Man* (Hay), 103
Prison reform movement, 4

## About the Editor

Lisa Tendrich Frank is an Independent Scholar who received her Ph.D. from the University of Florida. She has taught courses in the American Civil War and Women's History at various universities, including the University of North Florida, University of California, Los Angeles, and Occidental College. She is the author of numerous articles and is currently writing a book on the experiences of Confederate women and Sherman's March. She lives in Tallahassee, Florida.